THE OXFORD HISTORY OF A

General Editor: Rowan Strong

The Oxford History of Anglicanism, Volume I
Reformation and Identity, c.1520–1662
Edited by Anthony Milton

The Oxford History of Anglicanism, Volume II
Establishment and Empire, 1662–1829
Edited by Jeremy Gregory

The Oxford History of Anglicanism, Volume III
Partisan Anglicanism and its Global Expansion, 1829–c.1914
Edited by Rowan Strong

The Oxford History of Anglicanism, Volume IV
Global Western Anglicanism, c.1910–present
Edited by Jeremy Morris

The Oxford History of Anglicanism, Volume V
Global Anglicanism, c.1910–2000
Edited by William L. Sachs

The Oxford History of Anglicanism, Volume I

Reformation and Identity, c.1520–1662

Edited by
ANTHONY MILTON

OXFORD
UNIVERSITY PRESS

OXFORD
UNIVERSITY PRESS

Great Clarendon Street, Oxford, OX2 6DP,
United Kingdom

Oxford University Press is a department of the University of Oxford.
It furthers the University's objective of excellence in research, scholarship,
and education by publishing worldwide. Oxford is a registered trade mark of
Oxford University Press in the UK and in certain other countries

© Oxford University Press 2017

The moral rights of the authors have been asserted

First published 2017
First published in paperback 2019

All rights reserved. No part of this publication may be reproduced, stored in
a retrieval system, or transmitted, in any form or by any means, without the
prior permission in writing of Oxford University Press, or as expressly permitted
by law, by licence or under terms agreed with the appropriate reprographics
rights organization. Enquiries concerning reproduction outside the scope of the
above should be sent to the Rights Department, Oxford University Press, at the
address above

You must not circulate this work in any other form
and you must impose this same condition on any acquirer

Published in the United States of America by Oxford University Press
198 Madison Avenue, New York, NY 10016, United States of America

British Library Cataloguing in Publication Data
Data available

Library of Congress Cataloging in Publication Data
Data available

ISBN 978–0–19–963973–1 (Hbk.)
ISBN 978–0–19–882231–8 (Pbk.)

Links to third party websites are provided by Oxford in good faith and
for information only. Oxford disclaims any responsibility for the materials
contained in any third party website referenced in this work.

Acknowledgements

I am very grateful to all the contributors for their efficiency in producing their chapters, and for the good-natured forbearance with which they have tolerated editorial direction and interference. At an early stage of the project, many of us were able to meet to discuss the volume at a one-day symposium that took place in the Wren Suite at St Paul's Cathedral. I am very grateful to the Dean and Chapter of St Paul's for their hospitality, and to Professor Peter McCullough—Lay Canon (History) at St Paul's—for his kindness in organizing the event. I must also thank Karen Raith and Tom Perridge at OUP for all their help and advice, and the eagle-eyed Joanna North for her copy-editing prowess.

Contents

List of Illustrations	ix
List of Abbreviations	xi
List of Contributors	xiii
Series Introduction	xvii

1. Introduction: Reformation, Identity, and 'Anglicanism', c.1520–1662 — *Anthony Milton* — 1
2. The Emergence of the Church of England, c.1520–1553 — *Ethan H. Shagan* — 28
3. Settlement Patterns: The Church of England, 1553–1603 — *Peter Marshall* — 45
4. Unsettled Reformations, 1603–1662 — *Anthony Milton* — 63
5. Bishops, Church, and State, c.1530–1646 — *Andrew Foster* — 84
6. The Godly Magistrate — *Jacqueline Rose* — 103
7. Religion and the English Parish — *J. F. Merritt* — 122
8. Liturgy and Worship — *Bryan D. Spinks* — 148
9. Canon Law and the Church of England — *Gerald Bray* — 168
10. Art and Iconoclasm — *Felicity Heal* — 186
11. Confessional Identity — *Stephen Hampton* — 210
12. Cathedrals — *Ian Atherton* — 228
13. Ireland and Scotland, 1534–1663 — *John McCafferty* — 243

14.	North America to 1662 *Michael P. Winship*	266
15.	Perceptions of Christian Antiquity *Jean-Louis Quantin*	280
16.	Protestants and the Meanings of Church History, 1540–1660 *W. J. Sheils*	298
17.	The Church of England and International Protestantism, 1530–1570 *Diarmaid MacCulloch*	316
18.	Attitudes towards the Protestant and Catholic Churches *Anthony Milton*	333
19.	'Puritans' and 'Anglicans' in the History of the Post-Reformation English Church *Peter Lake*	352
20.	'Avant-Garde Conformity' in the 1590s *Peter McCullough*	380
21.	Early Modern English Piety *Jessica Martin*	395
22.	The Bible in Early Modern England *Lori Anne Ferrell*	412
23.	The Westminster Assembly and the Reformation of the 1640s *Chad van Dixhoorn*	430
24.	The Cromwellian Church *Ann Hughes*	444
25.	Episcopalian Identity, 1640–1662 *Kenneth Fincham and Stephen Taylor*	457

Index 483

List of Illustrations

10.1	Black-letter inscriptions, Puddletown, Dorset.	192
10.2	Lincoln College east window of the Lincoln College chapel.	197
10.3	Commandments board, St Saviour, Southwark.	200
10.4	Passenham church, chancel stalls.	202
10.5	Passenham church, chancel painting.	203
10.6	Plasterwork of East Knoyle church.	204
10.7	Brancepeth church interior.	205
10.8	St Katherine Cree, Leadenhall Street, London.	206

List of Abbreviations

BL	British Library
Bodl.	Bodleian Library, Oxford
CJ	*Journals of the House of Commons*
CSPD	*Calendar of State Papers, Domestic Series*
JEH	*Journal of Ecclesiastical History*
LJ	*Journals of the House of Lords*
ODNB	*Oxford Dictionary of National Biography*
RO	Record Office
RSTC	*Revised Short Title Catalogue*, 2nd edn. (3 vols., 1976–91)
SCH	Studies in Church History
TNA	The National Archives, London

Place of publication is London unless otherwise stated.

List of Contributors

Ian Atherton is Senior Lecturer in History at Keele University. He specializes in the history of religion, politics, and war in early modern Britain. He is the author of *Ambition and Failure in Stuart England: The Career of John, First Viscount Scudamore* (Manchester University Press, 1999) and co-editor of *The 1630s: Interdisciplinary Essays on Culture and Politics in the Caroline Era* (with Julie Sanders; Manchester University Press, 2006) and has written a number of essays and articles about the history of British cathedrals in the early modern period.

Gerald Bray is Distinguished Professor of Historical Theology at Knox Theological Seminary. He is the Research Professor of Divinity at Beeson Divinity School where he has taught Church History and Theology since 1993. His publications include *The Church: A Theological and Historical Account* (Baker Academic, 2016) and *The Books of Homilies: A Critical Edition* (James Clark & Co, 2016).

Chad van Dixhoorn is Chancellor's Professor of Historical Theology and Associate Professor of Church History at Reformed Theological Seminary. He is the editor of *The Minutes and Papers of the Westminster Assembly, 1643–1652* (Oxford University Press, 2012).

Lori Anne Ferrell is John D. and Lillian Maguire Distinguished Research Professor in the Humanities, and Director of the Kingsley and Kate Tufts Poetry Awards Program at Claremont Graduate University. Her research concentrates on the effect religious and political change had on early modern texts—theological, literary, theatrical, and practical—in the turbulent century before the outbreak of civil war in Britain. She is the author of *The English Sermon Revised: Religion, Literature and History, 1600–1750* (with Peter McCullough; Manchester University Press, 2000) and *The Bible and the People* (Yale University Press, 2009).

Kenneth Fincham is Professor of Early Modern History at the University of Kent. His research centres on politics, religion, and culture in early modern Britain. His publications include *Altars Restored: The Changing Face of English Religious Worship, 1547–c.1700* (Oxford University Press, 2007) and *Prelate as Pastor: The Episcopate of James I* (Oxford University Press, 1990).

Andrew Foster is Honorary Senior Research Fellow in History at the University of Kent. He has written chiefly about the early modern Church of England, with articles on bishops, clergy, dioceses, cathedrals, parishes, and churchwardens' accounts.

Stephen Hampton is Dean, Chaplain, Catechist, and Fellow in Theology at Peterhouse, Cambridge. He specializes in the development of Protestant theology between the Reformation and the Enlightenment. He is the author of *Anti-Arminians: The Anglican Reformed Tradition from Charles II to George I* (Oxford University Press, 2008).

Felicity Heal is Emeritus Fellow at Jesus College, Oxford, and formerly Fellow and Tutor in Modern History. Her research interests include British Reformations, the English gentry, 1500–1700, and gift exchange in early modern culture. She is the author of *Reformation in Britain and Ireland* (Oxford University Press, 2003) and *The Power of Gifts: Gift Exchange in Early Modern England* (Oxford University Press, 2014).

Ann Hughes is Professor of Early Modern History at Keele University. She is a historian of early modern England with particular interests in the culture, religion, and politics of the English civil war. Her publications include *Gender and the English Revolution* (Routledge, 2011) and *The Complete Works of Gerrard Winstanley* (with Thomas N. Corns and David Loewenstein; Oxford University Press, 2009).

Peter Lake is Professor of the History of Christianity at Vanderbilt Divinity School. His research focuses on post-Reformation English History with particular attention to the Elizabethan and early Stuart periods. His publications include *The Trials of Margaret Clitherow: Persecution, Martyrdom and the Politics of Sanctity in Elizabethan England* (with Michael Questier; Continuum, 2011), *The Antichrist's Lewd Hat* (Yale University Press, 2002), and *The Boxmaker's Revenge* (Stanford University Press, 2002).

John McCafferty is Professor of History at University College Dublin. His research focuses on church history and the history of belief in Ireland in the period from 1500 to 1700. As Director of the Mícheál Ó Cléirigh Institute he works in partnership with the Irish Franciscans whose transfer of manuscripts and rare books has been one of the most significant donations ever made to an Irish university. He is the author of *The Reconstruction of the Church of Ireland: Bishop Bramhall and the Laudian Reforms, 1633–1641* (Cambridge University Press, 2007) and co-editor of *The Origins of Sectarianism in Early Modern Ireland* (with Alan Ford; Cambridge University Press, 2005).

Diarmaid MacCulloch is Professor of Church History at St Cross College, Oxford. His research interests include the European Reformation 1490–1700 and Christian history in general. He is the author of *Silence: A Christian History* (Penguin, 2014), *A History of Christianity: The First Three Thousand Years* (Penguin, 2010), and *Reformation: Europe's House Divided 1490–1700* (Penguin, 2004).

List of Contributors

Peter McCullough is Sohmer Fellow, Tutor in English Literature, and Fellow Archivist at Lincoln College, Oxford. His research focuses on the Elizabethan, Jacobean, and Caroline periods of English literary history (1558–1649). He is the editor of *The Oxford Handbook of the Early Modern Sermon* (with Hugh Adlington and Emma Rhatigan; Oxford University Press, 2011), *The Oxford Edition of the Sermons of John Donne, Volume I: Sermons Preached at the Jacobean Courts, 1615–19* (Oxford University Press, 2015), and *Lancelot Andrewes: Selected Sermons and Lectures* (Oxford University Press, 2005).

Peter Marshall is Professor of History at the University of Warwick. He is a Fellow of the Royal Historical Society, a member of the Irish Research Council's International Advisory Board, and of the Council and the Editorial Committee of the Dugdale Society. He is also a founding editor of the monograph series *Religious Cultures in the Early Modern World*, published by Pickering & Chatto. He is the editor of *The Oxford Illustrated History of the Reformation* (Oxford University Press, 2015). He is the author of *Beliefs and the Dead in Reformation England* (Oxford University Press, 2002) and *The Reformation: A Very Short Introduction* (Oxford University Press, 2009).

Jessica Martin is currently priest-in-charge of five South Cambridgeshire parishes, and about to take up a new post as Canon Residentiary for Education at Ely Cathedral. She has published on Izaak Walton and early modern clerical life-writing. Most recently she edited and contributed to the volume *Private and Domestic Devotion in Early Modern England and Scotland*, with Alec Ryrie (Ashgate, 2012).

J. F. Merritt is Associate Professor of History at the University of Nottingham. Her research interests lie in the intersections between the social, religious, and cultural history of early modern England, with particular reference to the history of London. Her books include *Westminster 1640–1660: A Royal City in a Time of Revolution* (Manchester University Press, 2013), *The Social World of Early Modern Westminster* (Manchester University Press, 2005), and *Imagining Early Modern London: Perceptions and Portrayals of the City from Stow to Strype, 1598–1720* (Cambridge University Press, 2001).

Anthony Milton is Professor of History at the University of Sheffield. His publications include *Catholic and Reformed: The Roman and Protestant Churches in English Protestant Thought, 1600–1640* (Cambridge University Press, 1995), *The British Delegation and the Synod of Dort, 1618–1619* (Boydell, 2005), and *Laudian and Royalist Polemic in Seventeenth-Century England: The Career and Writings of Peter Heylyn* (Manchester University Press, 2007).

Jean-Louis Quantin is Professor of the History of Early Modern Scholarship at École Pratique des Hautes Études (Sorbonne, Paris). He is the author of *The Church of England and Christian Antiquity: The Construction of a Confessional Identity in the 17th Century* (Oxford University Press, 2009).

Jacqueline Rose is a lecturer at the University of St Andrews. Her teaching ranges broadly across early modern British history. She is the author of *Godly Kingship in Restoration England: The Politics of the Royal Supremacy, 1660–1688* (Cambridge University Press, 2011).

Ethan H. Shagan is Professor of History at the University of California Berkeley. His publications include *The Rule of Moderation: Violence, Religion and the Politics of Restraint in Early Modern England* (Cambridge University Press, 2011) and *Catholics and the Protestant Nation: Religious Politics and Identity in Early Modern England* (Cambridge University Press, 2009). He is the co-editor of *Religion in Tudor England: An Anthology of Primary Sources* (with Debora Shuger, 2016).

W. J. Sheils is Professor Emeritus in History and Leverhulme Fellow 2014–16 at the University of York. He has a long-standing interest in the social history of the English Reformation and of religion between 1500 and 1800. He is the author of *The English Reformation 1530–1570* (Longman, 1989). He is the co-editor of *Clergy, Church and Society in England and Wales, c.1200–1800* (with Rosemary C. E. Hayes; Borthwick Institute Publications, 2013) and *A History of Religion in Britain: Practice and Belief from Roman Times to the Present* (with Sheridan Gilley; Wiley-Blackwell, 1994).

Bryan D. Spinks is Bishop F. Percy Goddard Professor of Liturgical Studies and Pastoral Theology at Yale Divinity School. His research interests include East Syrian rites, Reformed rites, issues in theology and liturgy, and worship in a postmodern age. He is the author of *The Worship Mall: Contemporary Responses to Contemporary Culture* (SPCK, 2010) and *Do This in Remembrance of Me: The Eucharist from the Early Church to the Present Day* (SCM Press, 2013). He co-edited, with Teresa Berger, *The Spirit in Worship—Worship in the Spirit* (The Liturgical Press, 2009).

Stephen Taylor is Professor of Early Modern British History at Durham University. He is a specialist in the religious and political history of England in the seventeenth and eighteenth centuries, and his published work has touched on topics as diverse as the identity of Anglicanism, court culture, party politics, the circulation of news, and libertinism.

Michael P. Winship is Professor of History at the University of Georgia. His publications include *Godly Republicanism: Puritans, Pilgrims, and a City on a Hill* (Harvard University Press, 2012), *Seers of God: Puritan Providentialism in the Restoration and Early Enlightenment* (Johns Hopkins University Press, 1996), and *The Constitutional Convention: A Narrative History from the Notes of James Madison* (with Edward J. Larson; Random House, 2005).

Series Introduction

Rowan Strong

Even Henry VIII at his autocratic best could hardly have imagined that his Church of England would, nearly five centuries after he had replaced papal authority with his own, become a global Christian communion encompassing people and languages far beyond the English. Formally, Henry asserted his royal power over the national Church on a more global scale—on the imperial theory that 'this realm of England is an empire' asserted the Act in Restraint of Appeals (to Rome) in 1533. Yet this was sixteenth-century imperial theory serving a national end. England was an empire and therefore King Henry was an emperor, that is, a ruler who was the paramount earthly authority and consequently superior to the papacy. So Henry's Church of England was always a national project, meant first and foremost to be the Church of the English—all the English—who would, if necessary, be compelled to come in. That national politico-religious agenda—a Church of all the English with the monarchy as its supreme head—formed the thrust of the policy of all but one of the succeeding Tudor monarchs. However, that royal agenda of the inclusion of all the English lay at the heart of the problem of this national ecclesiastical project.

At no time since Henry VIII ushered in his religious revolution did all the English wish to be part of this Church of England, though for over two centuries the monarchy and the English ruling classes attempted to encourage, cajole, or compel everyone in England to at least attend their parish church on Sunday. In Henry's reign, religious dissent from this monarchical Church was disparate and small, partly because Henry ensured it was dangerous. So some advanced Evangelicals (as early Protestants were called), such as Robert Barnes and William Tyndale, were executed by the regime in the early years of the religious revolution. Later, some prominent conservatives influenced by Catholic reform, such as Bishop John Fisher, Sir Thomas More, and some members of particular observant religious orders, followed their Evangelical enemies to the scaffold or the block. As the Protestant Reformation unfolded, and Catholic reform began to gather definition, from the reign of Edward VI onwards, those among the English who dissented from, or who were dissatisfied with, this national Church began to increase in numbers. Even those within it argued among themselves as to what the Church of England stood for.

Consequently, the Church of England, and its later global Anglican expansion, was always a contested identity throughout its history. It was contested both by its own adherents and by its leadership. This series looks at the history of that contestation and how it contributed to an evolving religious identity eventually known as Anglican. The major question it seeks to address is: what were the characteristics, carriers, shapers, and expressions of an Anglican identity in the various historical periods and geographic locations investigated by the volumes in the series? The series proposes that Anglicanism was not a version of Christianity that emerged entire and distinct by the end of the so-called Elizabethan Settlement. Rather, the disputed and developing identity of the Church developed from Henry VIII's religious revolution began to be worked out in the various countries of the British Isles from the early sixteenth century, went into a transatlantic environment in the seventeenth century, and then evolved in an increasing global context from the eighteenth century onwards. The series proposes that the answer to 'what is an Anglican?' was always debated. Moreover, Anglican identity over time experienced change and contradiction as well as continuities. Carriers of this developing identity included formal ecclesiastical dimensions such as clergy, Prayer Books, theology, universities, and theological colleges. Also among such formal carriers of Anglican identity was the English (then the British) state, so this series also investigates ways in which that state connection influenced Anglicanism. But the evolution of Anglicanism was also maintained, changed, and expressed in various cultural dimensions, such as architecture, art, and music. In addition, the series pays attention to how Anglicanism interacted with national identities, helping to form some, and being shaped itself by others. Each volume in the series devotes some explicit attention to these formal dimensions, by setting out the various Anglican identities expressed in their historical periods by theology, liturgy, architecture, religious experience and the practice of piety, and its interactions with wider society and politics.

A word needs to be said about the use of the term 'Anglicanism' to cover a religious identity whose origins lie in the sixteenth century when the name was not known. While recognizing the anachronism of the term Anglicanism, it is the 'least-worst' appellation to describe this religious phenomenon throughout the centuries of its existence. It is a fallacy that there was no use of the term Anglicanism to describe the Church of England and its global offshoots before John Henry Newman and the Oxford Movement in the 1830s. Newman and his Tractarian *confreres* certainly gave wider publicity to the name by using it to describe the separate Catholic culture of their Church. However, its usage predates the Tractarians because French Catholic writers were using it in the eighteenth century. It has become acceptable scholarly usage to describe this version of Christianity for the centuries prior to the nineteenth, notwithstanding its admittedly anachronistic nature.[1] Into the nineteenth century

---

[1] John Spurr, *The Restoration Church of England* (New Haven, CT, 1991), pp. xiii–xiv; John Walsh, Colin Haydon, and Stephen Taylor (eds.), *The Church of England c.1689–c.1833*

contemporaries used the terms 'Church of England' or 'Churchmen' to encompass their Church, even in countries and colonies beyond England. However, these names are not acceptable or understood today with their formerly inclusive meaning. The latter is objectionable on gender terms; and the former, while used by Anglicans in a variety of different lands and cultures, only leads to confusion when addressing the Church of England beyond England itself. Consequently, it has long been recognized in the scholarly literature that there is a need for some term that enshrines both the Church of England in England, its presence beyond that nation, and for that denomination over its entire historical existence. The most commonly adopted term is Anglicanism, and has been used by a number of recent scholars for periods prior to the nineteenth century.[2] A less Anglo-centric term—'Episcopal' or 'Episcopalianism'—is widely used in some parts of world for the same ecclesiastical phenomenon—Scotland, North America, and Brazil. However, that term does not figure as widely as Anglican or Anglicanism in the historical literature, so it is the predominant usage in this series.

Consequently, Anglicanism is understood in this series as originating as a mixed and ambiguous ecclesiastical identity, largely as a result of its foundation by the Tudor monarchs of the sixteenth century who were determined to embrace the whole of the English nation within their national Church. It is, consequently, a religious community that brings together aspects of ecclesiastical identity that other Western Churches have separated. From an English Church that was predominantly Reformed Protestant in the sixteenth century, emerging Anglicanism developed a liturgical and episcopal identity alongside its Protestant emphasis on the Bible as the sole criterion for religious truth. The series therefore views Anglicanism as a Church in tension. Developing within Anglicanism over centuries was a creative but also divisive tension between Protestantism and Catholicism, between the Bible and tradition, between the Christian past and contemporary thought and society, that has meant Anglicanism has not only been a contested, but also at times an inconsistent Christian identity.

Within England itself, the Tudor project of a Church for the English nation became increasingly unrealistic as that Church encompassed people who were not English, or people who thought of themselves less as English than as different nationalities. But it has proved to have a surprisingly long life for the English themselves. The series demonstrates various ways in which the

---

(Cambridge, 1993), ch. 1; J. C. D. Clark, *English Society 1660–1832* (Cambridge, 2000 edn.), p. 256; Nigel Voak, *Richard Hooker, and Reformed Theology: A Study of Reason, Will, and Grace* (Oxford, 2003), pp. 1–5; Patricia U. Bonomi, *Under the Cope of Heaven: Religion, Society, and Politics in Colonial America* (Oxford, 2003 edn.), pp. 40–61.

[2] John Frederick Woolverton, *Colonial Anglicanism in North America* (Detroit, 1984); Thomas Bartlett, 'Ireland and the British Empire', in P. J. Marshall (ed.), *The Oxford History of the British Empire: The Eighteenth Century* (Oxford, 1998), p. 270.

Church over the centuries attempted to enforce, encourage, or cling to its national identity in England, with some degree of success, not least in retaining an enduring cultural appeal for some English who were only loosely connected to its institutional life, or barely to its theological or religious claims. Even today English cathedrals often attract audiences to daily Evensong that otherwise would not be there.

But for those in England and beyond for whom their Church was more central, contestation, and the evolution of identity it prompted, was probably inevitable in a Church that, after its first two supreme heads, was deliberately re-founded by Elizabeth I to be ambiguous enough in certain key areas to give a Church for all the English a pragmatic chance of being accomplished. But this was a loaded gun. A basically Protestant Church, aligned with the Swiss Reformation, but with sufficient traditional aspects to irritate convinced Protestants at home (though less so major European Reformers); but insufficiently Catholic to pull in reformed Catholics for whom papal authority was non-negotiable, simply pleased no one for quite a while. It was neither Catholic fish nor properly Protestant fowl, at least according to those English that wanted the Church of England to conform completely to the worship and polity of Geneva, by the later sixteenth century the pre-eminent centre of international Protestantism. Even Elizabeth's bishops were not entirely comfortable with the Church they led, and some of them tried to push the boundaries towards a properly Reformed Church modelled on that of the New Testament. Until, that is, they realized Elizabeth was having none of it, and made it clear she would not deviate beyond the Church and worship enacted by Parliament in 1558–9. In her mind, though probably in no one else's, those years constituted 'the settlement' of religion. When her archbishop of Canterbury, Edmund Grindal, refused to suppress the so-called 'prophesyings' of local clergy meeting for what would now be termed professional development, the queen simply suspended him for the rest of his life and put his functions into the hands of an appointed committee. Royal Supremacy was an undoubted component of the Church of England's identity, and Elizabeth and her successors for many years were not about to let anyone forget it, be they bishops or religiously interfering Members of Parliament.

The fact that Elizabeth emulated the long reigns of her father and grandfather, and not the short ones of her half brother and half sister, meant that her Church of England had time to put down local roots, notwithstanding the 'Anglican' puritans who sought to remake it in Geneva's image; or the zealous Catholic mission priests who hoped to dismantle it by taking Catholics out of it completely.

Where the English went their Church was bound to follow, though this intensified the unhappy situation of Ireland where the English had for centuries sought political domination undergirded by settlement. The consequence of legally establishing a Protestant Church of Ireland was to add religious difference to the centuries-old colonial condition of that island, whose Gaelic-speaking population remained stubbornly Catholic, in part because the Catholic Church was not English. Generally, the Irish wanted no part of this Church, aside from a small percentage of Irish who stood to gain from alliance with the prevailing Protestant power.

The following century saw the contest for the Church of England become more militant and polarized, until the English went to war to settle the issue among themselves. Perhaps the most surprising development was the emergence of a group of Anglicans who began to publicly advocate for the conservative aspects of the Church of England, a group that coalesced and became another sort of Anglican to the usual sort of Calvinist. This new variety of Anglican was particularly encouraged by specific royal patronage under the first two Stuart kings, James I and Charles I. These new contestants for the identity of the Church have been called by various names—Arminians, Laudians, avant-garde conformists—partly because they were not tightly defined but represented various agendas. Some sought, with the support of Charles I (the first Supreme Governor to be born into the Church of England), to bolster the independence and wealth of the Church; others, to oppose the Church's Calvinist theology and particularly the doctrine of predestination; others, to redress the lack of attention given to the sacraments and sacramental grace compared with the fervour for preaching among the more devout. But all were more or less agreed that the worship of the Church and the performance of the liturgy were woeful and needed to be better ordered, and churches should be more beautiful as aids to devotion and the fundamental significance of the sacraments.

But whether their agenda was liturgical, theological, or sacramental, to their puritan opponents this new Anglicanism looked like Catholicism, and that was the Antichrist from whose idolatrous and superstitious clutches the Protestant Reformation had released the English into true Christianity. They were not prepared to hand over the Church of England to a Catholic fifth-column. But while James I was cautious in his support for these avant-garde Anglicans, liking their support for divine-right monarchy but not their anti-Calvinism, his aesthetic, devout, and imperious son was markedly less so. The religious ball was in the royal court, particularly when Charles pulled off, in the 1630s, a decade of ruling without calling a Parliament, thereby silencing that body's uncomfortable and intolerable demands for royal accountability and religious reform.

The export in 1637 of Charles's particular version of the Church of England to his other kingdom of Scotland, in the form of a Scottish Prayer Book, not only stoked the fires of Scottish Presbyterian nationalism, but also released the pent-up energies of those within the Church of England who wanted an end to what they saw as royal absolutism and religious renovation by would-be papists. The rapid result of this intensification of political and religious contestation was the outbreak in 1642 of years of civil war in the royal Supreme Governor's three kingdoms. The internal Anglican quarrel, part of wider political differences, ended with the demise of the revolution begun by Henry VIII—the legal abolition of the Church of England, sealed in 1645 in the blood of the beheaded archbishop of Canterbury, William Laud; and followed by that of his Church's head, Charles I, in 1649. For the first time in its legal existence the Church of England (and the Church of Ireland) no longer officially existed.

Then an unexpected thing happened—some people continued to worship and practise their devotional lives according to the use of the defunct Church of England, demonstrating that its identity, though contested, was by this time a genuine reality in the lives of at least some of the English. They did this despite it being illegal, though the republican regime under Oliver Cromwell was not particularly zealous in its proscription of such activities. However, the diarist John Evelyn was present one Christmas Day when a covert congregation in London was dispersed by soldiers while keeping the holy day (proscribed by the regime) by gathering for Holy Communion according to the Book of Common Prayer.[3] Evelyn and others worshipped this way, and numbers of clergy used as much of the Prayer Book as they could in the parishes, notwithstanding that their leaders, the bishops, did little to set an example or to ensure the continuation of their illegal order. Anglican identity through worship and the ordering of the week and the year according to the Prayer Book and the Calendar of the Church of England was now being maintained, not by the state, but at the clerical and lay grassroots.

When Charles II landed in Dover in 1660 as the recognized king of England, after the rapid demise of the republican regime with its non-episcopal quasi-congregationalist Church following the death in 1658 of Lord Protector Oliver Cromwell, one outcome was the restoration of the legal monopoly of the Church of England. What that legal restoration did not do was to restore the spirituality, devotion, practice, and belief of the Church of England, because these had been ongoing in the period of the Church's official demise. Nevertheless, the legislation that brought back the establishment of the Church of England did newly define some ingredients of Anglican identity.

Before the Commonwealth the Church of England had not made ordination by bishops a non-negotiable aspect of Anglicanism. While it was certainly normal, there were exceptions made for some ministers who had been ordained in non-episcopal Churches elsewhere to minister in the Church of England without re-ordination. Now all clergy in the Church had to be episcopally ordained, with the sole exception of those clergy who came from Churches with a long historic tradition of episcopacy—the Roman Catholic,

---

[3] William Bray (ed.), *Diary and Correspondence of John Evelyn FRS* (1878, 4 vols.), I, p. 341 (25 Dec. 1657).

Orthodox, and the Church of Sweden. So from 1660 episcopacy became a basic characteristic of Anglicanism. The result was the expulsion of hundreds of clergy who would not conform to the requirement and to that of using only the Book of Common Prayer in worship. These dissenting clergy and laity, most of whom came from the previous Calvinist and puritan groups, now became permanent Nonconformists outside the Church of England. In 1662 a slightly revised Book of Common Prayer was passed by Parliament as the only authorized liturgy for the Church therefore reinforcing liturgical worship as a fundamental criterion of Anglican identity. Parliament again passed an Act of Uniformity and various other acts against Nonconformist worship. Uniformity was restored as an aspect of Anglicanism. So also was the royal supremacy.

However, while episcopacy has remained virtually unquestioned, and liturgical worship remained uncontested within Anglicanism until the late twentieth century, the same could not be said for the other dimensions of the 1662 resettlement of Anglicanism—legal establishment, the royal supremacy, and uniformity. These identifiers were to be victims of the global success of Anglicanism from the eighteenth century, as the Church of England expanded; first across the Atlantic into North American colonies, and then globally within and beyond the British Empire. The first to go was legal establishment when the Americans successfully ushered in their republic after their War of Independence with Britain and some Anglicans remained in the new state. No longer could these Anglicans be subject to the British crown, or be legally privileged in a country in which they were a decided minority, when the Americans had gone to so much trouble to jettison these things. So an Anglicanism—known after the Scottish precedent as Episcopalianism—came into existence for the first time in history without monarchical headship, but rather as a voluntary association. Even within the British Empire these legal and political aspects of Anglicanism, so much a part of its foundation in the sixteenth century, were in trouble by the 1840s. It was then that the bishop of a very new colony, almost as far away from England as you could get, started acting as though the monarchy and establishment were Anglican optional extras. Inspired by the United States precedent, Bishop Augustus Selwyn began unilaterally calling synods of his clergy just four years after New Zealand had been annexed in 1840 as a crown colony, and a few years later he was leading his Church into a constitution which made authoritative synods of laymen, clergy, and bishops. Voluntaryism was catching on in international Anglicanism.

Contestation and evolution continued to be a part of Anglicanism. One of its most enduring characteristics, the sole use of an authorized liturgical form for public worship, began to be challenged by two mutually hostile internal parties—Evangelicals and Anglo-Catholics. In some dioceses the latter succumbed to the temptation to use the Roman missal with the permission of sympathetic diocesan bishops. In contrast, encouraged by the global ambitions of the wealthy diocese of Sydney, some of the former had *de facto* abandoned the use of an authorized Prayer Book entirely. Into this recent Anglican contest has been thrown issues of human sexuality which have conflicted wider society, particularly in the West, but which have been accentuated for Anglicans by questions of how varieties of human sexuality conform or do not conform to the authority of Scripture. So these historical forces have not ceased to play their part within the dynamic of Anglican identity. The postcolonial era following the retraction of the British Empire has brought further criticism, from Anglicans themselves, about the extent to which their denomination was complicit in British imperialism, and that therefore their identity suffers from being an imperial construct. For such Anglican critics, necessary deconstruction has to occur which allows English markers of identity, even as basic as liturgical worship or episcopacy, to be questioned or even relinquished.

Since the nineteenth century and the effective end of the royal supremacy—whether that was exercised by the monarch or the British Parliament—emerging global Anglicanism was increasingly beset into the twenty-first century by the issue of authority. There has been no effective replacement for the royal supremacy, in part because of Anglicanism's historical origins in anti-papal national royalism. Beyond the purely diocesan level, the Anglican Communion struggled to find an operative replacement for the authority of the royal supremacy. Various attempts at authority by moral consensus, all bedevilled by anxiety that something akin to a centralized (i.e. papal) authority was being constructed, were tried. But all such central organizations of an emerging international communion were saddled with the original limitations imposed by Archbishop Longley when he agreed to call the first Lambeth Conference of diocesan bishops in 1867. By repudiating any real global authority, and opting for the consultative label of 'conference' rather than 'synod', Longley found a way to bring opposing parties of Anglicans together. But the emerging Anglican Communion, with its so-called 'Instruments of Unity'—be they the Anglican Consultative Council, or Primates' Meeting—tried to emulate Longley and both avoid the devil—papal centralism—and the deep blue sea—myriad manifestations that belied the claim to unity. True to its origins, Anglicanism perhaps remained more comfortable with its various national existences, than with its international one.

However, the history of Anglicanism is not merely the tracing of the evolution of a now global form of Western Christianity, important though that may be to tens of millions of contemporary Anglican adherents. As part of the historical turn to religion in recent academic interest, in the past two decades there has been a great increase of interest in the history and development of both the Church of England and its global offshoots. Scholars have investigated a plethora of facets of these religious phenomena, from the institutional to the popular, from formal theological belief and worship to informal, more diffusive faith. Other historians have looked at seminal Anglican figures and movements. As well as specifically religious history, other historians have been recapturing the pivotal importance of Anglicanism in wider social and political contexts.

There has been a general historiographical revision which might broadly be described as moving the Church of England (and religion generally) from the margins to the centre of major economic social, political, and cultural development in English, British, imperial, and global history from the sixteenth to the twentieth centuries. The Church of England, Anglicanism, and religion more generally are now seen to be seminal dimensions of these various historical periods. So, for example, the significance of religion in the British Empire has now been recognized by a number of important scholars.[4] However, the major religious denomination in that empire, the Church of England, has been only sparsely studied compared to Nonconformity and is just now beginning to be critically examined.[5] Belatedly religion is moving up the scale of historical importance in British, imperial, and global history, but it still lags behind the significance and attention that it has received from historians of England. There have been various studies of the Church of England in its national context, but these have not always been integrated into wider British and global studies.[6]

A number of studies of historical Anglicanism have focused on the narrative of the institutional and theological history of Anglicanism, either as the Church of England or as an Anglican Communion. These include Stephen Neil's now very dated *Anglicanism*, originally published in 1958. More recently, there have been William L. Sachs's *The Transformation of Anglicanism: From State Church to Global Communion* (1993), and Kevin Ward's *A History of Global Anglicanism* (2006). However, these scholarly histories are single-volume histories that inevitably provide insufficient depth to do justice to the breadth of scholarship on their subject. Anglicanism is now a subject of such complexity as both an institutional Church and a religious culture that sufficient justice cannot be done to it in a single-volume historical treatment.

But there is now sufficient international historical interest and extant scholarship to make an extensive, analytical investigation into the history of

---

[4] Andrew Porter, *Religion versus Empire? British Protestant Missionaries and Overseas Expansion, 1700–1914* (Manchester, 2004); Catherine Hall, *Civilising Subjects: Metropole and Colony in the English Imagination 1830–1867* (Chicago, 2002); Jeffrey Cox, *The British Missionary Enterprise since 1700* (Abingdon, 2008).

[5] Rowan Strong, *Anglicanism and the British Empire 1700–c.1850* (Oxford, 2007); Steven S. Maughan, *Mighty England Do Good: Culture, Faith, Empire, and World in the Foreign Missions of the Church of England, 1850–1915* (Grand Rapids, MI, 2014).

[6] Nancy L. Rhoden, *Revolutionary Anglicanism: The Colonial Church of England Clergy during the American Revolution* (Basingstoke, 2007); Rowan Strong, *Episcopalianism in Nineteenth-Century Scotland: Religious Responses to a Modernizing Society* (Oxford, 2000); Bruce Kaye (ed.), *Anglicanism in Australia* (Melbourne, 2002).

Anglicanism a feasible intellectual project. In undertaking such a challenge the scholars who embarked on the project back in 2012 understand that not only was Anglicanism a religious identity shaped by theological and ecclesiastical understandings, but Anglicans were also formed by non-religious forces such as social class, politics, gender, and economics. Anglicanism has, therefore, been an expression of the Christianity of diverse social groups situated in the differing contexts of the past five centuries—monarchs, political elites, and lower orders; landowners and landless; slave-owners and slaves; missionaries, settlers, and indigenous peoples; colonizers and colonized—and by their enemies and opponents, both within and without their Church.

1

Introduction

Reformation, Identity, and 'Anglicanism', c.1520–1662

Anthony Milton

Historians of Anglicanism often assert that it is 'a distinctive trajectory of faith and practice', and 'a recognizably distinctive form of Christianity' launched in the sixteenth century.[1] Its values are taken to be those of moderation, balance, equipoise, and order, with an instinctive avoidance of dogma and precise doctrinal formulation, a scepticism towards religious enthusiasm, and a tendency to preserve continuity with and a reverence for the past. Anglicanism is founded on 'the middle way'—characterized as a distinctive path between Roman Catholicism and Protestantism, avoiding the excesses of both. The first century following the beginning of the Henrician Reformation is therefore assumed to be the time when these unique values were established. Sixteenth-century England, it has been claimed, 'was not passionately stirred over confessional issues'. Instead, the period witnessed, as Henry Chadwick has called it, 'the historical shaping of Anglicanism in its middle path between Roman Catholicism and Protestantism'.[2] The celebrated English theologian Richard Hooker wrote in the 1590s of the 'calm and moderate' course of the English Reformation in contrast to that experienced on the continent, and Anglicans have often been prone to take him at his word.[3] Calm, order, and moderation are the watchwords of the English Reformation.

Relating this vision of Anglicanism to the actual events of the first century following the Reformation has, however, proved rather difficult. The Church of England in the sixteenth century can appear a confusing muddle. The

---

[1] W. P. Haugaard, 'From the Reformation to the Eighteenth Century', in S. Sykes, J. E. Booty, and J. Knight (eds.), *The Study of Anglicanism* (2nd edn., 1998), pp. 3, 6, 10.
[2] Haugaard, 'From the Reformation to the Eighteenth Century', p. 14; R. H. Bainton, *The Reformation of the Sixteenth Century* (Boston, MA, 1953), p. 183; H. Chadwick, 'Tradition, Fathers and Councils', in Sykes et al., *Study*, p. 105.
[3] Richard Hooker, *Of the Laws of Ecclesiastical Polity*, IV, xiv.6.

Reformation under Henry VIII—often misleadingly described as 'Catholicism without the Pope'—offered an uncomfortable mix of pragmatism, evangelism, and reactionary conservatism. There was a rejection of papal authority combined with an assault on some other central aspects of Catholic devotion, but other reforms that were reversed as royal support for Protestant ideas ebbed and flowed with political circumstances, and there was much that later Protestants would be anxious to forget. The short reign of his son Edward VI witnessed more emphatic and destructive Protestant reforms and the creation of most of the later Church of England's institutions, but again this was an evolving, radicalizing process, with a revised prayer book, destructive iconoclasm and an assault on church lands and property, and a reform of canon law (although this remained unimplemented). After a hiatus with the reversion to Catholicism under Edward's sister Mary, a further settlement under Elizabeth restored some but not all of the Edwardian reform programme, and left open significant areas of ambiguity and confusion, especially in matters of ecclesiastical authority. And as Peter Marshall observes in this volume, most of those involved in the Elizabethan Settlement would have been puzzled by the suggestion that this was indeed a definitive 'settlement' rather than part of an ongoing process of reformation. Elizabeth's motto of 'semper eadem' was manifested more in inertia than in principled consistency.

The seventeenth century then seems to witness a significant change of gear. The accession of James VI of Scotland to the throne in 1603 did not result in the further reforms that some English people hoped for, but did generate a new official vernacular bible (issued some seventy-two years after the first Great Bible of 1539). The reigns of James and his son Charles I witnessed a significant revival of the powers and standing of the clergy and church courts, and the emergence to prominence of churchmen who sought a renewed 'beauty of holiness', with greater attention to some of the more conservative survivals of the earlier Reformation settlements and some important revisions in understanding of the Church's identity, culminating in the 'Laudian' movement. The resulting backlash against Laudianism was one of the elements that helped to provoke a civil war in which both sides claimed to be fighting to defend 'true religion'. This itself helped to usher in a yet more dramatic reform of the Church in the 1640s and 1650s where most of its institutions were abolished, to be replaced by new liturgical, doctrinal, and governmental forms which nevertheless did not receive full ratification. It was only with the so-called 'restoration' of the Church in the 1660s that the Prayer Book (after further debate) reached what was to prove its final form.

In this series of different settlements there was no stable foundation of formularies. Over the course of 130 years of oscillating reforms and revisions, the authorities had managed to generate three different official vernacular bibles, four different prayer books (along with a Directory for Public Worship), three versions of the Ordinal, nine different sets of canons, an extraordinary number of different doctrinal statements (including the Ten, Thirteen, Six,

Forty-Two, Thirty-Eight, and Thirty-Nine Articles, and the Bishops' Book and King's Book), and two books of official homilies of varying character.

Amid such a heady mix of different formularies—all of which might be taken as authorities for rather different readings of 'Anglican' orthodoxy—there were other texts whose authority was simply unclear: the *Reformatio Legum Ecclesiasticarum* (a revision of canon law by a committee overseen by Cranmer, but rejected in Parliament); the Lambeth Articles of 1595 (drawn up by Archbishop Whitgift and blocked by the queen, yet incorporated into the Irish Articles of 1615); and the Canons of 1606 (drawn up by Convocation but not ratified by King James). It is therefore not clear at which point we should deem the English Reformation to have been definitively completed (so that further developments should therefore be regarded as unrepresentative and reversible alterations). As Ethan Shagan remarks in this volume, to present the resulting disarray of changes as a masterly equipoise is the equivalent of throwing darts at a wall and then drawing a bull's-eye around where they have landed.

There therefore seems to be a good deal of confusion, even schizophrenia, in the process of the English Reformation. But also much of the religious landscape of the English Church in the sixteenth century can appear very much more in tune with the Calvinist reformations of the continent than with later 'Anglican' ideals. There is, for example, the iconoclasm perpetrated under Henry, Edward, and Elizabeth (and enshrined in the official Homily against the Peril of Idolatry) and the ubiquitous virulent anti-Catholicism, with denunciations of the Pope as Antichrist by all levels of the clergy from parish preacher to archbishop of Canterbury. The Edwardian reforms, in which the foreign divines Peter Martyr and Martin Bucer (who both held professorial chairs) were involved, tied the Church of England very obviously to the orbit of the Reformed Churches abroad (which was unquestionably the vision and intent of Thomas Cranmer). We can also point to the pervasive influence of foreign Reformed Protestantism in the Elizabethan Church. This is visible in many areas—not least in the extraordinary popularity of the metrical psalms in the English Church that seem to breathe the spirit of Geneva. It can be seen further in the number of Elizabeth's first bishops who had strong links with Zürich, and the official promotion of two notable works: the *Decades* of that city's most famous divine Heinrich Bullinger (to be studied by all non-preaching parochial clergy every week by order of Archbishop Whitgift in 1586), and the Heidelberg Catechism (a staple of university teaching from the 1590s onwards). It is also evident in the prominence of Calvinist predestinarian doctrines in the universities, and the extraordinary popularity in England of the works of Calvin and of the Heidelberg divine Zacharias Ursinus.[4] The Church's Reformed identity would seem to be encapsulated in the attendance

---

[4] D. MacCulloch, 'The Myth of the English Reformation', *Journal of British Studies*, 30 (1991): 1–19; A. Milton, 'The Church of England and the Palatinate, 1566–1642', in P. Ha and P. Collinson (eds.), *The Reception of Continental Reformation in Britain* (2010), pp. 139–42.

of an official British delegation of churchmen at the international Reformed Synod of Dort in 1618–19. All these features of the early Church of England and its reformations seem very remote from the conservative, undogmatic, and non-confessional moderation of the English Church's supposedly unique and exclusive 'via media' between Rome and Protestantism beloved of so many later Anglicans, and which could seem rather more visible as the seventeenth century progressed.

This apparent discontinuity in the Church of England's religious character between the sixteenth and seventeenth centuries has prompted a variety of responses from Anglicans over the years. For nineteenth-century Tractarians, the easiest solution was to disown the chaotic sixteenth-century Reformation altogether, to treat the seventeenth century as the beginning of the true 'specific genius of Anglicanism', and to create bodies of sources from the later period (in the shape of the Library of Anglo-Catholic Theology) that could be taken to speak for 'true' Anglicanism. Working very much in this spirit, P. E. More explained his decision to focus his own later collection of sources entitled *Anglicanism* (1935) on the period 1594–1691 because 1594 marked the publication of the first four books of Richard Hooker's *Ecclesiastical Polity*, when 'first the Anglican Communion was made aware of itself as an independent branch of the Church Universal...with a positive doctrine and discipline of its own and a definite mission in the wide economy of Grace'.[5] Where More's marginalization of the Reformation and the Elizabethan Church was conscious but implicit, Victorian Anglo-Catholics were prepared to condemn them more directly. John Keble reflected that the reformers were 'of the same class with the puritans and radicals' and Hurrell Froude denounced even John Jewel (the author of the semi-official defence of the Elizabethan settlement—the *Apologia pro Ecclesia Anglicana*) as 'what you would call in these days an irreverent Dissenter', remarking that Jewel's book itself 'disgusted me more than any work I have read'. Nevertheless, certain features of the sixteenth-century Reformation such as the Prayer Book were still regarded as central to the Anglican tradition, although this was a salvaging exercise among acceptable fragments of the Tudor reforms.[6]

A different approach has been to embrace the Reformed aspects of the sixteenth-century English Reformations, to see these as the mainstream and indeed normative position of English Protestantism, to highlight foreign Reformed influences on the English Church, and to treat seventeenth-century developments—and the Laudians in particular—as an illegitimate move away

---

[5] P. E. More, 'The Spirit of Anglicanism', in P. E. More and F. L. Cross (eds.), *Anglicanism* (1935), p. xix.

[6] P. B. Nockles, 'A Disputed Legacy: Anglican Historiographies of the Reformation from the Era of the Caroline Divines to that of the Oxford Movement', *Bulletin of the John Rylands Library*, 83 (2001): 121–67 (pp. 129–33); P. B. Nockles, *The Oxford Movement in Context* (Cambridge, 1994), pp. 127–42.

from a true Reformed Church of England. This approach is visible in nineteenth-century Evangelical readings of the Reformation, and was enshrined in the publications of the Parker Society (to which the Library of Anglo-Catholic Theology was a belated response). It has been partly echoed in more recent historical works that have emphasized the degree to which puritan people, ideas, and practices played a central role in the Elizabethan and Jacobean Church and state.[7] Thus Patrick Collinson has written that 'It is hardly an exaggeration to say that it [puritanism] was the real English Reformation.'[8] In a sense, this approach is compatible with the Tractarian view in assuming that the sixteenth-century Church of England can be claimed for Evangelical churchmanship, and that the Laudian 'Caroline divines' of the seventeenth century marked a significant and elemental break from the Church of the English reformers. This is in some ways to turn puritanism into the 'Anglican' mainstream, and indeed some historians have even referred to 'Anglican Puritans' or 'Puritan Anglicans'.[9] Extending this puritan dominance into the Jacobean Church has enabled these historians to imply its normative status, so that the world of Laudianism can be portrayed as a strange and disastrous aberration that disrupted a settled 'Puritan Church'.[10]

A third approach, more typical of pre-Tractarian High Churchmen and of much historical scholarship of the twentieth century, has been to claim both the sixteenth and seventeenth centuries for 'Anglican' history by discerning distinctive 'Anglican' values throughout both centuries, which can be juxtaposed with 'puritan' ones.[11] These essential 'Anglican' values are seen (variously) as instinctive moderation and compromise, attachment to a 'middle way', respect for antiquity and continuity, a concern for order, and a reluctance to follow aspects of continental Protestantism. These values are then discerned in the Prayer Book and Ordinal, in some of the Homilies, in the retention of bishops and church courts, and in other of the more conservative aspects of the various settlements. The continuity of such values within the Church of England is traced via a series of selective and indeed proleptic readings of the works of Thomas Cranmer, Nicholas Ridley, John Jewel, and Matthew Parker. A continuity is thereby traced though the Henrician, Edwardian, and Elizabethan Reformations. This is a reformation defined not

---

[7] Nockles, 'Disputed Legacy', p. 160; P. Collinson, *The Religion of Protestants* (Oxford, 1982); C. H. and K. George, *The Protestant Mind of the English Reformation, 1570–1640* (Princeton, NJ, 1961); A. Ryrie, *Being Protestant in Reformation Britain* (Oxford, 2013).

[8] P. Collinson, *The Reformation* (2003), p. 117.

[9] A. G. Dickens, *The English Reformation* (2nd edn., 1989), p. 368; C. Russell, 'Introduction', in C. Russell (ed.), *The Origins of the English Civil War* (1973), p. 23; P. Christianson, 'Reformers and the Church of England under Elizabeth I and the Early Stuarts', *JEH*, 31 (1980): 463–82.

[10] Dickens, *English Reformation* (2nd edn., 1989), p. 362; Collinson, *Religion of Protestants*, p. 90.

[11] Nockles, 'Disputed Legacy', pp. 126–8, 134–62.

so much by doctrine as by temperament and national character. Thus, writing in 1964 (and restating this position in 1989), the distinguished historian of the English Reformation A. G. Dickens argued that, during the first half of the sixteenth century, the English were 'groping their way toward a Reformation of compromise and detachment... because these attitudes come naturally to the English temperament'. Dickens was emphatic in seeing 'the genesis of Anglicanism' in the 1530s rather than with Elizabeth and the 1559 Prayer Book. Henry VIII's reluctance to tie his church simply to Lutheranism thus became emblematic of an instinctive English 'middle way'. The idea that Henry VIII established a 'middle way' that shaped the future history of the Church and is traceable in later monarchs continues to be surprisingly tenacious in the work of some historians.[12] And this is a 'via media' that expressed an inherent national distaste for and temperamental aversion to (or even incapacity for) religious confessionalism. As Dickens wrote: 'As a people we have scarcely grasped the deepest implications of either Catholicism or Protestantism; we have tended to avoid the peaks and the abysses of both, and our greatest men have seldom found it easy to operate within the framework of either.'[13] Any elements of ambiguity, or the use of a language of a 'via media' in different settlements, can therefore be seized upon as either meaning essentially the same thing, or at least as being expressive of the same fundamental mindset, and it is implied that to use the term 'middle way' is itself distinctive and emblematic of English religion. Inconsistency, for example, is more consistently read as 'studied ambiguity'. This is often combined with the treatment of Erasmus as an honorary reformer and member of the Church of England: the official injunctions of Edward VI and Elizabeth that his *Paraphrases on the New Testament* should be kept in churches are seen as evidence that the Church of England was the natural home of his perceived theological and temperamental moderation. Erasmus's rhetorical vocabulary of peace, unity, and moderation (no matter how aggressively deployed in practice) is then seen as emblematic of 'Anglicanism'.[14]

In this schema there is therefore no break in thinking in the 1590s. Richard Hooker is seen as being in a clear line of descent from Cranmer and Jewel, restating rather than inventing 'Anglicanism'. Elizabethan and Jacobean Calvinism tend to be sidelined, with English participation in the Synod of Dort either ignored or seen as being reluctant and irrelevant. While this third

---

[12] Bainton, *Reformation*, pp. 208–9; G. Bernard, *The King's Reformation: Henry VIII and the Remaking of the English Church* (New Haven, CT, 2005); G. W. Bernard, 'Henry VIII: Catholicism without the Pope?', *History*, 101 (2016): 201–21 (p. 221).

[13] Dickens, *English Reformation* (1st edn., 1964, pp. 181–2; 2nd edn., pp. 205–6).

[14] R. H. Bainton, *Erasmus of Christendom* (New York, 1969), p. 279; H. R. Trevor-Roper, *Catholics, Anglicans and Puritans* (1987), pp. 42–9, 189; G. D. Dodds, *Exploiting Erasmus: The Erasmian Legacy and Religious Change in Early Modern England* (Toronto, 2009), esp. pp. 1–4, 76–7, 91–2, 223–6, 264–8.

approach differs from the Tractarian approach by its emphasis on the integrity of the sixteenth-century reformations, and its sense of continuity with the Henrician Reformation in particular, it does still sometimes encompass the idea of evolution, and the sense that an Anglican tradition was in the process of being worked out and refined, its implicit principles being fully realized over time. As Florence Higham wrote: while Elizabeth's settlement initially 'seemed... merely an expedient', the seventeenth century saw 'the emergence of Anglicanism as a living way'.[15]

A further twist to this third 'Anglican' approach may be observed among some recent historians who, struggling to find 'Anglican' moderation in the Elizabethan Church and political elite, have discovered it instead in the ways in which people on the ground muddled through, compromising and working together to avoid harmful religious division. This emphasis on avoiding dogma and embracing toleration then takes a step further to become a distinctively 'Anglican' approach. It can therefore be found in villages where English 'folk' adopted an instinctively tolerant syncretic approach towards religious divisions which is equally infused with an essential 'Anglicanism' (even if the term is not used directly).[16] This sort of 'Anglicanism' is mostly used by historians in either implicit or explicit juxtaposition with the divisive dogmatizing force of 'puritanism'. It presupposes an essential unity and coherent identity among those opposing 'puritanism', with the latter thereby representing an un-English dogmatism which ultimately reached its pre-ordained and de-legitimizing end in Dissent, after an unwarranted and violent seizure of power in the 1640s and 1650s.

The problem with all these three approaches is that each one assumes that there is a distinctive orthodox English Protestant position in the years before 1662 which can be identified and its adherents traced. All rely upon the idea that there was a high-point of 'Anglican' orthodoxy from which later developments represented a regrettable decline (thereby serving to de-legitimize other trends within the Church). In this volume, studying patterns of religious identity and practice in the period between the early Henrician Reformation and the Restoration, all the contributors have tried as much as possible to avoid using the terms 'Anglican' and 'Anglicanism' altogether when discussing religious views and practices in the period, as such words imply that the Church of England had a specific, settled identity (that people were either groping towards, achieving, or seeking to re-establish) whereas in fact no such thing existed. As Kenneth Fincham has pointed out, 'bar a few separatists, all English Protestants were "Anglican" before 1642, members of an inclusive

---

[15] F. M. G. Higham, *Catholic and Reformed* (1962), p. 1; Nockles 'Disputed Legacy', pp. 148ff.
[16] N. Jones, *The English Reformation* (Oxford, 2002); C. Marsh, *Popular Religion in Sixteenth Century England* (Basingstoke, 1998), esp. pp. 212–13.

national Church'.[17] This is not to suggest that questions of where orthodoxy lay, or what was the authentic and representative voice of the Church of England, were not important issues to contemporaries. Rather, it is to suggest that it is the struggle between competing claims in this period that should itself be the object of historians' attention, with the historian's task being to understand the struggle itself, rather than to adjudicate between the different sides on the basis of a preconceived notion of what should be considered orthodox or authentic English Protestantism.

Several chapters of this volume tackle the identities and roles played by contrasting religious groups in the Church of England's development. Peter Lake insists that puritanism must be part of the story of 'Anglicanism'. This is partly because puritans could see themselves as (and in the Elizabethan period often were) central to the political establishment, and because their competing claims to orthodoxy and the mainstream deserve respect. They were not trying to subvert the established national Church but to take it over, and to pursue their ideals within it. And even senior figures in the national Church were implicated in the puritan thought-world: not only was Archbishop Grindal a famous advocate for puritans and their activities, but as late as 1597 Archbishop John Whitgift had to reprimand his fellow archbishop Matthew Hutton of York (dubbed 'a puritan bishop' by Lake) for following the puritan practice of using the word 'Christ-tide' rather than Christmas in a letter to the Privy Council.[18] But in addition, and more fundamentally, Lake argues that the anti-evangelical positions often associated with later 'Anglicanism' themselves emerged as part of a tense dialectical relationship with puritanism. Indeed, he claims that this anti-puritan position was first fully articulated by its puritan opponents. That is not, of course, to say that the wellsprings of these forms of piety and religion were located in a polemical relationship, but rather that the non-puritan position was articulated, explained, and justified often in explicit dialogue with a puritan opposite. In other words, as an image of error and deviance, puritanism functioned as a 'defining other' that could help to formulate a positive conformist vision: it clarified non-puritan identity, and helped thereby to discredit (in conformist eyes) certain forms of religious argument, language, and behaviour, rendering them supposedly incompatible with the Church's orthodox religion.

Peter McCullough's chapter considers the usage of the recently coined term 'avant-garde conformity' to define forms of enhanced ceremonialism and anti-puritanism, associated most notably with Lancelot Andrewes and Richard

---

[17] K. Fincham, 'Introduction', in K. Fincham (ed.), *The Early Stuart Church* (Basingstoke, 1993), pp. 3–4.

[18] M. M. Knappen, *Tudor Puritanism* (Chicago, IL, 1965), p. 302n; P. Lake, 'Matthew Hutton: A Puritan Bishop?', *History*, 64 (1979): 182–204.

Hooker in the last decade of Elizabeth's reign and the first decade of James I. This term has been developed recently to distinguish the more enthusiastic and ideologically charged ceremonialist churchmanship of these clergymen from the low-key defence of the Church, based on the pragmatic acceptance of 'things indifferent', by earlier conformists such as John Whitgift. The 'conformist' position expounded by Whitgift and others lacked (as Lake comments) any 'spiritual and affective core'. The term 'avant-garde conformity' enables scholars to identify this newly emergent style of churchmanship while resisting any temptation to define its enhanced ceremonial emphasis as 'Anglican' (or to use the term 'Laudian' inappropriately to describe the pre-1630s period). The distinction between different types of 'conformist' also of course helps to challenge the more fundamental assumption that the defences of the Established Church constitute a single common and identifiable 'Anglican' thought-world stretching in a continuum from Cranmer through Jewel to Hooker and Andrewes. That being said, as McCullough notes, this 'avant-garde' position did not come out of nowhere: there were 'pockets of sentiment and practice' that anticipated these concerns, but they lacked the combination of favourable social and political circumstances that could facilitate their open expression and wider imitation. Such circumstances emerged and began to be exploited more in the 1590s (and much more fully in the Laudianism of the 1620s and 1630s). McCullough provides a valuable corrective in reminding us that Andrewes (so often associated with the Jacobean court) was as much an Elizabethan figure as Hooker. The more that we locate these trends unambiguously in the Elizabethan Church, the more difficult it becomes to brand them and later Laudianism as illegitimate (as opposed to contested) later readings of the Church of England. That being said, it would be wrong to treat 'avant-garde conformity' as inherently orthodox, and it is important to resist the Tractarian model in which Hooker helps Anglicanism to discover its own identity. As Lake has noted elsewhere, the combination of anti-Calvinist and ceremonialist views that found their voice in the 1590s did not carry all before them—indeed, as events changed they were forced to beat a chastened retreat for the time being.[19] This was a 'moment' that failed, but its time came again, with different inflections, in the Laudianism of the 1630s.

While there is no separate chapter on Laudianism in this volume, it should be clear from the foregoing discussion that, while key features of Laudianism (high church ceremonialism, vigorous clericalism, and the doctrinal repositioning of the Church vis-à-vis Rome and Reformed Protestantism) clearly marked a significant departure from the style and content of dominant modes of Elizabethan and Jacobean churchmanship, it nevertheless reflected a novel

---

[19] P. Lake, 'The "Anglican Moment"? Richard Hooker and the Ideological Watershed of the 1590s', in S. Platten (ed.), *Anglicanism and the Western Christian Tradition* (Norwich, 2003), pp. 91–112.

rethinking, highlighting, and extending of what had been pre-existing features of a pluriform English Reformation. Nor was Laudianism a bolt out of the blue. Rather, it built upon 'avant-garde conformist' emphases stretching back to the 1590s, and even older anti-puritan attitudes. It was in part a reaction against the integration of more evangelical modes of religion into the Church of England, and against the perceived damage that they were doing to the worship and institutions of the Established Church. As Lake says, both the public representation and polemical defence of Laudianism were a 'culmination of a dialectical process of challenge and response' with puritanism. To try to exclude it from English Protestantism is as unwarranted as to attempt to exclude puritanism itself.

'Anglicanism' is often assumed to have been distinctive in its view of the past and its use of tradition. Later Anglican commentators have often been tempted to read off these distinctive views from the polemical tactics and conservative survivals of the Tudor reformations, and to see them as being encapsulated in John Jewel's famous 'challenge' to his Roman Catholic opponents in which he laid claim to the authority of the primitive Church. Certainly, Tudor divines always combined to some degree the Protestant principle of *sola scriptura* with a respect for the testimony of the Church Fathers. Indeed, patristic proof-texts were always an important element in printed religious controversy with the Church of Rome. But such appeals to patristic testimony were not simply expressive of a distinctive English Reformation that was bent on preserving continuity with the past, nor were they the intellectual foundations of the preservation of medieval ecclesiastical government or liturgical forms. As Jean-Louis Quantin shows in his chapter, the English reverence for patristics was not notably different from that embraced by continental scholars. Jewel's famous challenge sermon in which he promised to yield to his Catholic opponents if they could provide clear evidence from Scripture, the Fathers, or early general councils to support a series of Roman Catholic positions, was not the declaration of a distinctive Elizabethan *via media*, but reflected the methods and scholarship of the continental divines among whom Jewel had been living in the immediately preceding years. Indeed, it is easy to find hardline Dutch Calvinists writing fifty years after Jewel who deploy a very similarly worded challenge against Roman Catholic opponents.[20] Moreover, Jewel's appeal was specifically for a revival of the purity of the primitive Church; he was not invoking a line of continued institutional succession. In the early seventeenth century, patristic study was just as prominent in the Rhineland Palatinate as it was in England; it was the uses to which it was put, and the status that it was accorded, that changed in

---

[20] Sibrandus Lubbertus, *De Principiis Dogmatum Replicatio* (Franeker, 1608), pp. 124–6, 299–300, 501–2, 527–8.

the seventeenth-century English Church. This is one of those areas of English religion where distinctive developments would appear to have taken place from the 1620s onwards. It was then that the idea of the Church of England as a 'primitive Church' started to acquire significantly different emphases and interpretations in some eyes, with more importance attached to apostolic traditions and an insistence that the Fathers, rather than modern divines, should form the foundation of theological study. And even then, the Huguenot theologian Jean Daillé's scepticism towards patristic authority may be discerned among the denizens of Great Tew, who are often seized upon in other contexts as emblematic of the liberal theology at the heart of 'Anglicanism'. As Quantin argues, it was only in the Restoration period that the use of antiquity as a basic yardstick for the interpretation of Scripture and ecclesiastical practice became fundamental to the Church of England's self-identity and that divines created 'a distinctly English theory of the appeal to the fathers'.[21]

A similar trajectory may be observed in English Protestant views of the medieval Church. A sense of dissociation from a corrupt medieval past was central to the Protestant self-image and, as Bill Sheils explains in his chapter, the most influential semi-official history of the church—John Foxe's famous *Actes and Monuments* (or 'Book of Martyrs')—provides a narrative where the national Church emerges from a succession of earlier true believers who were persecuted by the establishment. As Sheils observes, this could be problematic: Foxe's strictures against medieval error and the misdeeds of bishops could easily carry implicit condemnations of aspects of the Elizabethan Settlement and the behaviour of the current episcopate. Generally, though, Foxe's history dwelt in uneasy coexistence with other defences of the Church of England which emphasized its institutional continuity with the past (against Roman charges of schism and novelty). Archbishop Matthew Parker sponsored the *De Antiquitate Britannicae Ecclesiae et Privilegiis Ecclesiae Cantuariensis* (1572) which provided an account of all the past archbishops of Canterbury while demonstrating the continuity of the rights that they had enjoyed. Nevertheless, he also offered patronage to John Foxe, and indeed the *De Antiquitate* and the *Actes and Monuments* were published by the same man—John Day.[22] Some divines sought to locate Protestant doctrines in the medieval Church as a way of validating the search for institutional continuity and thereby reconciling these divergent tendencies. Other divines, however, increasingly sought to celebrate the devotional life and authority of the medieval Church, and to see the medieval centuries as models for contemporary emulation. We can also see this in the writings of nostalgic antiquaries and historians such as John Stow and William Camden, and later William Dugdale, where this tendency was combined with strong attacks upon the iconoclasm and sacrilege of the

---

[21] J.-L. Quantin, *The Church of England and Christian Antiquity* (Oxford, 2009), pp. 312–95.
[22] M. McKisack, *Medieval History in the Tudor Age* (Oxford, 1971), p. 44.

early Reformation. But it was among the Laudian divines that this tendency became most pronounced, and that these two ways of looking at the past—focusing on either doctrinal succession through a minority of true believers (often laypeople) or institutional succession through the medieval Church—were increasingly seen as incompatible.

The assumption that from the outset the Church of England had a distinctive reverence for the past has partly arisen from the undoubted fact that its sixteenth-century reformations still preserved significant elements of the structure of the pre-Reformation Church—notably in the shape of the canon law, church courts, and episcopacy. But, as Gerald Bray's chapter reminds us, this was often the result of inertia and the quirks of Tudor political history rather than of principled choice. The reformation of canon law (the *Reformatio Legum Ecclesiasticarum*) drawn up by Cranmer's committee failed to be formally approved due apparently to short-term political factors. It is especially ironic that the Church that was born out of Henry VIII's marital problems should thereby become the only Protestant Church in Europe to include no provision for divorce. The persistence of canon law was not unique to England, but in other countries it was usually blended into the law of the state. The continued independence of canon law from the common law in England made for long-term tensions, and unresolved arguments over the independent authority of Convocation and the legitimacy of canons passed therein. As in other areas of ecclesiastical government, the Jacobean Church witnessed a notable revival of canon law, as what was initially an unintended survival became the possible basis for the restoration of the fortunes of the ecclesiastical authorities. Indeed, Helmholz has argued that the late Elizabethan and early Stuart period was one of the greatest ages of 'flourishing canonical and civilian scholarship' in English history.[23]

The persistence of medieval administrative structures, as Andrew Foster's chapter demonstrates, was more a matter of accident than design. There were recurring proposals for the rationalization of the government of the English Church throughout this period. Elizabethan schemes include a plea for the establishment of 150 bishoprics, and proposals for a system of auxiliary superintendents (in effect, revived rural deans) who could exercise jurisdiction and preside with the bishop over diocesan synods (annual diocesan synods were proposed in the *Reformatio Legum Ecclesiasticarum*).[24] These were not simply manifestations of puritan opposition to the Established Church, but were more general reform programmes. In this respect, the upheavals of the 1640s can also be seen, not as a sudden attack on an established ecclesiastical system, but as the latest round in an ongoing struggle over the precise balance

---

[23] R. H. Helmholz, *Roman Canon Law in Reformation England* (Cambridge, 1990), p. 49.

[24] P. Collinson, *Godly People: Essays on English Protestantism and Puritanism* (1983), pp. 170–4, 181–2; G. Bray (ed.), *Tudor Church Reform* (Woodbridge, 2000), pp. 351–3, 365–9.

between secular and ecclesiastical forces in that Church, and the role that the ecclesiastical hierarchy should perform. Moreover, the persistence of medieval administrative structures also hides significant changes in the position of the clergy that took place in the first century following the Henrician Reformation. While the Erastianism of the Henrician Reformation—with the extraordinary powers exercised over the Church by the layman Thomas Cromwell as the king's 'vicegerent in spirituals'—is well known, it is less often appreciated that Elizabeth's reign (so often seen as marking the establishment of Anglican tradition) represented in some ways a high-water mark of the exclusion of the clergy from secular affairs. Elizabeth was still happy to give ecclesiastical posts to laymen, who were serving as deans as late as 1596. The restoration of the rights and privileges of the Church and clergy (as Bray and Foster argue) was very much an early Stuart development, reflected partly in the rising number of bishops serving on the Privy Council and the enormous increase of clerical justices of the peace. This retrenchment can also be observed in the rise of 'divine right' arguments for tithes and episcopacy from the 1590s onwards in the writings of a broad range of divines (not just avant-garde conformists). Yet it is not self-evident that these changing definitions and rationalizations of episcopacy were the inevitable or natural expression of an 'Anglican' norm, of an 'Anglicanism' discovering itself. Nor is it clear at what point in the first century following Henry VIII's Reformation we should judge clerical power in the Church of England to have reached its natural, normative position.

Of course, there were prominent physical remains of the medieval past in the post-Reformation Church of England, most notably in the shape of the cathedrals. But again, it is not evident that their mere survival is evidence itself of a distinctive Anglican reverence of and desire for continuity with the past. As always, there is a danger in seizing on anything in the Church of England that is different from other European reformations and imbuing it with especial significance as the key to explaining England's divergence from continental norms (and in fact there are instances where collegiate churches abroad survived the Reformation with their chapters, canons, and secular authority intact—Utrecht provides a striking example).[25] Certainly, the idea that cathedrals could have no function in a properly reformed Protestant Church was not necessarily accepted by contemporaries: Patrick Collinson and Julia Merritt have noted the role that a prominent cathedral like Canterbury and the pseudo-cathedral of Westminster Abbey could play as centres of preaching, and have observed the prominence of godly clergy (as well as more high church figures) among their prebendaries.[26] Ian Atherton's chapter builds

---

[25] R. Feenstra, 'Canon Law at Dutch Universities from 1575 to 1811', in R. H. Helmholz (ed.), *Canon Law in Protestant Lands* (Berlin, 1992), pp. 123–34 (pp. 129–30).

[26] P. Collinson, 'The Protestant Cathedral 1541–1660', in P. Collinson, N. Ramsay, and M. Sparks (eds.), *A History of Canterbury Cathedral* (Oxford, 1995), pp. 154–203, esp.

helpfully on this work, agreeing that there was nothing inevitable about cathedrals' association with Laudian high churchmanship (although it was hardly an unnatural development), while also making the intriguing suggestion that the notion that cathedrals embody the Church of England arguably dates more from their desolation in the 1650s. It was their very dissolution that enabled cathedrals to epitomize the pre-war Church and to encapsulate its restoration in the eyes of sympathetic contemporaries and later commentators.

The notion that the Church of England is naturally averse to formal doctrinal definitions and systematic theology is perhaps one of the most resilient features of Anglican self-identity. But, as Stephen Hampton shows in his chapter, the Thirty-Nine Articles were clearly intended as a confession of faith, a formal statement of the Church of England's beliefs, and were perceived as such by all parties at the time. He also demonstrates that on a range of practical and doctrinal issues, the Thirty-Nine Articles show the Church of England to be closer to the religion of Zürich than to that of Calvin's Geneva. That being said, people on both puritan and conformist sides felt that the Articles needed to be glossed further to prevent misreadings. There were regular appeals by conforming Calvinists and puritans alike that the Thirty-Nine Articles be supplemented—most famously in the Lambeth Articles and recurrent attempts to give these an official status. On the other hand, among those who rejected Calvinist readings of the Thirty-Nine Articles, there was an equivalent move to emphasize that the Articles must be interpreted only in the light of the Church's other formularies. These anti-Calvinists maintained that the Church of England's doctrinal position should be derived from the collectivity of the Articles, Book of Common Prayer, Ordinal, and Homilies— and in particular that it was the Prayer Book that should be used to gloss and determine the true meaning of the Thirty-Nine Articles.[27] The insistence that the Church of England's doctrine is contained in the Church's liturgy is a very distinctive one, and it is this argument which has ultimately triumphed among later commentators. Just as some modern historians and theologians have claimed that the English Reformation 'is not...to be primarily appraised in the field of doctrine' because 'its greatest distinction was in worship', where 'the spirit of Anglicanism' truly resides, so it has seemed only appropriate to them that its form of worship should prevail over the Articles as expressing true 'Anglican' beliefs. The inevitable result has been that even recent

---

pp. 156–7, 159, 178–84; J. F. Merritt, 'The Cradle of Laudianism? Westminster Abbey 1558–1630', *JEH*, 52 (2001): 623–46 (pp. 642–4); J. F. Merritt, 'Reinventing Westminster Abbey, 1642–1660: A House of Kings from Revolution to Restoration', *JEH*, 67 (2016): 122–38 (pp. 127–31).

[27] A. Milton, '"Anglicanism" by Stealth: The Career and Influence of John Overall', in K. Fincham and P. Lake (eds.), *Religious Politics in Post-Reformation England* (Woodbridge, 2006), pp. 159–76 (pp. 171–2).

historians can still be found affirming stoutly that the Thirty-Nine Articles are not a confession of faith and claiming that the Church of England was 'a national church unique in the Reformation era', because it did not ground its unity on 'a confessional statement' and was therefore 'a non-confessional church'. Modern Anglicans have been tempted to argue that the Articles should be seen more 'as one strategic lens of a multi-lens telescope through which to view tradition and approach Scripture, than to treat them as the single doctrinal foundation' of the Church of England.[28] But this is merely to replicate one contested early modern reading of the Reformation formularies.

Moreover, if the Prayer Book supposedly represents the 'spirit of Anglicanism', the obvious question is to which Prayer Book does this refer? As Bryan Spinks notes, the Church's liturgy went through a series of changes. In a sense, the conservative 1549 and more Reformed 1552 Prayer Books represented polarities between which English churchmanship oscillated (although, as MacCulloch has commented, there is no reason to assume that Cranmer would not have sought to revise the 1552 Book in due course).[29] Moreover, English churchmen—including those of the most ostensibly conservative variety—continued to toy with ideas of liturgical experimentation in the 1650s and in the discussions over Prayer Book reform in the early 1660s. Few believed that the liturgy should be preserved in aspic.

Judith Maltby has written powerfully of the ways in which the Prayer Book infused itself into the hearts of English parishioners in the Elizabethan and early Stuart Church, but this did not mean that it generated a single distinctive, coherent non-Reformed body of ideas and devotional practices. As Jessica Martin demonstrates in her chapter, English piety was shot through with tensions and ambivalences, but also with a surprising degree of 'eclectic confessional permeability', and she points to a widespread 'combination of Calvinist sensibility and a lively sense of liturgical efficacy in domestic observance'. Isaac Stephens has similarly talked of the 'Prayer Book puritanism' of such devout laypeople as Lady Elizabeth Isham.[30] But Martin rightly warns us not to fall into the trap of implying that the result was an undifferentiated shared piety in which puritanism was effortlessly integrated into a world of shared devotion. If devotional practices were borrowed from other religious traditions, this did not necessarily signify that they carried the same meaning for those who used them, nor need such borrowings reflect an 'Anglican' anti-confessional mindset, or an instinctive syncretism and aversion to the

---

[28] Bainton, *Reformation*, p. 209; Haugaard, 'From the Reformation to the Eighteenth Century', p. 14; L. Weil, 'The Gospel in Anglicanism', in Sykes et al., *Study*, pp. 55–84 (p. 65) and P. Toon, 'The Articles and Homilies', in Sykes et al., *Study*, pp. 144–54 (p. 153).

[29] D. MacCulloch, *Thomas Cranmer: A Life* (New Haven, CT, 1996), p. 618.

[30] J. Maltby, *Prayer Book and People in Elizabethan and Early Stuart England* (Cambridge, 1998); I. Stephens, 'Confessional Identity in Early Stuart England: The Prayer Book Puritanism of Elizabeth Isham', *Journal of British Studies*, 50 (2011): 24–47.

divisions in doctrine and churchmanship that were such a notable feature of English religious life in this period. Puritan piety had its own distinctive inflections, and while personal devotion may not necessarily have been simply shaped by divisions in doctrine and churchmanship, it was undoubtedly informed by those conflicts.

Christopher Haigh has used the term 'parish Anglicans' to describe non-puritan conforming members of the Church, seeing them as the 'spiritual leftovers of Elizabethan England', abandoned Catholics who were not really Protestants at all. While Maltby has provided them with more dignified and positive religious commitment and credentials and rechristened them as 'Prayer Book Protestants', there is still an assumption that they constitute a single coherent group with a common ideology to match (both anti-puritan and anti-Laudian).[31] There is a tendency here to essentialize both the use of the Prayer Book and involvement in parish religion, seeing them as imbuing and embodying specific religious values. As we have seen, Martin cautions us against assuming that there was a simple style of Prayer Book divinity. Julia Merritt's chapter warns against a view of the parish that treats it as the location of an unproblematic and fundamentally stable 'Anglicanism'. Instead, she reveals not a stable continuum of conservative values, but a dynamic, richly diverse, and multi-faceted parochial experience. She reminds us of the political, social, and cultural functions that the parish performed in theory and practice, before turning to the important variables that could shape the nature of Prayer Book worship and other religious activities in the parish. She notes the interplay of different views of what the parish was for with practical considerations that affected the tenor of religious life there, such as the control of the advowson, the churchmanship of the minister, and the role of vestries or leading notables in the parish. Her chapter reveals the tenacity of the parish as the focus of local society that commanded the allegiance and commitment of people of all shades of religious opinion, rather than the resilience of a specific, coherent form of 'parish religion'.

One variable in parochial religious life was church decoration, but here as in so many areas there was an active debate over what precisely was permitted by the Church. The keynote of Felicity Heal's study of images and iconoclasm in the Church of England is ambiguity: the unclear relationship between the emphatic language of the Homily against the Peril of Idolatry and the less specific 1559 Injunctions against 'abused' images. But there was ambiguity too in the status of the spaces in which biblical images were still permitted, such as in domestic settings and the 'quasi-private spaces of homes and chapels' where the private was also on public display. It was in domestic and college chapels that more elaborate decorative schemes were introduced before they partly

---

[31] J. Maltby, '"By This Book": Parishioners, the Prayer Book, and the Established Church', in Fincham (ed.), *Early Stuart Church*, pp. 115–37 (p. 117).

found their way into parish churches. But these were forms of beautification that met a variety of aesthetic and practical needs, and were founded on 'uncertain ideological grounds'. It was the Laudianism of the 1630s that provided a stronger ideological edge and brought this decoration more systematically into public churches. It should be emphasized that, if the Church of England's position on images displayed a certain ambiguity, then this was manifestly not a source of harmony and consensus. As Heal observes, it was the fact that the Church of England neither simply retained nor simply removed images which partly explains why (in contrast to other European countries) English people seem to have been so constantly agitated by the issue of idolatry, which led to a second sustained bout of iconoclasm in the 1640s. Like the uncertainty surrounding the status of the canon law, this ambiguity led to extremes, conflicts, and contestation. If a balance was achieved in the end, it was not by the softening of the English aversion to images, but rather by the abandonment of the more elaborate forms of figurative art amid the 'sober aesthetic' of the Restoration period. Even if the Laudian policy of railed altars became standard in the late seventeenth century, church decoration was more muted, with the lavishly decorated plasterwork and woodwork set against whitewashed walls and plain glass.[32] Church music seems to have followed a similar pattern. The Reformed Protestant style of worship was evident in the congregational use of the metrical psalms that had first established itself in Edward's reign and that became almost ubiquitous under Elizabeth and the Stuarts, with choirs mostly the preserve of the private chapels which had also retained more elaborate church interiors. While Laudianism brought in more elaborate musical settings (exploiting the haziness of the Church's liturgical directions) and provoked an inevitable reaction, the Restoration Church did not generally witness a return to Laudian-style music in most churches. Instead, there was predominantly a more pared-down style of musical accompaniment, although the picture is a mixed one, with organs gradually returning to urban churches and a notable revival of parochial choirs in the countryside.[33]

A plurality of forms and variety of messages can be found even in a text as central to the Church of England as the vernacular Bible. As Lori Anne Ferrell notes in her chapter, John Donne can be found citing six different versions of the Bible within a single sermon. Of these, three were different official vernacular translations (and one a very widespread unofficial one). It was

---

[32] K. Fincham and N. Tyacke, *Altars Restored: The Changing Face of English Religious Worship, 1547–1700* (Oxford, 2007), pp. 317, 347, 350.

[33] A. Ryrie, 'The Psalms and Confrontation in English and Scottish Protestantism', *Archiv für Reformationsgeschichte*, 101 (2010): 114–37; G. Parry, *Glory, Laud and Honour: The Arts of the Anglican Counter-Reformation* (Woodbridge, 2006), pp. 157–70; C. Marsh, *Music and Society in Early Modern England* (Cambridge, 2010), pp. 404–11; N. Temperley, *The Music of the English Parish Church*, 2 vols. (Cambridge, 1979), I, pp. 85–105.

this confused variety that prompted the creation of the King James Bible, published in 1611, but (as Ferrell argues) this was in a sense an attack upon the idea of private scriptural study, with its removal of the marginal notes that were prominent in the unofficial 'Geneva Bible', and a de-emphasis under the Stuart kings on the principle of *sola scriptura*. Even then, the King James Bible was not to the taste of some more hardline Laudian divines.[34]

Multiple and changing readings also characterized how English Protestants understood what was ostensibly one of 'Anglicanism''s most established features—the royal supremacy. Just as Quantin notes the existence of a wide variety of thinking about tradition and the Christian past, so Jacqueline Rose emphasizes the Church's many different interpretations of the power of the 'godly' civil magistrate. And this was true from the very beginning: Rose notes that the principal formularies of the Henrician Reformation—the Act in Restraint of Appeals, Act of Submission of Clergy, and Act of Supremacy—all contradict each other on the location of the royal supremacy and extent of the Church's independent jurisdiction. There was also a surprising lack of clarity regarding the precise authority of the monarch, and the roles of Convocation, Parliament (explicitly regarded by some as the 'body representative' of the Church of England, as opposed to Convocation),[35] and episcopacy. The role of the 'godly magistrate' on the national and local levels was central in the thinking of all religious groups, but this often had very different implications. Again, lack of clarity meant that a very broad range of opinion could feel that law and tradition supported their own reading of the authority of the magistrate, and that was not a recipe for a comfortingly vague agreement to differ, but for endless argument and division. No contemporaries celebrated such lack of clarity as 'studied ambiguity'. All tried to clarify such uncertainties to suit their own vision of the Church.

While different Anglican traditions have chosen to select and highlight very different aspects of the reformation settlements between Henry VIII and the early Stuarts, the decades of the 1640s and 1650s have performed a significant but very different role in histories of Anglicanism. The civil war and its aftermath were accompanied by the abolition of bishops, the Prayer Book, and deans and chapters, the ejection of royalist ministers, and (with the execution of Charles I) the abolition of the royal supremacy. With the removal of these fundamental features of the Established Church, this is seen as a time when the Church of England was temporarily disestablished, surviving underground as a voluntarist movement, its adherents united by their continued

---

[34] For example, Peter Heylyn, *Theologia Veterum* (1654), p. 441.

[35] Henry Burton, *A Tryall of Private Devotions* (1628), sig. M3v; M. P. Winship, *Godly Republicanism: Puritans, Pilgrims, and a City on a Hill* (Cambridge, MA, 2012), p. 72. Cf. canon 139 of 1604.

allegiance to a usurped Church and monarch, and sustained by private Prayer Book services.[36] That is certainly how some contemporary royalists saw themselves, and how the Church's later apologists presented events.

But this is a partial interpretation of what occurred. What happened in the 1640s was initially a further reformation of the Church. The immediate prewar period (1640-2) witnessed discussions across many shades of religious opinion about the reform of church government and ceremonies. When reforms began in earnest in 1643 with the calling of the Westminster Assembly it was initially concerned with a careful and moderate revision of the existing Thirty-Nine Articles. Other reforms, even as they involved a more radical rethinking of liturgy and government of the Church, still emphasized their sense of continuity with the earlier history of the Church of England and its Reformation, as Chad van Dixhoorn demonstrates in his chapter. Members were told that they were continuing the work of Henry VIII and Edward VI as part of a gradual ongoing reformation, and most seem to have believed it. Such has been the Church of England's determination to turn a blind eye towards and to marginalize the reforms of the 1640s that surviving records of the moderate initial changes to the Thirty-Nine Articles made by the Westminster Assembly are still misidentified and misdated, and assumed to be the work of earlier bishops.[37] If these measured deliberations can be read as the work of the Jacobean Archbishop Richard Bancroft, one is left to wonder at precisely which point the Assembly's continuing reforms should be considered to have ceased to be part of the history of the Church of England's ongoing reformation and to have become an irrelevant aberration. W. A. Shaw, writing in 1900, was emphatic that the Westminster Confession which the Assembly produced was 'of little further interest to our national history' because it had not been authorized by Parliament. But the same could of course be said of the 1604 canons, and it is notable that in more recent years Gerald Bray's decision to include the Confession in his edition of *Documents of the English Reformation* does not seem to have raised any eyebrows.[38]

This volume has therefore made a point of including histories of the Westminster Assembly (1643-52) and the Cromwellian Church of the 1650s among its essays, alongside an account of the struggles of episcopalians in these years. If Anglicans have often felt that the religious changes of the 1640s and 1650s cannot be considered to be part of the history of their own Church or as any true 'reformation', this has presumably been because of a number of

---

[36] For example, Haugaard, 'From the Reformation to the Eighteenth Century', p. 20; J. G. A. Pocock and G. J. Schochet, 'Interregnum and Restoration', in J. G. A. Pocock (ed.), *The Varieties of British Political Thought, 1500-1800* (Cambridge, 1993), pp. 146-79 (p. 156).

[37] For example, Lambeth Palace Library, Database of Manuscripts and Archives, Fairhurst MS 3472, fos. 43-4.

[38] W. A. Shaw, *A History of the English Church during the Civil Wars and under the Commonwealth, 1640-1660*, 2 vols. (1900), I, p. 366.

disturbing features which seem antithetical to 'Anglicanism'. These might include the fact that the reformers were an unrepresentative minority going against the conservative religious desires of the rest of the population; the alarming levels of iconoclasm, sacrilege, and destruction; the radical doctrines being expounded; the influence of foreign ideas and practices; the fact that Parliament rather than the Church played a prominent role in dictating religious change; and the intrusion of political events in dictating the shape and momentum of reform at a time of chronic political instability. Yet these were all features of the Tudor reformations too, and if we reject the idea that the Reformation was already complete and 'settled' a century earlier, then it becomes easier to see the events of the 1640s and 1650s as simply a further (albeit dramatic) development in the history of the Church of England. The face of the English Church was certainly altered very significantly by these developments, but this does not mean that the Church itself ceased to exist, or only continued to exist in underground groups. The 1640s and 1650s seem more obviously to represent a puritan takeover of the establishment and a sustained attempt at a magisterial reformation that would reshape the state Church according to the puritans' own precepts. As Ann Hughes comments in her chapter, if we associate the Church of England and 'Anglicanism' with establishment and the legal arrangements through which the national Church operated, then the Cromwellian Church could in a sense be seen as representing the 'Anglicanism' of the 1650s.

Moreover, it is among loyalists of episcopacy and the Prayer Book that we can find the more obvious forms of marginalized behaviour: as they became a persecuted religious minority, so it made practical sense that they adopt the same practices that radical puritans had in the pre-war period, including clandestine, extra-parochial meetings (or what one might term 'episcopalian congregationalism') where forbidden forms of worship were celebrated under the protection of sympathetic gentry and aristocrats. Otherwise, though, as Kenneth Fincham and Stephen Taylor note, episcopalian clergy did not all exist in splendid isolation from the Interregnum Church. Some were involved in county associations with Presbyterian ministers, signing up to articles which included a condition that no one disparage the Westminster Confession, and an acceptance of the claim that groups of ministers (without a bishop) have the power of ordination. And even those episcopalian ministers who did not comply with the authorities still did a good deal of rethinking about the royal supremacy, episcopacy, and the nature of the Reformation. The unusual situation of the 1640s and 1650s, when the normal arbiters of orthodoxy were absent and authoritative institutions had been discontinued, prompted new patterns of thinking among all English Protestants, and not just amid a radical fringe.[39]

---

[39] See A. Milton, *England's Second Reformation* (forthcoming).

This rethinking of the 1640s and 1650s also enables us to problematize the Restoration settlement. Because if the Church of England's identity had not been definitively settled under Elizabeth, and the 1640s and 1650s represented further reformations of the Church rather than its simple displacement underground, then it is difficult to talk in 1660 of a simple 'restoration' of what had been there 'before', or to assume that what emerged in the 1660s was in any ways inevitable or more 'authentic' than some other possible outcomes. Historians have long noted that there were very different settlements that were initially mooted, and in the end this was a very selective 'restoration' (indeed, the very term 'restoration' has itself tended to distort our understandings and memories of the preceding decades). Some significant developments that had flowed from the collapse of the old order, including 'reduced episcopacy' and the innovations in doctrine and worship contemplated or even embraced by royalists in the 1640s and 1650s, were purged from the collective memory of the Restoration Church. And, as Fincham and Taylor note, even though the 1662 Act of Uniformity saw the return of an episcopal system, a modestly revised Prayer Book, and mass ejections of those refusing subscription, those ministers who remained in the Church were a heterogeneous bunch. They included erstwhile Presbyterians or those who had happily cooperated with them, and many who had partially collaborated with the Cromwellian authorities.

If the 1640s and 1650s provide an important and unsettling angle on assumptions about 'Anglican' identity, then other versions of British Protestantism—in Ireland, Scotland, and North America—provide us with an instructive sense of how English Protestantism might evolve in different ways when confronted by different external conditions. Scotland provided both an inspiration and a warning to the godly English and their opponents—of what a further reformation could look like, and of how 'reduced episcopacy' could over time evolve back into a more coercive system of government. The Irish Church was more at the mercy of religious changes imposed from England, but could therefore act as a laboratory for potential English reforms. And as John McCafferty shows in his chapter, it could thereby sometimes anticipate English religious changes. The 1615 Irish Articles—with their incorporation of the Lambeth Articles and condemnation of the Pope as Antichrist—were a model for English Calvinists of how the English Church's doctrinal statements should be supplemented. The 1634 Irish Canons, with their imposition of east-end altars, anticipate the Laudian canons of 1640, and encapsulate the more untrammelled version of Laudianism that was experienced in Ireland. Laudian circles in England sometimes expressed a preference for the First Edwardian Prayer Book, but its restoration was specifically proposed in Ireland, and effectively imposed in Scotland in the shape of the 1637 Prayer Book. On the other hand, Ireland may also have offered partial inspiration for English schemes for 'reduced episcopacy' in the early 1640s proposed by Archbishop Ussher of Armagh, perhaps building on his own experience of accommodating Scottish Presbyterian ministers on a local level.[40] McCafferty also suggests that the defences of the disestablished episcopal Church of England that John Bramhall, bishop of Derry, published in the 1650s may have reflected his experience of belonging to a minority Church in 1630s Ireland.

The New World experience of English people also offered a distinctive spin on English Protestant ideas about the nature of the Christian community, as Michael Winship demonstrates, but it found some intriguing solutions when trying to knock 'large congregationalism' into shape to serve as a form of national Church. As such, it deserves to be studied as one strand in the complex genesis of English Protestant forms of church establishment. But the New World also witnessed a curious variation on more usual Church of England forms in those settlements such as Barbados and Virginia which preserved a parish-based system yet without episcopal supervision. In these cases it was the parish vestries—run by local notables—which were in effective control of local religion: thus even the more apparently conservative forms of Church of England religion had their own distinctive 'New World' character.[41] This part of the world also had its own forms of 'Anglican' survivalism and support for the Prayer Book during the 1650s which may offer fruitful contrasts and comparisons with the episcopalianism discussed in Fincham and Taylor's chapter.[42] As with Ireland and Scotland, New England also provided models (or warnings, depending on one's point of view) of alternative English reforms of Church and society. Indeed, it is impossible to understand English debates of the 1640s and 1650s without an awareness of the looming example of New England (manifested physically in those puritans who returned to the mother country in these years).

Oddly, the one body of historical scholarship where the idea that the Church of England pursued a unique reformation and distinctive style of religion remains stubbornly persistent is among historians of the European Reformation. Volumes covering early modern European history still include maps of the religious divisions of early modern Europe in which 'Anglican' features as a separate religion from 'Lutheran' or 'Calvinist', with its own separate colour.[43]

---

[40] A. Ford, *James Ussher* (Oxford, 2007), p. 243.

[41] J. D. Bratt, 'English, Dutch and Swedish Protestantism in the Era of Exploration and Early Colonization', in S. J. Stein (ed.), *The Cambridge History of Religions in America*, 3 vols. (Cambridge, 2012), I, pp. 219-38 (pp. 221-2).

[42] C. G. Pestana, *The English Atlantic in an Age of Revolution, 1640-1661* (Cambridge, MA, 2004), pp. 57-63, 125-6, 135.

[43] For example, T. A. Brady, H. A. Oberman, and J. D. Tracy (eds.), *Handbook of European History*, 2 vols. (Leiden, 1995), II, back cover; R. Mackenney, *Sixteenth-Century Europe: Expansion and Conflict* (Basingstoke, 1993), p. 196; S. Ozment, *The Age of Reform, 1250-1550* (1980), pp. 373, 417. Contrast D. MacCulloch, *Reformation: Europe's House Divided 1490-1700* (2003), p. 486.

So deeply rooted is this assumption that when Diarmaid MacCulloch's *The Later Reformation in England* (a book which distances itself unambiguously from the notion that there was a distinctively 'Anglican' religion) was published in German translation in 1998, its German publisher insisted on retitling it 'The Second Phase of the English Reformation and the Birth of the Anglican Via Media'.[44] English religious exceptionalism thus appears nowadays to be more of a dictum on the European continent than it does in England itself.

This is particularly strange because, as Diarmaid MacCulloch notes in his chapter, not only was the influence of Zürich decisive in the course of the English Reformation (and many of the Edwardian reforms make the Church of England look like a subset of other magisterial Reformed Churches), but some of the features that are most regularly seen as distinctively 'Anglican' may be observed in other European reformations. MacCulloch identifies several continental equivalents of Henry VIII's ambiguous reformation, while the subsequent English shift away from Lutheranism is also observable in the territories of Archbishop von Wied of Cologne and Countess Anna of East Friesland. The 'sacramentalist Lutheranism' in the litany and Church Order devised by the archbishop of Uppsala, Laurentius Petri Nericius, also reveals notable similarities with the English Prayer Book and the Ordinal.[45] And as Hampton observes, episcopacy was evident not just in Lutheran Churches, but also on the Reformed side in Poland-Lithuania and Hungary, while the Genevan forms of ecclesiastical jurisdiction independent of the civil magistrate were opposed not simply in England, but also in Zürich and elsewhere. If Cranmer aspired towards a 'reformed Catholicity', this was precisely what all the continental reformers sought as well.[46] It was not simply reflective of an instinctive and distinctive English anti-confessionalism to declare oneself to be a 'Christian Catholic' rather than a Protestant, and to reflect that Calvin was only a man and that his words should not be taken as inherently truthful: these are also standard sentiments observable in hardline continental Reformed circles.[47] MacCulloch also finds echoes of the views of Zürich's Heinrich Bullinger even in the writings of the apparently quintessentially English Richard Hooker. These are all useful reminders that we do not need to invoke a unique English mentality when explaining different trends in the Church of England. It is arguably more helpful (and accurate) to see

---

[44] D. MacCulloch, *Die Zweite Phase der Englischen Reformation (1547–1603) und die Geburt der Anglikanischen Via Media* (Münster, 1998).

[45] E. E. Yelverton, *An Archbishop of the Reformation* (1958), pp. 16–17, 83–5, 136–7; D. MacCulloch, 'Sixteenth-Century English Protestantism and the Continent', in D. Wendebourg (ed.), *Sister Reformations: The Reformation in Germany and in England* (Tübingen, 2010), pp. 1–14 (p. 14).

[46] MacCulloch, *Cranmer*, p. 617.

[47] For example, Lubbertus, *De Principiis*, pp. 6, 143; Sibrandus Lubbertus, *De Ecclesia* (Franeker, 1607), pp. 233, 237–8.

elements of English religion within a diverse European spectrum, rather than as uniquely separated from it.

It is also interesting to note the degree to which the supposedly most distinctive features of 'Anglicanism'—such as anti-Calvinist doctrines of grace, and the belief in *iure divino* (by divine right) episcopacy—owe part of their development to the input of foreign divines in the Elizabethan Church. It was the Flemish refugee Hadrian Saravia (later one of the translators of the King James Version) who made some of the most decisive early contributions to the English development of the doctrine of *iure divino* episcopacy (seeing this continuous form of church government from the apostles' time as 'a sacred canon') and who also linked his extreme clericalism to absolutist interpretations of royal authority in a manner that anticipated later Laudian developments.[48] Similarly, it was the Spaniard Antonio del Corro and the French Huguenot exile Peter Baro who led the way in opposing dominant Calvinist doctrines of grace in Elizabethan Oxford and Cambridge respectively, where they ran into opposition from the majority of native English divines who upheld Calvinist orthodoxy.[49] In the Jacobean Church, it was expatriates such as the Frenchman Isaac Casaubon and the ex-Roman Catholic archbishop of Spalato Marco Antonio de Dominis who first expressed the notion that the Church of England was uniquely faithful in its appeal to antiquity.[50] The Church of England's curious constitution arguably enabled certain forms of churchmanship to appear and develop with less impediment than in continental Churches, but the English were not necessarily the first to grasp the opportunities thereby offered.

Arguably what students of 'Anglicanism' need is a more informed sense of the sheer variety of early modern European Protestantism. This should enable English Protestantism to take its place among a dizzying spectrum of ideas and forms of organization, rather than remaining as an outside observer of a continental religious order that is too often assumed to be monolithic. There were significant disparities between the Reformed Churches in forms of church organization and government, Church–state relations, liturgical practices, and in doctrine and piety. As Hampton and MacCulloch observe, it is only if the Church of England is relentlessly measured against the example of Geneva that it seems less Reformed.[51] We have noted how far some supposedly distinctive Anglican elements were actually shared by other continental

---

[48] P. Lake, *Anglicans and Puritans? Presbyterianism and English Conformist Thought from Whitgift to Hooker* (1988), pp. 95–6, 117, 135–9.

[49] N. Tyacke, *Anti-Calvinists: The Rise of English Arminianism, c.1590–1640* (Oxford, 1987), pp. 29–30, 58–60; P. Lake, *Moderate Puritans and the Elizabethan Church* (Cambridge, 1982), pp. 227–42.

[50] Quantin, *Church of England*, pp. 142–54, 397.

[51] P. Benedict, *Christ's Churches Purely Reformed: A Social History of Calvinism* (New Haven, CT, 2002), esp. pp. 116–17, 282–7, 424–6.

Reformed Churches. But the picture is still richer and more interesting than that. In fact, the Church of England was in some ways more 'Calvinist' than the continent. Calvin's works were more popular in England in the later sixteenth century than in any other European country (including Calvin's native France), and it was the famous English divine William Perkins whose writings provoked the most important work opposing Calvinist predestinarianism by the Dutch theologian Jacobus Arminius.[52] As the events at the Calvinist Synod of Dort demonstrated, some European countries had more 'liberal' religious traditions in some respects than those displayed by the English delegates, and their representatives occasionally displayed a greater readiness than the English to accommodate their religious opponents.[53]

Another linked misconception is that the Church of England only differed from the continent in conservative forms of religious worship and government, which should therefore be deemed the sole criteria of 'Anglicanism' and as uniquely orthodox features of the English Church. It is certainly true that there was no shortage of foreign divines who were perplexed by some of these aspects of the Church of England. Not only, though, were defences of bishops and conservative religion not unique to English divines (as we have seen), but there were very distinctive elements of English Protestantism on the puritan side. If we look at what well-informed European contemporaries saw as distinctive of English religion, we find that they were convinced that it was practical divinity. In the 1630s the outside observers Samuel Hartlib (a Polish exile) and John Dury (a Scottish-born international irenicist) were emphatic that this was the case, and saw the active dissemination of this unique form of English religion as the key to international Protestant unity and reform. They racked their brains to find ways of creating for foreign consumption a complete body of puritan 'practical theology' combined with a comprehensive 'body of case-divinity', and arranged for petitions to be sent from foreign divines to the English clergy, pleading for such a work to be produced (although the deficiency would ultimately be supplied by the hundreds of editions of foreign translations of English puritan works).[54] Strict sabbatarianism was another area where the English made a very distinctive contribution. The celebrated Independent divine John Owen complained that hostile Dutch theologians referred to Sabbath doctrine as 'Figmentum Anglicanum', but more sympathetic Dutch clergy consciously embraced English teaching on the issue, and the Dutch Second Reformation (*nadere reformatie*), with its

---

[52] W. B. Patterson, *William Perkins and the Making of Protestant England* (Oxford, 2014), pp. 84–6.

[53] A. Milton (ed.), *The British Delegation and the Synod of Dort (1618-19)* (Woodbridge, 2005), pp. xxxvi–il.

[54] Sheffield University Library, Hartlib MSS 29/2, fos. 20v–21r; 29/3, fos. 19r, 24v, 50r–51r; John Dury, *The Earnest Breathings of Foreign Protestants...for a Compleat Body of Practicall Divinity* (1658).

strong emphasis on practical piety, was profoundly influenced by English puritanism, and by sabbatarianism in particular.[55] Congregationalism was another area of distinctive English religious development. In the early 1640s, the leading Congregationalist 'Independent' divines observed that foreigners granted (as Dury and Hartlib had done) that the 'power of godliness' had been more 'advanced and held forth' in England than on the continent. But they also laid claim to 'that light which the conflicts of our owne Divines (the good old Non-conformists)' had revealed. In other words, the conservative English religious settlement, in generating puritanism, had also generated new and distinctive thinking on church government, and revealed the truth of Congregationalism to the English before continental thinkers.[56] Similarly, it has been suggested that English Presbyterian thought in the 1640s created a unique reading of the Church and church government, different from all foreign Reformed Presbyterian writing.[57]

As we can see, then, to treat as truly 'Anglican' only certain forms of conservative ceremonialism and liberal theology is to look at only a few features of the distinctive religious developments that emerged from the incoherent English Reformation. It also argues implicitly that the more evangelical modes of doctrine, government, and piety promoted by English puritans were 'un-English' and unthinkingly reflective of continental norms, which was manifestly not the case.

As the chapters in this volume demonstrate, to seek to locate 'Anglicanism' within the first 130 years following Henry VIII's break with Rome is a quixotic enterprise. The period was one of multiple reformations, multiple settlements, and multiple trajectories of religious change. This means that different stages of this process can be seized upon to present very different readings of 'Anglican' identity. We began this Introduction with a view of the three prominent approaches to the first century of the Church of England that have adopted starkly different readings of 'Anglicanism' and its early history. One tendency (with the Evangelicals) has been to stress the Reformed aspects of the Tudor reformations as definitive, while another has been (with the Tractarians) to emphasize instead the seventeenth century as the time when 'Anglicanism' truly discovered itself. A third approach (with the pre-Tractarian High Churchmen) seizes upon elements of apparent principled moderation, reverence for the past, and the invoking of a 'middle way' in both the sixteenth and seventeenth centuries in order to trace a continuous

---

[55] C. Mather, *The Life and Death of the Reverend Mr John Eliot* (1694), p. 29; J. R. Beeke, *Assurance of Faith* (New York, 1991), pp. 105–38, 383–413.

[56] *An Apologeticall Narration* (1643), p. 4.

[57] H. Powell, *The Crisis of British Protestantism: Church Power in the Puritan Revolution 1638–44* (Manchester, 2015), esp. pp. 76–7.

tradition of 'via media' Anglicanism. All three of these tendencies are ones into which modern historians of the Church of England sometimes unconsciously (and in many cases only momentarily) drift, even when we eschew the specific word 'Anglican'. All three approaches have plentiful evidence to support their interpretations because of the essentially heterogeneous nature of the English Reformation. Yet none presents an adequate account of the Church of England's identity in the first century of her existence because each seeks to locate a single orthodox identity based upon a selective reading of the evidence. Some Anglicans have seized upon this very heterogeneity as evidence of an Anglican genius for comprehension and felicitous indecision. But this ignores the fact that this variety was generated by (and in itself helped to provoke) conflict and change, rather than emerging from any sort of native taste for principled irresolution. Few contemporaries embraced incoherence, uncertainty, and ambiguity as not only good things, but as inherently 'Anglican' things. This was a period when there was a 'struggle for Anglicanism' in the sense of a combat between many different groups to define what the contested Church of England identity truly was, and where English Protestant orthodoxy truly lay. The modern association of 'Anglicanism' with specific ideas and emphases—conservative, ritualistic, non-confessional, 'moderate'—reflects the triumph of those trends in the Church. We should not, though, read that particular victory and set of associations back into the Church's first century, when their triumph was far from assured, and their preponderance far from self-evident.

2

The Emergence of the Church of England, c.1520–1553

Ethan H. Shagan

When the Act of Supremacy asserted the existence of a 'Church of England' in November 1534, no one knew with any confidence what such a creature was. The statute, with typical Tudor bluster, proclaimed that English kings had always been supreme heads of their Church, so the law was merely 'for corroboration and confirmation thereof'.[1] But this language fooled no one. In point of fact, England had been Christianized by missionaries from Rome around AD 600 and for the subsequent nine hundred years had been an appendage of the Latin Church which called itself *catholic*, or universal. England had occasionally been near the heart of that Church's intellectual development, but, despite all the local variation that was sometimes possible, it had remained dependent upon Rome for its ecclesiastical governance, theology, liturgy, and law. To declare independence from Rome, then, was not unlike the later independence movements of so many colonies in the western and southern hemispheres, striking out boldly into the unknown, conjuring new polities into existence through an unstable combination of idealism and self-interest. But in this case, crown and Parliament conjured not only a new ecclesiastical polity but also, slowly but surely, a new pathway to salvation. The stakes, in other words, were very high.

The temptation to describe the thing they created as 'Anglican' is overwhelming. Such a nomination is technically accurate, both in the tautological sense that the *Ecclesia Anglicana* is Anglican by definition, and in the more substantive sense that most of the later features of Anglicanism can be located embryonically within it. But those elements were not the vital core of the Church of England at its inception, nor did they fit neatly together in opposition to other, competing strands. Rather, as befitting a Church created for largely contingent

---

[1] Gerald Bray (ed.), *Documents of the English Reformation* (Minneapolis, MN, 1994), pp. 113–14.

reasons, different and seemingly contradictory elements made strange bedfellows. A coherent Anglicanism only emerged much later, not through a peculiar genius that distilled core elements from this mixture, but through a very worldly process of negotiation and sometimes naked struggles for power.

The purpose of this first, introductory narrative is to suggest how diverse the Church of England was in its formative years and to delineate the process by which some of its ideas and institutions thrived while others withered on the vine. The resulting Church was not a triumph of compromise or a middle way between competing extremes but rather an unstable compound whose detonation was in many ways inevitable. To see in that Church the origins of Anglicanism is, paradoxically, both unquestionably correct and deeply misguided, something akin to the exercise of throwing darts at a wall and then drawing a bull's-eye around where they land.

The creation of the Church of England depended upon two parallel developments: first, the political revolution of the break with Rome; and second, the growth of a new theological position whose adherents could be counted upon to support that revolution. We shall take each in turn.

The story of Henry VIII's ill-fated marriage to his brother's widow, the Spanish princess Catherine of Aragon, has been told too many times to require much elaboration here. What must be stressed, however, is the intense awkwardness of the relationship between Church and state that made this marriage so complicated in the first place. Like all European monarchs of the early sixteenth century, the early Tudors imagined themselves as God's supremely powerful vicegerents on earth, but in practice they were extremely weak, unable to execute basic functions of sovereignty without securing cooperation from both internal and external competitors. They could not raise taxes without the support of the urban merchants and landed aristocracy, as Henry VIII's abortive attempt to raise the so-called Amicable Grant of 1525 proved. Their kingdom contained a series of holes or gaps, like the Palatinate of Cheshire, where the Tudors were merely feudal overlords rather than monarchs in a modern sense. The clergy and all of their lands lay outside the monarchy's jurisdiction, so not only were kings debarred from taxing clerics or suing them in civil court, but fugitives from royal justice could gain lifelong sanctuary if they escaped to monasteries or cathedrals. And, most important for the current purpose, a great swathe of public law in England—including family law—was the exclusive jurisdiction of the Church, outside common law, parliamentary statute, and royal decree. Thus, after his eldest son Prince Arthur died in 1502, Henry VII was incapable of arranging the marriage of his next son Henry to Arthur's widow without appealing to Rome for a papal dispensation, because under Church law it was illegal (within prohibited degrees of consanguinity, or, more colloquially, incest) and English princes were bound by the laws of Rome.

This condition of overlapping jurisdictions and contested sovereignties was entirely normal in the later middle ages, but normal does not mean uncontested. For generations, the kings of England, France, and Castile, as well as Holy Roman emperors and the republican and ducal rulers of Italian city-states, had fought to win concessions from the Church, considering it offensive to be beholden to a foreign power within their own borders. In perhaps the most famous example, Phillip IV of France had won significant control over ecclesiastical property in the early fourteenth century. But, because Rome was not only a foreign power but also held the keys of St Peter, and what the Pope bound on earth would be bound in heaven, there were limits beyond which temporal rulers usually could not go. Just to cite two infamous examples: the Holy Roman emperor Henry IV and the English king Henry II had both found themselves literally on their knees, begging forgiveness for their interference with the clergy in their realms.

So when Henry VIII found himself in a showdown with Pope Clement VII in 1527, it presented both risks and opportunities. Henry had convinced himself that his failure to produce a male heir was God's punishment for his invalid marriage to Catherine, hence the only solution was an annulment of their marriage, which would free him to take another wife. Clement was unable to grant Henry's request, whatever his own views on the matter, because Rome had just been sacked by Catherine's nephew, the emperor Charles V. This was a dilemma that called for delicacy, but for reasons beyond the scope of this essay—not unrelated to the king's lust for a young woman who was smart enough to refuse to become his mistress, but not smart enough to avoid him altogether—Henry VIII chose a path of confrontation rather than conciliation. The risks of this strategy were manifest: excommunication for himself, interdict for his realm, and deposition by the Pope, just as King John had suffered in the thirteenth century. But the potential opportunity that Henry recognized was the final solution to the problem of overlapping jurisdictions. By having Parliament declare him head of the Church within his realm, and the realm itself an empire subject to no external jurisdiction, Henry VIII could with a single stroke obliterate centuries of awkward and sometimes humiliating compromises between Church and state, while at the same time making him the final arbiter of his own marriage. The political utility of the break with Rome thus spawned the creation of the Church of England.

The statutory basis of the Church was relatively simple. Parliament, at the king's behest, first experimented in 1529 with passing laws to bind the clergy. Encountering little effective resistance, and egged on by the king, they declared in the 1533 Act in Restraint of Appeals that no legal case in England could be appealed outside the realm, thus paving the way for the archbishop of Canterbury to annul the king's marriage without fear of external interference. A year later, the Act of Supremacy formally eliminated papal authority in England and declared that Henry VIII was Supreme Head of something called the Church of England. Out of political expediency, and one man's obsessions, the Church of England had been born. But the relative ease of this legislative process belies the vicious power politics that facilitated it. The majority of the clergy went along because they were bullied, bribed, or blackmailed, and given that it was at least plausible to argue that no overtly theological issues were yet at stake in this jurisdictional battle, relatively few of them could rouse themselves to potentially deadly crises of conscience. In 1530-1, the king threatened the entire clergy of Canterbury province with prosecution for *praemunire*, the crime of obedience to a foreign power, punishable by forfeiture of goods and imprisonment at the king's pleasure; the clergy bought their pardon for around £100,000, a sum comparable to the annual income of the English crown, and effectively apologized for their past obedience to the Pope. In the 1532 'submission of the clergy', the Convocation of Canterbury renounced their authority to make Church law without royal approval and agreed to submit all existing canons to the king's assent; the day they submitted, Thomas More resigned as Lord Chancellor of England, even though his own elevation as the first layman ever to hold that office had been part of the same assault on the clergy that he now opposed. The culmination of this campaign of intimidation was the king's execution in June 1535 of the most outspoken enemies of the break with Rome, a group of Carthusian and Bridgettine monks along with Bishop John Fisher of Rochester. A month before Fisher's execution, the Pope had made him a cardinal, hoping to stop Henry from killing him. It had the opposite effect: Henry joked that instead of the Pope sending a cardinal's hat to England, he would send Fisher's head to Rome.[2]

Yet Henry VIII had virtually no capacity to impose his will without securing at least some cooperation from his subjects. Hence nothing could have come of Henry VIII's machinations against Rome if there had not been at least a quorum of interested parties willing to help him. This quorum came, in significant measure, from people whom we would be tempted to call 'Protestants'. But it is important to stress that the term is anachronistic for England in the 1530s. In Henry VIII's reign, they more often called themselves 'followers of the gospel' or 'gospellers'—Christians hoping to liberate the Bible from its suppression by Rome—and their theology was known to others as 'the new learning' or 'the German heresy'. Historians usually refer to them as 'evangelicals', a plausible modern synonym for gospellers, emphasizing their focus on the *evangelion*, or good news, of the New Testament.[3] The term 'Protestant' existed after 1529, but it was coined in the Holy Roman Empire to describe a

---

[2] *Letters and Papers of Henry VIII*, VIII, p. 876.
[3] See Peter Marshall, *Religious Identities in Early Modern England* (Aldershot, 2006), ch. 1; Diarmaid MacCulloch, 'Henry VIII and the Reform of the Church', in Diarmaid MacCulloch (ed.), *The Reign of Henry VIII: Politics, Policy and Piety* (New York, 1995), pp. 159-80.

political position in some ways nearly opposite from England's gospellers, whatever their theological similarities: 'Protestants' were those who 'protested' against the 1529 Diet of Speyer, which forbade German princes from reforming the Church against the will of the emperor. The point is significant: unlike in Germany, where the religious revolution made common cause with local rulers of cities and territories against imperial authority, in England the same religious revolution made common cause with imperial authority against the local resistance of cities and territories.

The continental Reformation had seeped slowly into England, via the port towns and universities, from 1520 onwards. The young Cambridge don Thomas Bilney, for instance, became a Lutheran by the early 1520s and converted several of his senior colleagues, notably the future bishop Hugh Latimer. Granted a preaching licence in 1525 by the oblivious bishop of Ely, he proceeded to make converts up and down East Anglia, as well as twice being ejected from his pulpit by mobs of parishioners. He was burned at the stake for heresy in 1531. John Frith left Cambridge in the early 1520s to become a junior canon of the new Cardinal College (soon to be renamed Christ Church) Oxford. He was tossed in prison after he participated in a public assembly in the college promoting the new religion; upon release he fled to the continent and personally attended the famous colloquy between Martin Luther and Huldrych Zwingli at Marburg in 1529. He was burned at the stake for heresy in 1533. William Tyndale was converted to the new religion at Oxford, then returned to his native Gloucestershire where he tutored the children of a local squire and preached in the pulpits of Bristol. He was accused of heresy but released, then moved to London where he tried but failed to win the support of Bishop Cuthbert Tunstall for his Bible translation project. All of this occurred before he left, semi-voluntarily, for Cologne in April 1524. He was burned at the stake for heresy in 1536.[4]

All these men shared similar trajectories. They were young university men in 1520, the up-and-coming generation of intellectuals at just the moment when Christian humanism—the previous fad for tenured radicals—yielded to the more dangerous ideas of Luther and Zwingli. They all experienced the excitement and danger of realizing that they had crossed the line dividing reform from revolution, and they all experienced persecution. They not only knew one another, they just as intimately knew their persecutors: men with whom they had studied and dined but who, for whatever reasons, remained loyal to the old religion. The young Turks who debated radical religious ideas at Cambridge's White Horse Inn (nicknamed 'Little Germany') in the early 1520s, for instance, included not only Frith, Bilney, Latimer, and Tyndale, but also Stephen Gardiner, a leading humanist who supported the break with

---

[4] *ODNB*, 'Bilney, Thomas (c.1495–1531)', 'Frith, John (1503–1533)', 'Tyndale, William (c.1494–1536)'; David Daniell, *William Tyndale: A Biography* (New Haven, CT, 2001).

Rome but ultimately refused to step over the line to heresy. As bishop of Winchester, Gardiner would play a role in the executions of many of his former friends. In such a small and inbred intelligentsia as the first generation of the Church of England's leadership, the politics of the Reformation were academic politics writ large.

In the years surrounding the 1534 Act of Supremacy, then, the surviving evangelicals, who had previously been hounded and hunted by Henry VIII's regime, now became its greatest allies, not because Henry VIII considered them anything other than heretics, but because the enemy of my enemy is my friend. In 1533, Thomas Cranmer, a virtually unknown Cambridge don and foreign ambassador, was raised from obscurity to become archbishop of Canterbury because his hatred of the papacy meant that he could be relied upon to support Henry's break with Rome; he brought with him to the primacy the Lutheran ideas he had picked up as ambassador in Germany. A decade later, the king jokingly referred to him as 'the greatest heretic in Kent', but he kept his man in place.[5] For another example, Robert Barnes did hard time in the Fleet prison and was nearly burnt for heresy in 1526; he temporarily escaped that grisly fate by abjuring his beliefs and then escaping to Wittenberg. But by the early 1530s, Barnes was back in England and in the king's good graces; he was employed by the crown as an intermediary and ambassador to the Lutheran princes of Germany, despite the complaints of Thomas More that he was a heretic (which, of course, he was) and he eventually burned for it when the political winds turned against him in 1540. More generally, adherents of the new religion wrote pamphlets supporting the Church of England, and mounted vigorous campaigns against suspected adherents of Rome, making themselves appear the most loyal subjects of a king who valued loyalty above all else, and suggesting as explicitly as they dared that in order to truly achieve independence from Rome, the king needed to banish not only the Pope's authority but also his theology.[6]

Everywhere in Europe, in order for the Reformation to succeed, the reformers had to hitch themselves to a political star. A core feature of the English Reformation, and one that would produce recurrent crises for generations of English Protestants, was that the reformers hitched themselves to the brightest star of all, the new Supreme Head of the Church, the king himself.

If supporters of the new religion had been the only supporters of Henry VIII's break with Rome, things would have been much simpler. But many opponents of the new religion—led by the king himself, who insisted that he hated heresy and remained Defender of the Faith—jumped on the bandwagon

---

[5] Diarmaid MacCulloch, *Thomas Cranmer: A Life* (New Haven, CT, 1996), p. 316.
[6] Richard Rex, 'The Crisis of Obedience: God's Word and Henry's Reformation', *Historical Journal*, 39 (1996): 863–94.

as well. Their reasons included loyalty, ecclesiology, and avarice in roughly equal measure. Loyalty was the lynchpin: it was relatively easy to argue that the king was due the undivided allegiance of his subjects, and it was convenient to support an immanent monarch over a transcendent pontiff, without granting that the new Church of England either could or should innovate in doctrine. Ecclesiology was a harder sell, but it was nonetheless significant to intellectuals raised in the Christian humanism of the previous generation, who already believed that Roman supremacy was a relatively late historical development. But the real innovation was avarice. Within two years of assuming plenipotential power over his Church, Henry VIII had already begun to confiscate its vast wealth for his own treasury, beginning with the smaller monasteries and moving quickly to the greater ones. This was perhaps predictable, but it was a stroke of genius to grant or sell much of this wealth to English laymen, who became literally invested in the success of the Church of England, whatever their theological opinions. The years between 1536 and 1540 saw the greatest redistribution of property in England since the Norman Conquest, transferring much of the Church's wealth to a gentry class whose privileged place in England over the subsequent three centuries was largely built upon this singular act of sacrilege.

Vast numbers of Henrician subjects who considered themselves pious traditionalists thus subsisted in the Church of England, alongside those who imagined the Church of England as an engine to overthrow the old religion. Indeed, part of the success of the Church of England under Henry VIII was that it was virtually impossible not to belong to it. Technically speaking, of course, the English government regarded certain persons as heretics on account of their doctrines (notably denying the real presence of Christ in communion), and it regarded others as traitors on account of their ecclesiastical preferences (notably denying the royal supremacy and maintaining the authority of the Pope). So, in some sense, many people did not belong to Henry VIII's Church of England at all. But, in another sense, virtually all of these people were nonetheless members of the *Ecclesia Anglicana*, in that they attended the services of the Church of England and no other, for there was simply no other to attend. Neither Protestants nor Catholics had as yet alighted upon the idea of separation: there were virtually no priests in England who were not priests of the Church of England, nor were there reformist alternatives for subjects whose priests happened to be traditionalists, nor were there Catholic alternatives for subjects whose priests happened to be reformers. To opt out of the Church of England would have meant, with rare exceptions, either forgoing the benefits of organized religion altogether, or else fleeing into exile (far harder in England than in Central Europe, where competing Churches dotted the landscape). Very few people opted out.[7]

---

[7] Marshall, *Religious Identities*, appendix.

The result was that the 'Church of England' covered a multitude of sins. A reformer who disapproved of the mass he attended might ostentatiously read an English bible as he sat through the elevation of the host, but sit through it he nonetheless did. A Roman Catholic who disapproved of her evangelical minister might protest that the Body of Christ had been desecrated, but nonetheless, since the sacrament worked through God's power rather than the priest's, she took communion anyway and grumbled about it later. All attended the same Church, and they all attended it together. Elsewhere in Europe, different Churches competed for members. In England, different members competed for their Church.

The fortunes of these different potentialities within the Church of England rose and fell with political circumstances. In the first stage, up to 1536, conservatives remained more or less ascendant, because the break with Rome was formally a jurisdictional rather than a spiritual battle. The gentry and nobility in Parliament went along because they saw the potential to limit the power of the clergy. Key members of the clergy went along because, like Bishop Stephen Gardiner of Winchester, they convinced themselves of the king's legitimate authority. Despite the bitter protests of many papal loyalists, who argued cogently that schism would always produce heresy, the Church of England could still be understood as an essentially conservative Church, nearly identical to the Church of Rome except for its administration.

That all changed with a series of nearly simultaneous manoeuvres in the summer of 1536, much to the disappointment of traditionalists who had hoped that the king's vicious destruction of his wife Anne Boleyn in May would herald the end of the English schism. The Ten Articles, the first doctrinal statement of the new Church of England, offered a theological compromise in which the majority of contested Catholic doctrines and practices were retained—like the veneration of saints, the existence of purgatory, and of course the real presence of Christ in the eucharist—but two important innovations were slipped in: a basically Lutheran understanding of justification, and the shrinkage of the sacraments from seven to three. Its most important novelty may simply have been claiming the authority to pronounce doctrine in the first place. The following month, Royal Injunctions were promulgated by Thomas Cromwell, a layman who in July was made the king's 'vicegerent in spirituals'.[8] The Injunctions offered what amounted to a radical interpretation of the Ten Articles, claiming that even those ceremonies allowed by the Articles could not be practised with 'superstition and hypocrisy' and therefore a great deal of the ceremonial apparatus of the Church, including images of saints and non-scriptural holidays, must be eliminated.[9]

---

[8] F. Donald Logan, 'Thomas Cromwell and the Vicegerency in Spirituals: A Revisitation', *English Historical Review*, 103 (1988): 658–67.

[9] Bray, *Documents*, pp. 175–8.

Finally, as backdrop to all of this, royal commissioners fanned out across the country to implement the March 1536 statute that dissolved England's smaller monasteries; by the autumn nearly 250 houses had been dissolved and a huge new bureaucracy called the Court of Augmentations had been created to receive and redistribute the plundered wealth of the Church. An enormous revolt in the north that autumn, euphemistically referred to by the rebels as a 'Pilgrimage of Grace', arose in October, intent upon stopping this revolution in its tracks; rebels attacked functionaries of the Church of England, defended monasteries, and demanded, among many other things, the extirpation of heresy. But their unwillingness to take the decisive step of marching south on London, combined with Henry VIII's duplicity in offering and then withdrawing pardon, spelled doom for the Pilgrimage. By spring, the king had found an excuse to declare martial law and execute scores of traitors; Catholic resistance in the north was crushed for a generation.

It was in the period 1536–8, therefore, that Protestant ideas made their deepest inroads into the official apparatus of Henry VIII's Church. It was in this period that many of the great relics of England's abbeys and cathedrals, like Thomas Becket's bones and the Blood of Hailes, were destroyed by government agents. It was in this period that the eminent preacher and future bishop of Ossory, John Bale, received government sponsorship to produce overtly evangelical plays with titles like *A Comedy Concerning Three Laws of Nature, Moses, and Christ, corrupted by the Sodomites, Pharisees, and Papists Most Wicked*. The high-water mark of this radical vision of the Church of England was the burning of the Franciscan friar John Forest for heresy at Smithfield in May 1538, in a fire fuelled by an image of St Derfel plundered from a Welsh shrine. This was the one and only instance in the English Reformation of a Catholic being burned for heresy.[10] It offered an extraordinary model, implying that the parents and grandparents of every English subject had been servants of Satan, and suggesting that all English subjects who refused to convert to the new religion were at least theoretically heretics themselves and liable to the same punishment. But in practice, the English government proved unwilling to establish this precedent—not even Calvin's Geneva ever came close to such an uncompromising claim—and in the end Forest's burning helped to end the radical phase and inaugurate a conservative reaction.

In November 1538, Henry VIII made this reaction official by personally overseeing the heresy trial of the evangelical John Lambert, who was subsequently burned at the stake. In 1539, at the king's behest, Parliament issued the so called 'Six Articles'—known to reformers as the 'whip with six strings'—which reinforced medieval heresy statutes to ensure that important orthodoxies,

---

[10] Peter Marshall, 'Papist as Heretic: The Burning of John Forest, 1538', *Historical Journal*, 41 (1998): 354–74.

especially transubstantiation, could not be challenged. It appeared that the English Reformation was dead on arrival. But in fact, there was less here than met the eye. Quite apart from the fact that the Six Articles did not result in the wave of heresy prosecutions that reformers feared, it is also noteworthy that much of importance was excluded from the statute. Where, for instance, was the issue of justification by faith versus the efficacy of works? This avoidance of doctrinal niceties contributed to the ongoing ambiguity of the Church of England, and the early 1540s would see a remarkably jumbled Reformation in which, for instance, the mass was kept intact but purgatory was attacked; in which priests could break their vows of obedience but not their vows of chastity; in which the superstitious use of traditional ceremonies was attacked even as the Church re-approved the same ceremonies. Perhaps most distressingly, by slowly chipping away at the medieval Catholic economy of salvation without ever approving a coherent alternative to replace it, Henry VIII's Reformation left his subjects seemingly bereft of any path to salvation.[11]

The Henrician Reformation established a series of patterns and precedents that would later become distinctively 'Anglican'. Among the most important of these were: the integration of the Church into the constitution of the realm; the Church's authority to enforce uniformity in worship; the dual authority of the bishops as simultaneously ordained prelates and officers of the crown; a devout ceremonialism that retained much of the traditional symbolic order of the medieval liturgy; and an abiding self-identification as a scion of the primitive Church of the apostles rather than the Church of Rome. A key point, however, is that these distinctively 'Anglican' features of Henry VIII's Church did not all line up neatly on one side of contemporary religious disputes, but rather could appear intensely incongruous or even incompatible.

Let us take as Exhibit A the writings of that great Anglican hero, William Tyndale. Tyndale's translation of the Bible was banned by royal proclamation in 1530, and Tyndale himself was burned at the stake in 1536. Yet in 1537, less than a year later, the English government gave official approval to the so-called 'Matthew Bible'—so called in a stroke of genius by Thomas Cromwell and John Rogers, who invented the fictitious translator 'Thomas Matthew' so as not to rub the king's nose in the fact that it was the heretic Tyndale's book that he had approved. Clearly, then, Tyndale enjoyed an ambivalent relationship with the Church of England. But an even deeper ambivalence surrounded questions of law and authority. Tyndale's 1528 *Obedience of a Christian Man*—a furious assault on the authority of Rome and a defence of the Christian's obligation to civil rather than ecclesiastical authorities—was slipped into Henry VIII's hands by Anne Boleyn and helped convince him

---

[11] MacCulloch, 'Henry VIII and Reform'.

that he was head of the Church. Two years later, Tyndale's *Answer unto Sir Thomas More's Dialogue* provided an authoritative new answer to the great ecclesiological question raised by the break with Rome—what is a Church if it is not the *Ecclesia Catholica* based in Rome? Tyndale argued that *a* Church is simply a company of Christians gathered together in a particular place—like the Church of Corinth in scripture—and *the* Church is therefore simply the body of such companies, 'the whole multitude of all them that receive the name of Christ to believe in him'.[12] This was to become a quintessentially Anglican position, as was Tyndale's interrelated claim that each particular Church was answerable to civil power and derived its worldly authority from law. Yet at the same time, Tyndale's *Answer* was deeply antithetical to other elements that would later be coded Anglican. He was intensely anti-ceremonial, for instance, stressing that sacraments and holidays were not binding. He wrote, 'we be lords over the Sabbath, and may yet change it into the Monday or any other day as we see need, or may make every tenth day holy... neither needed we any holiday at all, if the people might be taught without it'.[13] He opposed hierarchy in the Church, arguing that all ministers were equally bishops of their congregations. He so opposed the intrinsic authority of an ordained clergy that in one remarkable passage he argued that women could preach and minister the sacraments 'if necessity required'.[14] There was no *intrinsic* incongruity between these positions and Tyndale's proto-Anglican ecclesiology.

Another quintessentially Anglican development in Henry VIII's Church was the spiritual supremacy of each bishop in his own diocese, under the civil authority of the crown but each an heir of the apostles in his own right. This interpretation of the break with Rome was first floated by Bishop John Longland of Lincoln, a doctrinal conservative who, despite his hatred of the new religion, vigorously supported the Church of England on the grounds that he ought to enjoy a plenitude of apostolic authority and he did not want the pope telling him what to do any more than the king did.[15] If one version of Anglicanism would later consist of 'Catholicism without the Pope', and if the post-Restoration Church of England would place episcopal rather than royal authority at its core, then Longland could make a decent claim to be the first Anglican. Yet, at nearly the same time, the staunchly evangelical archbishop of Canterbury, Thomas Cranmer, used very much the same argument to eviscerate the old religion in Kent and replace it with a fully realized Reformed Protestantism. With full apostolic authority, he launched a furious

---

[12] Thomas Russell (ed.), *The Works of the English Reformers: William Tyndale and John Frith*, 3 vols. (1831), II, p. 13.
[13] Russell (ed.), *Works*, II, p. 101. [14] Russell (ed.), *Works*, II, p. 18.
[15] Margaret Bowker, *The Henrician Reformation: The Diocese of Lincoln under John Longland, 1521–1547* (Cambridge, 1981).

and arguably illegal assault on images in churches throughout his diocese, interpreting the law against 'abused' images—i.e. those that had been the object of pilgrimages and extravagant veneration—to effectively ban all images, since, he argued, abuse was inherent in the mere presence of images in worship. As supreme authority over ecclesiastical justice in his diocese, he refused to prosecute reformers who preached salvation by faith alone or denied the real presence of Christ in the sacrament. And as dispenser of ecclesiastical office, he appointed known heretics to positions of power, for instance his own brother Edmund, who as archdeacon personally hacked the arms and legs off the crucifix in St Andrew's, Canterbury.[16]

We think we know with hindsight that a radical Reformation was incompatible with Anglicanism. But at the time, it did not take much imagination to realize that royal supremacy over the Church—especially in the form of a bulldozer of a man who seemed to care not a whit for what anyone else thought—was in fact the *only* form of ecclesiastical governance that might have made genuinely radical reform practicable on a large scale. Tyranny was full of possibilities.

The death of Henry VIII in January 1547 yielded complicated consequences for the Church he had founded. On the one hand, the Church of England headed by Henry's young son Edward VI would prove the high-water mark of the Tudor Reformations and offered a series of precedents and examples for later Protestants. Yet on the other hand, Edward VI's Church of England was just as bedevilled by contradictions and crosswinds as his father's Church had been, and later English subjects who sought either more or less Reformation were equally able to trace their pedigree back to the 'pious imp' King Edward.

With Henry's death and the ascendancy of the new king's uncle, Lord Protector Edward Seymour, duke of Somerset, English Protestants were able to cease their subtleties and equivocations and effectively seize control of the Church. Of course, English Protestants were a diverse bunch, and even many who were hardly Protestants at all saw which way the wind was blowing and asserted the authority of 'the gospel' for their endeavours. There was no unitary agenda. But now the authority of the government was unambiguously harnessed for reformist ends, among the first of which was a vigorous iconoclasm. At the coronation of the nine-year-old Edward, Archbishop Cranmer compared him to King Josiah, the biblical King of Judea who took the throne when he was only eight years old and cleansed God's temple of idolatry. Soon thereafter, the government destroyed the stained-glass windows of Westminster Abbey, the opening salvo of a broad attack on religious images. In Shrewsbury, for instance, royal agents made a bonfire in the marketplace where they burned all the saints' statues from local churches. This official

---

[16] Ethan Shagan, *Popular Politics and the English Reformation* (Cambridge, 2003), ch. 6.

iconoclasm unleashed a wave of unlicensed attacks, as Protestants with undisguised glee released three decades' worth of frustration. So severe were the attacks in London that the Privy Council repeatedly had to restrain overzealous churchwardens.[17]

Concurrent with these attacks on images was a concerted plunder of the grandeur of the medieval Church. Every English parish possessed remarkable treasures, collected painstakingly over centuries to ornament Christian worship. Parishioners had contributed during their lives and at their deaths to help pay for beautiful churches and the fabric they housed: silver chalices and pyxes, carved wooden rood screens and altar pieces, silk copes and chasubles, and much else besides. The break with Rome had already technically made all of this the property of the crown, but it took real Protestant doctrine, redefining so much beauty as the bells and smells of superstition, to convince the crown to seize it. What had taken centuries to build took only a few short years to destroy as government commissioners, abetted by a minority of local Protestants in each parish and sometimes Catholics on the make, packed these treasures onto carts to be melted down or sold for scrap.

A particular target was anything that reflected the doctrine of purgatory, now unambiguously denounced by the Protestant regime as a fraud perpetrated by the Catholic Church to part fools from their money. Most importantly, medieval Catholics had routinely left bequests to the Church to pay for prayers for their souls after death. On a small scale this might mean cash or livestock to pay for temporary interventions, like the popular 'trental' that paid for thirty intercessory masses for the benefactor. On a grander scale it might mean a permanent endowment, funded by land bequests in perpetuity, to pay the salary of a mass priest and even to build an altar or freestanding chapel. All of this property—whether six cows in a barn or a thousand acres of land—was liberated from superstition by absorbing it into the royal treasury.

The reign of Edward VI also witnessed a concerted effort to make the Church of England the vanguard of international Reformed Protestantism. This was a period when the Reformation in Europe looked deeply threatened, and Archbishop Cranmer invited many of the great leaders of the continental Reformation to enjoy their exile in Oxford, Cambridge, and Canterbury. England, previously on the periphery of the Reformation, was now at its centre.

Two other official projects sponsored by Thomas Cranmer attempted thoroughly to transform the Church of England. The first was a new confession of faith, known as the 'Forty-Two Articles', which was perhaps the most systematic and advanced Reformed formulary yet created anywhere in Europe. It is easy to forget that this was such a revolutionary document, not only because its somewhat modified successor, the 'Thirty-Nine Articles',

[17] Diarmaid MacCulloch, *Tudor Church Militant: Edward VI and the Protestant Reformation* (2000).

overshadowed it after 1563, but also because by the 1560s a new wave of more strident Reformed confessions in Europe had already made the Edwardian confession seem tame by comparison. But in fact, with its strong attack on any real presence of Christ in the eucharist, it pushed far past Lutheranism; with its forthright affirmation of predestination, it set the stage for later debates over God's decrees; and with its remarkable article on 'Blasphemy against the Holy Ghost', asserting that opponents of the Reformation were guilty of the unpardonable sin, it at least imagined a future in which Catholics might be violently purged from England.[18] The Forty-Two Articles, however, were stillborn; they were promulgated on 6 June 1553, less than three weeks before Edward VI's death made them moot, and they were never subscribed by the clergy.

A second project was the revision of canon law known as the *Reformatio Legum Ecclesiasticarum*. The *Reformatio* was defeated in Parliament in 1553, despite the overwhelming support of church leaders, because of a political squabble between the bishops and the civil administration of John Dudley, Lord President of the Council. Hence the Church of England afterwards continued to use the old law of the Roman Catholic Church, except where new canons superseded it (as occurred in 1604), or where the old law was 'contrary and repugnant' to the civil laws of England (as when asserting papal supremacy). If the *Reformatio* had been accepted, much of the Church of England's future might have looked different. This would have empowered those who desired further reformation to pursue their goals without the assent of crown and Parliament.[19]

But the most influential and lasting achievement of the Edwardian Reformation was undoubtedly the 1549 Act of Uniformity and its great innovation, the Book of Common Prayer. The new rite was envisioned by its drafters as a progressive first step, a service that eliminated the most egregious errors of the past and helped smooth the way for a thoroughgoing Reformation, even if it still retained, for the sake of order, traditional elements that would ideally be eliminated in the fullness of time. The most significant novelty of the Prayer Book lay not in its content but in its form: it gave the Church of England a liturgy in English rather than Latin, laying bare the services of the Church and implicating the whole realm in a grand new project of communication with God. The Prayer Book was *common* not only in the sense that it was uniform across the country, but also in the sense that it was shared among the community for the common good, and in this sense it was precisely an evangelical project: an endeavour to spread the good news of the gospel.

Yet at the same time, the Act of Uniformity was also necessarily coercive, intended to enforce the new rite upon a conservative priesthood and

---

[18] Bray, *Documents*, pp. 284–311.
[19] Gerald Bray (ed.), *Tudor Church Reform: The Henrician Canons of 1535 and the Reformatio Legum Ecclesiasticarum* (Woodbridge, 2000).

population who, by and large, did not want it. Through the Act of Uniformity, then, the Book of Common Prayer was written into law: every word and gesture acquired binding statutory authority. At a stroke, this transformed the relationship between Church and state in England. It was not sufficient for the clergy to be officers of the crown; now, religious policy became civil rather than spiritual, the stuff of judges, juries, and assizes rather than excommunication and reconciliation. This was, minimally, in significant tension with the notion that common prayer belonged jointly to the people and the broader Protestant programme of what they called Christian liberty. While few in 1549 envisioned the enforcement of every jot—who would really want to drag before a grand jury a minister who performed a marriage with no wedding ring?—the statute introduced a virtually inexhaustible series of legal requirements that could be selectively enforced by authorities with different agendas. Within a year, this tension would become manifest when the famous preacher and controversialist John Hooper, citing conscience and Christian liberty, refused to be consecrated bishop of Gloucester wearing the vestments required by the Book of Common Prayer. Despite Cranmer's willingness to compromise, Bishop Nicholas Ridley of London refused to consecrate Hooper unless he fully conformed; Hooper was thrown into the Fleet prison, and after three weeks of stewing in his juices he reluctantly put on the offending garments and became a bishop, leaving bad blood all around.

Already woven into the first Edwardian Prayer Book of 1549, then, was the great contradiction that would plague all subsequent Acts of Uniformity and their enforcement for centuries: they froze in amber and raised to nearly scriptural status a religious structure that everyone acknowledged to be provisional, conventional, and incomplete. No one regarded the 1549 Prayer Book, or its successor in 1552, as finished; proposals for revision emerged before the ink was dry, sometimes from the drafters themselves. But once enshrined in law, they could be enforced at law, and this enforcement served important ends. To those who regarded the statutes as bulwarks of order against turbulent religious pluralism, strict enforcement became a way to protect the Church from the centrifugal forces that threatened to tear it apart. But to those who regarded the purpose of those same statutes as the emancipation of Christians from spiritual bondage, certain forms of prosecution—especially the use of these laws against godly Protestants rather than their intended target, the superstitious papists—became pharisaical enforcement of the letter rather than the spirit, a rearguard action by the Antichrist to stop the Reformation halfway. Neither of these two sides was doctrinally any more or less 'Protestant' than the other, but their emergent antipathy meant that within a generation, support for the Prayer Book would turn one hundred and eighty degrees, from a mark of radicalism to a mark of conservatism. Both positions—which would evolve into puritanism and conformity—were already present in 1549, and each regarded itself as the authentic position of the Church of England. Indeed, in Archbishop Cranmer's own desire to enforce obedience to the Prayer Book while pushing for revisions, imagining each new version as a gradual unfolding of God's plan to make England ready for the next stage of Reformation, we can see how hard it was to tell these positions apart. Cranmer can legitimately be interpreted as both the first Anglican and the first puritan.

The emergence of the Church of England can thus be envisioned along two tracks—corresponding to the two conditions of political expediency and evangelical zeal that produced that Church in the first place—and it is in the complex interactions between those tracks that we can find the origins of so much later conflict and confusion. The first track was legal and governmental, the emergence of *establishment*, the point of origin for the modern problem of Church and state in the Anglophone world. The Church of England is unthinkable without establishment: the unified church-state or ecclesiastical polity not only structured the conditions under which the Church of England grew but also redefined what a Church *was* around ideals of law and constitution. This track, organized around institutions rather than ideas, cast a wide enough net to pull in people of vastly different doctrinal leanings. The second track was evangelical, the English Reformation as a branch of the movement that began with Martin Luther and reorganized Christianity around salvation through faith, grace, and Scripture. The Church of England is equally unthinkable without evangelical Protestantism: no step in the Church's emergence would have been possible without the dedicated support of ideologically committed revolutionaries willing to risk their lives for their beliefs.

The relationship between these two tracks was so complicated precisely because so many people of so many different stripes hoped or imagined that establishment was God's gift to them. No religious position theologically required establishment; as the subsequent history of English religion down to 1689 would show, virtually every religious group, including 'Anglicans' in the 1650s, was capable of thriving under persecution. But in the early English Reformation, as establishment was invented and honed as a technology of religious governance, virtually every religious position worked productively within its boundaries and sought to be the 'Anglican' Church. As Edward VI lay dying in the summer of 1553, no one could have predicted which would succeed.

SELECT BIBLIOGRAPHY

Bernard, G. W., *The King's Reformation: Henry VIII and the Remaking of the English Church* (New Haven, CT, 2005).

Daniell, David, *William Tyndale: A Biography* (New Haven, CT, 2001).

Davies, Catharine, *A Religion of the Word: The Defence of the Reformation in the Reign of Edward VI* (Manchester, 2002).

Duffy, Eamon, *The Stripping of the Altars: Traditional Religion in England, 1400–1580*, 2nd edn. (New Haven, CT, 2005).

Duffy, Eamon, *The Voices of Morebath: Reformation and Rebellion in an English Village* (New Haven, CT, 2001).

Gray, Jonathan, *Oaths and the English Reformation* (Cambridge, 2013).

Haigh, Christopher, *English Reformations: Religion, Politics and Society under the Tudors* (Oxford, 1993).

Hoyle, R. W., *The Pilgrimage of Grace and the Politics of the 1530s* (Oxford, 2001).

MacCulloch, Diarmaid, *The Later Reformation in England, 1547–1603* (2nd edn., Basingstoke, 2001).

MacCulloch, Diarmaid, *Thomas Cranmer: A Life* (New Haven, CT, 1998).

MacCulloch, Diarmaid, *Tudor Church Militant: Edward VI and the Protestant Reformation* (2000).

Marshall, Peter, *Reformation England 1480–1642* (2003).

Marshall, Peter, *Religious Identities in Early Modern England* (Aldershot, 2006).

Marshall, Peter and Alec Ryrie (eds.), *The Beginnings of English Protestantism* (Cambridge, 2002).

Ryrie, Alec, *The Gospel and Henry VIII* (Cambridge, 2003).

Shagan, Ethan, *Popular Politics and the English Reformation* (Cambridge, 2003).

3

Settlement Patterns

The Church of England, 1553–1603

Peter Marshall

On the battlefield of English religion, the second half of the sixteenth century was not some time of 'post-Reformation' armistice, when smoke lifted, corpses were interred, and memorials raised by the victors. Rather, it was an era of continued and intensified conflict over the direction and identity of the Church, during which the body-count, figurative and sometimes literal, remained disconcertingly high.

Near the start of the period was what has come to be called 'the Elizabethan Settlement'. This did resemble a post-war treaty, insofar as it dictated a set of terms under which the English Church was henceforth to be governed and worship conducted. Some of these—royal governorship, episcopacy, the Book of Common Prayer—proved remarkably durable, and in retrospect look like foundation stones of 'Anglicanism'. But from the moment the ink was metaphorically dry, the meanings and intentions of the 'Settlement' were intensely contested—on specific issues, and on the wider question of whether the reformation of the Church was essentially finished, or whether the start of Elizabeth's reign was merely a way-station to further transformations.

Most historians now think that the phenomenon we call 'the Reformation' embraces, rather than precedes, the reign of Elizabeth I. Protestants of various stripes would have agreed that there was still much to do in the decades around 1560, in terms of converting 'papists' to the true faith, and instilling greater understanding into those who were arguably Protestant in name only. But there was little consensus about the instruments necessary to bring these objectives about, with respect to liturgy, church structures, or models of clerical ministry. Arguments about means tend to lead to reconsideration of ends. Increasingly, Elizabethan Protestants were divided, not just on how a reformed Church should look, but on the purpose of reformation itself. English Catholics, meanwhile, were not merely passive objects of potential conversion, but acted in their own plays of persuasion and reformation. The consequences of these rival visions were supremely disruptive, but also creative. Over the course of this period, English religion came to display itself along a spectrum of distinct and sharply contrasting colours.

That this should have happened is distinctly ironic. By European standards, sixteenth-century England was a unified and effectively governed monarchical polity. It possessed throughout an established state church, with a legal monopoly of adherence and attendance. Yet somehow this produced fertile soil, not for the growth of uniform and conformist confessional culture, but for a flowering of experiment and religious pluralism.

None of this was foreseeable in July 1553. Within a fortnight of Edward VI's death, the dreams of reformers were in tatters, as Catherine of Aragon's daughter Mary ascended the throne, having seen off an attempt to divert the succession to Jane Grey, Protestant great-granddaughter of Henry VII. Mary's priority was to reunite the English Church with the wider communion of Christendom. A once-prevalent opinion held this to be hopelessly anachronistic, a fortunately brief digression from the path to progress and modernity. Such interpretations still influence popular perceptions of the reign. But modern scholarship largely takes the view that there was nothing preordained about Mary I's failure. It owed more to the shortness of her life, and inability to give birth to an heir from her marriage to Philip of Spain, than any supposed unwillingness of the English or Welsh to accept the restoration of Catholicism. The speed at which—across large swathes of the country—the Latin mass was reinstituted, altars restored, and churches re-equipped for Catholic worship, suggests the existence of considerable reservoirs of popular support. There was less enthusiasm for papal supremacy, but anxieties here were economic rather than doctrinal. After guarantees were secured that landowners could hold on to ex-monastic lands, Parliament was happy enough to repeal religious legislation going back to 1529.

Mary's reign resolved dilemmas for English Christians while raising some new ones. For religious traditionalists, it seemed that the expedient of a non-Roman option had been tried and found wanting. Leading figures in Mary's Church, such as Bishops Stephen Gardiner, Cuthbert Tunstall, and Edmund Bonner, had been vocal supporters of Henry's royal supremacy, and a model of Christianity prefiguring the 'branch theory' of nineteenth-century Anglo-Catholicism. But under Edward, they had seen that same supremacy used to dismantle Catholic fundamentals. After 1553 they became born-again papalists, repudiating their Henrician phase.

Catholics, bruised and battered by the iconoclastic assaults of the Edwardian years, recovered their voice. The universities were thoroughly 're-Catholicized'. Reginald Pole, Cranmer's replacement at Canterbury, assisted by a revitalized and pastorally minded bench of bishops, oversaw a comprehensive programme of planned reforms. Some of these—insistence on episcopal residence, plans for diocesan seminaries and a vernacular catechism—anticipated key reforms of the Council of Trent. The Marian Church was not the ghost of the medieval past, but a vision of the Counter-Reformation future.

Not everyone was cheering as roods and altars were restored, although it is not possible to say how many English people were 'Protestants'—a word still not in general use at this time.[1] The most determined were forced into the open: around 1,000 went into continental exile, and nearly 300 were burned in an anti-heresy campaign which, by English standards, was exceptionally rigorous. Opinion remains divided over whether the persecution, had it continued, might have permanently eradicated the evangelical movement.

As it was, Marian persecution arguably saved Edwardian Protestantism from itself. Internal squabbles over matters such as vestments were temporarily forgotten, as erstwhile opponents like Bishops Ridley of London and Hooper of Gloucester went to the stake as fellow-martyrs. Their deaths, along with those of Cranmer, Hugh Latimer, and Robert Ferrar of St David's, helped anchor the notion that episcopacy might be a respectably, even heroically, Protestant institution. English reformed identity crystallized and clarified. Henrician evangelicals held a variety of views on the eucharist. But official rejection of 'real presence' in the Edwardian second Prayer Book was reinforced by the witness of the martyrs. The boundaries of doctrinal orthodoxy were drawn still closer by the endorsement of predestinarian theology by the clerical leadership, and a vigorous campaign—conducted even within Mary's prisons—to marginalize and silence 'free-willers' among the ranks.[2]

Persecution galvanized the Protestant movement, but did not quell its turbulent spirits. Tensions erupted among the exiles at Frankfurt, over whether to use the Edwardian Prayer Book in its entirety (as Edward's former tutor Richard Cox insisted) or whether (as a faction headed by John Knox desired) to omit unappealing elements like the litany of saints, and use of vestments. The defeated Knoxians, who had already adopted the practice of election of deacons and ministers, decamped to Calvin's Geneva.

The Marian exiles were small in number but big in impact. They remind us that the history of the English Reformation, and of 'Anglicanism', belongs in international context. In Basel, John Foxe began the compilation of what would become the single most important literary influence on English Protestant identity, his *Actes and Monuments* (*Book of Martyrs*). Counterparts in Geneva prepared a new scriptural translation (the Geneva Bible), which, with

---

[1] Peter Marshall, 'The Naming of Protestant England', *Past & Present*, 214 (2012): 87–128.
[2] Thomas Freeman, 'Dissenters from a Dissenting Church: The Challenge of the Freewillers 1550-1558', in Peter Marshall and Alec Ryrie (eds.), *The Beginnings of English Protestantism* (Cambridge, 2002), pp. 129–56.

its overtly Calvinist notes and introductions, would be the preferred version of 'godly' Protestants for many decades to come.

In addition, the exiles were brimming with advice for co-religionists in England, usually of an uncompromising nature. In particular, the message went out that 'it is not lawful for them to be present at the popish masses'.[3] This was whistling Calvin's tune. He had coined the derogatory term 'Nicodemite'—named after the Pharisee (John 3:1–2) who came secretly to Jesus at night—for supporters in France who outwardly adhered to Catholicism. Moral high ground was comfortably occupied by those fleeing the rising waters of state persecution. Things were less clear-cut for evangelicals—surely the vast majority—who remained in England, wading through boggy ground of compromise and conformity. Their numbers included Matthew Parker, who would succeed Pole as archbishop of Canterbury, William Cecil, who would serve as Elizabeth's chief minister for the best part of four decades, and Elizabeth herself, who was careful not to leave any traces which might allow enemies to accuse her of treason or heresy. Elizabeth's experience in Mary's reign—with its victory of pragmatism over principle, and sanctioning of a separation between outward performance of obedience, and inward motions of the heart—was to be a decisive factor for the future.

Elizabeth's accession in November 1558 is conventionally regarded as the moment of establishment for the modern Church of England: never again would that Church enter into formal communion with Rome, or (other than for a few years in the mid-seventeenth century) lose its status as an established national Church under the crown. Contemporaries, whether they welcomed it or not, were aware that this was a moment of decisive change. But what precise forms would change take? Not all options were on the table. There was little prospect of a return to the Henrician, non-papal Catholicism of the 1540s, though some lay elites might have welcomed an opportunity to keep both the mass and secure title to their monastic lands. Elizabeth signalled that this was not her preference, sweeping out of mass on Christmas Day 1558 when the bishop refused to omit the elevation of the host, and rebuking the monks of Westminster for bearing ceremonial candles at the opening of Parliament—'we see well enough!'[4] Such gestures heartened the returning exiles, and fed their hopes that Elizabeth would prove a new 'Deborah', Judge of Israel. The Catholic bishop of Winchester, by contrast, observed darkly in his funeral sermon for Queen Mary that 'the wolves be coming out of Geneva...and hath sent their books before'.[5]

---

[3] Peter Martyr Vermigli, *A Treatise of the Cohabitacyon of the Faithfull with the Unfaithfull* (Strassburg, 1555), fol. 17r.

[4] Martin A. S. Hume (ed.), *Calendar of State Papers, Spain, 1558–1567* (1892), no. 6; Rawdon Brown et al. (eds.), *Calendar of State Papers, Venetian*, 9 vols. (1864–98), VII, no. 15.

[5] John Strype, *Ecclesiastical Memorials*, 6 vols. (Oxford, 1822), III, ii, p. 542.

In fact, neither Genevans nor their books could expect a warm welcome from the new queen. Elizabeth was irritated with Calvin for having allowed the publication in Geneva of John Knox's *First Blast of the Trumpet Against the Monstrous Regiment of Women*, a misogynist attack on the exercise of power by the Catholic rulers Mary I and Mary Queen of Scots, appearing only a few months before the replacement of an English Catholic queen by a Protestant one. Knox might have been expected to foresee the event, if not the timing; tact was never his defining feature.

Elizabeth's coolness, however, provides little justification for the perennial myth that the parliamentary settlement enacted in the spring of 1559 was a careful 'via media' between Rome and Geneva, a masterly sifting of the best elements from Catholicism and Protestantism. To an objective eye, the Settlement looks more like a resurrection of the Edwardian Church Settlement as it had stood in the summer of 1553. An Act of Supremacy restored all the rights of the 'imperial crown' within the realm, and repudiated all claims of a 'usurped foreign power'. Ecclesiastical and lay office-holders were to swear an oath affirming this state of affairs. The accompanying Act of Uniformity restored a lightly revised version of the Edwardian Prayer Book of 1552, with a schedule of fines and imprisonment for clergy who refused to use it, and laypeople who refused to attend its services.[6]

The Catholic bishops fought a valiant rear-guard action against the legislation, but were unable to prevent it passing. Then, with the exception of the undistinguished Bishop Kitchen of Llandaff, they refused to take the Oath of Supremacy and were deprived of their dioceses. This unprecedented resignation *en masse* was a tribute to the high calibre of the Marian episcopate, and an indication of how issues of religious and confessional allegiance were becoming more clear-cut, at least for the educated elites. The pattern of refusal was replicated among many higher clergy and university dons, though to a much lesser extent among ordinary priests in the parishes. None of the refusenik bishops, however, was put to death. The new regime was at the outset careful not to make martyrs, mindful of the moral capital to be reaped from lamenting the cruel persecution of the preceding reign. There was cold comfort for Catholics in any aspect of the settlement, as they witnessed the mass again abolished, and Royal Visitors cleansing parish churches of their 'idolatrous' furnishings and decoration.

In particular, it is doubtful whether one noticeable difference from the Edwardian *status quo ante*—the designation of Elizabeth as 'Supreme Governor' rather than 'Supreme Head'—either intended or managed to conciliate conservatives. This was more plausibly a palliative to nagging anxieties about the new monarch's gender, and a salve to Protestant sensibilities about the

---

[6] Henry Gee and William Hardy (eds.), *Documents Illustrative of English Church History* (1896), pp. 442–67.

headship of anyone other than Christ. Legally, it made no difference to the queen's jurisdictional rights. Yet in an appendix to the Visitation Injunctions of 1559, Elizabeth laid down what was in effect a self-denying ordinance: no one was to believe malicious rumours that the monarch was empowered to 'challenge authority and power of ministry of divine offices in the Church', a statement she later elaborated to specify that the office of teaching belonged to 'archbishops, bishops, pastors, and such other ecclesiastical ministers and curates as by the ecclesiastical ancient policy used in the realm hath been in former ages ordained'.[7] She would not weigh in on doctrinal questions (as her father, overtly and ineptly, had sometimes tried to do). Yet if anyone thought that this was a promise that Elizabeth would defer to her bishops, and follow their guidance on matters of ecclesiastical policy, they were due to be rudely disabused.

Did the Settlement of 1559 reflect the young Elizabeth's own key priorities, or the agenda of a more resolutely Protestant bloc of advisers headed by the indispensable William Cecil? It is hard to be certain. But while the Settlement was unambiguously Protestant, it was ambiguous about the kind of Protestantism it was intending to settle. The Injunctions were a mandate for renewed iconoclasm, but were peppered with a cautious conservatism absent from the 1547 set on which they were based. They explicitly endorsed the 'laudable science of music' (Elizabeth was a fan of liturgical music, and notoriously employed Catholic composers, Byrd and Tallis, in the Chapel Royal). They reinstituted parochial processions at Rogationtide, and commanded reverent bowing when the Name of Jesus was uttered in church. This smelled a bit odd to advocates of thoroughgoing Reformation, as did the emphasis throughout on strict licensing of preachers. Non-licensed clergy were merely to say services, and to read out the extended Thoughts for the Day contained in the officially sanctioned Book of Homilies.[8]

And there were puzzling contradictions. The Prayer Book specified the use of ordinary bread for communion, but the Injunctions, 'for the more reverence to be given to these holy mysteries', ordered the use of traditional communion wafers (if a little thicker, and without embossed pictures). There was inconsistency too over the placing of communion tables. The Prayer Book envisaged them standing permanently in the body of the chancel, where communion services were now celebrated. But the Injunctions ordered that when not in use, they should be returned to the east end of the church 'and set in the place where the altar stood'. Eucharistic doctrine was a keystone of confessional identity in virtually all parts of Reformation Europe. But it seemed almost as if the Church of England was asking adherents to guess its doctrine from hints and clues in the rubrics and paraphernalia. Matters were not helped by what

[7] William Haugaard, *Elizabeth and the English Reformation* (Cambridge, 1968), pp. 270–1.
[8] Gee and Hardy, *Documents*, pp. 417–42.

ought to have been an overt declaration of meaning and significance—the 'words of administration' spoken by the minister as he delivered communion to the congregants. Curiously, the 1559 Prayer Book stitched together the forms of words used in the 1549 and 1552 services to produce a real liturgical mouthful: 'The body of our Lord Jesus Christ which was given for thee, preserve thy body and soul into everlasting life: and take and eat this, in remembrance that Christ died for thee, and feed on him in thy heart by faith, with thanksgiving.' This did not exactly affirm the real presence, as, arguably, in 1549, nor explicitly deny it, as the now-omitted 'Black Rubric' of 1552 had done, explaining that kneeling to receive the bread and wine did not imply any 'real and essential presence there being of Christ's natural flesh and blood'. It may well be that the intention here was to remain abreast of developments in continental Protestant theology since the late 1540s, a developing convergence of the teachings of Zürich and Geneva around the notion of a 'spiritual' presence rather than a bare memorialism.[9]

This seemed also to be the gist of the subsequent Article 28 (of the thirty-nine), which laid down that the Body of Christ was given and eaten 'only after an heavenly and spiritual manner'. The article strongly attacked transubstantiation, but left out a condemnation of belief in 'real and bodily' presence found in the corresponding article of 1553, along with a denial that Christ's body might 'be present at one time in many and diverse places'. The latter omission may have been a concession to the sensibilities of Lutherans, and their 'Ubiquitist' teaching that Christ's body might be really present in the eucharist because it was in fact present everywhere. But the bishops and other clergymen drawing up the Articles at the Convocation of 1563 showed no such sensitivity in drafting another article, affirming that unworthy communicants were in no way 'partakers of Christ'. This was a point of sharp controversy between Lutherans and Calvinists in Europe, and the article firmly aligned the English Church with the latter. When the Articles were presented to the queen, Elizabeth vetoed this one, fearing its impact on diplomatic relations with Lutheran powers, and perhaps feeling offence to her own views. So much for the royal promise not to challenge the teaching authority of ministerial office! In consequence, only thirty-eight articles were authorized in 1563, with the missing Article 29 restored, and the whole given parliamentary underpinning, only in 1571.[10] Needless to say, there was more than enough here for later Anglican theologians to construe various plausible versions of what the eucharistic doctrine of the Church of England actually was.

A more immediate cause for concern was the question of what ministers should wear while celebrating the eucharist and performing other priestly

---

[9] Diarmaid MacCulloch, *The Later Reformation in England, 1547–1603* (2nd edn., Basingstoke, 2001), pp. 26–7.
[10] Haugaard, *Elizabeth and the English Reformation*, pp. 247–54.

offices. The matter seems trivial to modern senses of priority, but this was an age in which externals mattered, testifying to unseen realities and providing pointers to the tone and direction of official policy. The Uniformity Act ducked the ball: clerical dress was to revert to forms used in the first year of Edward's reign, 'until other order shall be therein taken by the authority of the queen's majesty'. That order was supplied by the 1559 Injunctions: ministers were to wear 'such seemly habits' as were in use in the last year of Edward's reign. This meant wearing surplices for the celebration of services, and distinctive clerical square caps at other times.[11]

Vestments had proved a toxic subject for Protestants in Edward's reign, when the question was decided but not resolved by Cranmer and Ridley's hard-fought victory over Hooper's initial refusal to be consecrated bishop of Gloucester wearing them. None of the protagonists had an aesthetic or emotional attachment to vestments, in the manner of some nineteenth-century Anglo-Catholics. The issues were pragmatic, tactical. They were acceptable as a matter of uniformity, decency, and order, and to lubricate the transition while the populace as a whole was eased from popery. But behind the sartorial squabbling lurked larger and more intractable questions. Hooper, and many who thought like him, regarded vestments as irredeemably compromised by their association with sacrificial priesthood. He rejected the argument that such things were *adiaphora*—'indifferent' matters which might be mandated or omitted at the judgement of the Church. There was a tension here about the Church's relationship with its pre-Reformation past. But fundamentally this was a matter of authority, and of how far the conscience of the individual Christian might legitimately be constrained by the powers that be. Article 20 of the thirty-nine seemed definitively to settle the matter: 'the Church hath power to decree rites and ceremonies' (a phrase inserted on the queen's authority after initial drafting). But the article went on to say that it was not lawful for the Church 'to ordain anything that is contrary to God's Word written'.[12] Whether individual rites and ceremonies *were* contrary to Scripture was inevitably a matter of opinion, so this was a question-begging formula. And vestments, persistently and doggedly, were to be its principal test-case.

If we take together the Acts of Supremacy and Uniformity, the Prayer Book, the Injunctions, the Book of Homilies, the Articles of Religion, and perhaps also the polemical defences of the proceedings by Bishop John Jewel and others, as collectively constituting the 'Settlement'—the self-declaration—of the English Church, then we are looking at an unprecedented concentration of liturgical, doctrinal, and ecclesio-political creativity, which fully justifies the attention conventionally paid to it. Yet perhaps the principal reason why its

---

[11] Gee and Hardy, *Documents*, pp. 432, 466.
[12] Haugaard, *Elizabeth and the English Reformation*, pp. 253–4.

'character' or 'essence' has proved so difficult to capture is that most of those involved would have been puzzled and disturbed by the idea that this was a definitive 'settlement' at all. Rather, they believed that they were engaged on a series of steps to advance the reformation of English religion and society—a process that would inevitably be incremental and ongoing, and with no fixed end-point in view.

Here the irresistible force that was English Protestantism met the immovable object that was the English queen. Monarchs are not usually revolutionaries, and Elizabeth was inclined by instinct and experience to favour caution, and an orderly status quo; her motto was *semper eadem*, always the same. At the 1563 meeting of Convocation, the bishops prepared a package of measures for further reform, including the removal of controversial ceremonies, but Elizabeth scotched the plans. Thus far, and no further.[13] Elizabeth's conservatism was cultural and temperamental, as much as explicitly doctrinal. But it had the capacity to shock and dismay the returning exiles, whose appointment to bishoprics at the start of the reign may have owed more to the influence of William Cecil than to the queen herself. One of these, Edmund Grindal, was later appalled by Elizabeth's suggestion that three or four preachers in each shire were quite enough. For serious Protestants like Grindal, there needed to be a preacher in every parish.[14] In addition to her old-fashioned penchant for church music, Elizabeth made little secret of her distaste for clerical marriage; ministers wishing to marry had petty bureaucratic obstacles to overcome. While Royal Visitors swept parish churches clean of 'idolatrous' imagery, Elizabeth doggedly retained a crucifix and candles on the communion table in the Chapel Royal. Appropriately for someone who, as Francis Bacon famously said, misliked 'to make windows into men's hearts and secret thoughts', Elizabeth's true religious convictions remain somewhat mysterious.[15] But her determination not to budge beyond the arbitrary parameters of 1559–63 did more than any other factor to shape the development of religion in her reign. Was she, as has been suggested, 'the true progenitor of Anglicanism'?[16]

The conflict and religious instability of Elizabeth's reign did not, as used to be supposed, arise from the drama of a resolutely 'Anglican' establishment defending itself against the attacks of disenfranchised outsiders, 'papists', and 'puritans'. As we have seen, the ambiguous and incomplete 'settlement' was

---

[13] David Crankshaw, 'Preparations for the Canterbury Provincial Convocation of 1562-3: A Question of Attribution', in Susan Wabuda and Caroline Litzenberger (eds.), *Belief and Practice in Reformation England* (Aldershot, 1998), pp. 60–93.

[14] Patrick Collinson, 'The Elizabethan Church and the New Religion', in Christopher Haigh (ed.), *The Reign of Elizabeth I* (Basingstoke, 1984), p. 181.

[15] Francis Bacon, *The Works of Lord Bacon with an Introductory Essay*, 2 vols. (1838), I, p. 387.

[16] *ODNB*, 'Elizabeth I (1533–1603)'.

itself a mechanism for generating tensions. But the dissatisfaction of a range of groups with officially prescribed norms for worship and belief was undoubtedly a major factor in the formation of religious identities and solidarities across the last decades of the sixteenth century.

A history of Anglicanism is (perhaps) not the place for a full account of the travails of English Catholics. But that the Elizabethan Church of England failed to secure and maintain the allegiance of all mainstream English Christians, and that Catholicism remained an internal as well as external rival, was of great significance for its future development. It is likely that the majority of the population was in some sense 'Catholic' in 1560, but there was no reason not to hope that virtually all these traditionalists could over time be absorbed into the Church of England, encouraged to habituate its services by non-attendance fines prescribed in the Act of Uniformity, and gradually won over to its tenets by experience of vernacular common prayer and the persuasions of sermons and homilies. This did to a considerable extent happen—a distinctly mixed blessing to more ideologically driven reformers, far from convinced that all 'statute Protestants' had properly imbibed transformative teachings of justification by faith and predestination.

Indigenous Catholicism did not, however, experience a slow and lingering demise, as happened, for example, across much of Scandinavia in the early modern period. In part, this was due to Elizabeth's reluctance to sanction intensive policies of coercion and repression, even in the wake of a serious Catholic rebellion in the north in 1569, a reverberation from which was the papal bull of February 1570, excommunicating and deposing Elizabeth for imposing on her realm 'the profane mysteries and institutions which she had received and observed from the decree of Calvin'.[17] The softly-softly approach might have yielded results, but events proceeded to derail it. The arrival in England of the deposed Mary Queen of Scots in 1568 supplied a plausible Catholic reversionary hope, and a focus for a series of plots of varying degrees of danger. Meanwhile, the decision of the Catholic clerical exiles headed by William Allen to train priests in continental seminaries for missionary work at home supplied youthful and zealous replacements for the ageing former Marian priests beginning to die out in the 1570s. Advocating full withdrawal from heretical worship (recusancy), the seminarists were joined from 1580 by Jesuits, provoking a government backlash and a raft of repressive legislation.

Fuelled by government propaganda, the assiduously perpetuated memory of the Marian fires of Smithfield, and such decidedly real events as the 1572 Massacre of St Bartholomew in Paris, and the attempted Spanish invasion of 1588, anti-Catholicism took deep root in English culture. There was a reckoning in blood: between 1574 and the end of the reign, 124 missionary priests

---

[17] Robert Miola (ed.), *Early Modern Catholicism: An Anthology of Primary Sources* (Oxford, 2007), pp. 486–8.

were put to death, along with fifty-nine laypeople accused of helping them. But it is significant that Catholic belief as such was never construed as a capital crime. The Catholic victims of the Elizabethan state were executed for treason, not heresy, as William Cecil pedantically pointed out in his 1584 *The Execution of Justice in England*. With acknowledgement of the spiritual authority of the Pope, and obedience to his mandates, reckoned a treasonable offence, the distinction was rather moot. Yet the fact that the adolescent Church of England, as opposed to individual churchmen, never formally defined a range of Catholic tenets as heresy left possibilities for future contestation. It also left space for those who thought of themselves as Catholics to ignore Jesuit strictures on the absolute necessity of recusancy, and to continue to fulfil the 'civil' requirement of church attendance, with the attendant advantages, such as eligibility to hold office under the crown. To a considerable extent, such Catholic Nicodemism, known as 'church popery', was undertaken with the connivance of the Elizabethan state. On three occasions, mindful of Catholic consciences, Elizabeth vetoed parliamentary attempts to make reception of the Protestant communion, rather than mere bodily attendance at church, a requirement of statute law.[18] There could be no clearer indication that the regime, for all its repressive instincts, was not prepared to sanction a rigorous campaign to eradicate Catholicism and indoctrinate its adherents. Inner conviction was desirable, but outward compliance was enough. Affiliation, rather than affirmation, was the hallmark of Church of England membership.

To say that there were those in the Church who considered this state of affairs unsatisfactory would be an understatement. The most vocal critics were called by their enemies 'puritans', and historians do not need to suppose we are talking about a precisely delineated phenomenon to find the term useful. Puritanism—the name and perhaps also the thing—first emerged in the 'Vestiarian Controversy' of the mid-1560s. Scrupulous clergy, particularly in the capital, balked at donning the prescribed 'popish' surplice, and Elizabeth, hiding behind the authority of Archbishop Parker, ordered a crackdown in which thirty-seven London clergy were suspended.

It was the start of a pattern by which the bishops, themselves often impatient for an increased pace of reform, came to be seen by significant numbers of 'godly' Protestants as part of the problem rather than the solution to the Church's woes. For the Church as an institution, arguably the most significant achievement of the official reformations was what they left in place: the entire medieval structure of bishops, cathedrals, and diocesan church courts—an intact inheritance virtually unparalleled in Protestant Europe. This was not the practice of what former exiles and others tended to call 'the best reformed churches' (i.e. those of Zürich and Geneva). Calvin himself saw episcopacy as

---

[18] Alexandra Walsham, *Church Papists: Catholicism, Conformity and Confessional Polemic in Early Modern England* (Woodbridge, 1993), pp. 12, 87–8.

in some circumstances an acceptable model of church government. But a considerable number of Geneva's admirers in England regarded the Presbyterian system used there as the model mandated in the Acts of the Apostles: it was not, in other words, a matter of *adiaphora*. This was the case set out in 1570 by the Cambridge divinity professor Thomas Cartwright, arguing for the equality of all ministers, overseen by a system of presbyteries and synods. In 1571 there was (unsuccessful) agitation in Parliament to finally institute Cranmer's *Reformatio Legum*—the lost scheme for the establishment of that 'discipline' which many regarded as a necessary mark of the true Church—as well as to remove objectionable elements from the Book of Common Prayer. They were itemized by the ministers Thomas Field and John Wilcox in a rambunctiously satirical *Admonition to the Parliament* of the following year: the surplice, kneeling to receive communion, 'churching' women after childbirth, saints' days, the use of the sign of the cross in baptism, and of rings in the wedding service. These constituted a litany of long-standing puritan grievances. In the ensuing 'Admonition Controversy', John Whitgift, Master of Trinity College, Cambridge, sought to confound Cartwright, Field, and Wilcox in what has been called 'a struggle for the "soul" of mainstream Protestantism'.[19] Whitgift represented an emerging 'conformist' growth of Protestant opinion, tied to the trellis of uniformity, order, and ceremony, and watered by the favour of the queen.

It was no straightforward matter of 'Anglicans' versus 'puritans'. Whitgift, like virtually all bishops and front-rank theologians in Elizabeth's Church, was doctrinally Calvinist, as firm a believer as Cartwright in God's double decree of predestination (though Article 17, 'Of Predestination and Election'—in perhaps another concession to Lutheran sensibilities—spoke only of election to everlasting salvation, and not of its infernal corollary). Nor did Whitgift advocate *iure divino* episcopacy, the view—mirror image to scripturalist Presbyterianism—that governance of the Church by bishops was a positive ordinance of God. Puritans were undoubtedly what the Jesuit Robert Parsons called 'the hotter sort of Protestants'.[20] But they largely partook in what historians have termed a 'Calvinist consensus' about the doctrine of salvation. Nor were bishops deaf to the argument that there were matters in the Church requiring attention, in particular an ongoing shortage of well-qualified preaching ministers.

It was to remedy this that Edmund Grindal, Parker's successor as archbishop of Canterbury in 1575, gave his blessing to the movement for 'prophesyings'. These were not, as the name might suggest, occasions for outpourings of visionary ecstasy, but rather 'workshops', held regularly in market towns,

---

[19] Peter Lake, *Anglicans and Puritans? Presbyterianism and English Conformist Thought from Whitgift to Hooker* (1988), p. 24.

[20] Robert Parsons, *A Brief Discours containing Certayne Reasons why Catholiques Refuse to Goe to Church* (Douai [i.e. East Ham], 1580), fol. 39v.

Settlement Patterns: The Church of England, 1553–1603   57

where ministers would preach to fellow clergy and a few laity and receive constructive criticism. Elizabeth thought this a quasi-Presbyterian challenge to episcopal hierarchy, and ordered Grindal to suppress them. Remarkably, he flat refused: 'Bear with me, I beseech you, Madam, if I choose rather to offend your earthly Majesty than to offend the heavenly majesty of God.'[21] Elizabeth was offended, and suspended Grindal from office, an unflinching display of supreme governorship in action.

Grindal's successor was John Whitgift, and his accession in 1583 marked a more authoritarian tone to the Church's governance: 1584 was what puritans called 'the woeful year of subscription', when Whitgift demanded that all ministers set their names to a set of articles asserting, *inter alia*, that the Prayer Book 'containeth nothing... contrary to the word of God'.[22]

But the opposition, if we can call it that, was not cowed, and nonconforming ministers had friends in high places, including the queen's long-time favourite, the earl of Leicester. Even Cecil—much preoccupied with the Catholic threat, and Elizabeth's frustrating reluctance to deal with Mary Queen of Scots—thought Whitgift was going too far. In various parts of the south and Midlands, ministers were getting together in local conferences or *classes*, with synods at the county level. The motivations were often primarily pastoral, but these effectively Presbyterian structures were an implicit political challenge to the hierarchical status quo. That challenge became most explicit in the Parliament of 1587, with the introduction of legislation to abolish the Book of Common Prayer and to replace episcopacy with a Presbyterian structure. Speaking in favour of the bill, the zealous Warwickshire gentleman Job Throckmorton repeatedly insisted that 'dumb ministry' was the root cause of all the ills of the Church.[23]

Throckmorton had been instrumental in the compilation of county-based puritan 'surveys of the ministry'. The snapshots these contain, intended as indictments of inadequate pastoral provision, inadvertently offer insight into alternative, less dogmatic patterns of clerical ministry. Revealingly, ministers are sometimes accused of being 'subject to the vice of good fellowship'.[24] Puritans are some of our best, albeit hostile, witnesses for the temper and temperature of conformist parish religion. Character dialogues, such as the Essex minister George Gifford's *A Briefe Discourse of Certaine Points of the Religion which is among the Common Sort of Christians which may be termed*

---

[21] Patrick Collinson, 'The Prophesyings and the Downfall of Archbishop Edmund Grindal 1576–1583', in Melanie Barber, Stephen Taylor, and Gabriel Sewell (eds.), *From the Reformation to the Permissive Society* (Woodbridge, 2010), p. 23.
[22] Patrick Collinson, *Richard Bancroft and Elizabethan Anti-Puritanism* (Cambridge, 2013), p. 43.
[23] T. E. Hartley (ed.), *Proceedings in the Parliaments of Elizabeth I*, 3 vols. (Leicester, 1981–95), II, p. 203.
[24] Patrick Collinson, *The Elizabethan Puritan Movement* (1967), pp. 280–2.

the Countrie Divinitie, portray a rural world in which well-meaning churchgoers value neighbourliness above the rebuking of sin, and see good works as milestones to salvation. Allowing for an element of caricature, such assessments may not be too wide of the mark. The most thorough study of religious cheap print—ballads and chapbooks—in the later sixteenth and early seventeenth centuries finds an imaginative world from which Catholic saints have been excised, but in which traditional concerns about moral behaviour and preparation for death are very much present: a patchwork of beliefs that 'may be described as distinctively "post-Reformation", but not thoroughly "Protestant"'.[25] And in the best-selling of published catechisms—the principal printed means of Protestant instruction—historians have found a downplaying of the 'hard' doctrines of predestination and justification by faith.[26]

In the crowded congregation of Elizabethan religious typology, the godliest were the noisiest, but conformists were not always quiescent. They can sometimes be found in the court records, reporting puritan ministers for omitting to wear the surplice, leaving out Prayer Book ceremonies, or forbidding kneeling at communion. It is a moot point—debated at the time, and in modern historiography—whether such people can meaningfully be considered Protestants. It is likely that this is how most considered themselves, and we have rightly been warned against allowing '"Geneva" to fix the goal posts of Protestantism'.[27] But lay defenders of ceremonies and the Prayer Book in Elizabeth's reign never called themselves 'anglican', and it is not certain that we should look precisely here to find the well-spring of a later tradition. The most we can safely say is that English local Christianity was varied and pluriform, encompassing shades of godliness, recusancy, and church papistry, as well as dutiful conformity of various degrees of positive engagement.

Puritanism could be 'popular' too, and in a determination to demonstrate this, overplayed its hand at the end of the 1580s. A series of short, scurrilous, and hilarious pamphlets, the *Marprelate Tracts*, satirizing episcopacy and individual bishops, was published clandestinely in 1588–9. The mystery of their authorship has never been definitively solved, but the Warwickshire firebrand Job Throckmorton may have been principal mover. Their audacity lay in placing high matters of doctrine and church policy directly in front of a popular audience. 'Matters of religion', complained Francis Bacon, were 'handled in the style of the stage'.[28] Whitgift went on the offensive, cracking open the Presbyterian movement and arresting its leaders. The authorities

---

[25] Tessa Watt, *Cheap Print and Popular Piety, 1550–1640* (Cambridge, 1991), p. 327.

[26] Ian Green, *The Christian's ABC: Catechisms and Catechizing in England, c.1530–1740* (Oxford, 1996).

[27] Judith Maltby, '"By this Book": Parishioners, the Prayer Book and the Established Church', in Kenneth Fincham (ed.), *The Early Stuart Church, 1603–1642* (Basingstoke, 1993), p. 117.

[28] Joseph L. Black (ed.), *The Martin Marprelate Tracts: A Modernized and Annotated Edition* (Cambridge, 2008), p. xxvii.

decided to fight fire with fire, commissioning a succession of London literary types to answer 'Martin Marprelate' in the same populist vein. The result was an effusion of anti-puritan satire, whose echoes can be heard in the plays of Shakespeare and Jonson. Indeed, it has been argued, it was only with the development of a full-formed anti-puritan stereotype that puritanism itself can rightly be regarded as having started to exist, an instance of how hostile labelling and name-calling called into being a social reality it only imperfectly mirrored.[29] Whatever we think of that, it seems incontrovertible that a major influence on the construction of religious identities in Elizabeth's reign was the availability of an array of unvalued 'others', against whom self-perceptions could be drawn and measured: papists, church papists, puritans, neuters, atheists, 'cold statute Protestants', or (as Marprelate saw in the episcopal seats) 'petty popes and petty antichrists'.

Puritanism, or godly Protestantism, has a fair claim to be considered the conscience of the English Reformation, at the forefront of campaigns for solidarity with beleaguered co-religionists in Europe, and for moral reformation in the parishes at home. But in some quarters it was starting to be thought of in profoundly conspiratorial terms, as an intrinsically subversive threat to royal authority and episcopal government. That was the view of Elizabeth's court favourite, Lord Chancellor Sir Christopher Hatton (a possible crypto-papist). It was held more strongly still by his chaplain, Richard Bancroft, who in 1597 was elevated to the key strategic see of London, and shortly after Elizabeth's death would succeed Whitgift at Canterbury.

In the last decade of the reign, in an increasingly tense political context, as the question of the succession loomed, the doctrinal consensus of the earlier Elizabethan years began slowly to unravel. Puritan criticism of episcopacy and the Prayer Book inevitably provoked some churchmen to value them more highly. Episcopacy *iure divino*, by divine law, was argued for in 1587 by John Bridges, dean of Salisbury, in a weighty book provoking the first Marprelate tract. The still-novel idea was taken up by a clutch of writers patronized by Bancroft in the 1590s.[30] This was one less 'indifferent' thing about which compromises might be reached, one step away from European Protestants who lacked this necessary mark of a Church, and one step back towards the medieval Church which embodied the notion of apostolic succession.

Various signs of wistfulness about the lost medieval past can be detected as the century drew to a close: an antiquarian interest in tombs and monuments, and desire to protect them from the ravages of time and puritan iconoclasm, nostalgic regrets about the devastation inflicted on monastic houses and their

---

[29] Patrick Collinson, 'Ecclesiastical Vitriol: Religious Satire in the 1590s and the Invention of Puritanism', in John Guy (ed.), *The Reign of Elizabeth I: Court and Culture in the Last Decade* (Cambridge, 1995), pp. 150–70.

[30] Lake, *Anglicans and Puritans?*, pp. 90–7, 220–5.

priceless libraries.³¹ Meanwhile, more direct institutional continuity with that past was preserved in the elaborate round of sung services maintained in cathedral churches, and in that cathedral-in-all-but-name, the royal peculiar of Westminster Abbey, presided over from 1561 to 1601 by the highly conservative Dean Gabriel Goodman.³²

At the universities, the shibboleth of Calvinist predestinarianism itself was starting to be challenged by a handful of adventurous Protestant divines— William Barrett, Peter Baro, John Overall, Antonio del Corro—following the lead of the dissident Dutch theologian, Jacobus Arminius. 'Arminianism' was very much a minority opinion in the Elizabethan Church, and Whitgift sought to edge the dissidents back into line with the ultra-predestinarian Lambeth Articles of 1595, which removed all the ambiguity about double predestination adhering to Article 17. But this was a move beyond the Settlement of 1559–63, and, typically, Elizabeth refused to ratify them.³³

Yet for all his orthodox Calvinism, Whitgift was godfather of a new strain of divinity emerging in the late Elizabethan Church. He recommended his chaplain Richard Bancroft for the bishopric of London in 1597, noting—one might hope superfluously—that he was 'certainly no papist'.³⁴ Another chaplain was Lancelot Andrewes, a preacher favoured by the queen, whose sermons were openly critical of Calvinist doctrine and practice. Significantly, he succeeded Goodman as dean of Westminster in 1601. Andrewes was friends with Richard Hooker, a third Whitgift protégé, and safeguarded the manuscripts of his *Laws of Ecclesiastical Policy*, unfinished upon Hooker's death in 1600. The *Laws* is seen as the quintessentially 'Anglican' work of theology and ecclesiology, but it was distinctly outré for its day. Hooker moved beyond the earlier conformist view of ceremonies as theologically 'indifferent' matters of order and discipline to ascribe to them a positive spiritual value as instruments of edification and sanctification. More radically still, he broke with the notion— expressed in the millenarian historiography of John Bale and John Foxe—that the true Church was an invisible congregation of the elect, locked in cosmic antagonism with Rome. Instead, there was a clear line of succession from pre- to post-Reformation Church in England, and an inheritance in many respects to be proud of. Even the contemporary Roman Church, though undeniably corrupt, might claim to be a redeemable part of Christ's visible Church on

---

[31] Patrick Collinson, 'John Stow and Nostalgic Antiquarianism', in Julia Merritt (ed.), *Imagining Early Modern London: Perceptions and Portrayals of the City from Stow to Strype 1598–1720* (Cambridge, 2001), pp. 27–51.

[32] Julia Merritt, 'The Cradle of Laudianism? Westminster Abbey, 1558–1630', *JEH*, 52 (2001): 623–46.

[33] Nicholas Tyacke, *Anti-Calvinists: The Rise of English Arminianism c.1590–1640* (Oxford, 1987).

[34] Collinson, *Bancroft*, p. 26.

earth.[35] Such reflections were anathema to countless English Protestants who had grown up believing the Pope to be the Antichrist.

The leaders of the later Reformation in England preserved a medieval hierarchical Church in order to shape it to the political needs of a monarchical polity, all the while hoping, in varying degrees, to imbue it with energy as an instrument of evangelical Protestant conversion. It was an unstable agenda, containing incompatible ideals. In fact, having enacted a political and liturgical Reformation, Elizabethan authorities expended much of their energies trying to constrain a religious one, the grass-roots movement for further reform within the Church of England known to history as puritanism. But even to speak of the religious policies of 'the state' is to oversimplify a complex set of dynamics, in which various lay and ecclesiastical ministers protected particular individuals, and promoted particular priorities in response to changing political circumstance. Such 'consensus' as existed was not in the end primarily doctrinal, but focused upon the ideal of comprehension. Puritans wished to reform the Church of England from within, acting as the leaven in the lump; only a very few formally separated from it. A larger number of Catholics did, conscious of their obligations to a larger concept of Christian communion. But the authorities did remarkably little to force them to leave, and large numbers of people of broadly conservative instincts did in fact remain and apparently thrive. In some ways, the Elizabethan Church of England was a notable success, managing to retain, in a time of international turmoil, the formal allegiance of the vast majority of the English people. But the price of comprehension and unity was diversity and discord. That, perhaps, is the paradox and pride of 'Anglicanism' in its prefatory, pre-nominal and embryonic phase.

SELECT BIBLIOGRAPHY

Black, Joseph L. (ed.), *The Martin Marprelate Tracts: A Modernized and Annotated Edition* (Cambridge, 2008).
Collinson, Patrick, 'Ecclesiastical Vitriol: Religious Satire in the 1590s and the Invention of Puritanism', in John Guy (ed.), *The Reign of Elizabeth I: Court and Culture in the Last Decade* (Cambridge, 1995), pp. 150–70.
Collinson, Patrick, 'The Elizabethan Church and the New Religion', in Christopher Haigh (ed.), *The Reign of Elizabeth I* (Basingstoke, 1984), pp. 169–94.
Collinson, Patrick, *The Elizabethan Puritan Movement* (1967).
Collinson, Patrick, *Richard Bancroft and Elizabethan Anti-Puritanism* (Cambridge, 2013).

---

[35] Anthony Milton, *Catholic and Reformed: The Roman and Protestant Churches in English Protestant Thought, 1600–1640* (Cambridge, 1995), pp. 128–33, 146–50, 470–5.

Crankshaw, David, 'Preparations for the Canterbury Provincial Convocation of 1562–3: A Question of Attribution', in Susan Wabuda and Caroline Litzenberger (eds.), *Belief and Practice in Reformation England* (Aldershot, 1998), pp. 60–93.

Doran, Susan and Thomas S. Freeman (eds.), *Mary Tudor: Old and New Perspectives* (Basingstoke, 2011).

Duffy, Eamon, *Fires of Faith: Catholic England under Mary Tudor* (New Haven, CT, 2009).

Green, Ian, *The Christian's ABC: Catechisms and Catechizing in England, c.1530–1740* (Oxford, 1996).

Haugaard, William, *Elizabeth and the English Reformation* (Cambridge, 1968).

Jones, Norman L., *Faith by Statute: Parliament and the Settlement of Religion, 1559* (1982).

Lake, Peter, *Anglicans and Puritans? Presbyterianism and English Conformist Thought from Whitgift to Hooker* (1988).

Lake, Peter, 'Calvinism and the English Church 1570–1635', *Past & Present*, 114 (1987): 32–76.

Maltby, Judith, '"By this Book": Parishioners, the Prayer Book and the Established Church', in Kenneth Fincham (ed.), *The Early Stuart Church, 1603–1642* (Basingstoke, 1993), pp. 115–37.

Tyacke, Nicholas, *Anti-Calvinists: The Rise of English Arminianism c.1590–1640* (Oxford, 1987).

Walsham, Alexandra, *Church Papists: Catholicism, Conformity and Confessional Polemic in Early Modern England* (Woodbridge, 1993).

Watt, Tessa, *Cheap Print and Popular Piety, 1550–1640* (Cambridge, 1991).

4

Unsettled Reformations, 1603–1662

Anthony Milton

Unlike the reigns of the Tudors, where the advent of each monarch led to a significant national change of religious direction, the reigns of the first two Stuart kings did not begin with a new settlement that dramatically altered the country's religious identity. Historians have therefore tended to assume that the Elizabethan Settlement had already acquired a permanent, accepted status, with the result that the unprecedented upheavals of the civil wars seem a strange aberration in the Church's history. But if there was no significant dismantling of the Elizabethan Settlement in the years before the civil war, this did not mean that there was not a good deal of argument about the nature of that Settlement, and sustained pressure for further religious reform. Seen in this light, the convulsions of the civil war, Interregnum, and Restoration arguably form part of a continuous, ongoing debate over the religion of the Church of England.

The reign of James I began with hopes and fears of religious change. The Hampton Court Conference which met in January 1604 was called by the new king in response to a wave of puritan petitioning for religious reform—a 'highly professional campaign' which reflected the re-activation of Elizabethan puritan networks. The so-called 'Millenary Petition' sought to unite puritan opinion under a moderate banner of reform of the liturgy and church courts, rather than a wholesale challenge to episcopal church government.[1] In the event, although the king allowed the bishops to sweat while complaints were aired, he ultimately threw his weight behind the existing Settlement. Some puritan concerns were addressed—in the promises that bishops should promote 'the planting of a learned and painful minister in every parish' and that the king would issue a new catechism and a new Bible translation, and abolish lay baptism—while the set of canons that were issued soon afterwards explained at length that the prescribed use of the sign of the cross in baptism

---

[1] P. Collinson, *The Elizabethan Puritan Movement* (1967), pp. 452–7.

was not superstitious and formed 'no part of the substance of this sacrament'. Nevertheless, the key point was that no further reform was intended, and a royal proclamation in July 1604 emphasized that on examination it was clear that there was no reason to change the Prayer Book and church discipline and that it was therefore everyone's duty to conform. Most memorably, in his observation 'no bishop, no king', James made plain his rejection of Presbyterianism and his endorsement of episcopacy. After the conference, ministers were compelled to subscribe to Whitgift's Three Articles of 1583, and between seventy-three and eighty-three beneficed clergy were deprived for refusing to do so.[2]

Nevertheless, it is important not to underestimate the continuing appetite in some quarters for further religious change. The conference might have curtailed further agitation for significant liturgical reform (the Prayer Book and its ceremonies ceased to be areas of mainstream complaint for the time being), but it marked only the beginning of sustained struggles not just over the best means of combating pluralism and non-residence among the clergy, but also over the power of the Church to make canons and to prosecute dissenters. The next seven years witnessed persistent conflicts in Parliament, and set-piece debates between the new archbishop Richard Bancroft and his supporters on the one hand, and the forces of Parliament and the common law on the other.[3] Older generations of historians wrote of 'the reconstruction of the Church of England' in the first decade of James's reign at the hands of Bancroft, and there is no doubt that these years did witness a significant retrenchment of the Church's power and authority, with the systematic codifying of the 1604 canons, the imposition of clerical subscription, the reassertion of the authority of church courts, and the defence of the powers of the Court of High Commission. But these were strongly contested reforms: Parliament refused to recognize the authority of the canons passed without its assent, and would continue to do so in subsequent decades. The *ex officio* oath (in which the accused swore a religious oath to answer questions truthfully before knowing what those questions were), the legality of the Court of High Commission, the authority of bishops to conduct visitations in their own names, the power of Convocation to meet and decree ceremonies independent of Parliament: all of these were vehemently and continually opposed. Lay concerns were prompted by the increasing role being played by the clergy in secular affairs—from the Privy Council down to the local bench of JPs—which they could do nothing to prevent. It was royal authority alone that underpinned much of this 're-establishment' under the first Stuart kings. The complaints over the legal powers of the Church that marked the opening of the Long Parliament (1640)

---

[2] G. Bray, *The Anglican Canons 1529–1947* (Woodbridge, 1998), p. 307; K. Fincham and P. Lake, 'The Ecclesiastical Policy of King James I', *Journal of British Studies*, 24 (1985): 169–207 (pp. 173–4); K. Fincham, *Prelate as Pastor: The Episcopate of James I* (Oxford, 1990), p. 323.

[3] S. B. Babbage, *Puritanism and Richard Bancroft* (1962), esp. chs. 8–10.

were not therefore a sudden hostile explosion but merely the crescendo of a concern that had rumbled constantly in the background.

The Jacobean Church has in recent years been spoken of as having been dominated by a 'Calvinist consensus', and by the absorption of puritans into the heart of the establishment. Certainly Calvinist theology was a dominant force in English Protestantism in these years, helping to bind puritans doctrinally to the Established Church, although most Jacobean theologians retreated from the hardline supralapsarian doctrines of the 1590s (which made the decrees of divine predestination apply to man before the Fall). So prominent were puritan preaching and patterns of piety in the Established Church that some historians have tended to talk of evangelical puritanism in almost 'Anglican' terms in these years. Thus Patrick Collinson maintained that by the early decades of the seventeenth century it is preferable for historians 'to consider puritanism as embodying the mainstream of English Protestantism'.[4] Certainly puritans had been absorbed in some senses. The end of Presbyterian agitation made it easier for puritans to forge alliances with prominent evangelical bishops who were willing to grant degrees of practical toleration to puritan nonconformity, while puritans and puritan sympathizers could be found preaching everywhere from market town lectureships to the Chapel Royal. Even the notorious 'prophesyings' that had alarmed Queen Elizabeth continued in the form of 'exercises' or 'lectures by combination', which could be formally permitted by bishops under Canon 72 of 1604.[5] The minister Richard Bernard provides a perfect example of the effective integration of committed puritanism into the English Church in these years. Initially ejected for refusing to subscribe in 1605, Bernard flirted with separatism, but was won back to the Church by the godly archbishop Tobie Matthew and promptly wrote several attacks upon separatism, offering a firm defence of the Church of England and of set forms of prayer. Nevertheless, this was more in the nature of a ceasefire than of a conversion. While he continued to enjoy the patronage and protection of the godly bishops James Montague and Arthur Lake in Bath and Wells diocese, Bernard did not fully conform, and was presented at different times for refusing to use the sign of the cross in baptism and for not wearing a graduate hood. The implicit agreement was that a blind eye would be turned to occasional nonconformity if puritans did not directly oppose the Church's ceremonies and episcopal government. Similarly, John Rogers, the celebrated puritan lecturer at Dedham, condemned ministers who spoke out against ceremonies and church government, which were issues 'beyond our reach', rather than focusing on 'the Doctrine of Faith, Sanctification, Love, etc.', but he still systematically avoided wearing the

---

[4] P. Collinson, *Godly People: Essays on English Protestantism and Puritanism* (1983), p. 534.
[5] Collinson, *Godly People*, pp. 473–83.

surplice.⁶ The later Presbyterian Constant Jessop remembered how his father forbade public or even private discussion of issues relating to church government, so that he would not be drawn to express his true feelings regarding episcopacy and could continue to exercise his ministry.⁷ But changing defences of episcopacy meant that this often required a willing suspension of disbelief. The growing importance of the claim that episcopacy existed *iure divino* ('by divine right')—which enjoyed the status of a semi-official orthodoxy in the early Stuart Church—potentially undermined the rationale behind the puritans' acceptance of the Church of England's government as a temporary infelicity which would be reformed in due course. A degree of practical toleration of occasional puritan nonconformity was observed, then, but blind eyes needed to be turned by bishops and puritans alike for this to work. And this was a long way away from meaning that puritans were indeed members of the establishment, or part of a straightforward mainstream.

That being said, some erstwhile puritan nonconformists did make their way into higher office in the Established Church. Samuel Ward and William Bedell were close friends who conducted an anxious correspondence regarding subscription after the passage of the 1604 canons, with Bedell seeking to convince Ward that if subscription was necessary to secure the freedom to continue preaching then this was an acceptable compromise. Ultimately Bedell would end up as a bishop in Ireland working in uneasy partnership with Archbishop Laud, and Ward—whose earlier diary reveals a clear sense that he was a member of the community of the godly—became an archdeacon and pluralist as well as Master of Sidney Sussex College, Cambridge and Lady Margaret Professor of Divinity. Ward defended compliance with the Caroline Book of Sports on the grounds of obedience and order, and by 1641 clearly had a more exalted view of episcopacy than that held by his friends Bedell and James Ussher, who were bishops themselves. Both Ward and Bedell continued to use their positions to push for godly reforms or to defend Calvinism against 'Arminian' onslaughts.⁸ Nevertheless, Bedell and Ward arguably exemplify a broader process of 'conformist drift' in this period, in which godly individuals could find the logic of their defence of conformity (and opposition from erstwhile puritan colleagues) drawing them into a more wholehearted defence of the Established Church and its ceremonies, and a retreat from some hardline Calvinist and anti-Catholic positions.⁹

---

⁶ *ODNB*, 'Bernard, Richard (1568–1642)'; T. Webster, *Godly Clergy in Early Stuart England: The Caroline Puritan Movement, c.1620–1643* (Cambridge, 1997), pp. 191–2.

⁷ *The Angel of the Church of Ephesus* (1644), sig. A2v.

⁸ M. Todd, '"An Act of Discretion": Evangelical Conformity and the Puritan Dons', *Albion*, 18 (1986): 581–99; M. Todd, 'Puritan Self-Fashioning: The Diary of Samuel Ward', *Journal of British Studies*, 31 (1992): 236–64; Sidney Sussex College, Cambridge MS O/3.

⁹ A. Milton, *Catholic and Reformed: The Roman and Protestant Churches in English Protestant Thought, 1600–1640* (Cambridge, 1995), pp. 535–7.

Unsettled Reformations, 1603–1662

But the Jacobean Church was not simply characterized by the embedding of 'puritan' evangelical attitudes in Church and state. This was only one element of the story, and the partial integration of puritanism may in itself have been responsible to some extent for generating a reactionary backlash. From the 1590s a number of divines—dubbed in recent years 'avant-garde conformists'— were gaining in importance and disseminating a vision of the English Church that sought to attack its perceived over-emphasis on the importance of preaching. Instead they urged a significantly enhanced view of the importance of public worship and of the capacity of ceremonies to be spiritually efficacious. This was a vision that was consciously inimical to the Calvinism and the word-based piety and preoccupations of puritanism, and to the sacrilege that this had allegedly promoted. Spokesmen for this position, such as Lancelot Andrewes and John Overall, came close to the heart of the establishment in the first decades of James's reign. Some of them pursued an anti-puritan agenda in their dioceses (Canon 72 made the existence of combination lectures dependent on the approval of the bishop, which could be withheld), while those at court promoted more elaborate ritual in worship, and often played a key role in the creation of conservative, semi-official definitions of the identity and doctrines of the Church of England. An example is the preface to the new edition of the collected works of Jewel, where Overall described the separation from Rome at the Reformation in a restrained, passive fashion, and emphasized continuity with the pre-Reformation Church.[10]

As a result, two strands of churchmanship—evangelical and avant-garde conformist—unfolded simultaneously during the reign of James I, and could lead to the Church seeming to speak in two very different voices at the same moment. This was not just the case in James's English Church. The Irish Articles of 1615 were an unambiguous assertion of mainstream Calvinism in their incorporation of the 1595 Lambeth Articles when expounding the doctrine of predestination, their implacable anti-Catholicism (they are almost unique among Protestant confessions of faith in identifying the Pope as the Antichrist), and their conscious omission of references to episcopal consecration and ordination, and to baptismal regeneration.[11] Yet in James's kingdom of Scotland, episcopacy increasingly reasserted itself, and the Articles of Perth (issued just three years after the Irish Articles) introduced ceremonial innovations including episcopal confirmation and kneeling at communion to the Scottish Church. James himself issued instructions that the Chapel Royal at Holyrood should have a richly decorated altar with carved and gilded figures

---

[10] A. Milton, '"Anglicanism" by Stealth: The Career and Influence of John Overall', in K. Fincham and P. Lake (eds.), *Religious Politics in Post-Reformation England* (Woodbridge, 2006), pp. 159–76.

[11] A. Ford, *James Ussher: Theology, History, and Politics in Early Modern Ireland and England* (Oxford, 2007), ch. 4.

of apostles and evangelists. Although, after warnings from the Scottish bishops, James ultimately agreed not to insist on the erecting of images, this was with the characteristically Jacobean face-saver that this was for practical reasons, 'not for ease of their hearts, or confirming them in their error'.[12] While passing through Cheshire on his return from his trip to Scotland in 1617 (attended by a number of avant-garde conformist divines), James also issued the notorious Book of Sports, by which parishioners received official permission to enjoy lawful recreations on the Sabbath (with the aim of curbing the overzealous puritan JPs whose sabbatarian initiatives were accused of hindering the conversion of local Catholics).

By contrast, the same year that witnessed the national publication of the Jacobean Book of Sports (1618) also saw an apparently emphatic official expression of the Church's Calvinist identity when James dispatched official delegates to attend the Reformed Synod of Dort in the Netherlands. Not only was the decision to attend significant in itself, but the king's choice of ecclesiastical representatives was especially notable—all good Calvinists with no avant-garde conformists to be seen. However, this selection was made by the king to fit a particular foreign policy objective: the decisive defeat of the Dutch Arminians was necessary to bolster the power of the Prince of Orange. And just as notable as the English Calvinist presence at Dort was the increasing willingness of those with avant-garde conformist views to condemn the same synod. Moreover, while foreign policy considerations prompted a symbolic manifestation of the Church of England's links with the Reformed Churches by sending a delegation to the Synod of Dort, they also led to the opposite with the outbreak of the Thirty Years War. Popular support for the king's daughter Elizabeth and her husband the Elector Palatine—the champions of continental Reformed Protestantism and the most notable victims of the early stages of the war—was combined with hostility towards the projected Spanish marriage for James's son Charles which was the king's preferred solution to the ensuing confessional warfare. This opposition pushed James's support towards those court divines who were more hostile towards entanglements with foreign Reformed Protestantism and more accommodating (or at least pragmatic) in their attitudes towards Roman Catholicism.[13]

If the evangelical nature of the Jacobean Church had been characterized by a 'Calvinist consensus', then it was natural that arguments over the doctrine of predestination would become part of the battleground between these different factions in the Church. This was not least because Dutch events had tarred Arminians as crypto-Catholics, and the defeat of them at Dort by

---

[12] C. C. Rogers, *The History of the Chapel Royal of Scotland* (Edinburgh, 1882), pp. cxxi–cxxiv, cxxvi.

[13] Fincham and Lake, 'Ecclesiastical Policy', pp. 198–202; A. Milton (ed.), *The British Delegation and the Synod of Dort (1618–1619)* (Woodbridge, 2005), pp. xxii–xxx.

representatives of the Church of England meant that upholders of Calvinist orthodoxy could claim to speak for the authorized Church of England. The fact that the Church's most prominent divines over the previous decades could also be characterized as supporting 'Calvinist' views further bolstered the conformist, 'orthodox' credentials of those defending the Calvinist position. What ensued was a very public struggle over the identity of the Church of England, particularly focused on the writings of one of the most outspoken advocates of 'avant-garde conformity', Richard Montagu. Montagu's notorious two books—the *New Gagg* and *Appello Caesarem* (the latter dedicated to King James)—famously opposed the claim that Calvinist doctrines were those of the Church of England: a stance that positively invited the charge of 'Arminianism'. But this was part of Montagu's broader argument that most of the attacks that Catholics levelled against the Church of England's doctrines and practices were misapplied, as the points being targeted were not formal positions upheld by the Church, but rather were the unrepresentative opinions of 'puritans'. In the process, Montagu not only considerably reduced the areas of division between the Church of England and Roman Catholicism, but he also marginalized as 'puritan' much of the doctrinal common ground between puritans and the Established Church. He did this not only with reference to Calvinist predestinarianism, but also to the doctrines 'that onely Faith justifieth', 'that the Pope is Antichrist', and 'that no good workes are meritorious', along with many other staples of anti-Catholic controversial literature.[14] It is notable that Montagu's assailants in print included not just puritans but also his own diocesan bishop, while the House of Commons and archbishop of Canterbury also weighed in against him.

The response to Montagu's ideas was further complicated by the accession of Charles I in 1625. There was no Millenary Petition and no requests for church reform at the beginning of the new reign, although (perhaps anticipating calls for reform and seeking to remind readers how these had been rejected by the previous monarch) the king's printer republished the official account of the Hampton Court Conference. However, MPs did debate a bill to allow silenced ministers to preach without subscribing to the 1604 canons (although tellingly it was remarked that 'moderate bishops' would allow this anyway).[15] More generally, Parliament would appear to have been content with the state of the Church itself, but felt the need to support it in rooting out men such as Montagu, as part of its broader concern to stamp out Roman Catholicism (and anything that resembled it). Initially the reaction to Montagu saw the Calvinist Church and state united: MPs were happy to

---

[14] Richard Montagu, *A Gagg for the New Gospell? No: A New Gagg for an Old Goose* (1624), esp. sigs. A2–A4.

[15] M. Jansson and W. B. Bidwell (eds.), *Proceedings in Parliament 1625* (New Haven, CT, 1987), pp. 247–8.

entrust the matter of Montagu's books to the Calvinist Archbishop Abbot, although Abbot's failure to act decisively in the matter led to the Commons seeking to intervene more directly themselves, both in prosecuting Montagu and in drawing up bills to ratify the canons of Dort 'as part of the doctrine of the Church of England' and to give joint statutory authority to the Thirty-Nine Articles and the Irish Articles.[16] A theological conference at York House in 1626—attended by divines and members of the House of Lords—was another attempt to resolve the disputes in a fashion that avoided raising awkward questions about where authority lay in resolving doctrinal disputes. But the failure of the conference, and the increasingly provocative behaviour of Montagu's friend and ally John Cosin in promoting extreme ceremonialist practices in Durham Cathedral, meant that events escalated into a more general assault on avant-garde conformity and its supporters clustered around the circle of Bishop Neile (the king's Clerk of the Closet) at Durham House in the Strand. Cosin—who was Neile's chaplain—exacerbated the existing tensions when he also published his *Collection of Private Devotions*, which were organized according to the hours of prayer and included prayers for the dead in its first version. The more elaborate styles of churchmanship practised hitherto by Lancelot Andrewes were now being advocated in a much more confrontational fashion. By 1628, opponents of Montagu and Cosin such as the puritan William Prynne had already lost hope that Convocation would be capable of acting to uphold doctrinal and ceremonial orthodoxy. The suspension of Archbishop Abbot from exercising his metropolitical authority in 1627–8 made it even more clear that the so-called 'Durham House Group' could not be vanquished by opponents within the Church hierarchy, and that attacks would have to be entrusted to Parliament alone.

With the death of Abbot in 1633 and the king's support for his new archbishop William Laud, the 1630s saw the full flowering of this style of churchmanship, when the epithet 'Laudianism' becomes an appropriate description. The policies pursued by Laud and his supporters in this decade comprehended a number of different elements. Principal among these was the restoration of the 'beauty of holiness'—a conviction that the church building was God's house and should be treated as such, reflected in the more elaborate decoration of church interiors and furniture, and an enhanced importance placed upon the inherent 'edifying' value of the public worship and ceremonies conducted within. The flipside of this was a de-emphasis on preaching, and indeed a suggestion that it could afford to be curtailed in favour of a greater emphasis upon the sacraments as channels of grace. This took its most visible form in the Laudian altar policy—the placing of the communion table altarwise at the east end of the church, encompassed by rails. While there were

---

[16] N. Tyacke, *Anti-Calvinists: The Rise of English Arminianism c.1590–1640* (Oxford, 1987), pp. 149–52, 154.

some precedents for this arrangement it was certainly not required by the canons, and its implementation throughout the country was unprecedented.[17] It was accompanied by a preference for the sustained use of the terms 'altar', 'priest', and 'sacrifice' in officially approved tracts and sermons. Such language not only reflected a readiness to rethink aspects of the sacrament of the Lord's Supper, but also a greater reverence for and willingness to imitate the words and practices of the pre-Reformation past. The enthusiastic ritualism of some of the Church Fathers was embraced more wholeheartedly than before, with a greater emphasis placed upon such works as providing a model and yardstick for Church of England worship, while Old Testament examples of Solomon's Temple were enlisted as direct precedents for ceremonial worship, rather than as forerunners of more figurative worship. This was combined with a less allergic response to the religion of the medieval centuries, an emphasis on the importance of continuous tradition, and an avoidance of outspoken anti-Catholicism. More generally, Laudian divines showed a greater preoccupation with the sin of sacrilege rather than that of idolatry (Rom. 2:22 was a favourite Laudian text).[18]

This greater sense of identity with the medieval Church also reflected the fact that at the heart of the Laudian movement lay a determination to reverse some of the trends that the Reformation had initiated (especially those of increasing lay control and the diminishing power of the church courts). They sought instead to rebuild the power, wealth, and legal authority of the Church and of its clerical representatives vis-à-vis the laity. The revival of the Jacobean Book of Sports—which defended the use of certain recreations on the Sabbath—was as much about curbing the powers of puritan JPs in religious affairs as it was about promoting lawful recreations or preventing Sunday afternoon sermons. Hence also Laud's determination to crush the Feoffees for Impropriations (a group of lay and clerical trustees with strong puritan connections, who purchased impropriations and advowsons in order to present livings to 'godly' clergymen of their own choice). Where puritan clergy were concerned, the Laudian Church marked a decisive shift from earlier policies in its determination to enforce both subscription *and* ceremonial conformity on the clergy, and its distaste for the compromises that earlier evangelical bishops had overseen. When Laud declared at his trial for treason in 1645 that 'unity cannot long continue in the church, where uniformity is shut out at the church door' he spelt out both the rationale of his policies and the inevitability of their failure.[19]

---

[17] K. Fincham, 'The Restoration of Altars in the 1630s', *Historical Journal*, 44 (2001): 919–40.
[18] P. Lake, 'The Laudian Style: Order, Uniformity and the Pursuit of the Beauty of Holiness in the 1630s', in K. Fincham (ed.), *The Early Stuart Church, 1603–1642* (Basingstoke, 1993), pp. 161–85; Milton, *Catholic and Reformed*, pp. 63–77, 274–6, 310–21.
[19] J. S. McGee, 'William Laud and the Outward Face of Religion', in R. L. DeMolen (ed.), *Leaders of the Reformation* (Selinsgrove, PA, 1984), pp. 318–44; *The Works of William Laud*, ed. W. Scott and J. Bliss, 7 vols. (Oxford, 1847–60), IV, p. 60.

While some contemporaries and modern historians have been tempted to brand Laudian policies as 'Arminian', it should be clear that there was a great deal more to Laudianism than an 'Arminian' rejection of Calvinist predestinarianism, even if the emphasis placed upon the sacraments and public worship might betoken a non-Calvinist doctrine of grace.[20] The king's declarations in 1626 and 1628 had imposed silence on any debates over predestination, but while this made it difficult actively to promote Arminian doctrines, nevertheless the silencing of Calvinist ones enabled the ceremonies and liturgy of the Church of England to be promoted without being implicitly undercut by predestinarian qualifications (and Laud at least would appear to have been happy to rest with that).

Here then was a desire to revive ecclesiastical authority that echoed Archbishop Bancroft's earlier efforts, but combined with a much broader agenda to reform church worship and to revisit the Reformed and anti-Catholic doctrinal emphases of the English Protestant tradition. Moreover, if Laud was still careful to secure the legal basis for his interventions, his junior and more exuberant supporters had fewer reservations in embracing neglected ceremonies and doctrines. Laudianism had a momentum that was constantly pushing against the boundaries of accepted Protestant orthodoxies.[21]

An emphasis on restoring the powers of the Church, and undoing some of the sacrilege of the early Reformation, meant that Laudianism could appear to hostile observers as if it was opposed to the Reformation itself. Laud himself described what he was doing as returning the Church 'to the rules of its first reformation', but this could also mean reviving non-canonical conservative forms of devotion such as bowing towards the altar that had swiftly died out after the Reformation (those rites and ceremonies 'daily and ordinarily practised in the past albeit without any rule or law for the observation of the same', as the preface to the 1640 canons put it).[22] There was a pronounced tendency among Laudian divines to seek to establish the status quo at the very beginning of the Elizabethan Settlement. The logic of the Laudian position often led them to reject many of the dominant practices and writings in the Church of England in the decades *since* the Settlement, and implicitly to see all subsequent Protestant developments as a process of decline. Their perspective on the Tudor reformations tended to be highly selective, avoiding aspects of the Henrician and Edwardian Reformations in particular (whose more radical elements could be blamed on avaricious courtiers and the baleful influence of

---

[20] Tyacke, *Anti-Calvinists*, pp. 198–244.
[21] A. Milton, 'The Creation of Laudianism', in T. Cogswell, R. Cust, and P. Lake (eds.), *Politics, Religion and Popularity in Early Stuart Britain* (Cambridge, 2002), pp. 177–84.
[22] Laud, *Works*, VI, p. 42; Bray, *Canons*, p. 554.

John Calvin), and disregarding sections of the Elizabethan Book of Homilies that they found less attractive.[23]

Historians have sometimes been tempted to treat Laudianism as a bizarre anomaly—a sudden calamitous subversion of a flourishing evangelical Church by an unrepresentative high church minority. But this is misleading in a number of ways. Firstly, many of Laudianism's preoccupations had earlier roots and precedents, for example in the 'avant-garde conformity' espoused by Lancelot Andrewes as early as the late 1580s, and in some of the emphases in Richard Hooker's writings. It also built upon a broader movement of distaste for the iconoclastic excesses of the Reformation and a nostalgia for the past that is evident in a range of lay authors, from the historian William Camden and the legal antiquarian Henry Spelman to the avid recorder of funeral monuments John Weever. It also drew upon a groundswell of popular opposition to puritanism. Although many of the elements of the Laudian programme can be glimpsed in earlier writings and policies, Laudianism was however distinctive in the ways in which these features were combined, and the force with which they were translated into a sustained programme of reform. Also characteristic of Laudianism was its strongly anti-puritan edge, combined with the assumption that the Church's evangelical traditions and Calvinist doctrines were incompatible with a reverence for the past and the 'beauty of holiness'.[24]

Another reason why Laudianism should not be portrayed as a mere aberration is the fact that the Laudian movement also attracted a wide range of followers. There was a 'Laudian moment' as well as movement, and in the polarized religious world which Laudians perceived and partly helped to generate, there were plenty of hitherto 'Calvinist' clergymen who found themselves perforce on the Laudian side and prepared to speak with the requisite Laudian accent where ceremonies were concerned. These included two erstwhile delegates at Dort—Thomas Goad and Walter Balcanquahall. There were also other divines who for many years had silently opposed the prevalent godly culture and who now spoke out, emerging after decades in the shadows, or others who either avidly converted to the newly dominant theme of the 'beauty of holiness', or who were careerists eager to embrace what appeared to be the route to successful promotion.[25] Laypeople might also find the elaborate forms of Laudian worship and decoration more to their religious and secular taste. Through a mixture of careerism, conversion, grudging and sometimes enthusiastic compliance, the Church of England

---

[23] A. Milton, *Laudian and Royalist Polemic in Seventeenth-Century England* (Manchester, 2007), pp. 83–8; Milton, *Catholic and Reformed*, pp. 331–6.

[24] K. Fincham and and N. Tyacke, *Altars Restored: The Changing Face of English Religious Worship, 1547–c.1700* (Oxford, 2007), pp. 66–125.

[25] Milton, 'Creation of Laudianism', pp. 176–7.

had acquired a Laudian face by the end of the decade—certainly, the majority of parish communion tables had been converted into east-end altars and railed in by 1640.

But what of the opposition to Laudianism? Initially this was often framed in a conservative mode—in a sense, this represented a confrontation between different elements of the earlier English Reformation. The Commons' Resolutions on Religion of 1629, attacking the novelties in doctrine and practice, struck a purely conservative note. They condemned the new ceremonies advanced by Cosin and his colleagues at Durham, the spread of Arminian doctrine and publishing of 'points of Popery' by Montagu and others, and urged as sources of orthodox predestinarian doctrine not just the Lambeth and Irish Articles and the official doctrinal submission by the British delegates at Dort, but also the Prayer Book, Homilies, and Catechism, along with the works of John Jewel. Their appeal was simply for 'the orthodox doctrine of our Church, in these now controverted points' to be 'established and freely taught, as it hath been hitherto generally received'.[26] Similarly, the Laudian policies of the 1630s were attacked by their opponents as innovations, and a raft of homilies, episcopal authors, and official Elizabethan injunctions were cited against them. If Laudians were nostalgic for the pre-Reformation Church, their opponents were nostalgic for the doctrinal rigours of the Calvinist bishops and clergy of the Elizabethan and Jacobean Church. The Book of Homilies—and in particular the Homily against the Peril of Idolatry—had never been more popular among puritan writers. In a sense, both sides were appealing to different parts of a shared English Reformation past, and in the process undeclared inconsistencies and incompatibilities in English Protestants' readings of the Reformation started to be spelt out more clearly.

There was, however, a more radical edge to anti-Laudianism. Complaints against Laudian innovations were combined with those against ceremonies such as bowing at the name of Jesus which was already required by the 1604 canons but was simply being imposed more systematically than before. Moreover, in anti-Laudian pamphlets, early Jacobean objections against the legitimacy of the Court of High Commission and episcopal authority were combined with complaints against more recent innovations by Laudian bishops. This more radical edge was strengthened when Charles directed the imposition of a new Prayer Book and canons in the Scottish Church. The critical Scottish response soon encompassed attacks upon the Articles of Perth (which included ceremonies enshrined in the 1559 English Prayer Book) as well as the more recent innovations of the New Scottish Prayer Book. This was swiftly combined with an attack upon the institution of episcopacy. The

---

[26] S. R. Gardiner, *Constitutional Documents of the Puritan Revolution 1625–1660* (Oxford, 1906 edn.), pp. 77–83.

radical edge of Scottish anti-Laudianism soon found its way into English anti-Laudian works too.[27]

The Short Parliament (April–May 1640)—called by Charles in 1640 in the wake of the inconclusive end to the First Bishops' War against the Scottish rebels—prefigured later clashes in its concerns about Laudian innovation, but also in arguments concerning the role of Convocation. Convocation's plan to draw up new canons was generating opposition in Parliament even before the added provocation that Convocation continued in session after the Short Parliament had been dissolved. Not only did the resulting 1640 canons enshrine the new altar policy as now legally approved, but they also introduced the notorious 'etcetera' oath that required the acceptance of the existing church government 'as by right it ought to stand', and as containing all things necessary to salvation. This could imply the *iure divino* status of bishops (and of all other existing church officers), and that was certainly how critics interpreted it. It seemed to offer the worst possible combination of establishing the freedom of the Church to bring in new ceremonies, while at the same time requiring the acceptance of hitherto-resented elements of church government as unalterable. For many, this was the last straw.

The meeting of the Long Parliament in November 1640 was greeted by clarion calls for religious reform, after the disastrous defeat of Charles's forces in the Second Bishops' War with the Scots. The number of petitions against the clergy, and the early emergence of the petition to remove episcopacy 'root and branch' in December 1640, have tended to give historians the impression of an unstoppable puritan steamroller working inevitably towards the destruction of the existing post-Reformation Church, opposed only by petitioners fighting a rearguard action to defend the Prayer Book and episcopacy and the established ecclesiastical status quo. Yet it is easy to miss the degree to which there were desires all round to see a less drastic reform of the Church, despite the reforming energies of puritan critics and the radicalizing force of the emerging political crisis. The oft-expressed desire to 'reduce' episcopacy did not necessitate its removal, and was not incompatible with a wish to adhere to the Prayer Book (while seeing some of its errors and perceived infelicities reformed). Schemes for reduced episcopacy generally proposed a church structure where weekly meetings of parish officials were supplemented by a hierarchy of monthly deanery and annual diocesan synods. It is notable that many of the principles behind this proposed 'reduction' and the reform of the Prayer Book had been raised before, at the beginning of James's reign and earlier. Similarly, the removal of the Court of High Commission and the reform of church courts had long been a goal of MPs who had not questioned other aspects of the settlement. In fact, the period 1640–2 witnessed what

---

[27] A. Milton, *England's Second Reformation* (forthcoming).

might be called an 'abortive reformation', when senior members of the Established Church were not only prepared to outlaw Laudian doctrines and practices and to reassert pre-Laudian doctrinal orthodoxies, but also to consider significant reforms, such as abandoning the sign of the cross in baptism. Indeed, a subcommittee of bishops, deans, and other clergymen chaired by Bishop Williams was empowered by the House of Lords 'to examine all Innovations in Doctrine or Discipline introduced into the Church without Law *since the Reformation*' (i.e not just under Laud). It was also stipulated that if their lordships then thought it necessary for the good of Church and state then they should 'examine after that the Degrees and Perfection of the Reformation it self'.[28] Reforms of episcopacy were also certainly on the table during this time, and the most publicized scheme for 'reduced episcopacy' was the work of an archbishop—James Ussher—and attracted considerable interest.[29]

In the end, this attempted reformation collapsed due to the erosion of political consensus, and the radicalization of opinion on both sides. Yet many of the proposals and reforms being debated in the period 1640–2 were (as has been stressed) entirely familiar, echoing Elizabethan reform proposals, and need not be seen as harbingers of the destruction of the later 1640s and 1650s. In many ways, they are best seen as a continuation of the debates conducted in the first years of James's reign, and reforms that might have been implemented then if King James had not then thrown his weight against them. One disappointed MP lamented in 1642 what he saw as the betrayal by radicals of this 'blessed Reforming' and 'the losse of such a Glorious Reformation, as being the revived image of the best and purest ages, would with its Beauty and Piety have drawn the eye and heart of all Christendome unto us'.[30] The fundamental point to be emphasized here is that the reforms of 1641–2 did not represent an unnatural departure or temporary aberration from a previously stable 'Anglican' position. Similarly, the conservative petitions drawn up throughout the country in defence of episcopacy and the Prayer Book at this time were not simply traditional defences of an unchanging 'Anglican' orthodoxy purged of Laudian elements, but were themselves hotly contested and carefully orchestrated. Their content was monitored and sometimes subtly altered to procure maximum numbers of signatories.[31]

---

[28] John Hacket, *Scrinia Reserata* (1692), pt. 2, p. 147 (my italics); *A Copie of the Proceedings of Some Worthy and Learned Divines* (1641).

[29] Ford, *Ussher*, pp. 240–1. [30] Edward Dering, *A Collection of Speeches* (1642), p. 164.

[31] For example, J. Walter, 'Confessional Politics in Pre-Civil War Essex: Prayer Books, Profanations and Petitions', *Historical Journal*, 44 (2011): 677–701; R. Cust, 'The Defence of Episcopacy on the Eve of Civil War: Jeremy Taylor and the Rutland Petition of 1641', *JEH*, (forthcoming); P. Lake, 'Puritans, Popularity and Petitions: Local Politics in National Context, Cheshire, 1641', in Cogswell et al. (eds.), *Politics, Religion and Popularity*, pp. 259–89.

The two sides in the civil war that followed came to stand for different attitudes towards the Church of England, but both saw themselves as upholders of English Protestant orthodoxy against those undermining the true Reformation. On the royalist side, there were consistent attempts to elide the defence of monarchy with the defence of the episcopal Church, but the increasing attempts by Charles I (and later his son) to reach a deal which would actually sacrifice elements of the Established Church created a crisis in the royalist view of the royal supremacy. Already the king had agreed to exclude bishops from Parliament (a state of affairs which continued in the royalist Parliament at Oxford). More generally, royalist churchmen found themselves struggling with royalist Erastians who were unwilling to see a new possible church settlement jeopardized by the bishops' opposition. If the king in his posthumously published (and possibly ghost-written) collection of devotions, *Eikon Basilike*, blamed his sufferings on God's judgement upon him for his abandoning of the Church, some royalist churchmen at least may have agreed, and drew the obvious conclusion when Charles II's alliance with the Scottish Covenanters in 1651—the ultimate betrayal of the episcopal Church—led to abject military defeat.[32]

On the other side, parliamentary religious policy was most obviously characterized by destruction. Instruments of Laudianism such as the Court of High Commission were suppressed, and Laud himself was executed for treason in 1645, followed by the abolition of bishops, deans and chapters, and the Book of Common Prayer. There was literal destruction in the iconoclasm unleashed in cathedrals and parish churches, while holy days including Christmas and Easter were also abolished. This period witnessed the largest-ever purging of ministers from the Church—the famous expulsions of 1604 and even 1662 pale numerically before those of the 1640s. Nevertheless, creativity sprang from the work of the reforming body established by Parliament—the Westminster Assembly (1643–52)—with its creation of a new Westminster Confession of Faith, two official catechisms, a new Directory for Public Worship, a new directory of ordination, and the attempt to introduce a Presbyterian system of church government. Moreover, most parliamentarian reformers did not see themselves as being in an antagonistic relationship with the past. Instead, their task was—as they saw it—to perfect the earlier Reformation ('to reform the Reformation it self' in Edmund Calamy's memorable phrase). Indeed, the 1640s reform of the Church had begun with what was intended to be a mere revision of the Thirty-Nine Articles, but with the entry of the Scots on the parliamentarian side this

---

[32] A. Milton, 'Anglicanism and Royalism in the 1640s', in J. Adamson (ed.), *The English Civil War: Conflict and Contexts, 1640–49* (Basingstoke, 2009), pp. 70–3, 80; A. Milton, '"Vailing his Crown": Royalist Criticism of Charles I's Kingship in the 1650s', in J. McElligott and D. L. Smith (eds.), *Royalists and Royalism during the Interregnum* (Manchester, 2010), p. 99.

escalated into the drawing up of a new confession of faith. Similarly, the Prayer Book was not initially a focus of hostility, and the preface of its replacement, the Directory for Public Worship, gives thanks for 'the Blessed Reformation' of 'our wise and pious Ancestours' in drawing up the Book of Common Prayer. In fact, the preface insists that this 'further Reformation' was conducted by the current reformers 'not from any love to Novelty, or intention to disparage our first Reformers', claiming that had they still been alive 'they would joyne with us in this work', and acknowledging them to be 'Excellent Instruments raised by God'. And ultimately, because the Directory for Public Worship was more a set of rubrics than a prayer book or fixed liturgy, the eminent puritan clergyman and prominent member of the Westminster Assembly John Ley can be found appealing in the 1650s for a set form of prayer for church services to be reintroduced into the Church (albeit not the Book of Common Prayer itself, and with its use to be commended rather than required).[33]

In the end, the Westminster Assembly's plans were complicated by the interference of Parliament, which was determined to resist the establishment of independent clerical authority, and in particular to prevent the exclusion of individual laypeople from communion. What emerged was an Erastian settlement in which Parliament acted decisively to modify what the Assembly proposed, and to emasculate the new form of church government. The intended Presbyterian settlement was never effectively imposed, and its requirements never made compulsory. As a result, a system of provincial assemblies was only properly operational in London and Lancashire (although one wonders how much of the Elizabethan Settlement would have been implemented in the sixteenth century if it had had to rely solely on the voluntary actions of local authorities). The fact that this settlement was decisively shaped by the intervention of the secular magistrate was, of course, entirely consistent with the manner of England's earlier reformations (albeit the monarch was absent this time).

But if Parliament had acted to curb the clericalist pretensions of the Assembly, the intended Presbyterian settlement was also critically undermined by divisions among the puritan clergy themselves. In the Assembly this took the form of actions by a very small minority (the 'Dissenting Brethren', or 'Independents' to their enemies) who objected to the Presbyterian elements of the proposed settlement and instead urged a Congregationalist model of self-governing churches of the godly. The Presbyterian Reformation was ultimately defeated by the fact that these Independents enjoyed crucial influence within the army, which itself came to play an increasingly decisive role in the political situation. But even these Independents were not simply

---

[33] Edmund Calamy, *Englands Looking-Glasse, Presented in a Sermon Preached before the Honorable House of Commons* (1642), p. 46; *A Directory for the Publique Worship of God* (1645), pp. 1, 3; John Ley, *A Debate concerning the English Liturgy* (1656), pp. 24–6.

antagonistic towards pre-war English Protestantism. Their *Apologeticall Narration* adopted a typically 'Anglican' ploy of presenting their position as a moderate 'middle way' (in this case between Presbyterianism and separatism). They also emphasized their indebtedness to the writings of previous generations of anti-separatist puritans, 'our owne Divines, the good old Nonconformists'. Moreover, for all their stress on the independence of individual congregations, many of them attached great importance to the role of the civil magistrate in promoting true religion, and were supportive of attempts to promote godly preaching and moral reform on a national scale.[34]

With the execution of Charles I in 1649 the Church of England moved into unknown territory—along with the abandonment of so many of its other pre-war features there was now no royal supremacy. But under the new Commonwealth there was still an assumption that the civil magistrate should play a major role in overseeing the effective performance of the Church. There were proposals to reform the more unwieldy parish divisions and to augment parish livings, while under Cromwell a system of Triers and Ejectors was erected to approve the appointment of clergymen, and to direct the removal of any deemed unsatisfactory. There was also a national programme of godly reformation in the localities which embraced the efforts of a broad cross-section of ministers, including Independents and Presbyterians, while some episcopalians also cooperated with Presbyterians in regional associations. While the September 1650 Toleration Act abolished the requirement to attend parish church, parishes nevertheless continued to function. Congregationalist ministers who held parish livings still observed a parochial as well as a more exclusive ministry, and the theoretically intimidating restrictions on access to the sacrament often resulted in parishes simply avoiding the parochial celebration of the divisive sacrament altogether. Despite some determined attacks, tithes remained as a fundamental source of clerical income. While use of the Book of Common Prayer was theoretically forbidden, the King James Bible was still used by all contending parties, and the Thirty-Nine Articles were still frequently cited in tracts as orthodox doctrine.

With the execution of the king, royalist episcopalians in some cases rethought the role of the civil magistrate, especially in cases where the civil power sought to interfere with the exercise of episcopal authority. This could be as true of monarchs such as Charles II (who agreed to sign the anti-episcopal Covenant in 1650) and his father (who had curbed episcopal authority and agreed to its temporary suspension) as of a Presbyterian or Independent Parliament. The royalist divine Herbert Thorndike wrote that, in cases where the sovereign forbade the exercise of the ecclesiastical power needed to preserve the unity of the Church (i.e. episcopal authority), then

---

[34] *An Apologeticall Narration* (1643), pp. 4–5, 19, 24.

'those that are trusted with the Power of the Church' should not only 'disobey the commands of the Sovereign, but... use that Power, which their quality in the Society of the Church gives them, to provide for the subsistence thereof, without the assistance of Secular Powers'. In cases where the bishops and the sovereign power disagreed, and it was not clear who was in the right, it behoved Christians 'at their utmost perils' to 'adhere to the Guides of the Church, against their lawful Soveraigns'.

Episcopalians who would not conform to the new regime were often forced to cultivate a non-parochial form of religious organization. Bishops were (with some notable exceptions) inactive, and people from many different parishes might gather in private houses or chapels for clandestine religious services—and they admitted it. In 1657 Dr Edward Hyde commented in print: 'In these times, when conscientious Ministers cannot officiate in the church, conscientious Christians cannot go to church, customary Christians go thither to little purpose... 'tis fit the Church should come to private houses.'[35] Indeed, we might suggest that a wide range of English Protestants participated in what was a 'congregationalist moment' in the 1650s. In a sense, as episcopalians became a persecuted religious minority, so practical logic dictated that they embrace some of the activities that we associate more with radical puritans in earlier decades, with religiously sympathetic gentry and aristocrats offering patronage and protection, illegal lecturers being smuggled in to give sermons, clandestine private meetings for proscribed forms of worship, and 'martyrologies' of persecuted colleagues being composed. There was also much rethinking of doctrinal orthodoxies: while sectarian groups famously challenged basic Christian orthodoxies, episcopalian clergy also toyed with anti-trinitarianism or rejected the doctrine of original sin.[36]

While royalists contemplated innovative approaches to doctrine and church government, parliamentarians who were associated with radical positions fashioned their own curious hybrids of conventional and heterodox churchmanship, and few more intriguingly than John Tombes. A firm opponent of infant baptism in voluminous publications and decades of public debates, Tombes was in other respects a dedicated upholder of the principle of an Established Church, and a determined anti-separatist (he would later publish in support of taking the oath of supremacy at the Restoration and would dedicate books to Charles II's chief minister the earl of Clarendon). Tombes had first struggled to find texts to support infant baptism when reading the catechism lecture in Magdalen Hall, Oxford in 1627, but it was the upheavals of the early 1640s which encouraged him, on the issue of infant baptism at

---

[35] Herbert Thorndike, *Discourse of the Right of the Church in a Christian State* (1649), pp. 234–5; Edward Hyde, *Christ and his Church* (1657), sig. A2r.

[36] Milton, 'Anglicanism and Royalism', p. 76; Christ Church College, Oxford, Allestree Papers, MS M.3.6, fos. 148v–149v.

least, to pursue the matter further and to rethink first principles. In being prompted by the disruptions of the 1640s to reconsider theological basics he was far from alone.[37] With the normative structures of religious authority and orthodoxy in abeyance, all groups—episcopalian royalists included—participated in a remarkable explosion of theological creativity which deserves its place in all histories of English religion, whatever their particular denominational focus. Religious radicalism was not simply the spiritual journey of a few notorious sectarians; it was a *national* experience.

The restoration of the Church of England could have gone in a variety of directions, and there was nothing inevitable about the eventual settlement that emerged. Presbyterians were mostly firmly royalist, and shades of a very different potential settlement can be discerned throughout 1660. Two months before Charles II's re-entry into London, the restored Long Parliament had re-established the Solemn League and Covenant and the Westminster Confession. The promise in Charles II's Declaration of Breda (issued on 4 April) of 'a liberty to tender consciences' perhaps implied toleration of different views rather than a settlement comprehensive enough to accommodate Presbyterian desires. Nevertheless, there were certainly contemporaneous discussions aimed at creating a settlement that would accommodate Presbyterians on the basis of 'a Moderate Episcopacy'. Indeed, Ussher's earlier scheme for 'reduced episcopacy' was republished and formally proposed as a model by Presbyterian representatives. There were also offers of bishoprics and deaneries made to a number of the most prominent Presbyterians, and proposals that disputed ceremonies such as the cross in baptism and kneeling at communion should not be imposed as necessary. The fact that the Commons passed the Act for Confirming Ministers (which recognized the legitimacy of ordination by non-bishops) in September might also have signalled that a comprehensive settlement was on the cards. The Worcester House Declaration issued on 25 October has recently been dubbed 'the highwater-mark of plans for comprehension for the Church of England between the Reformation and the present day'. Among many concessions, it provided for presbyters to play a role in episcopal jurisdiction, and proposed the meeting of an equal number of divines 'of both Persuasions' to agree alterations to the Prayer Book, but with ministers still having the option of using alternative set forms of public worship. In November 1660 a *Humble and Grateful Acknowledgement*, signed by many Presbyterians, applauded the Declaration and signified their acceptance of modified episcopacy.[38]

---

[37] *ODNB*, 'Tombes, John (1602–1676)'; John Tombes, *An Apologie for the Two Treatises* (1646), pp. 6–8.
[38] *LJ*, XI, pp. 179–82; N. H. Keeble, 'Introduction: Attempting Uniformity', in N. H. Keeble (ed.), *'Settling the Peace of the Church': 1662 Revisited* (Oxford, 2014), pp. 3–11; B. Till, 'The Worcester House Declaration and the Restoration of the Church of England', *Historical Research*, 70 (1997): 203–30.

The failure of the Declaration to receive a second reading in the Commons in November 1660 undoubtedly marked a decisive turning-point in the Restoration settlement, but the ground had already been prepared for several months for this reverse, ever since Charles II's return to England. Prominent clergymen and courtiers moved swiftly to establish a more reactionary settlement: episcopal government and cathedrals were already being re-established on the ground, and bishops were implementing a coordinated national policy of demanding re-ordination of those with Presbyterian orders before they could be confirmed in their livings.[39] When reform of the Prayer Book was finally deliberated at Savoy House in 1661, the puritan delegates' position was that of supplicants, analogous to that of the puritans at the Hampton Court Conference, and their objections were similarly disregarded. By 1662 all the elements of a reactionary settlement were in place. It was inevitable that whatever emerged would be deemed to be a 'restoration' of earlier orthodoxy, and would crystallize a specific reading of what was the true nature of the pre-war Church of England too. But we might ponder whether a more evangelical settlement, based on the Worcester House Declaration, would have led us to talk of the inevitable and indelible 'puritan' identity of the Church of England.

By 1662, over one thousand beneficed ministers, schoolteachers, and university fellows chose to give up their positions rather than accept the Act of Uniformity. The later history of the Church of England invested this event with historic import, but there was no immediate reason to see it as an inevitable and irreversible division between conformity and dissent. After all, these numbers were significantly smaller than the more than 2,000 clergymen purged during the great wave of ejections in the 1640s (and the ejection of royalist clergy has not in the eyes of historians permanently removed them *ipso facto* from the right to consider themselves to be mainstream English Protestants).[40] Certainly, contemporaries did not see the event in such definitive terms. Plenty of those ejected still considered themselves to be loyal members of the Church of England, and still continued to practise occasional communion in parish churches. Like the royalist episcopalians of the 1650s, many of these Presbyterians were forced to become *de facto* Congregationalists by default rather than out of ecclesiological preference or conviction. As Richard Baxter put it, their 'Congregations were, through necessity... of Independent and Separating Shape, and outward Practice, though not upon the same Principles'.[41] Rumours and plans of comprehension continued to be

---

[39] K. Fincham and S. Taylor, 'The Restoration of the Church of England, 1660–1662: Ordination, Re-ordination and Conformity', in S. Taylor and G. Tapsell (eds.), *The Nature of the English Revolution Revisited* (Woodbridge, 2013), pp. 213–26.

[40] I. M. Green, 'The Persecution of "Scandalous" and "Malignant" Parish Clergy during the English Civil War', *English Historical Review*, 94 (1979): 507–31 (p. 508).

[41] M. Sylvester, *Reliquiae Baxterianae* (1696), III, p. 43, cited in Keeble, 'Introduction', p. 25.

heard through the 1660s. The creation of a single 'nonconformist' identity ruptured from the established 'Anglican' Church was a process that was long, drawn-out, painful, and far from inevitable. In fact, it was a process as troubled, extended, and unpredictable as the creation of an 'Anglican' identity from which puritans were excluded.

SELECT BIBLIOGRAPHY

Babbage, S. B., *Puritanism and Richard Bancroft* (1962).
Bosher, R. S., *The Making of the Restoration Settlement* (1951).
Collinson, P., *The Religion of Protestants: The Church in English Society 1559–1625* (Oxford, 1982).
Fincham, K. (ed.), *The Early Stuart Church, 1603–1642* (Basingstoke, 1993).
Fincham, K., *Prelate as Pastor: The Episcopate of James I* (Oxford, 1990).
Fincham, K. and P. Lake, 'The Ecclesiastical Policy of King James I', *Journal of British Studies*, 24 (1985): 169–207.
Fincham, K. and N. Tyacke, *Altars Restored: The Changing Face of English Religious Worship, 1547–c.1700* (Oxford, 2007).
Keeble, N. H., 'Introduction: Attempting Uniformity', in N. H. Keeble (ed.), *'Settling the Peace of the Church': 1662 Revisited* (Oxford, 2014), pp. 1–28.
Lake, P., 'The Laudian Style: Order, Uniformity and the Pursuit of the Beauty of Holiness in the 1630s', in K. Fincham (ed.), *The Early Stuart Church, 1603–1642* (Basingstoke, 1993), pp. 161–85.
Milton, A., 'Anglicanism and Royalism in the 1640s', in J. Adamson (ed.), *The English Civil War: Conflict and Contexts, 1640–49* (Basingstoke, 2009), pp. 61–81.
Till, B., 'The Worcester House Declaration and the Restoration of the Church of England', *Historical Research*, 70 (1997): 203–30.

5

Bishops, Church, and State, c.1530–1646

Andrew Foster

The ruthless imposition of state power over the Church, accompanied by some devastation of its wealth and authority, is most usually associated with the English Reformations presided over by Henry VIII and his son Edward. A more equitable *via media* is seen as emerging in the aftermath of Elizabeth's accession to the throne. Here, the familiar story runs, the 'Anglican' balance of Church and state was successfully established, with clergy and monarch playing mutually supportive roles. Bishops and clergy tuned their pulpits to preach obedience, help raise taxation, and employed the diocesan courts to assist in maintaining order in the provinces. If there were problems under Elizabeth, these stemmed from the growing need to control Catholic recusants, while also staunching puritan criticism and calls for 'further reformation'. In this general scenario it was James I—and more particularly his son Charles I—who upset the balance and brought about a breakdown for both Church and monarchy. Perhaps because bishops throughout this period were so frequently the objects of envy and criticism, it has been underestimated how far their status in 'government' fell after 1558, only to be restored to something like earlier times after 1603.[1] In investigating the interaction of bishops, Church, and state over a long timescale, and looking closely at structure and practice rather than theory or doctrine, this essay seeks to demonstrate that the 'Elizabethan Settlement' may not have been as settled or as helpful for Church and state as has been supposed.

The clerical establishment available to the state in the 1530s was sizeable: two archbishops, twenty-one bishops serving England and Wales, nineteen cathedral deans, just under 500 cathedral canons, sixty-one archdeacons, and countless parish priests serving some 9,000 parishes; added to which there

---

This essay is dedicated to the memory of Brett Usher.

[1] A. Foster, 'The Clerical Estate Revitalised', in K. Fincham (ed.), *The Early Stuart Church, 1603–1642* (Basingstoke, 1993), pp. 139–60.

were around 7,000 clergy in religious orders, headed by a senior echelon of some 300 abbots and priors.[2] Fifty clergymen sat in the House of Lords in 1529; over 580 attended the Canterbury and York Convocations that year.[3] At no stage before 1558 were there fewer than three prelates on the Privy Council, which invariably included the sitting archbishops of Canterbury and bishops of Winchester and Durham.[4] The Lord Chamberlain, a layman, headed a small phalanx of clergymen—the Lord High Almoner, dean of the Chapel Royal, and a Clerk of the Closet—who exercised great control over court ceremonial and access to the monarch.[5] In 1529, Bishop Cuthbert Tunstall was Keeper of the Privy Seal and Archdeacon John Taylor was Master of the Rolls.[6] All four of the Lord Chancellors under Henry VII were bishops, two under Henry VIII, one under Edward VI, and two under Mary. That pattern was broken on the accession of Elizabeth I.[7]

Clergymen in the 1530s served several masters: God, the crown, and the papacy, with the roles of the latter two leaving them often open to abuse. It was characteristic of the period 1530–58—regardless of shifting theological climes—that Henry VIII, Edward VI, and Mary treated their bishops as civil servants. Henry VIII employed Archbishops Warham and Wolsey as Lord Chancellors and Bishops Fox, Ruthall, and Tunstall as Keepers of the Privy Seal.[8] Bishop Gardiner was frequently on missions abroad, while Wolsey became the most notorious clerical pluralist of the day.[9] The Vatican, meanwhile, exploited English bishoprics for its ambassadors and took lucrative revenues from England. The see of Worcester suffered badly, being held between 1497 and 1535 by a succession of non-resident Italians. Such 'political' appointments affected at least nine English and Welsh dioceses between 1500 and 1558.[10]

Both crown and Vatican happily employed their bishops as civil servants, diplomats, and ambassadors, prizing them for administrative experience and canon law training, rather than for their theology. The break with Rome changed

---

[2] These optimum numbers represent posts not people (thus ignoring pluralities), yet fit contemporary estimates: R. M., *The Parson's Vade Mecum* (1693), p. 64; R. Bernard, *A Short View of the Prelaticall Church of England* (1641), pp. 7–9.

[3] S. Lehmberg, *The Reformation Parliament 1529–1536* (Cambridge, 1970), pp. 36–48, 64–75; M. A. R. Graves, *Elizabethan Parliaments 1559–1601* (2nd edn., 1996), p. 2.

[4] D. Gladish, *The Tudor Privy Council* (Retford, 1915), pp. 18, 140–3; P. Williams, *The Tudor Regime* (Oxford, 1979).

[5] E. Chamberlayne, *Angliae Notitia or The Present State of England* (14th edn., 1682), pp. 141–5; P. McCullough, *Sermons at Court: Politics and Religion in Elizabethan and Jacobean Preaching* (Cambridge, 1998), pp. 60–76.

[6] M. Powicke and E. Fryde (eds.), *Handbook of British Chronology* (2nd edn., 1961), p. 93; *ODNB*, 'Taylor, John (d. 1534)'.

[7] Powicke and Fryde, *Handbook*, p. 86.

[8] Powicke and Fryde, *Handbook*, pp. 86, 93.

[9] G. Redworth, *In Defence of the Church Catholic: The Life of Stephen Gardiner* (Oxford, 1990); P. Gwyn, *The King's Cardinal: The Rise and Fall of Thomas Wolsey* (1990).

[10] Powicke and Fryde, *Handbook*, p. 262.

everything, ridding England of the papacy, and intruding laymen like Thomas Cromwell into senior positions (such as vicar-general) within the Church. It gave supremacy to the crown, trimmed the number of clergy, and—most dramatically, for financial as well as spiritual consequences—rid England and Wales of the monastic orders and their monasteries. Not surprisingly, the size of the ecclesiastical establishment available to support the state was cut, although this would have been felt chiefly in the provinces. In 1640, for example, there were still two archbishops, now twenty-five bishops, twenty-four cathedral deans and around 490 senior cathedral figures, and sixty-two archdeacons available to the crown, apart from court chaplains. Yet the political power of this top echelon had been clipped: clerical representation in Parliament had been cut to twenty-six, while the size of Convocation had been reduced by over two-thirds.[11]

Bishops thus commonly served Catholic and Protestant monarchs alike in major roles in central and regional government until 1559. Bishops on the borders, for example, served on the Councils in the Marches and of the North.[12] Four bishops were active presidents of the Council of the North between 1530 and 1599 (Cuthbert Tunstall [1530–3, 1537–8], Robert Holgate [1538–50], Thomas Young [1564–8], and Matthew Hutton [1595–9]). The Council in the Marches was even more dominated by bishops: six succeeded in succession as Lord Presidents between 1473 and 1549, when John Dudley, duke of Northumberland, took office. Nicholas Heath, bishop of Worcester, served as Mary's Lord President in the Marches between 1553 and 1555. Gilbert Bourne, bishop of Bath and Wells, served briefly as her last President, losing office in February 1559. No bishop served as president of this council after this date.[13]

While Henry VIII's Reformation witnessed losses, it also yielded six new dioceses (Westminster, Peterborough, Chester, Gloucester, Oxford, and Bristol) of which five survived (Westminster reverted to London in 1550). These were tender plants that had to undergo many vicissitudes before they became fully part of the establishment. Cathedrals of the old monastic foundations were remodelled, and so too eventually were the foundations of all of the cathedrals.[14] The nine principal cathedrals were vast concerns in theory: up to sixty-two senior clergymen at Lincoln, while twelve, or below, was a more common number in places like Worcester and Ely.[15] The crown took control

---

[11] Graves, *Elizabethan Parliaments*; G. Bray, *Convocation Facts and Figures* (Beeson Divinity School, Samford University, USA, 2004), p. 105; J. W. Joyce, *England's Sacred Synods: A Constitutional History of the Convocations of the Clergy* (1855).

[12] R. R. Reid, *The King's Council in the North* (1921); F. W. Brooks, *The Council of the North* (1953, rev. edn., 1966).

[13] P. Williams, *The Council in the Marches under Elizabeth I* (Cardiff, 1958).

[14] S. Lehmberg, *English Cathedrals: A History* (2005); S. Lehmberg, *The Reformation of Cathedrals: Cathedrals in English Society, 1485–1603* (Princeton, NJ, 1988).

[15] J. Le Neve, *Fasti Ecclesiae Anglicanae* (1716), edited by T. D. Hardy in 1854, subject to further revision by Joyce Horn's team at the Institute of Historical Research, London.

of the appointment of twenty-four deans, and rights to appoint to seventy other posts, leaving the vast majority in the hands of the bishops.[16] The royal supremacy, control over visitations, a regular income from first fruits and tenths, together with subsidies and benevolences, meant that crown control of the Church had increased greatly by the time Elizabeth reached the throne. Yet it was a ramshackle structure of complex and often competing jurisdictions.

The end of Mary's reign finally ensured a widespread departure to the continent of intellectual talent from the two universities of Oxford and Cambridge.[17] Henry VIII had already appreciated the importance of the universities to his regime in the creation of celebrated regius professorships and the allocation of cathedral funds to finance the growth in student numbers that soon ensued.[18] The importance of education was not lost on the changing political establishment; it was imperative to police what happened in the colleges while promoting the new Protestant Church. The year 1558 again marks a turning point for the role of clergy in this process. Before this, William Warham, archbishop of Canterbury, John Langland, bishop of Lincoln, Richard Cox, dean of Christ Church, Sir John Mason, dean of Winchester, and Cardinal Pole had all served as successive chancellors of Oxford University. Elizabeth, however, relied resolutely on her lay nobility, notably Robert Dudley, and bishops did not figure again as Oxford chancellors until Archbishop Bancroft (1608–10), and more famously, William Laud, bishop of London and then archbishop of Canterbury, between 1630 and his resignation in 1641.[19] Cambridge was less entwined with the Church, although John Fisher, bishop of Rochester, was chancellor between 1504 and 1535, before Thomas Cromwell took over. Stephen Gardiner, bishop of Winchester, served between 1540 and 1547 and again after 1553; Cardinal Pole—showing the importance of the universities to Mary—took over in 1556 until his death in 1558.[20] It was lay control thereafter, with William Cecil taking the reins.

The significance of the universities to the state was also registered when the colleges were subject to Royal Visitations, along with the dioceses, in 1549 and again in 1559.[21] Elements of ecclesiastical control remained evident thanks to

---

[16] Le Neve, *Fasti Ecclesiae Anglicanae*.

[17] E. Duffy, *Fires of Faith: Catholic England under Mary Tudor* (New Haven, CT, 2009), pp. 196–207.

[18] Charles Knighton, 'The Provision of Education in the New Cathedral Foundations of Henry VIII', in D. Marcombe and C. Knighton (eds.), *Close Encounters: English Cathedrals and Society since 1540* (Nottingham, 1991), pp. 18–42.

[19] *Fasti Ecclesiae Anglicanae*, ed. T. D. Hardy, 3 vols. (Oxford, 1854), III, pp. 468–9.

[20] *Fasti Ecclesiae Anglicanae*, ed. Hardy, III, pp. 601–2; Claire Cross, 'The English Universities, 1553–58', in E. Duffy and D. Loades (eds.), *The Church of Mary Tudor* (Aldershot, 2006), pp. 57–76.

[21] W. H. Frere and W. M. Kennedy (eds.), *The Visitation Articles and Injunctions of the Period of the Reformation*, 3 vols. (1910), II, pp. 134–50; Cross, 'English Universities', p. 74.

the appointment of bishops as Visitors of five of the eight Oxford colleges founded between Brasenose in 1509 and Pembroke in 1624.[22] The crown naturally took that position for Christ Church, while the earl of Pembroke did likewise for his foundation. Significant involvement of bishops in Oxford affairs might be one reason why Queen Elizabeth felt comfortable in leaving the diocese vacant for long periods in her reign. There was less scope for clerical involvement in Cambridge after 1558 even though Ely and Peterborough were close at hand for ordinations. There were fewer colleges, and if one counts the re-founding of Gonville and Caius in 1557, seven were founded between 1505 and 1662. Of these, all were assigned to the crown as Visitor, apart from St John's College in 1511 that seems to have involved the bishop of Ely.[23] As Visitor of Peterhouse and Jesus College, the bishops of Ely were the most conspicuous bishops in Cambridge, although the bishops of Lincoln may have influenced King's, as they certainly did under James and Charles.

Important training centres though they were, the queen does not seem to have appreciated the full political potential of her universities, and they were not on royal progress routes as often as they came to be under the Stuarts.[24] Levers of power were strengthened with oaths on admission and graduation, together with periodic re-drafting of rules of best governance, but it was not until the 1620s and 1630s that these levers were pulled in a fashion that led to problems for the ecclesiastical authorities involved, sufficient to provoke a backlash in the 1640s. As in other matters, it was 1604 that proved to be a turning point, with Canons 17 and 23 of that year requiring students in colleges to wear surplices in times of divine service and to receive communion at least four times a year; all enforced by subscription campaigns soon afterwards.[25]

ELIZABETH UNDERVALUES AND UNDERCUTS HER CHURCH, 1558–1603

Elizabeth's accession in 1558 thus marked the theoretical acquisition of great power for the crown. Royal supremacy was ratified once more; the crown controlled all senior Church appointments, and indeed the advowsons of many lesser livings. And through the device of taking income from sees left vacant, not to mention the flurry of forced land exchanges that accompanied

---

[22] P. Williams, 'Elizabethan Oxford: State, Church and University', in J. McConica (ed.), *The History of the University of Oxford*, vol. III: *The Collegiate University* (Oxford, 1986), pp. 404–5; V. Morgan, *A History of the University of Cambridge, 1546–1750* (Cambridge, 2004), p. 97.
[23] Morgan, *History*, pp. 116, 156.
[24] Mary Hill Cole, *The Portable Queen: Elizabeth I and the Politics of Ceremony* (Amherst, MA, 1999), p. 229.
[25] G. Bray (ed.), *The Anglican Canons, 1529–1947* (Woodbridge, 1998), pp. 287, 293.

many new appointments, the crown proceeded to milk much income.[26] The Royal Visitation of 1559 exemplified this power in practice. Archbishop Heath, Mary's Lord Chancellor, was deprived of his posts in July 1559. Elizabeth now had a blank canvas, but she proceeded to fill bishoprics slowly, had little time for clergy, and seemed indifferent to the needs of her new Church. This was abundantly clear at court where her Lord Almoners have been described as 'not particularly pre-possessing', her Clerks of the Closet likewise undistinguished, and she only bothered to appoint one dean of the Chapel Royal in her entire reign—the conservative survivor and noted pluralist, George Carew.[27] Such scant regard makes the success of those under her in stabilizing the Church almost without her even more remarkable.

In her defence, however, it should be noted that we have probably underestimated the task of reconstruction/construction that confronted everyone at the start of the reign. For too long, our attention has been diverted by the arguments over the making of the Acts of Supremacy and Uniformity, and the celebrated Thirty-Nine Articles, and we have been lured into a false sense of security by the sophisticated rhetoric of Bishop Jewel and later Richard Hooker.[28] The success of the Protestant Reformation in England—the so-called *via media* beloved of Anglican hagiographers—has come to be taken for granted and reduced to a matter of how it was achieved and when. It is perhaps too easy to underestimate the extent of the shock that those in the Church must have experienced in the 1560s.

Yet the devastation of the Church structure in the years 1558–9 was truly remarkable. Twenty-six out of twenty-seven dioceses required new bishops, fifteen out of twenty-four cathedrals new deans, while several hundred new canons were needed to staff the cathedrals, slimmed down though these had been in recent years. Meanwhile, in Oxford and Cambridge around 80 per cent of the heads of colleges needed replacing, not to mention a vast number of fellows. The process of rebuilding was painfully slow, hampered by the very limited supply of qualified, experienced clergymen who were both willing to take posts, and acceptable to the queen and her advisers. Not all sees had bishops even by 1562, and of the new appointments, twenty-three were consecrated—in other words they were novices. For comparison with another great crisis for the Church of England, eighteen of the new bishops appointed

---

[26] C. Hill, *Economic Problems of the Church from Archbishop Whitgift to the Long Parliament* (Oxford, 1956), pp. 14–38.
[27] F. Heal, *Of Prelates and Princes: A Study of the Economic and Social Position of the Tudor Episcopate* (Cambridge, 1980), p. 278; McCullough, *Sermons at Court*, pp. 69–70; J. Bickersteth and R. Dunning, *Clerks of the Closet in the Royal Household* (Stroud, 1991).
[28] W. P. Haugaard, *Elizabeth and the English Reformation* (1968); N. Jones, *Faith by Statute: Parliament and the Settlement of Religion 1559* (1982).

in the 'crisis' of 1660 were consecrated.[29] The sees of Bristol and Gloucester were yoked together under Bishop Cheney in April 1562, highlighting the insecurity of at least two of the new Henrician dioceses, and Oxford was not filled until 1567. Episcopal posts catch the headlines, but thirty-eight out of sixty-two archdeaconries—a crucial level in the administrative structure— required new archdeacons at this time. Only three of these new archdeacons had any experience of the role, and larger dioceses like London and Lincoln required a completely new team of five and six archdeacons respectively. The situation was slightly better with regard to diocesan chancellors, the key civil lawyers who led a bishop's administrative team, yet even here seventeen new appointments were required out of twenty-six dioceses, excluding Sodor and Man. And this would have had implications for many years to come as new people took time to get adjusted.[30] This wholesale turnover of key personnel represented a major crisis for the Church as an organization, whatever might be said about eager Protestants waiting to step into the breach. This was worse than the crisis faced by the Church in 1660, for the task in 1558 entailed *establishing* a new national Church, not just restoring one. The new Elizabethan bishops had neither the time nor the experience to perform major service for the state.

The diocese of Chichester reveals the story in microcosm: it needed a new bishop, three-quarters of the cathedral chapter, two new archdeacons, a new diocesan chancellor, and out of 282 parish livings it looks as if there were fifty-seven deprivations, thirty-four resignations, and ninety-seven livings vacant owing to death.[31] If this is correct it represents a staggering turnover of around two-thirds of the diocese. No wonder contemporaries and later critics talked about the appearance of 'mechanics and young boys' to fill vacancies and kept reporting 'dumb dogs'.[32]

Doubly confusing to contemporaries was what might be described as a massively changed 'landscape of power'. Unleashed by the Reformation and the dissolution of the monasteries, the crown had embarked upon a huge asset-stripping exercise, led by Henry VIII, Edward VI, and their courtiers. Famously made worse by the Act of Exchanges of 1559, Elizabeth did nothing to stop the rot whereby her bishops were systematically robbed of their prime assets over the course of the sixteenth century. Bishops were either forced to give up property completely, to offer long leases, or to exchange land for

---

[29] I. Green, *The Re-establishment of the Church of England 1660–1663* (Oxford, 1978), pp. 81–98.
[30] A. Foster, *The Dioceses of England and Wales, c.1540–1700* (forthcoming).
[31] T. McCann, 'The Clergy and the Elizabethan Settlement in the Diocese of Chichester', in M. Kitch (ed.), *Studies in Sussex Church History* (1981), pp. 99–123; <http://www.theclergydatabase.org.uk>.
[32] J. Collier, *An Ecclesiastical History of Great Britain*, 2 vols. (1708), II, p. 436.

impropriations, which was much more vulnerable to inflation.[33] It has been variously calculated that in this process the number of residences available to the bishops fell from around 300 to fewer than 100 properties by 1603.[34] Whether they wished to aid the state or not, bishops found their capacity for hospitality and influence severely curtailed. This would have stood out dramatically in the capital. Whereas a Londoner and visitor alike would have been overawed by the sight of around twenty-five large episcopal and monastic residences straddling the Strand in 1529, after 1559 these had been reduced to a handful: abbots and priors lost out, and so too did the majority of the bishops.[35] It must have represented one of the largest wholesale transfers of prime real estate in the history of London.

In the decade following 1542, virtually every diocese in England and Wales lost property to the crown and courtiers. While these exchanges may not have cost the Church as much financially as was once thought—and were spread out over a long period and not the responsibility of one monarch—it is undeniable that by the time James I put a stop to the rot in 1604, the Church had lost much property. This 'sacrilege' was commented upon by contemporaries and picked up throughout Elizabeth's reign by complaining bishops. Bishops after 1559 could never exercise the financial muscle of some of their predecessors, even if they were 'still rich and powerful enough to be envied'.[36] Attempts to regain some of their lost financial rights in the 1630s played some part in the downfall of Archbishop Laud and his colleagues, for they had inherited a Church that was deeply flawed from top to bottom. As Archbishop Whitgift remarked ruefully in the 1590s, relatively few benefices could properly support a clergyman.[37]

The financial plight of her bishops—and any resulting lack of political clout—does not seem to have bothered Queen Elizabeth. It is well known that she left sees vacant for many years while she took the revenues, notably Oxford (1568–89) and Ely (1581–1600). In total she left sixteen out of twenty-seven dioceses vacant for more than one year in her reign. This contrasts with eight sees so treated between 1500 and 1558 (ignoring other abuses such as absentee Italian bishops), none by James, and only three by Charles. The general story of financial ruin has been softened by Felicity Heal and the late Brett Usher, but his research revealed that virtually no bishop paid full first fruits and tenths on

---

[33] Hill, *Economic Problems*, pp. 14–38; Heal, *Prelates*, pp. 202–311; B. Usher, *William Cecil and Episcopacy* (Aldershot, 2003), pp. 69–90.

[34] P. Hembry, 'Episcopal Palaces, 1535 to 1660', in E. Ives, R. Knecht, and J. Scarisbrick (eds.), *Wealth and Power in Tudor England* (1978), pp. 146–66.

[35] A. Emery, *Greater Medieval Houses of England and Wales: 1300–1500*, 3 vols. (Cambridge, 1996–2006), III, pp. 216, 230–4; Hembry, 'Episcopal Palaces'; R. S. Rait (ed.), *English Episcopal Palaces (Province of Canterbury)* (1910), R. S. Rait (ed.), English *Episcopal Palaces (Province of York)* (1911); M. W. Thompson, *Medieval Bishops' Houses in England and Wales* (Aldershot, 1998).

[36] Hill, *Economic Problems*, p. 39.   [37] Hill, *Economic Problems*, p. 205.

gaining his diocese throughout her reign: it was tacitly acknowledged that they had all become poorer.[38] It is also telling that the bishops of two-thirds of all the dioceses of England and Wales were granted dispensation to hold livings *in commendam* to augment their poor incomes during Elizabeth's reign. Meanwhile, the first generation of bishops found themselves with a large taxation bill.[39] No general revaluation of benefices was undertaken during this period, but this was not a matter for rejoicing for hard-pressed clergymen.

What did Elizabeth want of her cathedral clergy? Again the picture is unclear, apart of course from her supposed dislike of wives in the closes. The rearrangement of cathedral establishments noted earlier gave her much control, but this was oddly distributed: ten out of twelve Worcester posts and seven out of eight respectively at Gloucester and Bristol; nine out of ten in Oxford, but no say whatsoever in the four Welsh dioceses, not even over the two deans of Bangor and St Asaph. Nor is there much evidence of real care in her appointments to the deaneries. Like others before, she was happy to abuse the Church by giving posts to laymen, most notably at Carlisle, where the small establishment was rendered even smaller by the appointment of Sir Thomas Smith as dean between 1559 and 1577, then Sir John Wooley, and in 1596 Christopher Perkins. No wonder that letters from the bishop of Carlisle in Rose Castle often have a beleaguered feel to them, concerned about his isolation, the Scots, and the lack of adequate clergy.[40]

The abuse occurred elsewhere; the deanery of Wells being held *in commendam* successively by the laymen Robert Weston, Valentine Dale, and John Herbert. Cathedral posts were frequently used as sinecures to provide senior clergy with enhanced incomes. No fewer than eleven out of twenty-four cathedral deaneries were held *in commendam* between 1558 and 1603. It should be no surprise to learn that many still contemplated the abolition of cathedrals in the latter part of Elizabeth's reign; they were hardly secure places. Frequent calls for structural reforms must have made many clergy uneasy. In 1572, Lord Keeper Nicholas Bacon suggested a plan to devolve more power to rural deaneries, a definite rebuke for the bishops.[41] While radicals debated the benefits of 'classes', others wondered about rural deaneries and archdeaconries, similarly smaller units of jurisdiction that might improve discipline and quality. These debates never faded, and in 1589 Anthony

---

[38] Usher, *William Cecil and Episcopacy*, appendix I, pp. 187–216; B. Usher, *Lord Burghley and Episcopacy, 1577–1603* (Farnham, 2016), appendix I, pp. 195–238.

[39] P. Carter, '"Certain, Continual and Seldom Abated": Royal Taxation of the Elizabethan Church', in S. Wabuda and C. Litzenberger (eds.), *Belief and Practice in Reformation England* (Aldershot, 1998), pp. 98–9.

[40] H. Birt, *The Elizabethan Religious Settlement* (1907), pp. 341–2.

[41] P. Collinson, 'Episcopacy and Reform in England in the later Sixteenth Century', reprinted in P. Collinson, *Godly People: Essays on English Protestantism and Puritanism* (1983), pp. 154–89.

Bridgeman from Gloucestershire proposed that cathedrals be scrapped to divert funds to ameliorate problems stemming from pluralities and non-residence.[42] Even in 1604, Sir John Harington wondered whether the new diocese of Oxford would survive.[43]

Schemes for diocesan reform were still circulating at the accession of James I.[44] It is hardly surprising that Sir John Neale felt 'religion was a creeping paralysis in Elizabeth's Parliaments'.[45] To be fair, the bishops too were concerned about the quality and quantity of clergy that they had at their disposal. This is well captured as we come to learn more about the 'Parker Certificates' (requests for details of serving parish incumbents that were required from archdeacons in the 1560s).[46] Prompted by puritan surveys later, Archbishop Whitgift was still collecting such information in 1589, 1593, and 1597. The clerical establishment did not feel secure even at the end of the reign.

What transpired was a developing interest among clergy and laity alike in the importance of the pastoral function of bishops, much discussed by the late Patrick Collinson and well illustrated for the Jacobean period by Kenneth Fincham.[47] It is almost as if—deprived of a political voice—this was all that was permitted, although of course, Grindal was famously not permitted! We pick up these concerns in virtually every Parliament of the reign, with calls for further reformation and complaints about the supply and quality of the ministry. One initiative that might have helped, namely the use of suffragan bishops, was allowed to lapse under Elizabeth. A total of thirty bishops served as suffragans in the early sixteenth century while England was still under the papacy. They were partly used to ameliorate some of the damage caused by *commendams* already cited, and their use extended to thirteen dioceses.[48] Mindful of keeping what had worked before—and possibly because it boosted the availability of 'bishops' for other services—Henry VIII maintained his right to appoint suffragan bishops through an Act of 1534. This was invoked for twelve dioceses after the break with Rome. Of these, several ran into the reign of Elizabeth but only three suffragan bishops were subsequently appointed under her authority: Richard Barnes consecrated bishop of Nottingham in 1567; Richard Rogers, bishop of Dover in 1569; and John

---

[42] Collinson, 'Episcopacy and Reform'; TNA, SP/12/222/70; F. Heal, *Reformation in Britain and Ireland* (Oxford, 2003), p. 396.
[43] J. Harington, *Nugae Antiquae*, 3 vols. (1779), I, p. 174.
[44] W. Stoughton, *An Assertion of true and Christian Church Policie* (Middleburg, 1604).
[45] J. Neale, *Elizabeth I and her Parliaments*, 2 vols. (1965), II, p. 162.
[46] 'The Parker Certificates: The State of the English Clergy in 1559': a major project based at the University of Reading.
[47] Collinson, 'Episcopacy and Reform'; K. Fincham, *Prelate as Pastor: The Episcopate of James I* (Oxford, 1990).
[48] Powicke and Fryde, *Handbook*, pp. 268–9, 271–2.

Sterne, bishop of Colchester in 1592.[49] The first two were appointed to assist the archbishops of Canterbury and York respectively, while the latter was probably appointed to aid the ailing bishop of London, John Aylmer.[50] At least two of these suffragans played a prominent role in ordinations, suggesting that their work was to supplement that of the archdeacons in the care of the clergy. Neither Queen Elizabeth nor her immediate successors seem to have valued suffragan bishops, for on the death of Sterne in 1608 the role was not revived until 1870.[51]

None of this gainsays improvements for the Church over Elizabeth's reign. The quality of the clergy improved dramatically—if judged by educational qualifications—even if Archbishop Whitgift still had to carry out surveys to counter puritan criticisms in the 1590s.[52] Ralph Houlbrooke and Martin Ingram showed long ago how successful the civil lawyers were in reviving the fortunes of the church courts and placing the administration of dioceses on a firmer footing.[53] Study of churchwardens' accounts reveals that the rebuilding, repair, and redecoration of parish churches was underway before the big survey of churches requested by Whitgift in 1602. That survey did, however, give such initiatives a push that would be carried forward under James I, before being given a controversial slant under Charles and Laud in the 1630s.[54]

There was never a full complement of Elizabethan bishops in Parliament as there was never a full bench, and many bishops felt disinclined to attend.[55] There was never a full cathedral establishment without some post vacant or mortgaged elsewhere. There was never a full workforce of archdeacons, as several of those were effectively lost to *commendams* over the period, as for example in Bangor. There was never a full set of operational diocesan chancellors as these key figures were often quite illustrious, multi-tasking, multi-post holders, and therefore used surrogates about whom we would like to know more. Even though key sees, like Durham and Carlisle, had special border responsibilities, they were never fully supported. Only after it was strictly necessary to worry about the Scots did James I grant the title of Lord

---

[49] Powicke and Fryde, *Handbook*, p. 272.

[50] *ODNB*, 'Aylmer, John (1520/21–1594)', 'Sterne, John (c.1545–1607/8)'.

[51] Fincham, *Prelate as Pastor*, pp. 15–16.

[52] R. O'Day, *The English Clergy: The Emergence and Consolidation of a Profession, 1558–1642* (Leicester, 1979).

[53] R. Houlbrooke, *Church Courts and the People during the English Reformation 1520–1570* (Oxford, 1979); M. Ingram, *Church Courts, Sex and Marriage in England, 1570–1640* (Cambridge, 1987); R. B. Outhwaite, *The Rise and Fall of the English Ecclesiastical Courts, 1500–1860* (Cambridge, 2006).

[54] A. Foster, 'Churchwardens' Accounts of Early Modern England and Wales', in K. French, G. Gibbs, and B. Kumin (eds.), *The Parish in English Life 1400–1600* (Manchester, 1997), pp. 74–93; K. Fincham and N. Tyacke, *Altars Restored: The Changing Face of English Religious Worship, 1547–c.1700* (Oxford, 2007), pp. 176–226.

[55] Graves, *Elizabethan Parliaments*, pp. 29, 35.

Lieutenant of County Durham to Bishop Richard Neile in 1617 in recognition of his military role in that Palatinate.[56]

If Matthew Parker was a hero of the early Elizabethan Church—'statesman' as some might say—John Whitgift is a candidate later, together with their key allies, William Cecil (later Lord Burghley) and Sir Christopher Hatton.[57] Burghley clearly played a critical role in most of the episcopal appointments of the reign and steered the Privy Council on religious matters. Archbishop Matthew Parker is surely in the frame, because the task of rebuilding or recreating the Church of England was greater than we have been led to believe.[58] If the Roman Catholic Church needed the Council of Trent to reconsider its faith, ceremonies, and structures, how much more did a new Church of England need to work out similar issues? The celebrated Acts of Supremacy and Uniformity, together with later work in Convocation, did not offer much practical guidance on what roles were now open to bishops, how dioceses were managed, or how the ecclesiastical courts were to run without reference to Rome. This had to be thought through by people largely new to the posts, guided by a few with experience of an old regime. Ironically, the queen's negligence may have worked to the advantage of those building afresh.

While Parker gathered together a team of bishops and soon ran into problems in gaining conformity on ceremonial, those at a lower rank must have pulled their weight: there are unsung heroes among the diocesan chancellors, cathedral deans, and archdeacons who laboured to assemble the Church of England.[59] The diocesan chancellors in 1559 were clergymen; many had been archdeacons. They knew how to manage clergy and also how to run the church courts. Neglected as the Church may have been, particularly during the early years of the reign, these people went about recreating a system without Rome. While their importance has been acknowledged in the past—and highlighted by Patrick Collinson—attacks on these figures by puritans and Presbyterians have perhaps been exaggerated.[60] They may indeed have formed a particularly highly qualified rump of lawyers with adherence to canon law, but they were the essential bureaucrats who kept the Church running as an institution.[61] And big changes in their background and status did not materialize until the early seventeenth century. Even in 1603,

---

[56] *ODNB*, 'Neile, Richard (1562–1640)'.   [57] Usher, *William Cecil and Episcopacy*.
[58] D. Crankshaw, 'Ecclesiastical Statesmanship in England in the Age of the Reformation', in D. Wendebourg (ed.), *Sister Reformations: The Reformation in Germany and in England* (Tübingen, 2010), pp. 271–303.
[59] *ODNB*, 'Wotton, Nicholas (c.1497–1567)', 'Yale, Thomas (1525/6–1577)', 'Mowse, William (d. 1588)', 'Harvey, Henry (d. 1585)'.
[60] Collinson, 'Episcopacy and Reform', pp. 166–75.
[61] B. P. Levack, *The Civil Lawyers in England 1603–1641: A Political Study* (Oxford, 1973), pp. 158–95.

ten out of twenty-six diocesan chancellors were still clergymen.[62] Yet the 1603 tranche of chancellors did reveal elements of things to come: nineteen were Justices of the Peace, while nine were Members of Parliament.[63] This marks their progress during the reign and is evidence of 'professionalization' outside the ranks of clergy (where this process has more commonly been noted).[64] This parallels the emergence of other officials, such as secretaries and registrars, within a bishop's household.[65] It is also significant that the post of chancellor slowly gained supremacy in most dioceses during the latter part of the sixteenth century, as their role subsumed those of official principals and vicar-generals (as is evident in the dioceses of Lincoln, Carlisle, and Exeter). Taking the long view, however, Collinson was correct in emphasizing the process of secularization, for by 1640 only three chancellors were clergymen.

Bishops, their clergy, lawyers, and churchwardens had always carried responsibilities for reporting heretics; under Elizabeth the task was enlarged to embrace Catholic 'recusants'. This enhanced role in 'state security' could prove embarrassing, for it entailed working with local Justices of the Peace whose own loyalty was often suspect. Hence the famous enquiries of 1564 in which the dioceses of Carlisle, Durham, York, Worcester, Hereford, and Exeter were thought to be most adverse to the religious changes.[66] 'State security' provides a link to a line of continuity within royal proclamations over the period. While those of the 1520s had reinforced statutes against 'heresy', an increasing stream over the sixteenth and seventeenth centuries concerned the discovery and ejection of Roman Catholic priests and the circulation of 'seditious books'. What is noteworthy about royal proclamations after the 1530s, however, is just how far the state intruded in matters of religion—exercised the royal supremacy no less—as for example reinforcing 'injunctions' in 1547, silencing disputes over the eucharist in the same year, ordering bishops to destroy old service books in 1549, and appointing homilies to be read in churches in 1559. A proclamation enforcing the Act of Uniformity and use of the Book of Common Prayer in October 1573 represented orders to bishops and archdeacons that would previously have come from within the Church hierarchy.[67]

Bishops clearly felt that they had inadequate powers to conduct this new role of locating and reporting potential religious deviants, for they clamoured

---

[62] Foster, *Dioceses of England and Wales*.   [63] Foster, 'Clerical Estate'.
[64] O'Day, *English Clergy*.
[65] R. O'Day, 'The Role of the Registrar in Diocesan Administration', in R. O'Day and F. Heal (eds.), *Continuity and Change: Personnel and Administration of the Church in England, 1500–1642* (Leicester, 1976), pp. 77–94.
[66] M. Bateson (ed.), 'A Collection of Original Letters from the Bishops to the Privy Council, 1564 with returns of the justices of the peace and others within their respective dioceses, classified according to their religious convictions', *Camden Society Miscellany*, 9 (1895).
[67] P. L. Hughes and J. F. Larkin (eds.), *Tudor Royal Proclamations*, 3 vols. (New Haven, CT, 1964–9), I, pp. 287, 296, 300, 353; II, p. 461; III, p. 599.

for new ecclesiastical commissions to buttress their own courts.[68] Such commissions had commenced under Thomas Cromwell, the first for the province of Canterbury being granted to him in April 1535. A commission for Canterbury was granted quite speedily in the reign of Elizabeth in July 1559, one having already been granted for York a month earlier. Whereas bishops and clergy had played a major role on such commissions prior to 1559, it is significant that the laity dominated them for many years after that date.[69] It was not until 1584 that clergy formed more than half of all the commissioners, and that soon dropped again so that even under the Stuarts (who trusted them more than Elizabeth had done) clergy never formed a majority on these commissions. Who carried out the bulk of the work might of course be another matter.[70]

By the 1590s Archbishop Whitgift, and Bishops Bancroft and Aylmer, are rightly associated with a new-found clerical confidence and assertiveness among the episcopate that established a platform for the following reigns. Clerics at all levels in the Church were now better educated and qualified than for some time since the Reformation and they had a new-found sense of self-assurance.[71] Many were attracted to new thinking about ceremonial and the sacraments, the rituals of the Church, and aspects once associated with Rome: such thinking became discussed and controversial in Cambridge in the 1590s and fed what became stigmatized as 'Arminianism'.[72] In reviving the fortunes of the church courts, civil lawyers contributed to that revival of confidence. Certainly, the Church as an organization was in far better shape by 1603 that it had been in 1558. Elizabeth valued Whitgift's advice and finally took him into her Privy Council in 1586, but she still had no truck with novelty in her Church. It is salutary to note that Whitgift apparently used to ask that the Council clerks only schedule him for attendance regarding matters of the Church; he did not wish to intrude on other work.[73] Equally telling is Thomas Fuller's summary that, like a bad housemaid, Elizabeth 'had swept the Church of England, and left all the dust behind the door'.[74]

---

[68] R. Usher (Intro. P. Tyler), *The Rise and Fall of the High Commission* (Oxford, 1968), pp. 284–304.
[69] Usher, *Rise and Fall*, pp. 345–61.
[70] For example, P. Clark, 'The Ecclesiastical Commission at Canterbury: 1572–1603', *Archaeologia Cantiana*, 89 (1974): 183–97; R. Manning, 'The Crisis of Episcopal Authority during the Reign of Elizabeth I', *Journal of British Studies*, 11 (1971): 1–25; Heal, *Reformation in Britain and Ireland*, pp. 398–9.
[71] Foster, 'Clerical Estate'; Collinson, 'Episcopacy and Reform'.
[72] N. Tyacke, *Anti-Calvinists: The Rise of English Arminianism, c.1590–1640* (Oxford, 1990).
[73] Hamon L'Estrange, *The Reign of King Charles* (2nd edn., 1656), p. 189.
[74] Thomas Fuller, *Pulpit Sparks*, ed. M. Fuller (1886), p. 142.

JAMES AND CHARLES OVER-PROMOTE THEIR CHURCH, 1603–1649

What changed everything once more was the accession of King James I in 1603.[75] Here was a king who liked and valued the company of bishops: he was happy to have them at court and pleased to employ them once more on foreign embassies and as civil servants in the provinces, a counterweight to the county authorities. He appointed six bishops as members of his Privy Council between 1603 and his death in 1625: Richard Bancroft, George Abbot, Thomas Bilson, Lancelot Andrewes, James Montague, and John Williams. In his old country of Scotland the episcopate had been thoroughly reinstated and gained even greater place in helping to run the country through their representation on the Privy Council.[76] Most significant of all—in both material senses and the message it sent to others—was his reversal of the Elizabethan Act of Exchanges, ratified by Act of Parliament in 1604.[77] James I never left a single see vacant for more than one year and (as we have noted) his son Charles only left three (Ely, Winchester, and Exeter) vacant in the financial exigencies of the years 1626–8.

The operation of his court exemplifies the changes under James I. The deanery of the Chapel Royal was given to James Montague, a moderate Calvinist, while the Clerkship of the Closet went to Richard Neile of a more proto-Arminian cast of mind. Both were keen on decorum in court worship and both played their part in organizing the preaching rotas. 'Court bishops' became a common sight at court and Neile eventually became the longest serving Clerk of the Closet for two centuries. Under Neile the 'position metamorphosed from a Tudor sinecure to a crucial Stuart point of political contact'.[78] Nothing better captures the change from Elizabeth's reign, however, than the fact that where she had been attended at her funeral by seventeen chaplains, James I was attended by sixty-two.[79] He really did value the company of his clergy!

The first two years of the reign of James in England were marked by a flurry of activity as top posts were filled—eight bishops (two filling long-standing vacancies) and four deans—while Whitgift's survey of parish churches had initiated a campaign for church restoration that soon had the church bells ringing (quite literally) to welcome the new age.[80] Puritan complaints in the Millenary Petition were successfully headed off and after some moments of concern it became clear at the Hampton Court Conference that James really did mean 'no bishop, no king'. Convocation in 1604 passed 141 canons

---

[75] Foster, 'Clerical Estate'.   [76] Foster, 'Clerical Estate', p. 142.
[77] Hill, *Economic Problems*, pp. 3–38.   [78] McCullough, *Sermons at Court*, p. 110.
[79] McCullough, *Sermons at Court*, p. 116.
[80] Foster, 'Churchwardens' Accounts'; D. MacCulloch, 'The Myth of the English Reformation', *Journal of British Studies*, 30 (1991): 1–19; J. F. Merritt, 'The Social Context of the Parish Church in Early Modern Westminster', *Urban History Yearbook*, 18 (1991): 20–31.

and the Church that had once been but 'half-formed', now seemed secure at last.[81] Bancroft's succession as archbishop of Canterbury was praised by Harington because he was 'a man more exercised in affairs of the state' than his rival Tobie Matthew, 'so learned a man, and so assiduous a Preacher'.[82]

The pastoral tradition that had emerged as a key function of bishops under Elizabeth—partly by inclination, partly by the reduction of other roles and temptations, and also in response to external criticism—continued under James.[83] This might seem to harken back to Bishop Ponet's discussion of bishops as 'superintendents' in their dioceses, and the rhetoric of the earlier generation of bishops who had returned from exile and spoke of being 'first amongst equals'.[84] It would also serve as a model for those who argued for 'reduced episcopacy' in the 1640s.[85] But another tradition had been rekindled under Whitgift, however, namely that of the 'administrator bishop', which, when coupled with the revival of interest in ceremony and the sacraments that characterized the 'Arminian faction', offered James I an attractive alternative vision of the Church.[86]

Bishops, and indeed lower ranking clergymen, found themselves pressed back into the role of loyal civil servants. Elizabeth's practice of leaving sees vacant had resulted in some areas of the country having no clerical representation at quarter sessions. In 1604, eleven out of fifty-seven jurisdictions had no clerical Justices of the Peace. A further nineteen areas had just one cleric, usually the bishop, and throughout England and Wales only ten clergymen below the rank of dean were magistrates. This all changed after 1604 as all bishops and deans were pressed into service, while the number of clergy Justices below that rank jumped to seventy-eight by 1622.[87] Caveats need to be noted, but the basic case remains that clergy at all levels started to play a bigger role in regional government after 1603, and possibly even earlier.[88] Bishops too found their workload increasing: they had always been used as regional agents when sent orders from the Privy Council, and that too increased over a range of matters from reporting recusants to opening bridges and supervising land improvements as in the Fens. The bishops of Durham commanded the local militia and supervised the defences of Newcastle upon Tyne and Berwick on Tweed in the 1620s and 1630s.[89]

---

[81] R. Usher, *The Reconstruction of the English Church*, 2 vols. (New York, 1910); S. B. Babbage, *Puritanism and Richard Bancroft* (1962).
[82] Harington, *Nugae Antiquae*, I, p. 12.   [83] Fincham, *Prelate as Pastor*.
[84] Collinson, 'Episcopacy and Reform', pp. 164n, 171–3.
[85] Collinson, 'Episcopacy and Reform', p. 189.
[86] A. Foster, 'The Function of a Bishop: The Career of Richard Neile, 1562–1640', in O'Day and Heal (eds.), *Continuity and Change*, pp. 33–54; Tyacke, *Anti-Calvinists*; Fincham, *Prelate as Pastor*, pp. 276–91.
[87] Foster, 'Clerical Estate', pp. 148–50.
[88] C. Haigh and A. Wall, 'Clergy JPs in England and Wales, 1590–1640', *Historical Journal*, 47 (2004): 233–59.
[89] *ODNB*, 'Neile, Richard (1562–1640)', 'Morton, Thomas (1564–1659)'.

Throughout the period 1604 to 1640, bishops also played a considerable and responsible role sitting as peers in the House of Lords, serving actively on committees and speaking on a wide range of topics, fully integrated into the government of the day.[90] In contrast to the reign of Elizabeth, a full complement of bishops eligible to serve in the Lords was usually available between 1604 and 1640, Abbot's suspension in 1628 being a notable exception. It has been calculated that between 1603 and 1614, three-quarters of the bishops, but only one-half of the lay peers attended the Lords.[91] And they were not as bashful in speaking out as they might have been under Elizabeth. They did of course speak largely for the royal prerogative, as with Bishop Thornborough as early as 1604, and Bishop Neile, more notoriously, in 1614. They obligingly voted for subsidies, including one of their own after the failure of the Addled Parliament of 1614. And the clergy of Charles I became notorious for speaking in defence of the Forced Loan of 1627.[92]

The return of bishops to powerful offices of state was not universally welcomed, but sinister overtones were not voiced generally until the breakdown of authority and rows in the Long Parliament after 1640. It was argued that Bishop John Williams was appropriate to act as the king's conscience on his appointment as Lord Keeper in 1621.[93] And who could be more honest than Bishop Juxon as Lord Treasurer in 1636? Fears mounted once the relatively balanced Privy Council of James I was replaced by representatives of a more factional element of the Church of England in the shape of Bishops Neile, Laud, Harsnett, and Juxon. This had been made particularly obvious when members of this group presided over Canterbury during the brief sequestration of Archbishop Abbot between October 1627 and December 1628.

Tinged with Arminianism, as many clerical attitudes were even before the accession of Charles I in 1625, a renewed confidence amongst the clergy may be discerned after 1603. Clergy and civil lawyers became open not only in their defence of ecclesiastical law and their courts, but also in asserting their rights to tithes, and in the case of some bishops, their *iure divino* status.[94] Bishops became more evident on the hated Court of Star Chamber, something that Elizabeth had limited to only one bishop at a time.[95] The civil lawyer Dr Cowell went too far for many in favouring royal absolutism in his *Interpreter* published in 1610. Clergy lined up to speak critically about the sacrilege of past 'robbery' of the Church. George Carleton dedicated his *Tithes*

---

[90] Foster, 'Clerical Estate', pp. 143–7; E. Cope, 'The Bishops and Parliamentary Politics in Early Stuart England', *Parliamentary History*, 9 (1990): 1–13.
[91] A. Britton, 'The House of Lords in English Politics, 1604–14', DPhil thesis, University of Oxford, 1982, cited in Cope, 'Bishops', p. 2.
[92] Foster, 'Clerical Estate', pp. 144–6; Cope, 'Bishops'.
[93] Foster, 'Clerical Estate', p. 141.   [94] Foster, 'Clerical Estate', pp. 150–1.
[95] H. Phillips, 'The Last Years of the Court of Star Chamber 1630–41', *Transactions of the Royal Historical Society*, 4th ser., 21 (1939): 103–31.

examined and proved to bee due to the clergie by a divine right to Bancroft in 1606, knowing that it would be well received. This picture of renewed clerical confidence in fighting their cause suggests that John Selden's more famous *Historie of Tithes* published in 1618 can now be seen as actually a rather cautious venture into the debate that was not designed to cause offence.[96]

Concern with 'sacrilege' informed many of the policies pursued under Archbishop Laud, and he won the support of King Charles for his campaigns, whether over the recovery of property and rights, or the pursuit of conformity and due reverence for ceremony. Curiously, the combined efforts of Laud and Charles led to a further blurring of the boundaries between Church and state. In his demand for the production of annual reports from his bishops after 1629, Charles exercised the royal supremacy in a manner never required by Queen Elizabeth.[97] She demanded loyalty, obedience, and information from her bishops, but never in such an officious manner, and never displaying the attention that King Charles did for the details. In the reign of Charles I it must have appeared to many that the wheel had come full circle, and with some extra unpleasant features. Bishops were common at court, they sat on the Privy Council, and some seem to have had privileged access to the king. Juxon was Lord Treasurer after 1636 and Laud had become chancellor of Oxford University in 1630. Here were distinct echoes of the early sixteenth century.

What did contemporaries think about all this? In his classic *Church History*, published in 1655, the judicious Thomas Fuller bemoaned the invention of the puritan bogeyman and recognized the problems of a Church 'but half-reformed'. By contrast, Peter Heylyn and his Laudian colleagues exaggerated continuities with the reign of the popular Queen Elizabeth in order to demonstrate their conservatism and reject charges of novelty.[98] Yet James almost inadvertently, and Charles more purposefully, were drawn into supporting a new vision of the Church. It is difficult to discern how angry people were that bishops had returned to some positions of secular power; it may have provided a convenient smokescreen for wider anger that would capture more attention than the niceties of Arminian theology. What is apparent is that speakers such as Nathaniel Fiennes in the Long Parliament made no bones about complaining about the 'confusion of the Spirituall sword with the Temporall'.[99] Yet MPs were tapping into folk memory rather than hard facts. None of

[96] Foster, 'Clerical Estate', pp. 150–1.
[97] K. Fincham (ed.), 'Annual Accounts of the Church of England, 1632–1639', in M. Barber, S. Taylor, and G. Sewell (eds.), *From the Reformation to the Permissive Society* (Woodbridge, 2010), pp. 63–149.
[98] A. Milton, *Laudian and Royalist Polemic in Seventeenth-Century England: The Career and Writings of Peter Heylyn* (Manchester, 2007); C. Lane, *The Laudians and the Elizabethan Church* (2013).
[99] Nathaniel Fiennes, *A Speech of the Honourable Nathanael Fiennes...concerning Bishops* (1641), pp. 14–15; Foster, 'Clerical Estate', p. 139.

that generation had lived under the early Tudors. They were creating a mythology about the likes of Cardinal Wolsey and Bishop Gardiner, reliant on a good grounding in the work of John Foxe the martyrologist. They smeared Archbishop Laud and his associates as 'crypto-Catholic' and 'abnormal', when in fact it would have appeared entirely 'normal' to encounter Catholic and Protestant bishops alike in the corridors of power in the first half of the sixteenth century. It is a comment on how radically different things had been in the reign of Queen Elizabeth I that this had been conveniently forgotten. The ambiguities of the reign of Elizabeth and her 'settlement' created a continuing power struggle within the Church of England and it is no accident that all sides appealed to precedents, whether they concerned interpretations of the Thirty-Nine Articles, rights to hold visitations, or matters such as the placing of altars. While Henry VIII, Edward VI, and Mary used their bishops and clergy to buttress their respective states, Elizabeth destabilized her Church to such an extent that when the balance shifted again under James I and his son Charles it all seemed too much, to many of the clergy as well as to a wider population.

SELECT BIBLIOGRAPHY

Birt, H., *The Elizabethan Settlement of Religion* (1907).
Carleton, K., *Bishops and Reform in the English Church, 1520–1559* (Woodbridge, 2001).
Collinson, P., 'Episcopacy and Reform in England in the Later Sixteenth Century', in *Godly People: Essays on English Protestantism and Puritanism* (1983), pp. 154–89.
Collinson, P., *The Religion of Protestants: The Church in English Society 1559–1625* (Oxford, 1982).
Fincham, K. (ed.), *The Early Stuart Church, 1603–1642* (Basingstoke, 1993).
Fincham, K., *Prelate as Pastor: The Episcopate of James I* (Oxford, 1990).
Haugaard, W., *Elizabeth and the English Reformation* (Cambridge, 1968).
Heal, F., *Of Prelates and Princes: A Study of the Economic and Social Position of the Tudor Episcopate* (Cambridge, 1980).
Heal, F., *Reformation in Britain and Ireland* (Oxford, 2003).
Hill, C., *Economic Problems of the Church from Archbishop Whitgift to the Long Parliament* (Oxford, 1956).
O'Day, R., *The English Clergy: The Emergence and Consolidation of a Profession, 1558–1642* (Leicester, 1979).
Usher, B., 'New Wine into Old Bottles: The Doctrine and Structure of the Elizabethan Church', in S. Doran and N. Jones (eds.), *The Elizabethan World* (2011), pp. 203–21.
Usher, B., *William Cecil and Episcopacy, 1559–1577* (Aldershot, 2003).
Usher, R., *The Reconstruction of the English Church*, 2 vols. (New York, 1910).

6

The Godly Magistrate

Jacqueline Rose

In the ideal early modern polity, every magistrate from the prince to the parish constable would be a godly magistrate. Richard Hooker's famous fusion of Church and commonweal exemplified the partnership of magistrate and pastor to secure the salvation of all subjects.[1] That the ruler had a duty to uphold true religion was a principle established long before the sixteenth century. But the English Reformation drastically changed the scope of these powers, while schism and confessional fragmentation meant that the meaning of true religion was now an open question. While the godly magistrate's jurisdiction was widened, their authority was increasingly laid open to question. The distinction between the godly and ungodly magistrate was subjective, unstable, and yet fundamental to securing religious and civil peace.

The Reformations out of which the Church of England emerged appear to have created the godly magistrate *par excellence* in the royal supremacy. That the king or queen of England was on earth the supreme head or governor under Christ of the Church of England was a fundamental starting point for any discussion of the nature of the Church and the direction it should take—its identity and reformation. Supremacy was both an institutional fact of England's constitution in its long Reformation and a piece of conceptual terrain—an idea whose precise interpretation was open to question. Much of what follows will, therefore, outline the royal supremacy and its implications. But we should not forget that most other religious groups had their own version of godly rule. This chapter will therefore also take note of Catholic, Presbyterian, and Independent notions of the godly magistrate. Only by placing the Established Church's[2] godly magistrate against a matrix of alternative interpretations of the office can we try to identify anything specifically

---

[1] Richard Hooker, *Of the Laws of Ecclesiastical Polity*, VIII.1.2.
[2] This will be used as shorthand for the Church of England, although it was of course unestablished from 1644 to 1662 and the establishment was Catholic from 1553 to 1558.

'Anglican' about the 'Anglican' godly magistrate. Who could lay claim to this position? Who were their allies and their enemies? What happened if they turned ungodly and who could do anything about this? Most fundamentally of all, who counted as a magistrate and whose godliness should they foster?

ESTABLISHING AND RE-ESTABLISHING THE GODLY MAGISTRATE

Arguments about the godly magistrate reflected both the remarkably prolonged Reformation process and the particular nature of each phase of that experience. This section briefly outlines those phases.

The founding moment was the Henrician schism of the 1530s. Supremacy was invented to secure Henry's immediate dynastic aims; there was no grand design for what it might include or the Church it might create. Three crucial statutes—the Act in Restraint of Appeals (1533), the Act of Submission of the Clergy (1534), and the Act of Supremacy (1534)—all contradicted each other. The Act of Appeals depicted the clergy and laity as two independent jurisdictions under the king; the Act of Submission subjected Convocation and canon law to the king and perhaps to Parliament (since extant canons were to be reviewed by a committee half of which was comprised of MPs and Lords). The terse Act of Supremacy perpetuated rather than clarified the fuzziness between the supremacy of the king and of the 'imperial crown of this realm'.[3] For Henry, his godly magistracy included expelling the Pope but excluded evangelical reform. Those around him thought otherwise, resulting in an idiosyncratic hotchpotch, especially as Henry backpedalled after 1539.

Henrician quirks are an important reminder that the supremacy was not originally and inherently Protestant. It was a notable success of Edwardian propaganda to make it seem so.[4] While a number of prominent Catholics (most famously Thomas More and John Fisher) had opposed Henry's supremacy, others had endorsed it. Only during the reign of Edward VI—a royal minority in which urgent reform was carried out initially by royal injunctions and only thereafter by statute—did this change. Edward's reign fused supremacy with evangelism. Overtly disowning supremacy, Mary I was not above using it to restore Catholic bishops.[5] But, as will be shown, the Catholic godly magistrate was a somewhat different beast.

---

[3] 24 Hen. VIII c.12; 25 Hen. VIII c.19; 26 Hen. VIII c.1.

[4] Diarmaid MacCulloch, *Tudor Church Militant: Edward VI and the Protestant Reformation* (1999); Stephen Alford, *Kingship and Politics in the Reign of Edward VI* (Cambridge, 2002).

[5] David Loades, 'The Last Years of Cuthbert Tunstall, 1547–1559', *Durham University Journal*, NS 35 (1973): 10–21.

The Elizabethan Settlement of 1559 famously changed supreme headship of the Church to supreme governance. Why this change occurred is frustratingly obscure, since we know only that the Marian exile Christopher Lever 'put such a scruple in the queen's head that she would not take the title of supreme head'. However, as John Parkhurst (future bishop of Norwich) explained to the Swiss theologian Heinrich Bullinger, 'she willingly accepts the title of governor which amounts to the same thing'.[6] Although Catholics in Parliament attacked the first supremacy bill (which did include headship) for granting a woman supremacy, this was not their main reason for rejecting it, nor was gender crucial in the subsequent debate. It was Elizabeth's lay status which invalidated her claim to supreme governance and it was this point which the Injunctions of 1559 sought to refute. Elizabeth sought 'soueraigntie & rule', she did not 'chalenge auctoritie and power of ministrie of divine offices'.[7] Supremacy meant jurisdictional governance, not sacerdotal powers. The Act which the regime forced through in 1559 was the last foundational statute of the established godly magistrate. The Act in Restraint of Appeals, Elizabethan Act of Supremacy, and Elizabethan Injunctions were the major reference points of later debates.

For many, Elizabeth's supremacy was but halfly godly. She froze the Church as it was settled in the early years of her reign, never reviving the urgent Swiss reform of the Edwardian Church. As will be shown below, this allowed hotter Protestants to advocate a godlier version of supremacy while permitting countervailing claims for *iure divino* episcopacy to develop in partnership with a more 'absolutist' interpretation of temporal government. In one sense James VI and I's supremacy continued this pattern: incorporating—more intentionally than Elizabeth—a range of positions within the Established Church. The debate sparked by the Oath of Allegiance of 1606 meant that Protestants could rally round an attack on the papal deposing power. But the debates in Parliament and among lawyers about who exactly authorized ecclesiastical law, the arguments over *iure divino* episcopacy and (increasingly) theology, and James's reluctance to overtly intervene in confessional warfare were ever more difficult to contain by the 1620s.

Charles I's partisan backing of the Laudian movement newly tied supremacy to a particular theology, ecclesiology, and version of ritual practice. Ironically, in the 1630s the supreme governor and his archbishop of Canterbury worked in perfect partnership: magistrate and minister united in enforcing their vision of godliness. The problem was their interpretation of this as high ceremony, the revitalization (financially and politically) of the clerical estate, and hardline enforcement of those positions. Dismantling

---

[6] Claire Cross, *The Royal Supremacy in the Elizabethan Church* (1969), pp. 136–7; Norman Jones, *Faith by Statute: Parliament and the Settlement of Religion, 1559* (1982).

[7] *Iniunctions geuen by the Quenes Maiestie* (1559), sig. D3r.

the Laudian reconstitution of the Church, Parliament in the 1640s seized supremacy—depriving Laud, overseeing synods and excommunication, and threatening the Westminster Assembly with *praemunire* (the crime of clerical subversion of royal power) when it displeased them. In effect supremacy was appropriated by the new parliamentary sovereign. Yet even the Interregnum unwillingness to enforce a compulsory form of church membership was not simply a rejection of supremacy, but another reinterpretation of what godly magistracy meant. As will be shown, Independents had their own temporarily dominant account of godly rule.

Thus each phase of England's long Reformation—a concept which should be taken to include the failed Laudian endeavours of the 1630s and abortive Cromwellian godly reform of the 1650s—invented its own version of the godly magistrate. But there were underlying continuities. This was partly for legal reasons—the practical necessity of repealing earlier statutes—and partly due to a mentality where history was a fount of authority. Increasingly the Tudor Reformations themselves became a source of legitimacy alongside Israelite and Constantinian models. But constant recollection of earlier developments was ingrained most of all because of the advantages of the way in which the period up to 1662 provided a set of multiple and contradictory godly magistrates which various groups could exploit. The godly magistrate was a chameleon-like creature, ever changing to fit in with which magistrate and whose godliness one preferred.

THE CASE FOR SUPREMACY

At its simplest, the royal supremacy was a fusion of ideas about the nature of the Church, what was fundamental and indifferent in religion, and the division of jurisdictional and spiritual authority. In breaking from Rome, Henry VIII had to justify his Church as a jurisdictionally self-sufficient body. The Act in Restraint of Appeals therefore spoke of the Church as juridically 'sufficient and meet of itself'. Instead of the universal Church being a single body under the aegis of a pope or general council, Christendom was conceived of as some sort of federation of independent Churches whose borders happened to coincide with different countries. These were *national* Churches—the idea was not quite the same as the later High Church notion of a confederation of sees held together, on a patristic model, by letters communicatory between bishops. The claim that the English Church was a national branch of Christianity suited Henry's perception of himself as pruning away papal jurisdiction while remaining a good orthodox Christian. But it was an argument which echoed throughout polemic from the 1530s to the 1660s (and beyond). 'The same men, which in a temporal respect make the Commonwealth, do in a spiritual make the Church', declared Laud: 'both are but one Jerusalem'. 'When the Church is incorporated into the Commonwealth, the chief authority in a Commonwealth as Christian, belongs to the same to which it doth as a Commonwealth', Edward Stillingfleet argued in 1660.[8] Given that all the members of the national Church were also members of the kingdom, then logically the king must preside over the Church and clergy just as he did the laity. The theologically conservative defender of Henrician supremacy Stephen Gardiner could perceive 'no cause why any man shoulde be offended that the kinge is called headde of the churche of Englande rather than the headde of the realme of Englande'.[9]

In the 1530s and late 1550s Henry VIII's supreme headship and Elizabeth I's supreme governance—a distinction without a difference—were therefore presented as logical symmetries of royal governance of the laity. This had been usurped by medieval popes and surrendered by supine kings such as John. Because of the Oath of Allegiance controversy, Jacobean works such as George Carleton's *Iurisdiction regall, episcopall, papall* (1610) were especially concerned to chart the rise of papal power. Throughout the early modern period, history remained a vital justification for supremacy. The ecclesiastical powers of Old Testament kings, early Christian emperors, and medieval monarchs were all frequently cited. (Authors variously emphasized medieval papal usurpation or resistance to it.) The monarch's right to govern religion was defended through immense historical scholarship on the early Church and its councils. But it was also displayed through deeply dubious myths such as that of King Lucius, the early British ruler who had been informed by the Pope of his status as 'vicar of God in your kingdom', not because of papal warrant but *ipso facto* as its king.[10] This striking combination of scholarship and storytelling performed the important legitimating function of making the supremacy look like a restoration of old Christian values, not an innovation—a pejorative word. Henrician statutes always 'declared' the king's status as supreme head; they never 'created' it anew and the Elizabethan Act 'restored... ancient jurisdiction'. The latter was glossed by the lawyer Edward Coke as 'not a statute introductory of a new law, but declaratory of the old'.[11]

None of this actually helped define what fell within the remit of the royal supremacy. Here the notion of 'matters indifferent' was vital. These *adiaphora* included questions of religious practice which were not specified in the Bible, especially ceremonies such as bowing, kneeling, making the sign of the cross,

---

[8] William Laud, *Works*, ed. William Scott and James Bliss, 7 vols. (Oxford, 1847–60), I, p. 6; Edward Stillingfleet, *Irenicum* ('1661' [1660]), p. 127.

[9] Stephen Gardiner, 'De Vera Obedientia Oratio', in Pierre Janelle (ed.), *Obedience in Church and State* (Cambridge, 1930), p. 93.

[10] Felicity Heal, 'What Can King Lucius Do for You? The Reformation and the Early British Church', *English Historical Review*, 120 (2005): 593–614.

[11] 77 Eng. Rep. 10, 5 Co. Rep. 8a (*R. v. Caudrey*).

and the use of vestments, especially the surplice. 'Decency and order' required their usage, but not if it gave offence to weaker brethren (1 Corinthians 14:40; Romans 14). Attitudes to these items demarcated enthusiastic ceremonialists, conformists, moderate puritans willing to comply but wishing the offending objects were removed, and hotter puritans unwilling to acquiesce in using such 'popish rags' irreparably contaminated by their pre-Reformation Catholic use. The royal supremacy clearly encompassed decisions on these questions, which were neither doctrinal nor (everyone agreed) necessary for salvation. Even puritans tended to admit royal governance of *adiaphora*—not least because they persistently, if vainly, hoped monarchs would be more lenient than bishops about enforcing them. Being a layman, the supreme governor should not meddle in theological fundamentals, but he (or she) might well decide whether to enforce conformity in *adiaphora*.

The question became more contentious when the sphere of *adiaphora* widened. Most importantly, it was unclear whether the Bible prescribed a particular form of church government. Scriptural vagueness meant that it was possible to claim that church government was *adiaphorous*, up to the supreme magistrate to decide. In 1660 Stillingfleet moved from noting the shared headship of Church and commonwealth to claiming that the form of church polity 'is wholly left to the prudence of those in whose power and trust it is to see the peace of the Church', and any *obligatory* form must be determined by the magistrate, as only civil authority had coercive power.[12] Whereas early Elizabethan clergy seemed to have no problem with this argument, it became increasingly untenable in the later sixteenth century as divisions between Presbyterians and episcopalians hardened. Different types of church government were now defended with divine-right claims. When in 1660 Stillingfleet made the above claim about church polity as a way to try to reconcile Presbyterians and supporters of episcopacy, he came under attack from the latter and had to write an appendix 'clarifying' his views. As will be shown, the godly magistrate's wobbles over church government made it increasingly vital from the 1640s that defenders of episcopacy exclude it from the sphere of indifference.

ALLIES AND ENEMIES

Although the royal supremacy divorced England from a traditional Catholic ecclesiology, under the supreme head the Church's pre-Reformation structure survived. Archbishops, bishops, and archdeacons manned a top-down system

---

[12] Stillingfleet, *Irenicum*, pp. 3, 44–8.

of ecclesiastical enforcement. This did not mean that the episcopate was homogeneous: it included Latimers and Grindals as well as Whitgifts and Bancrofts, Jacobean preaching prelates and Laudian enforcers of ceremonial conformity. It was certainly the godly magistrate's duty to take heed of clerical advice and maintain godly clergy, less clear that church government had to be episcopal. Yet arguments about the nature and origin of church government naturally affected perceptions of the magistrate. This section explores a debate prevalent throughout the early modern period: were bishops the allies of supremacy, or did the defence of episcopal government, especially on *iure divino* grounds, limit the magistrate?

The Church of England was eager to assert episcopal authority as more pure and primitive than papal power. Yet she was initially reluctant to criticize her non-episcopal European Protestant brethren. It was right for the English Church to have retained episcopacy, but that did not invalidate non-episcopal Churches.[13] Indeed, Archbishop Parker said it was the queen's decision whether 'you will haue any Archbisshoppes or bisshops or howe you will haue them ordered'.[14] Perhaps Parker knew that there was no chance that Elizabeth would ever turn Presbyterian. Yet the period from 1570 to 1640 saw the defence of episcopacy pushed into firmer, less compromising territory. Because Presbyterians insisted on the biblical warrant for their form of church government—leaving the godly magistrate no choice but to obey the scriptural determination of Presbyterianism—their opponents had perforce to match their arguments. The case for *iure divino* episcopacy only gradually emerged. It began with claiming that episcopacy was apostolic, evidenced in the Acts and Epistles. Whitgift combined this with saying that church government was a matter indifferent, to be decided by the magistrate.[15] But the argument for episcopacy moved from interpreting the proof text for papal authority (Matthew 16:18) as Christ giving power to all the apostles equally (a well-established line in the 1530s) to insisting on Christ's distinction between the twelve apostles and seventy disciples (Luke 6 and 10). Richard Hooker and John Bridges insisted on the divine appointment or approbation of episcopacy. Yet Hooker still argued that it was possible for the Church to alter government in a case of necessity.[16] It was Hadrian Saravia, Thomas Bilson, and Matthew Sutcliffe who finally endorsed episcopacy as 'not to bee repealed'.[17] This restraint on any adaptation of church polity naturally affected magisterial powers.

---

[13] John Whitgift, *The Defense of the Aunswere to the Admonition* (1574), p. 169. See also Chapter 18, 'Attitudes towards the Protestant and Catholic Churches', in the present volume.
[14] BL, Lansdowne MS 17, no. 93.
[15] Whitgift, *Defense*, pp. 210–11, 304, 313, 215, and tract 8.
[16] John Bridges, *A Defence of the Government Established* (1587), pp. 277, 280; Hooker, *Laws*, VII.1.4, VII.5.3, VII.5.10, VII.5.8.
[17] Hadrian Saravia, *The Diuerse Degrees of Ministers of the Gospell* (1592), p. 55.

Divine-right episcopacy thus theoretically constrained royal supremacy. Opponents of prelacy made much of this. The bishops subverted royal authority! Episcopacy was a form of *praemunire*! Taken at its most abstract, this was true: the magistrate could not change *iure divino* church government. But in practice it was false, for it was not until the 1640s that there was any chance that an English ruler would do so. The potential conflict between magistrate and episcopate was not actualized until political circumstance required it. Even then, there was confusion about whether Caroline divines were stooges of absolutism or cunning manipulators who plotted to overthrow royal power. Such confusion was evident in the quarrels over the 'etcetera oath' in the canons of 1640. Swearing to uphold 'archbishops, bishops, deans and archdeacons, etc' both endorsed episcopal government as unalterable and wrote the supreme governor out of the hierarchy. The Laudian clergy of the 1630s might be as guilty of treasonable *praemunire* as they were of absolutism.

Those needing to protect episcopacy from magisterial abolition while upholding supremacy had to respond to several opponents in the 1640s. The most obvious were the parliamentarians and their Presbyterian allies who abolished episcopacy in 1646. But there were other threats. Henrietta Maria's circle of royalists urged Charles to jettison the episcopal Church and forge a Catholic alliance to gain military victory, while even their 'constitutional royalist' opponents disliked Laudian *iure divino* episcopacy.[18] Were constitutional royalist defences of bishops along *iure humano* lines of royal choice and custom sufficient safeguards? Most worryingly of all, in the late 1640s and early 1650s, both Charles I and Charles II showed themselves willing to permit Presbyterianism in order to regain their thrones. Divine-right arguments thus flourished in the Interregnum as the easiest way to protect the Church from Catholic, Presbyterian, and monarchical attack. Their proponents tended to say less about the role of the magistrate, seeking to re-found Anglican identity in episcopacy, the Prayer Book, and the early Church rather than on Constantinian foundations. That the royal supremacy was not sacerdotal appeared as one of the minor questions of John Bramhall's polemical writings, although as ever it was the Elizabethan Injunctions which provided the evidence for this.[19]

But where episcopalians did debate the interstices of their relationship to their supreme governor, they tended to continue their predecessors' claims of a doubly asymmetrical partnership. This perpetuated the third crucial line of argument about supremacy: that it was jurisdictional and not sacerdotal. The magistrate held juridical power over the clergy—necessarily so, for they ought

---

[18] David L. Smith, *Constitutional Royalism and the Search for Settlement, c.1640–1649* (Cambridge, 1994).

[19] John Bramhall, *Schisme Garded and Beaten Back* (1658), p. 170; John Bramhall, *A Just Vindication of the Church of England* (1654), p. 269.

to purge the Church of ungodly pastors. But the clergy held spiritual authority over the ruler, with the right to counsel and admonish them for their religious failings. Church of England clergy thus constantly told rulers of their faults while denouncing anyone who justified rebellion on religious grounds. Again, at their most extreme the two views were incompatible, as shown by the argument between Elizabeth and Archbishop Grindal in 1576.[20] But this was driven by a particular religious concern (suppression or allowance of puritan prophesyings) and by the personalities of the participants. Only particular circumstances caused theories about the Church to come into conflict.

English monarchs were generally fortunate in their bishops; surprisingly so, given that they inherited their predecessors' bishops, unlike their councillors whom they could change on their accession. It was fortunate for Elizabeth that Cardinal Pole and a number of Marian bishops died in 1558–9; it was fortuitous for Charles I that he could promote Laudians to vacant sees. The system offered enough flexibility to allow rulers to promote the clergy they liked and to quietly sideline others (as Charles did Archbishop Abbot, for example). Nevertheless, the period after 1640 showed that when monarchs posed an existential threat to bishops, the two could quickly turn from allies to enemies. Political and religious pressures could alter ecclesiological alignments, depending on whose godliness was *de rigueur* at the time.

WHICH MAGISTRATE?

The prevalence of the defence of godly magistracy derived in part from its flexibility. When Henry VIII broke with Rome, his vision—as far as he had one—was of the enhancement of royal authority. This was signalled in the Act of Appeals's description of 'plenary, whole, and entire' authority, an echo of papal plenitude of power. Many defences of supremacy rested on the nature of royal authority and cited monarchical models—Israelite kings and Constantine. There was nothing in the Old Testament, Henry Stubbe snidely wrote in the 1670s, which suggested Parliament had a role in supremacy.[21]

Yet other theorists did envisage a less monarchical version of supremacy (and found biblical support for it, the Sanhedrin being one obvious, though ambiguous, example). From the very beginning, the possessors of godly rule were pluriform. Henry used Parliament to declare his supremacy for practical reasons—the authority of statute, its ability to impose oaths, capital and corporal punishment, and the veneer of consent it offered. Yet enacting

---

[20] See Chapter 3, 'Settlement Patterns: The Church of England, 1553–1603', in the present volume.
[21] TNA, SP 29/319/220, fo. 330.

supremacy meant that later rulers had to use Parliament to unpick or adjust the Henrician revolution. Even if Parliament only declared rather than created the king's godly rule, only a statute could undo a statute. But Henrician legislation contained ambivalent phrases and contradictory messages, as was only natural in a series of piecemeal Acts passed after significant redrafting. The Act of Appeals spoke of the imperial 'crown' and empire of the 'realm', something rather more than the monarch. While it suggested that the spiritualty and temporalty were two independent jurisdictions under the king, the Act of Submission firmly subordinated Convocation and canons to lay control.[22]

But which layman? By the Act of Submission, the king was to summon Convocation, license its debates, and ratify its canons. But since this was legislated by statute, Parliament might assert its power to control ecclesiastical legislation. From the later sixteenth century, MPs began to articulate this argument, a discourse which reached its full flowering in the early Stuart era. In 1610, a bill was drafted to limit execution of canons not ratified by Parliament.[23] In 1640, MPs and lawyers denounced Convocation for sitting after the Short Parliament had been dissolved, as well as for the content of the canons it had passed. This episode is telling: the latent ambiguity of the Act of Submission—which the common lawyer Edward Bagshaw quoted in defence of his argument that Parliament shared supremacy with the king—was only fully dissected when Parliament was engaged in a battle with the king over the nature of the Church.[24] Theoretical incoherence mattered when it had immediate political implications. Its legacy involved Parliament curbing the debates of the Westminster Assembly of Divines and governing Presbyterian excommunication in the 1640s.[25] The Anglican royalist Parliament of 1661 calmly accepted Convocation's changes to the Book of Common Prayer, but it was not so chastened as to avoid noting that such changes 'might...have been debated', had Parliament so wished.[26]

That it was lawyers as much as MPs who were in the vanguard of exposing the ambiguities of supremacy should not surprise us. Although it is necessary to remember that many practitioners upheld a monarchical incarnation of godly rule, the first writer to suggest that ecclesiastical oversight lay in the hands of king-in-Parliament was the common lawyer Christopher St German

---

[22] Conrad Russell, 'Whose Supremacy? King, Parliament, and the Church, 1530–1640', *Ecclesiastical Law Journal*, 4 (1996–7): 53–64.

[23] Elizabeth Read Foster, *Proceedings in Parliament, 1610*, 2 vols. (New Haven, CT, 1966), I, pp. 85, 124n2.

[24] Edward Bagshaw, *Two Arguments in Parliament* (1641), p. 10; Jacqueline Rose, *Godly Kingship in Restoration England* (Cambridge, 2011), pp. 70–3.

[25] See Chapter 23, 'The Westminster Assembly and the Reformation of the 1640s', in the present volume.

[26] *CJ*, VIII, p. 408.

in the 1530s.[27] Again this had a practical dimension, being part of the point-scoring in the turf wars between common lawyers and ecclesiastical courts. While anti-clericalism is now debunked by historians as a cause of Reformation, a specific self-interested judicial strand of it seems to have been alive and well in the early Tudor Inns of Court. Arguing that English monarchs held *politicum dominium et regale*, St German stated that Parliament interpreted Scripture, for it represented all the people of England and therefore the Church of England. It was ecclesiastical treachery to conceive of the Church as purely a clerical entity.[28] St German wavered over exactly who held supremacy: the king alone, or assisted by Parliament or lawyers.[29] But the fact that his *Doctor and Student* (albeit not the most interesting of his writings from the point of view of this chapter) was read in the Inns of Court well into the seventeenth century makes it likely that his Fortescuean account of mixed rather than mere monarchy was suggestive for later legal thinkers. Edward Coke naturally cited it; so did Edward Bagshaw.[30] The prolific polemicist William Prynne probably knew it. All shared St German's sense that it did not matter exactly which layman governed the Church, as long as the clergy were kept under control, for all sometimes attributed supremacy to the king alone, sometimes to crown-in-Parliament. Thus Coke could produce a strongly monarchist account when upholding High Commission in Caudrey's Case of 1593 and a mixed monarchist version in his early seventeenth-century *Institutes*.[31] Similarly, Prynne could attack Charles I for lazy surrender of his imperial monarchy to Laudian prelates, go on to denounce civil war Presbyterians for clerical tyranny manifested in excommunication, and end by pouring out his distress at being excluded from receiving communion by divines in the restored Church of England. Prynne's belief that manipulation of excommunication was one of the ways in which clergy tyrannized over the laity linked an 'Erastian' concern about excommunication with the broader meaning the epithet was acquiring as state control of the Church. But while Congregationalists and Erastians allied in the mid-1640s to defeat Presbyterianism, their views were not the same. Congregationalists' concern was with the type of godliness that the magistrate would patronize, Erastians' concern was with his power to crush clerical tyranny. Godly rule was distinct from, though it overlapped with, Erastianism.

That many MPs were lawyers helps explain how conceptions of the godly magistrate which encompassed king-in-Parliament, or the king supported by

---

[27] John Guy, 'Thomas More and Christopher St German: The Battle of the Books', in Alistair Fox and John Guy (eds.), *Reassessing the Henrician Age* (Oxford, 1986); Christopher Brooks, *Law, Politics and Society in Early Modern England* (Cambridge, 2008), ch. 3.
[28] Christopher St German, *An Answere to a Letter* (1535), sigs. G4v–G6v, B2v.
[29] Rose, *Godly Kingship*, pp. 34–9.
[30] Edward Coke, *The Fourth Part of the Institutes* (1669), p. 343; BL, Stowe MS 424, fo. 2r.
[31] 77 Eng. Rep. 9–11, 5 Co. Rep. 8a–9a; Coke, *Fourth Part of the Institutes*, p. 328.

his judges, spread from the Inns of Court to Parliament. But the gentry who enjoyed a smattering of legal education played a role in local as well as central government. Their legislative role as MPs was complemented by their position as Justices of the Peace, and both offices offered them a chance to play the godly magistrate. Godly rule at the centre could not produce a new Israel were it not enforced locally. Such men were crucial in fostering (or thwarting) Reformation locally. As patrons with the right to appoint local preachers and ministers, as the probable lay elders in any Presbyterian church, and as magistrates able to enforce social and moral discipline, the gentry could be conceived of as the godly magistrate in their locality.

The local godly magistrate faced many of the same issues as his central counterpart. He had to determine which religious groups to support and punish. How strictly should he enforce the laws against recusants and Dissenters? Could he promote a puritan godly society, even in the teeth of monarchical dislike? He had to foster a good working relationship with the ministers of the area, and find ways of accommodation if he discovered that he disagreed with them, or with the archdeacons and bishops who came on periodic visitations. Above all, he had to balance the competing demands of divisive discipline—either in a puritan moral and social sense, or in a Laudian one of ceremonial conformity—with the desire to maintain good neighbourliness with all religious persuasions.

WHOSE GODLINESS?

The advancement of God was 'the especyall office of euery good Christen prince', declared John Christopherson in 1554.[32] Godly rule, and godly obedience, was a theme of his work, as of many in this period. But Christopherson praised a godly magistrate who was Catholic, not Protestant. His work is an apt reminder that evangelicals did not have a monopoly on the language of godly rule. Many Marian supporters engaged in this sort of praise, depicting Mary as God's handmaid, providentially preserved to restore Catholic truth to England.[33] How distinctive was their version of the godly magistrate?

Some of the depictions of Edward VI echoed in portrayals of Mary and her husband. The Protestant Solomon was Edward, the Catholic one Philip; Edward's death was God's punishment on a world too ungodly for the godly ruler, so too was Mary too good for the earth. Yet the scope of the Catholic godly ruler was narrower, and less fully discussed, than that of the evangelical

---

[32] John Christopherson, *An Exhortation to All Menne to Take Hede and Beware of Rebellion* (1554), sig. P5v.
[33] Christopherson, *Exhortation*, sigs. M1v, Q4r.

one. The leader of Mary's Church, Cardinal Pole, insisted on the need for papal headship to build Solomon's Temple, while John White's funerary panegyric to Mary emphasized her *rejection* of the supremacy as evidence of her learned godliness. 'She could say, How can I, a Woman, be Head of the Church, who by Scripture am forbidden to speak in the Church?... Authoritys of Scripture she was able to alledg, why she could not be *Caput Ecclesiae*, and by Learning defended the same.'[34] Depiction here departed from the reality of Mary's use of such powers to deprive Edwardian bishops.

The Catholic interpretation of the godly magistrate was not the only alternative depiction available to those discontented with the Established Church. Those demanding further Protestant reform, whether of a Presbyterian or more radical variety, also offered competing versions of the office. As Peter Lake has shown, Elizabethan Presbyterians were in part forced to pay lip service to the royal supremacy in order to prove their loyalty even as they challenged the queen's preferred Church. Yet they tended to deprive the ruler of any substantive powers, limiting the sphere of royal action by restricting *adiaphora* and by their ecclesiology.[35] Thomas Cartwright's vision of the English constitution as one of mixed rather than absolute monarchy further encouraged parliamentary interference in royal godly magistracy.[36] Urging the magistrate to crush episcopal tyranny could thus take the form of appeals to Elizabeth (as for John Penry) or to parliamentary statute (as for William Stoughton).[37] Both methods would become entrenched ways of seeking further reformation.

But although Presbyterian ecclesiastical loyalism was partly lip service, it also included a genuine adherence to a vision of godly magistracy. The most expansive account was Richard Baxter's *Holy Commonwealth* (1659), a paean to the godly rule of Richard Cromwell. Baxter declared that a true commonwealth was not a mere hierarchy of sovereign and subjects, but an organization of relationships for the purpose of pleasing God. The man who felt Charles I's fundamental failure was neglect of, if not complicity in, the popish threat naturally insisted that the Long Parliament 'never made it the Old Cause to disown their power in matters of Religion'.[38] Indeed: the Westminster Assembly's description of the magistrate's limits exactly repeated the 1559

---

[34] John Elder, *The Copie of a Letter Sent into Scotlande* (1555), fos. D7r–8v; John Strype, *Ecclesiastical Memorials*, 3 vols. (1721), III, appendix, p. 284.

[35] Peter Lake, *Anglicans and Puritans? Presbyterianism and English Conformist Thought from Whitgift to Hooker* (1988), pp. 75–6, 51–2.

[36] Peter Lake, '"The Monarchical Republic of Queen Elizabeth I" (and the Fall of Archbishop Grindal Revisited)', in John F. McDiarmid (ed.), *The Monarchical Republic of Early Modern England* (Aldershot, 2007), pp. 129–47.

[37] John Penry, *An Hvmble Motion with Svbmission* (Edinburgh, 1590); William Stoughton, *An Abstract of Certain Acts of Parliament* (1583).

[38] Richard Baxter, *A Holy Commonwealth*, ed. William Lamont (Cambridge, 1994), pp. 68–9, 23.

Injunctions.[39] Baxter depicted a partnership of magistrate and minister, differing in roles, but virtually converging in their ultimate goals: 'so twisted together, that they may concur and co-operate, without any invasion of each others' Offices, but for mutual help'.[40] The ability of the ruler to punish erring pastors came very close to royal supremacy, although it remained distinct from the episcopalian version of it given Baxter's unwillingness to call the king *imperator* and ministerial control of excommunication. (He just about allowed sovereigns to be excommunicated.) Baxter's description of the limits of godly magistracy[41] could sound very close to the way some Church of England men discussed supremacy. Yet one feels that the Church working with Baxter's godly magistrate would have looked rather different to the episcopal one—as shown by Baxter's growing antipathy to 'French' as well as 'Italian' popery (conciliarism as well as papalism).[42] However, the potential convergence of moderate Presbyterianism and moderated episcopacy over the godly magistrate was not yet theoretically impossible. Perhaps the practical convergence on specific details was the ultimate barrier, only discovered to be so when Presbyterians and episcopalians sat down to negotiate the mechanics of the Restoration Church.

That Presbyterians proffered their own version of the godly magistrate is unsurprising, for they firmly upheld the idea of a national Church. That more radical groups who questioned the very notion of a compulsory establishment also suggested a type of godly ruler is more surprising. Although the Independent incarnation of godly magistracy was proposed most forcefully in the years after 1662, earlier traces of it can be detected.[43] It could be used to appeal to the ruler over the heads (or mitres) of the bishops, or it could—especially in the civil wars—be manipulated to praise new rulers like Cromwell who would patronize the sects and quash intolerance in whatever guise (or vestments) it appeared. Again, therefore, the godly magistrate's role was both to protect and fund godly preachers, and to crush opponents of the favoured type of piety.

Separatist groups were a tiny minority in the Tudor era, and they frequently rejected magisterial meddling in religion. The 'anabaptist' epithet with which they were slandered linked them to the European radical Reformation of the 1520s which rejected the social, political, and religious establishments in favour of theocratic anarchy. This association was unfortunately fostered by those who in 1583 obliterated the royal coat of arms in the parish church of Bury St Edmunds, painting underneath the text from Revelation 3:16 on God

---

[39] Alex F. Mitchell and John Struthers (eds.), *Minutes of the Sessions of the Westminster Assembly of Divines* (Edinburgh, 1874), p. 224.
[40] Baxter, *Holy Commonwealth*, pp. 129–32, 160.
[41] Baxter, *Holy Commonwealth*, ch. 10.
[42] William Lamont, *Richard Baxter and the Millennium: Protestant Imperialism and the English Revolution* (1979).
[43] Rose, *Godly Kingship*, ch. 4.

spewing the lukewarm Laodicean church out of his mouth. It was fatally cemented in 1591 by William Hacket, Edmund Coppinger, and Henry Arthington's plot to depose Elizabeth and free jailed Presbyterian leaders.[44] All these episodes usefully allowed the government to condemn those wanting further reformation—including Presbyterians and puritans—as dangerously subversive. But other reformers appealed to royal supremacy in order to crush episcopal intolerance.[45]

The early Stuart years were unhappy times for separatists. They were persecuted by the government, forced into unwilling exile, and discovered just how bitterly divided they were from more conservative puritans. Their chance seemed to come during the civil wars of the 1640s. Then Independency grew because of the failure of Presbyterian discipline, but it might have seemed under threat from new forms of intolerance. The Independents' appeals to Parliament and army leaders allowed them to seize the initiative after the regicide. Their godly magistrate prevailed in the 1650s, permitting them to openly uphold his authority.[46] This did not mean that the Interregnum godly magistrate held the same powers as the antebellum one. Part of their godliness lay in their restraint—the *lack* of interference in belief. There would be no *compulsory* national Church, no canons to ratify or Convocation to oversee, no hierarchy of bishops to head. Parishes were fraternally linked by informal bonds of mutual advice, not a hierarchy of synods. And believers were to be left to seek divine truth, not compelled to plod along the government's chosen pathway to heaven. Yet there was a positive role for the magistrate too. There was a Cromwellian Church in which approved preachers would be salaried. Lay godly magistrates included central Triers and local Ejectors, who inspected clergy for godliness. The godly ruler might promote reconciliation between Presbyterians and Independents. And he policed the boundaries of toleration: no episcopalians, no papists, no Socinians were to threaten his godly people.[47] The ruler was thus given a religious role in Interregnum constitutional experiments. This culminated in 1658, when the Savoy Declaration pronounced that the magistrate was 'bound to encourage, promote and protect the professors and profession of the Gospel' but should exercise 'indulgency and forbearance' to those of differing opinions. Such a ruler 'doth therein discharge as great a faithfulness to Christ [as...] any Christian magistrate'.[48]

---

[44] Alexandra Walsham, '"Frantick Hacket": Prophecy, Sorcery, Insanity, and the Elizabethan Puritan Movement', *Historical Journal*, 41 (1998): 27–66.

[45] Henry Burton, *For God and the King* (1636); William Prynne, *A Breviate of the Prelates Intollerable Usurpations* (1637).

[46] Jeffrey R. Collins, *The Allegiance of Thomas Hobbes* (Oxford, 2005).

[47] See Chapter 24, 'The Cromwellian Church', in the present volume.

[48] Gerald Bray (ed.), *Documents of the English Reformation* (Minneapolis, MN, 1994), pp. 537, 533.

THE UNGODLY MAGISTRATE

One of the major impacts of the European Reformations was their effect on political thinking. Whether in the formal channels of 'political thought', the out-of-doors politics of riot and rebellion, or merely vaguer attitudes to the legitimacy of rulers, the Reformations destabilized magistracy. Rulers gained significant power, but also acquired extra responsibilities as the Reformation opened up new arenas for criticism. If godly rule was, as Bishop Hugh Latimer told Edward VI, 'a dygnity wyth a charge' and tyranny was, as Thomas Hobbes put it a century later, nothing but monarchy 'misliked',[49] then religious policy was a crucial determinant of obedience or resistance. Dislike of religious policy could be worse than that of temporal decisions because it was impossible to compromise on the salvation of one's soul and the souls of one's fellow subjects, in the way one might on taxes, socio-economic troubles, or political grievances. If the ruler was an ungodly tyrant, then surely deposing and killing them was a godly act. The Reformation era was therefore one in which the physical tools of dagger, poison, or handgun became appropriate means to achieve a spiritualized political end.

The ungodly tyrant was at one and the same time the polar opposite and the disturbingly proximate neighbour of the godly magistrate. While the godly ruler upheld true religion, the ungodly despot persecuted it. The former made policy according to the advice of knowledgeable and expert divines and preachers; the latter scorned the prophetic counsel of churchmen. But what counted as true religion and good counsel? Under Mary I Protestant exiles in Europe complained of the evil policies of the Catholic Jezebel, while Catholic exiles denounced Elizabeth I in remarkably similar terms only a decade later. Do not think that political office is possessed in order to enforce the rule of a wicked woman, the Marian exile Christopher Goodman told his fellow Englishmen. Rather, it was to uphold godliness even against the queen.[50] Writing in defence of the papal deposition of Elizabeth I and the Spanish Armada in 1588, Cardinal William Allen appealed in particular to the nobility and gentry as having a duty to free their country from Elizabethan tyranny—as their ancestors had done.[51] Such appeals to 'lesser magistrates' to correct and if need be depose the chief magistrate were characteristic of Reformation political thinking.

But the language which these writers used to attack the godly ruler could easily be manipulated. It might be appropriated by a group of people who held

---

[49] Hugh Latimer, *The Seconde[-seventh] Sermon...Preached before the Kynges Maiestie* (1549), sig. [K3]v; Thomas Hobbes, *Leviathan*, ed. R. Tuck (Cambridge, 1996), p. 130.

[50] Christopher Goodman, *How Superior Powers Oght to be Obeyd of their Subiects* (1558), p. 95.

[51] William Allen, *An Admonition to the Nobility and People of England* (1588), pp. vii–viii.

The Godly Magistrate

no magistracy at all. As late as 1680, the Sanquhar Declaration declared war on the 'tyrant' Charles II for having 'forfeited' the throne 'by his perjury and breach of covenant both to God and His Kirk'.[52] Even more disturbingly, the rhetoric could be seized on by any spiritually inspired individual to legitimize their own defence of religion. Godly individuals like Phineas in the Old Testament had wielded the *ius zelotarum* to save the Israelites. If the monarch shifted from a Josiah or Hezekiah or Deborah to a Nebuchadnezzar or Ahab or Jezebel, modern zealots might revive Israelite assassination principles. Early modern rulers were perhaps less threatened by large armadas than by lone assassins: William the Silent, Henri III, and Henri IV all fell to the latter. And political theorists found it remarkably difficult to prohibit the spiritual zeal of such individuals. Both Goodman and, eventually, John Knox fell back on popular rebellion if the lesser magistrates 'cease to do their duetie'.[53]

Over time, another problem loomed. What if it were possible to live under a magistrate who, though ungodly, refrained from interfering too much with the lives of the godly? Against all the ingrained assumptions that religious difference implied disloyalty, might it be feasible to offer temporal loyalty to a sovereign of a different religion? By the later sixteenth century, this question had irredeemably divided the English Catholic community. 'Church papists' attended Protestant services to avoid the penal laws and sometimes sought ways to prove their loyalty to Elizabeth. Sir Thomas Tresham wanted to fight for the English government against the Armada.[54] Other Jesuits insisted that such Nicodemism and compromise with heretics was impossible. But in 1580 Gregory XIII had to allow Catholics temporary respite from their duty in *Regnans in excelsis* to assassinate Elizabeth.

From the later sixteenth century, the Established Church of England took pride in distancing itself from such 'Jesuitical' and 'fanatical' principles of sedition. From Richard Bancroft's sermon at Paul's Cross in 1589, which first associated Catholic and Calvinist political principles, to David Owen's *Herod and Pilate Reconciled* (1610) and 'Lysimachus Nicanor''s *Epistle* to the Covenanters of 1640, Catholic and Calvinist resistance theories were jointly rejected. (Many other works of course aggressively refuted one or the other.) Thus the Church of England began to claim an identity for herself as peculiarly obedient to magisterial authority, the feature 'which distinguishes ours from all other communions'.[55] This was not a lame Erastian submission to royal whim, for the Church proudly insisted on her principles of passive resistance to ungodly commands. But she resisted the commands, not the commander.

---

[52] Andrew Browning (ed.), *English Historical Documents, 1660–1717* (1953), pp. 243–4.
[53] Goodman, *Superior Powers*, p. 185.
[54] Thomas M. McCoog, *The Society of Jesus in Ireland, Scotland, and England, 1589–1597* (Farnham, 2012), p. 336; Alexandra Walsham, *Church Papists: Catholicism, Conformity and Confessional Polemic in Early Modern England* (1993).
[55] Samuel Parker, *A Reproof to the Rehearsal Transprosed* (1673), p. 305.

The strategy of non-cooperation was the chosen way to disable distasteful policies. It was an effective strategy in a pre-modern society with no standing army, no police force, and no great bureaucracy, and it certainly worked in 1688. Anglican identity was here associated with a particular political stance.

Furthermore, the Church insisted that she had her own preferred strategy for getting the recalcitrantly godly magistrate back on the straight and narrow—namely, counsel.[56] Advising them to rectify mistaken decisions and admonishing them when they got policies wrong was the route to exercising what was called 'directive', not 'coactive' authority. Directive authority channelled decisions the right way by moral guidance, without the coactive or coercive use of legal or constitutional (let alone physical) restraint. Of course, spiritual counsel was not exclusive to Anglicans, but their insistence on the importance of giving it privately, not publicly, and on the inability to practise active resistance if the ruler failed to heed it, did demarcate a distinctive ecclesiological and political attitude. Whether Church of England men in practice adhered to their self-denying ordinance was, of course, another matter.

From 1530 to 1662, the idea of the godly magistrate was strikingly prevalent because of its remarkably heterogeneous nature. Almost every religious group was able to construct a ruler whose duty was to defend true religion and to compel dissenters into their preferred Church. The most prominent and officially 'established' of these interpretations was a magistrate holding jurisdictional authority over a national episcopal Church—the type re-established in 1662. But, as events over the next thirty years would show, legislative triumph did not equate to an intellectual monopoly over interpretations. For almost all religious groups, getting one's own godly magistrate in post was the route to determining identity and imposing reformation. After more than a century of religious change, both remained open questions in 1662.

SELECT BIBLIOGRAPHY

Collins, Jeffrey R., *The Allegiance of Thomas Hobbes* (Oxford, 2005).
Cross, Claire, *The Royal Supremacy in the Elizabethan Church* (1969).
Figgis, John Neville, 'Erastus and Erastianism', *Journal of Theological Studies*, 2 (1901): 66–101.
Fox, Alistair and John Guy (eds.), *Reassessing the Henrician Age: Humanism, Politics, and Reform 1500–1550* (Oxford, 1986).

---

[56] Jacqueline Rose, 'Kingship and Counsel in Early Modern England', *Historical Journal*, 54 (2011): 47–71.

Guy, John, 'The Elizabethan Establishment and the Ecclesiastical Polity', in John Guy (ed.), *The Reign of Elizabeth I: Court and Culture in the Last Decade* (Cambridge, 1995), pp. 126–49.

Lake, Peter, *Anglicans and Puritans? Presbyterianism and English Conformist Thought from Whitgift to Hooker* (1988).

Lamont, William, *Godly Rule: Politics and Religion, 1603–1660* (1969).

Nicholson, Graham, 'The Act of Appeals and the English Reformation', in Claire Cross, David Loades, and J. J. Scarisbrick (eds.), *Law and Government under the Tudors* (Cambridge, 1988), pp. 19–30.

Rose, Jacqueline, *Godly Kingship in Restoration England* (Cambridge, 2011).

Russell, Conrad, 'Whose Supremacy? King, Parliament, and the Church, 1530–1640', *Ecclesiastical Law Journal*, 4 (1996–7): 53–64.

7

Religion and the English Parish

J. F. Merritt

The historiography of the early modern English parish has pursued curiously divergent paths in recent decades. Some studies have considered parishes chiefly in religious terms, and have tended to see them as embodying cohesive, conservative, and inclusive values. Others, by contrast, have studied them principally in social terms, and have presented a starkly different picture of socially divided communities, defined in terms of social differentiation and the emergence of a ruling oligarchy monopolizing local power.[1] Each approach has tended to regard the other as reductionist in its assumptions, and as a result two incompatible images of the early modern parish have emerged from scholarship that run parallel but seldom intersect, often drawing upon different types of sources. To study the religious experience of the early modern parish effectively, though, it is vital to take an approach that considers the interaction of the social and the religious more fully, with an eye to the specific political context, and informed by factors that could also be cultural or administrative. This is especially necessary in the context of this volume, as 'parish religion' has tended to assume a very special role in the development of 'Anglicanism'. It is often portrayed as conveying and encapsulating a conservative and inclusive type of Protestantism inculcated by the overriding influence of the Prayer Book. But views of the parish as a heartland of unproblematic 'Anglican' values carry presuppositions not only about the ideological impact of the Prayer Book on local men and women but also tacit assumptions about the underlying homogeneity of the English parish and its cohesive character. The multi-faceted reality of English parishes in this period, though, means that religious historians must not discount the significance of wide differences in the social, geographical, and political make-up

---

[1] For example, C. W. Marsh, '"Common Prayer" in England 1560–1640: The View from the Pew', *Past & Present*, 171 (2001): 66–94; K. Wrightson, 'The Politics of the Parish in Early Modern England', in P. Griffiths, A. Fox, and S. Hindle (eds.), *The Experience of Authority in Early Modern England* (Basingstoke, 1996), pp. 10–46.

of individual parishes, and the complex ways in which religion interacted with them.

This chapter does not seek to provide a simple description or evocation of church services nor even primarily a discussion of the sociability surrounding church-going. Instead it aims to analyse the factors that made the religious experience of parishioners distinctive in this period, particularly in relation to the impact of national religious policy. The study of the parish takes us to the heart of the early modern Church of England and people's daily religious experiences, and reveals not a stable continuum of conservative values, but a dynamic, richly diverse, and multi-faceted parochial experience.

THE EARLY MODERN PARISH COMMUNITY

Our discussion of religion within the parish must begin, however, by recognizing the parish's secular role as a unit of government within post-Reformation society, with a number of vital administrative and social duties to perform. Even if the parish church was no longer the focus of the extensive and elaborate communal ceremonies that characterized the pre-Reformation church, the parish itself had an ever more central role as the lynchpin of Elizabethan religious and social policy. The Tudor state imposed increasing duties on the parish. For example the parish (and its officers) were often named explicitly in parliamentary statutes as those responsible for implementing legislation, and their responsibilities included local poor relief and the punishment of vagrants, the levying of local rates, and providing arms for the militia and support for maimed soldiers.[2]

In matters concerning the church and religion, the parish was the level at which the state implemented its legal requirement for all inhabitants to attend church (which they did, beneath the prominently displayed royal arms where prayers were offered for the reigning monarch). Church attendance was thus a mark of political loyalty and obedience. This meant that the religious function of the parish was necessarily inclusive, although it was attendance rather than belief that was monitored. Here, despite some ambiguous evidence and regional variation, an improving picture of attendance seems to emerge from the 1590s.[3] The presupposition of universal church attendance had an impact in various ways. The fact that the whole community theoretically

---

[2] B. Kümin, *The Shaping of a Community: The Rise and Reformation of the English Parish c.1400–1560* (Aldershot, 1996), chs. 2–3; E. J. Carlson, 'The Origins, Function and Status of Churchwardens', in M. Spufford (ed.), *The World of Rural Dissenters 1520–1725* (Cambridge, 1995), pp. 164–207.

[3] M. Ingram, *Church Courts, Sex and Marriage in England, 1570–1640* (Cambridge, 1987), pp. 107–8; F. Heal, *Reformation in Britain and Ireland* (Oxford, 2003), p. 466.

gathered in the parish church meant that church services also offered an opportunity for the state to interact directly and regularly with its subjects. These were the occasions when royal declarations and state prayers were read out, official news announced, plague regulations disseminated, and the community exhorted to give thanks for Protestant military victories and royal births, to fast for God's protection against the plague, dearth, or Catholic plots, and to contribute to collections ranging from the relief of English prisoners abroad to the rebuilding of St Paul's.[4]

The parish also regulated a wide range of the social as well as the religious behaviour of its inhabitants, reporting anti-social or immoral behaviour to the church courts. The monitoring of church attendance was entrusted to the locally selected churchwardens, but wardens were not just to report to their archdeacon on matters such as parishioners being absent from communion or behaving in a disorderly fashion in the church, but also about the conduct of church officials including the minister himself, and on the state of the church fabric.[5]

The parish may thus have been a unit of administration, answering to two chains of command—one secular and one ecclesiastical—but it was obviously much more than that. The early modern parish also inherited a whole body of broader assumptions about the social role that the church would perform in promoting Christian fellowship, social harmony, and order. In the medieval period such ideas were reinforced in myriad forms of ritual and festive activity that brought the community together. While many of these potentially unifying activities disappeared at the Reformation because of their 'superstitious' associations, some remained, and the model of the parish church as the spiritual heart of the community, promoting cohesion, and as the forum for socially ameliorative activities, was still deeply ingrained.

This can be observed in the sacrament of communion. This was one of only two sacraments to be retained within the Church of England (along with baptism), and participation was a requirement overseen by the churchwardens and minister. The significance attached to the ceremony blended deeply spiritual elements with important social ones, despite changes to its theological underpinnings within the English Church. The ceremony assumed that all eligible inhabitants were physically present, as well as symbolically united, in a 'feast of charity', and, significantly, charitable collections in church tended to peak at Easter communions. Parishioners were theoretically required to take communion three times a year, but in practice it was often taken only once, at Easter. Before taking the sacrament, the Prayer Book stipulated that

---

[4] N. Mears, A. Raffe, S. Taylor, and P. Williamson (eds.), *National Prayers: Special Worship since the Reformation*, vol. 1 (Woodbridge, 2013); J. Peacey, *Print and Public Politics in the English Revolution* (Cambridge, 2013), pp. 77–8.

[5] J. Spurr, *The Post-Reformation 1603–1714* (Harlow, 2006), pp. 240–1.

parishioners should be 'in charity' with their neighbours, a proviso that many took very seriously and there is also plentiful evidence that ministers were prepared to bar from communion those who were in dispute with their neighbours, or any who were 'an open and notorious evil liver, so that the Congregation by him is offended' (as the Prayer Book put it). Although attendance levels at communion might vary, this does not seem to have reflected indifference to the sacrament. It is also clear that to be *excluded* from communion (less common after 1604) could be a deeply distressing experience, with both spiritual and social ramifications.[6] Communal norms could thus be strengthened by acts of temporary exclusion, and there were other rituals of exclusion too, in the public shaming and loss of 'credit' of those convicted of drunkenness or Sabbath-breaking, who might be required to admit their fault publicly in church after morning prayer on Sunday, while those convicted of sexual misdemeanours performed public penance in church with a white sheet.[7]

As we have noted, collective ritual activities were undoubtedly attenuated compared with the pre-Reformation parish: the extraordinary medieval round of feast-days and processions were severely curtailed as part of general restrictions on saints' days and the removal of elements of superstition. Nevertheless, among those rites that did survive, those associated with the life-cycle—such as baptism, churching, marriage, and funerals—were important public, sociable activities as well as marking the entry and departure of parishioners from the Christian community.[8] Even in times of plague, Church and secular authorities struggled to prevent families and neighbours from organizing and attending public funerals, events that often included doles to the parish poor.[9] When parishioners were sick, prayers could be solicited from the community assembled in church. In 1630s London it was reported that petitions for prayers for named individuals were printed as 'bills' and handed to the minister to read out.[10] Other rituals and festivities punctuated the calendar year, such as the Rogationtide perambulation of the parish, which

---

[6] A. Hunt, 'The Lord's Supper in Early Modern England', *Past & Present*, 161 (1998): 39–83 (pp. 41–51); J. F. Merritt, *The Social World of Early Modern Westminster: Abbey, Court and Community 1525–1640* (Manchester, 2005), p. 292; C. Haigh, 'Communion and Community: Exclusion from Communion in Post-Reformation England', *JEH*, 51 (2000): 721–40 (pp. 722, 724, 738–40).

[7] Ingram, *Church Courts*, pp. 53–4; 336–7. For example, London Metropolitan Archives (hereafter LMA), DL/C/617, n.f. (March 1604/5, May 1605); DL/C/306, fos. 55b, 383; Westminster Archives Centre, E19, fo. 46v.

[8] D. Cressy, *Birth, Marriage, and Death: Ritual, Religion, and the Life-Cycle in Tudor and Stuart England* (Oxford, 1997); C. Gittings, *Death, Burial and the Individual in Early Modern England* (1984); R. Houlbrooke, *Death, Religion, and the Family in England, 1480–1750* (Oxford, 1998); P. Marshall, *Beliefs and the Dead in Reformation England* (Oxford, 2002), ch. 4.

[9] Robert Hill, *The Pathway to Prayer and Piety* (1613), pp. 146–7; P. Slack, *The Impact of Plague in Tudor and Stuart England* (1985), pp. 210, 234, 296–8.

[10] Peter Heylyn, 'A Brief Discourse Touching the Form of Prayer Used Before Communion', in *Ecclesia Vindicata* (1657), pp. 340–1; Thomas Edwards, *Gangraena* (1646), pt. 3, sig. [Ii4r].

not only confirmed parish boundaries for legal and financial purposes, but also encompassed processions involving young and old, the distribution of charity, and festive eating and drinking.[11] The festive aspects of Christmas Day itself, of course, were just one of the many reasons that it attracted the ire of puritans in the 1650s.[12] In addition to these traditional holidays, this period also saw the emergence of a 'Protestant calendar', with bells, bonfires, and feasting accompanying days that commemorated significant dates for the Protestant Church and state, such as the monarch's birthday and the commemoration of the foiling of the Gunpowder Plot. Needless to say, these events were also routinely associated with special sermons and prayers.[13]

Other local feasts and customs survived more patchily, and were often discontinued due to fears of 'popery' or disorder.[14] Among the more notable of these were parish feasts to celebrate the anniversary of the dedication of the church, and so-called 'church ales', where ale was brewed and sold (principally to meet the costs of church repair and other parish expenses). It was reported of Somerset in the 1630s that these feasts were not only popular there, but also that they promoted charitable giving to the poor, hospitality from the rich, and 'the increase of love and unity', such that 'many suites in law have bin taken up at these feasts by mediation of friends, which could not have bene soe soone ended in Westminster Hall'. More generally, the repair, rebuilding and decoration of the parish church could often involve many inhabitants working collectively, with the parish here acting as a focus of charity, identity, and cultural endeavour.[15]

The parish also maintained its communal identity by manufacturing and sustaining a sense of continuity, and by fostering collective memory (albeit locked in a complex dialogue with its pre-Reformation past). The focus of memorialization in the medieval Church had been particularly linked to prayer and masses for the dead. In the post-Reformation period these patterns of memorialization changed but were still prominent, evidenced in the commemoration of parish benefactors in funerary monuments, painted boards, and stained glass, in sermons, and sometimes in elaborate ritual acts of commemoration where bequeathed alms were distributed. Such acts of charity and remembrance were still upheld in roughly de-Catholicized rather than

---

[11] R. Hutton, *The Rise and Fall of Merry England: The Ritual Year 1400–1700* (Oxford, 1994), pp. 34–6, 142–3, 175–6; F. Heal, *Hospitality in Early Modern England* (Oxford, 1990), ch. 9; Merritt, *Social World*, pp. 208–12; A. Walsham, *The Reformation of the Landscape: Religion, Identity, and Memory in Early Modern Britain and Ireland* (Oxford, 2011), pp. 252–62, 267.

[12] R. Hutton, *The Stations of the Sun: A History of the Ritual Year in Britain* (Oxford, 1996), chs. 1–6.

[13] D. Cressy, *Bonfires and Bells: National Memory and the Protestant Calendar in Elizabethan and Stuart England* (1989), pp. 50–7; Hutton, *Rise and Fall*, pp. 146–51, 186–7.

[14] For example, P. Collinson, 'The Shearman's Tree and the Preacher', in P. Collinson and J. Craig (eds.), *The Reformation in English Towns 1500–1640* (Basingstoke, 1998), pp. 205–20.

[15] TNA, SP 16/250, fo. 56r-v; J. F. Merritt, 'Puritans, Laudians, and the Phenomenon of Church-Building in Jacobean London', *Historical Journal*, 41 (1998): 935–60 (pp. 940–50).

confessionally specific form, while parish customs were supported by a ubiquitous and still powerful rhetoric of things being done 'time out of mind'.[16] This was underpinned by the parish's continuous legal status and by the fact that parishioners often acted as guardians of things held in common (such as common land or benefactions). Despite the depredations of the Reformation period, the parish still acted as the receptacle for community interests on a local level: thus, after the dissolution of the chantries, endowments that funded 'non-superstitious' purposes such as education or poor relief were protected, while in other cases parishes acted promptly to obtain a communal resource. Thus the parish of St Botolph Aldersgate almost immediately gained possession of the hall of the dissolved Trinity fraternity to serve as a venue for parish meetings.[17]

THE PARISH AND RELIGION

As we can see, the parish could thus in theory perform a whole range of roles in building and sustaining the local community—its identity, customs, values, and memory. But we cannot assume that parochial *religious* activities were therefore an uncomplicated reflection of these cohesive forms of communal endeavour and ritual activity, not least because the post-Reformation parish also had an urgent evangelical task to perform. In the century following the Reformation, the Church of England faced the task of building a Protestant nation, of teaching the true Protestant religion and instilling its values in the beliefs and practices of parishioners. This raised a basic question of what religious functions the parish could and should serve, given that the state's concern was focused on church attendance rather than belief. The challenge for Protestant ministers, in particular, was to decide how far the social and administrative functions of the parish might aid or frustrate the attempt to improve the religious lives of the community. Could parochial structures, rituals, and traditions facilitate Protestant pastoral, evangelical aspirations, or did they merely serve to impede them? Who controlled the parish's religious life in practice, and how might this affect the role that religion played in the local community?

Before discussing how parochial religious experience was shaped by individuals and institutions, we must note some of the ways in which the ideal of

---

[16] I. Archer, 'The Arts and Acts of Memorialization in Early Modern London', in J. F. Merritt (ed.), *Imagining Early Modern London: Perceptions & Portrayals of the City from Stow to Strype, 1598–1720* (Cambridge, 2001), pp. 89–113; Merritt, *Social World*, pp. 273–9; Marshall, *Beliefs and the Dead*, p. 304.

[17] *London and Middlesex Chantry Certificate, 1548*, ed. C. J. Kitching (London Record Society, 16, 1980), pp. x, xxxii; *Parish Fraternity Register: Fraternity of Holy Trinity and SS Fabian and Sebastian*, ed. P. Basing (London Record Society, 18, 1982), p. xxvi.

the cohesive parish community gathered together in church was often impossible to realize. One hindrance relates to the size of parishes, since the Reformation did nothing to reshape the geographical pattern of medieval parishes, which sometimes extended over large areas. The role of the parish as the cornerstone of local society, inculcating Protestant ideas and maintaining some form of moral and religious discipline, was also affected by the government's subsequent failure to adjust the number and size of parishes to reflect changes in population. The sixteenth and seventeenth centuries witnessed tremendous demographic expansion as well as changes to the distribution of population, in particular the striking growth of the capital and other urban centres. In towns this resulted in parishes where it was impossible to assemble the whole body of parishioners in church at any one time. At the same time, in rural areas (especially in the north) parishes were often too large for their scattered populations, making regulation of conformity more difficult and potentially impeding the regular preaching and catechizing that facilitated the word-centred piety of Protestantism.[18] However, from the 1590s onwards, some parts of northern England gained chapels of ease, while programmes of church refurbishment in urban areas were accompanied by campaigns to enlarge churches, adding galleries and refiguring interiors in order to accommodate larger numbers. Significant amounts of money were spent on these building projects and some churches in the capital were substantially rebuilt. Parishes in the capital also adopted practices such as 'Easter' communions that were staggered over many weeks to ensure fuller participation by inhabitants.[19] There were episodic attempts to create new parishes in the pre-civil war period, and some subdivisions and amalgamations of parishes in the Interregnum, but the uncertainties of the 1650s meant that these anomalies were still unaddressed at the Restoration. In any case, enormous tenacity was needed to set up new parishes, since this required an Act of Parliament as well as large sums of money to build a new church and to provide an income for a minister. The case of St Paul Covent Garden (a parish created *ex nihilo* in the 1630s) perhaps illustrates why the solution of creating new parishes was so rarely attempted, with countless complications and acrimonious disputes—over local rates, ecclesiastical patronage, architectural style, allocation of pews, and control of the vestry—that stretched well into the Restoration period.[20]

---

[18] For example, M. Clark, 'Northern Light? Parochial Life in a "Dark Corner" of Tudor England', in K. L. French, G. Gibbs, and B. Kümin (eds.), *The Parish in English Life 1400–1600* (Manchester, 1997), pp. 66–7.

[19] Heal, *Reformation*, p. 444, Merritt 'Church-Building'; J. P. Boulton, 'The Limits of Formal Religion: The Administration of Holy Communion in Late Elizabethan and Early Stuart London', *London Journal*, 10 (1984): 135–54.

[20] J. F. Merritt, '"Voluntary Bounty and Devotion to the Service of God"? Lay Patronage, Protest and the Creation of the Parish of St Paul Covent Garden, 1629–41', *English Historical*

The ideal model of the whole community assembled in the parish church was a powerful one, of course, and drew upon familiar discourses of the body politic, but it could also be frustrated in other ways. There was always a certain number of parishioners who did not attend their parish church at any given time. It is more helpful, however, to think of these as more fluid, fluctuating groups rather than as simple 'blocs' of non-attenders. Such behaviour might vary across the individual's position in the life-cycle. Evidence from church court records and indeed much contemporary comment particularly draws attention to the patchier attendance of the young, too easily tempted by the rival attractions of the alehouse or fiddlers, pipers, and dancing. Also absent from the church were the small numbers who had been excommunicated, although few people seem to have remained contumacious for long, beyond highly mobile groups, such as servants.[21] But the group whose relationship with the parish was most truly problematic were Roman Catholics. Scholarship specifically on the English parish has often tended to overlook this group, leaving them to more specialist recusant history. Yet throughout our period, many parishes, especially in parts of the north and Midlands, counted Catholics among their inhabitants. Their presence was potentially ambiguous. Laws against popish recusancy encouraged many Catholics to slip in and out of conformity, with perhaps the head of the household attending the parish church as necessary to avoid prosecution.[22] This meant that Protestant parishioners, including the godly, could be forced to attend the same services and sermons as their so-called 'church papist' neighbours (Catholics who attended Protestant services only to avoid statutory fines), while known Catholics were sometimes buried in the local churchyard or commemorated by monuments in the parish church. Few Catholics, though, were quite as audacious as Lady Wotton, who was fined £500 by High Commission in 1633 for placing a 'bold epitaph' on her husband's monument at Boughton Malherbe, stating that he had died a true Catholic of the Roman Church.[23]

Review, 125 (2010): 35–59; C. Cross, *Church and People: England 1450–1660* (2nd edn., Oxford, 1999), pp. 204–5.

[21] For example, W. Hale (ed.), *A Series of Precedents and Proceedings in Criminal Causes* (1847), pp. 218, 219, 235, 242; P. Collinson, *The Religion of Protestants: The Church in English Society, 1559–1625* (Oxford, 1982), pp. 206–7, 224–6; Ingram, *Church Courts*, p. 365; C. Haigh, *The Plain Man's Pathways to Heaven: Kinds of Christianity in Post-Reformation England, 1570–1640* (Oxford, 2007), pp. 68–9, 72.

[22] A. Walsham, *Church Papists: Catholicism, Conformity and Confessional Polemic in Early Modern England* (Woodbridge, 1993), p. 95; M. Questier, 'Conformity, Catholicism and the Law', in P. Lake and M. Questier (eds.), *Conformity and Orthodoxy in the English Church, c.1560–1660* (Woodbridge, 2000), pp. 237–61.

[23] P. Marshall, 'Confessionalization and Community in the Burial of English Catholics, c.1570-1700', in N. Lewicky and A. Morton (eds.), *Getting Along? Religious Identities and Confessional Relations in Early Modern England* (Farnham, 2012), p. 62; L. E. C. Evans, 'The Wotton Monuments', *Archaeologia Cantiana*, 87 (1972): 15–30 (p. 25).

Though periodically the prosecution of recusants loosened or tightened (often in response to the international situation), in some regions enforcement was known to be more slack. Some light is shed on forms of coexistence, however, by the Jesuit Henry Garnet's advice to fellow Catholics that it was permissible for them to accompany the bodies of their Protestant neighbours to burial, as long as they held back from the service. However, in other areas of the north (and especially in Lancashire) the high numbers of relatively unmolested Catholics more consistently stirred up puritan opposition and resulted in more polarized communities.[24]

Even when most inhabitants did indeed gather in the parish church this did not, of course, guarantee harmony and sometimes it generated precisely the opposite. The very fact that the church was the one place where the entire community gathered inevitably meant that it was also a place for social display and competition, which was reflected in the location of one's seat and place of burial. Seating within the church was also seen as a symbolic representation of a theoretically fixed local hierarchy, delineated by social and economic status as well as by age and gender. But the finer gradations of such hierarchies were often changing or open to dispute, and acrimonious conflicts could lead to confrontations in church (where churchwardens or vestries allocated pews according to custom) and thence into the church courts.[25] At other times, clergymen might fret that the obligations of social deference were interfering with parishioners' religious duties: the Laudian John Swan urged parishioners not to interrupt their prayers by standing up and acknowledging when their social superiors entered the church, as 'there bee other times and other places to shew your dutie and respect to Man'.[26]

Further practical problems could sometimes interfere with the religious use of the parish church. The religious message implicitly conveyed by the church interior had been one of the key targets of Protestant reform, resulting in whitewashed churches, purged of 'superstitious' church goods. However, the architecture of medieval churches, with their side-chapels and processional routes, still reflected the ceremonial and sacramental character of medieval Catholicism. English churches gradually—and more or less successfully—transformed their interiors from ones designed primarily for ceremonial purposes into spaces for preaching the word of God and the administration of communion in both kinds to parishioners. Nevertheless this was sometimes a protracted process. The location of the communion table, pulpit, and reading

---

[24] A. Walsham, *Charitable Hatred: Tolerance and Intolerance in England, 1500–1700* (Manchester, 2006), chs. 3–6; Marshall, 'Confessionalization and Community', p. 69.

[25] Merritt, *Social World*, pp. 214–23; C. W. Marsh, 'Sacred Space in England, 1560–1640: The View from the Pew', *JEH*, 53 (2002): 286–311; N. Alldridge, 'Loyalty and Identity in Chester Parishes, 1540–1640', in S. Wright (ed.), *Parish, Church and People: Local Studies in Lay Religion, 1350–1750* (1988), pp. 94–7.

[26] John Swan, *Profano-mastix* (1639), pp. 44–5.

desk (regardless of later disagreements among Protestants regarding the religious significance of their disposition) and the ways in which the reception of communion was arranged, often required adaptation to the surviving architecture of the church, which could make the experience of worship vary considerably in different communities. Parishioners of St Martin in the Fields were ultimately forced to move pillars in the church in 1596 'that the People may better here [sic] the Preacher'.[27]

Faced with both practical problems that could hinder the transition to Protestant worship, and with the religiously ambiguous inheritance of parochial rituals, how was the religious experience of the parish shaped in the post-Reformation period? As we shall see, the parishioners themselves could make a decisive contribution, but a central role was obviously performed by the individual clergyman.

On a basic level, the presence or absence of a resident clergyman was a key variable in English parishes. The poverty of many livings encouraged pluralism, non-residence, and the employment of poorly qualified curates, which inevitably limited contact between laity and their vicar, and inhibited access to the regular services and preaching needed to promote Protestantism. Complaints over non-residency and 'dumb dog' ministers prompted the many puritan surveys of the clergy in the Elizabethan period, although standards seem to have improved significantly by the reign of James.[28] Nevertheless, delicate and socially awkward matters of finance and dependency could loom large over the minister's relationship with his parish and also affected his potential impact in religious affairs. For example, how tithes were paid, and how insistent the clergyman was in collecting them, even in times of dearth, often exacerbated tensions between the minister and his flock regardless of other religious disagreements.[29] The Laudian Brian Walton's ceremonialism might in itself have alienated his congregation at St Martin Orgar in the 1630s, but his behaviour on arrival in the parish would not have helped to win them over. This included seizing the profits from a recent successful but longstanding parish lawsuit and then claiming sole credit for it, which he commemorated with an inscription in the church.[30] Equally, disagreements over

---

[27] W. Harrison, *The Description of England*, ed. G. Edelen (Washington, DC, 1994), pp. 33–6; Heal, *Reformation*, pp. 442–3; R. Whiting, *The Reformation of the English Parish Church* (Cambridge, 2010); *St Martin in the Fields: The Accounts of the Churchwardens 1525–1603*, ed. J. Kitto (1901), p. 484.

[28] Heal, *Reformation*, pp. 405–8; Ingram, *Church Courts*, pp. 86–7.

[29] C. Hill, *Economic Problems of the Church from Archbishop Whitgift to the Long Parliament* (Oxford, 1956), pp. 157–8.

[30] LMA, P69/MTN2/B/001/MS0959/001, fos. 119r, 133r, 144v, 149v, 164v, 165r, 167r, 177v, 181r, 188v; TNA, SP16/302/49; *The Articles and Charge proved in Parliament against Doctor Walton, Minister of St. Martins Orgars in Cannon Street* (1641).

church fees for baptisms, marriages, and burials were significant flashpoints. This income could be vital to the clergy, but could encourage unscrupulous conduct. The royal Commission on Fees in the 1620s and 1630s uncovered a number of examples of ministers destroying old tables of fees in order to raise charges. The curate of St Giles in the Fields went even further: he was accused of refusing to bury one parishioner who had opposed him in parochial affairs, and declining to conduct a pauper burial until he had been paid in advance.[31]

When a minister was resident, his own religious attitudes—especially if he was a puritan—could obviously have a profound impact on the character of public worship in the parish (a point to which we shall return). Although it is important not to pit an exclusively 'sermon-centred' piety against a 'sacrament-centred' piety in this period, the relative emphasis that ministers placed upon the word and sacraments undoubtedly varied, and contemporaries were certainly capable of placing them in hostile juxtaposition.[32] A minister of puritan instincts might also bring a distinctive approach to his pastoral duties. The puritan George Gifford's fictional dialogue between 'Atheos' and 'Zelotes' memorably invoked the distinction between a minister who mixes easily with his parishioners, above all promoting good fellowship and reconciling neighbours over a game of cards or a drink, as opposed to the godly minister who specifically avoids such activities and concentrates instead on spending time in his study preparing his sermon. At the heart of the ministry extolled by the puritan minister Zelotes was the division between the godly and ungodly, based on particular readings of the doctrine of grace and predestination. Zelotes accepts the complaint that the true minister brings division into the local community ('whereas before they loved together, now there is dissention sowne among them') by denying the ultimate primacy of peaceful coexistence and good fellowship: 'Woulde yee have God and the Divell agree together? woulde ye have the godlie and the wicked for to bee at one?'[33] The model of godly minister presented by Gifford was certainly familiar to contemporaries. We can find ministers such as Stephen Dennison in London and Richard Bernard in Batcombe, Somerset, introducing publicly divisive elements into parishes by denouncing specific local sinners from the pulpit, a practice known as 'particularizing'.[34] The popular Nonconformist minister Samuel Hieron was among those who sowed division in his Devon

---

[31] TNA, E215/58F, pp. 114–15, 122; E215/1232/1 and 1232/2; Hill, *Economic Problems*, pp. 182–6.

[32] A. Hunt, *The Art of Hearing: English Preachers and their Audiences, 1590–1640* (Cambridge, 2010), pp. 52–4; J. Maltby, *Prayer Book and People in Elizabethan and Early Stuart England* (Cambridge, 1998), pp. 67–8.

[33] George Gifford, *A Briefe Discourse of Certaine Points of the Religion which is Among the Common Sort of Christians, Which may bee Termed the Countrie Divinitie* (1582), sigs. A1–A3, 46v.

[34] P. Lake, *The Boxmaker's Revenge: 'Orthodoxy', 'Heterodoxy' and the Politics of the Parish in Early Stuart London* (Manchester, 2001), pp. 65, 311–14; Haigh, *Plain Man's Pathways*, pp. 21–4.

parish still further by using the occasion of funeral sermons to condemn the sins of the deceased, although the practice was defended in print by puritan authors as a means of instruction to the living.[35]

This being said, while the picture emerging from printed literature of the period (including Gifford's dialogue) tends to suggest a sharp contrast between puritan ministers and those wedded to a more traditional role promoting social cohesion, the reality appears to have been more complex.[36] Firstly, the extent to which godly men and women truly held themselves aloof from their neighbours in practice has rightly been queried. When around 1630 the redoubtable John White of Dorchester devised a covenant for his congregation as a condition of their receiving communion, he did not include a provision to avoid the company of the ungodly.[37] In addition, puritan ministers were not necessarily averse to fulfilling the traditional social role of promoting reconciliation among their parishioners, as the notable efforts of the famously godly but pastorally sensitive puritan minister Richard Greenham testify.[38] The informal role of ministers across the religious spectrum in reconciling members of their flocks and arbitrating in lawsuits is also frequently alluded to in church court records. Reconciliation could, of course, form part of a larger puritan agenda in preparing the godly to receive communion: one notable puritan pastor provided his congregation with a list of no fewer than eight questions through which individuals could test themselves to ensure that 'you are so reconciled, that you love your brother'.[39] But here the different social and religious imperatives for reconciliation were likely to have been mutually supportive.

Some historians have argued that puritan-inflected Protestantism purveyed an unpalatable and divisive message that was also virtually impossible for ministers to convey to their flocks.[40] But the career of Robert Hill, which largely unfolded in Jacobean London, suggests otherwise. There can be no question that Hill's message from the pulpit was a rigorously Calvinist one. In the 1590s, this disciple of William Perkins specifically attacked John Overall (later dean of St Paul's) for having suggested that predestinarian doctrine should be modified to make it more palatable for a lay congregation. Yet Hill was also famous for his pedagogical gifts: he excelled in the popularization of

---

[35] Samuel Hieron, *The Worldling's Downfall* (1618), 'To the Christian Reader' (preface); Emmanuel Utie, *Matthew the Publican. A Funeral Sermon, preached in St Stephen Walbrook the 11 of March 1615* (1616), 'To the Christian Reader' (preface).

[36] For example, Ingram, *Church Courts*, pp. 118–23.

[37] Collinson, *Religion of Protestants*, pp. 272–3.

[38] Samuel Clarke, *The Lives of Two and Twenty English Divines* (1660), p. 15; K. L. Parker and E. Carlson, *'Practical Divinity': The Works and Life of Revd Richard Greenham* (Aldershot, 1998), pp. 81–3.

[39] Ingram, *Church Courts*, p. 111; Hill, *Pathway*, ii, p. 27.

[40] C. Haigh, 'The Taming of Reformation: Preachers, Pastors and Parishioners in Elizabethan and Early Stuart England', *History*, 85 (2000): 572–88.

puritan doctrines via homely images and simple catechetical formats. Hill's message was clear but also subtly nuanced. If his predestinarian doctrine was unequivocally polarized, he nevertheless presented election as a universal aspiration, and talk of 'brethren' and 'community' was woven into his discourse in ways that could speak to a godly elite but also to the broader parish population. Hill essentially offered a vision of the community that recognized the godly and their special duties without severing them from their neighbours.[41] The stark binary division between the godly and the ungodly invoked by Gifford and others may have been rhetorically appealing, but it is not only Hill's example that suggests that puritan ministers could in practice adopt a more nuanced and complex approach to their role as pastor. Describing his parochial congregation in the 1650s, Richard Baxter (albeit in the context of restricted communions) divided his flock into no fewer than twelve different groups, and was optimistic that even some of those who 'seem to be ignorant of the very Essentials of Christianity' were yet 'tractable and of willing minds'.[42]

An effective ministry was also crucially dependent on the clergyman securing the effective support of at least a portion of his flock, although this was complicated by the fact that the views of parishioners were generally not taken into consideration in clerical appointments. After the Reformation, many advowsons (the right of presentation to a living) previously exercised by religious houses passed to the crown. In Essex, for example, nearly half the advowsons in the county passed to the crown at the dissolution, although about half of these were granted away within a few years. This large-scale acquisition of advowsons by laymen was an important feature of the Reformation, with the patronage rights acquired by many gentry along with the purchase of manors.[43] Advowsons thus provided opportunities to advance clergy of a particular religious complexion, a strategy famously pursed by the puritan Feoffees for Impropriations under Charles I, and reflected in the great puritan patronage networks that depended on noble and gentry families in East Anglia and the Midlands, where individual noblemen might control a formidable number of advowsons. In Elizabethan West Suffolk, for example, the radical puritan Sir Robert Jermyn controlled ten livings and Sir John Higham, another four, while puritan gentry and noblemen including Lord North and Sir Nicholas Bacon presented to at least thirty more Suffolk parishes.[44] But lay patronage was not

---

[41] J. F. Merritt, 'The Pastoral Tightrope: A Puritan Pedagogue in Jacobean London', in T. Cogswell, R. Cust, and P. Lake (eds.), *Politics, Religion and Popularity in Early Stuart Britain* (Cambridge, 2002), pp. 143–61.

[42] Richard Baxter, *Confirmation and Restoration, The Necessary Means of Reformation and Reconciliation* (1658), pp. 157–65.

[43] J. E. Oxley, *The Reformation in Essex to the Death of Mary* (Manchester, 1965), pp. 263–4; Hill, *Economic Problems*, pp. 56–7.

[44] P. Collinson, *The Elizabethan Puritan Movement* (1967), pp. 337–8.

always used for godly ends. In some cases, lay patrons neglected the needs of parishioners and simply left livings unfilled, as was the case in several parishes in Colchester at the end of Elizabeth's reign, or imposed crippling bonds on prospective ministers to maximize their financial advantage.[45] Other factors that might dictate the choice of ministers included family ties, an institutional link, or mere simony, while many livings remained in the hands of the crown and bishops. Others, though, were controlled by organizations such as colleges and corporations, and the latter often tended to be puritan or anti-Laudian in their sympathies, although in these cases advowsons were less common than the sponsoring of a lectureship.[46] In Ipswich, though, there was a long pre-Reformation tradition of parochial nomination of clergy, and after the Reformation five livings came directly into the hands of parishioners, who proceeded to both nominate and to oust their clergyman. In the capital, at least thirteen parishes controlled their own advowson.[47]

Parishes that held their own right of presentation echoed the general Presbyterian principle that the minister should be chosen by his congregation (albeit that in Reformed Churches abroad this was usually on the recommendation of the *classis*). This was an ideal that was sometimes gestured towards in puritan circles even in cases where the parishioners did not themselves own the advowson. Thus when the godly gentleman Sir Robert Harley—who possessed the Herefordshire advowson of Brampton Bryan—appointed a new minister in 1634, it was emphasized that this was with the parishioners' consent (and specifically that the local bishop's permission was irrelevant).[48] The possibility of parishioners (or indeed lay patrons) acquiring the right to appoint their own minister also troubled William Laud, and when he was presented with schemes for new chapels and churches in the 1620s and 1630s he monitored them closely and sometimes intervened to prevent what he called a 'popular nomination' (as in the case of Hammersmith in 1629).[49]

But parishioners did not need to control the patronage of the living in order to exert a significant influence on local religious affairs. The exercise of lay power in parishes by vestries—bodies typically consisting of twelve or twenty-four of the principal inhabitants of the parish—became more widespread over

---

[45] R. D. Smith, *The Middling Sort and the Politics of Social Reformation: Colchester 1570–1640* (New York, 2004), p. 133; Hill, *Economic Problems*, pp. 63–7.

[46] P. Seaver, *The Puritan Lectureships: The Politics of Religious Dissent 1560–1662* (Stanford, CA, 1970), p. 89.

[47] F. Grace, '"Schismaticall and Factious Humours": Opposition in Ipswich to Laudian Church Government in the 1630s', in D. Chadd (ed.), *Religious Dissent in East Anglia* (Norwich, 1996), pp. 104–5; Seaver, *Puritan Lectureships*, p. 138.

[48] Collinson, *Elizabethan Puritan Movement*, pp. 338–40; J. T. Cliffe, *The Puritan Gentry: The Great Puritan Families of Early Stuart England* (1984), p. 188.

[49] Merritt, 'Voluntary Bounty', pp. 41–2; J. F. Merritt, 'Contested Legitimacy and the Ambiguous Rise of Vestries in Early Modern London', *Historical Journal*, 54 (2011): 25–45 (pp. 39–43); Hill, *Economic Problems*, pp. 59, 299.

this period, although they were principally concentrated in towns. Vestries are generally seen as a post-Reformation phenomenon, although there is little doubt that medieval parishes depended on their 'chief parishioners' to carry out many duties. The term 'vestry' was used as early as 1507 in the London parish of St Christopher le Stocks, and the use of the term by Bishop Grindal in 1567 in a circular letter to the London clergy demonstrates that its meaning was already assumed to be familiar. Vestries gained a higher profile as they undertook the wider range of tasks increasingly allocated to parishes by parliamentary statute in the sixteenth century. As such tasks grew in volume and complexity, so quotidian parish government increasingly became the preserve of a more narrow body of administrators, and a distinction becomes apparent between a small body of inhabitants meeting more regularly for day-to-day administration, and larger meetings of the whole parish to elect parish officers every Easter.[50] It is too simplistic to see this merely as a matter of oligarchical usurpation: the image of the vestry as the paternalistic embodiment of the parish and custodian of its legal and financial interests was crucial both to the vestry's self-identity and to local acceptance of its authority as a bulwark of parochial order and unity. The formal creation of a vestry in All Hallows Staining in 1574 specifically noted how the lack of good orders and government were the cause of 'varience strife and enemitie...Betweene parishioners neighbours and Frendes'.[51] While they constituted a decision-making body whose members formed a self-selecting elite, vestries were nevertheless meant to reflect local opinion more broadly. Yet the vestry's executive oversight of the parish meant that it regularly took crucial decisions on issues surrounding parish worship, such as changes to the church fabric, furniture, and decoration, as well as acting with churchwardens in their response to directives and enquiries from episcopal authorities.

Crucial to the religious experience of the parish was therefore the nature of the relationship between the vestry and the local clergyman (who did not always attend vestry meetings), and this could be problematic. The extent of vestry powers, and the ecclesiastical authorities' concern to protect the rights and authority of the minister, is suggested in the set of limitations contained in new vestry faculties granted by the bishop of London from 1612 onwards. Among other things, these forbade vestries from summoning before them any clergyman, or from 'intermeddling' with the churchwardens' bill of presentment.[52] Nevertheless, it is not difficult to find vestries brokering agreements with their parish minister that demonstrate where effective power lay, and the

---

[50] Lambeth Palace Library, CM VII/69; S. and B. Webb, *English Local Government (The Parish and the County)* (1906, rpr. 1924), pp. 38–9n, 178, 183; S. Hindle, 'The Political Culture of the Middling Sort in English Rural Communities, c.1550–1700', in T. Harris (ed.), *The Politics of the Excluded c.1500–1850* (Basingstoke, 2001), p. 127.

[51] LMA, P69/ALH6/B/001/MS04957/001 (unfoliated).

[52] Merritt, 'Contested Legitimacy', p. 31.

ease with which they could wrest control of parochial religion. Thus in 1624, the vestry of St Olave Jewry paid off the debts of their minister, Thomas Tuke, on condition that 'the divinity lecture shall henceforth be freely read, without his interruption, and also that the choice of the person to read the same lecture shall also forever hereafter rest wholly in the election of the parishioners without molestation or intermeddling herewith'.[53]

Parish lectureships represented a very effective way in which parishioners could obtain preaching attuned to their religious tastes, especially if these differed from those of their parish minister. Although lectureships had originated as a means of supplementing preaching more generally, they were also frequently seen as a vehicle for promoting puritan preaching and the furtherance of godly programmes of social regulation.[54] Ideally, of course, minister and lecturer would support each other, and there are certainly cases where this happened perfectly amicably. But the example of Thomas Tuke shows that the lectureship could also be a means of circumventing a minister unsympathetic to the vestry's preferences. The manner in which vestries superintended the creation of parish lectureships was almost calculated to arouse the anxieties of the ecclesiastical authorities. Vestries auditioned candidates to compare their preaching and then voted for their preferred candidate. The fact that lecturers were chosen by election, paid an annual salary decided by the parishioners, and could be dismissed at will inevitably set alarm bells ringing.[55]

Beyond any role that the lecturer might perform, it was still the parish minister's personal style of churchmanship that could have a decisive impact on the performance of Prayer Book worship that parishioners experienced. A zealous puritan preacher might disregard aspects of the official service, as well as seldom wearing the surplice or omitting the sign of the cross in baptism, or turning a blind eye to those who failed to kneel at communion. Equally, he could merely provide a context in which Prayer Book ceremonies were implicitly downgraded by the importance attached to the sermon and to extemporary prayers. By contrast, a more ceremonialist minister might seek to emphasize the sacraments and the more ritualistic aspects of the liturgy, resembling, as Edward Boughen wrote in 1638, an 'Angel of light... in his white vestment, behaving himselfe with... gravity, and reverence, and decency', presiding over the whole congregation, 'decently kneeling, rising, standing, bowing, praising, praying altogether... like men of one mind and religion in the house of God'.[56] Just as decisive, though, could be the precise

---

[53] LMA, P69/OLA2/B/001/MS04415/001, fo. 16r.
[54] Seaver, *Puritan Lectureships*, chs. 3–4.
[55] Merritt, 'Contested Legitimacy', pp. 28, 43; Seaver, *Puritan Lectureships*, pp. 165–70 and ch. 8.
[56] Edward Boughen, *A Sermon concerning Decencie and Order in the Church* (1638), pp. 10–11.

balance between the influence and views of the minister, those of the lecturer (if there was one), and the role played by the vestry and other parishioners. We therefore need to be particularly careful to avoid the assumption that the religious experience of parishioners was defined simply by the text of the Prayer Book service. Not only was the message of the service crucially dependent upon the context and style in which it was read, but the actual content of the Prayer Book service could also vary significantly from parish to parish. We know, for example, that services were not standardized, with the minister often juggling parts of the service (such as the position of the sermon, and the inclusion of psalms), while some parishioners came late or attended only part of the service.[57] There was, then, no generic 'parish Anglican' experience.

It is also problematic to assume that it was the Prayer Book alone that had the greatest influence on the religious sensibility of parishioners. Not only does this reduce our sense of the vital role played by the sermon, but it disregards the importance of other religious exercises conducted in the church and also elsewhere. Not the least of these was metrical psalm singing, in which all the congregation participated, and which was clearly enormously popular in this period.[58] Outside the services of public worship, public catechizing was one of the minister's critical pastoral duties, which the 1604 canons required to take place every Sunday before evening prayer. Although puritans were sometimes attacked for neglecting catechizing in favour of preaching sermons (a charge that is implicit in the 1629 royal instructions that directed the conversion of afternoon sermons into catechizing), in fact puritan writers were emphatic that preaching without catechizing was fruitless. Indeed, they were the most energetic composers of catechisms, which sold in huge numbers (three-quarters of a million of the unofficial catechisms were probably in circulation by the early 1600s). Official catechizing also became more systematic, and was particularly emphasized by Archbishop Bancroft in his metropolitical visitation of ten dioceses in 1605. Problems tended to arise more from parishioners not presenting themselves to be catechized, rather than ministers refusing to catechize them.[59] Nevertheless, the manner in which the minister chose to conduct his catechizing could provide another important variable in the parochial religious experience.

---

[57] A. Ryrie, *Being Protestant in Reformation Britain* (Oxford, 2013), pp. 317–19; P. Collinson, 'Shepherds, Sheepdogs and Hirelings: The Pastoral Ministry in Post-Reformation England', in his *From Cranmer to Sancroft* (2006), pp. 50–1, 60, 64–6; *Holinshed's Chronicles* (6 vols., 1807), I, p. 232; Collinson, *Religion of Protestants*, pp. 208–9.

[58] A. Ryrie, 'The Psalms and Confrontation in English and Scottish Protestantism', *Archiv für Reformationsgeschichte*, 101 (2010): 114–37.

[59] G. Bray (ed.), *The Anglican Canons 1529–1947* (Woodbridge, 1998), p. 349; K. Fincham (ed.), *Visitation Articles and Injunctions of the Early Stuart Church*, 2 vols. (Woodbridge, 1994, 1998), I, p. xxiii; II, p. 38 (cf. pp. 85, 103, 106, 108, 124, 135, 198, 210, 231); I. Green '"For Children in Yeeres and Children in Understanding": The Emergence of the English Catechism under Elizabeth and the Early Stuarts', *JEH*, 37 (1986): 397–425 (p. 425); Ingram, *Church Courts*, pp. 89–90; Haigh, *Plain Man's Pathways*, pp. 26–30, 60–3.

The high sales of printed catechisms also attest to the popularity of religious instruction in private households, and the importance of household worship in complementing (or even undercutting) parochial worship needs to be remembered. Not only were private prayer and household worship important strands in people's religious lives,[60] but parishioners could also organize themselves to participate in other forms of collective religious activity. This had also been true in the medieval Church, where some parishioners had additionally joined fraternities, not all of which were parish-based. Although after the Reformation informal forms of voluntary religious association are most often associated with puritans, they could also be found even among more conservative parishioners, such as the group of 'understanding Soules'— a Jacobean devotional group that met in Southwark under the auspices of William Austin, a layman whose tastes accorded with those of the Laudians.[61] More common, though, were the supplementary forms of religious exercises in which puritans (lay and clerical alike) shared. While puritans undoubtedly sought to control the institutional framework for local religious practice provided by the parish (as we have seen), at the same time they also devoted time and energy to the fostering of the 'community of the godly'.[62] Distinctive forms of puritan lay piety emerged that helped to foster this special sense of community and to support those whose mode of living and forms of recreation differed from most in their locality. Examples include the style of household worship famously documented in the daily round of activities recorded by Lady Margaret Hoby in Yorkshire. More generally, puritan sociability included meetings for Bible-reading, sermon repetition (something of a misnomer, since it required reflection and discussion and was designed to evoke a spiritual response), the sharing of stories of individual conversion, and fasting. Ministers were in theory not allowed to appoint or keep fasts either publicly or in private houses without licence from the bishop, but fasting nevertheless continued to perform an important role in private and public puritan piety.[63]

These activities were normally supplementary to parochial religion rather than in direct competition with it (although for some of its participants these may have been more central to their religious experience than was collective parish worship). Sometimes a combination of religious fervour and sense of estrangement from their neighbours might lead 'godly' parishioners to enter

---

[60] Ryrie, *Being Protestant*, chs. 6–8, 14.

[61] G. Parry, *The Arts of the Anglican Counter-Reformation: Glory, Laud and Honour* (Woodbridge, 2006), pp. 121–3.

[62] P. Collinson, 'Elizabethan and Jacobean Puritanism', in C. Durston and J. Eales (eds.), *The Culture of English Puritanism, 1560–1700* (Basingstoke, 1996), pp. 51–4; *Diary of Lady Margaret Hoby*, ed. D. M. Meads (1930), pp. 73–5; Hunt, *Art of Hearing*, pp. 72–7; Ryrie, *Being Protestant*, pp. 359–60; Heal, *Reformation*, pp. 471–2.

[63] Bray, *Canons*, p. 363; Collinson, *Religion of Protestants*, pp. 261–3; Ryrie, *Being Protestant*, pp. 195–9, 342–4.

into a formal covenant between themselves. Nevertheless, such covenants did not necessarily undermine the parish. Clergy involved in these covenanted groups specifically attacked separation from the Church of England and 'withdrawing from the publick places of Assembly, or from any part of Gods Worship there used'.[64] At Worksop, about one hundred 'voluntary professors' entered into a covenant 'to watch over one another, to admonish one another... and thereupon to receive the Lord's Supper' under the auspices of their minister, Richard Bernard, but it was said he did so 'in policy' to dissuade them from joining the schismatic Baptist John Smyth.[65]

It should be clear from the foregoing, then, that it is difficult to talk of 'parish Anglicans' or 'Prayer Book Protestants': there were too many variables in the religious experience of parish congregations and Prayer Book usage for these to make sense as categories of behaviour or belief. More generally we find a fair degree of eclecticism in the parochial religious experience and its forms of public and private expression. In addition, it is very rare to find a religiously uniform parish. The parish of St Margaret Westminster—one of the most conservative parishes in the country in its religious style—had puritan parishioners, but it is notable that they were not involved in parish activities and directed their religious patronage outside the parish.[66] The Essex village of Terling has provided a famous example of a place where social, economic, and religious forces of differentiation worked together in the emergence of a puritan oligarchy exerting strict moral control over the local community. But later scholarship has emphasized Terling's unusual and unrepresentative character, and has stressed that the religious configuration of parishes was often more unstable, while social differentiation did not necessarily have a straightforward and predictable impact on the religious life of a parish.[67] In addition, the enormous geographical diversity of parishes defies any simple categorization of the parochial cultural experience, encompassing as it did differences not only between urban and rural parishes, but also between areas such as fens and uplands, and lowland nucleated settlements. More fundamentally, social factors could affect religious practice in unpredictable ways. The motivations behind rebuilding or decorating churches, for example, potentially reflected a complex range of incentives on the part of many different actors within a parish, and could include questions of taste and fashion, local identity, and a desire to ensure a venue in which local elites could assert their status.[68]

---

[64] Samuel Clarke, *The Lives of Thirty-Two English Divines* (1677), p. 57; Collinson, *Religion of Protestants*, p. 271.

[65] Collinson, *Religion of Protestants*, pp. 270–1.   [66] Merritt, *Social World*, p. 323.

[67] K. Wrightson and D. Levine, *Poverty and Piety in an English Village: Terling, 1525–1700* (New York, 1979), esp. ch. 6; Ingram, *Church Courts*, pp. 95, 112–13, 116, 166–7.

[68] Spurr, *The Post-Reformation*, pp. 250–1; Merritt, 'Church-Building', pp. 944–6, 950–5.

Models of post-Reformation parish religion must also accommodate the fact that in this period there was significant change over time. Parish communities themselves experienced substantial social and economic change over the sixteenth and early seventeenth centuries. The congregations over which ministers presided also began to alter, with increasing literacy levels and greater exposure to print culture, which held important implications for pastoral endeavours. As we have noted, the potential of the parish to fulfil evangelical and pastoral needs seems to have improved significantly by the Jacobean period as the qualifications and availability of graduate clergy increased, and there was a notable decline in non-residence and pluralism.[69] At the same time, however, certain forms of parochial ritual activity were undergoing a significant revival. The first decades of the seventeenth century, for example, are notable for the sustained revival of Rogationtide processions, and also of the practice of 'festival communions' at Christmas, Whitsun, All Souls, Michaelmas, and Midsummer Day.[70] How far these concurrent trends aided or undermined each other was, of course, a matter of context. Each parish would experience its own unique (and often precarious) solution to the problem of balancing the needs of the godly and ungodly, and reconciling the evangelical imperative with cohesive communal rituals. But these solutions would come under significant extra pressure from the reign of Charles I onwards.

LATER DEVELOPMENTS

The interplay of these various elements in parish religion was further complicated by developments in national religious policy from 1625 onwards. The first of these was the impact of the policies of Archbishop Laud and his supporters. Laudianism had its most direct impact in the interiors of parish churches, where the communion table was required to be removed to the east end of the church and railed in, alongside an intensified programme of the beautification of church interiors, summarized in the term 'the beauty of holiness'.[71] As we have already noted, for some communities, decorating and preserving the local church may have appealed to a sense of 'seemliness'

---

[69] Ingram, *Church Courts*, pp. 86–9; Collinson, *Religion of Protestants*, ch. 3.
[70] Hutton, *Rise and Fall*, pp. 175–7.
[71] P. Lake, 'The Laudian Style: Order, Uniformity and the Pursuit of the Beauty of Holiness in the 1630s', in K. Fincham (ed.), *The Early Stuart Church, 1603–1642* (Basingstoke, 1993), pp. 161–85; A. Foster, 'Church Policies of the 1630s', in R. Cust and A. Hughes (eds.), *Conflict in Early Stuart England: Studies in Religion and Politics, 1603–1642* (Harlow, 1989), pp. 203–6; K. Fincham and N. Tyacke, *Altars Restored: The Changing Face of English Religious Worship, 1547–c.1700* (Oxford, 2007), chs. 5–6.

and parochial pride, and need not have been inherently objectionable, without there being a need to categorize such parishioners as 'lay Laudians' (a misleading umbrella term—especially before the 1630s—that imposes a false coherence on a complex range of lay motives for church beautification and ceremonialism).[72] By the end of the 1630s the country seems to have displayed fairly high levels of compliance with the policy of railed east-end altars, although some of this must have been reluctant.[73] Other aspects of the Laudian reforms may have prompted greater opposition. More elaborate forms of worship (including the observance of ceremonies that may have been seen as popish, such as bowing at the name of Jesus), and the enhancing of the status of the minister, could generate unease on a number of levels. More generally, it was the Laudian drive for ceremonial and architectural uniformity (including the cutting down of pews to a uniform size) that potentially rode roughshod over the many idiosyncrasies of local worship and religious expression, and doubtless alienated broader bodies of opinion.[74] The authorities' more intensive regulation of clerical behaviour—imposing ceremonial conformity, disciplining puritan ministers, and suspending lectureships—not only interfered with local religious activities, but was part of the ecclesiastical authorities' increasing desire to restrict the exercise of power by laypeople over the clergy. Overall, Laudianism threatened many of the ways in which local people had customized aspects of worship and religious life in each parish, as well as potentially altering relations between ministers and parishioners.[75]

The downfall of Laudianism in 1640 ushered in a period of dramatic change in local and national religion and politics. The national Church was dismantled, with the abolition of bishops, deans and chapters, and church courts, but their replacement was less clear. On the local parish level there was the ejection of over 2,000 clergymen, while church buildings themselves were subject to bouts of iconoclasm, stone fonts were abandoned, and parish churches lost the word 'Saint' from their titles. Prayer Book services were also replaced by more extemporary services, following the broad-brush outlines and suggestions of the Directory for Public Worship.[76]

---

[72] Merritt, 'Church-Building', pp. 942–6, 953–6; M. Reynolds, *Godly Reformers and their Opponents in Early Modern England: Religion in Norwich c.1560–1643* (Woodbridge, 2005), pp. 14–15, ch. 9; Fincham and Tyacke, *Altars Restored*, pp. 253–73.

[73] Fincham and Tyacke, *Altars Restored*, pp. 172–210.

[74] A. Walsham, 'The Parochial Roots of Laudianism Revisited: Catholics, Anti-Calvinists and "Parish Anglicans" in Early Stuart England', *JEH*, 49 (1998): 620–51 (pp. 622–3); D. Cressy, 'Conflict, Consensus and the Willingness to Wink: The Erosion of Community in Charles I's England', *Huntington Library Quarterly*, 61 (1998): 131–49 (pp. 144–6, 149); Foster, 'Church Policies', pp. 200–10, 215–16; P. Marshall, *Reformation England 1480–1642* (2nd edn., 2012), pp. 227–8.

[75] Cliffe, *Puritan Gentry*, pp. 158–64, 169–71; Merritt, *Social World*, pp. 344–8.

[76] J. Spraggon, *Puritan Iconoclasm during the English Civil War* (Woodbridge, 2003), chs. 4–5; F. McCall, *Baal's Priests: The Loyalist Clergy and the English Revolution* (Farnham, 2013).

But amid all this change, parish structures proved remarkably resilient. Even when there were attempts in the 1640s to establish a Presbyterian church government, the features of the traditional parish—especially urban ones—could actually support Presbyterianism very easily. Vestries had been accused in the 1620s of introducing Presbyterianism by stealth, and could naturally assume the function of presbyteries. Similarly, it was observed in Westminster Assembly debates that elders could grow naturally out of the roles performed by churchwardens.[77] The hierarchy of synods that was initially intended rarely assembled outside London and Lancashire, and as a result parishes continued to be run much as before, albeit now without episcopal overview. Vestries were in effect as active as ever. And by the 1650s it is possible to observe a gradual pattern of the revival of earlier forms of collective ritual activity in parishes, and even the name 'Saint' started to return to parish documents.[78]

The decisive change for local communities was the explosion of nonconformity and different sects. The ideal of local religious unity was in some senses abandoned, and attendance at a single local parish church was no longer required (in contrast to the pre-1640 period, when members of sects such as the Family of Love continued to play important roles within their local parish).[79] But there was still a national Church settlement of sorts, and it has been observed that 'all research suggests that most English people attended parochial worship rather than a gathered congregation or a sect'. The parish remained a key administrative unit, and the parish church remained a principal focus of the local community, continuing to act as the local school, storehouse, and arsenal, and as the venue for many types of local meetings and announcements (and sometimes court sessions).[80]

The abolition of Christmas and the implementation of a stringent Sabbatarian discipline were perhaps some of the most immediately visible changes that parishioners encountered.[81] But there were also more creative developments: in some places, ministers sought to revivify the parish's pastoral engagement by means of ambitious programmes of lecture exercises. However, initially the puritan urge to separate godly and ungodly seems to have been given free rein within the parish community, with a greater stress on exclusion from communion, but the tension this created with the parish's social role soon became

---

[77] A. Milton, *Laudian and Royalist Polemic in Seventeenth-Century England* (Manchester, 2007), p. 96.

[78] J. F. Merritt, *Westminster 1640-60: A Royal City in a Time of Revolution* (Manchester, 2013), pp. 248-54.

[79] C. W. Marsh, *The Family of Love in English Society, 1550-1630* (Cambridge, 1994), pp. 96, 170-3, 182-97.

[80] A. Hughes, '"The Public Profession of These Nations": The National Church in Interregnum England', in C. Durston and J. Maltby (eds.), *Religion in Revolutionary England* (Manchester, 2006), p. 96.

[81] B. Capp, *England's Culture Wars: Puritan Reformation and its Enemies in the Interregnum, 1649-1660* (Oxford, 2012), esp. pp. 20-4, 100-10.

apparent. Occasionally inhabitants refused to pay the poor rate if they were excluded from communion. The pragmatic solution adopted by some clergy was to not celebrate communion at all, rather than initiating socially divisive distinctions on the calculation of relative sincerity of belief.[82] Instead, they retained some of the more inclusive parochial rituals, such as perambulation (although the opponents of Presbyterians jeered that they did so simply to ensure that the boundaries caught as many people as possible in the net of tithe-payers). The Essex minister Giles Firmin thought it absurd that Presbyterian ministers could exclude half the parish at communion, yet also felt bound to baptize all the children. In Ralph Josselin's parish, people claimed that paying tithes and rates entitled them to a place in church, even if they were not especially 'godly' or in sympathy with the minister.[83] However, not only did Presbyterian ministers continue to fulfil normal parochial duties, but most Congregational churches in the 1650s existed in a parochial format, with Congregationalist ministers holding a parish living and operating what was essentially a two-tier pastorate. That is, access to the sacraments was restricted to covenanted 'saints' (who alone constituted the true 'church') but fellowship, prayer, preaching, and psalm-singing were open to all the parish, and Congregationalist ministers were committed to preaching the gospel and promoting reformation within the parish system.[84]

By contrast, upholders of earlier Prayer Book worship may sometimes have been willing to abandon parochial structures, especially when their own parish was taken over by a puritan minister. The image of the persecuted Anglican John Evelyn attending clandestine Prayer Book services is a familiar one. Similarly, when in the 1650s Sir John Bramston went to seek out a church service in the capital for his elderly father 'where the orthodox clergie preacht and administered the sacraments', he managed to stumble across one in Milk Street (he also describes better-known venues which had the disadvantage of 'the soldiers often disturbing those congregations').[85] But while these accounts show that such services might be available, including in private houses, they also demonstrate that devotees of the Prayer Book often worshipped *outside*

---

[82] Merritt, *Westminster 1640–60*, pp. 234–7, 240–3; E. Vernon, 'A Ministry of the Gospel: The Presbyterians during the English Revolution', in Durston and Maltby (eds.), *Religion in Revolutionary England*, pp. 115–36.

[83] S. Hardman Moore, *Pilgrims: New World Settlers and the Call of Home* (New Haven, CT, 2007), p. 137; Abraham Boun, *The Pride and Avarice of the Clergie* (1650), pp. 51, 168–72; Collinson, 'The English Conventicle', in Collinson, *From Cranmer to Sancroft*, pp. 170–1.

[84] J. Halcomb, 'A Social History of Congregational Religious Practice during the Puritan Revolution', PhD thesis, University of Cambridge (2009), pp. 101–15; Hardman Moore, *Pilgrims*, pp. 132–7, 140; J. Coffey, 'Church and State, 1550–1750', in R. Pope (ed.), *T&T Clark Companion to Nonconformity* (2013), p. 59.

[85] *The Autobiography of Sir John Bramston K.B.*, ed. P. Braybrooke (Camden Society, 32, 1845), pp. 91–2; *Diary and Correspondence of John Evelyn*, ed. W. Bray, 4 vols. (1850), I, pp. 323, 326, 333, 334.

parish structures. Ironically, the existence of royalist 'congregations' in London and elsewhere suggests that such episcopalians were implicitly undermining the idea of a common 'parish' community (even if they would have preferred to return to parish-based worship).

At the Restoration, though, the settlement saw parish religion more rigorously based around acceptance of the Prayer Book, the exclusion of nonconforming clergy (with some 1,760 English clergy forced to leave their parishes between 1660 and 1663),[86] and the later formalization of Dissent. The idea that the local religious and social community were coextensive was effectively abandoned. Nevertheless, the 1660s witnessed a series of awkward compromises, with moderate puritans still attending their local church, while the ideal of a parish whose religious inclusivity would match its all-encompassing civil jurisdiction was still remarkably tenacious. Even Presbyterian clergy taking out licences to be permitted free public worship under the 1672 Declaration of Indulgence claimed that this was not about embracing schism, and that they were assisting parish ministers and extending the scope of the local ministry. By licensing dissenting ministers, it was suggested, the king was incorporating them into the Church national: these were quasi-parishes.[87]

CONCLUSION

As should be clear, 'parish religion' was in this period the outcome of the shifting combination of a whole range of different social, religious, and political forces, whose precise configuration was unique to each individual parish. The challenge of making the parish work as both a social and a religious institution exposed different assumptions about what constituted true 'order' and what the scope of the religious community truly was. This was a world in which many polarities loomed: between the godly and ungodly, laity and clergy, public and private religion, collective and exclusive views of religious fellowship, cohesive and divisive visions of the minister's message, communal and oligarchic forms of local governance. The parochial experience was shaped by the ways in which these potential divisions were negotiated, by the minister, by the vestry, and ultimately by the individual parishioner. The English parish in this period was the arena in which these variously balanced forces operated, and where implicit or explicit compromises were devised, negotiated, or rejected. It was not the receptacle of a simple 'parish

---

[86] Spurr, *Post-Reformation*, p. 147.
[87] M. Goldie, 'Toleration and the Godly Prince in Restoration England', in J. Morrow and J. Scott (eds.), *Liberty, Authority, Formality: Political Ideas and Culture, 1600–1900* (Exeter, 2008), p. 64.

Anglicanism'. Rather, what emerges from a study of the parish in the century or more following the Henrician Reformation is the extraordinary tenacity with which the parish continued, despite all the revolutionary changes, to be central to the social identity and experience of early modern English men and women. But the precise religious implications of that social experience would vary significantly, and cannot be subsumed within an ideology of 'Anglicanism', no matter how capaciously defined.

SELECT BIBLIOGRAPHY

Boulton, J. P., 'The Limits of Formal Religion: The Administration of Holy Communion in Late Elizabethan and Early Stuart London', *London Journal*, 10 (1984): 135–54.

Collinson, P., *The Religion of Protestants: The Church in English Society, 1559–1625* (Oxford, 1982).

Craig, J., 'Psalms, Groans and Dog-Whippers: The Soundscape of Sacred Space in the English Parish Church, 1547–1642', in W. Coster and A. Spicer (eds.), *Sacred Space in Early Modern Europe* (Cambridge, 2005), pp. 104–23.

French, K., G. Gibbs, and B. Kümin (eds.), *The Parish in English Life 1400–1600* (Manchester, 1997).

Hill, C., *Economic Problems of the Church from Archbishop Whitgift to the Long Parliament* (Oxford, 1956).

Hindle, S., 'Beating the Bounds of the Parish: Order, Memory and Identity in the English Local Community, c.1500–1700', in M. Halvorson and K. Spierling (eds.), *Defining Community in Early Modern Europe* (Aldershot, 2008), pp. 205–28.

Hunt, A., 'The Lord's Supper in Early Modern England', *Past & Present*, 161 (1998): 39–83.

Ingram, M., *Church Courts, Sex and Marriage in England, 1570–1640* (Cambridge, 1987).

Kümin, B., *The Shaping of a Community: The Rise and Reformation of the English Parish c.1400–1560* (Aldershot, 1996).

Maltby, J., *Prayer Book and People in Elizabethan and Early Stuart England* (Cambridge, 1998).

Marsh, C. W., '"Common Prayer" in England 1560–1640: The View from the Pew', *Past & Present*, 171 (2001): 66–94.

Merritt, J. F., 'Contested Legitimacy and the Ambiguous Rise of Vestries in Early Modern London', *Historical Journal*, 54 (2011): 25–45.

Merritt, J. F., 'Puritans, Laudians, and the Phenomenon of Church-Building in Jacobean London', *Historical Journal*, 41 (1998): 935–60.

Merritt, J. F., *The Social World of Early Modern Westminster: Abbey, Court and Community 1525–1640* (Manchester, 2005).

Walsham, A., *Charitable Hatred: Tolerance and Intolerance in England, 1500–1700* (Manchester, 2006).

Wright, S. (ed.), *Parish, Church and People: Local Studies in Lay Religion, 1350–1750* (1988).

Wrightson, K., 'The Politics of the Parish in Early Modern England', in P. Griffiths, A. Fox, and S. Hindle (eds.), *The Experience of Authority in Early Modern England* (Basingstoke, 1996), pp. 10–46.

8

Liturgy and Worship

Bryan D. Spinks

Liturgical scholars have long been aware that the texts that form much of their subject material are more like a musical score or a play than a textbook or essay; they were designed for performance, and require a 'cast' of players, a space, movement, symbolic gesture, and material culture as well as individual reflection and interpretation that always exists alongside official interpretations. For the formative decades of the Church of England from its separation from Rome in the 1530s to its emergence as 'Anglican' in 1662 we have plenty of legal documents, liturgical texts, and some clergy accounts, all of which give us considerable insight into what was intended and hoped for. The sources fall short for any such fuller comprehension and so our picture is at best partial. With such limitations acknowledged, we must nevertheless piece together those parts of the story that we have.

THE HENRICIAN INDEPENDENT 'HUMANIST' CATHOLIC CHURCH

In his Preface to the 1549 Book of Common Prayer Archbishop Thomas Cranmer wrote:

> And where heretofore, there hath been great diversitie in saying and synging in churches within this realme: some folowynge Salsbury use, some Hereford use, same the use of Bangor, some of Yorke, and some of Lincolne: Now from hencefurth, all the whole realme shall have but one use.[1]

---

[1] Brian Cummings (ed.), *The Book of Common Prayer: The Texts of 1549, 1559, and 1662* (Oxford, 2011), p. 5.

It is of course true that the bedrock of parish worship in the Church of England was the Book of Common Prayer which, in the words of Gregory Dix, 'with an inexcusable suddenness, between a Saturday night and a Monday morning at Pentecost 1549' overturned a thousand years of English liturgical tradition.[2] The Act of Uniformity of 1549 replaced the Romano-Western liturgical synthesis that by the tenth century had established itself across practically the entire Western Church. Yet as drastic as this undoubtedly was, it was only one further piece in a drastic process that had begun in the 1530s. Robert Parkyn, the conservative priest of Aldwick the Street, Doncaster compiled his own narrative of the Reformation which is probably to be dated c.1555. There he asserted: 'Thus in Kyng Henrie days began holly churche in Englande to be in greatt ruyne as it appearide daly.'[3] It is clear from Parkyn's narrative that like many English folk, he regarded the destruction of the shrines of the saints as the beginning of the 'ruyne', and it was the attack on popular worship and devotion to the saints that marked a first and significant break not only with the medieval Church, but with an ancient Christian tradition that had its origins at least in the second century, if not before. The studies of Ramsey MacMullen indicate that in most cities and towns in antique Christianity, only the elite gathered for worship in a church building on a Sunday.[4] Most 'ordinary' Christians made for the cemeteries to be near the tombs of the martyrs and the remains of their own loved ones. In a religion that proclaimed the resurrection of the dead, and whose sacred scripture told that a trumpet would sound and the dead would arise from their graves, it made perfect eschatological sense to many to gather near the departed rather than in churches. Bishops answered the problem by building churches over the graves of the martyrs or by moving the martyrs' remains into the churches. This was not some late superstitious practice, but seems to have been universal in east and west.[5] The English Church had its own relics and bodies, from those brought by St Augustine of Canterbury to the remains of St Augustine himself and of St Cuthbert to the shrines of Anglo-Saxon royal saints such as Æthelburh and Æthelthryth (some of whom acquired the title by simply being royalty), to St Swithun, and the newer Norman saints such as Becket of Canterbury and William FitzHerbert of York. Durham not only boasted the body of St Cuthbert, but also the remains of his teacher, St Boisil, as well as the head of St Oswald and the bones of the Venerable Bede. Pilgrimage to and prayers at these shrines were an important part of English Christian devotion,

---

[2] Gregory Dix, *The Shape of the Liturgy* (1945), p. 686.
[3] A. G. Dickens, 'Robert Parkyn's Narrative of the Reformation', *English Historical Review*, 62 (1947): 58–83 (p. 66).
[4] Ramsay MacMullen, *The Second Church: Popular Christianity AD 200–400* (Atlanta, GA, 2009).
[5] Ann Marie Yasin, *Saints and Church Spaces in the Late Antique Mediterranean: Architecture, Cult, and Community* (Cambridge, 2009).

and the saints were acknowledged in public liturgical rites.[6] Contemporary Anglicans and other Protestants, having developed a spiritual culture devoid of shrines and relics, may well regard this as an unnecessary add-on and extra-liturgical. Those who lived in England from the seventh through to the early sixteenth centuries would not have regarded these as add-ons, but were conditioned to see them as a crucial and normative part of faith. Saints' bodies and relics were a witness that Christianity worked. Many were no doubt fakes, but many were not. Furthermore, depiction of the saints was not regarded as a violation of the second commandment; they were the 'family' portraits and sculptures. This 'Second Church', as MacMullen has called it, lived fully integrated with the Church of learned clergy and scholars, and intelligent laypersons whose faith was less invested in eschatological bones. Such was the Church that was referred to in the Act of Supremacy, 1534, in which the Parliament enacted 'that the King, our Sovereign Lord, his heirs and successors, kings of this realm, shall be taken, accepted, and reputed the only Supreme Head in earth of the Church of England, called *Anglicana Ecclesia*'.[7]

The Royal Injunctions of 1536 reiterated and emphasized the supremacy of the king's authority, as did the Convocation Act for the abrogation of certain holy days. This latter seems to have been for economic rather than theological reasons, since the days were still observed liturgically, though without solemnity, and were no longer public holidays. However, the Injunctions noted:

> Besides this, to the intent that all superstition and hypocrisy, crept into divers men's hearts, may vanish away, they shall not set forth or extol any images, relics, or miracles for any superstition or lucre, nor allure the people by any enticements to the pilgrimage of any saint, otherwise than is permitted in the Articles lately put forth by the authority of the king's majesty and condescended upon by the prelates and clergy of this his realm in Convocation.[8]

The further Injunctions of 1538 discouraged alleged superstition such as 'wandering to pilgrimages, offering of money, candles, or tapers to images or relics, or kissing or licking the same'.[9] No candles, tapers, or images of wax were to be set before any image or picture, and there was to be no extolling of pilgrimages, feigned relics, or images. The honouring of the 'family portraits' and their mortal remains was prohibited.

Although this seems to be a reasonable humanist attack on superstitious practice rather than a direct assault on the saints and their remains, it should be noted that the same Injunctions began by requiring that the Great Bible in

---

[6] John Crook, *English Medieval Shrines* (Woodbridge, 2011).
[7] Gerald Bray (ed.), *Documents of the English Reformation 1526–1701* (Cambridge, 2nd edn., 2004), p. 114.
[8] Henry Gee and William John Hardy, *Documents Illustrative of the History of the English Church* (1896), p. 271.
[9] Bray (ed.), *Documents*, p. 180.

English be set in some convenient place in churches. In the preface to the Great Bible, Cranmer described Holy Scripture as 'the most precious jewel and most holy relic that remaineth on the earth'.[10] If all churches had this most precious relic, then they would have no need of any other. One further instruction in the Injunctions is noteworthy:

> Item, where in times past men have used in divers places in their processions to sing *Ora pro nobis* to so many saints that they had not time to sing the good suffrages following, as *Parce nobis Domine*, and *Libera nos Domine*, it must be taught and preached that better it were to omit *Ora pro nobis*, and to sing the other suffrages.[11]

The year 1538-9 saw Canterbury's most recent revered St Thomas Becket demoted, removed from the liturgical books, his shrine dismantled, and the bones burnt. Lehmberg notes that other shrines soon met the same fate, even though they were dedicated to saints who could not be charged with having opposed the monarchy.[12] On 21 September 1538, St Swithun's shrine was destroyed.[13] The bodies of Edward the Confessor at Westminster, and St Cuthbert at Durham were some of the few to have survived this destruction of the material culture of worship and devotion. It is indisputable that economic motives were involved: it was the Treasury that received the confiscated precious metals and jewels. Liturgically, however, the sidelining of the saints was highlighted by the issue of the first official public liturgical composition in English, namely the Litany of 1544. The traditional litany was used rarely in full except for the three Rogations days and St Mark's Day, and was supplicatory and penitential, and this vernacular version was issued as a *processio causa necessitatis vel tribulacionis* (procession in times of necessity or tribulation) as Henry relaunched his war with France. A prescribed homily was first read, and then a procession with the litany and suffrages. Compared with its Latin precursors it was much abbreviated, and as Roger Bowers has rightly observed, 'The principal casualty of the practical need for abbreviation was the invocation of saints. The three invocations of the Virgin Mary were compressed into one; all the individual invocations of the saints were suppressed, and eight generic invocations were aggregated into two. The whole of the blessed company of heaven was still bidden to "pray for us"; now, however, this was undertaken by category, not by name.'[14]

---

[10] Preface to the Great Bible. <http://www.bible-researcher.com/cranmer.html>.

[11] Gee and Hardy, *Documents*, pp. 280-1.

[12] Stanford E. Lehmberg, *The Reformation of Cathedrals: Cathedrals in English Society, 1485-1603* (Princeton, NJ, 1988), p. 71.

[13] Thomas Wright (ed.), *Three Chapters of Letters Relating to the Suppression of Monasteries* (Camden Society 26, 1843), p. 218.

[14] Roger Bowers, 'The Vernacular Litany of 1544 during the Reign of Henry VIII', in George W. Bernard and Steven J. Gunn (eds.), *Authority and Consent in Tudor England* (Aldershot, 2002), pp. 151-78 (p. 160).

On 15 October 1545 this Litany was prescribed for use on all Wednesdays, Fridays, and Sundays. Bowers has argued that it did not replace the processions that preceded mass and some of the offices on certain festivals on the grounds that it, like its precursors when used in full, was a separate liturgical event and not used for the liturgical processions.[15] In Bowers's view, parts of the Latin litanies traditionally used before and after the mass were retained alongside the King's Litany which would have been a quite separate service. This is debatable, mainly because we lack firm evidence either way. However, the King's Litany found its way into the King's Primer of 1545 which was intended to replace all other primers (whether it succeeded is beside the point), and thus it may be that the Litany was intended to replace all other litanies. What is not in question is that both in the public Litany and its private recitation from the Primer, the invocation to fifty-nine individual saints had vanished. In the light of the Injunctions of 1538 and the dismantling of shrines, something more than abbreviation was going on. Contrasting the petitions for the monarch with the suppression of the saints in the Litany, J. P. D. Cooper has remarked that the crown had supplanted the saints in parish prayer.[16] Henry's *Anglicana Ecclesia* was a very different Church from the one he had been born into, and part of the liturgical tradition of a thousand years had already been overturned.

THE EDWARDIAN LITURGICAL REFORMS

Gordon Jeanes has commented that what was unusual in the English Reformation was the use of the liturgy as the central plank.[17] The architect of liturgical reform in the English Church was Archbishop Thomas Cranmer. Others were involved in the committees, but the majority of the authoring was his. Cranmer's interest and abilities in liturgical reform is demonstrated by BL Royal MS.7B.IV which contains two drafts of schemes to revise the Divine Office. They were designated Schemes A and B, with A being a more radical departure from the rite then in use. It seems that A dates from 1538 during Henry's 'Lutheran' period, whereas B represents the king's more conservative Catholic reaction of the period *c*.1543. In both schemes Cranmer drew on the breviary compiled by Cardinal Quignon, which in many ways represented a

---

[15] Terence Bailey, *The Processions of Sarum and the Western Church* (Toronto, 1971); Bowers, 'Vernacular Litany'.

[16] J. P. D. Cooper, '*O Lorde Save the Kyng*: Tudor Royal Propaganda and the Power of Prayer', in Bernard and Gunn (eds.), *Authority and Consent*, pp. 179–96 (p. 182).

[17] Gordon Jeanes, 'The Tudor Prayer Books: That "the Whole Realme Shall Have But One Use"', in Stephen Platten and Christopher Woods (eds.), *Comfortable Words: Polity, Piety and the Book of Common Prayer* (2012), pp. 20–34 (p. 22).

Catholic humanist Renaissance reform.[18] The King's Litany (which has already been noted), authored by Cranmer, encapsulated the attack on and demise of the cult of the saints in the English Church. Henry, however, neither allowed nor encouraged any further liturgical reform. Only with Henry's death were the floodgates opened. In 1547 further assaults on images were undertaken, with the destruction of many roods. In 1548 a vernacular communion devotion was issued with a royal proclamation. This communion preparation was to be inserted into the Latin mass prior to where communion was intended to take place. Much of the material of this devotion had been taken from the *Simplex ac Pia Deliberatio* prepared by Martin Bucer and Philip Melanchthon for Archbishop Hermann von Wied of Cologne. Published first in German, and then Latin, an English translation was printed by John Day in 1547.[19] Cranmer's *The Order of the Communion* consisted of the following:

1. An exhortation giving notice of communion and the need for preparation
2. Directions for preparation of sufficient bread and wine
3. An exhortation to worthiness
4. A warning not to communicate if unworthy
5. Invitation to confession
6. General confession
7. Absolution
8. Comfortable words of Scripture
9. Prayer of approach—'We do not presume to come to this thy table'
10. Directions for communion, and words of delivery—bread and wine
11. A blessing.

The Order provided communion in two kinds, but there was little in this document to suggest any great departure from traditional doctrine. The Proclamation requested that the Order be received 'quietly', and such reception would encourage those in authority to 'further to travail for the Reformation and setting forth of such godly orders'.[20] Those who waited patiently for further reformation did not have to wait long. A new godly order appear in 1549—the Book of Common Prayer mentioned earlier—and it was accompanied by an Act of Uniformity which replaced all the older Latin 'Uses' with the new services contained all in the one book and in English. The old service

---

[18] Bryan D. Spinks, 'Renaissance Liturgical Reforms: Reflections on Intentions and Methods', *Renaissance and Reformation*, 7 (2005): 268–82.
[19] Geoffrey Cuming, *The Godly Order: Texts and Studies Relating to the Book of Common Prayer* (1983), pp. 68–90; Bryan D. Spinks, 'German Influence on Edwardian Liturgies', in Dorothea Wendebourg (ed.), *Sister Reformations: The Reformation in Germany and in England* (Tübingen, 2010), pp. 175–89.
[20] See the facsimile edition, *The Order of the Holy Communion*, ed. H. A. Wilson (Henry Bradshaw Society 34, 1908).

books were to be surrendered for destruction. The final text of the 1549 services may not have been seen even by a committee drawing up the new liturgy which had apparently met at Chertsey Abbey, since the Wanley Part Books witness to musicians working with a slightly different liturgical text from that which was finally published.[21]

The nature of the 1549 Book of Common Prayer was ambiguous. Already in 1547/8 ceremonies such as ashes on Ash Wednesday and the blessing and procession of palms on Palm Sunday had been abolished. The new book retained the word 'mass' for the communion, and retained the traditional vesture and ornaments. On the other hand it forbade the elevation of the bread and wine which was an important focal point in the traditional Latin mass.[22] Sacrifice and offering had also been important concepts in the old mass, and any concept of offering other than of prayers, alms, and 'our souls and bodies' was entirely omitted. The doctrine of transubstantiation was bitterly attacked by all serious reformers, and Cranmer was no exception. He had written:

> But what availeth it to take away beads, pardons, pilgrimages, and such other like popery, so long as the two chief roots remain unpulled up?... The rest is but branches and leaves... but the very body of the tree, or rather the roots of the weeds, is the popish doctrine of transubstantiation, of the real presence of Christ's flesh and blood in the sacrament of the altar (as they call it), and of the sacrifice and oblation of Christ made by the priest, for the salvation of the quick and the dead.[23]

Although a concept of presence of Christ in the eucharistic elements was certainly suggested by phraseology in the communion service, it is certain that by this date Cranmer no longer held either the Catholic or Lutheran ideas of real presence, and there is ambiguity in the phraseology. For example, where the old mass had petitioned God that the bread and wine be the body and blood of Christ, the new mass asked that 'they may unto us' suggesting a subjective understanding rather than an objective change. The conservative bishop Gardiner, in the Tower for his resistance to the changes, declared that the doctrine in this book was not too distant from the Catholic faith, and Cranmer answered in a long essay arguing that is was very distant from the old doctrines.[24] Gordon Jeanes has shown that in compiling his baptismal rite Cranmer used three German sources, two of them Lutheran and the third

---

[21] Gordon P. Jeanes, *Signs of God's Promise: Thomas Cranmer's Sacramental Theology and the Book of Common Prayer* (2008), pp. 132–5; Peter le Huray, *Music and the Reformation in England 1549–1660* (New York, 1967), pp. 172–6.

[22] For the background see Bryan D. Spinks, 'The Roman Canon Missae', in *Prex Eucharistica Vol. III. Studia, Pars prima* (Fribourg, 2005), pp. 129–39.

[23] J. I. Packer and G. E. Duffield (eds.), *The Work of Thomas Cranmer* (Philadelphia, PA, 1965), p. 57.

[24] Jeanes, *Signs of God's Promise*.

being the *Simplex* of Hermann. In addition he used a now lost Spanish source, the old Visigothic, which he may have acquired earlier in his diplomatic career which had taken him on the king's business to Spain. Like the old rite, that of 1549 was divided into two, the first part taking place at the church door. Like the 1544 Litany, it seemed to many an abbreviation of the old, and like the 1544 work, the litany of saints in the old baptismal service was discarded. The rite retained anointing and the use of the chrisom (white baptismal garment).[25] The emphasis in this rite was forgiveness of original sin and engrafting into the 'ark' of Christ's Church. The Divine Office reduced the eight offices of the Latin rite to two, morning and evening prayer. Services such as churching of women after childbirth as well as confirmation were very close translations of their Latin antecedents.

These new vernacular services were met with varied responses. Parkyn's view was that 'tholly masse was subdewyde and depposside by actt of parliamentt, and noyne to be uside, butt only a communion'.[26] In Cornwall, the Cornish-speaking regarded English as more foreign than Latin, and perhaps referring to the need to put alms into the poor man's chest, Cornish rebels described the new communion as a 'Christmas game'.[27] On the other hand, John Hooper was offended that vestments had been retained, and had to be persuaded by a spell in prison to wear them for his consecration as bishop. Prominent continental reformers now in England, Martin Bucer and Peter Martyr Vermigli, being appointed as regius professors at Cambridge and Oxford respectively, each were invited to write a critique of the book, which they did. For many Protestants it was still far too Catholic. Conservative parish priests celebrated the new mass as much like the old as they could, whereas those of a more Protestant bent made their own extra reforms to ensure that the new services were celebrated in a different manner from the old.

At Easter in 1551 it was reported of Nicholas Ridley, bishop of London, that he

> altered the Lordes table that stoode where the high aulter was, and he removed the table beneth the steepps into the middes of the upper quire in Poules, and sett the endes east and west, the priest standing in the middest at the communion on the south side of the bord, and after the creed song, he caused the vaile to be drawen, that no person shoulde see but those that receaved, and he closed the iron grates of the quire on the north and sowth side with bricke and plaister, that non might remaine in at the quire.[28]

Music must have been a problem. Many churches had relied on chantry priests to supplement or to actually be the choir, but with the dissolution of the

---

[25] Jeanes, *Signs of God's Promise*.   [26] Dickens, 'Parkyn's Narrative', p. 69.
[27] Nicholas Pocock, *Troubles Connected with the Prayer Book of 1549* (Camden Society NS 37, 1884), p. 169.
[28] W. D. Hamilton (ed.), *A Chronicle of England during the Reigns of the Tudors from A.D. 1485 to 1559 by Charles Wriothesley*, 2 vols. (Camden Society NS 11, 20, 1875–7), II, p. 47.

chantries, this came to an end. Cathedrals and large parish churches with a competent musician probably set the English text to plainsong, but it was not until 1550 that John Merbecke provided a simple setting for the communion service that could be used by less musically skilled congregations.

The 1549 liturgy was itself short-lived. It was replaced in 1552 with a second Book of Common Prayer accompanied by new Act of Uniformity. The new Act drew attention to the fact that 'divers doubts for the fashion and manner of the ministration' of 1549 had arisen, because of 'the curiosity of ministers and mistakers' so that now in this new order the former is 'explained and made fully perfect'.[29] It was clear from the new rubrics and liturgical texts that the 'mistakers' had been the conservatives who tried to make the 1549 rites like those of the medieval Latin liturgies. In the 1552 Prayer Book, the traditional vestments for the mass were abolished, and only the surplice, tippet, and hood were to be worn. Any hint that the bread and wine in the communion are in any sense the body and blood of Christ was removed. At communion the words of administration were 'Take and eat this in remembrance that Christ died for you, and feed on him in your hearts by faith with thanksgiving'. The communion service is divided into two distinct parts, with a move from the nave into the chancel to kneel around the table when there was a communion. Anointing disappeared from baptism and confirmation. A confession and declaration of forgiveness of sins precedes the 1549 forms of morning and evening prayer. The new book was unmistakably Protestant. The old altars were to be removed and destroyed and replaced by a wooden communion table. Ornaments were defaced and walls whitewashed to blot out the wall paintings that survived. However, unlike some of the continental Reformed Churches, some vesture and the sign of the cross in baptism were retained, as was the use of a ring in marriage. In 1552/3 Cranmer had invited a number of leading continental Protestant divines to come to England, with the hope of holding some ecumenical Protestant council to rival the Catholic Council of Trent. Such a council never happened, but it may be that Cranmer viewed this unmistakably Protestant liturgy as a middle way between the Lutherans and the Reformed. A new primer was also issued for lay use, which excluded any invocation of Mary or the saints, and excluded prayer for the dead. The contemporary commentator Charles Wriothesley recorded:

> This day all copes and vestments were put downe through all England... After the feast of All Saintes, the upper quire in St. Pawles Church, in London, where the high aulter stoode, was broken downe and all the quire thereabout, and the table of the communion was set in the lower quire where the preistes singe.[30]

---

[29] Bray (ed.), *Documents*, p. 282.   [30] Hamilton (ed.), *Chronicle*, II, pp. 78–9.

These more obviously Protestant reforms were short-lived. Edward VI died on 6 July 1553, the Protestant regime rapidly crumbled, and the Catholic Mary Tudor was proclaimed queen. Wriothesley recorded:

> Thursdaye, the 24 of August and St. Bartholomews daye, the olde service in the Latin tongue with the masse was begun and sunge in Powles in the Shrowdes, now St. Faythes parishe. And likewise it was begun in 4 or 5 other parishes within the Cittie of London, not by commaundement but of the peoples devotion.[31]

Commandment soon followed. New altars were built, new rood screens erected, and the traditional vesture and ceremonies were reintroduced. Relics that had been hidden away reappeared, but since so many mortal remains had been destroyed, the centre of the 'second' Church had gone forever from the English Church.

THE ELIZABETHAN SETTLEMENT

Mary's restoration of the English Church to communion with Rome ended shortly after her death in 1558. Her half-sister Elizabeth made it clear that she preferred English to Latin, and since all but one of the Marian bishops refused to cooperate, Elizabeth had to rely on those of varied Protestant sympathies for leadership of the Church. The Henrician legislation was re-enacted, breaking the legal ties with Rome, though whereas Henry took the title 'Supreme Head' of the Church of England, Elizabeth settled for 'Supreme Governor'. Elizabeth's own vision for the English Church is shrouded in a certain ambiguity. On the one hand she seems to have wanted to retain rood screens and the roods themselves, but in fact the latter were ultimately removed and destroyed. It is conjectured by some that she would have preferred the 1549 Book of Common Prayer, and that her own Chapel Royal composers did write some compositions for the text of that liturgy.[32] But by 23 March 1559 it was clear that the Elizabethan liturgy would in fact be that of 1552, though with some ambiguous changes. A rubric before the order of morning prayer required the ornaments of the churches (adornments of the altar/table, and vesture) be that of the second year of the reign of Edward VI, which technically allowed the traditional mass vestments, candles, and crosses on the altar, and even the use of incense. In practice it seems that few if any contemporaries (other than perhaps some

---

[31] Hamilton (ed.), *Chronicle*, II, p. 101.
[32] William P. Haugaard, 'The Proposed Liturgy of Edmund Guest', *Anglican Theological Review*, 46 (1964): 177–89; Roger Bowers, 'The Chapel Royal, the First Edwardian Prayer Books, and Elizabeth's Settlement of Religion, 1559', *Historical Journal*, 43 (2000): 17–44. Contrast Diarmaid MacCulloch, Review of Heal, Felicity, *Reformation in Britain and Ireland*. H-Albion, H-Net Reviews. September, 2003. <http://www.h-net.org/reviews/showrev.php?id=8172>.

ultra-conservative rural priests) ever obeyed the rubric. In the communion service the words of administration of 1549 were now prefixed to those of 1552. Third, the so-called 'Black rubric' that had explained kneeling for communion but denied any real or essential presence in the elements was omitted. Commissioners toured the dioceses collecting and confiscating the traditional mass vestments, but Elizabeth's intention was to have copes worn over the surplice at communion. Ultimately it was difficult enough to insist on the surplice, and copes were enforced only in the cathedrals. Elizabeth herself had candles and a cross on the holy table in her chapel, and insisted officiating clergy wore copes. Section 13 of the Elizabethan Act of Uniformity had given the queen authority to 'ordain and publish such further ceremonies or rites as may be most for the advancement of God's glory, the edifying of his Church and the due reverence of Christ's holy mysteries and sacraments'.[33] Under this section the queen authorized by letters patent of 6 April 1560 the *Liber Precum Publicarum*, a Latin edition of the Book of Common Prayer for use in the chapels of Oxford, Cambridge, Eton, and Winchester. However, the translator, thought to be Walter Haddon, drew on the Latin version of the 1549 Book of Common Prayer. Amongst its differences to the 1559 English book was provision for an epistler and gospeller, vested in copes at the communion; reservation of the sacrament; a fuller calendar of saints; a service commemorating college benefactors; and provision for a requiem communion. Protestant scholars were not slow to note the differences, and it was reported that most Cambridge colleges refused to use it. A Primer was published in 1559, being a reissue of the 1551 edition of Henry's 1545 Primer. Whereas the Prayer Book provided two offices of morning and evening prayer, the Primer gave an English version of the more traditional eight offices, suggesting a more conservative Catholic trend. In 1560 the *Orarium* was published, giving the eight offices in Latin and it included Latin hymns.[34] It is these elements that suggest an ambiguity about Elizabeth's ideal for her Church. The ambiguity was reflected in the varied performance of the prescribed rites.[35]

In the cathedrals and collegiate churches and chapels where there was provision for choirs, a fine repertoire of music developed to accompany morning and evening prayer, the litany, the communion service, and other offices such as burial. In most parish churches, however, music tended to be confined to the metrical psalms of Sternhold and Hopkins of 1562.[36] In many

---

[33] Bray (ed.), *Documents*, p. 334.
[34] Bryan D. Spinks, 'The Elizabethan Primers: Symptoms of an Ambiguous Settlement or Devotional Weaning?', in Natalie Mears and Alec Ryrie (eds.), *Worship and the Parish Church in Early Modern Britain* (Farnham, 2013), pp. 73–87.
[35] John Strype, *The Life and Acts of Matthew Parker* (1711), Book II, p. 152.
[36] Peter Phillips, *English Sacred Music 1549–1649* (Oxford, 1991); Beth Quitslund, *The Reformation in Rhyme: Sternhold, Hopkins and the English Metrical Psalter, 1547–1603* (Aldershot, 2008).

parish churches communion became limited to a monthly, quarterly, or tri-annual celebration and the main Sunday services of the Elizabethan Church were morning prayer, the litany, and the first part of the communion service with a sermon; and evening prayer with catechism. A contemporary account was given by the historian Raphael Holinshed in 1586.[37]

However, a good number of godly churchmen felt that the Prayer Book was too close to its Roman parent, and they looked forward to, and agitated for, a more Protestant reform. Some of these 'puritans' were extremely hostile to many features of the liturgy. Some objected to the surplice, and wore only a black gown. Some omitted pieces of the liturgy they did not like. The liturgical complaints of the more radical puritans were presented in *An Admonition to the Parliament*, 1572, authored by John Field and Thomas Wilcox. Comparing their understanding of the early Church with the Elizabethan settlement, they objected to copes, surplices, the use of the cross in baptism, and the mandatory use of a ring in the marriage rite.[38] A bill of 1572 proposed allowing clergy to omit parts of the Book of Common Prayer and also to allow use of the liturgies of the 'Stranger' Churches—the Dutch and French Protestant congregations who had found asylum in England. The latter respectively used liturgies of Petrus Datheen, 1564 and Valerand Poullain's edition of Calvin's liturgy for Strassburg.[39] There are also so-called 'puritan' editions of the Book of Common Prayer where the word 'minister' is substituted for 'priest', and references to celebrating at the north side were omitted, although Ian Green has argued that these are simply the abbreviation of printers and more to do with sales than doctrine.[40] Other godly ministers and groups used prayers from the 1556 *Form of Prayers*, the later household prayers of which were contained in editions of the Sternhold and Hopkins metrical psalter used in most parish churches. This liturgy had been compiled for the English exiles in Geneva by John Foxe, William Whittingham, John Knox, and Anthony Gilby, and it was recommended for use in the Church of Scotland in 1562 (and reaffirmed in 1564).[41] Twice in Elizabeth's reign there were attempts in Parliament to enact editions of this liturgy in place of the Book of Common Prayer, under the title *A Book of the Form of Common Prayers, Administration of the Sacraments: &c. Agreeable to God's Word, and the Use of the Reformed Churches*. These two editions, the Waldegrave Book of 1584 and the Middleburg Book 1586, were

---

[37] Raphael Holinshed, *The Chronicles of England, Ireland and Scotland, 1586*, 6 vols. (1807–8), I, p. 232.
[38] W. H. Frere and C. E. Douglas (eds.), *Puritan Manifestoes* (1907), pp. 14, 29–30.
[39] Bryan D. Spinks, *From the Lord and 'The Best Reformed Churches': A Study of the Eucharistic Liturgy in the English Puritan and Separatist Traditions 1550–1633* (Rome, 1984).
[40] A. Elliott Peaston, *The Prayer Book Tradition in the Free Churches* (1964), pp. 31–2; Ian Green, '"Puritan Prayer Books" and "Geneva Bibles": An Episode in Elizabethan Publishing', *Transactions of the Cambridge Bibliographical Society*, 11 (1998): 313–49.
[41] Spinks, *From the Lord*.

presented respectively in bills in 1584 (introduced by Dr Peter Turner) and in 1587 (introduced by Peter Wentworth and Anthony Cope). In keeping with the Reformed tradition, there were no versicles and responses. The main Sunday morning service consisted of a greeting, confession of sins, a psalm, a prayer for illumination, the Lord's Prayer, a scripture reading, a sermon, a prayer for the Church, the Apostles' Creed, the Decalogue, the Lord's Prayer (again), a psalm, and a blessing. When there was a communion, the words of institution were read after the final psalm, followed by an exhortation, a eucharistic prayer (derived in part from a liturgy Knox drew up for Berwick-on-Tweed), communion, followed by a thanksgiving, a psalm, and the blessing. Both attempts were quashed by royal intervention. Elizabeth insisted that her bishops enforced conformity, and those more extreme 'nonconformist' puritans were often deprived of their livings or had their licences revoked. No doubt some ministers made their own ad hoc emendations and omissions, but no official further reforms were authorized. Rather different were the extreme separatists such as Henry Barrow and John Greenwood. They rejected the idea of a national Church, however reformed it might be, and they rejected what they termed 'stinted' liturgy, that is, any set forms of prayer, be it the Book of Common Prayer or the *Form of Prayers*. Since these groups did not write prayers, we have little information about their worship other than passing remarks in their polemical theological writings. A deposition before a magistrate outlined the Lord's Supper as celebrated by a Barrowist congregation in London:

> Beinge further demaunded the manner of the Lord's Supper administred emongst them, he saith that five whight loves or more were sett vppon the table and that the pastor did breake the bread and then delivered yt unto some of them, and the deacons delivered to the rest, some of the said congregacion sittinge and some standing aboute the table and that the pastor delivered the cupp unto one and he an other, and soe from one to another till they had all dronken, usinge the words at the deliverye therof according as it is sett downe in the eleventh of the Corinthes the xxiiiith verse.[42]

Barrow and Greenwood refused to conform or repent and were executed for sedition.

Though at the beginning of Elizabeth's reign there were many who were theologically and devotionally attached to the traditional Latin rites, Judith Maltby has shown how by the last decades of Elizabeth's reign, most English people had become devoted to the new English Prayer Book, and had absorbed its spirituality.[43] Daniel Swift has illustrated how its prose is reflected in

---

[42] Leland H. Carlson (ed.), *The Writings of John Greenwood and Henry Barrow 1592–1593* (1970), p. 307.

[43] Judith Maltby, *Prayer Book and People in Elizabethan and Early Stuart England* (Cambridge, 1998).

Shakespeare's plays, and Sophie Read has noted some of its direct and indirect influence on the poetic imagination in early modern England.[44]

THE JACOBEAN AND CAROLINE CHURCH

With Elizabeth's death the crown passed to James VI of Scotland. Many of the puritan-minded divines hoped that the Stuart monarch would conform the Church of England to the Church of Scotland model, whose polity was Presbyterian, and whose liturgy was the Genevan *Form of Prayers*. On his way from Scotland to London, James had been presented with the Millenary Petition which renewed the demands of the Elizabethan puritans for further reformation of the English Church in its worship, polity, and canon law. The liturgical demands included the removing of the sign of the cross in baptism and the ring in marriage, and the abolition of confirmation.[45]

James responded by calling the Hampton Court Conference which met in 1604. Representing the signatories were Laurence Chaderton of Cambridge, John Rainolds of Oxford, John Knewstubbs, rector of Cockfield, Suffolk, and Dr Thomas Sparkes, rector of Bletchley. James met with them, and separately he met with nine bishops and seven deans who represented the status quo. Patrick Galloway, a Scottish minister from Perth, was also in attendance. An account of the conference was made by Dean William Barlow, but another 'anonymous' account has also survived, and these accounts differ. It is generally thought that Barlow gives a version more favourable to the bishops whereas the 'anonymous' account suggests that James sided on a number of things with the puritan divines. Whatever was or was not agreed at the conference, it appears that even fewer concessions were made in the final emendation of the Prayer Book by the bishops. There were restrictions on midwives baptizing babies in danger of death, and a new canon required the repetition of the words of institution if the consecrated elements were exhausted. The catechism in the Prayer Book was expanded to cover the sacraments. The most important outcome of the conference was the undertaking of a new translation of the Bible, giving rise to the Authorized Version of 1611. James seems to have approved of the idea of some conformity between the two Churches in his kingdoms, though it was in the reverse direction from that expected by the puritans. He restored bishops to the Church of Scotland, and through the Five Articles of Perth James attempted

---

[44] Daniel Swift, *Shakespeare's Common Prayers: The Book of Common Prayer and the Elizabethan Age* (New York, 2013); Sophie Read, *Eucharist and the Poetic Imagination in Early Modern England* (Cambridge, 2013).
[45] Gee and Hardy, *Documents*, p. 509.

unsuccessfully to impose the observance of Christmas and Easter as well as kneeling for communion in the Scottish Church. His bishops also worked on a revised liturgy, three drafts of which have survived, but the attempt was abandoned.[46]

There was, however, a growing polarization amongst English divines during his reign. Most may be described as 'Calvinist conformists'. They largely shared a theology with the Reformed Churches (as against the Lutheran Churches) and saw the Church of England as part of the Reformed family. Others, however, regarded the English Church as quite distinct from other Protestant Churches, and distanced themselves from some of the prevailing Reformed theology, particularly 'double' predestination. These 'avant-garde' conformists, or 'Patristic Reformed Churchmen', valued the continuity in liturgy, custom, and canons with the medieval Church, regarding these things as guaranteeing continuity with the Church of Augustine of Canterbury.[47] Some felt that the 1549 liturgy was preferable to that of 1559/1604, and they also had a concern for decency and order in worship. They particularly emphasized worship as the beauty of holiness, and liked aesthetically pleasing furnishings. They regarded the sacraments as equally if not more important than preaching, and they liked some limited ceremonial in worship. A leading figure in this was Bishop Lancelot Andrewes. In his chapel he laid out the furnishings with a 'theology' that may have been suggested by the Eastern Orthodox Church, and he carefully furnished the altar and burnt incense. Special vessels were procured for the communion, and he added certain prayers, scripture sentences, and formulae to the official liturgy. Following his friend Bishop John Overall, he used the post-communion 'prayer of oblation' in its 1549 place, immediately after the words of institution.[48]

As dean of the Chapel Royal, Andrewes had some considerable influence, and his protégé Richard Neile, bishop of Durham, continued these interests in a group he gathered around himself, known as the Durham House Group. Amongst this group were John Cosin, to become a prebendary of Durham, and later Master of Peterhouse, Cambridge, and also William Laud the future archbishop of Canterbury. Many of Neile's protégés gained preferment under Charles I and they used their new authority to encourage and impose their views. This was particularly marked by John Cosin's development of ceremonial and music at Durham Cathedral, and later in Peterhouse Chapel in

---

[46] Bryan D. Spinks, *Sacraments, Ceremonies and the Stuart Divines: Sacramental Theology and Liturgy in England and Scotland 1603–1662* (Aldershot, 2002), pp. 58–62.

[47] Peter Lake, *Anglicans and Puritans? Presbyterianism and English Conformist Thought from Whitgift to Hooker* (1988); Peter Lake, 'Lancelot Andrewes, John Buckeridge and Avant-Garde Conformity at the Court of James I', in Linda Levy Peck (ed.), *The Mental World of the Jacobean Court* (Cambridge, 1991), pp. 113–33; Spinks, *Sacraments*, p. 81.

[48] Peter McCullough, 'Absent Presence: Lancelot Andrewes and 1662', in Platten and Woods (eds.), *Comfortable Words*, pp. 49–68.

Cambridge. According to the vitriolic sermon preached by an older prebend of Durham, Peter Smart, Cosin developed 'Altar-ducking, Cope-wearing, Organ-playing, piping and singing, crossing of Cushions, and kissing of Clouts, oft starting up, and squatting downe, nodding of heads, and whirling about, till their noses stand Eastwards... Setting Basons on the Altar, Candlesticks and Crucifixes; burning Waxe-candles, in excessive number, when and where there is no use of Lights.'[49]

By the reign of Charles I there was a more general move to place communion tables permanently where the old altar had stood, and to rail them so they could not be moved out into the chancel and placed table-wise.[50] Laud's biographer wrote that by 1635

> Many things had been at *Cambridge*... as beautyfying their Chappels, furnishing them with Organs, advancing the Communion Table to the place of the Altar, adorning it with Plate and other Utensils for the Holy Sacrament, defending it with a decent Rail from all prophanations, and using lowly Reverence and Adorations, both in their coming to those Chappels, and their going out.[51]

This was attempting to impose the ceremonial of the Chapels Royal on not only the cathedrals, but also on parish churches.[52] But not everyone felt so enthusiastic. Robert Woodford who lived in the 'puritan' parish of Northampton wrote in his diary for 17 March 1638: 'The Com[munio]n Table is raylinge in to the top of the Chancell & the seates there pulled downe. O Lord destroy sup[er]stit[i]on.'[53]

James was an astute monarch and kept a balance amongst his English bishops. His son Charles was less astute and promoted the Durham House divines, or 'Laudians' as they were called, and their enforcement of ceremonial through the ecclesiastical courts led to the growing unpopularity of them, and of the monarch. In 1636 Scottish bishops attempted to revise and impose a liturgy in place of the Geneva *Form of Prayers*. The precise details are somewhat obscure, but they were urged by Archbishop Laud to adopt the English 1604 Book of Common Prayer. In the event, they compiled a Prayer Book that recycled material from the 1549 liturgy, and it was published for use

---

[49] Peter Smart, *A Sermon Preached in the Cathedrall Church of Durham, July 7 1628* (1640), p. 23.

[50] Bryan D. Spinks, 'The Seventeenth Century Context of Peterhouse Chapel and Latin Books of Common Prayer' (forthcoming); Graham Parry, *The Arts of the Anglican Counter-Reformation: Glory, Laud and Honour* (Woodbridge, 2006); Kenneth Fincham and Nicholas Tyacke, *Altars Restored: The Changing Face of English Religious Worship, 1547–c.1700* (Oxford, 2007).

[51] Peter Heylyn, *Cyprianus Anglicus* (1668), pp. 314–15.

[52] Bryan D. Spinks, 'Durham House and the Chapels Royal: Their Liturgical Impact on the Church of Scotland', *Scottish Journal of Theology*, 67 (2014): 379–99.

[53] John Fielding (ed.), *The Diary of Robert Woodford, 1637–1641* (Camden Society 5th ser. 42, 2012), p. 188 (entry for 17 March 1638).

in 1637. It attempted a Scottish flavour—it referred to Pasch for Easter, and Yule for Christmas, as well as presbyter rather than priest. However, it reintroduced a blessing of the water in baptism, and for the communion service a rubric directed:

> The holy Table, having at the Communion time a carpet and a fair white linen cloth upon it, with other decent furniture meet for the high mysteries there to be celebrated, shall stand at the uppermost part of the Chancel or Church, where the Presbyter, standing at the north side one end thereof, shall say the Lord's Prayer with the Collect following for due preparation.[54]

The prayer setting apart the bread and wine was now given a title, 'the Prayer of Consecration', and the words of administration were just those of the 1549 book. Though the work of the Scottish bishops, it reflected the theology of the 'Laudians' and because of Laud's approval of the book, it was regarded as an English episcopal imposition of popery.

A carefully orchestrated revolt against the Book's introduction ensured that it was rejected. The events that followed—the expulsion of bishops from the Scottish Church, and the invasion of England—gradually exploded into the English civil war.[55] Bishops and their ceremonial policies were held responsible for the state of affairs, and the parliamentarians abolished episcopacy, and through the Westminster Assembly of Divines, replaced the Book of Common Prayer with A Directory for Public Worship, 1644. This book of directions was inspired by the Genevan *Form of Prayers*, but a Scottish radical party and the emergence of a well-connected Independent party, both of whom objected to the use of set prayer, ensured that no liturgy—not even Knox's or Calvin's—was adopted, but merely a guide for what ministers might pray in public worship. At morning worship, for example, the minister was advised to begin by praying a prayer expressing the majesty of God and the vileness of humans, and to ask for pardon and assistance, especially to hear the Scriptures. At baptism the old fonts were not to be used, and the minister was to begin by giving an instruction on the nature, use, and ends of the sacrament, and then to admonish the people to repent. At the Lord's Supper directions included the need to warn about unworthy eating, while permission was given for reception at the table (as in the Church of Scotland) or sitting about it (in pews, as was the Independents' practice). Although parishes were required to purchase the Directory, the sales suggest that many did not, and although the use of the Book of Common Prayer was subject to legal penalties, it appears that it was more widely used, even if in a modified form, than was once thought to be

---

[54] Gordon Donaldson, *The Making of the Scottish Prayer Book of 1637* (Edinburgh, 1954), p. 183.

[55] David Cressy, *England on Edge: Crisis and Revolution 1640–1642* (Oxford, 2006).

the case.[56] However, it was the Book of Common Prayer that was outlawed, and not necessarily set forms of prayer. Jeremy Taylor, in his capacity as a private chaplain, prepared elaborate liturgies which he published in 1658 under the title *A Collection of Offices, or Form of Prayer in Cases Ordinary and Extraordinary*. He drew on the older Roman rite for his baptismal rite, and the Syrian Orthodox version of the Liturgy of St James, together with some borrowing from the Byzantine Liturgy of St Basil for his communion service.[57] He gave the communion rite a three-fold structure of ante-communion, communion, and post-communion, each part beginning with the Lord's Prayer.

The death of Oliver Cromwell led to the demise of the Commonwealth and Protectorate, and an invitation was issued to Charles II to return as king. In 1660 Charles issued the Declaration of Breda, promising liberty to those of tender conscience, and some of the Presbyterian-minded English clergy presented Charles with an address, asking him not to reintroduce the Book of Common Prayer. The Worcester House Declaration of October 1660 stated that although the king thought the English liturgy the best he had ever seen, nevertheless he would appoint an equal number of divines from the episcopal and puritan sides to debate the issue of liturgy. A royal warrant of 25 March 1661 established a commission to discuss liturgical reform. This commission met at the Master's Lodge of the Savoy, and hence is known as the Savoy Conference. The episcopal side announced that they were content with the Book of Common Prayer, and invited their puritan brethren to list their objections. This they did and their list, known as the Exceptions, made them look like nit-pickers. One of their number, Richard Baxter (who would decline the offer of a bishopric), undertook to draw up an alternative liturgy to the Prayer Book. He appears to have expanded his use of the Directory at Kidderminster. It was rather a verbose piece of work, but its theology of the eucharist certainly had much in common with the Durham House Group, even though their preferred liturgical texts were poles apart.[58] In the event, the Savoy Conference ended without agreement, and the business of revision passed to the newly restored Convocation.

---

[56] Paul S. Seaver, *The Puritan Lectureships: The Politics of Religious Dissent, 1560–1662* (Stanford, CA, 1970), pp. 276–9; John Morrill, 'The Church in England 1642–9', in John Morrill (ed.), *Reactions to the English Civil War 1642–1649* (1982); Judith Maltby, '"Extravagencies and Impertinencies": Set Forms, Conceived and Extempore Prayer in Revolutionary England', in Mears and Ryrie (eds.), *Worship and the Parish Church*, pp. 221–43.

[57] Spinks, *Sacraments*.

[58] Bryan D. Spinks, *Freedom or Order? The Eucharistic Liturgy amongst the English Independent or Congregationalist Tradition 1645–1980* (Alison Park, PA, 1984); Spinks, *Sacraments*; Glen Segger, *Richard Baxter's Reformed Liturgy: A Puritan Alternative to the Book of Common Prayer* (Farnham, 2014).

It was Gilbert Sheldon, bishop of London, who steered the Restoration Church of England, and his political outlook, shared by Parliament, was that none of the troublemakers that led to the civil war would be rewarded or appeased. This meant that the Presbyterian-puritan faction, and the Durham House extremes, would be ignored. Indeed, the preface of the Prayer Book that emerged in 1662 stated that it represented the mean between two extremes, and that the general aim was 'not to gratify this or that party in any of their unreasonable demands'. There was thus no alternative text such as Baxter's proposal. However, Bishop Matthew Wren who had been imprisoned in the Tower of London had spent some of his time drawing up suggestions for revision, known as the Advices, and John Cosin had also made suggestions for revision in the margins of a 1619 edition of the Prayer Book, known as the Durham Book. This latter suggested a number of elements from the 1549 and 1637 Prayer Books. There was, however, no restoration of 1549 or the Scottish 1637 book. The 'Laudians' were well represented in the revision, being mostly in the hands of Matthew Wren, John Cosin, and Robert Sanderson, and some of the 'Laudian' preferences were incorporated by rubric rather than prayer. That of the 1662 Book of Common Prayer updated some of the language of Cranmer's prose, clarified ritual by additional rubrics, and provided some new prayers. In baptism, provision was made for explicit blessing of the water: 'sanctifie this water to the mysticall washing away of sin'. The prayer in the communion service that included the words of institution was unaltered, but now had the title that had been used in the 1637 Scottish book, 'the Prayer of Consecration'.

The new Annexed book, printed as the 'sealed books' (certified under the Great Seal) was signed by Convocation on 21 December 1661 and given the royal assent on 19 May 1662. It was to come into use no later than 24 August, St Bartholomew's Day, 1662. Clergy unwilling to assent to its use were ejected from their livings. The text was little altered from its predecessors reaching back to 1552. Brian Cummings has aptly noted:

> The new edition of 1662 is thus not an act of acclamation so much as one of conscious cultural retrieval...It was designed to give a sense of uninterruptedness while it also enacted a suppression of any genuinely new alternatives. For those who resuscitated it, this was an act of emotion as much as will. And religious emotion is just as much evident in those who demurred.[59]

---

[59] Brian Cummings, 'The 1662 Prayer Book', in Platten and Woods (eds.), *Comfortable Words*, pp. 69–82 (pp. 72–3).

SELECT BIBLIOGRAPHY

Bernard, George W. and Steven J. Gunn (eds.), *Authority and Consent in Tudor England* (Aldershot, 2002).

Cuming, Geoffrey, *The Godly Order: Texts and Studies relating to the Book of Common Prayer* (1983).

Cummings, Brian, *The Book of Common Prayer: The Texts of 1549, 1559, and 1662* (Oxford, 2011).

Donaldson, Gordon, *The Making of the Scottish Prayer Book of 1637* (Edinburgh, 1954).

Jeanes, Gordon P., *Signs of God's Promise: Thomas Cranmer's Sacramental Theology and the Book of Common Prayer* (2008).

Maltby, Judith, *Prayer Book and People in Elizabethan and Early Stuart England* (Cambridge, 1998).

Mears, Natalie and Alec Ryrie (eds.), *Worship and the Parish Church in Early Modern Britain* (Farnham, 2013).

Platten, Stephen and Christopher Woods (eds.), *Comfortable Words: Polity, Piety and the Book of Common Prayer* (2012).

Segger, Glen, *Richard Baxter's Reformed Liturgy: A Puritan Alternative to the Book of Common Prayer* (Farnham, 2014).

Spinks, Bryan D., *From the Lord and 'The Best Reformed Churches': A Study of the Eucharistic Liturgy in the English Puritan and Separatist Traditions 1550–1633* (Rome, 1984).

Spinks, Bryan D., 'Renaissance Liturgical Reforms: Reflections on Intentions and Methods', *Renaissance and Reformation*, 7 (2005): 268–82.

Spinks, Bryan D., *Sacraments, Ceremonies and the Stuart Divines: Sacramental Theology and Liturgy in England and Scotland 1603–1662* (Aldershot, 2002).

9

Canon Law and the Church of England

Gerald Bray

INTRODUCTION

Few people may have realized it at the time, but when the English Parliament passed the Act in Restraint of Appeals in 1533, making it illegal for any English person to appeal a court case to Rome after Easter (5 April) 1534, it changed the history of the English Church for ever.[1] For nearly a millennium, since the arrival of Augustine of Canterbury in 597, the Church had maintained close and generally harmonious relations with the Apostolic See.[2] Modern research in the papal archives has shown that about a quarter of all the cases heard before the Roman curia were of English provenance, evidence both of the litigiousness of the English and of their confidence in the papal courts. At home, the competence of the church courts had been defined in the *Articuli cleri* of 1316, which would remain essentially unchanged until the mid-nineteenth century.

The break which occurred in 1534 need not have been permanent, and it was reversed for a time during the reign of Mary I (1553–8), but the clock could not be turned back. Forces in favour of reform had been gathering even before the crisis over Henry VIII's desire to annul his marriage to Catherine of Aragon broke in 1529. The papacy was not needed to operate the Church's legal system, and when relations with it were broken off, little if anything changed. In the longer term, however, the source of its jurisdictional authority had been removed and it remained to be seen what effect that would have. Would the canon law be laicized and merged into the English common law, or

---

[1] G. L. Bray (ed.), *Documents of the English Reformation 1526–1701* (2nd edn., Cambridge, 2004), pp. 78–83.
[2] R. H. Helmholz, *The Oxford History of the Laws of England*, vol. I: *The Canon Law and Ecclesiastical Jurisdiction from 597 to the 1640s* (Oxford, 2004), pp. 95–100; Robert E. Rodes, *Lay Authority and Reformation in the English Church: Edward I to the Civil War* (Notre Dame, IN, 1982), pp. 59–66.

could it be re-established on a new foundation and allowed to continue its separate existence? In other Protestant countries the medieval canon law was often absorbed into the law of the state, but that was relatively easy because those countries had already 'received' Roman civil law in the fifteenth century.[3] In England the Roman canon law had to compete with a native common law that was not superseded and that would increasingly encroach on its jurisdiction. The abolition of the canon law faculties in Oxford and Cambridge (1535) helped to further this process, and although the canonists continued to operate and even to consolidate and expand their business to some degree in post-Reformation England, they could never escape this threat.[4]

Students of the English Reformation have generally concentrated on its political and religious aspects and ignored ecclesiastical law—a clear example of how modern perspectives influence the writing of history. For more than 300 years after the break with Rome, the ecclesiastical courts continued to administer the matrimonial and testamentary jurisdictions that they had inherited from the Middle Ages, giving them an importance that genealogists have always recognized and that social historians have now rediscovered.[5] But since 1858 these courts have been confined to internal church matters, making them of little interest to most modern historians. Only with the revival of Anglican canon law since 1945 has the significance of the sixteenth-century ecclesiastical jurisdiction been properly appreciated, and the sterling work of the Ecclesiastical Law Society has done more than anything else to stimulate scholarly interest in the subject.

This is long overdue, because in many respects it was the canon law and its limitations that provoked the English Reformation in the first place, and that continued to be the motivating force behind most of the controversies that disturbed the English Church for the next century and a half. The word 'canon' is simply the Greek for 'rule' and was applied to the law of the Church because it was based largely on rules (or canons) that had been adopted by ecclesiastical synods in the early centuries of Christianity. These canons followed the general pattern of ancient Roman law, with modifications due either to Christian influence (like the restrictions placed on divorce) or to compromise with local customs. Many of them were ad hoc responses to particular problems in one part of the Christian world or another, and for many centuries there was no overall control or consistency among them.

That began to change in the twelfth century as the power of the papacy grew and established its jurisdiction over the Western Church. About 1140 an

---

[3] R. H. Helmholz (ed.), *Canon Law in Protestant Lands* (Berlin, 1992).
[4] R. H. Helmholz, *Roman Canon Law in Reformation England* (Cambridge, 1990).
[5] E. J. Carlson, *Marriage and the English Reformation* (Oxford, 1994); R. Houlbrooke, *Church Courts and the People during the English Reformation, 1520-1570* (Oxford, 1979); M. Ingram, *Church Courts, Sex and Marriage in England, 1570-1640* (Cambridge, 1987).

Italian monk called Gratian attempted to reduce the canons to order in his magisterial textbook, the *Concordantia Discordantium Canonum* ('Concordance of Discordant Canons'), more usually known today as the *Decretum*. Gratian approached his subject by proposing various possible court cases and working out how they should be adjudicated. In the process he incorporated the canons of the major Church councils that had been held up to his time and provided his students with a pattern of reasoning that would become the foundation of canon law practice.

Gratian's work was supplemented by a series of papal decretals compiled and subdivided into five books by Pope Gregory IX in 1234. This is known to us as the *Liber Extra* (*X*) and it was in turn supplemented by another collection made by Pope Benedict VIII in 1298 and known to us as the *Liber Sextus* (*VI*) or 'sixth book'. There were further collections made by Pope Clement V in 1313, by Pope John XXII in 1325, and finally by the printer Jean Chappuis in 1503. Taken together, these collections are now known as the *Corpus Iuris Canonici* which formed the basis of the Church's law at the time of the Reformation.[6] The *Corpus* was abolished in most of Protestant Europe in the sixteenth century and replaced in the Roman Catholic Church in 1917, but by a quirk of history it remains valid in the Church of England to the extent that it has not been superseded by subsequent legislation.

To this universal law of the medieval Western Church must be added legislation that was peculiar to England. For practical purposes this consisted of the legatine decrees of Otho (1237) and of Othobon (1268), two cardinals who had been sent to England as papal legates charged with sorting out the internal affairs of the Church. These decrees were commented on by John of Atton (Ayton) around 1340 and his commentary became a standard source for English canonists. In 1430 William Lyndwood, the archbishop of Canterbury's chancellor since 1414, compiled a digest of the province's canons to which he added his own commentary. This work, known to us as the *Provinciale*, was published in 1433 and printed in 1505, with a final edition (the one usually cited today) in 1679.[7] The commentary grew and changed somewhat as the law developed, but it remained recognizably the same work and was accepted as foundational for English canon law. Lyndwood did not include the canons of the northern province of York, but his compilation was adopted there in 1462 insofar as it did not conflict with local legislation. In 1514 Thomas Wolsey, the newly appointed archbishop of York, put together a *Provinciale* for the north which survives in manuscript, but was never published.[8]

---

[6] E. Friedberger, *Corpus Iuris Canonici*, 2 vols. (Leipzig, 1879).

[7] W. Lyndwood, *Provinciale* (Oxford, 1679).

[8] G. L. Bray (ed.), *Records of Convocation*, 20 vols. (Woodbridge, 2005–6), XIV, pp. 493–9.

ECCLESIASTICAL JURISDICTION AND ADMINISTRATION

In 1534 the Church of England possessed a range of ecclesiastical courts belonging to its archbishops, bishops, and archdeacons. Theoretically these dignitaries were supposed to preside over them in person but they seldom did, leaving everyday administration to their vicars-general or officials principal. Originally these were separate offices but by 1500 they had generally coalesced into one. A case could be brought to the lowest of these courts (the archdeacon's) and then appealed to the bishop and the archbishop, but it was also possible to skip these intermediate steps and go straight to the top. As a result, the archbishops' courts became far more important than the others, which tended to fade into insignificance. From 1504 the official principal of Canterbury was invariably also the dean of the arches, a group of thirteen parishes in London centred on St Mary-le-Bow (hence the 'arches') where his court met. His equivalent in the northern province was the auditor of York and the two offices were finally merged in 1874. The lawyers who served these courts were known as advocates (barristers) and proctors (solicitors) and were trained in the faculties of canon law that existed in the universities of Oxford and Cambridge until they were abolished in 1535. Many of these advocates and proctors also had a degree in (Roman) civil law to which canon law was closely related and after the Reformation they staffed both the High Court of Admiralty and the High Court of Chivalry in addition to the ecclesiastical courts.[9] From about 1511 a separate law society known as Doctors' Commons was formed to provide a professional body for canon lawyers, which it did until it was dissolved in 1865.[10] Initially the doctors of canon and/or civil law were clergymen, but that ceased at a very early stage and since 1559 the dean of the arches has been a layman, with the single exception of Bishop Kenneth Elphinstone (1976–80).

The ecclesiastical courts had jurisdiction over two distinct groups of people. First came the 'spiritualty', consisting of the ordained clergy, as well as monks and nuns. They claimed exemption from the secular courts on the grounds that they belonged to a different estate of the realm, though this was disputed by the common lawyers who believed, with some justification, that the ecclesiastical courts were too lenient. After 1534 there was no question of granting the clergy exemption from the common law, but the original claim was preserved in the so-called 'benefit of clergy' by which any literate person could claim privileged treatment in the secular courts. Benefit of clergy was

---

[9] See G. D. Squibb, *High Court of Chivalry: A Study of the Civil Law in England* (Oxford, 1959).
[10] G. D. Squibb, *Doctors' Commons: A History of the College of Advocates and Doctors of Law* (Oxford, 1977).

frequently abused by being granted to anyone who could sign his name, but it was not finally abolished until 1827. The second group the courts had jurisdiction over was the lay population, who were directly affected in matrimonial and testamentary matters as well as in tithe and defamation suits.[11] The Church continued to claim the right to impose canon law and its penalties on the laity until that was struck down by the chief justice in 1736, but long before then, it had become customary for the common law courts to issue writs of prohibition, which prevented a case being taken to the church courts. Such prohibitions became widespread in the early seventeenth century and were a major bone of contention between the different legal jurisdictions until the suppression of the ecclesiastical courts in 1646. The overall effect of these prohibitions was to put the ecclesiastical courts on the defensive and to increase the common law jurisdiction, though it would be more than two centuries before the common law triumphed completely.

The abolition of appeals to Rome was compensated for by the creation of a Court of Delegates to hear appeal cases.[12] This was an ad hoc body, convened when necessary, but it never made much impression. It last sat in 1750 and was formally abolished in 1832. More significant and far better known were the Courts of High Commission, originally established in 1559. Their task was to monitor the progress of the Reformation at parish level and ensure that the royal injunctions were being observed. Under Elizabeth I they functioned fairly smoothly and gradually increased their range and influence. After about 1610 they policed the Church of England with such rigour that their very existence became one of the main causes of the opposition to the Personal Rule of Charles I. The abolition of these courts on 1 August 1641 was greeted by many as a triumph for liberty, and memories of their excesses played a significant part in hastening the decline of the ecclesiastical jurisdiction.[13]

Before the Reformation, English canonical legislation had been enacted by the provincial synods of Canterbury and York. The desire of the crown to tax the clergy had led to the creation of parliaments in the thirteenth century, to which the bishops and the clergy were invited. Very soon, the Church began to demand the right to tax itself because the hierarchy were afraid that lay resentment of their wealth and privileges would be taken out on them in the form of punitive taxation. This led to the emergence of tax convocations which were summoned by royal writ and met in each province to vote a subsidy to the crown when requested to do so. By 1400 they had merged with the provincial synods, which were now popularly referred to as convocations. The archbishops never relinquished the right to summon their synods, but

---

[11] R. B. Outhwaite, *The Rise and Fall of the English Ecclesiastical Courts, 1500–1860* (Cambridge, 2006).
[12] Helmholz, *History*, pp. 211–12.
[13] R. G. Usher, *The Rise and Fall of the High Commission* (Oxford, 1913).

they rarely did so, the last occasions being in 1509 (Canterbury) and 1515 (York), though the latter did not meet. In the 1520s, Thomas Wolsey, archbishop of York and the king's chief minister, tried to unite the clergy in a single national synod, using his powers as papal legate to do so, but this was resisted by Canterbury and after Wolsey's fall no more was heard of this. In 1529, Henry VIII summoned the Canterbury Convocation to meet at the same time as Parliament, but its northern counterpart was suspended because the disgraced Wolsey was still archbishop of York and it did not meet until 1531, after Wolsey's death.[14]

The king's strategy was to get Parliament to accuse the convocations of misgoverning the Church and to persuade them either to reform or to forfeit their jurisdiction. The bishops were able to show that these accusations were either groundless or grossly exaggerated, which enraged the king.[15] In response, he demanded the immediate submission of the Convocation which, after a few days' debate, he received on 15 May 1532, provoking Sir Thomas More's resignation as chancellor the following day. There then followed a long period of uncertainty when the convocations continued to meet but their future and functions remained in doubt. In 1536 Thomas Cromwell, keeper of the privy seal, imposed himself as president of the Canterbury Convocation, representing the king and symbolizing the royal supremacy over the Church, but this experiment was not repeated. In 1540 the two convocations met together, but that too proved to be ephemeral. The only enduring legacy of this period was that from 1545 the Canterbury Convocation was summoned to meet on the day after the opening of Parliament and both bodies were dissolved at the same time, an arrangement that was to last (with one notable exception in 1640) until 1966. The York Convocation was normally summoned a few days after the Canterbury one and dissolved along with it.

The convocations continued their deliberations throughout this time, but Church reforms were enacted either by Parliament or by a series of royal injunctions issued by Henry VIII in 1536 and again in 1538, and then by each of his successors until the accession of Elizabeth I.[16] Apart from those of Mary I in 1554, which sought to reverse the changes made in the previous reign, these reforms all enjoined a radical restructuring of the parish churches, pushing the pattern of devotion in a clearly Protestant direction. By 1559 it was clear that the worship and doctrine of the Church would be legislated by Parliament, with or without the approval of the convocations, though members of the latter (especially bishops) were usually asked to prepare the legislation. A semblance of clerical order was thereby preserved, even though the crown and its advisers remained in firm control.

---

[14] S. E. Lehmberg, *The Reformation Parliament, 1529–1536* (Cambridge, 1970).
[15] Bray (ed.), *Documents*, pp. 57–70.
[16] Bray (ed.), *Documents*, pp. 175–83, 247–57, 315–17, 335–48.

After 1559 however, the Canterbury Convocation came back to life and began to enact new canons for the Church, which it submitted to the queen for ratification (canons were prepared in 1571, 1575, 1584, and 1597).[17] Royal ratification was refused until 1597, for reasons that are not clear. The queen was always very cautious in religious matters, and perhaps she did not want to risk a confrontation with Parliament that might have resulted if she had ratified the Convocation's canons without its consent. What we know for certain is that when she finally relented there was no opposition from Parliament and the legality of the 1597 canons was not questioned.

The accession of James I in 1603 provided an opportunity to renew the canon law, which was deemed to have lapsed on the demise of the previous sovereign. James entrusted this task to John Whitgift, who was still archbishop of Canterbury, though Whitgift died before he could do anything. The commission was renewed on 20 March 1604 (1603 Old Style) and given to Richard Bancroft, then still bishop of London but soon to succeed Whitgift at Canterbury. Bancroft was the major figure behind a series of measures that James I took to strengthen the Church of England, not least by restoring a degree of financial independence and clerical discipline that had been neglected under Elizabeth. Bancroft saw the canons as a major part of this project, and did everything he could to ensure that they would be as traditional (and traditionalist) as possible. Puritan discontent with this was expressed mainly through the House of Commons, which for the first time challenged the legality of the procedure whereby the king could ratify canons devised by the Canterbury Convocation without their consent. The stage was set for confrontation and the canons of 1604 may be seen as the first step in a journey that would lead eventually to the civil war and the sundering of the unity of the Church of England.

Having said that, there is no doubt that the 1604 canons were much more detailed and systematic than anything that had appeared since the Reformation.[18] They incorporated most of what had been adopted since 1571 and included elements from the royal Injunctions and the *Corpus Iuris Canonici*. They were ratified by the king and by the York Convocation as well (in 1606) but not by Parliament, a fact that was later used as justification for claiming that they were not binding on the laity. However, the Reformation Parliament had forbidden the convocations from making any canons that were contrary to the laws of the realm, and many observers believed that only Parliament could decide whether particular canons were repugnant to its legislation or not. The king, however, ratified them independently and the bishops proceeded to enforce them, much to the chagrin of many puritans, who felt that they were being unfairly targeted.[19] Nevertheless, the 1604 canons remained

---

[17] G. L. Bray (ed.), *The Anglican Canons, 1529–1947* (Woodbridge, 1998), pp. 172–257.
[18] Bray (ed.), *Anglican Canons*, pp. 258–453.
[19] S. B. Babbage, *Puritanism and Richard Bancroft* (1962), esp. pp. 99–102.

in force (apart from the period of the civil war and Interregnum), with only minor alterations, until they were superseded in two stages, in 1964 and 1969, and so they have come to be regarded as the 'classical' form of English canon law.

At the time, however, their permanence could not have been foreseen and it was not long before further suggestions were being proposed. In 1606 a series of canons were drawn up and presented by the prolocutor of Convocation, the dean of St Paul's John Overall, that advanced an extreme form of royal supremacy supposedly based on the Bible.[20] James I wisely rejected them, but they resurfaced in 1690 and were acknowledged (if not formally adopted) by the non-jurors who refused to accept the Williamite succession. In the next reign, a disastrous attempt was made to impose a highly conservative set of canons on the Scottish Church (1636) which was followed by the promulgation of new canons for England in 1640.[21] These were passed by the Canterbury Convocation which was kept in session after the dissolution of Parliament, but because this procedure was unprecedented, their legality remained in doubt until they were formally abolished in 1969, and the bishops never tried to enforce them.

THE FAILURE OF CANON LAW REFORM

The Convocation that was summoned to meet in tandem with the 1529 Parliament was not immune to the spirit of reform and thought that it could meet the demands of the Church's critics by legislating for a stricter observance of the Church's traditional laws and practices. Bishops were enjoined to reside in their dioceses, particularly at Easter, so that they would be able to consecrate the holy chrism used in baptism and distribute it to their clergy. This had been an important sign of episcopal authority in the medieval Church, but the Convocation's insistence on it is typical of its backward-looking approach. Within a few years the whole rite would be abolished by the Reformers, who regarded it as a superstitious addition to the pure gospel. Other proposed measures included upgrading clerical education, which had become notoriously inadequate and the abolition of letters dimissory, by which one bishop could allow another to ordain a man from his diocese. These were all recognized abuses, but putting them right would have done little more than scratch the surface of the underlying problems and so it is not surprising that these canons got lost in the politics of the next few years and were never enacted.

[20] Bray (ed.), *Anglican Canons*, pp. 454–84.
[21] Bray (ed.), *Anglican Canons*, pp. 532–78.

What the king wanted was control of the Church, and that could only be achieved by a much more fundamental process of change. The submission of the Canterbury Convocation in 1532 was a first step along the way, as was the progressive dismantling of the Church's remaining links with the papacy. Once that was achieved, a thorough overhaul of the Church's law could be envisaged. Henry VIII began by dissolving the canon law faculties at Oxford and Cambridge, a move which effectively laicized the ecclesiastical legal profession. In the articles of submission the king had promised to establish a commission which would prepare a revised set of canons for use in a non-papal Church, and work on this was begun in mid-1534. The resulting 'Henrician canons' were ready by October 1535.[22] In essence they appear to be a digest of the canons that were actually in force at the time, and in many cases they do no more than extract texts verbatim from Lyndwood or the *Corpus Iuris Canonici*. Only occasionally are they modified in any way, and then it is usually to specify something that had previously been regarded as a matter of custom. For example, suspension from duties was a common canonical punishment for misdemeanours but the length of time it was to last was not specified. The compilers of the Henrician canons tended to add that it should be for a three-year period (*per triennium*), which we assume was already fairly standard practice. The project was soon abandoned, however, and the king probably never saw the canons, which disappeared from view and were not rediscovered until 1974.

The canon law commission was renewed in 1536 and again in 1544, but when Henry VIII died in 1547, nothing had been done. A new commission was formed in October 1551 and set to work, though it is not clear how many of the commissioners took part in the deliberations.[23] What is certain is that a draft was prepared in the course of 1552 under the direction of Archbishop Thomas Cranmer. It made use of the Henrician canons to some extent, but it was essentially a new work that incorporated the teaching of the Forty-Two Articles and the revised Book of Common Prayer, both of which appeared in the same year. But whereas the Articles and the Prayer Book both received royal sanction, the canon law, later dubbed the *Reformatio Legum Ecclesiasticarum*, was blocked in the House of Lords and disappeared.[24] An attempt was made to revive it in 1571, and again in 1640, but they both failed to make any impression. By then things had moved on to the point where a further major revision would have been necessary, and rather than attempt that, the whole project was allowed to lapse. Had the *Reformatio* been adopted it would have allowed for divorce in the modern sense, which did not appear in England

---

[22] G. L. Bray (ed.), *Tudor Church Reform* (Woodbridge, 2000), pp. 4–143.
[23] Bray (ed.), *Tudor Church Reform*, pp. xli–liv.
[24] Bray (ed.), *Tudor Church Reform*, pp. 150–743.

until the nineteenth century.[25] As it was, the *Reformatio* acquired a kind of surrogate authority thanks to Edmund Gibson, who included several of its provisions in his *Codex Iuris Ecclesiae Anglicanae*, which first appeared in 1713.[26]

A final attempt at canonical reform was made by Cardinal Reginald Pole in his capacity as papal legate during the reign of Mary I. Pole had been involved in similar reform projects in the German dioceses of Cologne, Mainz, and Trier, and he brought them with him to England. His canons were adopted by a legatine synod on 10 February 1556 and remained in force until the queen's death on 17 November 1558, but whether they were ever applied remains a mystery.[27] An attempt to do so was made by the Canterbury Convocation in 1558, but by then it was too late. Whatever their intentions may have been, both Mary and Pole have gone down in history as persecutors of the Church and not as reformers, and whatever they achieved died with them.

THE ELIZABETHAN CANONS

In 1563 Queen Elizabeth I allowed the Canterbury Convocation to produce the Thirty-Nine Articles, a revision of the Forty-Two Articles which had received royal sanction in 1553, though probably without Convocation's approval.[28] In 1566 she addressed the controversy over clerical vestments in the so-called 'Advertisements', which are generally seen as a conservative reaction to proposals being put forward by more advanced Protestant ministers.[29] Following the queen's excommunication by the Pope in 1570, she was forced to strengthen her support base in the Church by leaning in a more Protestant direction. The Thirty-Nine Articles were revised and the Canterbury Convocation passed a series of canons that were clearly Protestant in character.[30] A particular concern of these canons was to define the scope of excommunication, which had become the standard censure for all manner of offences, including contempt of an ecclesiastical court. Abuse of this was a particular fear of the laity and the willingness of the Church authorities to satisfy them shows how far things had moved since 1529.

The 1571 canons were the first to make it clear that preachers were to teach nothing that could not be proved from the Old and New Testaments, a provision that clearly upheld the Protestant principle of *sola scriptura*, and they were to interpret the text along the lines laid down in the ancient councils

---

[25] L. Dibdin, *English Church Law and Divorce* (1912), pp. 3–79.
[26] Bray (ed.), *Tudor Church Reform*, pp. cvi–cxiii, 773–82.
[27] Bray (ed.), *Anglican Canons*, pp. 68–161.
[28] D. MacCulloch, *Thomas Cranmer* (New Haven, CT, 1996), p. 536.
[29] Bray (ed.), *Anglican Canons*, pp. 163–71.
[30] Bray (ed.), *Anglican Canons*, pp. 172–209.

and creeds of the Church.[31] They were also obliged to subscribe to the Articles of Religion and to accept that the Book of Common Prayer (as revised in 1559) and the Ordinal contained nothing that was not compatible with Holy Scripture. It was this last provision that was to cause trouble later on, because many puritans believed that the Prayer Book (in particular) required further revision in order to eliminate any remaining vestiges of 'popery'.

The canons also tried to insist on a learned ministry who would reside on their benefices and teach their parishioners in a systematic fashion, but this was more easily said than done. It was practically impossible to eject ministers who were already in post, or to provide enough university graduates to meet the need. As a result the canons compromised on the standards required, but they were adamant that the regulation clerical dress imposed in 1566 should be worn at all services. If the inward substance could not be immediately attained, then at least the outward forms would be observed, an approach which infuriated the puritans and sowed the seeds of future conflict. The long-term impact of this should not be underestimated. Even today, Anglicans tend to be obsessed with clerical dress in a way that other Christians find peculiar, and it is perhaps symptomatic of this that the effective abolition of control over this in recent times has led to the proliferation of both extremes with no consensus in the middle.

The inadequacy of the provisions made for preachers in the 1571 canons is fully revealed by the next set, which was approved by the Canterbury Convocation that met in February–March 1576.[32] These were composed mainly by Archbishop Edmund Grindal, who was a well-known advocate of a preaching ministry. It is clear from their tenor that the standard of preachers had not improved and all licences for preaching that had been issued before 8 February 1576 were withdrawn. Only graduates resident in their home dioceses would henceforth be ordained and all candidates would have to demonstrate that there was a benefice or other ecclesiastical office that wanted them. The problem of non-preaching ministers was to be dealt with by insisting that they should all acquire a New Testament and be periodically examined on it by the archdeacon or other competent official. An interesting touch here is that the New Testament could be in Latin, English, or Welsh—the first time that a minority language was specifically mentioned in a canon.

Most of the other canons of 1576 merely tighten up existing provisions, but it must be noted that one designed to restrict private baptism and another that would have permitted the solemnization of marriage at any time of the year, were omitted from the final version, presumably because the queen objected to them. If so, this is the first clear indication we have that she was putting the brakes on 'puritanism', an impression that would be confirmed the following

---

[31] Bray (ed.), *Anglican Canons*, pp. 196–9.
[32] Bray (ed.), *Anglican Canons*, pp. 211–15.

year when Archbishop Grindal was sequestered and relieved of his duties because of his support for preaching conferences at which the clergy would help each other to improve their sermon techniques. Elizabeth suspected any gatherings of the clergy that she did not control, an attitude that was bound to get her into trouble with the more convinced Protestants sooner or later.

The next series of canons was adopted in 1584, shortly after John Whitgift became archbishop of Canterbury.[33] Unlike Grindal, Whitgift was on good terms with the queen and defended her policies, with the result that his prescriptions for the reform of the Church met with greater acceptance at court. Like the canons of 1571 and 1576, those of 1584 show a continued concern for standards in the ministry and raised the bar higher than it had been before, since candidates would henceforth have to give an account of their faith in Latin before being ordained. In effect this meant expounding the Thirty-Nine Articles and providing the biblical evidence on which they were based. How far this was put into practice is hard to say, but it is notable that the first full-length commentary on the Articles was produced the following year by Thomas Rogers (d. 1616), a puritan clergyman who later became a staunch defender of the establishment.[34] Furthermore, penalties for instituting unqualified persons were introduced for the first time, though this was made less effective by the deletion of a clause which would have penalized patrons for doing this. As so often, powerful vested interests, in this case those of William Cecil, Lord Burghley, could (and did) thwart widely desired reforms.

The remaining canons deal with the now familiar abuses that seemed impossible to eradicate. Marriage without banns was severely restricted, excommunication was once more tightened up, pluralism was tolerated (as it had not been in 1571) but only for those able to serve more than one parish at a time, and ecclesiastical fees were fixed at their 1558 level. To ensure compliance with this, a table of fees was to be set up in every parish church, and the survival of a number of these indicates that the order was actually carried out.

The last set of canons to be passed in Elizabeth's reign were those of the Convocation of 1597, which re-enacted the canons of 1584 and added a number of extra provisions.[35] One of them was an insistence that beneficed clergy should not only reside on their benefices but provide hospitality—essentially poor relief—there, which had not appeared anywhere in earlier legislation. Deans and canons in cathedral churches were also obliged to preach there from time to time, and further restrictions were placed on marriages without the reading of banns.

[33] Bray (ed.), *Anglican Canons*, pp. 216–31.
[34] Thomas Rogers, *The English Creede, Consenting withe the True Ancient Catholique, and Apostolique Church in al the Pointes, and Articles of Religion which Everie Christian is to Knowe* (1585–7).
[35] Bray (ed.), *Anglican Canons*, pp. 232–57.

The 1597 canons are especially interesting because they treat of 'divorce' for the first time after the Reformation. There had been no divorce in the modern sense in the medieval Church, which granted only annulments and legal separations. In 1597 this traditional position was reaffirmed and accompanied by instructions as to how it should be applied. Annulments were not to be granted except when there was clear proof that they were justified, and separated couples were to live celibate lives, something that had not previously been specified.

The canons also demanded regular church attendance on pain of excommunication, a provision that was specifically designed to counter the growing threat of recusancy at both ends of the theological spectrum. Roman Catholics were the obvious target, but so too were puritan separatists, who had become a factor to be reckoned with in the years after the failure of the Spanish Armada in 1588. These puritans had grown tired of waiting for the queen to die so that her ecclesiastical settlement could be revised and some of them were starting to form conventicles of their own, outside the bounds of the Established Church. There is also a long section on the payment of fees, which were now to be reported to the bishop. These transcripts still survive in most cases and provide a useful back-up for information about baptisms, weddings, and funerals that may have been lost at parish level. There had clearly been some laxity in the keeping of parish registers, and this too was censured, much to the delight of modern genealogists who generally find that parish record-keeping improved after this date.

The ratification of the 1597 canons was effectively also a ratification of those published in 1584 and included many of those from 1571 as well. It had taken a long time, but in the end, the Elizabethan canon law entered the life of the Church of England and remained enforceable at law, even after the canons of a later date were declared to be inapplicable to the laity.

THE EARLY STUART CANONS

When James VI of Scotland ascended the English throne as James I there were high hopes among the puritans that finally their demands for change would be heard. James appreciated their Calvinist theology and largely shared it, but he did not like their radical programme for the Church and did his best to maintain as much of the Elizabethan Settlement as he could. Indeed, in his desire to unite the Churches of England and Scotland, he was inclined to go the other way and introduce English practices into his homeland. Scotland was stony ground as far as that was concerned and James was wise enough not to push his compatriots too far, but his son Charles I had no such scruples and his attempts to impose conformity of religion across the British Isles on the English model led him and his three kingdoms to disaster.

James inherited a Church in which Roman canon law had continued to exert a certain influence, and by the time he came to the throne this could be openly acknowledged with little protest.[36] The chief conduit for this influence was the growing body of literature on procedure in the ecclesiastical courts and treatises written by the advocates who practised in them. Foremost among them was Francis Clerke's *Praxis in Curiis Ecclesiasticis*, which he wrote in 1596 and which soon became a standard work all over England. It is, however, symptomatic that it was not printed until 1666 (in Dublin), although numerous manuscript copies survive. Many of them contain notes taken from continental sources, which proves that they were still being read and consulted.[37]

The king also discovered that both John Whitgift and his successor Richard Bancroft were determined to restore the rights and privileges of the Church which had been seized by the crown and distributed to various lay interests after the Reformation. In many cases, essential tithe revenue had been alienated and unless it could be recovered, a preaching ministry in every parish could not be sustained.[38] Their campaign received the king's support, but it was contested by powerful interests in Parliament, which did not want to lose the revenue that had been diverted to the landowning classes. Eventually, much of what the archbishops fought for was won, especially after 1613, when Sir Henry Spelman produced a book warning people of the dire fate that awaited those who were guilty of sacrilege. Spelman's views were challenged by John Selden, but although Selden's criticisms would eventually triumph (in 1836!), it was Spelman who carried the day at the time.[39] Surprising as it might seem today, Spelman's censures persuaded several laypeople to surrender their tithe impropriations and the Church's finances were gradually put on a sounder footing. It was in this climate of a reorganization that was designed to strengthen the administrative machinery of the Church, that the shape and significance of the 1604 canons must be understood.

The 1604 canons begin with a section (Canons 1–13) devoted to the royal supremacy, the legitimacy of the Church of England, and a series of censures against those who called its worship and doctrine into question. In theory this hit Catholics as much as Protestant nonconformists, but the canons directed against opponents of episcopacy, promoters of 'schism' within the Church and members of 'conventicles' made it clear where the emphasis lay.

After the opening section there is one dealing with worship and the administration of the sacraments (Canons 14–30), which enjoins the use of the prescribed forms of service on Sundays and holy days and even orders

---

[36] Helmholz, *Roman Canon Law*, pp. 41–51.
[37] Helmholz, *Roman Canon Law*, pp. 128–31.
[38] C. Hill, *Economic Problems of the Church from Archbishop Whitgift to the Long Parliament* (Oxford, 1956).
[39] Henry Spelman, *De Non Temerandis Ecclesiis: A Tract of the Rights and Respect due unto the Churches* (1613); John Selden, *The Historie of Tithes* (1618).

students to wear surplices in college chapels. Church members were expected to receive holy communion at least three times a year (and students four times) and in cathedral churches copes were to be worn by the celebrants. The clergy were expected to 'fence the table' by barring notorious offenders, schismatics, and strangers from communion, and much was said about the use of the sign of the cross in baptism. These things were regarded by the puritans as useless rituals verging on popery and they were initially very hostile to them. Over time, however, they moderated their opposition and even appealed to them against what they saw as the excesses of Archbishop Laud.

The next section (Canons 31–76) deals with the ordained ministry, beginning with their ordination and proceeding from there to the details of their institution to a benefice and then to what was expected of them once they were in the parish. Most of this material is unexceptional, though it is set out with a degree of orderly logic not hitherto found in any comparable document. Only occasionally does an anti-puritan note sound, but when it does it is unmistakable. Canon 53 enjoins ministers not to criticize one another in the pulpit, and puritans were prone to condemn the laxity of their colleagues. Canon 54 voids the preaching licences of those who refuse to conform to the rules of the Church, another puritan foible. Laypeople were not to refuse to receive communion from ministers who were not licensed to preach (Canon 57), which only puritans would be inclined to do, and the surplice makes another appearance in Canon 58, where it is prescribed for any minister leading divine service or administering the sacraments. Puritans, of course, preferred the black Geneva gown and tended to regard the surplice as a relic of popery. It is true that Canon 66 enjoins ministers to remonstrate with Roman Catholic recusants and to urge them to conform to the Established Church, but the canon is fairly weak and cannot have been easy to enforce. Private ministry of all kinds is forbidden, a provision that cut both ways, and in all things ministers were to defer to the forms of service authorized by the Church, which most of them did.[40]

There then follows a short section dealing with schoolmasters (Canons 77–9), who are included because the Church was responsible for educational provision. After that comes a section (Canons 80–8) dealing with the church building and its fabric, which had to be kept in good repair. This seems sensible enough to us but these canons could be interpreted to suggest that outward decoration was more important than inward spiritual commitment, and so a subtle anti-puritan bias can be detected here as well.

Next come canons dealing with churchwardens, sidesmen, and parish clerks (Canons 89–91), all of whom were now laymen, followed by a long section (Canons 92–138) dealing with the ecclesiastical courts and their officers. Most

---

[40] K. Fincham, *Prelate as Pastor: The Episcopate of James I* (Oxford, 1990), p. 323.

of these canons are unremarkable, although there are a number that oblige the churchwardens or other responsible people to present delinquents to the Church authorities for punishment. This procedure, which was commonly followed in the ecclesiastical courts, was directly contrary to the common law and caused enormous resentment because of the obvious opportunity it offered for abuse. Few things were as deeply resented as presentments, and with the revival of the High Commission courts and their zeal for imposing stricter discipline, the door was open to all kinds of misuse.

The last canons (139–41) deal briefly with the dignity and prestige of synods, by which the Convocation of Canterbury was especially meant. Rather remarkably, given the canonists' attention to protocol, that Convocation is even called 'the sacred synod of this nation' (Canon 139) as if its northern counterpart did not exist. Criticism of the synod's behaviour was treated as an offence, and since such criticism was largely of puritan origin, it is easy to detect an anti-puritan bias here as well.

The last set of canons to be adopted by the Canterbury Convocation were those of 1640.[41] Though only seventeen in number, they touched on matters of great controversy at the time and were divisive from the start. The first two deal with royal authority and prestige, which the Church was expected to uphold at a time when the king was rapidly squandering them. Popery was duly condemned and so was Socinianism, a unitarian heresy that had appeared since 1603, but as might be expected, the bulk of the remainder are devoted to opposing 'sectaries', in other words puritans, who were on the verge of seizing control of Parliament. The canon most deeply objected to was the sixth one, which enjoined an oath on the clergy that promised total obedience to the Church as it then stood. After listing certain obvious particulars, the oath includes the words 'et cetera', which theoretically left the door open to the inclusion of anything that the administrator of the oath might deem to belong to the proper order of the Church. Such a blank cheque was sure to be misused by people who were used to the procedures of the High Commission courts, and so it became the focus around which discontent with these canons gathered.

From the start, Parliament objected to these canons and frustrated their implementation. Before long, the High Commission courts were abolished, the archbishop of Canterbury was arrested, and the country slid into a civil war that led to the overthrow of both the crown and the Established Church. When the Church was reconstituted in 1660 it was no longer possible to impose the kind of discipline that the authorities had envisaged a generation earlier, despite some attempts to do so. The old order returned in form but not in substance, not least because the younger generation of clergy and canon

---

[41] Bray (ed.), *Anglican Canons*, pp. 553–78.

lawyers had lost the sense of continuity with the traditional Church that had existed before 1640. The Convocations were revived but after hammering out the settlement of 1662, they gave up their traditional right to tax themselves and quickly faded into obscurity. The Canterbury Convocation was allowed to meet again from 1701 to 1717, but was eventually suspended because of internal squabbling, and apart from a brief flurry of activity in 1742, it was not revived until 1852. The York Convocation, on the other hand, slumbered on uninterruptedly until 1861, when it too re-emerged. The church courts continued to exist but they were shadows of their former selves and the canon law was honoured as much in the breach as in the observance. Nonconformity, a word which derives its meaning from the puritan attitude to the canons, had come to stay, and although it would be a generation before it was tolerated and a further 150 years before it acquired legal standing, it could never again be ignored or uprooted. The Church of England lost its monopoly and could no longer impose its teachings on a nation that was free to worship elsewhere—or not at all.

CONCLUSION

The history of English canon law from 1529 to 1662 is the story of how an ancient institution adapted to the changing circumstances brought about by a theological revolution. The new was embraced and initially looked as though it would overpower the old, but as time went on, much of the old returned and found its place alongside what was new. Some of what was done had an ephemeral life and soon disappeared, but the canons of 1604 lasted into the second half of the twentieth century and have marked Anglicanism more than we realize. That the canon law was manipulated for political ends that eventually split the Church is a misfortune whose effects the Church of England still feels, but which must be understood if we are to make any sense of modern Anglicanism and of its relations with the other Protestant Churches of English origin.

SELECT BIBLIOGRAPHY

Baker, J. H., *Monuments of Endlesse Labours: English Canonists and their Work, 1300–1900* (1998).

Bray, G. L. (ed.), *The Anglican Canons, 1529–1947* (Woodbridge, 1998).

Bray, G. L. (ed.), *Documents of the English Reformation 1526-1701* (2nd edn., Cambridge, 2004).

Bray, G. L. (ed.), *Records of Convocation*, 20 vols. (Woodbridge, 2005–6).
Bray, G. L. (ed.), *Tudor Church Reform* (Woodbridge, 2000).
Carlson, E. J., *Marriage and the English Reformation* (Oxford, 1994).
Helmholz, R. H., *The Oxford History of the Laws of England*, vol. I: *The Canon Law and Ecclesiastical Jurisdiction from 597 to the 1640s* (Oxford, 2004).
Helmholz, R. H., *Roman Canon Law in Reformation England* (Cambridge, 1990).
Houlbrooke, R., *Church Courts and the People during the English Reformation, 1520–1570* (Oxford, 1979).
Ingram, M., *Church Courts, Sex and Marriage in England, 1570–1640* (Cambridge, 1987).
Lehmberg, S. E., *The Reformation Parliament, 1529–1536* (Cambridge, 1970).
Marchant, R. A., *The Church under the Law: Justice, Administration and Discipline in the Diocese of York, 1560–1640* (Cambridge, 1969).
Outhwaite, R. B., *The Rise and Fall of the English Ecclesiastical Courts, 1500–1860* (Cambridge, 2006).
Rodes, R. E., *Lay Authority and Reformation in the English Church: Edward I to the Civil War* (Notre Dame, IN, 1982).
Usher, R. G., *The Rise and Fall of the High Commission* (Oxford, 1913).

10

Art and Iconoclasm

Felicity Heal

'Better it were that the arts of painting, plastering, carving, graving, and founding, had never been found nor used, than one of them, whose souls in the sight of God are so precious, should by occasion of image or picture perish and be lost.'[1] Thus the 'Homily against the Peril of Idolatry' (1563) weighed the sacred arts against the danger of image worship, reflecting in the aftermath of the Elizabethan Settlement on a battle that was only half-won by the Protestant clergy. Campaigns against idolatry had been waged in the 1530s, in Edward VI's reign, and during and after the Royal Visitation of 1559. In 1547 the Injunctions ordered the removal of 'abused' images, to be followed in 1548 by the more comprehensive insistence that 'images, shrines, candlesticks, trindals or rolls of wax, pictures, paintings' be utterly 'abolished and destroyed'. But in 1559 the royal Injunctions tempered the bluntness of this second Edwardian prohibition, ordering destruction without specific mention of images, and returning to an emphasis on abuse. There should be no preaching extolling the dignity of 'abused images, relics or miracles', no retention of 'abused' images in houses.[2] Though the queen's Visitors did their best to interpret these injunctions in the light of the accompanying articles that explicitly ordered the removal and destruction of all images, there was here a studied ambiguity which gave countenance to those, led by Elizabeth, who saw the visual representation of the holy as an acceptable part of Protestant worship. The specific conflict between the monarch and her new bishops concerned the retention of the crucifix and candlesticks in the Chapel Royal.[3] Her choice could not have

---

[1] John Griffiths (ed.), *The Two Books of Homilies Appointed to be Read in Churches* (Oxford, 1859), p. 243.

[2] W. H. Frere and W. M. Kennedy (eds.), *Visitation Articles and Injunctions of the Period of the Reformation* (hereafter *VAI*), 3 vols. (1910), II, pp. 114ff.; III, pp. 9, 16, 21; Margaret Aston, *England's Iconoclasts: Laws against Images* (Oxford, 1988), pp. 298–303.

[3] William P. Haugaard, *Elizabeth and the Reformation: The Struggle for a Stable Settlement of Religion* (Cambridge, 1968), pp. 183–200; Aston, *England's Iconoclasts*, pp. 306–9, 313–14.

been more damaging to the cause of reform for, as Edwin Sandys wrote to Peter Martyr in 1560, 'the ignorant and superstitious multitude are in the habit of paying adoration to this idol before all others'.[4]

The unresolved conflict of 1559 to 1560 explains why the attack on idolatry became such a key defining feature of the early Elizabethan Church. The prelates and other zealous reformers looked back on the stripping of the altars under Edward as the time when the nation had been bound in godly covenant, and had turned away from the false worship of images. Since then the Church had once again been polluted by religious iconography and saint cults, and yet the opportunity for complete cleansing was now denied. It was in this environment that the second edition of the Homilies contained its extremely lengthy and detailed attack on idolatry, and, as Margaret Aston has shown, that the famous painting of Edward VI trampling popish idolatry while the dying Henry VIII urged him onwards, was produced.[5] It seems that the Church of England was even more exercised about image worship than its continental neighbours: Lutheranism had largely made its peace with non-abused images; most of the Reformed churches had briskly removed all sign of such visual stimulus.[6]

We can trace the doctrinal development of the attack on images in England, but explaining the intensity of hostility to paintings on the wall, pictures in stained glass, and even free-standing carvings of Christ and the saints is less easy.[7] The Homilies adopted a variety of approaches—that Scripture ordained the removal of images; that they had been assailed by the Fathers; that their legitimate role as aids to memorializing individuals in private houses had gradually allowed them to creep into churches and be reverenced; that true preachers of the Word were costly and could not compete with icons that could be purchased and adorned with little money. The scriptural obligation to act emanated, of course, from the Second Commandment, which in its fully developed Protestant form began, 'Thou shalt not make unto thee any graven Image, or any likeness of anything that is in heaven above, or that is in the earth beneath'. No Elizabethan schoolboy could fail to learn the catechetical lesson that images were idolatrous: 'he [God] first forbiddeth us to make any images to expresse or counterfeit God...and secondly he chargeth us not to worship the images themselves'.[8]

---

[4] Hastings Robinson (ed.), *Zurich Letters*, 2 vols. (Cambridge, 1842), I, p. 74.

[5] Margaret Aston, *The King's Bedpost: Reformation and Iconography in a Tudor Group Portrait* (Cambridge, 1991).

[6] Carlos M. N. Eire, *War Against the Idols: the Reformation of Worship from Erasmus to Calvin* (Cambridge, 1986).

[7] John Phillips, *The Reformation of Images: Destruction of Art in England, 1535–1660* (Berkeley, CA, 1973); Aston, *England's Iconoclasts*, pp. 343–480.

[8] Alexander Nowell, *A Catechisme, or First Instruction and Learning of Christian Religion* (1571), fol. 8r.

At the heart of contemporary fears was the conviction, expressed in the Homilies, that an image, especially a free-standing statue, 'enticeth the ignorant, so that he honoureth and loveth the picture of a dead image that hath no soul'. The episodic survival of defaced statues and paintings suggests that the hostility of the iconoclasts was often directed to the head and hands of the saints, attacking those aspects of the image that were feared to embody the spirit of the holy figure.[9] 'Executing' a statue, in the way that the Lady Chapel carvings in Ely Cathedral were decapitated, reflected a fear that observers thought the saint somehow alive and threatening.[10] In an interesting argument about the relationship between icons and literacy Ellen Spolsky suggests that the reformers were right to fear the embodied power of the image. Current cognitive models suggest that the brain processes physical images very differently from abstract ideas, and that representations that are constantly reinforced construct deep networks of association. 'To take away the statue', she says, 'would be like teaching people to play basketball, then taking away the ball and expecting them to keep playing'.[11] In this sense, popular attachment to images was deeply embedded in the mind, and, especially if located in a crucial setting such as the altar, they could stimulate a veneration that was a form of worship. To leap from this form of association to an understanding based upon the word was a formidable challenge, employing aspects of the brain that were inevitably underdeveloped in many Tudor men and women in the pew. Theologians had some understanding of the importance of this brain patterning. Thomas Aquinas had recognized that the saints would 'be stronger in our memory when they are represented daily to the eyes'.[12] Nicholas Sander, writing against the iconoclasts in his *A Treatise of the Images of Christ* (1567), argued that 'we can not learne, know, or understand any thing without conceiving the same in some corporal Image or likenes'.[13]

When Protestant preachers worried about the possibility of men lapsing into idolatry, they were acknowledging the power of visual perception and the difficulty of escaping from the image formed and reinforced in the mind. The mind has such imagination that it is, to quote Calvin, 'a perpetual factory of idols...the mind begets an idol; the hand brings it forth'.[14] So idols of the

---

[9] C. Pamela Graves, 'From an Archaeology of Iconoclasm to an Anthropology of the Body: Images, Punishment and Personhood in England, 1500–1660', *Current Anthropology*, 49 (2008): 35–60.

[10] Ann Kibbey, *The Interpretation of Material Shapes in Puritanism* (Cambridge, 1986), pp. 45–50.

[11] Ellen Spolsky, 'Literacy after Iconoclasm in the English Reformation', *Journal of Medieval and Early Modern Studies*, 39 (2009): 305–30 (quotation at pp. 309–10).

[12] Quoted in Margaret Aston, 'Gods, Saints and Reformers: Portraiture and Protestant England', in Lucy Gent (ed.), *Albion's Classicism: The Visual Arts in Britain, 1550–1660* (New Haven, CT, 1995), p. 186.

[13] Nicholas Sander, *A Treatise of the Images of Christ* (Louvain, 1567), fol. 43r.

[14] John Calvin, *Institutes of the Christian Religion*, trans. John Allen, 3 vols. (Philadelphia, PA, 1909), I, pp. 104–5.

mind combined with the statues and paintings arrayed in the church to defraud the ear of its rightful primacy over the eye, and the intellect over all the senses.[15] 'The nature of man', alleged the puritan Samuel Hieron, 'is very enclinable to affect rather that which some outward shew offereth it selfe unto the eie, than to content it selfe with the bare and naked instruction of the eare'. Some godly preachers, committed to the centrality of hearing, even feared that the deaf might be excluded from an understanding of their salvation.[16] It is this insistence that the ear was the organ through which individuals had to reach an understanding of salvation that explains the Protestant/puritan obsession with preaching. Whilst the attack on images was in part an assertion that the Word, and only the Word, was the key to the regenerate life, it meant for many the priority of the heard Word, delivered in lively faith to the assembled congregation by the preacher.

This shift from the visual to the spoken was the shared objective of most Protestant divines before the end of the sixteenth century. And, despite Elizabeth's determination to defend her cross and candlesticks, regular episcopal visitations and the gradual spread of reformed ideology did much to empty English churches of their images and 'popish' art. It is usual here to appeal to the testimony of William Harrison, the Essex parson whose 1577 *Description of England* offers a rare description of the state of the Church. Harrison claimed that 'all shrines, tabernacles, rood lofts and monuments of idolatry are removed, taken down, and defaced', leaving only stories in some glass windows, which were slowly being replaced by white glass as they decayed.[17] This seems reasonably accurate, at least as far as the southern part of the kingdom is concerned, though the destruction must at times have been fairly superficial to judge by how much was left for the civil war iconoclasts to attack. Even on William Dowsing's East Anglian tours in 1643 and 1644, long lists of 'superstitious' items remained to demolish.[18] Sixteenth-century attacks seem to have focused on the intercessory functions of the saints, and manifestations of prayer for the dead, leaving in place much else perceived as ornamental.[19] The godly feared that too often this left paintings which were 'slubbered over with a white wash... standing like a Dianaes shrine for a future hope and daily comforte of old popish beldames and yong perking papists'.[20]

---

[15] Arnold Hunt, *The Art of Hearing: English Preachers and their Audiences, 1590-1640* (Cambridge, 2010), pp. 22-30.
[16] Samuel Hieron, *Sixe Sermons* (1608), sig. Bivr; Hunt, *Art of Hearing*, pp. 24-5.
[17] William Harrison, *Description of England*, in Raphael Holinshed, *Chronicle of England, Scotland and Ireland* (1577 edn.), fo. 76v.
[18] Trevor Cooper (ed.), *The Journal of William Dowsing* (Woodbridge, 2001).
[19] Eamon Duffy, *The Stripping of the Altars: Traditional Religion in England 1400-1580* (New Haven, CT, 1992), pp. 494-6.
[20] Albert Peel (ed.), *The Seconde Parte of a Register*, 2 vols. (Cambridge, 1915), I, p. 239.

The dramatic rupture with the Catholic past was traumatic, and recognized as such by the leaders of Elizabeth's Reformation. 'What shall we now do at church', says the imagined goodwife in the 'Homily of the Place and Time of Prayer', 'since all the saints are taken away, since all the goodly sights we were wont to have are gone?'[21] The answer, of course, was to turn to the Word spoken and read. We should not, however, conclude that the consequence was a total absence of Protestant religious art, since important representations were to be found outside churches. Within consecrated buildings the continuities do seem almost non-existent: the only legitimate aesthetic opportunities being the structure of the building and its formal furniture of communion table, pulpit, and perhaps pews. Major repair and rebuilding was unusual under Elizabeth, so it was in practice the woodwork that offered almost the only scope for 'comeliness' or 'sumptuousness' (as can be seen in surviving Devon examples at Braunton, Alwington, and Tawstock).[22] There is also, however, that limited form of decoration that was approved by the Established Church—funeral monuments, the royal arms, and the writing of Scripture on the walls. Monuments are a complex case. In the high years of iconoclastic enthusiasm they risked being caught up in the attack on superstition, either because they included iconography that offended Protestants, or simply because there was slippage between the idea of sacred and of secular representation. Fearing that the honouring of the dead might become veneration, some reformers cited Wisdom 14:15–16, which describe how a father's image of his dead son gradually led to his worship. Lest this should be projected onto modern tombs and legitimate an attack upon them, Elizabeth issued a proclamation in 1560 'against breaking or defacing monuments of antiquitie, being set up in Churches'.[23] Seventy years later John Weever, in his *Ancient Funerall Monuments*, lamented that the proclamation did little good, proving his point by citing the second proclamation on the subject in 1572.[24] However, there is no doubt that wholesale destruction was avoided, and that the elite quickly returned to memorializing themselves and their families within the church. In many parishes tombs with figural arrangements, and even in time with freestanding effigies of classical and Christian virtues, became the nearest proxy for traditional sacred ones. It was rare indeed for any Elizabethan tomb maker to represent scriptural figures: when Melchior Sallabass did so on a painted triptych, dated 1588, for the Cornwall family in Burford, Shropshire, he added

---

[21] Griffiths, *Homilies*, pp. 349–50.

[22] Bridget Cherry and Nikolaus Pevsner, *The Buildings of England: Devon* (2nd edn., 1989).

[23] Philip L. Hughes and J. F. Larkin (eds.), *Tudor Royal Proclamations*, 3 vols. (New Haven, CT, 1964–9), II, pp. 146–7; Peter Sherlock, *Monuments and Memory in Early Modern England* (Aldershot, 2008), pp. 166–71.

[24] John Weever, *Ancient Funerall Monuments Within the United Monarchie of Great Britaine* (1631), pp. 51–4.

the precautionary legend 'regard not these pictures, but follow the Lord: as did the Apostles in lyffe and word'.[25]

More interesting is the visual role played by the two elements positively encouraged by the settlement—the royal arms and scriptural writing on the walls. At the simplest level an elaborate painted version of the royal arms provided a much-needed splash of colour above the chancel arch. The arms, by their positioning, also obliterated the familiar doom paintings of the arch, just as the scriptural texts covered the whitewashed images in the rest of the church. The obligation to provide a board of the Ten Commandments was a particularly confrontational challenge to the old idolatries: a royal order of 1561 required that special texts should be fixed to the wall above the communion board, and from the late 1560s episcopal injunctions ordered that the east end should be 'hanged with a fair cloth' and the Decalogue fixed to it.[26] The Second Commandment against making graven images was to be placed above the site where Christ's body had hung in sight of the congregation. In 1561 Elizabeth, characteristically, required that the texts should 'give some comlye ornament' to the chancel as well as edify; the canons of 1604 made visibility the only requirement.[27] The survival of black-letter texts has been too little studied and is probably too patchy for confident generalization, but it became common to think like the queen. Words were 'framed' and 'pictured', utilizing strap-work borders copied from pattern books or bible illustration.[28] By the early seventeenth century there were certainly elaborate attempts to integrate the black letter into an aesthetic scheme for a church. At Puddletown in Dorset, where there was a parochial agreement in 1634 that the church should be 'beautified', there are several such texts, including one written on an open bible held by two hands (Fig. 10.1).[29] Such examples were offering more than the simple substitution of word for image and, at least for the literate, belonged in a category not wholly alien from the images they replaced, stimulating meditation, pointing to moral action, and edifying the spirit. The Dutch Reformed Church explicitly encouraged the painting of religious texts as a new form of church decoration.[30]

---

[25] Nigel Llewellyn, *Funeral Monuments in Post-Reformation England* (Cambridge, 2000), p. 255 and fig. 55.

[26] *VAI*, III, pp. 109, 165, 301.

[27] Edward Cardwell (ed.), *Documentary Annals of the Reformed Church of England*, 2 vols. (Oxford, 1844), I, p. 296; Gerald Bray (ed.), *The Anglican Canons 1529–1947* (Woodbridge, 1998), pp. 376–7.

[28] Tessa Watt, *Cheap Print and Popular Piety, 1550–1640* (Cambridge, 1991), pp. 217–18; Kenneth Fincham and Nicholas Tyacke, *Altars Restored: The Changing Face of English Religious Worship, 1547–c.1700* (Oxford, 2007), pp. 247–9.

[29] *Royal Historical Monuments Commission: Dorset*, III, pt. 2 (1970), p. 225.

[30] Mia Mochizuki, 'Supplanting the Devotional Image after Netherlandish Iconoclasm', in A. McClanan and J. Johnson (eds.), *Negotiating the Image: Case Studies of Past Iconoclasms* (Aldershot, 2004), pp. 137–57.

Fig. 10.1 Black-letter inscriptions, Puddletown, Dorset.

The search for a more figurative Protestant religious art must take us outside the church building. What was permitted in a domestic environment was markedly different from the public space of the church and slippage between categories of representation was more acceptable. Even here, however, there were constraints upon Protestants. The Second Commandment was interpreted as forbidding the representation of the deity, or of other persons of the Trinity. Calvin expressed this most powerfully: 'God's majesty is sullied by an unfitting and absurd fiction, when the incorporeal is made to resemble corporeal matter.'[31] William Perkins articulated the view common among English Protestants: 'we hold it not lawfull to worship God in, or at, any image... the name of the thing signified is given to the signe, as upon a stage he is called a King that representes the King'.[32] The solution was to substitute the letters of the tetragrammaton for the painting of an old man in the clouds and, in theory, the IHS for the person of Christ, though the latter was a bitterly contested representation given its use by the Jesuits. On the other hand, Perkins took the view that representation of itself was not inherently sinful, and that civil art and even biblical narrative was acceptable, provided that it was displayed outside the church building. Most famously he conceded that 'we think the histories of the Bible may be painted in private places'.[33] William Fulke had earlier tried to be more precise about where religious art could be located: 'in clothes or galleries etc', which 'were in no use of religion and without all daunger of worshipping'.[34]

Tara Hamling and Tessa Watt have shown that this licence to employ biblical images in a domestic setting was widely accepted in all the decorative arts.[35] Representation of biblical stories reached well down the social scale, and was used by families of most ideological persuasions. Old Testament scenes appeared in plasterwork, on fireplaces, bed heads, and walls: New Testament narratives were less common, though by no means unknown. One of the best-known is the unique set of painted cloths of the life of St Paul that were commissioned by Bess of Hardwick.[36] While most of the examples cited by Hamling avoid controversial representations of Christ (especially his sacrificial role) the sacrifice of Isaac, and brazen serpent were popular as types that foreshadowed Christ and as such central portrayals of the scheme of sin and salvation. Or the Nine Worthies, heroic figures from the classical, Old Testament and medieval past, were acceptable to Protestants and a useful substitute for images of the apostles.[37] Even in book production, where visual anorexia associated with iconophobia became common in the later sixteenth century, it

---

[31] Calvin, *Institutes*, I, p. 98.
[32] William Perkins, *A Reformed Catholike: or a Declaration Shewing How Neere we may come to the Present Church of Rome* (Cambridge, 1598), pp. 183–4.
[33] Perkins, *Reformed Catholike*, p. 172.
[34] William Fulke, *D. Heskyns, D. Sanders and M. Rastell... Overthrowne and Detected of their Severall Blasphemous Heresies* (1579), p. 598.
[35] Tara Hamling, *Decorating the 'Godly' Household: Religious Art in Post-Reformation Britain* (New Haven, CT, 2010); Watt, *Cheap Print*, pp. 178–216.
[36] Anthony Wells-Cole, *Art and Decoration in Elizabethan and Jacobean England* (New Haven, CT, 1997), pp. 275–85.
[37] Watt, *Cheap Print*, pp. 212–14.

was still possible to illustrate not only the Bishops' Bible (1568), but also the Geneva version, with Old Testament scenes and maps.[38]

So there was a Protestant art, even under Elizabeth. What was lacking was a distinctive English aesthetic. Anthony Wells-Cole has shown convincingly that most decorative art, religious or otherwise, was deeply dependent on foreign models, especially those provided in print by the books of pattern and engraving that became readily available from the middle of the sixteenth century. The influence of Netherlandish engravers, in particular, can be traced throughout productions intended for the elite, and probably trickled down even to those decorating quite ordinary households. Antwerp Mannerism, in Wells-Coles's words, became 'inseparably grafted on to what was essentially a late-medieval architectural stock'.[39] One consequence of this deep continental influence was that much of the representation in English books and homes had been produced in the pluralistic religious environment of the Low Countries, some by Catholic engravers, others by those sympathetic to Lutheranism or inclining to reform. But more significant than their religious background was a shared adaptation of the classical conventions of Italian art to biblical narrative: to presenting the stories in ways that were distanced from medieval imagery.

There is a sense of liminality about the decoration of the godly household. Although it occurred in space that the state did not normally touch, and upon which the Church was hesitant to tread, it was not merely private as we would define the term. The surviving images are largely from the houses of the elite and the wealthy, houses which were often accessible to a local community, and in which worship would be conducted for household members and their visitors. Thus the separation described by Perkins between sacred and secular space was less absolute than the language might suggest. Prayers in the hall might be conducted, as at Burton Agnes in Yorkshire, under the eye of an over-screen of apostles and Old Testament patriarchs so elaborate that it can be compared to a late medieval reredos.[40] Or worship might be held in a parlour or great chamber with plasterwork ceiling of biblical scenes, and an over-mantel emphasizing spiritual meditation. But the most interesting for iconographic slippage was the domestic chapel. It is ironic that Archbishops Neile and Laud were often reluctant to consecrate private chapels because of the risk of nonconformity, while much of the revived ritualism of the Church of England in the early seventeenth century occurred in precisely this protected space.

---

[38] Patrick Collinson, *From Iconoclasm to Iconophobia: The Cultural Impact of the Second English Reformation* (Reading, 1986); Margaret Aston, 'The *Bishops' Bible* Illustrations', in Diana Wood (ed.), *The Church and the Arts* (SCH 28, Oxford, 1995), pp. 267–85.

[39] Wells-Cole, *Art and Decoration*, pp. 298–9 (quotation at p. 95).

[40] Hamling, *Decorating the 'Godly' Household*, pp. 124–7.

The example was, of course, set from above, when Elizabeth defied the bishops about the crucifix and candlesticks in the Chapel Royal. She continued to hold that this was her personal ideological territory, excoriating the unfortunate Dean Nowell when he preached before her on idolatry, renewing at least part of the communion table furniture after each attack, and maintaining that table altar-wise for services.[41] The crucifixion may have remained on a tapestry behind the communion table. William Fuller noted in 1586 that there were undefaced images of the saints, the Trinity, and the Virgin in the chapel at Whitehall, providing an 'ill example and permission' to subjects throughout the realm.[42] If the godly thought that such popish remnants would be swept away under Elizabeth's successor, they had a rude awakening. James retained ceremonialism, and from 1617, when Lancelot Andrewes became dean of the chapel, actively encouraged the renewal and development of Whitehall and later Greenwich, providing schemes of wall-paintings with figures and reintroducing the silver crucifix.[43] His most dramatic gesture was his refitting of the Chapel Royal at Holyrood ahead of his 1617 visit: organs, stalls, and freestanding statues of the apostles and evangelists were prepared in London and shipped north. The horrified Scottish Church protested, and James conceded just so far as to exclude the 'idolatrous' carvings, while maintaining the rest of his scheme.[44] When in 1624 the Commons accused Harsnett, bishop of Norwich, of countenancing images, the king was dismissive: the charge of idolatry involved 'nothing but the pictures of the Apostles and such like as I have in myne owne chappell'.[45] There was political intention behind much of this—forcing obedience upon the Scots; impressing the negotiators for Charles's Spanish marriage—but they also provided a signal that the days of extreme iconoclasm had passed.[46]

The position of the Chapels Royal might be unique, especially in the relative continuity of their elaborate pattern of worship throughout the late sixteenth century. However, as the anxiety about idolatry diminished in some circles in the early Jacobean years, the owners of other chapels not directly subject to the public discipline of the Church began to experiment with figural art and more elaborate visual settings for worship. The earl of Salisbury's chapel at Hatfield, completed in 1611, is a key example of the changes that had become

---

[41] Peter McCullough, *Sermons at Court: Politics and Religion in Elizabethan and Jacobean Preaching* (Cambridge, 1998), pp. 46–7.
[42] Peel, *Seconde Parte of a Register*, II, p. 53; Fincham and Tyacke, *Altars Restored*, pp. 80–2.
[43] McCullough, *Sermons at Court*, pp. 16, 31–4.
[44] McCullough, *Sermons at Court*, p. 29. David Calderwood, *History of the Kirk of Scotland*, ed. T. Thomson, 8 vols. (Edinburgh, 1842–59), VII, p. 244.
[45] Quoted in Annabel Ricketts, *The English Country House Chapel: Building in a Protestant Tradition* (Reading, 2007), p. 138.
[46] Anthony Milton, '"That Sacred Oratory": Religion and the Chapel Royal during the Personal Rule of Charles I', in Andrew Ashbee (ed.), *William Lawes (1602–1645): Essays on his Life, Times and Work* (Aldershot, 1998), pp. 69–96.

acceptable since the death of Elizabeth. The windows were filled with twelve large biblical scenes in painted glass, each being a narrative moment that could be said to figure the New Testament—Jonah and the whale, the sacrifice of Isaac, and so on. The inscriptions make it clear that these narratives pre-figure Christ, while not directly displaying him. By the time the chapel was complete, however, it had been decided to paint the New Testament parallels along with patriarchs and prophets on the walls.[47] At the same time Salisbury was updating the chapel in his Strand house and adding painted glass, though we know nothing about the scheme.[48]

Hatfield may have been a more significant example to elite patrons even than the Chapels Royal. Henry Peacham, in his commentary on art *The Gentleman's Exercise* (1612) gives specific praise to the chapel, while acknowledging that imagery continues to be controversial.[49] Within a few years the earl of Northampton, or his executors, had commissioned an important pictorial window for the chapel of Trinity Hospital, Greenwich, showing scenes from the life of Christ—the agony in the garden, the crucifixion, and the ascension—which would previously have been denounced as idolatrous.[50] Before the end of James's reign other private chapels, such as Wilne in Derbyshire, Little Easton, Essex, and Abbott's Hospital in Guildford, had been given painted glass. Abbott's Hospital may have been confined to the Old Testament: scenes from the life of Jacob survive and these would be appropriate for a moderate Calvinist patron. In the other cases, and at Apethorpe church in Northamptonshire where the Mildmay chapel, with full painted window, is treated as separate from the body of the church, New Testament scenes predominate. The Apethorpe window (dated 1621), narrates the whole biblical story from the Fall to the Resurrection.[51] Sir Henry Slingsby had his Red House chapel in Yorkshire glazed by Richard Butler with a crucifixion scene and the twelve apostles.[52]

Private chapels are indicative of a shift of religious sensibility which was even better exemplified in the college chapels of Oxford and Cambridge. Many of the changes there date from the 1630s, and can be associated directly with Laudianism, but at Oxford they were under way earlier, and were not necessarily funded by patrons who were sympathetic to Laud. Wadham College

---

[47] Claire Gapper, John Newman, and Annabel Ricketts, 'Hatfield: A House for a Lord Treasurer', in Pauline Croft (ed.), *Patronage, Culture and Power: The Early Cecils 1558-1612* (New Haven, CT, 2002), pp. 88-93.

[48] Michael Archer, 'Richard Butler, Glass-Painter', *Burlington Magazine*, 132 (May 1990): 307-9.

[49] Henry Peacham, *The Gentleman's Exercise* (1612), pp. 7, 13-14.

[50] Geoffrey Lane, 'A World Turned Upside Down: London Glass-Painters 1600-1660', *Journal of Stained Glass*, 29 (2005), p. 50.

[51] Lane, 'A World Turned Upside Down', p. 51; Hamling, *Godly Household*, pp. 57-9.

[52] *The Diary of Sir Henry Slingsby*, ed. D. Parsons (1836), pp. 3-4; Archer, 'Richard Butler', pp. 310-11; Ricketts, *Country House Chapel*, pp. 140-8.

Fig. 10.2 Lincoln College east window of the Lincoln College chapel. Used by permission of Lincoln College.

chapel was consecrated in 1613 and had richly painted windows to north and south installed around the same time. The great east window, showing the passion figured in ten scenes, was paid for by John Strangways and completed in 1622.[53] Laud began the beautification of St John's chapel with scenes from the life of John the Baptist in 1619.[54] At the end of the 1620s Lincoln College chapel was edified by John Williams, bishop of Lincoln, and given an east window of similar type and ambition. That beautiful Van Linge window may stand as exemplar of the quality and nature of the work (Fig. 10.2).

The story of the pre-Laudian chapels at Oxford is one that combines the newly permissive attitudes of leading divines, with an interest in formality and order in worship, and willingness to invest in foreign expertise, or at least to

---

[53] Graham Parry, *The Arts of the Anglican Counter-Reformation: Glory, Laud and Honour* (Woodbridge, 2006), pp. 59–62.

[54] John Newman, 'The Architectural Setting', in Nicholas Tyacke (ed.), *The History of the University of Oxford*, vol. 4: *The Seventeenth Century* (Oxford, 1997), p. 164.

study foreign patterns when employing native craftsmen. Permissive attitudes can be traced from the 1590s through developing avant-garde anti-Calvinist conformity. Richard Hooker is always invoked as a proponent of 'comeliness' in the church, and of the 'majestie and holiness of the place where God is worshipped', while Lancelot Andrewes is presented as the patron saint of the new order.[55] There are, however, others who are worth consideration: for example John Howson, who preached three key sermons on the need for reverence in caring for church buildings, and 'sumptuousness' in worship; and John Overall, who Anthony Milton has shown was a firm defender of the role that images could play in stirring up devotion.[56] The willingness to rebuild and invest in foreign expertise can be attributed in part to the relative religious security of James's reign after the uncertainty of the succession and the economic difficulties of the 1590s. It surely owed something to a growing competitive impulse within the University of Oxford. The Van Linge brothers, Bernard and Abraham, arrived in England in the 1620s, and swiftly fulfilled commissions at Wadham, followed by Lincoln's Inn in London.[57] By the late 1620s, when the Lincoln commission was undertaken, their Flemish style of painted glass had become a highly valued commodity, introducing bold images of prophets and evangelists, and above all focusing the chapels upon the east end with windows that expressed programmes of redemptive theology. Chapels were also refitted to underline greater formality in worship: ante-chapels were separated more explicitly from the inner sacred space, the east end was elevated, and fine vestments provided.[58] By the time University College and Queen's were employing Abraham Van Linge in the 1630s this style had become associated with full Laudian ritualism, but it is important to recognize that this was not its beginning.

The visual expression of 'avant-garde conformity' found in the quasi-private spaces of houses and chapels was only one strand in the aesthetic revival of the early seventeenth century. The refurbishing of churches, after a long period of neglect, was the ambition of the hierarchy, and of some parishioners, especially in London. In June 1602 Archbishop Whitgift sent out a general enquiry on the physical state of all churches, claiming that the queen was concerned that many 'are very ondecentlie kept within'.[59] The

---

[55] Richard Hooker, *Of the Laws of Ecclesiastical Polity*, V, 5.32, 15.57, 16.61; Parry, *Anglican Counter-Reformation*, pp. 14–21; Fincham and Tyacke, *Altars Restored*, pp. 111–35.

[56] John Howson, *A Sermon Preached at Paules Crosse* (1597); John Howson, *A Second Sermon Preached at Paules Crosse* (1598), pp. 22, 24–5. Anthony Milton, '"Anglicanism" by Stealth: The Career and Influence of John Overall', in Kenneth Fincham and Peter Lake (eds.), *Religious Politics in Post-Reformation England* (Woodbridge, 2006), pp. 159–65.

[57] Michael Archer, Sarah Crewe, and Peter Cormack, *The English Heritage in Stained Glass: Oxford* (Oxford, 1988), pp. 25–9.

[58] John Hacket, *Scrinia Reserata* (1693), pt. ii, p. 35.

[59] C. W. Foster (ed.), *The State of the Church in . . . the Diocese of Lincoln* (Lincoln Record Society, 23, 1926), p. 220.

survey was to be national: it was followed in 1604 by a canon ordering triennial inspections of buildings.[60] The impact can be seen most explicitly in London where as many as twenty-two parish churches had undergone significant repairs by 1610, and sixty-three by the end of James's reign.[61] The objective of Whitgift's letter was to improve church fabric, rather than determining a particular aesthetic. However, the new initiative came at a time when the fear of icon worship had diminished for some, and many congregations in the metropolis had developed a strong sense of their own ideological identity. Much of the repair and renewal that Anthony Munday's supplement to Stow's *Survey of London* chronicles involved more comfortable and elegant furnishings—pews, pulpits, and reading desks—as well as much structural change as churches were enlarged and beautified.[62] It is the nature of that beautification that is controversial. In the Jacobean years it could articulate an ideological stance. Puritan parishes could refurbish pulpits, pews, and black-letter texts, as an expression of the centrality of the Word. Congregations like that of Christ Church, Newgate Street, identified even in the 1590s as 'backward in matters of religion' might be expected to welcome the opportunity to use stained glass and painting as an expression of greater formality in worship, as they relished music and organs.[63] There is something in this: yet, as with the college chapels, the situation is more complex. A godly congregation like that of St Saviour, Southwark, could accept an extraordinary display at the west end of the church, with a Commandments board, replete with images of themselves at worship, with Moses and Aaron above (Fig. 10.3). At St Mildred, Bread Street, stained glass windows lauded the 'Protestant cause' from the Armada to 1625.[64] Even saints and martyrs could prove acceptable in the new climate: the windows installed at St Stephen, Walbrook, in 1613, included images of St Stephen being martyred and eight other 'personages', and were a parochial effort partly funded by men with impeccably Calvinist wills.[65]

It is easy to overstate the degree of consensus that is demonstrated by the refurbishing of London churches and the beautification of private and collegiate churches. Like the supposed Jacobean ecclesiastical consensus in general it rested on uncertain ideological grounds and was accepted because there was often an urgent need for renovation of church fabric. While the heat of the debate about images may have temporarily diminished, the godly would not have accepted Henry Hammond's later polemical observation that 'the

---

[60] Bray, *Canons*, p. 381.
[61] Fincham and Tyacke, *Altars Restored*, pp. 92–3; Julia Merritt, 'Puritans, Laudians and the Phenomenon of Church Building in Jacobean London', *Historical Journal*, 41 (1998): 935–60 (pp. 941, 944).
[62] *The Survey of London... Begunne First by... John Stow*, enlarged by Anthony Munday and others (1633), pp. 819–86.
[63] Fincham and Tyacke, *Altars Restored*, pp. 94–9.   [64] Munday, *Survey*, p. 859.
[65] Fincham and Tyacke, *Altars Restored*, pp. 100, 102–3.

Fig. 10.3 Commandments board, St Saviour, Southwark.

worship of images or any thing but God, is not a thing to which English Protestants... (especially the Catechized and knowing) have generally had any strong temptations'.[66] Meanwhile an increased interest in the beautification of churches was being subsumed into the more explicit programme which is conventionally labelled Laudianism. This can be differentiated from more general concerns for dignity in worship by its intense sacramentalism, with the altar policy at its heart. The history of its development can be traced from Lancelot Andrewes's arrangement of his private chapel, via Laud's introduction of the east-end altar at Gloucester Cathedral in 1617, and John Cosin's refurbishment at Durham at the end of the 1620s, to the full enforcement of altar rails and the east-end communion table after Laud succeeded to Canterbury in 1633.[67] In these developments spiritual and aesthetic preferences for imagery and formality already seen in chapels and churches were assimilated to a liturgical and doctrinal programme. It was the intensity of belief in the sacrosanct nature of ecclesiastical space and the divine presence in the sacraments that set the ritualists apart from many of those who had pursued comeliness and beauty in the previous decades. 'It is the highest advancement a Christian hath to be fed at God's board and with Christ's very body', as John Yates expressed it.[68]

An important aesthetic consequence of this sacramentalism was an intensified focus upon the chancel as the site of the eucharist. The Oxford and Cambridge colleges continued the development of chapels of the new kind—now under official pressure as well as ideological enthusiasm. Peterhouse's complete chapel refurbishment during Cosin's mastership (1635–44), involved a raised east end, lavish angel roof over the sanctuary, great east-end crucifixion window by one of the Van Linge brothers, and supporting hangings and liturgical objects. All this set the highest Laudian standard, though its full impact had to be supported by ephemeral objects like painted cloth, the music, and the gestures of the priests.[69] The process begun earlier at Oxford continued in a number of colleges, with new glass, free-standing statuary, and new elaborate vestments as some of its manifestations. The surviving west window of Magdalen College, the Last Judgement painted in black on white glass (even though heavily restored) conveys something of the ambitious visual impact of Christocentric art that was now acceptable. Elite patrons followed some of these developments in their chapels. For example at Temple Newsam, Leeds, Sir Arthur Ingram not only installed glass, paintings of prophets, and organs in the mid-1630s, he commissioned paintings on canvas, one of which was a copy of Titian's *Supper at Emmaus*.[70]

---

[66] Henry Hammond, *Of Idolatry* (1646), p. 22.
[67] Fincham and Tyacke, *Altars Restored*, pp. 176–226.
[68] John Yates, *A Treatise of the Honour of God's House* (1637), p. 63; Peter Lake, 'The Laudian Style: Order, Uniformity and the Pursuit of the Beauty of Holiness in the 1630s', in Kenneth Fincham (ed.), *The Early Stuart Church, 1603–1642* (Basingstoke, 1993), pp. 161–85.
[69] Parry, *Anglican Counter-Reformation*, pp. 77–9.
[70] Parry, *Anglican Counter-Reformation*, p. 107.

Fig. 10.4 Passenham church, chancel stalls.

Parish churches were rarely transformed in this way, since only a determined ritualist patron was likely to invest much beyond the mandatory movement and railing of the communion table and the removal of impediments to sacramental worship cluttering the chancel. But rare survivals, or recorded examples, indicate the ambitions of the few. At Passenham, Northamptonshire, Sir Robert Banastre, father-in-law of the Laudian supporter Lord Maynard, restored the church between 1621 and 1628, rebuilt the chancel, and gave it a fine set of choir stalls, backed by niches which probably originally carried free-standing statues of apostles and evangelists. If so, he was challenging one of the greatest anxieties of the iconoclasts, that free-standing statues were the most likely inducement to image worship. Banastre also commissioned wall paintings of the foretelling prophets and the evangelists for the chancel walls and the figures of Joseph of Arimathea and Nicodemus, participant in the burial of Christ, to flank the east-end communion table (Figs. 10.4 and 10.5). Other known examples of elaborate east-end furnishing, with painting and stained glass pointing to Christ's sacrifice include St Chad's, Shrewsbury, Glenfield, Leicestershire, and Viscount Scudamore's reconstruction of Abbey Dore, Herefordshire.[71] The most complete surviving chancel scheme is the plasterwork of East Knoyle, Wiltshire, where the incumbent, Matthew Wren's brother Christopher, devised the scheme in 1639. Its complex

---

[71] Fincham and Tyacke, *Altars Restored*, pp. 259–64; Ron Shoesmith and Ruth Richardson (eds.), *A Definitive History of Dore Abbey* (Almeley, 2000), pp. 163–94.

Fig. 10.5 Passenham church, chancel painting.

iconography celebrates the dream and sacrifice of Jacob, linking earth and heaven, and the offering of prayer and praise that will secure the return of sacramental grace (Fig. 10.6).[72]

---

[72] Louise Durning and Clare Tilbury, '"Looking unto Jesus": Image and Belief in a Seventeenth-Century English Chancel', *JEH*, 60 (2009): 490–513.

Fig. 10.6 Plasterwork of East Knoyle church. Used by permission of Historic England.

Even within the ranks of Laudian ritualists we should note differences of aesthetic choice. The beauty of holiness did not attach to one dominant form of art, and patrons rarely showed evidence of concern about disparity between medieval and classical styles of church building, furnishing, or window painting. The best of past style and of modern influences from Europe could

Fig. 10.7 Brancepeth church interior. Used by permission of Historic England.

coexist, as at Passenham or St Katharine Cree, London (rebuilt 1621–30) because Laudians both looked back to continuities with past Christianity and outwards to reconciliation with aspects of Catholic devotion (Fig. 10.7). Medievalism had powerful appeal to some, for example the young John Cosin in his furnishing of Brancepeth church. There the chancel screen so faithfully reproduced a gothic enclosure that it appeared to exclude lay observation—the necessary corollary of the sacralization of chancel space (Fig. 10.8). On the other hand, classical structure could underline formality and decorum, and, as at St Katharine's, allow the drama of the eucharist to be displayed in an open and theatrical context. Eclecticism was often the result. The crucial issue for the ritualists was not precise artistic form, but the functions of the newly splendid context of worship: the turning of men to prayer and devotion, and the enhancement of the priesthood in the sacraments. Painted windows might 'moderate that bright light, which is a hinderance to devotion'; chancel roofs should be adorned with azure and gilded stars 'so in colour it resembled the Hemisphear of the Heavens'.[73]

---

[73] R.T., *De Templis, a Treatise of Temples Wherein is Discovered the Ancient Manner of Building, Conserving and Adorning of Churches* (1638), pp. 196–8.

Fig. 10.8 St Katherine Cree, Leadenhall Street, London. Used by permission of Conway Library, The Courtauld Institute of Art, London. Photograph by A. F. Kersting.

Opposition to these aesthetic changes was, of course, muted but not undermined in the 1630s. As soon as political circumstances offered any liberty, the controversialists resumed their attack. The literary assault followed patterns already defined by a century or more of denunciation of idolatry. John Vicars wrote against picturing Christ's humanity and Edmund Gurnay against images in churches: the primary innovation of the latter being direct criticism of tombs and monuments.[74] The management of iconoclasm also owed much to the past. After the initial bursts of attacks on altar rails and breaking of windows the Long Parliament moved swiftly to control unlicensed activity. In September 1641 the Commons ordered 'the Suppression of Innovations', most explicitly aimed at Laudian worship, removing altar rails, levelling chancels, and taking away 'scandalous pictures'. This was followed by orders in 1643 and 1644, which extended the scope of the earlier one to include roods and rood lofts, images of angels as well as saints and the Trinity, crosses, and organs. Even symbolic representations of the divine were prohibited.[75] The licensed cleansing of churches that followed is best documented in William Dowsing's assault on East Anglia, beginning with his sweep through Cambridge and its colleges. This may have begun as a removal of 'late idolatry': it quickly became a mission for completing the task that earlier reformers had left undone. Remnants like angels, which had often survived sixteenth-century destruction, fell to Dowsing. And private chapels, not usually touched by previous regimes, were now seen as parallel to public churches. At Little Wenham Hall, Suffolk, for example, Dowsing ordered the removal of a picture of the Trinity 'and the lady promised to do it'.[76] While Dowsing's record is unique, there were other zealous agents of reform, such as Robert Harley and Richard Culmer, who ensured the destruction of idolatry in cathedrals, and churches, and at market crosses.[77]

Laud mounted a defence of images and the beauty of holiness at his trial, focusing on his own Lambeth Palace chapel, whose picture windows might instruct the laity and offended none 'but such as would have God served slovenly and meanly'. He was also attacked for sanctioning the use of 'idolatrous' images in bibles.[78] Meanwhile the iconoclastic storm raged, and defenders of the arts of the Church could only accept and perhaps hide treasures against better times. Ordinary parishes responded with the full range of enthusiasm or reluctance to Parliament's orders. Some took down their rails ahead of official action, and could exceed official expectation, as in the case of Chatham, where cleansing was extended to the scriptural sentences

---

[74] John Vicars, *The Sinfulness and Unlawfulness of Making or Having the Picture of Christ's Humanity* (1641); Edmund Gurnay, *An Appendix Unto the Homily Against Images in Churches* (1641).

[75] Julie Spraggon, *Puritan Iconoclasm during the English Civil War* (Woodbridge, 2003), pp. 64–79.

[76] Cooper, *Journal of Dowsing*, p. 238.

[77] Spraggon, *Puritan Iconoclasm*, pp. 83–98, 178, 182–5.

[78] William Prynne, *Canterburies Doome... a Compleat History of the Commitment, Tryall, Condemnation, Execution of William Laud* (1646), p. 462; George Henderson, 'Bible Illustration in the Age of Laud', *Transactions of the Cambridge Bibliographical Society*, 8 (1982): 173–204.

on the walls because of the 'anticke painted worke about them'.[79] Yet beyond the parliamentary heartlands there is a sufficient survival of communion rails, and even of stained glass, to show that many sought to avoid the eyes of the committees and the military.

So, was there an 'Anglican' form of art in the early seventeenth century sufficiently robust to lie concealed during the Commonwealth and re-emerge with the triumph of 1660? Elements of the early seventeenth-century vision certainly survived. The alignment of college chapels is one example: the formality of their chancel-type stalls survived in the universities and became a model for many private chapels. Altar rails were enjoined again in a number of dioceses, and 'a more muted version' of the beauty of holiness returned to many churches, especially those London ones built by Wren after the fire.[80] Cathedrals sometimes flaunted their restored standing: as at Durham where Cosin brought back a highly ostentatious form of worship.[81] The Commandment boards, enjoined by the bishops, and extensive wall inscriptions found in many parishes, showed another sort of aesthetic continuity. But much did not return. The figural art of the 1630s seems to be extremely rare after 1660, except in private chapels, and stained glass was uncommon, though things hidden were often restored. The vivid arts of the earlier revival generally gave way to a more sober aesthetic influenced by a more formal classicism and employing a symbolic language which no longer looked backwards to medievalism or stirred the old iconoclastic passions.

SELECT BIBLIOGRAPHY

Aston, Margaret, *England's Iconoclasts*, vol. 1: *Laws Against Images* (Oxford, 1988).
Aston, Margaret, 'God, Saints and Reformers: Portraiture and Protestant England', in Lucy Gent (ed.), *Albion's Classicism: The Visual Arts in Britain, 1550–1660* (New Haven, CT, 1995), pp. 181–220.
Cooper, Trevor (ed.), *The Journal of William Dowsing* (Woodbridge, 2001).
Fincham, Kenneth and Nicholas Tyacke, *Altars Restored: The Changing Face of English Religious Worship, 1547–c.1700* (Oxford, 2007).
Hamling, Tara, *Decorating the 'Godly' Household: Religious Art in Post-Reformation Britain* (New Haven, CT, 2010).
Lake, Peter, 'The Laudian Style: Order, Uniformity and the Pursuit of the Beauty of Holiness', in Kenneth Fincham (ed.), *The Early Stuart Church, 1603–1642* (Basingstoke, 1993), pp. 161–85.

---

[79] Spraggon, *Puritan Iconoclasm*, p. 104. I am grateful to Catharina Clement for drawing this example to my attention.

[80] Fincham and Tyacke, *Altars Restored*, pp. 305–7, 347–50 (quotation at p. 306).

[81] Stanford Lehmberg, *Cathedrals under Seige: Cathedrals in English Society, 1600–1700* (Exeter, 1996), pp. 58–61.

Merritt, Julia, 'Puritans, Laudians and the Phenomenon of Church Building in Jacobean London', *Historical Journal*, 41 (1998): 935–60.
Parry, Graham, *The Arts of the Anglican Counter-Reformation: Glory, Laud and Honour* (Woodbridge, 2006).
Spolsky, Ellen, 'Literacy after Iconoclasm in the English Reformation', *Journal of Medieval and Early Modern Studies*, 39 (2009): 305–30.
Spraggon, Julie, *Puritan Iconoclasm during the English Civil War* (Woodbridge, 2003).
Thomas, Keith, 'Art and Iconoclasm in Early Modern England', in Kenneth Fincham and Peter Lake (eds.), *Religious Politics in Post-Reformation England* (Woodbridge, 2006), pp. 16–40.
Watt, Tessa, *Cheap Print and Popular Piety, 1550–1640* (Cambridge, 1991).

11

Confessional Identity

Stephen Hampton

In the foreign series of the State Papers there is a copy of a memorandum from Queen Elizabeth I which was handed by her ambassador, Robert Beale, to the Elector Palatine, Louis VI, during the autumn of 1577. The English government had become aware that pressure was being brought to bear on the Protestant princes of Germany to endorse the Formula of Concord, a confessional statement drawn up by some Lutheran theologians earlier that year. The government was alarmed by the effect such an endorsement might have on the cause of Protestant unity, and on any attempt to build a defensive alliance of Protestant states, a diplomatic goal which the queen had pursued, albeit fitfully, since her accession.[1] The memorandum warned that the Formula was condemning, unheard, the Churches of England, Ireland, Scotland, Poland, and Switzerland, along with the Reformed Churches of Germany. And it reminded the Elector, in forceful terms, that theology was not merely a matter of local concern:

> If Your Highness, thinks this matter of divines to be a private affair of Germany, whose constitutions permit only two religions, Her Majesty judges very differently. We believe the Church of Christ to be universal, and matters affecting it should be universal and not particular. Nothing prejudicial can be done to the churches in Germany who embrace the same confession as we, without affecting us.[2]

Such an explicit identification of the Church of England with the Reformed Churches of mainland Europe might come as a surprise to those who prefer to muddy the waters of her confessional identity, whether by suggesting that the Elizabethan Church was a kind of Protestant *tertium quid*, neither Reformed nor Lutheran, but something in between;[3] or by suggesting that the

---

[1] *ODNB*, 'Beale, Robert (1541–1601)'.
[2] TNA, SP 81/1/23; *Calendar of State Papers, Foreign Series, 1577–1578* (1901), pp. 215–17.
[3] William Haugaard, *Elizabeth and the English Reformation: The Struggle for a Stable Settlement of Religion* (Cambridge, 1968), pp. 261–2, 264–6. Paul Avis, *Anglicanism and the Christian Church* (Edinburgh, 1989), p. 28.

Elizabethan Church of England was not even straightforwardly Protestant.[4] Nonetheless, the memorandum reflects the views of the leading churchmen of England at the time and of their contemporaries abroad, whether Protestant or Roman Catholic.

In the correspondence between a number of Elizabethan bishops and the leaders of the Reformed Church in Zürich, the Reformed identity of the English Church is made explicit;[5] as is the corresponding hostility of English churchmen such as John Jewel to aspects of Lutheranism.[6] The Reformed identity of the English Church was acknowledged on mainland Europe as well. When Jean-François Salvart produced the *Harmonia Confessionum Fidei* (1581), to demonstrate the doctrinal consensus of the Reformed Churches, in response to the Formula of Concord, the statement of faith from Jewel's *Apologia*[7] was included as the 'English Confession'. It is clear, therefore, that Salvart held the Church of England to stand with the Reformed, rather than those he calls 'the brethren of the confession of Augsburg',[8] even if Salvart's ultimate intention was to downplay Protestant division. This assumption that the Church of England was part of the Reformed family of Churches was given tangible expression in the presence of an English delegation at the Synod of Dort (1618-19).[9]

Roman Catholic writers generally accepted this identification as well. One of the most formidable critics of the English Church, the Spanish Jesuit Francisco Suarez, certainly numbered her alongside Rome's Reformed, rather than Lutheran, adversaries. In 1613, Suarez published his *Defensio Fidei Catholicae et Apostolicae adversus Anglicanae sectae errores*. This was a rejoinder to James I's claim that he was entitled to call himself a catholic Christian.[10] Unsurprisingly, Suarez disagreed; and to establish his case, he traced the history of the English Reformation from the reign of Henry VIII, pointing out that, 'after the death of Henry, against his declared will, during the time of King Edward, the Zwinglian heresy prevailed in the kingdom. After that time, Calvinism was introduced by Elizabeth, and the same persists into the present day, whether wholly, or to a great extent' ('Post Henrici mortem, contra eius voluntatem, Edwardi Regis tempore, Zwingliana haeresis in regno praevaluit. Postea vero tempore Elizabethae Calvinismus introductus est,

---

[4] Diarmaid MacCulloch, 'The Myth of the English Reformation', *Journal of British Studies*, 30 (1991): 1-19.

[5] Hastings Robinson (ed.), *The Zürich Letters*, 2 vols. (Cambridge, 1842-5), I, p. 135.

[6] Robinson (ed.), *The Zürich Letters*, I, p. 123.

[7] John Ayre (ed.), *The Works of John Jewel*, 4 vols. (Cambridge, 1845-50), III, pp. 58-66.

[8] Jean-François Salvart, *An Harmony of the Confessions of Faith of the Christian and Reformed Churches* (Cambridge, 1586), Preface.

[9] Anthony Milton (ed.), *The British Delegation and the Synod of Dort (1618-1619)* (Woodbridge, 2005), pp. xvii-xxii and il-lv.

[10] King James I, *Works* (1616), p. 301.

212   *Stephen Hampton*

idemque usque in hunc diem, vel omnino, vel majori ex parte perseverat').[11] And since Calvin was a heresiarch, Suarez contends, the 'English sect, which is Calvinist' ('Sectam Anglicanam, quae Calviniana est'), must be heretical too and, consequently, not Catholic, whatever King James might believe.[12] So, although Suarez was alert to the changing theological flavour of English Protestant theology during the sixteenth century, he nonetheless tarred the Church of England with a Reformed brush.

The identification of the Church of England as a Reformed Church finds ample warrant in her confessional statement, the Thirty-Nine Articles of Religion. Before examining that warrant, however, it is necessary to establish the role which the Articles played within the Elizabethan and early Stuart Church; because there has been a widespread tendency to downplay their significance. It has been argued, for example, that the Church of England never became a 'confessional' Church,[13] and that, within the Church of England, there was no theological system to which adherence was sought.[14] But that is certainly not how it appeared at the time. In fact the bands of confessional discipline in England were steadily tightening around the Articles throughout the sixteenth and early seventeenth centuries.

English statements of faith had been produced since the time of Henry VIII, although during that reign they retained a decidedly conservative character. Even the Ten Articles of 1536 made only a limited gesture towards the Protestant view of justification. In 1553, however, the Edwardian government issued the Forty-Two Articles, and they were undoubtedly a Reformed confession. Nowhere was this clearer than in 1553 Article 29, which denied 'the real and bodily presence (as they term it) of Christ's flesh and blood in the sacrament'.[15]

But the Edwardian Articles also exhibited a degree of anxiety about the heterodox doctrinal trajectories which had emerged from more radical forms of Protestantism during the early days of the European Reformation. Article 8 points out that the Anabaptists have revived the ancient error of Pelagius. Article 40 condemns the idea that the souls of the dead sleep until the general resurrection, an idea maintained by Michael Sattler, who had chaired the Anabaptist meeting that produced the Schleitheim Confession. 1553 Article 41 condemns millenarianism, which had coloured the Anabaptist reformation in Munster in 1534–5. Article 42 condemns the doctrine of universal salvation,

---

[11] Francisco Suarez, *Omnia Opera*, 26 vols. (Paris 1856–66), XXIV, p. 109.
[12] Suarez, *Omnia Opera*, XXIV, p. 109.
[13] Haugaard, *Elizabeth and the English Reformation*, p. 338; Avis, *Anglicanism and the Christian Church*, p. 28.
[14] Geoffrey Rowell, Kenneth Stevenson, and Rowan Williams (eds.), *Love's Redeeming Work: The Anglican Quest for Holiness* (Oxford, 2001).
[15] Gerald Bray (ed.), *Documents of the English Reformation* (Cambridge, 1994), pp. 284, 302.

which had allegedly been taught by the Anabaptist leader Hans Denck, during the 1520s.[16]

The Forty-Two Articles also directed their fire at the scholastic theology of the Roman Catholic Church. 1553 Article 23 ascribed the erroneous doctrine of purgatory to 'school-authors', while 1553 Article 26 explicitly condemned the idea that the sacraments work *ex opere operato*, a dogma which had recently been endorsed at the seventh session of the Council of Trent in 1547. At the same time, however, 1553 Article 5 offered a qualified endorsement of non-scriptural traditions, suggesting that they might be received by the faithful as 'godly and profitable for an order and comeliness'. This endorsement did not survive into the reign of Elizabeth I. The Edwardian Articles also offered a ringing defence of the revised English liturgy. 1553 Article 35 insisted that both the Book of Common Prayer and the Ordinal were 'godly, and in no point repugnant to the wholesome doctrine of the gospel, but agreeable thereunto, furthering and beautifying the same not a little'.[17] In a number of respects, therefore, the Edwardian Articles struck a more polemical tone than the document that succeeded them.

In 1563, Archbishop Parker used Edward's Forty-Two Articles as the basis for Elizabeth's Thirty-Nine; revisions to the earlier document having been hammered out through Convocation, and in negotiation with the Privy Council. In the process, 1553 Article 29's denial of the real presence was eliminated, and the overtly polemical elements already mentioned were abandoned. At the same time, the 1553 Articles' teaching about the Incarnation, the Fall, and Justification were all clarified. 1553 Article 36 was extended to make clear that the assertion of royal supremacy did not make the monarch a Christian minister; and its claim that the monarch was 'supreme head in earth, next under Christ, of the Church of England and Ireland' was toned down somewhat, leaving the monarch with just 'chief power in this realm of England'.[18]

In 1566, Archbishop Parker's *Advertisements* instructed that 'all they which shall be admitted to preach shall be diligently examined for their conformity in unity of doctrine established by public authority'.[19] The canons of 1571 echoed this injunction, commanding that every minister, before taking up his charge, 'shall subscribe to all articles of Christian religion which were agreed upon in Convocation, and whensoever the bishop shall command, shall declare his conscience to the people, what he thinketh of those articles and the whole doctrine'.[20] Those ministers who taught doctrine contrary to the

---

[16] Bray (ed.), *Documents*, pp. 290, 309–10.
[17] Bray (ed.), *Documents*, pp. 287, 297, 300–1, 306–7.
[18] Bray (ed.), *Documents*, pp. 301–2, 307–8.
[19] Gerald Bray (ed.), *The Anglican Canons 1529–1947* (Woodbridge, 1998), p. 164.
[20] Bray (ed.), *Anglican Canons*, p. 187.

Articles were thenceforth to be excommunicated.[21] In 1583, Archbishop Whitgift launched a campaign to enforce clerical discipline in England, which exacted subscription to the Thirty-Nine Articles, as well as to the royal supremacy and the Book of Common Prayer. Political pressure soon forced Whitgift to moderate this campaign,[22] but the requirement to subscribe to the Articles was reiterated in the canons of 1604. Canon 5 enjoined that 'Whosoever shall hereafter affirm, that any of the Nine and Thirty Articles... are in any part superstitious or erroneous, or such as he may not with good conscience subscribe unto; let him be excommunicated ipso facto, and not restored, but only by the Archbishop, after his repentance, and public revocation of such his wicked errors.' In 1622, during the controversy over predestination in England, King James I issued directions 'that no preacher under the degree and calling of a bishop, or dean of a cathedral or collegiate church (and they upon the king's days only and set festivals) do take occasion by the expounding of any text of scripture whatsoever, to fall into any commonplace... which shall not be comprehended or warranted in essence, substance or natural inference, within some one of the Articles of religion... or in one of the homilies set forth by authority'.[23] And in 1628, King Charles I issued a *Royal Declaration for the Peace of the Church*, in which he underlined

> That the Articles of the Church of England, which have been allowed and authorized heretofore, and which our clergy generally have subscribed unto, do contain the true doctrine of the Church of England agreeable to God's word; which we do therefore ratify and confirm, requiring all our loving subjects to continue in the uniform profession thereof, and prohibiting the least difference from the said articles.[24]

It is clear, therefore, that the authorities in both Church and state understood the Thirty-Nine Articles to be the authoritative statement of the Church of England's beliefs. This view was accepted by her clergy as well. In his commentary on the Articles, *The English Creede* (1585), Thomas Rogers (later chaplain to Richard Bancroft) described them as 'the badge of English Christians, whereby we are known to the universal world not only to agree with all the godly that ever have been or do live at this present... but also to disagree from the Jews, Turks, Papists and Anabaptists and all other profane men'.[25]

---

[21] Bray (ed.), *Anglican Canons*, p. 189.
[22] Kenneth Fincham, 'Clerical Conformity from Whitgift to Laud', in Peter Lake and Michael Questier (eds.), *Conformity and Orthodoxy in the English Church, c.1560–1660* (Woodbridge, 2000), p. 131.
[23] Barry Coward and Peter Gaunt (eds.), *English Historical Documents 1603–1660* (Abingdon, 2010), p. 281.
[24] Coward and Gaunt (eds.), *English Historical Documents*, pp. 285–6.
[25] Thomas Rogers, *The English Creede* (1585), Preface.

He made the same point in the 1607 revision of that work, asserting that 'the purpose of our church is best known by the doctrine which she doth profess, the doctrine by the 39 Articles established by Act of Parliament'.[26] In their university lectures, John Prideaux (the regius professor of divinity in Oxford) and Samuel Ward (the Lady Margaret professor of divinity in Cambridge) both referred repeatedly to the Articles as 'our confession', and used them to guide their theological teaching.[27]

Theologians of all parties recognized that there was a qualitative difference between the theological authority of the Articles and the opinions of private writers, no matter how distinguished. So when, in his *Appello Caesarem* (1625), Richard Montagu was defending his teaching that a justified believer might ultimately fall from grace, he averred that: 'I determine nothing in this question positively ... resolving upon this, not to go beyond my bounds, the consented, resolved and subscribed articles of the Church of England', and he went on to suggest that Article 16 supported his view. Anticipating his adversaries' objections to this, he wrote: 'Haply you will quarrel the sense of the Articles: but then you must remember, that the plain words sound to the meaning for which I have produced them, and that until the church itself expound otherwise, it is as free for me to take it according to the letter, as for you to devise a figure.'[28] When George Carleton replied to Montagu, in his *Examination* (1626), he also knew that he had to take his stand on the Articles, and he duly contended that 'our author's words cross the words of the 17th Article, which he professeth to maintain'.[29] So although these two men disagreed about what the Articles meant, they both acknowledged that they were the authoritative statement of what the Church believed. And the same is true of those rather less inclined to conformity than either Montagu or Carleton: which is why, as we shall see, the godly interest repeatedly attempted to have the Articles amended.

It is clear, therefore, that the Thirty-Nine Articles were accepted as the normative statement of the Church of England's beliefs. So if we want to locate the Church of England within the Protestant fold, it is to the Articles that we should look: they simply hold more theological weight than the opinions of individual churchmen. And since the principal point of contention between Lutheran and Reformed theologians concerned the Lord's Supper, any assessment of the confessional identity of the English Church will be focused there.

---

[26] Thomas Rogers, *The Faith, Doctrine and Religion, Professed and Protected in the Realme of England* (Cambridge, 1607), Preface.

[27] John Prideaux, *Viginti-duae Lectiones* (Oxford, 1648), pp. 11, 118, 263, 297, 330, 357; Samuel Ward, *Opera Nonnulla* (1658), pp. 1, 19, 61, 63, 100, 103.

[28] Richard Montagu, *Appello Caesarem* (1625), pp. 29–30.

[29] George Carleton, *An Examination of Those Things Wherein the Author of the Late Appeale Holdeth the Doctrines of the Pelagians and Arminians to be the Doctrines of the Church of England* (1626), p. 38.

When it is, the Reformed character of the Articles soon becomes clear, despite the alterations made in 1563. The queen was therefore telling no more than the truth, when she told the Elector that the Church of England held the same confession as the continental Reformed.

Central to the Lutheran conception of the eucharist, as codified in the Formula of Concord, was the claim that 'in the holy supper the body and blood of Christ are truly and essentially present, and are truly distributed and received with the bread and wine'. Christ's words of institution are to be understood literally, and not symbolically, so 'the body and blood of Christ are received not only spiritually, by faith, but orally'. It follows from this that 'not only the genuine believers and those who are unworthy but also the unworthy and the unbelievers receive the true body and blood of Christ', a claim colourfully summarized as 'the chewing of the unfaithful'—*manducatio impiorum*. The Formula of Concord consequently anathematizes the assertion 'that in the holy sacrament the body of Christ is not received orally with the bread, but that with the mouth we receive only bread and wine and that we receive the body of Christ only spiritually by faith'.[30] Admittedly, when the Thirty-Nine Articles were composed, the Formula of Concord was still a number of years in the future, but the insistence of Lutheran theologians such as Jacob Andreae and Johann Brenz upon the physical presence of Christ in the Lord's Supper and upon its logical corollary, the *manducatio impiorum*, was clear well before then.[31] And it was the views of such men that were eventually reflected in the Formula of Concord.

The sections of the Thirty-Nine Articles which address the Lord's Supper offer no leeway for a Lutheran understanding of the sacrament, whatever the revised Book of Common Prayer (1559) might have hinted, with its studiedly ambiguous words of administration: 'The body of our Lord Jesus Christ which was given for thee, preserve thy body and soul unto everlasting life: take and eat this in remembrance that Christ died for thee, and feed on him in thy heart by faith with thanksgiving.' Article 28 insists upon the purely spiritual nature of the believer's communion with Christ in the sacrament: 'The body of Christ is given, taken and eaten, in the supper, only after and heavenly and spiritual manner. And the mean whereby the body of Christ is received and eaten in the Supper is faith.' And if that were not enough, Article 29 specifically denies the *manducatio impiorum*: 'The wicked, and such as be void of a lively faith, although they do carnally and visibly press with their teeth (as Saint Augustine saith) the sacrament of the body and blood of Christ, yet in no wise are they partakers of Christ: but rather to their condemnation, do eat and drink the

---

[30] Theodore Tappert (ed.), *The Book of Concord: the Confessions of the Evangelical Lutheran Church* (Philadelphia, PA, 1959), pp. 482–5.

[31] Jill Raitt, *The Colloquy of Montbéliard: Religion and Politics in the Sixteenth Century* (Oxford, 1993), pp. 24, 27, and 29.

sign or sacrament of so great a thing.' Such theological clarity was not entirely welcome to the Elizabethan government, however, since the queen was trying to build an alliance with the Lutheran princes even as her Convocation was condemning their theology.[32] So Article 29 did not appear in any printed edition of the Articles until 1571.[33] But the fact that it was first suppressed in the interests of confessional diplomacy, and then restored, demonstrates that the government was fully aware of how clearly it identified the English Church with the Reformed, an awareness reflected in the government's reaction to the Formula of Concord. Furthermore, the Articles' combination of affirming the spiritual nature of Christ's presence in the Lord's Supper whilst denying the *manducatio impiorum* was paralleled in near-contemporary Reformed confessions, including the Belgic Confession (1561)[34] and the Second Helvetic Confession (1566).[35]

Whilst acknowledging that the Church of England chose to place itself with the Reformed, and against the Lutherans, on the matter of the Lord's Supper, it is important not to overplay that sense of distinction.[36] Certainly, many English theologians were prepared to follow John Jewel in condemning the Ubiquitarianism which they saw as the root of Lutheran error about the sacrament. Others, however, including Richard Hooker, were prepared to interpret the Lutheran position more charitably, suggesting that the divine person underlying the human nature of Christ might indeed be said to be in every place.[37] But, even here, they were actually following a Reformed precedent: Girolamo Zanchi had taken a similar line in his *De Dissidio in Coena Domini* (1563), and had been cited to that effect in Richard Field's attempt to show that the Lutheran and Reformed positions were not irreconcilable.[38]

It has sometimes been suggested that the Reformed identity of the Church of England is brought into question by the Thirty-Nine Articles' teaching on predestination, and it is true that the doctrine of predestination became an increasingly significant point of contention between Lutheran and Reformed theologians after the Colloquy of Montbéliard (1586). Article 17 asserts that 'Predestination to life is the everlasting purpose of God, whereby (before the foundations of the world were laid) he hath constantly decreed by his counsel

---

[32] David Scott Gehring, *Anglo-German Relations and the Protestant Cause: Elizabethan Foreign Policy and Pan-Protestantism* (2013), pp. 150–3.

[33] Hirofumi Horie, 'The Lutheran Influence on the Elizabethan Settlement', *Historical Journal*, 34 (1991): 519–37 (p. 534).

[34] Arthur Cochrane (ed.), *Reformed Confessions of the Sixteenth Century* (Louisville, KY, 2003), p. 216.

[35] Cochrane (ed.), *Reformed Confessions*, pp. 221, 286–7.

[36] Anthony Milton, *Catholic and Reformed: The Roman and Protestant Churches in English Protestant Thought, 1600–1640* (Cambridge, 1995), pp. 384–95.

[37] Richard Hooker, *Ecclesiastical Polity (Books I to V)*, ed. Ronald Bayne, 2 vols. (1922), II, pp. 222–4.

[38] Richard Field, *Of the Church five bookes* (Oxford, 1628), p. 822.

secret to us, to deliver from curse and damnation those whom he hath chosen in Christ out of mankind, and to bring them by Christ to everlasting salvation, as vessels made to honour.' Since there is no mention of a decree of reprobation here, it is sometimes argued that the Articles come close to the Lutheran position, which asserts a single predestination to salvation, rather than a double predestination of some to salvation, and others to condemnation.[39] However, this argument is predicated on an inadequate grasp of both Lutheran and Reformed teaching on the subject.

The orthodox Lutheran position requires not only the assertion of single predestination, but also the denial of double predestination. The Formula of Concord, for example, lays down that 'Predestination or the eternal election of God... is concerned only with the pious children of God in whom he is well pleased'; it also condemns the view 'that God does not want everybody to be saved, but that merely by an arbitrary counsel, purpose and will, without regard to their sin, God has predestined certain people to damnation, so that they cannot be saved'.[40] In Article 17, by contrast, while double predestination is not asserted, it is not condemned either. In this, the Article reflects most closely the position of the Second Helvetic Confession, which similarly embraces single predestination, but without denying double predestination, stating simply that 'From eternity God has freely, and of his mere grace, without any respect to men, predestinated or elected the saints whom he wills to save in Christ.'[41]

Of course there are a number of Reformed confessions which, under the influence of John Calvin and Theodore Beza, do indeed assert double predestination. The French Confession (1559), for example, affirms that 'from this corruption and general condemnation in which all men are plunged, God, according to his eternal and immutable counsel, calleth those whom he hath chosen by his goodness and mercy alone in our Lord Jesus Christ, without consideration of their works, to display in them the riches of his mercy; leaving the rest in this same corruption and condemnation to show in them his justice'.[42] It would, though, be a mistake to claim that this was the only orthodox view within the Reformed fold. Heinrich Bullinger, for example, habitually asserted only single predestination,[43] and the Reformed Church in Bern preferred a prudent reserve on the issue.[44]

This diversity of Reformed teaching about predestination reflects the diversity of the Reformed tradition more generally. The Reformed tradition was not

---

[39] Haugaard, *Elizabeth and the English Reformation*, pp. 262–3.
[40] Tappert, *Book of Concord*, pp. 495, 497.
[41] Cochrane (ed), *Reformed Confessions*, p. 241.
[42] Cochrane (ed), *Reformed Confessions*, p. 148.
[43] J. Wayne Baker, *Heinrich Bullinger and the Covenant: The Other Reformed Tradition* (Athens, OH, 1980), pp. 30 *et seq.*
[44] Raitt, *Colloquy of Montbéliard*, pp. 23, 59.

as uniform or monolithic as is sometimes assumed, even by those sympathetic to it. This is an important point, because it is only possible to make sense of the claim that the Church of England was, in confessional terms, a Reformed Church, if the diversity of the Reformed tradition is properly acknowledged. If the model of Geneva, and the theology of John Calvin or Theodore Beza, is taken as the benchmark for Reformed identity, then the assertion that the English Church, under Elizabeth and the early Stuarts, was a Reformed Church begins to look problematic. This is the reason why some scholars deny that the Elizabethan Church ever became a properly Reformed Church.[45] However, it is now widely recognized that the theology and polity of Geneva cannot be taken as the normative expression of Reformed identity. The Reformed tradition flourished in a wide range of places, and under the influence of many different theologians.[46] In fact, the very diversity of the Reformed tradition is reflected in the arguments over the shape of the English Church during the early modern period, because English churchmen of every hue could point to Reformed precedents which supported their arguments. And although it is often assumed that those urging further reform within the Church of England were better able or more willing to call upon foreign Reformed examples, this is not the case. Conformist writers were quite as adept as their opponents at ransacking the volumes of Reformed divinity for supportive opinions.

Those English churchmen agitating for further reform within the Church—whom their opponents often called 'puritans'—pointed to various aspects of her life which, they suggested, distanced the Church of England from Reformed practice elsewhere. These included aspects of the English liturgy as well as organizational matters such as the absence of a disciplinary structure under the exclusive control of the Church's ministers, and the retention of an episcopal hierarchy to govern the Church. It was therefore vital for those defending the English Church's established practice to show that these characteristics could find warrant within the Reformed world. Otherwise, the claim that the Church of England was inadequately reformed—a claim which lay at the heart of the case for further innovation—would begin to look convincing.

The Church of England's distinguishing features were all, to some extent, rooted in the Thirty-Nine Articles. That is why those who were sympathetic to further reform attempted to restrict the requirement for subscription to those Articles which dealt with doctrine, rather than to those Articles which dealt with matters of polity. As a result of puritan pressure, for example, the Ordination of Ministers Act (1571), which imposed clerical subscription to

---

[45] Scott Wenig, *Staightening the Altars: The Ecclesiastical Vision and Pastoral Achievements of the Progressive Bishops under Elizabeth I, 1559–1579* (New York, 2000), pp. 10, 81.

[46] Philip Benedict, *Christ's Churches Purely Reformed: A Social History of Calvinism* (New Haven, CT, 2002), pp. xx–xxi.

the Articles as a matter of secular law, specified that subscription need only be made to 'all the articles of religion which only concern the confession of the true Christian faith and the doctrine of the sacraments'.[47] The bishops, however, simply imposed subscription to all thirty-nine using canon law instead.[48] At the Hampton Court Conference (1604), the leader of the puritan delegation, John Rainolds, renewed the request that the clergy be asked to subscribe only 'according to the statutes of the realm',[49] i.e. only to the doctrinal articles. The king refused to countenance this, saying, according to William Barlow, 'I will have one doctrine and one discipline, one religion in substance and in ceremony.'[50]

Three articles, in particular, anchored the Church of England's distinctive, and to puritans objectionable, practices within her public confession: Articles 36, 37, and 20. Article 36 establishes that 'The book of consecration of archbishops and bishops, and ordering of priests and deacons, lately set forth in the time of Edward the Sixth, and confirmed at the same time by authority of Parliament, doth contain all things necessary to such consecration and ordering: neither hath it anything that of itself is superstitious and ungodly.' Since the Edwardian ordinal stated, in its preface, that 'It is evident unto all men, diligently reading holy scripture, and ancient authors, that from the Apostles' time there hath been three orders of ministers in Christ's Church, bishops, priests and deacons', Article 36 is implicitly asserting the legitimacy of the Church of England's episcopal hierarchy. Consequently, subscription to the Articles implied acceptance of an episcopal polity, an objection articulated in *The First Admonition to Parliament* (1572).[51] That, of course, made subscription uncomfortable for those English churchmen persuaded by the widespread Reformed insistence on the fundamental parity of Christian ministers (ministerial parity was enjoined by the French Confession, the Belgic Confession, and the Second Helvetic Confession),[52] let alone for those who felt that Calvin's quadripartite model was the pattern of ecclesiastical polity found in the New Testament, an opinion reflected in the *Second Admonition to Parliament* (1572).[53]

Fortunately for those defending the Church of England's established polity, the Reformed position on bishops was far from uniform. Indeed, references to positive assessments of episcopal government by Calvin, Zanchi, and other Reformed writers from across Europe, became staples of conformist apologetic. Such references were useful to the conformist cause, because they demonstrated that a Reformed theological identity was by no means

---

[47] 13 Eliz. c.12, s.4.   [48] Haugaard, *Elizabeth and the English Reformation*, p. 257.
[49] William Barlow, *The Summe and Substance of the Conference* (1625), p. 60.
[50] Barlow, *Summe and Substance*, p. 73.
[51] Ian Archer and Douglas Price (eds.), *English Historical Documents 1558–1603* (2011), p. 180.
[52] Cochrane (ed.), *Reformed Confessions*, pp. 155, 212, 274.
[53] Archer and Price (eds.), *English Historical Documents 1558–1603*, pp. 183–9.

inconsistent with the retention of an episcopal polity, whatever puritans might have claimed. The openness of the Reformed tradition to a variety of church polities perhaps explains why Salvart simply presented Jewel's endorsement of episcopacy without comment in the *Harmonia Confessionum*,[54] although he routinely made critical observations about the confessions he included, when he felt the need: an entire section of the *Harmony* was devoted to just such 'Observations'.[55] This point is reinforced when it is recognized that the Churches of England and Ireland were not, in fact, the only Reformed Churches to retain a hierarchical structure: the Churches of Poland-Lithuania and Hungary did so as well.[56] So, whilst the episcopal commitment of Article 36 might irritate those churchmen who wanted England to look more like Geneva, it did not sever the English Church from the wider Reformed world.

The shape of the Church's ministry was closely related, in the Reformed mind, to the practice of ecclesiastical discipline; and ecclesiastical discipline was accepted by all Reformed theologians as fundamental to the well-being of the Church. Theologians such as Martin Bucer and Theodore Beza went even further, arguing that discipline was essential to the existence of the Church. The longer of the Church of England's two official catechisms, written by Alexander Nowell, underlined the importance of ecclesiastical discipline, reminding the catechumen that, in a Church, 'if it be well ordered, there shall be seen to be observed a certain order and manner of governance, and such a form of ecclesiastical discipline, that it shall not be free for any that abideth in the flock, publicly to speak or do anything wickedly or in heinous sort, without punishment'.[57] Nowell's catechism was first published in 1570, and the canons of 1571 gave it official sanction, alongside the shorter catechism contained in the Book of Common Prayer. Given such a widespread concern with discipline, the Articles troubled those churchmen who felt that the Church should possess a structure for imposing that discipline on the faithful which was independent of the magistrate, and their opinion was expressed in the *Second Admonition to Parliament* (1572).[58] Article 37, by contrast, stated that 'The Queen's majesty hath the chief power in this realm of England, and other her dominions, unto whom the chief government of all estates of this realm, whether they be ecclesiastical or civil, in all causes doth appertain', thus placing the Church's disciplinary jurisdiction under the explicit control of the magistrate.

---

[54] Salvart, *Harmony*, p. 359.   [55] Salvart, *Harmony*, sigs. Kkiiiir–Mmviiir.
[56] Benedict, *Christ's Churches*, pp. 269, 276, 280.
[57] Alexander Nowell, *A Catechisme, or First Instruction and Learning of Christian Religion* (1570), 46v.
[58] Archer and Price (eds.), *English Historical Documents 1558–1603*, pp. 187–9.

Here, however, the Church of England found herself on one side of a long-running, but clearly intra-Reformed dispute. The Swiss Reformed theologians of Zürich and Bern, as opposed to the French Reformed of Geneva, had always rejected the idea that the Church should have a jurisdiction independent of the magistrate. Indeed, the Swiss Reformed Churches had actively resisted the establishment of independent ecclesiastical jurisdictions, successfully in the Pays de Vaud during the 1550s, and unsuccessfully in the Palatinate during the 1560s.[59] Once again, the Reformed tradition proved itself sufficiently diverse to encompass the monarch's supreme authority over the English Church. Indeed, Richard Hooker saw the English conflict between puritans and conformists in England as merely the latest front in the Europe-wide battle over Genevan discipline.[60]

Those churchmen who agitated for an independent ecclesiastical jurisdiction generally took exception to various aspects of English liturgical practice as well. The aspects of ceremony which caused them most concern included the requirement that the minister sign a cross on the child's forehead during baptism, the requirement that the communicant kneel to receive the sacrament, and the requirement that the clergy wear liturgical vestments to conduct services. Such practices were indirectly rooted in the Church's confessional statement through Article 20, which opens with this statement: 'The church hath power to decree rites or ceremonies, and authority in controversies of faith.' This clause seems to have been added late in the production of the Articles, probably by the Privy Council, so although it appears in the official Latin edition published in 1563, it was not in several other editions from Elizabeth's reign.[61] As a result, its authenticity was hotly contested by those who objected to English liturgical use.[62] Certainly, the Second Helvetic Confession expressed more caution about the Church's right to impose ceremonies: 'For if the Apostles did not want to impose upon Christian people ceremonies or rites which were appointed by God, who, I pray, in his right mind would obtrude upon them the inventions devised by man? The more the mass of rites is increased in the church, the more is detracted, not only from Christian liberty, but also from Christ, and from faith in him.'[63] The French and Belgic Confessions echoed these concerns.[64]

A number of Elizabethan bishops were themselves unhappy about the ceremonies which the Church of England had maintained. Referring to the

---

[59] Charles Gunnoe, *Thomas Erastus and the Palatinate: A Renaissance Physician in the Second Reformation* (Leiden, 2011), p. 172.
[60] Hooker, *Ecclesiastical Polity*, I, 91–2.
[61] Charles Hardwick, *A History of the Articles of Religion* (1876), pp. 140–4.
[62] Cornelius Burges, *No Sacrilege nor Sin to Alienate or Purchase Cathedral Lands* (1660), Postscript; John Pearson, *An Answer to Dr Burges* (1660), p. 16.
[63] Cochrane (ed.), *Reformed Confessions*, p. 296.
[64] Cochrane (ed.), *Reformed Confessions*, pp. 155–6, 212.

ongoing arguments between puritans and conformists, Edmund Grindal wrote to Bullinger in 1568, claiming that 'we who are now bishops, on our first return, and before we entered on our ministry, contended long and earnestly for the removal of those things that have occasioned the present dispute'. Grindal added, however, that 'as we were unable to prevail, either with the Queen or the Parliament, we judged it best, after a consultation on the subject, not to desert our churches for the sake of a few ceremonies, and those not unlawful in themselves, especially since the pure doctrine of the gospel remained in all its integrity and freedom'.[65] The ongoing struggle with the puritans over liturgical conformity appears to have hardened the bishops' resolve; and, in their defence of the controversial ceremonies, conformist churchmen were once again able to draw on some powerful Reformed support, not least because the theologians of Zürich entered the lists on the conformist side.[66] In 1570, a pamphlet was published containing the opinions of Bullinger, Rudolf Gwalther, Martin Bucer, and Peter Martyr Vermigli, all of whom supported the Church's right to impose liturgical ceremonies for the sake of order and beauty. Vermigli's opinion, dating back to the Edwardian Vestiarian Controversy during the 1550s, even anticipates Richard Hooker's defence of the English liturgy on the grounds of natural law. Observing that some elements of Old Testament worship 'had some respect to comeliness, to order and to some commodity', Vermigli went on, 'and these, I judge, may be restored and retained, as things agreeing to the light of nature, and inducing to some profitable use'.[67] Conformist clergy could therefore demonstrate that the controverted ceremonies did not actually undermine the Church's Reformed identity, any more than the royal supremacy, or the retention of episcopal government did. The warrant which the Articles provided for such aspects of the Church's life did not therefore prevent them from being an authentically Reformed confession.

The assumption that the Thirty-Nine Articles were the authoritative declaration of the Church of England's doctrine and practice—the *Confessio Anglicana*—did not keep churchmen from seeking to improve them, particularly when new opinions were voiced to which they took exception. Andrew Willet observed, for example, that 'there are many unsound doctrines which, because they are omitted, are not opposite to the articles of religion established', and urged Parliament to consider amplifying the Articles as a result.[68] At the Hampton Court Conference, John Rainolds suggested that the Articles should be supplemented, in order to rule out certain opinions which he held to

---

[65] *Zürich Letters*, I, p. 169.
[66] W. J. Torrance Kirby, *The Zürich Connection and Tudor Political Theology* (Leiden, 2007), pp. 209–10.
[67] Anon., *Whether it be Mortall Sinne to Transgresse Civil Lawes* (1570), p. 69.
[68] Andrew Willet, *Limbo-mastix* (1604), Dedicatory Epistle to Parliament.

be inconsistent with the right understanding of predestination. In particular, he requested that Article 16 should be altered to make clear that a justified believer could not fall finally from grace, and that the 'nine assertions orthodoxal' be included in the articles of religion.[69]

The 'nine assertions orthodoxal'—commonly known as the Lambeth Articles—had been issued by Archbishop Whitgift in 1595, in order to settle an academic dispute in Cambridge about predestination. They offered a more detailed statement of predestination than those found in the Thirty-Nine Articles or the Second Helvetic Confession; explicitly endorsing double predestination, the indefectibility of the elect, and the incapacity of some to be saved. When the queen discovered that the Lambeth Articles had been issued without her authority she ordered them to be recalled and suppressed. However, the doctrine which they expressed enjoyed widespread support amongst the English clergy. This was partly because John Calvin's writings had become much more influential in England,[70] and partly because the assertion of double predestination was becoming increasingly normative amongst the Reformed Churches of mainland Europe. At the Colloquy of Bern (1588), for example, all the Churches of Switzerland had endorsed double predestination, including those which had previously been rather reticent on the subject.[71] Against this background, the Thirty-Nine Articles' teaching on predestination, which had been unexceptional within the Reformed theological world of the 1560s and 1570s, began to look insufficiently precise to a number of English churchmen.

When the matter was raised during the Hampton Court Conference, however, King James expressed a preference for concise confessional statements, and refused to add the Lambeth Articles to the existing Thirty-Nine.[72] As a result, English theologians desirous of greater clarity about predestination could only refer to the Lambeth Articles as explanatory guides to the Church's official teaching, as John Prideaux did in a lecture of 1616.[73] British attendance at the Synod of Dort did not change this situation, since the canons of Dort were never considered binding on the English Church.[74] Samuel Ward, for example, although he was confident that nothing had been defined at Dort which was contrary to the doctrine and discipline of the English Church, nonetheless agreed with Richard Montagu that no English churchman was bound to assent to the Synod's decisions, beyond what he judged consonant with Scripture and the Thirty-Nine Articles.[75]

---

[69] Barlow, *Summe and Substance*, p. 24.
[70] Nicholas Tyacke, *Anti-Calvinists: The Rise of English Arminianism c.1590–1640* (Oxford, 1987), pp. 1–8.
[71] Benedict, *Christ's Churches*, p. 304.   [72] Barlow, *Summe and Substance*, p. 39.
[73] Prideaux, *Viginti-duae Lectiones*, p. 11.   [74] Milton, *British Delegation*, pp. il–l.
[75] Ward, *Opera Nonnulla*, p. 114.

Matters were rather different in the Church of Ireland, however. For when that Church drew up its confessional statement in 1615, the Lambeth Articles were included, alongside a number of other concessions to puritan opinion.[76] And since the Churches of England and Ireland were so closely allied, some English churchmen argued that the Irish Articles could appropriately be used to explain the English ones.[77] Some theologians, however, interpreted the Church of England's repeated failure to enshrine double predestination in her confessional statement as giving licence to hold a range of opinions on the subject. That was clearly Richard Montagu's position, as we have seen.[78] In the *Royal Declaration* of 1628, King Charles effectively lent his sanction to the existing latitude, by prohibiting any attempt to show that the Articles should be interpreted in a particular way.[79]

Theologians sympathetic to the Reformed tradition were not, however, the only people who felt that the Articles needed a degree of clarification; and deploying the Lambeth Articles was not the only way that they could be made to speak with a different emphasis. As we have seen, Richard Montagu accepted the authority of the Articles but they were not, for him, the only source of authority within the Church. The Book of Common Prayer stood alongside them. Montagu made this clear at the beginning of *Appello Caesarem*, where he wrote, 'unto the public doctrine of the Church of England do I appeal, contained in those two and by all subscribed books of the Articles and divine services of the Church'.[80] He was consequently able to deploy the Prayer Book baptism service against the Reformed idea that the truly justified would never fall from grace. Edmund Reeve argued along similar lines in his *The Christian Divinitie contained in the divine service of the Church of England* (1631). Reeve viewed the Articles as just one of a long sequence of authoritative documents, that began with the Prayer Book and included the *Constitutions and Canons Ecclesiastical* (1604),[81] and he constructed a complete systematic theology—a 'sum of divinity' as he called it—by weaving them all together. Reeve even argued that the clergy ought not to 'expound any place of scripture so as it may make against the harmony of the Church doctrine'. To the Reformed harmony of confessions, in other words, he was proposing an alternative harmony of solely English religious authorities.[82]

Godly dissatisfaction with the Articles was given somewhat freer rein during the Westminster Assembly, when the delegates were at first instructed

---

[76] Alan Ford, *James Ussher: Theology, History and Politics in Early Modern Ireland and England* (Oxford, 2007), pp. 85–103.
[77] Ford, *James Ussher*, p. 102. [78] Montagu, *Appello Caesarem*, pp. 29–30.
[79] Coward and Gaunt (eds.), *English Historical Documents 1603–1660*, p. 286.
[80] Montagu, *Appello Caesarem*, p. 9.
[81] Edmund Reeve, *The Christian Divinitie contained in the Divine Service of the Church of England* (1631), p. 390.
[82] Edmund Reeve, *The Communion Book Catechisme Expounded* (1636), sig. C2r.

to focus on the Articles, in order 'to free and vindicate the doctrine of them from all aspersions and false interpretations'.[83] They duly did so for a number of months, adding scriptural citations, as well as revising and extending a number of articles in a more scrupulously Reformed direction. Before the work had been completed, however, the Commons ordered the Assembly to desist, and draw up, instead, a confession suitable for all three kingdoms. The Westminster Confession which resulted was both much longer than the Thirty-Nine Articles and also replete with biblical references. It also systematically addressed the shortcomings that the godly had seen in the Articles. Chapter 3 was explicit in its commitment to double predestination; Chapter 17 denied that those effectually called can finally fall from grace. Chapter 20 proclaimed liberty of conscience from all human additions to God's Word, and Chapter 21 underlined that the Bible was the sole and sufficient rule for Christian worship. Chapter 30 laid down that civil and ecclesiastical government were quite distinct and that only Church officers had authority to suspend or exclude people from Holy Communion. The Westminster Confession, in other words, was what the godly had been demanding for decades.

The spotlight returned to the Thirty-Nine Articles only at the Restoration, when their re-imposition was being discussed. In that debate, Cornelius Burges, who had been the effective prolocutor of the Westminster Assembly, and would be ejected for nonconformity in 1662, reiterated the classic godly position that they needed revision and expansion. John Pearson, by contrast, who served as Lady Margaret professor of divinity in Cambridge, after the Restoration, and later as bishop of Chester, answered him, defending the clarity and orthodoxy of the Articles, and underlining that 'the book of articles is not, nor is pretended to be, a complete body of divinity, or a comprehension of all Christian doctrines necessary to be taught; but an enumeration of some truths which upon and since the Reformation have been denied'.[84] As a result, Pearson argued, there was no need whatever to revise the public doctrine of the Church of England before subscription was once again imposed.

The Thirty-Nine Articles were accepted on all sides as the authoritative statement of the Church of England's faith, even by those who wished to see them revised. They hold, as a result, a privileged position in any attempt to discern that Church's confessional identity. The teaching which the Articles embrace, with regard to the Lord's Supper, places the Church of England unambiguously alongside the Reformed Churches of Europe; and this was recognized both in England and elsewhere. The Reformed tradition was, however, a diverse one; and the Articles enable the Church of England to be placed more precisely within it. Most obviously, the Articles endorse the

---

[83] *The Proceedings of the Assembly of Divines upon the Thirty-Nine Articles of the Church of England* (1647), Preface.
[84] Pearson, *Answer*, p. 9.

legitimacy of episcopal polity, a polity which only a handful of Reformed Churches retained. They also show that, on a range of issues, both practical and doctrinal, the Church of England was rather closer to the Reformed Church of Zürich, than to the Reformed Church of Geneva. This was, of course, a cause for regret amongst those English churchmen who held Geneva to be the benchmark of Reformed orthodoxy. But conformist churchmen were able to resist the pressure to make England more like Geneva, not least by exploiting the very diversity of the Reformed tradition of which they were a part. To that extent, the struggle between puritans and conformists should best be seen, perhaps, not as a debate about 'Anglicanism'—a concept foreign to both parties—but as an exploration of the breadth of the Reformed tradition.

SELECT BIBLIOGRAPHY

Anon., *The Proceedings of the Assembly of Divines upon the Thirty-Nine Articles of the Church of England* (1647).
Benedict, Philip, *Christ's Churches Purely Reformed: A Social History of Calvinism* (New Haven, CT, 2002).
Hardwick, Charles, *A History of the Articles of Religion* (1876).
Kirby, Torrance, *The Zürich Connection and Tudor Political Theology* (Leiden, 2007).
MacCulloch, Diarmaid, 'The Myth of the English Reformation', *Journal of British Studies*, 30 (1991): 1–19.
Milton, Anthony, *Catholic and Reformed: The Roman and Protestant Churches in English Protestant Thought, 1600–1640* (Cambridge, 1995).
Pearson, John, *An Answer to Dr Burges* (1660).
Rogers Thomas, *The Faith, Doctrine and Religion, Professed and Protected in the Realme of England* (Cambridge, 1607).
Salvart, Jean-François, *An Harmony of the Confessions of Faith of the Christian and Reformed Churches* (Cambridge, 1586).
Tyacke, Nicholas, *Anti-Calvinists: The Rise of English Arminianism c.1590–1640* (Oxford, 1987).

12

Cathedrals

Ian Atherton

Cathedrals have often been seen as oddities within the Church of England, sitting uneasily alongside parochial structures or the worship of the people. In 1918 Hensley Henson, newly consecrated as bishop of Hereford, opined that 'the right use to be made of the cathedral foundations has long perplexed the bishops, and constitutes a problem which none has yet succeeded in solving'. Enquiring of a solution, like any self-respecting gentleman he found more sense uttered by his butler than by any churchman.[1] Henson did not reveal his servant's wisdom, leaving modern responses to English cathedrals to take one of three forms. The first has been to ignore them altogether. Bereft of the services of their own Jeeves, some have found it easier to ignore cathedrals than to fit them into their understanding of the Church of England. One handbook to the history and ethos of the Anglican communion makes no mention of cathedrals in its 450 pages.[2] A version of this oversight is to take cathedrals as a given, consign them to their own mental world, safely isolated from the rest of the Church, and then overlook them. Henson, after all, only began to wonder about the role of a cathedral on his elevation to the episcopate; he had not bothered with that question in the previous two decades while he was parish priest, canon of Westminster, or dean of Durham.

A second, diametrically opposed perspective sees cathedrals as an essential part of the Church of England. In the words of a modern Anglican report, they are the church's 'shop windows', the cathedral or choral service 'one of the most significant contributions made by this country to European culture'.[3] The peculiarities and distinctiveness of cathedrals are celebrated as the very embodiment of the Anglican *via media* between Rome (with its cathedrals)

---

[1] H. H. Henson, *Retrospect of an Unimportant Life*, 3 vols. (1942–50), I, p. 272.
[2] S. Sykes and J. Booty (eds.), *The Study of Anglicanism* (1988).
[3] *Heritage and Renewal: The Report of the Archbishops' Commission on Cathedrals* (1994), pp. 17, 51.

and Protestantism (seen as lacking them).[4] Beyond church circles, the secular analogue of this point is that from dairy products to tourism, cathedrals are the essence of Englishness: the country's best-selling brand cheese is named 'Cathedral City', while cathedrals are among the most visited tourist attractions in England.[5]

A third perspective sees cathedrals nostalgically, representing the past. That view can be positive and wistful, cathedrals as symbols of the glories of earlier achievements: legions of guidebooks recount the history of a cathedral not as an institution or a community but as a building understood through its medieval architecture. Cathedrals are also seen positively as symbols of unchanging truth, as in Isaac Williams's High Church poem 'The Cathedral', in which the various parts of an idealized Gothic cathedral prompt meditations on religious doctrine, symbolizing the 'catholic' axis of the Anglican oxymoronic understanding of itself as 'catholic and reformed'.[6] A backward-facing view of cathedrals can also be negative, casting them as bastions of privilege and tradition holding back modernity and change, as in Anthony Trollope's Barchester chronicles or debates about church reform in the 1830s and 1840s;[7] or they are seen as upholding a flawed Establishment, as in protests at St Paul's Cathedral by socialists and others in the 1880s and by anti-capitalist protesters in 2011–12.[8] Whether positive or negative, such perceptions share an image of cathedrals as conservative and resistant to change.

These perspectives matter because all have shaped, and continue to shape, the ways in which both historians and the Church of England itself have thought about the history and role of cathedrals. They matter also because these blind spots and assumptions derive from the history of those cathedrals in the century after the Reformation. The idea of cathedrals as institutional oddities separate from an essentially parochially organized church is written through the structure of so many individual cathedral histories which treat the cathedral in isolation from the diocese or wider church. The idea of cathedrals as conservative is the basis of the most influential interpretation of their post-Reformation role: Diarmaid MacCulloch has argued that after the

---

[4] M. Chapman, *Anglicanism: A Very Short Introduction* (Oxford, 2006), p. 49.

[5] 'Named: Britain's most powerful brands...but can you spot the big cheese?', *Independent*, 12 July 2012; Visit England, 'Annual Survey of Visits to Visitor Attractions', <http://www.visitengland.org/insight-statistics/major-tourism-surveys/attractions/Annual_Survey/> (accessed 1 May 2014); *Spiritual Capital: The Present and Future of English Cathedrals* (2012), pp. 10–11, 14.

[6] [Isaac Williams], *The Cathedral, or the Catholic and Apostolic Church in England* (Oxford, 1838).

[7] W. L. Mathieson, *English Church Reform 1815–1840* (1923), pp. 67–70, 149–53.

[8] *The Standard*, 27 Mar. 1883, p. 4; *Illustrated Police News*, 27 Oct. 1883, p. 4; *Pall Mall Gazette*, 28 Feb. 1887, p. 5; 'Dean Ison reflects on Occupy—one year on', <http://www.stpauls.co.uk/News-Press/News-Archive/2012/Dean-Ison-reflects-on-Occupy-one-year-on> (accessed 1 May 2014).

Reformation cathedrals were 'fossils' from a Catholic past which formed a 'liturgical fifth column' within the Protestant Church, preserving, nourishing, inspiring, and, by the early seventeenth century, spreading conservative, choral, and ceremonial worship. As hothouses of what historians know as 'Laudian' (or high church) Protestantism, cathedrals were fundamental in reshaping the character of the Church of England, and were therefore crucial in the creation of a distinctive Anglicanism as a third way between Rome and Geneva.[9]

Such views find powerful support from three quarters. The first is the parallel of Scotland, where a more thoroughly Calvinist Reformation saw the abolition of cathedrals (and bishops). In 1560 the *First Book of Discipline* of the Scottish kirk declared that all cathedrals were, like monasteries and friaries, 'monuments and places' of idolatry and so should be 'utterly suppressed', while the *Second Book of Discipline* (1578) reinforced the message, demanding that cathedral chapters 'be uterly abrogate and abolished'.[10] Scottish cathedrals were either converted to parochial use (which usually meant the congregation retreating into a part of the building) or completely abandoned.[11] The Scottish example (seconded by Calvinist Churches in continental Europe) suggested that fully reformed Protestantism had no place for cathedrals. The second implication that England's continuing cathedrals are a sign that the Church was but halfly-reformed is the fact that all were abolished in 1649 during England's second Reformation. For the next eleven years the public profession of the nation sought its most intensely Protestant expression without the benefit of deans, prebendaries, or singing men, while cathedral buildings were abandoned, threatened with demolition, or put to other uses.[12]

The third suggestion that cathedrals were incompatible with fully reformed Protestantism comes from the strains of puritan critique that echoed so loudly through Elizabethan England, and which has informed many historians' views of cathedrals. The early stages of the English Reformation had seen criticism of prebendaries' supposed greed, idleness, and failure to preach—but these were swipes at particular individuals or invective against Catholic cathedrals, rather than an assault on the existence of such institutions in a reformed Church.[13] The growth of a more radical, Presbyterian sentiment in England from c.1570,

---

[9] D. MacCulloch, 'The Myth of the English Reformation', *Journal of British Studies*, 30 (1991): 1–19 (pp. 8–9); D. MacCulloch, 'Putting the English Reformation on the Map', *Transactions of the Royal Historical Society*, 6th series, 15 (2005): 75–95 (pp. 90–2).

[10] *The First and Second Booke of Discipline* ([Amsterdam], 1621), p. 26.

[11] R. Fawcett, *Scottish Cathedrals* (1997), pp. 97–8, 100–1, 112–17.

[12] I. Atherton, 'Cathedrals and the British Revolution', in M. J. Braddick and D. L. Smith (eds.), *The Experience of Revolution in Stuart Britain and Ireland* (Cambridge, 2011), pp. 96–112.

[13] [Henry Brinkelow], *The Complaynt of Roderyck Mors* [Strassburg, 1542?], p. 47; William Turner, *The Hunting of the Romyshe Vuolfe* [Emden, 1555?], sigs. [Dviii^v], Fii.

Cathedrals

however, questioned the very existence of a cathedral, and in 1572 a call for their abolition was publicly launched in *An Admonition to the Parliament*:

> Cathedrall churches, the dennes... of all loytering lubbers, wher master Deane, master Vicedeane, master Canons or Prebendaries the greater, master pettie Canons, or Canons the lesser, master Chanceller of the churche, master treasurer, otherwise called Judas the purssebearer, the cheefe chauntor, singin men speciall favourers of religion, squeaking queresters, organ players, gospellers, pistelers, pentioners, readers, vergerirs. etc. live in great idlenesse, and have their abiding. If you would knowe whence all these came, we can easely answere you, that they came from the Pope, as oute of the Troian horses bellye, to the destruction of Gods kingdome.[14]

Radical puritan critique of cathedrals in the 1570s and 1580s coalesced into two strands. One saw cathedrals as a damaging drain on the Church, parasites on the parochial ministry, with continuing condemnation of idle, greedy canons as non-residents and non-preachers, 'loitering fat fed great Residentiaries', 'wicked belligods', and 'Idle singing men', who 'sing badlie, rather of Custome then devocion'.[15] Linked to these complaints was trenchant criticism that much of cathedrals' wealth was in the form of impropriations and was therefore at the expense of parishes, so that while canons were 'well fed and enriched with the spoiles of divers the fattest benefits therabouts', parishes were served by 'leane Curats' or 'Idoll Shepheards and sielie bare readers', so encouraging the growth of popery.[16] The other strand of criticism, distinct but related, saw cathedrals as strongholds of popish practices. The use of copes and the images to be found in many cathedrals were seen as idolatrous,[17] but most censure was directed against organs and singing, 'tossinge of psalms from side to side in the quyer' which was 'a mockerie of Gods trewe worship'.[18] In the late 1580s an intemperate diatribe united these two branches of criticism:

> These are indeede verie Dennes of Theves, where the tyme and place of Gods service, preaching, and praier, is moste filthily abused In pyping with Organnes, in singing, ringing and Trowling of the Psalmes from one side of the Quiar to another, with squealing of Chaunting Queresters, disguised, (as are all the reste) in white surplesses, others in cornered capes and filthie Coapes, in pistelling and gospelling with such vaine Mockeries, contrary to the commaundment of God and true worshipping of God, Imitating the Manners and fashions of Antechriste the pope, that man of Synne and childe of perdition, with his other rable of miscreaunts and shavelings... These unprofitable members, for the moste parte Dumme Doggs, Unskilfull sacrificing priestes, Destroyeing Drones, or rather

---

[14] W. H. Frere and C. E. Douglas (eds.), *Puritan Manifestoes* (1954), p. 33.
[15] A. Peel (ed.), *The Seconde Parte of a Register*, 2 vols. (Cambridge, 1915), I, p. 178; II, pp. 8, 12, 15, 44; Bodleian Library, MS Perrot 1, fos. 25v, 94v, 105, 110v.
[16] Peel, *Seconde Parte*, I, pp. 178, 255; II, pp. 12, 17–18, 96, 195, 199.
[17] Peel, *Seconde Parte*, I, p. 198; II, pp. 53, 191.
[18] Peel, *Seconde Parte*, I, pp. 151, 199, 259; *A Briefe and Plaine Declaration, Concerning the Desires of all those Faithfull Ministers* (1584), pp. 67–8.

Caterpillars of the Word, they consume yerly, some £2500, some £3000, some more, some lesse, whereof no profit, but rather great hurte, commeth to the Churche of God and this commonwealth. They are Dennes of Lazie Loytering Lubberds, the verie harboroures of all disceitfull and Tymeserving hippocrites.[19]

In 1589, seeking to act upon such criticisms, a bill was presented to the Commons for the dissolution of cathedrals: since cathedrals were full of 'Idell persons' who 'spend all yt they haue in feasting, banqueting and entertaining such as haue no need therof... and in dysing, carding, gaming and vnchaste living', they should be dissolved and their wealth used to maintain the parochial ministry, education, the relief of the poor, and other good works.[20] The bill made no progress.

Radical puritans have preoccupied historians, but far greater threats to the existence of cathedrals came from two very different directions, though these hazards were informed by the above strains of Protestant criticism. The first was founded on the crown's financial problems, especially the dramatically rising costs of warfare. Cathedrals looked wealthy and appeared to some ripe for plucking. Those who had doubts about how well the Church used its wealth included Archbishop Thomas Cranmer, who in 1539 defined a prebendary as a 'good viander' who spent his time and income 'in much idleness and... superfluous belly cheer'.[21] Consequently, almost every time the crown went to war between the 1530s and the 1640s, proposals circulated either to put down cathedrals, or to strip them of their wealth, and apply the proceeds to raise troops. Such calls came c.1534 at the time of rebellion in Ireland,[22] in 1549 against military intervention in Scotland,[23] and during war against Spain in the 1580s[24] and 1620s.[25] Despite a few minor losses of estates, cathedrals survived until 1649, and it was the bishops who suffered the greater losses.[26] And yet the threat to cathedrals was real: one of Elizabeth's senior judges worried c.1580 that with the monasteries pulled down by her father, 'cathedrall churches shall be next'.[27]

An even more serious and immediate challenge to many cathedrals came from the hunters of concealed lands. The dissolution of monasteries and

---

[19] Peel, *Seconde Parte*, II, p. 211.   [20] BL, Additional MS 48066, fos. 8–11.

[21] Thomas Cranmer, *Miscellaneous Writings*, ed. J. E. Cox (Cambridge, 1846), p. 396.

[22] L. Stone, 'The Political Programme of Thomas Cromwell', *Bulletin of the Institute of Historical Research*, 24 (1951): 1–18 (pp. 9–10).

[23] BL, Cotton MS Galba B xix, f. 19r.

[24] BL, Lansdowne MS 45, f. 99r; Additional MS 48066, fos. 1v, 14; Inner Temple Library, Petyt MS 538, fos. 122–4.

[25] Northampton RO, Finch-Hatton MS 105, fos. 1–3; John Hacket, *Scrinia Reserata* (1693), pp. 203–6.

[26] F. Heal, *Of Prelates and Princes: A Study of the Economic and Social Position of the Tudor Episcopate* (Cambridge, 1980); I. Atherton and B. A. Holderness, 'The Dean and Chapter Estates since the Reformation', in I. Atherton, E. Fernie, C. Harper-Bill, and A. Hassell Smith (eds.), *Norwich Cathedral: Church, City and Diocese, 1096–1996* (1996), p. 666.

[27] John Harington, *Nugae Antiquae*, 2 vols. (1804), II, p. 7.

chantries had produced a confused situation in which it was believed that much former ecclesiastical land which should have reverted to the crown continued to lie concealed, encouraging speculators to obtain licences from Elizabeth to hunt out such land in the hope of rewards from a grateful queen. From the 1570s such men turned their attention to a number of cathedrals, claiming that deficiencies in their royal charters meant that they lacked a legal footing or did not, in law, exist at all. The cathedrals of Norwich, Ely, and Wells; the vicars choral of Hereford; and Manchester collegiate church were all individually threatened between the 1570s and 1604, but all cathedrals, especially those founded or refounded by Henry VIII, were vulnerable. A series of unedifying legal wrangles which consumed and threatened to dissolve cathedrals were only partly ended by a statute of 1593.[28]

The intellectual justification for so much apparently self-interested greed in seeking to devour cathedrals and their wealth was that they had lost their principal function at the Reformation. Medieval cathedrals had been, above all, factories of prayer, machines generating in as elaborate a fashion as possible the *opus Dei*, the ceaseless round of prayer and praise that was the highest calling of the Church. On the eve of the Reformation, Lincoln Cathedral had, for example, twenty-seven altars at which were celebrated perhaps forty masses a day, besides the eight daily offices.[29] The Protestant reinterpretation of the roles of the clergy and the Church itself from sacrifice to preaching raised fundamental questions about the role of cathedrals. Historians have suggested that the question of what a Protestant cathedral, prebendary, or chorister was for went unanswered between the 1540s and 1590s until small numbers of cathedral clergy began exploiting some of the unintended consequences of Cranmer's prayer book to emphasize the importance of elaborate ritual, ceremonial, and music in liturgy and worship. These high church or 'avant-garde conformists', associated especially but not exclusively with Westminster Abbey, were to the seventeenth-century English Church what the Oxford movement was to the nineteenth, and hence have been christened the Westminster movement. They rediscovered a role for cathedrals as diocesan mother churches, exemplars of ceremonial worship and the beauty of holiness and hence, so it is argued, cathedrals became the midwives

---

[28] A. Hassell Smith, *County and Court: Government and Politics in Norfolk 1558–1603* (Oxford, 1974), pp. 265–75; Huntington Library, EL 1983, 1986–7; I. Atherton, 'The Dean and Chapter, Reformation to Restoration: 1541–1660', in P. Meadows and N. Ramsay (eds.), *A History of Ely Cathedral* (Woodbridge, 2003), pp. 182–3; H. E. Reynolds, *Wells Cathedral* (Leeds, [1880]), pp. 243–78; C. L. Hunwick, 'Who Shall Reform the Reformers? Corruption in the Elizabethan Church of Manchester', *Transactions of the Lancashire and Cheshire Antiquarian Society*, 101 (2005): 85–100.

[29] D. Lepine, *A Brotherhood of Canons Serving God: English Secular Cathedrals in the Later Middle Ages* (Woodbridge, 1995), pp. 7–9.

of Laudianism that swept through (or was rammed down the throats of) parishes in the 1630s.[30]

That view of cathedrals in the century between the Reformation and the civil war, however, faces three problems. The first is that it is far from clear that Laudian ceremonialism emerged from cathedrals or that cathedrals were the midwives of Laudianism.[31] William Laud and others argued that churches should have a railed, east-end, altar-wise communion table because that was the practice of cathedrals since the Reformation;[32] but that precedent was a convenient fiction, as Laud's fiercest critic, William Prynne, delighted in exposing.[33] No cathedral had kept a railed, east-end table under Elizabeth.[34] Moreover, before 1617 and Laud's changes at Gloucester and Richard Neile's at Durham Cathedral (moving the communion table, enforcing bowing to that table, and improving both the fabric and conduct in services) no cathedral lived up to the Laudian ideal. Indeed, it took Laud and Neile as bishops and archbishops many years of persuading, hectoring, and cajoling to make all cathedrals fit the Laudian mould of altar-wise table, ceremonious worship, and beautified fabric. Many cathedrals such as Rochester, Worcester, Hereford, and Chester did not make the changes until 1633–4, just in time for the bishops then to impose the use of the diocesan mother church on parishes.[35] Although a programme of the 'beauty of holiness' that anticipated many of the priorities of the Laudian movement in the 1630s was enthusiastically instigated between 1617 and 1628,[36] cathedrals as a whole were not the seedbeds of the Laudian revolution in which ceremony had grown in the half century after the Reformation before bursting forth gloriously under the early Stuarts. Cathedrals had to be frog-marched by a handful of zealots into the new Laudian order.

The second problem with an understanding of post-Reformation cathedrals as fossils, medieval relics that survived into the Protestant age, is that of explaining their survival. Historians have generally been at a loss to understand why Protestant England kept its cathedrals when so many other ecclesiastical institutions—shrines, pilgrimage, monasteries, chantries—were so easily and so speedily abolished. The continuance of cathedrals has variously

---

[30] MacCulloch, 'Myth', pp. 8–9; R. Houlbrooke, 'Refoundation and Reformation, 1538–1628', in Atherton et al. (eds.), *Norwich Cathedral*, pp. 538–9; J. Merritt, 'The Cradle of Laudianism?: Westminster Abbey, 1558–1630', *JEH*, 52 (2001): 623–46.

[31] I. Atherton, 'Cathedrals, Laudianism, and the British Churches', *Historical Journal*, 53 (2010): 895–918.

[32] S. Eward (ed.), *Gloucester Cathedral Chapter Act Book, 1616–1687* (Gloucestershire Record Society, 21, 2007), p. 3; C. Wren, *Parentalia* (1750), p. 75.

[33] W. Prynne, *A Quench-Coale* ([Amsterdam], 1637), p. 161; W. Prynne, *Canterburies Doome* (1646), p. 77.

[34] Atherton, 'Cathedrals, Laudianism', p. 902.

[35] Atherton, 'Cathedrals, Laudianism', pp. 900–2.

[36] K. Fincham and N. Tyacke, *Altars Restored: The Changing Face of English Religious Worship, 1547–c.1700* (Oxford, 2007), p. 232.

been described as 'one of the great puzzles of the English Reformation', 'surprising', and 'strange'; 'somehow, over and over again, the cathedrals were not abolished'.[37] Some historians admit bewilderment over their survival: to the question 'Why do we have cathedrals?', Haigh candidly gave a recursive answer: 'Because they are here—they're here because they're here because they're here because they're here because they're here!'[38] Others turn to the whims of Queen Elizabeth, who saved them out of a personal preference for choral worship.[39] While that is an argument with a long pedigree—as early as 1572, John Bossewell suggested that were it not for the queen, choirs would have completely disappeared from the English Church[40]—it posits a religious settlement which was imposed against the queen's wishes, rather than one that she actively helped to shape. It also relies on a simplistic, binary notion of religion and politics that pits the queen against almost everyone else, rather than a more sophisticated depiction of shades of opinion and shifting alliances within government.[41]

The third problem of the current view of the perplexing survival of cathedrals as the Trojan horse of conservative practices and ideas is that it not only sees cathedrals as static and homogeneous between the Reformation and civil war, but also views them only through the lens of puritan critique. Historians have been too easily dazzled by the vitriolic, shrill, and eminently quotable invective directed against cathedrals, and have swallowed too easily puritan claims about cathedrals. A fresh look at cathedrals suggests, by contrast, that they were neither monochrome, nor static, nor functionless, nor necessarily conservative.

Far from being unchanging, the early stages of the Reformation had seen the most significant changes to England's cathedrals since the Normans had reorganized sees and cathedrals and rebuilt cathedral churches. Those changes had left the English and Welsh Church with twenty-three cathedrals for twenty-two dioceses, for the dioceses of Bath and Wells, and of Coventry and Lichfield, had two cathedrals each, while tiny Sodor and Man had no cathedral foundation. Thirteen were secular cathedrals, governed by chapters of secular clergy; the remaining ten were monastic cathedrals, governed by a prior and a convent of monks—an almost uniquely English experiment in cathedral governance. In the later 1520s Cardinal Wolsey opened negotiations

---

[37] D. MacCulloch, *The Later Reformation in England, 1547–1603* (2nd edn., Basingstoke, 2001), p. 79; C. Cross, '"Dens of Loitering Lubbers": Protestant Protest against Cathedral Foundations, 1540–1640', in D. Baker (ed.), *Schism, Heresy and Religious Protest* (SCH, 9, 1972), p. 237; C. Haigh, *Why Do We Have Cathedrals? A Historian's View* (St George's Cathedral Lecture, no. 4, Perth, 1998), pp. 4, 6.

[38] Haigh, *Why Do We Have Cathedrals?*, p. 6.

[39] MacCulloch, 'Putting the English Reformation on the Map', p. 91.

[40] J. Bossewell, *Workes of Armorie* (1572), f. 14r.

[41] N. Jones, *Faith by Statute: Parliament and the Settlement of Religion 1559* (1982).

with Rome to augment the number of English dioceses and cathedrals, since many dioceses such as Lincoln or Coventry and Lichfield were very large.[42] Wolsey's fall in 1529–30 ended these proposals, but the plans were dusted off in the later 1530s as the monasteries were being dissolved, and although grandiose schemes for a cathedral and diocese for each English county or pair of counties were abandoned, between 1540 and 1542 Henry VIII created six new cathedrals and dioceses: Bristol, Chester, Gloucester, Osney (rapidly relocated to Oxford), Peterborough, and Westminster. At the same time the ten monastic cathedrals were rationalized. Two were dissolved as superfluous (Bath and Coventry), so that each bishop had only one cathedral, while the remaining eight were converted to the government of a dean and chapter of secular clergy.[43] Experimentation and change did not stop in 1542. In 1545 Henry oversaw legislation abolishing collegiate churches (another form of capitular body like cathedrals, and sometimes mistaken for cathedrals); Edward VI completed the task, and within a few years around 170 collegiate churches had been dissolved, leaving but a handful including Brecon and Windsor.[44] Edward then established a new cathedral at Newcastle-upon-Tyne, but Mary rescinded the plan before any changes were implemented.[45] Edward also stripped Westminster of its diocese, merging it back into London, but left the cathedral intact; it survived a further six years to 1556 when Mary converted it back into a Benedictine abbey. She also re-established three collegiate churches dissolved by her brother: Manchester, Southwell, and Wolverhampton (James I refounded Ripon minster, another collegiate church, in 1604).[46] In 1560, Elizabeth dissolved this second abbey at Westminster, turning it into a collegiate church that was commonly but erroneously known as Westminster Abbey.[47] Barring the short-lived abolition of episcopacy in the 1640s and 1650s, the years between 1538 and 1560 thus witnessed the most significant changes to the institutional structure of not only cathedrals but the whole English Church between the Normans and the reforms of the Victorian Ecclesiastical Commission.

---

[42] *Letters and Papers of Henry VIII*, IV, nos. 80, 56-7-8; Thomas Rymer, *Foedera*, 20 vols. (1704–35), XIV, pp. 291–4.

[43] S. E. Lehmberg, *The Reformation of Cathedrals: Cathedrals in English Society, 1485–1603* (Princeton, NJ, 1988), pp. 81–8.

[44] P. Jeffery, *The Collegiate Churches of England and Wales* (2004); J. J. Scarisbrick, 'Henry VIII and the Dissolution of the Secular Colleges', in C. Cross, D. Loades, and J. J. Scarisbrick (eds.), *Law and Government under the Tudors* (Cambridge, 1988), pp. 51–66.

[45] D. Loades, 'The Dissolution of the Diocese of Durham, 1553–54', in D. Marcombe (ed.), *The Last Principality: Politics, Religion and Society in the Bishopric of Durham, 1494–1660* (Nottingham, 1987), pp. 105–12.

[46] J. M. Horn, D. M. Smith, and P. Mussett, *Fasti Ecclesiae Anglicanae 1541–1857*, 13 vols. (1969–2013), VII, pp. 65–6; Jeffery, *Collegiate Churches*, p. 39.

[47] C. S. Knighton, 'Westminster Abbey Restored', in E. Duffy and D. Loades (eds.), *The Church of Mary Tudor* (Aldershot, 2006), pp. 79–82, 100, 105.

Henry's reorganization left the English Church with three types of cathedral. The secular cathedrals (also henceforth known as the cathedrals of the old foundation) usually had large chapters: Lincoln had fifty-eight prebendaries, Wells forty-nine, and Salisbury forty-six, for example. With such large chapters, the daily running of the cathedral was in the hands of the dean and a small number of dignitaries (chancellor, precentor, and treasurer) and a similarly restricted number of residentiary canons. There were great disparities of wealth between individual prebends, and between the incomes of different cathedrals. By contrast, the chapters of the Henrician or new foundation cathedrals were much smaller, ranging from twelve canons at the wealthiest cathedrals (such as Canterbury and Durham) down to only four at the poorest (Carlisle). Canons at a new foundation cathedral received the same basic income, but the wealth of each cathedral varied significantly.[48] The third kind of cathedral was not technically a cathedral at all, but collegiate churches were capitular bodies that shared many of the same functions of cathedrals (and were often mistaken by contemporaries for cathedrals).[49]

Diversity was the hallmark of the system. Heterogeneity is significant because it disturbs simplistic notions of cathedrals as medieval institutions that merely needed to weather the storm of the Reformation so that the Anglican idea of a cathedral and the cathedral service could emerge fully formed under Elizabeth. Variety within the system also helps to explain why Protestant England kept its cathedrals except for the eleven years between regicide and Restoration, 1649–60. For if there was a cathedral system in England, it was part of the wider system of learning and higher education within the Church. Cathedrals should be seen not as a distinct oddity or the spiritual left-overs of the Reformation, but as cousins of the universities. In addition to Christ Church, Oxford, which was both a cathedral and a university college, three aspects make the point. Cathedrals were regularly considered as centres of learning, and John Whitgift merely made a familiar point when he claimed that cathedrals were 'the chiefe and principall ornaments of this Realme, and next to the vniuersities, chiefest mainteyners of godlinesse, religion, and learning'.[50] Henry VIII had stressed the link between cathedrals and learning by ordaining that his new foundations should maintain divinity students at universities, and although that stipulation was soon rescinded,[51] the idea of a cathedral as connected to a university was reinforced

---

[48] Lehmberg, *Reformation of Cathedrals*, pp. 88–9, 166–7.
[49] Jeffery, *Collegiate Churches*; William Sanderson, *A Compleat History of the Life and Raigne of King Charles* (1658), p. 888; Matthew Stevenson, *Florus Britannicus* (1662), p. 42.
[50] John Whitgift, *An Ansvvere to a Certen Libel Intituled, An Admonition to the Parliament* (1572), p. 225.
[51] C. S. Knighton, 'The Provision of Education in the New Cathedral Foundations of Henry VIII', in D. Marcombe and C. S. Knighton (eds.), *Close Encounters: Cathedrals and English Society since 1540* (Nottingham, 1991), pp. 26–34.

in several plans to formalize links between chapter and university preferment. These included suggestions of c.1539 to attach readers in divinity, Greek, Latin, Hebrew, civil law, and physic to each cathedral, and a scheme to refound Ripon minster in the 1590s as a university college, with lecturers in subjects ranging from biblical and modern languages to law, medicine, and music.[52] Although such schemes did not bear fruit, Charles I did annex the Lady Margaret professorship of divinity at Oxford to a prebendal stall at Worcester.[53]

That annexation formalized, and was an expression of, existing links between chapter personnel and college fellows. Cathedral preferment was a common perquisite of academics, and cathedrals were sometimes justified on the grounds that they were a reward for learning.[54] There was considerable cross-over between cathedrals and universities. In 1590, for example, seven of the eleven members of the Worcester chapter were, or had been, university fellows, including two heads of houses and one vice-chancellor.[55] Cathedrals, collegiate churches, and universities were bound together as senior clergy held several positions in plurality. From the late 1560s William Chaderton had a distinguished career in Cambridge University as regius professor of divinity and president of Queens' College; he was also a prebendary of both York and Westminster. He resigned all of these preferments on consecration as bishop of Chester in 1579, but the following year he also became warden (head) of Manchester collegiate church. His kinsman Laurence Chaderton was master of Emmanuel College, Cambridge, from 1584, holding that post from 1598 in combination with a prebend at Lincoln Cathedral. That he held the latter despite Presbyterian views which had seen him claim that deans were abhorred by the Church and were 'members and partes of the whore and strumpet of Rome' shows that cathedral preferment was more a useful supplement to their income for many people, rather than an essential part of their ministry or identity.[56]

The third link between cathedrals and universities was choral worship. Although cathedrals attracted considerable odium for their continuance of choral worship, choirs and organs were not unique to cathedrals. A few

---

[52] H. Cole (ed.), *King Henry the Eighth's Scheme of Bishopricks* (1838), pp. 1–27, 60–1; F. Bussby, 'An Ecclesiasticall Seminarie and College General of Learning and Religion, Planted and Established at Ripon', *JEH*, 4 (1953): 154–61.

[53] Horn, *Fasti*, VII, p. 125.

[54] Westminster Abbey Library, Muniment Book 15, f. 93r; Lambeth Palace Library, MS 2016, f. 25v.

[55] Horn, *Fasti*, VII, pp. 110–33; J. Venn and J. A. Venn, *Alumni Cantabrigienses...from the Earliest Times to 1900*, 4 vols. (Cambridge, 1922–7); J. Foster, *Alumni Oxonienses... 1500–1714*, 4 vols. (Oxford, 1891).

[56] *ODNB*, 'Chaderton, Laurence (1536?–1640)' and 'Chaderton, William (d. 1608)'; Horn, *Fasti*, IX, pp. 70–1; P. Lake, *Moderate Puritans and the Elizabethan Church* (Cambridge, 1982), pp. 25–35.

parishes had them,[57] but so too did a number of university colleges: in addition to Christ Church, at Oxford All Souls, Corpus Christi, Magdalen, New, and St John's colleges kept their choirs after 1559 (although that at St John's was abolished in 1577), while King's and Trinity at Cambridge retained theirs.[58] Cathedrals were neither unique nor anomalies in the post-Reformation English Church. They bore strong kinship with the colleges of the two universities, and should be bracketed with collegiate churches and the three Elizabethan and early Stuart foundations of Gresham College (1597), Chelsea College (1609), and Sion College (1630), established to spread learning, encourage preaching, and foster clerical discussion and sociability.[59] The survival of cathedrals through and after the Reformation was never assured, but it owed more to their similarities with other vital institutions of English learning, and rather less to the whims of a capricious queen.

The idea of a Protestant cathedral was not, therefore, an oxymoron; but there was no consensus on precisely what the essentials of such a Protestant institution should be. No agreed balance between the competing roles and contradictory pressures placed on cathedrals was reached. Cathedrals had several roles to perform. Chapters were the bishop's council, required to consent to episcopal grants.[60] Cathedrals were meant to promote learning and preaching. Royal and episcopal injunctions emphasized preaching at cathedrals, and by the early 1570s most cathedrals had established the post of divinity lecturer,[61] while cathedrals—or open-air pulpits in their precincts (as at St Paul's and Norwich)—staged set-piece sermons, frequently to the city corporation.[62] Chapters often sponsored a grammar school, most famously Westminster Abbey, whose school was known as 'the Kings Nurseries'.[63] Cathedrals also had important charitable roles: hospitality was enjoined on the dean and chapter commensurate with their income, while new foundation

---

[57] J. Willis, *Church Music and Protestantism in Post-Reformation England* (Farnham, 2010), pp. 90–131.

[58] John Scot, *The Foundation of the Vniuersitie of Oxford...1622* (1622); John Scot, *The Foundation of the Vniversitie of Cambridge...1622* (1622); P. M. Gouk, 'Music', in N. Tyacke (ed.), *The History of the University of Oxford*, vol. IV: *Seventeenth-Century Oxford* (Oxford, 1997), pp. 627–8.

[59] I. R. Adamson, 'The Administration of Gresham College and its Fluctuating Fortunes as a Scientific Institution in the Seventeenth Century', *History of Education*, 9 (1980): 13–25 (pp. 14–16); Thomas Faulkner, *An Historical and Topographical Description of Chelsea*, 2 vols. (1829), II, pp. 218–34.

[60] Edward Coke, *The Reports* (1658), p. 198.

[61] W. H. Frere and W. P. M. Kennedy (eds.), *Visitation Articles and Injunctions*, 3 vols. (1910), II, pp. 125, 137–8; III, pp. 78, 318; J. Saunders, 'The Limitations of Statutes: Elizabethan Schemes to Reform New Foundation Cathedral Statutes', *JEH*, 48 (1997): 445–67 (pp. 458–9).

[62] M. Morrissey, *Politics and the Paul's Cross Sermons, 1558–1642* (Oxford, 2011); I. Atherton and V. Morgan, 'Revolution and Retrenchment: The Cathedral, 1630–1720', in Atherton et al. (eds.), *Norwich Cathedral*, pp. 547–8; Carlisle RO, D&C 1/6, 39, 56–63, 500–2.

[63] William Camden, *Annales* (1625), p. 64.

cathedrals supported almsmen and fixed charitable donations for roads and to the poor.[64] Cathedrals were also to maintain the cycle of worship, though that was a role rarely justified under Elizabeth or James, and the 1604 grant refounding Ripon minster as a collegiate church conflated worship and the more common Protestant idea of instruction: the inhabitants of Ripon 'henceforth may be piously and religiously in a better manner instructed, trained, and informed to the true worship of God'.[65] The Protestant abolition of the *opus Dei* left a question mark hanging over the purpose of cathedral worship, where there was often little or no congregation, meaning that cathedrals no longer had an agreed central purpose. How should their other, hitherto lesser roles, be managed? If preaching was now their central function, to what extent should a cathedral be reorganized as a preaching college, as some schemes envisaged, such as those of Dean Simon Heynes of Exeter, probably from the 1540s, or Prebendary George Gardiner of Norwich of c.1569?[66] If a bishop were not to act alone in diocesan affairs, was he better advised by his chapter (many of whom might come from outside the diocese), or by senior parish clergy within the diocese, as schemes for 'reduced' episcopacy suggested?[67] If a cathedral was to be a centre of learning, where should the balance lie between a prebend as a reward for past endeavours and a canonry that gave the occupant space for further study? If a cathedral was about study, how could it avoid the dangers of idleness which featured so heavily in Protestant attacks on Roman Catholicism, and how could it ensure that prebendaries remained active pastors and preachers? Above all, how should a Protestant cathedral ensure that its members fulfilled their callings in both parishes and cathedral while avoiding criticisms of pluralism and non-residence? That, finally, was the circle which no one could square.

The idea of a Protestant cathedral was, nonetheless, a reality, and these tensions were held in creative balance until the Laudian capture of cathedrals and the wider Church in the 1620s and 1630s. Moderate puritan prebendaries like Andrew Willet at Ely, famous for his controversial works against popery, or Edmund Bunny at York, renowned for his devotional works and indefatigable preaching, were not uncommon in Elizabethan and Jacobean England, and one defence of choral music was left lamenting that there were so many nonconforming puritan prebendaries.[68] The 1630s, however, saw a dramatic

---

[64] I. Atherton, E. McGrath, and A. Tomkins, '"Pressed Down by Want and Afflicted with Poverty, Wounded and Maimed in War or Worn Down with Age"? Cathedral Almsmen in England 1538–1914', in A. Borsay and P. Shapely (eds.), *Medicine, Charity and Mutual Aid: The Consumption of Health and Welfare in Britain, c.1550–1950* (Aldershot, 2007), pp. 11–34.

[65] Brotherton Library, Leeds, MS Dep 1980/1 1.1.

[66] G. Oliver, *Lives of the Bishops of Exeter* (Exeter, 1861), pp. 477–83; BL, Stowe MS 128, fos. 3r, 5v–7r.

[67] BL, Additional MS 48066, fos. 8–15; James Ussher, *The Reduction of Episcopacie* (1656).

[68] BL, Royal MS B xix, f. 6r.

shift as cathedrals were converted or captured by Laudians and turned into showcases for ceremony and the beauty of holiness.[69] The godly began to see cathedrals as fatally compromised, irredeemably infected by crypto-popery and inextricably yoked to episcopacy, another institution which had by 1640 become intolerable in the eyes of many puritans. Further damaged by the zealous royalism of many vocal prebendaries in the 1640s, MPs tried to abolish cathedrals from 1641 onwards and finally succeeded in 1649.[70]

Parliamentarian opposition to cathedrals transformed their fortunes in other, surprising ways. Their institutions attacked and finally dissolved by the Parliament, their personnel turned out, their fabric the frequent target of iconoclastic attack by Roundhead troops and widely reported to be the victim of shocking acts of desecration such as animal baptism or the stabling of horses, their buildings put to profane use or given over to radical congregations, in the eyes of many episcopalian royalists cathedrals came to symbolize all their sufferings and all that had gone wrong in England, and became analogues of their martyred king.[71] In the Interregnum the first books of views of cathedrals were published (showing idealized pictures of how they had been, not what they had now become),[72] and the first history of St Paul's was published.[73] Cathedrals, far more than bishops, came to embody the Church of England, not just in its sufferings, but also in the hopes of restoration—a print of Lichfield Cathedral of 1655 not only ignored the ravages of war and the collapse of the central spire but bore the motto 'Resvrgam' ('I will rise again').[74] Hence, when Restoration came in the summer of 1660, cathedrals were rapidly restored on a wave of popular enthusiasm, and deans and chapters began functioning often many months before the bishop returned to his *cathedra*. Their rapid reinstatement was not down to the anxiety of tenants seeking to secure their tenure of chapter lands (as Ian Green has argued);[75] instead, it was a function of what few in the century since the break with Rome could have foreseen, that cathedrals had come to represent the English Church. In the mid-sixteenth century, the Church of England had many competing ideas about but no agreement regarding the place or role of its cathedrals; a century later, having been swept away in 1649

---

[69] Atherton, 'Cathedrals, Laudianism'.

[70] Atherton, 'Cathedrals and the British Revolution', pp. 98–104.

[71] Atherton, 'Cathedrals and the British Revolution', pp. 109–14; *Mercurius Melancholicus*, no. 25, 25 Dec. 1648–1 Jan. 1649, pp. 1–3.

[72] Roger Dodsworth and William Dugdale, *Monasticon Anglicanum* (1655); Daniel King, *The Cathedrall and Conventuall Churches of England* (1656).

[73] J. Broadway, '"The honour of this Nation": William Dugdale and the *History of St Paul's* (1658)', in J. McElligott and D. L. Smith (eds.), *Royalists and Royalism during the Interregnum* (Manchester, 2010), pp. 194–213.

[74] Thomas Fuller, *The Church-History of Britain* (1655), frontispiece.

[75] I. M. Green, *The Re-establishment of the Church of England 1660–1663* (Oxford, 1978), pp. 61–79, 99–116.

and apparently providentially restored in 1660, cathedrals had secured a permanent place in the Church of England that remained unassailable until the nineteenth century.

SELECT BIBLIOGRAPHY

Atherton, I., 'Cathedrals and the British Revolution', in Michael J. Braddick and David L. Smith (eds.), *The Experience of Revolution in Stuart Britain and Ireland* (Cambridge, 2011), pp. 96–112.

Atherton, I., 'Cathedrals, Laudianism, and the British Churches', *Historical Journal*, 53 (2010): 895–918.

Atherton, I., E. Fernie, C. Harper-Bill, and A. Hassell Smith (eds.), *Norwich Cathedral: Church, City and Diocese, 1096–1996* (1996).

Aylmer, G. E. and R. Cant (eds.), *A History of York Minster* (Oxford, 1977).

Collinson, P., N. Ramsay, and M. Sparks (eds.), *A History of Canterbury Cathedral, 598–1982* (Oxford, 1995).

Keene, D., A. Burns, and A. Saint (eds.), *St Paul's: The Cathedral Church of London 604–2004* (New Haven, CT, 2004).

Lehmberg, S. E., *Cathedrals under Siege: Cathedrals in English Society, 1600–1700* (University Park, PA, 1996).

Lehmberg, S. E., *The Reformation of Cathedrals: Cathedrals in English Society, 1485–1603* (Princeton, NJ, 1988).

MacCulloch, D., 'The Myth of the English Reformation', *Journal of British Studies*, 30 (1991): 1–19.

Marcombe, D., 'Cathedrals and Protestantism: The Search for a New Identity', in D. Marcombe and C. S. Knighton (eds.), *Close Encounters: English Cathedrals and Society since 1540* (Nottingham, 1991), pp. 43–61.

Merritt, J., 'The Cradle of Laudianism? Westminster Abbey, 1558–1630', *JEH*, 52 (2001): 623–46.

Willis, J., *Church Music and Protestantism in Post-Reformation England* (Farnham, 2010).

13

Ireland and Scotland, 1534–1663

John McCafferty

In the millennium and more during which Christianity was practised in Britain and Ireland before 1530, people, their rulers, and their clergy arrayed the countryside with buildings. These ranged from simple hermit cells to elaborate cloisters to gargantuan cathedrals. Who has possession of those buildings today? The cells are long gone or deserted and, with a minuscule number of exceptions, the friaries, nunneries, and monasteries which so dominated city and country on both islands are either unroofed ruins, mere stumps, or utterly obliterated. Parish churches and cathedrals tell a different story. In England, where not deconsecrated, they now belong to the still-established Church of England. In Scotland they belong to the Presbyterian Church of Scotland. In Ireland they are in the hands of the disestablished (1869) Church of Ireland. Before 1530, Ireland, England, and Scotland were provinces of the Western Church divided into dioceses. The persistence or otherwise of those medieval units tells a different story from the ecclesiastical buildings. In England, the ancient titles are the sole preserve of the Church of England. In Ireland (with some short intermissions) Roman and Anglican incumbents have been using the same styles and titles since the 1530s. This early modern anomaly—like the anomaly of Dublin's two medieval cathedrals—has become so natural that it passes unremarked. In Scotland, however, the old dioceses persist only in the minority Episcopal Church and have vanished from the Church of Scotland. The Church of Ireland's modern similarity to the Church of England in infrastructure, organization, liturgy, and theology is a lingering reminder of its emergence and fortunes from 1530–1662. That there is and has been a counter-hierarchy in communion with Rome functioning across the entire island and making a claim to national allegiance serves as a reminder of the conditions in which the Church as by law established functioned in its first century and a half. In Scotland both the national structure of the Established Church and a claim to be an essential part of that kingdom's identity have their roots in what transpired under the Stuart monarchs before and after 1603. The very existence of an episcopal Church also points to the manner in which issues of church organization both galvanized and stymied Scottish Protestantism.

What this little game of steeples and titles demonstrates is that Ireland experienced Anglophone, English-style, imported religious change during the sixteenth and seventeenth centuries. Scotland underwent Anglophone, indigenous religious change in those same years. Scottish reform so re-moulded an entire society that its Church became the most comprehensive religious body across all three kingdoms. Ireland's Protestant reformation was driven predominantly by English affairs and English exigencies producing, by the reign of Charles II, the least comprehensive (though not the least powerful) religious establishment in both islands. Its trajectory was the hapless driver of a Catholic reform that worked. The Englishness of Ireland's Established Church and the Scottish or, to begin with, the Lowland Scottishness of the Reformed Church there was widely recognized by contemporaries. Writing in the early 1640s Nicholas Archbold, a Capuchin priest from south county Dublin, attempted a taxonomy of Protestantism in Western Europe. For the 'spatious countrie of Germany' there was, in the main Lutheranism, labelled just so. France was the home of the 'Hugonoticall sect'. Switzerland, the Netherlands, and Scotland seethed with 'insolent Calvinists'. Those conforming to the Churches of England and Ireland he labelled simply 'Protestants'. The big danger, as far as Archbold was concerned in 1643 was that 'Henrician Protestancie [is] turning daily into Calvinistical Puritanitie'.[1] John Knox, whose *Historie of the Reformation of the Church of Scotland* was reprinted in 1644, devoted the long preface of that work to an articulation of Scottish identity which found itself most fully in the practice of the Reformed faith. Like his Irish Catholic counterparts he made an equivalence of nationality and confession. In his lengthy preface covering the period from early Christianity up to the 1530s Knox predictably excoriated the alleged introduction of episcopacy by the fifth-century legate Palladius but he also took a swipe at Henry VIII's settlement, dismissing it as a kind of devolved papalism: 'I called a little before the title Head of the Church, used by the Pope, and then given to Henry, *blasphemous*'.[2] The friar and the minister agreed that England's Church was Erastian and Scotland's Calvinist. Although writing eighty years apart they were *ad idem* in believing the *Ecclesia Anglicana* to be neither Lutheran nor Calvinist nor to be emulated. There the agreement ended; the Capuchin feared a Calvinist Britain while the evangelical prayed for it to come to pass. They would have conceded, if asked, that Tudor state-building in

---

[1] Nicholas Archbold, *Historie of the Irish Capuchins*, Bibliothèque Municipale, Troyes, MS 1103 (1643), p. 53.
[2] John Knox, *The Historie of the Reformation of the Church of Scotland* (Edinburgh, 1644), sig. g1r.

England and Wales had had an intimate effect on religious affairs north and west of that realm. In the 1530s, kings of England still aspired to the French throne and maintained pales in Wales, Ireland, and Calais. By 1662 Charles II may have been in the pay of France but Wales had long been absorbed into England, Ireland had been a kingdom for over a century, and Scotland was his by virtue of the dynastic union. England had invaded Scotland and had been invaded by the Scots. Ireland had been conquered by English forces and invaded by Scottish ones. All three realms had experienced civil wars. Ireland endured a cascade of confiscation and plantation over 130 years affecting over 80 per cent of the land and 100 per cent of the population.[3] Although piloted by the Catholic Mary I, land transfer on the smaller island came to be explicitly associated with creed. This union of Protestantism with landholding is a good reminder of how the medieval mesh of politics and religion, of the sacred and secular, became finer and tighter even as religious identity itself frayed and fragmented. Accordingly the spiritual disposition of the rulers of Ireland, Scotland, England, and Wales worked directly on the consciences of their subjects and on their participation in civic life and on their properties and goods. No windows into the soul, perhaps, but panopticon polities that marked how each subject worshipped and precisely where they went on Sundays.

By 1662 Christians on both islands had the blood of martyrs to cry up. Religious turmoil left piles of burnt, beheaded, pressed, and quartered bodies in its wake. Charles I (1649, London), Patrick Hamilton (St Andrews, 1528), Bishop Cornelius O'Devany (1611, Dublin)—all judicially executed—were all appropriated by their co-religionists to stiffen, resolve, and argue their righteous suffering. Their blood was held to have lubricated great engines of history and prophecy at work among the inhabitants of the three kingdoms. This air of destiny wafted into Tridentine masses, Prayer Book services, kirk sessions, and conventicles alike. But behind the ritualized and, indeed, sanctified violence of block, gibbet, and pyre lay an uglier truth. This was the unceasing interpenetration of armed conflict and confessional choice. The pikeman was at prayer all over the lands, soldiers sang the psalms everywhere. Twice—in 1560 and after 1638—Scotland's Church was settled by armed revolution. In Ireland, the bloodshed attendant on the Baltinglass revolt (1581), the Nine Years War, or in the spectacular eruption of October 1641, quickened a counter-reformation which had the extraordinary but unstable effect of uniting, over time, the crown's most loyal Irish subjects, the Old English, with their ancient enemies and allies, the Gaelic Irish. Costs and damages associated with foreign armies, French or English, pushed the prosperous elites of Edinburgh and Dublin in opposite directions—the former away from the old religion and the latter more comprehensively towards it.

---

[3] S. J. Connolly, *Contested Island: Ireland 1460–1630* (Oxford, 2007), ch. 7.

In 1534 Henry VIII intended extending his overthrowing of papal jurisdiction to the Irish Lordship. In the event, the statutory inception of the Church of Ireland had to wait two years because in June 1534, Lord Thomas (Silken Thomas) Fitzgerald, vice-deputy of Ireland and son of the earl of Kildare, launched a rebellion. Fitzgerald's decision to couple his insurrection with protestations of loyalty to Rome may have been opportunistic but it raised a ghost that would not settle until 1829, the year of Catholic Emancipation. The Kildare rebellion also paved the way for the almost uninterrupted exercise of viceroyalty in Ireland by Englishmen and a constitutional overhaul in 1541. The new kingdom of Ireland, entirely dependent on the crown of England, would come to bear directly on the question of religious reform across the island. Both those who sought to promote the Established Church and those who sought to oppose it acknowledged the interrelationship. Protestantism was irrevocably tangled up with English dominion. Even Oliver Cromwell could not escape a trap unwittingly devised by his namesake Thomas Cromwell, architect of the *Act for Kingly Title*. The 1536 supremacy statute, its ancillary acts, and the 1541 constitution all rested heavily on the same rhetoric of recovery of ancient authority that had echoed through Westminster a couple of years earlier. The Dublin legislation simply substituted Irish names and titles for English ones, noting only Ireland's dependency on the imperial crown of England. This was not a perfect process. In one instance, a failure to substitute 'Armagh' for 'Canterbury' left a legal kink that plagued the Church of Ireland for a long time.[4] While the niceties of ecclesiastical jurisdiction are of marginal interest, perhaps, a practice of always borrowing ribs from the side of the Church of England to build an Irish establishment proved to be tricky. This was, after all, an island where more than three-quarters of the population did not speak English and where Dublin Castle was unswervingly committed to a total anglicization of the populace. The 1541 Act also had the deleterious effect of erasing the origin myth of the Old English, by declaring the papal bull *Laudabiliter*, Henry II's charter for invasion in 1172, irrelevant.[5] So at the outset the Church of Ireland was framed as a western extension or replication of reforms found necessary for England; no indigenous reasons were advanced for its creation. It took dissolution of the existing Convocation house (or house of clerical proctors) in Parliament, along with pardons for those who had risen in 1534, to push through the supremacy and dissolution bills.[6] The king eventually got what he wanted, as he had done in England. The snag was that he was a very different monarch in Ireland. Loyalty had brought

---

[4] W. N. Osborough, 'Ecclesiastical Law and the Reformation in Ireland', in Richard H. Helmholz (ed.), *Canon Law in Protestant Lands* (Berlin, 1992), pp. 223–52.

[5] Brendan Bradshaw, *The Irish Constitutional Revolution of the Sixteenth Century* (Cambridge, 1979).

[6] Henry Jeffries, *The Irish Church and the Tudor Reformations* (Dublin, 2010), ch. 4.

the Church of Ireland into being, but could loyalty both in and beyond the Pale make flesh of its claim to national jurisdiction?

Limited jurisdiction was immediately made manifest to all since only just over half of all monasteries were suppressed by the time of Henry VIII's death. Revenues and benefices ended up in the hands of lords whose sons and grandsons did not conform but who diverted some of the money into the hands of recusant clergy. There is good evidence, too, that the popular and influential Franciscan Observants, forewarned by the fate of their outspoken confrères in England, staged a withdrawal from their houses in the Pale, and regrouped in the west and north.[7] On hearing of Martin Luther, Leo X is supposed to have quipped that the incipient reformation was no more than a quarrel among friars. While prominent in England and Scotland, ex-mendicant reformers did not manifest in Ireland. The ex-Augustinian George Browne, archbishop of Dublin, was appointed to effect the changes but he was English. Through many shifts and slips in policy under Tudor and Stuart monarchs, Whitehall would cling to importation as the preferred means of filling the episcopal bench. English policy in both Church and state was heavily dependent on an apparent elixir of outsiders. By Easter 1538, two years into his incumbency, Browne had succeeded only in issuing a 'Form of Beads' to be read in parishes to promote the supremacy. Iconoclasm began and ended with official destruction of high-profile shrines like that of Our Lady of Trim. There was no sign of motion from below nor was there anything other than very isolated enthusiasm from clergy. Application of the conservative Six Articles of 1539 created further drag and once against demonstrated that the Irish Church would be moved by the rhythms of its English progenitor.[8] Yet to say that the Church of Ireland was wholly unattractive to all of the inhabitants of the island would be to deny those people agency. Some individuals and some families, Gaelic Irish and Old English alike, did discern a reforming message and did adhere to it. State papers right into the middle years of Elizabeth's reign commend conforming 'natives' and talk up apparent green shoots in places like Kilkenny, Limerick, and Galway. Church papistry was initially common enough among the burghers of the chartered towns but it gradually crumbled away and fell into the sea after Elizabeth's excommunication by Pius V in 1570. Under Edward VI liturgical and theological changes were either by *de facto* extension or by proclamation. Protestants, as another English ex-friar, John Bale, discovered were isolated individuals. Cardinal Pole's legatine register contains only one Irish supplicant seeking absolution

---

[7] Colm Lennon, 'The Dissolution to the Foundation of St. Anthony's College, Louvain, 1534–1607' in Edel Bhreathnach, Joseph MacMahon, and John McCafferty (eds.), *The Irish Franciscans 1534–1990* (Dublin, 2009), pp. 3–26.

[8] James Murray, *Enforcing the English Reformation in Ireland: Clerical Resistance and Political Conflict in the Diocese of Dublin, 1534–1590* (Cambridge, 2009).

from heresy, from Kilkenny as it happens, the seat of Bale's diocese of Ossory and home of a short-lived movement of godly youth.[9] There was no cohort of Irish Marian exiles to be radicalized on the continent. When Mary acceded to the Irish throne she did deprive some married clergy (including Archbishop Browne himself) and restore a tiny number of religious houses. The main ecclesiastical effect of her reign was a papal ratification of Ireland's status as a kingdom. Her entirely secular plantation of counties Laois and Offaly, memorialized toponymically in King's County and Queen's County, initiated a vogue for 'civilizing' land transfer which Elizabeth, James VI and I, Charles I, the Long Parliament, *and* Oliver Cromwell would all attempt to wield as an instrument of Protestantization.[10] This would, in turn, yoke the extension of Dublin Castle's jurisdiction (island-wide by 1609) to confiscation. The Church of Ireland, reliant on imported clergy, attuned to the dynamics of the English settlement, was well on the road at Elizabeth's accession to becoming a service Church for incoming administrators and settlers. To borrow a term from England itself, it was becoming something like a very large official 'stranger church' on Irish soil.

Scotland, by contrast, ended up with a national Church inclined to condescension towards its southern neighbour Church. Contemporary observers initially predicted that the kingdom would remain Roman as a rejoinder to English heresy.[11] James V certainly liked to tease Henry VIII with this prospect but his abrupt death in 1542 changed the weight of the Scottish dice. Henry's 'rough wooing' at the end of the 1540s, with all of its anti-papal, anti-regular strut, did indeed confirm the auld alliance with France but, paradoxically, weakened the structures of Catholicism. England's shiftings in religion did not replicate themselves across the border but they did have direct effect. Scots reform was built on English bibles. Scottish laity and clergy read English books. The vernacular catechism issued in the 1550s by the Catholic Church in an attempt to initiate reform contained, for example, material from the English *King's Book* of 1543.[12] The Reformed swerve of Edward VI's reign not only emboldened Scots exiles in Geneva, France, and Germany, not to mention London and north-east England, but freed up John Knox to preach against the mass and by implication, those Scots clergy who were dabbling with the 1549 Prayer Book. In short, Scots read English material and watched English trends closely. They were influenced, even if they came to show little relish for imitating the Church of England.

If coupling of land and religion in Ireland had a big effect there, dynastic politics had a profound effect on Scotland's religious history. Mary of Guise's

---

[9] Jeffries, *The Irish Church*, p. 115.
[10] Nicholas Canny, *Making Ireland British 1580–1650* (2001).
[11] Alec Ryrie, *Origins of the Scottish Reformation* (Manchester, 2006), pp. 37–48.
[12] Ryrie, *Origins of the Scottish Reformation*, p. 100.

Ireland and Scotland, 1534–1663

call for an invasion of England in 1557 pushed the Scottish nobles—Hamilton, Campbell, Douglas—over the line. From this point on, dynastic considerations, aristocratic interest, and religious outlook went into an ongoing chemical reaction with each other, fuelling the ecclesiastical politics of Scotland through the reign of James VI, the union of crowns, and on into the Interregnum and to the Restoration. The Protestant, self-styled 'Lords of the Congregation' began by looking for a liturgical change—use of the English Prayer Book—and ended up accepting aid from an English force in 1560. Scottish ecclesiastical revolution was achieved by arms and in the teeth of the king (Francis I) and queen (Mary) of France. It was continentally inspired but transplanted and adapted for native soil. Scotland's Parliament, egged on by its nobles and returned exiles, bounced the court into a reformation. In Ireland, the crown believed reformation would bolster the structures of authority. In Scotland, the revivalistic fervour of Parliament gave rise to a Church which reserved the right to dispense with the monarch as supreme moderator in order to have direct dealing with God himself.[13]

On her accession Elizabeth I, Supreme Governor of the Church of Ireland, reverted to her father's practice of passing English statutes through the Irish Parliament. For the first time, though, a discernible difference became apparent. Irish uniformity of 1560 permitted a *Liber Precum Publicarum* (Book of Common Prayer) in *all* parishes on grounds of the difficulty in procuring Gaelic translations. This, along with permission for vestments as at 2 Edward VI, made such a significant sop to conservatives that all but two of the Marian bishops took the new oath of supremacy.[14] If nothing else, this settlement gave rise to an alluring idea of an Irish establishment which was English in origin, but somewhat localized in delivery, and that somehow Ireland's Church could set the speed and trajectory of its orbit around an English star. Alluring ideas were abundant during Elizabeth's long reign. Her reluctance to spend money caused one viceroy after another to advance eye-catching but essentially unrealizable programmes for resolution of the 'Irish problem'. The upshot was an extended, haphazard, and extremely expensive conquest that left the population traumatized and uncertain. Government by strategic plan did not relegate the Church of Ireland to the rear of political and military affairs. They were often bundled together. In 1567 Lord Deputy Henry Sidney promulgated the Twelve Articles (Parker's Eleven Articles of 1561 minutely adjusted) as a juridical prequel to filling the depleted bench of bishops. He also hoped to establish an Irish university on a statutory basis and he sponsored the first reformed foray into Gaelic—Seáan Ó Cearnaigh's *Aibidil Gaeilge agus Caiticiosma* (Dublin, 1567). This primer and catechism included a translation of

---

[13] Ryrie, *Origins of the Scottish Reformation*, p. 100; Ian B. Cowan, *The Scottish Reformation* (1982).
[14] Jeffries, *The Irish Church*, ch. 7.

the Twelve Articles. Sidney's efforts to give the national Church substance beyond statutes was killed by both Old English and New English interests and buried by his recall in 1571. During his second deputyship, starting in 1575, Sidney tried the prerogative road by erecting a court of faculties which aggregated key aspects of episcopal jurisdiction to itself. In 1577 he also established and packed a High Commission court designed to be used on conservative clergy and influential recusants alike. Opposition to his plans to pay for the army by permanent cess made another graveyard of his plans for the Church of Ireland. In theory lords deputy had both the powers and the incentive to promote religious reform; in reality though they were constrained by interest groups, obdurate parliaments dominated by Old English members, and the crown's belief that quick progress might be made at virtually zero cost.[15]

Patchy progress was not in itself toxic to the Church of Ireland. By the 1590s the Church was replacing an old guard with new Protestant preaching clergy. There was an overall structure and there were congregations using the Prayer Book in English. In 1594 there was also the bright promise of a Dublin university as nursery of reform. The citizens of that city, though, now chose to educate their sons on the continent, had ebbed away from church services, and could bear the 12d a week fine for absence when it was applied. Ó Cearnaigh's *Aibidil* had been printed in Dublin in an elegant type which emulated the high status penmanship of Gaelic scribes but only two hundred copies were printed. A Gaelic New Testament did not appear until 1602 and Uilliam Ó Domhnaill's (William Daniel) adroitly godly translation of the Prayer Book was issued in 1608.[16] An Irish Old Testament was begun in the 1630s but not finished until 1685.[17] Vernacular far later than Wales, perhaps, but more swiftly than Gaelic Scotland. The problem for the Church of Ireland was that most of its clergy and conforming laity did not think it a problem at all. They did not speak Irish, so they could not do what clergy in the highlands and islands did—make *ex tempore* translations of texts for their people. From the 1536 Act for the English Order, Habit and Language to the Irish canons of 1634 and beyond, the Church kept covenant with the medieval colony by insisting that any use of Gaelic was a temporary halt on a road to universal English speech and manners. Ironically Catholic clergy, who were so exuberantly insistent on Latinity, preached and composed devotional poetry and prose in Gaelic, and published in the vernacular, just as their counterparts were doing in Latin America and Asia. They also came to promote a cultural

[15] Ciaran Brady and James Murray, 'Sir Henry Sidney and the Reformation in Ireland', in Elizabethanne Boran and Crawford Gribben (eds.), *Enforcing Reformation in Ireland and Scotland, 1550–1700* (Aldershot, 2006), pp. 14–39.
[16] William Daniel, *Leabhar na nUrnaightheadh gComhchoidchiond* (Dublin, 1608).
[17] Nicholas Williams, *I bprionta i leabhar: na protastúin agus pros na Gaeilge, 1567–1724* (Baile Átha Cliath, 1986).

reconfiguration inspired by Iberian precedent by persuading both Gaelic Irish and Old English populations that their own deepest identity and that of the very island itself lay in fealty to Rome. A Protestant rejoinder, James Ussher's *Religion Anciently Professed by the Irish and British* (1631) met this challenge head-on. Ussher was one of the rare members of Dublin's oligarchy whose family had conformed and he was one of the first fruits of the new Trinity College Dublin. His pellucid picture of an early Irish Church—bibliocentric, Calvinistical, puritanical—drew water from the same well as John Jewel and Matthew Parker. It is redolent of the godly atmosphere of Protestant Dublin in Elizabeth's dying years and the early years of James I. Here was a Church without the Thirty Nine Articles, without canons, a Church where English exiles from the vestiarian crisis, and from the likes of Bancroft, could find a congregational berth. Ussher's essay at historio-theological patriotism, a pre-Henrician origin myth, of the kind that had struck real roots across the Irish Sea, got nowhere in persuading his Old English contemporaries to conform.[18] They had been persuaded that the only ancient religion was the Roman one. The majority of adherents to the Church of Ireland needed Ussher's construct, clever as it was, no more than they needed Gaelic liturgy.

James VI and I took care to mention Ireland during the Hampton Court Conference.[19] The tweaks made there to the English settlement were carried over into Ireland but the 1604 canons were not. Instead, during its first national Convocation in 1613-15, the Irish Church produced a confession of 104 articles which should be read as a Reformed reflection on the Thirty-Nine Articles spliced with the Lambeth Articles that Elizabeth had refused in 1595. Robust on double predestination, these Articles anticipated the 1647 Westminster Confession by stoutly affirming (Article 80) that the Pope was 'that man of sin foretold in the holy scriptures whom the Lord shall consume with the spirit of his mouth and the brightness of his coming'.[20] This went further than any English formulary. There was a view, though, and members of the Westminster Parliaments of 1626 and 1628 took it, that the Irish Articles showed the English Church what it could and should be. A rare inversion.[21]

The 1613-15 Convocation was, from the point of view of its membership, an overwhelmingly English affair. There were also three Scottish bishops and between twenty and twenty-five Scots in the Lower House. Following the flight of the Ulster earls to Catholic Europe in 1607, vast tracts of land in the north of the island were escheated. The new Scottish king of England nurtured imperial

---

[18] Alan Ford, *James Ussher: Theology, History and Politics* (Oxford, 2007), ch. 6.
[19] William Barlow, *Summe and Substance of the Conference... at Hampton Court* (1638 edn.), p. 98.
[20] Gerald Bray (ed.), *Documents of the English Reformation* (Cambridge, 1994), pp. 437-52.
[21] Nicholas Tyacke, *Anti-Calvinists: The Rise of English Arminianism c.1590-1640* (Oxford, 1987), pp. 154-5.

ambition and determined that the confiscated lands should be the inauguration site of a new British Protestant people. Tudor settlements had left the Church of Ireland saddled with never fewer than twenty-five dioceses between 1541 and 1641. James would make thirty-seven Irish bishops during his reign. Starting with a scant sixteen (ten Irish-born and six English-born), episcopal resurgence—both in tandem with Scotland and in the face of Roman rivalry—left Ireland with twenty-five prelates in 1625. This was a considered bench, pregnant with policy. There were fourteen English, three Irish-born, five Scots, and three Welsh. Scots bishops were concentrated in the north and west. Andrew Knox, architect of the king's 'civilizing' statutes of Iona, even held Raphoe (Donegal) and the Scottish Isles simultaneously from 1610–19. This was a striking, much overlooked royal *fiat* by the first ruler of all three kingdoms. The appointment of a diverse bench and the literally hundreds of orders and grants James made in their favour demonstrate his desire for an episcopally driven Briticizing reformation for Ireland. Lavish endowment in the Ulster plantation was designed not only to sustain a graduate preaching ministry for thousands of newcomers but also to serve as a regional harbinger of a national Church. Many of his bishops, preachers, and controversialists were personally known to the king. James lent vigour and lucre to an old solution—reformation by immigration. In doing so he ensured that the Church of Ireland had sufficient congregations and political clout through the new parliamentary boroughs to be sustainable.[22]

The Stewart dynasty faced multiple challenges in their dealings with the Church of Scotland during the second half of the sixteenth century. As in Ireland, finance was a running sore in the Church in Scotland. During her personal reign Mary Queen of Scots attempted to manage an odd hybrid of an ambitious new reformed Church running alongside the extensively gutted structure of the old one. All the while she heard mass herself in Edinburgh Castle, thus fanning the apoplectic apocalyptic of John Knox. While Mary nursed an ambition of succession and while Elizabeth refused to name her heir, Knox's *First Blast against the Monstrous Regiment of Women* (1558) had already impacted on the Church of England. It caused Elizabeth to set her face against Geneva, an effect deplored by Calvin himself.[23] During the civil war that followed upon Mary's death, Protestant England's military might was once again decisive, this time in securing the throne for James VI and his adherents. But once again, intervention was unmatched by any desire to emulate its ecclesiastical settlement.

---

[22] John McCafferty, 'Protestant Prelates or Godly Pastors? The Dilemma of the Early Stuart Episcopate', in Alan Ford and John McCafferty (eds.), *The Origins of Sectarianism in Early Modern Ireland* (Cambridge, 2005), pp. 54–72.

[23] Felicity Heal, *Reformation in Britain and Ireland* (Oxford, 2003), p. 354; *ODNB*, 'Knox, John (c.1514–1572)'.

Conflict between episcopacy and Presbyterianism saturates all ecclesiastical histories of Scotland, whether written in the early modern period or more recently. The Concordat of Leith (1572), the Black Acts (1584), and the Golden Act (1592) constitute a set of see-saw displays which have easily distracted from the growing conviction of the growing man and king James VI. He became convinced that the Scottish Church needed to be controlled by the crown more than it was by the ministers, their synods, and their General Assembly. When in 1598 James assured the General Assembly that his bishops would be neither 'papistical' nor 'Anglican' he had nonetheless made an irrevocable decision that these 'constant moderators' would, whether in Parliament, synod, or assembly, be first and foremost royal agents. This Scottish compromise, this limited episcopacy, was not modelled on England or on Ireland but on the king's sense of what was desirable and feasible. Still, when the king of Scotland came to be a communicant in the Church of England, the style and title of 'bishop' was present in all three establishments. If Patrick Adamson, archbishop of St Andrews, could go to England in December 1583 to confer with Whitgift, who had begun a subscription drive against puritan clergy, what other ideas might be brought up from the south? The union of crowns sparked fears of an incorporating union which were only heightened by postponement of a scheduled General Assembly until 1605. The fate of the Millenary Petition and the minimal adjustments to the Church of England after Hampton Court were well known in Scotland.[24]

In 1606 Scottish bishops were restored to their ancient temporalities; substantive jurisdiction over clergy was prised from the presbyteries and handed back to the prelates. A full complement was restored—thirteen bishops—all beholden to the king. Seventeen ancient abbacies now all in the hands of noble families were erected into temporal lordships. The long-standing disdain of kirkmen for the English settlement and their contention that the Negative Confession (1581) forbade episcopacy was rewarded with a serious slap. In the wake of the abortive and unsanctioned General Assembly of 1605, eight ministers were summoned to England, arriving in London in August 1606. Over the following months they were subjected to sermons and addresses by English bishops and royal chaplains that exalted episcopacy and denigrated presbytery. Andrew Melville's emotive response to this barrage—he grabbed Archbishop Bancroft's surplice and declared it part of the mark of the Beast—landed him in the Tower and then permanent exile in France. There was now, literally, no room left to criticize the Church of England settlement. Episcopacy, in Alan MacDonald's memorable phrase, 'was drip-fed into the [kirk] system via the commission of the General Assembly and ecclesiastical representation in parliament'.[25] The General Assembly of 1610

---

[24] Alan MacDonald, *The Jacobean Kirk 1567–1625: Sovereignty, Polity, Liturgy* (Aldershot, 1998).
[25] MacDonald, *The Jacobean Kirk*, p. 120.

was the most tightly controlled yet. Members were treated to guest preachers including Christopher Hampton, royal chaplain, and future archbishop of Armagh. He reworked the stock King Lucius myth to give the authority claimed by James VI and I a British, not merely English, pedigree.[26] Providential histories had traced godly lineages through the centuries by dint of 'saved remnants' but ultimately placed most weight on God's direct action in recent and contemporary affairs. These were the kind of books written by John Foxe, John Knox, and to a lesser extent James Ussher. This world-view was now under pressure from discourses like Hampton's or John Spottiswoode's *History of Scotland from the year of Our Lord 203 to... 1625* (written in the 1630s, published 1655) which privileged the *longue durée*, the slow but orderly turn of the wheel. In these works the king of heaven worked most on living souls via kings on earth not by preachers, not by prophets.[27] The year 1610 also saw the establishment of two Courts of High Commission, of the Canterbury and York kind, whose wide powers included oversight of any who preached against the established order of the Church of Scotland. In December 1610 the archbishop of Glasgow and the bishops of Brechin and Galloway were consecrated in London by the bishops of Ely, London, Worcester, and Rochester. In a curious half-nod to Scottish sensitivities neither of the two English primates, Bancroft of Canterbury or Matthew of York, was present, nor did Gledstanes of St Andrews make the journey south. The three Scots then went home to consecrate their peers and so, for the first time, there was a non-Roman episcopate claiming apostolic succession extant across the three kingdoms.[28]

In 1615, the year which came to be romanticized as that of maximum latitude for the Church of Ireland, 'Articles required for the service of the Church of Scotland' were sent up from court. These were a blueprint for convergence with England through a set liturgy and prayers, a confession of faith to agree 'so neir as can be' with the southern kingdom, and set forms for baptism, marriage, communion, and ordination. Canons were also planned as Scotland, like Ireland, had no code. This programme was put to the now-chastened General Assembly in 1616 and accepted. The king's 'salmon-like' return to his native land in 1617 was, in ecclesiastical terms, a visit by the Supreme Governor of the Church of England. The chapel royal at Holyrood was entirely renovated with organ, desks, stalls, and images. The anxieties of the Scottish bishops only provoked the monarch, whose entourage included

---

[26] Charles W. A. Prior, *Defining the Jacobean Church: the Politics of Religious Controversy* (Cambridge, 2005), pp. 215–18.

[27] See my unpublished paper 'Colmcille (Columba): A Fragmenting Patron', given at the third Lives & Afterlives Conference, UCD, April 2006.

[28] John S. Morrill, 'A British Patriarchy? Ecclesiastical Imperialism under the Early Stuarts', in Anthony Fletcher and Peter Roberts (eds.), *Religion, Culture and Society in Early Modern Britain* (Cambridge, 1994), pp. 209–37; Alan MacDonald, 'James VI & I, the Church of Scotland and British Ecclesiastical Convergence', *Historical Journal*, 48 (2005): 885–903.

three English bishops and William Laud. James used the Prayer Book, an altar-wise table, candles, surpliced clergy, choristers, and a £400 organ shipped from London.[29] The king's promotion of the Prayer Book picked up on a tradition of emulation interrupted in the 1560s. By his death in 1625 the Common Prayer was heard by all aspirant ministers, since it was required in full or part in the chapels of the Scottish universities and became standard liturgy in some Scottish cathedrals and the Chapel Royal. James was not telling the Scottish Church to become the Church of England but he was commanding it to listen to his adoptive Church and highly commending its services and structures. In 1618 Scottish theologians would have noticed the failure to send any kirkmen as part of the 'British' delegation to the Synod of Dort, the Reformed international. Coming from a king who fancied himself a new Constantine and promoter of Protestant unity this was a marked relegation. There was more. In 1616 James had consented to withhold 'Five Articles' until he had visited his birthplace. These articles were ratified at a General Assembly in Perth in August 1618. They struck at the very heart of the Sabbatarian, psalm-singing, sermonizing Church. They mandated kneeling for communion. Scots had sat at long trestles, banquet-wise. They licensed private communion for the sick and dying. The Lord's Supper had been a communal, strictly regulated affair since 1560. They condoned private baptism in cases of necessity. This was considered by many to be both anti-communal and verging on the superstitious. Catechesis of children was to be made subject to episcopal instruction and blessing. It was even presented as confirmation purged of its Romish sacramentalism. Finally, the very fabric of time was to be altered by punctuating Scotland's linear Sabbatarianism with a pared-down liturgical cycle through reintroduction of Christmas, Good Friday, Easter, Ascension Day, and Pentecost.[30] Even though the Church's financial and hierarchical workings had remained unsettled for six decades, its reconfiguration of Lowland society by means of kirk session had been immensely successful. The Articles of Perth could be construed to pick at or even tear at the fabric of that godly society, to exalt the prince beyond his divinely ordained bounds and to shove Scotland closer to the quasi-popery of the Church of England. The Scottish bishops tested the waters after Perth, found them hot, and withdrew from enforcement. James, however, threatened to bring up English clergy to replace the ministers he would deprive for non-compliance. The result was mass resistance and (quite shockingly for Scotland) the reappearance of 'conventicles' or 'privy kirks'—a separation not seen since the 1540s and 1550s.[31] The king went to his deathbed still pushing the Five Articles while his subjects disliked his display of power, its theological direction, and its southward gaze.

---

[29] MacDonald, 'James VI & I', pp. 877–8, 894.
[30] Gerald Bray (ed.), *The Anglican Canons 1529–1947* (Woodbridge, 1998), pp. 823–4.
[31] MacDonald, *The Jacobean Kirk*, p. 169.

Many, if not all of them, conflated the three. During the first twenty-two years of dynastic union, the Church of Scotland was pushed closer to the Church of Ireland in one very obvious but frequently overlooked way: both realms, both Churches, were in the hands of an absentee monarch. That monarch had strong opinions and thought far more about them—and the Church of England—than they thought about each other.

In 1622 a royal commission of inquiry into the state of Ireland issued a series of 'Orders and directions concerning the State of the Church of Ireland'.[32] These recommended use of the Gaelic Prayer Book and New Testament where practicable and made detailed proposals concerning the leasing of church land, impropriations, and clergy salaries. The Irish Church desperately needed a functioning ministry at parish level if it was ever to live up to its very title. At the opening of Charles I's reign the omens were not good as the Ulster plantation itself had stuttered into peculation and non-compliance. The tendency of the Irish kingdom to become an issue in foreign relations seriously disrupted any plans for punitive action against Catholic recusants. Beginning with the abortive Spanish Match and moving on to the French one, initiatives by Dublin Castle or by Irish bishops were either dropped or stifled because the crown needed to reassure Catholic majesties or propitiate Old English moneyed interests. This in turn reinforced the tendency that had brought forth Irish Article 80 in 1615. The more the king tolerated, the more Irish churchmen condemned the Antichrist. A declaration by a large group of Irish bishops in 1626 maintained: 'to consent that they [Catholics] might freely exercise their religion, and profess their faith and doctrine, is a grievous sin'.[33] Seven years later in 1633, though, a brash new tone would be heard in Dublin. On 4 August, John Bramhall, treasurer of Christchurch and chaplain to Lord Deputy Thomas Wentworth, took the pulpit to preach on Matthew 16:18: 'Tu es Petrus' ('You are Peter'). He declared the 'Church of Rome to be only schismatical and the Pope to be a Patriarch'.[34] Backed by Wentworth, Bishop William Laud of London, and ultimately the king himself, Bramhall's arrival and rapid promotion to the see of Derry heralded an attempt to create, mainly by prerogative instruments, a functioning Church of twenty-six dioceses manned by a formalist, subscribing, obedient clergy. Over the next eight years the state's church policy both enticed and confused veteran Irish ministers. A salvo of statutes passed in the 1634–5 Parliament, backed by proclamations and special hearings at the Irish Privy Council relentlessly prised the patrimony of the Church out of the hands of landed gentry, Catholic and Protestant alike, and back into the hands of the dioceses. Following a series of

---

[32] Marsh's Library, Dublin, MS Z 3.1.3.
[33] *Protestation of the Archbishops and Bishops of Ireland [1626]* (1641).
[34] Mark Empey (ed.), 'The Diary of Sir James Ware, 1623–66', *Analecta Hibernica*, 45 (2014), p. 95.

exemplary cases, including a vast multi-tentacled action against Richard Boyle, earl of Cork, the richest man in the three kingdoms, Ireland's elite rushed to settlement. The Church of Ireland was effectively re-endowed but there were many strings attached. Bishops found themselves subject to more minuscule oversight, or saddled with new deans directly appointed by Dublin Castle, or both.[35]

Bramhall's 1633 sermon mirrored a fashionable downgrade of the Pope from Antichrist to overreaching patriarch and so, in this regard, he was merely importing an English fashion to Ireland in the time-honoured manner.[36] There was more though. It began to dawn on both Bramhall and his patron Laud that the Irish Convocation might open the way towards some anticipatory actions. They spotted what the English MPs of 1626 and 1628 had spotted—the possibility of a reverse flow. Things might be done in Ireland that were not yet come to pass in England itself. The Irish Church would get a new confession of faith and a new set of canons between 1633 and 1635. The story of the Irish Convocation in these years is muddled, just like its predecessor, by the loss of any official record but a number of things are clear. First, the Thirty-Nine Articles of 1563 were adopted with the clear intent of superseding the 1615 ones. This move, just like the reception of the Perth Articles, did not go unresisted. Second, a need to mollify James Ussher, godly hero, led to the jettisoning of an original scheme to adopt the English canons of 1604 in their entirety. Instead Ireland emerged with a negotiated compromise which allowed auricular confession and demanded an altar-wise communion table at the east end, accompanied by precious vessels. In Ireland beauty of holiness was now not by injunction nor visitation article nor individual initiative but instead by enforceable canon law. The first four Irish canons, those to which clergy were to subscribe, tipped the establishment in an unmistakably sacerdotal direction. The Prayer Book, in the hands of the priest, along with the current order and hierarchy of the Church were now both symbol and test of uniformity. These canons required clergymen to declare the king's supremacy four times but also, in effect, to assent to the proposition that reformation was both perfect and complete. This was a new and highly compressed standard of conformity. As far as its gleeful sponsors were concerned Ireland now pointed the way forward for England and maybe even Scotland.[37]

By 1637 Ireland, Scotland, and England had overlapping codes that shared about forty canons. The effects of compression were beginning to be felt. While the Irish laity were more than irked by an aggressive temporalities

---

[35] John McCafferty, *The Reconstruction of the Church of Ireland: Bishop Bramhall and the Laudian Reforms, 1633–1641* (Cambridge, 2007), ch. 2.
[36] Anthony Milton, *Catholic and Reformed: The Roman and Protestant Churches in English Protestant Thought, 1600–1640* (Cambridge, 1995), chs. 2 and 3.
[37] McCafferty, *Reconstruction*, ch. 3.

campaign, Irish clerics were disconcerted that internal Protestant doctrine and order appeared to be a greater priority for the viceroy than tackling the further growth and confidence of popery. If they had seen a private position paper (almost certainly composed by Bramhall and filed by Wentworth for consideration) mooting a revival of the 1549 Prayer Book as a *vade mecum* to Catholics they would have been even more perturbed.[38] Outrage, though, was plain in Scotland where Charles I had commenced his rule by announcing a revocation (a long-standing device for recovering royal lands alienated during Scotland's frequent minorities) in July 1525. Given his age, a scant month inside the legal maximum, and the fact that this hastily devised scheme appeared to aim at recovery of all church land secularized since 1540, revocation alarmed Scottish lords. Charles would, in fact, alter course in 1627 by aiming directly at impropriators but it was pretty clear that, as in Ireland, ecclesiastical re-endowment was on the cards.[39] The king's journey to Edinburgh in 1633 for his Scottish coronation jangled nerves not just because of the eight-year delay but because it was a reprise of his father's visit in 1617. An even more shocking visit by a royal member of the Church of England ensued. Holyrood now boasted a railed stage, an altar-wise communion table with candles, and a tapestry decorated with a crucifix. Like James, here was a king accompanied by English clergy and Prayer Book, but now in 1633 six *Scottish* bishops emerged clad in rochets with golden copes. The king was crowned in the English manner and undertook a new oath to defend bishops and the churches under their government. Episcopacy itself, as Charles would later point out, was part of his personally covenanted duty as king. Again like his father, Charles issued instructions for use of the English liturgy—in the Chapel Royal, universities, and bishops' oratories: 'till some course be taken for making one, that may fit the custom and constitution of that church'.[40] This kind of language easily tickled the reflexive anti-Englishness of most Scots who were prone to perceive all interventions as invasive expressions of Anglo-hegemony. By the exact same token many contemporary English people identified Presbyterianism as quintessentially Scottish and rejected it on the same xenophobic basis.

Royal creation of a new diocese of Edinburgh (1636) mirrored the re-establishment of the tiny late medieval Irish diocese of Cloyne (1637), and campaigns to renovate St Paul's in London, Christchurch in Dublin, and St Giles in Edinburgh all suggested synchronization. For these and so many other things, fingers were pointed at William Laud, archbishop of

---

[38] McCafferty, *Reconstruction*, pp. 97–8.

[39] Allan Macinnes, *Charles I and the Making of the Covenanting Movement 1625–1641* (Edinburgh, 1991), ch. 3.

[40] Leonie Wells-Furby, 'A Re-appraisal of the Career and Reputation of William Laud, Archbishop of Canterbury, with specific reference to Scotland 1633–1640', PhD thesis, University of Kent, 2009, pp. 35–7.

Canterbury since 1633. Laud's known (and admitted) involvement in the direction of Irish and Scottish affairs is commonly linked to his primacy. But Canterbury's labour was not a vainglorious revival of Archbishop Lanfranc's twelfth-century dream of hegemony over both islands; it was instead a truly seventeenth-century business. What he did was only possible because monarchy had come to matter most in Britain and Ireland. His work, he joked, might well make him into a *universalis episcopus* but he understood himself as the ecclesiastical agent of his master.[41] During his trial he was entirely correct in maintaining that he had exercised no jurisdiction over Scotland or Ireland. But while this was true in a strictly formal sense he had, in fact, exercised power, patronage, and control. Even if his actions and mandates had been everything that Andrew Melville, James Ussher, or even John Pym might have desired, this phenomenon of, to borrow a phrase from Henry VIII's time, an informal 'vicegerent' in spirituals as a singular extension of royal will in the government of the Churches would have been a big problem in any circumstances.

The Scottish canons of 1636 were as remarkable as the Irish ones though for different reasons. The General Assembly may have been leaned on for the Perth Articles but neither synods nor General Assembly were consulted even once about this code. Instead its drafting was the fruit of shuttle correspondence and meetings in Scotland and England between English and Scots clerics, most of them bishops. This was innovation in itself but the canons went on to erect English-style supremacy. They were utterly silent on the customary sinews of the Scottish Church—assemblies, synods, and kirk sessions. Like the Irish canons they shifted power over to the episcopal ordinary, but unlike Ireland they did so by pretending that other bodies simply did not exist. If Ireland's code tightened conformity, Scotland's transformed its very nature. The canons reached into every household in the kingdom. For example, Sunday fasts, so characteristic of Scotland, were proscribed and all discretion on public fasts was to be henceforth vested in the crown. Like their Irish counterparts, the Scottish bishops succeeded in introducing modifications for local conditions but it is clear that they were simultaneously intimidated by the royal will and fearful of public reaction. They found themselves between a rock and a hard place both of which were about to become far more unyielding with the advent of the Scottish Prayer Book. The canons, just like the infamous 'et cetera' oath in the English canons of 1640, were a blank cheque as they mentioned a Prayer Book that had not yet been published. The overall tenor of the code, not to mention the circumstances of their composition, predisposed godly Scots to think that there was a great deal to fear from the new liturgy.[42]

---

[41] William Laud to Thomas Wentworth, 3 July 1634 in W. Scott and J. Bliss (eds.), *The Works of... William Laud*, 7 vols. (Oxford, 1847–60), VI, p. 385.

[42] Wells-Furby, 'A Re-appraisal', ch. 3.

The significance of the choice of Aberdeen as the place of printing for the canons, under the direction of Robert Baron, professor of divinity at Marischal College, has not been noticed by historians until recently.[43] Baron was one of six 'Aberdeen doctors' who would be deposed a few years later for alleged Arminianism and moral turpitude. These academics were entirely orthodox Calvinists but what made them different in the Scottish context was that they were prepared like very many of their Irish and English counterparts to accept that anything not directly repugnant to the fundamental word of God might be classified as a 'thing indifferent'. Their Presbyterian and future Covenanting opponents took their stand on the premise that everything must be measured against God's will as explicitly stated in Scripture.[44] The storm presaged by the canons did not take long to break. In October 1636 a proclamation required conformity to the as yet invisible liturgy. The Prayer Book, like the canons, had been composed by an English–Scottish committee. When riots did break out at St Giles's on 23 July 1637 they were well-orchestrated as offcuts of the new book (so heavily dependent on the 1549 Prayer Book) had been circulating as wrapping paper for weeks beforehand. The very same Prayer Book that Dublin Castle had secretly pondered as a sweetener drove Scottish Protestants to conclude that this Romish–English assault required nothing less than a re-tying of the fundamental bond between God and His people of Scotland. This was the purpose of the National Covenant first signed by nobles at Greyfriars kirk on 28 February 1638. The prop and stay of that covenant was the Negative Confession of 1581 forswearing Catholicism. God's people were not unanimous though. The Aberdeen Doctors mounted a spirited propaganda initiative against a backdrop of subscription campaigns. There was an alternative King's Covenant—a flop—and apocalyptic preaching redolent of the days of John Knox himself. The Glasgow General Assembly of August 1638 was, in effect, an armed ecclesiastical coup which proclaimed the policies of the last two Stuart kings null and void, repudiating supremacy, bishops, canons, Prayer Book, and the Five Articles. It was, and was meant to be, a reprise of 1560. A year later, following the ingrained Church tendency to comprehensiveness, the Assembly would order compulsory subscription to the National Covenant and declare episcopacy to be contrary to the will of God.[45]

During his first visit to Ulster in 1634, John Bramhall had dismissed the settlers there as 'the very ebullition of Scotland'.[46] The National Covenant triggered not only subscription in that province, but a tithe strike, resurgent conventicles, and, by the winter of 1638, lockouts of conformist clergy from

---

[43] Wells-Furby, 'A Re-appraisal', p. 122.

[44] John Ford, 'The Lawful Bonds of Scottish Society', *Historical Journal*, 37 (1994): 45–64; Wells-Furby, 'A Re-appraisal', ch. 3.

[45] John Morrill (ed.), *The Scottish National Covenant in its British Context* (Edinburgh, 1990).

[46] John Bramhall to William Laud, 20 December 1634, E. P. Shirley (ed.), *Papers relating to the Church of Ireland, 1631–9* (1874), p. 41.

their churches. Despite strong links between Scottish clerics on both sides of the narrow sea, such as Bishops Henry Leslie of Down and Connor and John Maxwell of Ross, the force of covenanting combined with the effect of Lord Deputy Wentworth's anti-Covenant 'Black Oath' would introduce a dangerous and irremediable instability into the Church of Ireland. In July 1639 a Scots minister, John Corbet, who was author of the inflammatory anti-Covenanter pamphlet *The Epistle Congratulatorie of Lysimachus Nicanor* went to see his compatriot Archibald Adair about a benefice in the former's diocese of Killala. A row between them about payment of lingering medieval tax on incumbents—the *quarta pars episcopalis*—degenerated into a shouting match. Adair, taunting Corbet, declared he 'had rather subscribed the Covenant' than leave his wife and children behind him in Scotland. Corbet's riposte so goaded Adair that he yelled: 'I do not regard the bishops of Scotland. I wish they had all been in hell when they did raise the troubles in Scotland.'[47] Adair was promptly dragged through High Commission, formally deposed from his see in June 1640 and, in a stinging slap-down, saw Killala granted to the refugee Maxwell of Ross. Yet in July 1641 as the crown tried to propitiate some of its opponents, he was provided with the diocese of Waterford and Lismore. Adair's fortunes are a useful microcosm of those of the Church of Ireland. He fell victim to Scottish troubles which also propelled Scots Commissioners to London where they assisted with and promoted the Root and Branch petitions against bishops. The very High Commission that toppled Adair was itself overturned by a temporarily united Irish Parliament whose land-holding members were keen to dismantle each of the prerogative instruments involved in the temporalities campaign overseen by Bramhall.[48] All three architects of reconstruction—Laud, Wentworth, and Bramhall—found themselves impeached in collusive actions undertaken by both Westminster and Dublin Parliaments. Enhanced conformity in three realms, incarnated in bishops and coterie politics, presented a highly compact target for its enemies. By 1649, king, viceroy, and archbishop had all been judicially executed. 'Henrician Protestancie', as Nicholas Archbold had dubbed it, was in serious jeopardy.

Neither Ireland nor Scotland witnessed the Prayer Book petitions that pulsed through the Long Parliament in England. In Ireland's case this had to do with the weakness of the settlement in the first place and also because 'Britishness' had rapidly broken down into its constituent parts. In early 1642 a Scottish army commanded by Robert Munroe established the first presbytery in Carrickfergus. Overt, organized Presbyterianism would permanently alter Ireland's confessional map. In Scotland, both the English Prayer Book and the stillborn Scottish Book were swallowed up because the Church was so strong, so close to being a total establishment. The Covenanters turned out to be as

---

[47] John Corbet's deposition, 10 August 1639, TNA, SP 63/257/28.
[48] McCafferty, *Reconstruction*, pp. 210-22.

insensitive to English ways as Charles I had been to theirs. In this respect the 'British' Solemn League and Covenant turned into a pyrrhic victory because when Scots opted to recognize their 'covenanted' monarch Charles II's title to all three kingdoms they precipitated the very form of incorporative union they had feared since 1603. Cromwell's congregationalist liberties were gall and wormwood to the Scottish Church. The lesson of the 1640s was that godly convergence was just as elusive as the conformist kind. In Ireland the Established Church had resorted to the older trope of anti-popery in a bid to stave off the collapse of the gains of the 1630s but found itself facing the erasure of the whole structure of establishment itself. While Root and Branch was never extended to Ireland, Westminster increasingly regarded its own authority as sufficient for the neighbouring island. At home, the churchmen found themselves facing an alternative establishment in the shape of the Catholic Confederation of Kilkenny. Their Supreme Governor's endless exigencies brought on one crisis after another. Ireland's first Old English viceroy for a century, James Butler, duke of Ormond was himself, though Protestant, involved in a skein of negotiations which might pave the way for toleration of Catholicism (actually a recognition of conditions on the ground in large paths of Ireland) or even a lurch towards quasi-establishment. Catholics had certainly reoccupied and re-consecrated many of the medieval buildings to the dismay of remaining Church of Ireland clergy.[49] In August 1646, eleven of the bishops remaining in Ireland ruefully praised Ormond for his defence of the 'true reformed religion according to the liturgy and canons so many years received in the church, which with sad and bleeding hearts we say, is more than we know to be in any part of the three dominions'.[50] Within twelve months they were dealing with the parliamentary commissioners who required them to use the Directory. Their request to retain the Prayer Book is couched in stock language but has two striking features. The first is their attempt to argue for the Church of Ireland as 'a free Nationall church'—a bid to work around the unpicking of the Church of England.[51] The second is that there was only one episcopal signatory—Lewis Jones of Killaloe. War brought out one of the flaws inherent in a policy of importation of personnel. When it came, they tended to go home. Many clergy and bishops returned to England while some others settled down to quiet accommodation with parliamentary and then

---

[49] Tadhg Ó hAnnracháin, *Catholic Reformation in Ireland: The Mission of Rinuccini 1645-1649* (Oxford, 2002); Micheál Ó Siochrú, *Confederate Ireland, 1642-1649* (Dublin, 1999).

[50] *The Humble Remonstrance of the Archbishops, Bishops, and the Inferior Clergy of the Kingdom of Ireland* (1646), in John Wilkins (ed.), *Concilia Magnae Britanniae et Hiberniae*, 5 vols. (1737), IV, pp. 555-6.

[51] *A Declaration of the Protestant Clergy of the City of Dublin, showing Reasons Why they Cannot Consent to the Taking Away of the Book of Common Prayer, and Comply with the Directory* (1647), p. 4.

Commonwealth regimes in a country where the broad badge of Protestant had once again become more important than the narrower label of conformist.

Following his release from confinement in early 1642 John Bramhall made his way to England where he attached himself to William Cavendish, marquess of Newcastle. After Marston Moor, Bramhall sailed with Newcastle to Hamburg in 1644. Apart from a spell in Munster and south Connacht in 1649, Bramhall spent the entire Interregnum on the continent. He was active in ordaining clergy and administered communion to a kneeling Charles II at Breda in 1650 and confirmed James duke of York, Henry duke of Gloucester, and Princess Mary. Between 1649 and 1658 he wrote seven books of which several, beginning with his *Answer to M. de la Millitière* (The Hague, 1653), were devoted to the defence of the Churches of England and Ireland. On a more practical level Bramhall devised a strategy for sustaining episcopacy had the royal exile lasted longer. From 1652 onwards he suggested direct nomination to Irish sees where no chapter election was necessary. The consecrated bishops could then be translated to English sees. This technical expertise was not the only way in which his Irish experience equipped him for exile. A near decade spent in Ireland as a serving prelate in an established but minority Church gave him the kind of perspective necessary to make a defence of both English and Irish settlements based on conciliarist thought and shorn of the need to invoke Antichrist as an efficient cause for reform. Ireland from 1541 to 1641 was, just like the fragmentary Church gathered in exile and in secret during the 1640s and 1650s, an English settlement transplanted. That fact allowed him to essay a definition of what came to be called Anglican. At Bramhall's funeral in 1663, Jeremy Taylor duly lined him up with Hooker, Jewel, and Andrewes, so proposing a narrative giving the Church of England an intellectual arc and pedigree that made a virtue of the starts and shifts of the Tudor and Stuart monarchs.[52]

On 27 January 1661 two archbishops and ten bishops were consecrated in St Patrick's Cathedral, Dublin to the strains of a specially composed anthem:

> Angels look down and joy to see
> Like that above, a monarchy
> Angels look down and joy to see
> Like that above, an hierarchy.[53]

While Charles II remained vague and uncommitted in the early months of 1660, both James Sharp, agent of the Scottish Church, and the commissioners of the General Convention of Ireland realized during that hot summer in London that whatever was settled in England would become the standard for

---

[52] *ODNB*, 'Bramhall, John (1594–1663)'.
[53] Dudley Loftus, *The Proceedings Observed in Order to, and in the Consecration of the Twelve Bishops at St. Patrick's Church Dublin* (1661), p. 7.

the other kingdoms as well. The Solemn League and Covenant vanished into the ether as did the halfway house of modified episcopacy. The angels invoked in Dublin were being invited to witness a celebration of restored hierarchy as stability incarnated, of an ecclesiastical restoration conceived and deployed in predominantly secular terms. The nobles of Scotland and both the pre- and post-1641 settlers of Ireland countenanced episcopacy as part of a package designed to procure a lasting settlement in the multiple monarchy of Britain and Ireland. Nascent Anglican identity nurtured by exiled and displaced divines was useful in that it put monarchy at the very centre of the insular orrery.[54]

From the outset the Church of Ireland worked like a modern time zone. Normally it was about an hour 'behind', waiting to catch up with English trends. Occasionally it moved 'ahead', whether in the 1615 Articles or with the 1634 canons. Yet all of these were recognizably English affairs, by-products or foreshadowings of that kingdom's shiftings in religion. From 1536–1662 the Church of Ireland rarely spoke in Gaelic. When it did, it was with a puritan inflection coloured by the anti-popery made more urgent by Rome's sway over the majority of the king's Irish subjects. Restoration would forge a Protestant Ascendancy exclusive of two sets of dissenters—Irish Catholics and Ulster-Scots Presbyterians. Scotland was different. It sat, perhaps, on the other side of the international date-line. The Scottish Church occasionally warmed to English arms but cooled to its Church. Scots would never stop reading English books but could never bring themselves to adopt English styles of churchmanship. The Aberdeen Doctors were not displaced Laudians nor were Scots Presbyterians English Presbyterians—separatism was a rare beast in Scotland. That Church's moment of stability, however, would not arrive until after the Glorious Revolution.

In 1534 Henry VIII had put the crown at the head of the Church in England and in Ireland. From 1576 and after 1603 James VI had essayed the same for Scotland. In and after 1662 the king-in-church, that is, the person of the monarch, his or her presence in the establishment pew, was deemed vital to the constitution. Espousers of an Anglican polity so needed the king to be where they wanted him to be that they were prepared to depose James II in 1688. They were even prepared to bind the kingdoms to Protestant succession in perpetuity. The 1660s also witnessed another Christian reality. After a century of switchback religious change there was, across both islands, a great scatter of confessions and sects. Yet despite this array of opinion and worship one late medieval idea still had a firm grip on the vast bulk of the population.

---

[54] Julia Buckroyd, *Church and State in Scotland 1660–1681* (Edinburgh, 1990); James McGuire, 'Policy and Patronage: The Appointment of Bishops 1660–61', in Alan Ford, J. I. McGuire, and Kenneth Milne (eds.), *As by Law Established: The Church of Ireland since the Reformation* (Dublin, 1995), pp. 112–19.

This was the notion that correct communion was synonymous with full and free participation in civil society. In each realm, plenitude of liberty still depended on performance of conformity.

SELECT BIBLIOGRAPHY

Boran, Elizabethanne, and Crawford Gribben (eds.), *Enforcing Reformation in Ireland and Scotland, 1550–1700* (Aldershot, 2006).
Ford, Alan, *The Protestant Reformation in Ireland* (Dublin, 1997 edn.).
Heal, Felicity, *Reformation in Britain and Ireland* (Oxford, 2005).
Jeffries, Henry, *The Irish Church and the Tudor Reformations* (Dublin, 2010).
McCafferty, John, *The Reconstruction of the Church of Ireland: Bishop Bramhall and the Laudian Reforms, 1633–1641* (Cambridge, 2007).
MacDonald, Alan, *The Jacobean Kirk, 1567–1625: Sovereignty, Polity, Liturgy* (Aldershot, 1998).
Mullan, David, *Scottish Puritanism, 1590–1638* (Oxford, 2000).
Murray, James, *Enforcing the English Reformation in Ireland: Clerical Resistance and Political Conflict in the Diocese of Dublin, 1534–1590* (Cambridge, 2009).
Ryrie, Alec, *Origins of the Scottish Reformation* (Manchester, 2006).
Ryrie, Alec, *The Age of Reformation: The Tudor and Stewart Realms 1485–1603* (Harlow, 2009).
Todd, Margo, *The Culture of Protestantism in Early Modern Scotland* (New Haven, CT, 2002).
Wells-Furby, Leonie, 'A Re-appraisal of the Career and Reputation of William Laud, Archbishop of Canterbury, with specific reference to Scotland 1633–1640', PhD thesis, University of Kent, 2009.

14

North America to 1662

Michael P. Winship

Church of England members of all persuasions, from radical puritans to Laudians, crossed the Atlantic during this period. The Church of England's resources and personnel, however, had been badly depleted by the Reformation, and the Church was lethargic about rising to the formidable task of projecting itself across the ocean. In the absence of episcopal support and supervision and of formal channels to recruit clergy, most colonies scarcely had a comprehensive institutional church structure of any sort. Few ministers reached the West Indies, where the largest colony, Barbados, had a population of around 10,000 by 1640 and six parishes. Visitors to the island were struck by the low attendance at church services, the general religious apathy, the sectaries, and the public drunkenness and brutality.[1] Virginia's General Assembly in this period gradually created the legal outline for a conformist, parish-based church system. By 1640 it had created twenty-three parishes for its widely dispersed population of around 10,000. But there were only six clergymen, some with puritan leanings, others with dubious reputations, and six churches in the colony. As in Barbados, county courts handled offences like Sabbath-breaking and slander with varying degrees of zeal. This ecclesiastical decentralization increased in 1643 when the General Assembly gave parish vestries the power of selecting their own clergy.[2] Tiny Bermuda was owned by the puritan-dominated Somers Islands Company and provided refuge for a few puritan ministers. But ecclesiastical control of the colony, except in the unsettled mid-century period, remained firmly with the company in England,

---

[1] Richard S. Dunn, *Sugar and Slaves: The Rise of the Planter Class in the English West Indies, 1624–1713* (New York, 1973), p. 55; P. F. Campbell, *The Church in Barbados in the Seventeenth Century* (St Michael, Barbados, 1982), pp. 32, 48, 51–2, 65.

[2] James B. Bell, *Empire, Religion and Revolution in Early Virginia, 1607–1786* (Basingstoke, 2013), p. 41; Edward L. Bond, *Damned Souls in a Tobacco Colony: Religion in Seventeenth-Century Virginia* (Macon, GA, 2000), pp. 129–30, 131, 133–4.

whose main concern was profits, not with shaping an alternative to the dominant form of Anglicanism in England.[3]

New England was the only British American region whose settlers had the motivation and personnel to create a comprehensive alternative to the government and parishes of the Church of England. Their sustained attempt and mixed results provide a distinctive angle on the tortured relationship between 'establishment' and 'sectarianism' within puritanism, while the effort affected the development of the Church of England itself. Seventy-six puritan clergy, some of them prominent, were among the 13,000 to 21,000 settlers who arrived before emigration dried up in 1640.[4] The establishment of Harvard College in 1636 ensured a sufficient continuing supply of clergy, who, uniquely among the colonial church establishments, were ordained by local churches rather than by an English bishop. The New England colonies were, like their Churches, self-governing, except for the small, transient proprietary colonies to the north-east of Massachusetts, which was by far the largest and most important New England colony. The region's magistracy was committed to godly reformation.

New England's church establishment started to take shape in 1629 and 1630 with the formation of the first four Massachusetts Churches. All of them were created broadly along Congregational lines. There is no evidence that the colonists had worked out a clear ecclesiastical agenda before emigrating. Contemporary sources agree that the separatist Congregational Church at hard scrabble, tiny Plymouth Plantation, founded in 1620, was the most significant influence on their Churches. Congregationalism had been created by separatists in the 1580s as a sharp modification of puritan Presbyterianism, and it had already been embraced and adapted by a few English puritans at the beginning of the seventeenth century.[5]

Congregationalism represented the ecclesiastic opposite of much that puritans loathed about the Church of England. Congregational churches were set up virtually as the antitheses of parish churches. They were entirely voluntary. They came into existence when a small group, eventually standardized at seven men, took a church covenant. Prospective members appeared before the old ones and demonstrated that they were doctrinally informed 'visible saints'. If approved, they took the church covenant themselves. In a mid-1630s Massachusetts innovation, the admission standard was raised to include an account of the process by which God had worked grace in a prospective

[3] Gregory Edwin Shipley, 'Turbulent Times, Troubled Isles: The Rise and Development of Puritanism in Bermuda and the Bahamas, 1609–1684', PhD thesis, Westminster Theological Seminary, 1989.

[4] Susan Hardman Moore, *Pilgrims: New World Settlers and the Call of Home* (New Haven, CT, 2007), pp. 22, 55.

[5] Michael P. Winship, *Godly Republicanism: Puritans, Pilgrims, and a City on a Hill* (Cambridge, MA, 2012), chs. 2, 3, 6.

member's soul.⁶ A Church was untouchable by any higher ecclesiastical power, for there was no such power, not even the synods that the Presbyterians favoured; each Church was an independent polity. Ministers and other church officers were elected by the male church members, and none of those officers had any power, sacramental or otherwise, outside their own church. A Church's responsibility to the rest of the population extended only to allowing it to attend services. Marriages were conducted by magistrates, and there were no funeral services. Initially, ministers were paid by voluntary contributions and there were no laws requiring attendance.⁷

Congregationalists shunned any sort of liturgy, leaving no opening for the Book of Common Prayer, which was loathed by radical puritans. New England services consisted of a minister's preaching and praying, both for more than an hour, interspersed with Scripture exposition and communal psalm singing, and followed occasionally by baptism or the Lord's Supper. There were two such services on Sundays, with variations at other times, when days of fasting were called to appease God's wrath or days of thanksgiving to thank Him for His mercies or when a minister gave a weekday lecture.⁸

While the dominant faction within the Church of England attempted to impose its version of Anglicanism through legally enforced articles and canons, New England Congregationalists emphasized consultation and consensus. Congregational churches were created after lengthy conferences, prayer, and fasting. In an important modification of Presbyterianism, all important business in these churches was conducted in front of the congregation and needed to be approved by it. If a substantial majority felt strongly enough that biblical rectitude was on their side to force a conclusion, dissenters could either defer to the judgement of the majority or face admonition for obstinately defying the rule of Scripture. Consensus was then created by declaring the dissenters' votes nullified, although this was a rare procedure (a lay majority could not override church officers, however).⁹

Churches, although autonomous, frequently consulted other churches, and ministers met regularly for shop talk. Like Presbyterians, Congregationalists recognized synods as scriptural and important vehicles for collectively discerning the mind of God. But it was no less foundational for Congregationalists that no group of churches could compel an individual church. Churches

---

⁶ Charles E. Hambrick-Stowe, *The Practice of Piety: Puritan Devotional Disciplines in Seventeenth-Century New England* (Chapel Hill, NC, 1982), pp. 127–8; Edmund S. Morgan, *Visible Saints: The History of a Puritan Idea* (New York, 1963).

⁷ Winship, *Godly Republicanism*, ch. 2.

⁸ Hambrick-Stowe, *Practice of Piety*, ch. 4.

⁹ James F. Cooper, Jr., *Tenacious of Their Liberties: The Congregationalists in Colonial Massachusetts* (New York, 1999), pp. 39–40; John Davenport, *An Answer of the Elders of the Severall Churches in New-England* (1643), p. 72; Richard Mather, *Church-Government and Church-Covenant Discussed* (1643), pp. 60–2.

could withdraw fellowship from a church that insisted on following error, but they could not coerce it.[10]

Ideally, however, the issue of coercion would not arise. Massachusetts puritans anticipated that godliness and consensus would go hand in hand. 'God's people are all marked with one and the same mark', Salem's governor John Endicott wrote to Plymouth's in 1629, '...and where this is, there can be no discord'. Nonetheless, the creation and preservation of New England's church establishment depended on sympathetic political structures. The general courts and governors of all the colonies were elected by male settlers approved by the courts. Massachusetts and New Haven required church membership for the franchise. It was argued in these latter colonies that the 'saints' should only be ruled by fellow-saints and that this franchise was vital to the long-term survival of their reformations. Righteous magistrates would preserve the purity of the churches and those churches' members would only elect righteous magistrates.[11]

New England puritans, like English Presbyterians, conceived of Church and state roughly as two equally important governments whose authority lay in separate spheres. The state was supposed to protect the churches, but it was not supposed to interfere spiritually with them. The colonies' general courts passed strict Sabbath and moral legislation, mandated maintenance for ministers, helped churches resolve their quarrels, and prevented the formation of non-Congregationalist Churches. Unlike English clerics, church elders could not serve in public offices; the churches could not fine or imprison, and excommunication had no secular consequences.[12]

How far governments could intervene when ecclesiastical consensual mechanisms failed to contain religious disputes was always a fraught issue. In 1634 Roger Williams from his Salem pulpit demanded a colony-wide cessation of a radical list of what he regarded as excessive religious entanglement with the world. The colony's religious and political leaders almost unanimously agreed that Williams's demands, in their vehemence, extremism, and visibility, were dangerous for both religious and pragmatic reasons. Yet public and private debates and conferences failed to restrain him, and his church refused to disavow or sanction him. A collision between the General Court and the Salem church was averted only when Williams further demanded that the Salem church break its fellowship with the other churches or he would break his fellowship with it. A majority of the church rejected Williams, making it straightforward for the General Court to convict him of contempt of their authority in October 1635 and to banish him.[13]

---

[10] Hambrick-Stowe, *Practice of Piety*, p. 127; Cooper, *Tenacious of Their Liberties*, pp. 18–22.
[11] Winship, *Godly Republicanism*, pp. 142, 197–200.
[12] Winship, *Godly Republicanism*, p. 217; Joseph B. Felt, *The Ecclesiastical History of New England*, 2 vols. (Boston, MA, 1855).
[13] Winship, *Godly Republicanism*, pp. 206–24.

The Massachusetts Churches had barely recovered from that controversy when a new one arose. In early 1636, some critics thought they detected echoes of antinomian and spiritist heresies in the increasingly unconventional preaching of the colony's most prominent minister John Cotton. The critics' suspicions were heightened because some members of Cotton's Boston congregation, most famously Anne Hutchinson, were quietly disseminating such doctrines under the cloak of Cotton's name, while attacking all the other ministers for preaching false doctrine. After a tumultuous spring, New England's first synod in the summer of 1637 managed to paper over the theological differences between Cotton and the other ministers while condemning the more radical lay opinions. The synod gave the General Court enough breathing space to banish Hutchinson and two others of the most vocal Boston partisans. Others left with them. New England Congregationalists would not face another significant theological controversy until a few ministers began flirting with Arminianism in the 1730s.[14]

The banishments resulted in settlements south of Massachusetts that would evolve into Rhode Island, a semi-anarchic handful of towns committed to religious liberty and minimal government. As Rhode Island demonstrated, the ease with which people could move away from each other was an important element in maintaining peace among the New England Churches. Besides Cotton, the two most important ministers to come to New England, John Davenport and Thomas Hooker, founded New Haven and Connecticut. It is not coincidental that the Congregationalism of these colonies had different inflections than Massachusetts's.[15]

Despite those different inflections, the minister Richard Mather was broadly correct when he wrote to his English brethren in 1639, 'For ought we know there is no materiall point, either in constitution, or government, wherein the Churches in N. E. ... do not observe the same course'.[16] These self-selected religious zealots, on the rebound from the unprecedented Laudian effort to wring puritanism out of the Church of England, had anchored an effort to create a properly reformed Christian society to Churches that bordered on sectarianism in their consensual decision-making, exclusivity, and resistance to interference by governments or any kind of higher earthly authority. By the mid-1630s, some Congregationalists were pleased enough with their accomplishment to look upon their churches as harbingers of the millennium.[17]

Except in separatist Plymouth, New England Congregationalists claimed that they had not separated from the Church of England. What they meant was that even though the hierarchy of the Church of England was false, as were

[14] Michael P. Winship, *Making Heretics: Militant Protestantism and Free Grace in Massachusetts, 1636–1641* (Princeton, NJ, 2002).
[15] Winship, *Making Heretics*, pp. 233–4.   [16] Mather, *Church-Government*, p. 82.
[17] Winship, *Godly Republicanism*, pp. 229–32.

most of its parish churches, there were at least some parish churches with a puritan minister and enough puritan members to qualify as true Churches in spite of their corruptions of worship and government. From those parish churches alone, the Congregational Churches had not separated. But it was a theoretical recognition, since the Congregationalists shunned all parish churches sacramentally. Like the separatists, they would not allow the members of any parish churches to receive the sacraments with them until they joined a local church, nor would they participate in the sacraments in parish churches on return visits to England.[18]

In 1641, the seemingly unstoppable Laudian juggernaut collapsed. The removal of the restraint of Laudianism was felt across the American colonies. Parliament attempted to repress Book of Common Prayer worship and encourage godliness in the colonies, with varying success. In 1644, three of the four ministers in Bermuda staged a Massachusetts-inspired church coup by creating a Congregational church from which the majority of the population found itself barred. The resulting intense struggles between Congregationalists and less extreme puritans in Bermuda did not die down until the 1650s. Virginia puritans were emboldened by the shifting political climate to ask Massachusetts to send them three ministers in 1642, which it did. But Virginia's newly appointed royal governor Sir William Berkeley was a Laudian and fervent royalist. Acts mandating conformity in 1643 and 1647 succeeded in driving many of Virginia's most committed puritans to New England or to neighbouring Maryland, which was set up as a refuge for Catholics. Virginia officially abandoned its royalism and Prayer Book worship in 1651 upon surrendering to a Commonwealth fleet. The fleet would soon work its will on Barbados, where Cavaliers had recently seized the government and instituted Prayer Book worship. In the mid-1650s, Maryland's new puritan residents, chafing under the burden of having to tolerate Catholics, seized control of the government for a few years.[19]

The lifting of Laudian repression brought about the climax of American Congregationalism's impact on the Church of England. In the 1630s its example and influence had revived the moribund English Congregationalist movement and invested it with millennial fervour.[20] At the same time, less extreme English puritans were increasingly offended and alarmed by the American Congregationalists' practice of sacramental shunning. In a fraught manuscript exchange between once- and future English Presbyterians and their former ministerial colleagues and friends in Massachusetts, the English

---

[18] Winship, *Godly Republicanism*, pp. 154, 156–7.
[19] Campbell, *Church in Barbados*, pp. 56–7; Shipley, 'Turbulent Times', chs. 6, 7; Bond, *Damned Souls*, pp. 153–5, 157–9; Carla Gardina Pestana, *The English Atlantic in an Age of Revolution, 1640–1661* (Cambridge, MA, 2004), pp. 75–85, ch. 3.
[20] Winship, *Godly Republicanism*, pp. 229–32.

rejected Congregationalism as being too atomistic in its conception of the Church, too restrictive in its conception of the ministry, too spiritually elitist in its admission standards, too democratic in its government, and too disordered and too separatist in practice. The manuscript exchange ended with one of the English ministers publishing a book pronouncing Congregationalism to be a sinful schism. That book was timed for the opening of the Short Parliament and the revival of hope for church reform. It was intended to nip in the bud a version of puritanism that turned its back on the parishes and rejected the very idea of a national Church.[21]

The exchange bled into the ones between English Congregationalists and Presbyterians that almost immediately broke out in the 1640s, often involving the same people and issues. American treatises often served as surrogate voices for the English Congregationalists, and Scottish ones for the English Presbyterians. Presbyterians were predictably no more successful at coming to terms with the handful of Congregationalists at the Westminster Assembly than they had been in the exchanges of the 1630s, and that failure hamstrung the effort to create a Reformed Church of England. Thereafter relations between American and English Congregationalists cooled somewhat as the latter grew more comfortable with religious toleration.[22]

One consequence of temporary Presbyterian English political dominance in the 1640s was the emboldening of like-minded puritans in New England. One Congregational church at Newbury, Massachusetts, adopted a Presbyterian type of government in 1643 after liberalizing admissions standards. The Newbury church continued to stay in communion with the other churches, although on its own, sometimes awkward terms. Its ministers were well respected and had influential friends in England—all good reasons for the Congregationalists to leave them alone. In 1646 Robert Child and six others presented a petition to the Massachusetts General Court calling for a remodelling of the government more along English lines and asking that either all members of the Church of England be made members of Massachusetts churches or that they be permitted to set up Presbyterian churches. There was no groundswell of support for the Child petition, and the subsequent political collapse of Presbyterianism in England shut down the English path for redress of local moderate puritan grievances.[23]

---

[21] Michael P. Winship, 'Straining the Bonds of Puritanism: English Presbyterians and Massachusetts Congregationalists Debate Ecclesiology, 1636–40', in Crawford Gribben and R. Scott Spurlock (eds.), *Puritans and Catholics in the Trans-Atlantic World 1600–1800* (Basingstoke, 2015), pp. 89–111.

[22] Pestana, *English Atlantic*, pp. 53–75; Winship, *Godly Republicanism*, pp. 234–5; Hunter Powell, *The Crisis of British Protestantism: Church Power in the Puritan Revolution, 1638–44* (Manchester, 2015), chs. 5, 6.

[23] Robert Emmet Wall, *Massachusetts Bay: The Crucial Decade, 1640–1650* (New Haven, CT, 1972), ch. 5; Cooper, *Tenacious of Their Liberties*, pp. 74–5.

Although Presbyterianism itself made little impact on New England, there was steady slippage from the initial 1630s ideal of anti-parish churches, pure, exclusive, voluntary, and decoupled as much as possible from state-enforced compulsion. Already in 1638 a Massachusetts law made support of a town's minister mandatory, even for non-church members, who had no say in selecting him and enjoyed none of his services except preaching. In 1646, another law mandated fines for non-attendance at services. The other puritan colonies in the 1640s and 1650s passed variations of these laws.[24]

Among church members, there was growing sentiment that too many people were being excluded from their ranks. The children of the churches were maturing, and when the time came for them to demonstrate convincingly to their churches as adults that they were among the predestined saved, they were holding back. Some way was needed of keeping these adult children and their offspring at least minimally within the churches. Some of the laity and ministers also wanted people outside the churches to gain access at least to baptism.[25]

It was in large measure to settle the swelling disagreements about baptism that the Massachusetts General Court called a synod of the New England churches in 1646. The professed goal was to write a confession for their churches. The result, published in England, was the Cambridge Platform of 1649, the closest New England Congregationalism ever got to formal Church of England statements like the Thirty-Nine Articles or the Canons of 1604.[26]

This innovation of a church platform almost died stillborn. The call for the synod occurred shortly after a Presbyterian platform had been drawn up by the Westminster Assembly and approved by Parliament. That platform was being used by English moderate puritans to attempt to snuff out English Congregationalism. Thus, the novel American ministerial/magisterial call to formalize New England Congregationalism could be and was seen by other suspicious Congregationalists as itself an un-Congregationalist effort to assert illegitimate control over the churches, with incipient Presbyterianism and/or Erastianism lurking behind it. Members of the General Court challenged the Court's power to call the synod, and two important churches, Boston and Salem, initially refused to send delegates. In 1651, the Court officially voted its 'testimony' that the now-completed Platform 'for the substance thereof... is that we have practiced and doe believe' while reiterating that it did not intend to impose the platform on any churches. Yet even this toothless affirmation of

---

[24] David D. Hall, *The Faithful Shepherd: A History of the New England Ministry in the Seventeenth Century* (New York, 1974), 147; Felt, *Ecclesiastical History*, I, p. 587; II, pp. 37, 72, 185.
[25] Williston Walker, *The Creeds and Platforms of Congregationalism* (New York, 1893), p. 160.
[26] Stephen Foster, *The Long Argument: English Puritanism and the Shaping of New England Culture, 1570–1700* (Chapel Hill, NC, 1991), p. 169.

what was only an idealized description of standard New England practices was opposed by fourteen Court members. Eventually for some Congregationalists the Cambridge Platform acquired a patina of informal authority. But it was never perceived as having binding force.[27]

That such an innocuous document could seem like a coercive imposition explains why the Cambridge Platform ducked the one specific issue that the General Court wanted tackled: baptism. At the synod, the majority wished to work out conditions for the children of the church who could not demonstrate that they were among the saved to have their own children baptized. Their intentions were derailed by a handful of ministers who were unwilling to degrade the purity of voluntary churches by adding to them a perpetual succession of birthright members unable to offer satisfactory signs of salvation. In the absence of consensus, the synod left the status quo intact in the Cambridge Platform. The synod had preserved the façade of Congregational unity by dodging the issue where unity was most under strain.[28]

In principle, individual churches should have been able to adjust their baptismal standards even if the Congregationalists collectively could not. Yet the Congregationalist culture of consensus hobbled the efforts of individual churches to expand baptism. In the 1650s, churches wanting to do so expressed their concern about 'walking alone'. Those churches that did raise the issue were cautioned not to press it. In any given church, it only took a handful of vociferous opponents to prevent change.[29]

This log-jam gave signs of breaking in 1656. The Connecticut General Court received a petition that year requesting liberalized baptizing. It sent out a call to the legislatures of the other colonies asking for a meeting of elders to discuss the issue. The Massachusetts General Court responded positively in the autumn. New Haven colony, which wanted no change in baptismal practices, warned that behind the petition was a plot to alter Church and state in New England and create communion with the corrupt English parish churches. It refused to send any delegates to the meeting.[30]

The meeting was something of a damp squib. Around twenty ministers, mostly from Massachusetts, gathered in Boston in 1657. Lacking any lay representatives, in Congregational terms, they were only an informal expert advisory group, not a meeting of churches; they had no special spiritual authority. The meeting, with the exception of two or three attendees, endorsed

[27] Walker, *Creeds*, p. 188; Cooper, *Tenacious of Their Liberties*, pp. 75–87.
[28] Walker, *Creeds*, pp. 169, 253; Charles Chauncy and others, *Anti-Synodalia Scripta Americana* (1662), p. 10.
[29] Robert G. Pope, *The Half-Way Covenant: Church Membership in Puritan New England* (Princeton, NJ, 1969), pp. 32–7; Increase Mather, *The First Principles of New-England, Concerning the Subject of Baptisme & Communion of Churches* (Cambridge, MA, 1675), pp. 9, 13, 24; Mather, *Magnalia*, II, p. 99.
[30] Walker, *Creeds*, pp. 257–61.

expanding baptism. Only a few churches acted on its recommendation. Ministers and many laity were willing in other churches, but in a system that did not work on majority rule, they were not prepared to override the adamant resistance of others.[31]

To some extent, the issue of baptism festered because the churches and magistrates were facing more immediate problems. Congregationalism's lack of internal policing mechanisms meant that the general courts had to regularly and clumsily intervene in church quarrels. The most prominent dispute, in the Hartford, Connecticut church, stretched over six years, from 1653–9. It dragged in successive church councils gathered from Connecticut, New Haven, and Massachusetts, whose advice the parties only heeded when it suited them, along with the Connecticut General Court, who had no more success, while it polarized towns up and down the Connecticut River Valley. These church controversies and the baptism log-jam prompted the prominent minister John Norton to warn the Massachusetts General Court in 1661 that spectators were raising the 'sad Query... Whether the Congregational-way be practicable, yea or not?'[32]

What appeared at first to be a greater threat to Congregationalism than its own internal lack of organization came with the arrival of Quaker missionaries in 1656. Driven by an apocalyptic conviction that they were to take over the world, Quakers were successful in establishing themselves in Rhode Island. From there, they created toeholds in Plymouth and Massachusetts that provided bases for further missionizing in those colonies. As in the Caribbean and the Chesapeake, the orthodox New England colonies quickly enacted laws against them. Massachusetts's, the harshest, called for whippings, mutilations, imprisonment, banishments, and, finally, for returning Quakers, execution. After hanging four Quakers between 1659 and 1661, Massachusetts ceased its executions not in response to widespread popular revulsion, for which there is no evidence, but because it faced a potentially even graver threat to New England's Congregational establishment: the restoration of Charles II in 1660. Virginia passed an adaptation of Massachusetts's laws in 1660, but the only Quaker who died there did so from the brutality of his treatment in jail.[33]

Since there had last been a functioning king, the British Atlantic world had expanded and grown more closely knit. The New England puritans were well

---

[31] Pope, *Half-Way Covenant*, pp. 25–6, 33, 38; Walker, *Creeds*, pp. 261–2.

[32] Timothy J. Sehr, *Colony and Commonwealth: Massachusetts Bay, 1649–1660* (New York, 1989), pp. 257–60; Francis J. Bremer, *Building a New Jerusalem: John Davenport, a Puritan in Three Worlds* (New Haven, CT, 2012), pp. 258–62; John Norton, *Three Choice and Profitable Sermons Opened and Applyed* (Cambridge, MA, 1684), p. 13.

[33] Stephen B. Weeks, *Southern Quakers and Slavery: A Study in Institutional History* (Baltimore, MD, 1896), pp. 16–17, 118; Monica Najar, 'Sectarians and Strategies of Dissent in Colonial Virginia', in Paul Rasor and Richard E. Bond (eds.), *From Jamestown to Jefferson: The Evolution of Religious Freedom in Virginia* (Charlottesville, VA, 2011), p. 118.

aware that they had located themselves on the losing side of the 'puritan revolution'. It was obvious that Connecticut and Plymouth would have to be accommodating to the new English regime, since both were squatter colonies; neither had a royal charter to give it firm legal existence. Moreover, neither colony tied the franchise to church membership, so their reformations had less to lose from royal interference than the more ambitious ones of Massachusetts and New Haven. Massachusetts had what it considered to be an inviolable charter, and it put off proclaiming Charles II until August 1661. New Haven was even more defiant, but it was absorbed into Connecticut under the royal charter negotiated by that colony in 1662.[34]

Even in Massachusetts, there were deep theo-political divisions about how to respond to the new king. The opponents of expanded baptism viewed the Congregational churches as besieged by a hostile world. The Restoration and renewed repression of puritanism in England were European manifestations of this. In New England, that hostile world was lapping up to the doors of the churches in the form of the unconverted children of the churches. Even worse, it was represented within Congregationalism itself by the ministers and laity who wanted to let those children in. Expanded baptism would not only pollute the churches, it would lead to an inevitable erosion of standards for full membership and eventually to communion with the English parish churches now being fully restored to their old corruption. The best response was to pull up the drawbridges and trust to God in the brief span of days remaining before the downfall of Antichrist and the coming of the millennium; to accommodate the king no further than to remind him that Massachusetts had the right by its charter to rule itself, while at home to resist all attempts to dilute the purity of the churches.[35]

Not all supporters of expanded baptism favoured seeking accommodation with the king, but for those who did, the transatlantic political regime and expanded baptism were bound together. As the Quaker onslaught across the Atlantic demonstrated, the English Atlantic world needed order. Hopefully a monarch would be able to provide that order better than the English puritan regimes of the previous two decades; New England as a society needed to be sheltered under the moral and spiritual order that expanded baptism would provide; Congregationalism itself badly needed more order, as the recent church disputes and the refusal of many of the laity to line up behind the vast majority of ministers in favour of expanded baptism demonstrated.[36]

---

[34] Thomas Hutchinson, *The History of the Colony and Province of Massachusetts-bay*, ed. Lawrence Shaw Mayo, 2 vols. (Cambridge, MA, 1936), I, pp. 182, 186; Bremer, *Building a New Jerusalem*, ch. 18.

[35] Isabel Macbeath Calder (ed.), *The Letters of John Davenport, Puritan Divine* (New Haven, CT, 1937), pp. 139–40; Foster, *Long Argument*, pp. 201–2.

[36] Foster, *Long Argument*, pp. 200–1.

In December 1661, after sharp internal debates, the Massachusetts General Court made a broad effort to get the colony's internal and external affairs in order. It narrowly agreed to send two agents to King Charles.[37] At the same time, it finally called a synod to settle the issue of baptism. To that synodical agenda, Massachusetts ministers added another item—consociations—regular meetings of the churches to provide stability through a regular, although not coercive, oversight that Congregationalism badly lacked. The 1662 synod was the last effort to define and affirm a unified New England Congregationalism. To the extent that the effort was driven by fear of social and religious disorder and disunity, it bore a relationship to the contemporaneous drive in the Church of England to create its own unified Anglicanism through the Clarendon Code, and it was no more successful.

At the synod, the call for consociations proved uncontroversial. As for baptism, the synod resolved that the children of church members were members in their own right and could have their own children baptized and themselves stay under discipline as long as they were 'nonscandalous' and doctrinally well versed and were willing to own their church's covenant. The requirements for access to the Lord's Supper and the right to vote in church affairs remained unchanged. The synod also affirmed that 'nonscandalous' visitors from other 'orthodox' churches could have their children baptized. The parish churches were included among those orthodox churches. Those propositions moderated the independence of each church, endorsed, in effect, church birthright membership, and opened the New England churches to the larger community of Protestant Churches. As such, they represented an impressive stride back to the conventional imperatives of a church establishment. The synod was profusely and repeatedly praised by the prominent moderate English puritan Richard Baxter, no lover of English Congregationalism, as an important step towards restoring unity among the godly.[38] Congregationalism had finally come in from the sectarian and schismatic cold, at least in Baxter's mind.

However, Congregational synods could propose anything they wanted; adoption still remained up to individual churches. For much the same reasons that Baxter praised the synod's conclusions, some New England Congregationalists, including a few leading ministers, bitterly attacked them. Consociations were never implemented, nor, as far as is known, were visitors from parish churches ever welcomed to the sacraments. Expanded baptism, sometimes well beyond the boundaries delineated by the synod, eventually became

---

[37] Hutchinson, *History*, I, p. 192.
[38] Walker, *Creeds*, pp. 313–39; John Allin, *Animadversions Upon the Antisynodalia Americana* (Cambridge, MA, 1664), p. 7; Norton, *Three Choice and Profitable Sermons*, sig. Gr; Richard Baxter, *A Defence of the Principles of Love* (1671), pp. 6–7, 46, 157–9; Richard Baxter, *A Christian Directory* (1673), p. 926; M. Sylvester, *Reliquiae Baxterianae* (1696), I, pp. 104, 137, 298, 387.

generally accepted, but it took a decade of heated political and religious struggle after the synod before New England Congregationalists resigned themselves to the fact that baptism was a subject on which they would have to agree to disagree.[39]

During this period, these Congregationalists realized a long-standing Church of England ambition and began missionizing among the Indians. In 1646 Massachusetts's government pushed local ministers to take up the task. For one of them, John Eliot, it grew into a vocation. Eliot became convinced that the only way to convert Indians was to anglicize them. They would move into new towns where English social mores would be enforced by law, and where some of them would become missionaries themselves. The Indians would run those towns, supervised by the English, as theocratic republics—prototypes of a form (Eliot believed in the aftermath of Charles I's execution) that would rapidly spread in preparation for the imminent millennial reign of the world's only legitimate monarch, Christ. The first of fourteen Praying Indian towns, Natick, was founded in 1650, with three streets of native-style dwellings, a fort, and an English building that served as meeting house, school, and warehouse. Funds for supplies, missionary work, Indian lay preachers and school teachers, and books and bibles that Eliot published in the local Algonquin dialect came from the New England Company, an English charity incorporated for this purpose in 1649.[40]

Indians came to Natick for a variety of reasons: protection from hostile Indian tribes, availability of English goods and craft skills, land that was secure (or so the Indians hoped) from further English expansion, and because their own gods were proving inadequate to the challenges of the English invasion. Once in Natick, they were exposed to the many religious exoticisms of Christianity through preaching, catechizing, Sunday worship services, and Christian civic moral discipline. In 1659, eight Indian males gave convincing accounts of their conversions before Eliot's Roxbury church, were accepted as members, and were baptized. They then formed their own church at Natick, as autonomous as any other Congregational church. The Indians chose not to elect one of their own as their minister, and Eliot, at their request, administered the sacraments. To Eliot and the Praying Indians' dismay, other local churches were not willing to acknowledge that the Indians were indeed genuine Christians by practising sacramental communion with the Natick church. A parallel missionizing effort, although with much more Indian control, was taking place on the New England island of Martha's Vineyard.[41]

---

[39] Pope, *Half-Way Covenant*, ch. 2.

[40] Richard W. Cogley, *John Eliot's Mission to the Indians before King Philip's War* (Cambridge, MA, 1999), pp. 44–97, 105–8, 119–24.

[41] Cogley, *John Eliot's Mission*, pp. 124–39; John Eliot, 'Eliot's Account of Indian Churches in New-England, 1673', *Massachusetts Historical Society Collections*, 1st. ser., 10 (1809), pp. 126–7;

In the rest of British America at the time of the Restoration, institutional Christianity remained catch as catch can. Virginia, for example, now had fifty-four parishes for its widely scattered population of around 27,000 but only eight church buildings and nine active ministers. Most ministers offered only one Sunday service, and none at all on days that were too hot or cold.[42] Barbados over the previous two decades had undergone a rapid, brutal transition to a sugar, slave-based economy. Its population was perhaps 20,000 Europeans, mostly English, and an equal number of Africans. The Europeans in their eleven parishes were served by nine ministers or preachers, four of whom were probably unordained. Only the Quakers on the island took a sustained religious interest in the slaves, which was counted among their many offences by their fellow colonists.[43]

SELECT BIBLIOGRAPHY

Bell, James B., *Empire, Religion and Revolution in Early Virginia, 1607–1786* (Basingstoke, 2013).

Bond, Edward L., *Damned Souls in a Tobacco Colony: Religion in Seventeenth-Century Virginia* (Macon, GA, 2000).

Foster, Stephen, *The Long Argument: English Puritanism and the Shaping of New England Culture, 1570–1700* (Chapel Hill, NC, 1991).

Hall, David D., *Worlds of Wonder, Days of Judgment: Popular Religious Belief in Early New England* (Cambridge, MA, 1990).

Hambrick-Stowe, Charles E., *The Practice of Piety: Puritan Devotional Disciplines in Seventeenth-Century New England* (Chapel Hill, NC, 1982).

Pestana, Carla Gardina, *The English Atlantic in an Age of Revolution, 1640–1661* (Cambridge, MA, 2004).

Shipley, Gregory Edwin, 'Turbulent Times, Troubled Isles: The Rise and Development of Puritanism in Bermuda and the Bahamas, 1609–1684', PhD thesis, Westminster Theological Seminary, 1989.

Winship, Michael P., *Godly Republicanism: Puritans, Pilgrims, and a City on a Hill* (Cambridge, MA, 2012).

David J. Silverman, *Faith and Boundaries: Colonists, Christianity, and Community Among the Wampanoag Indians of Martha's Vineyard, 1600–1871* (New York, 2005), ch. 1.

[42] Bell, *Empire, Religion and Revolution*, pp. 41, 43–4.
[43] Dunn, *Sugar and Slaves*, pp. 75–6, 103–7; Campbell, *Church in Barbados*, p. 70.

15

Perceptions of Christian Antiquity

Jean-Louis Quantin

In the nineteenth and twentieth centuries, especially in the circles most influenced by the Oxford movement, it was axiomatic that Anglicanism nourished a special devotion to Christian antiquity, which made it a *via media* between Roman Catholicism and continental Protestant Churches. The entire history of the Church of England since the Reformation was read in this perspective. Recent scholarship has largely exploded this view and, more generally, the very notion of a unique 'spirit of Anglicanism'. It is nonetheless true that the perception of the Church of England as a 'primitive Church' has its roots, if not in the sixteenth, at least in the seventeenth century, where its emergence went hand in hand with the construction of a distinct confessional identity. Attitudes towards Christian antiquity were both a factor in, and an indicator of, religious change.

THE STATUS OF CHRISTIAN ANTIQUITY IN THE REFORMED CHURCH OF ENGLAND

As far as principles were concerned, the authority ascribed to Christian antiquity was a major fault-line in the age of the Reformations. In his 1521 *Assertio Septem Sacramentorum*, Henry VIII repeatedly confronted Luther with patristic authority. The marginal note—on the question of auricular confession—'Submit to the Fathers, Luther' might be taken as the motto of the book.[1] Luther complained in his reply that, while he kept 'shouting: The Gospel, the Gospel, Christ, Christ', his adversaries opposed him 'nothing but statutes of men, glosses of Fathers, practices or rites of past ages'.[2]

---

[1] Henry VIII, *Assertio Septem Sacramentorum aduersus Martinum Lutherum*, ed. Pierre Fraenkel (Münster in Westfalen, 1992), p. 155.

[2] Martin Luther, *Contra Henricum Regem Angliae* [1522], in *D. Martin Luther's Werke*, 91 vols. (Weimar, 1883–2009), X, 2 (1907), pp. 182–3.

After it broke with Rome, the Henrician Church quickly moved away from a notion of unwritten traditions as a second source of revelation, of equal authority with Scripture. This doctrine had been taught by some late medieval theologians and subsequently appeared to be canonized by the Council of Trent (which decreed in 1546 that truth was to be found 'in the written books and in the unwritten traditions which, received by the Apostles from Christ's own word of mouth, or transmitted by the Apostles themselves, by the dictation of the Holy Ghost, as it were from hand to hand, have come down to us').[3] It had been propounded in Henry's own *Assertio*, which claimed—in words almost identical to the future Tridentine decree—that some actions and sayings of Christ, which had not been recorded in the gospels, had been 'transmitted, as it were from hand to hand, from the very time of the Apostles, and had come down to us'. If no gospel had ever been written, 'there would still remain the Gospel written in the hearts of the faithful'.[4] In all the doctrinal formularies and official pronouncements of the Henrician Reformation, by contrast, 'word of God' and 'canon of the Bible' were taken as synonymous. In 1537, Thomas Cromwell, in his capacity as royal vicegerent, summoned a synod to prepare a new doctrinal statement (the Bishops' Book). According to the testimony of the Scottish Lutheran Alexander Alesius, who attended the debates, Cromwell, in his opening speech, instructed bishops, in the king's name, to 'conclude all things by the word of God'. 'Neither, he insisted, will his magesty suffer the scripture to be wrested and defaced by any glosys, any papistical lawes, or by any auctoryte of doctors or councels, and moche lesse wil he admit any articles or doctrine not conteyned in the scripture but approved only by contynuance of tyme and old custome and by unwritton verytes as ye were wont to doo.' John Stokesley, bishop of London, tried in vain to defend the authority of unwritten apostolic traditions in the case of confirmation.[5]

At the same time, however, the Henrician Church referred to the 'three Creeds' inherited from antiquity (the Apostles' Creed, the Nicene Creed, and the so-called Creed of St Athanasius). The first of the Ten Articles adopted by Convocation in July 1536 (the earliest doctrinal statement of the Henrician Church) insisted that people 'ought and must most constantly believe and defend all those things to be true, which be comprehended in the whole body and canon of the Bible, and also in the three creeds, or symbols', and interpret Bible and Creeds 'according to the selfsame sentence and interpretation, which the words of the selfsame creeds or symbols do purport, and the holy approved

---

[3] *Enchiridion Symbolorum, Definitionum et Declarationum de Rebus Fidei et Morum*, ed. Heinrich Denzinger and Adolf Schönmetzer, 36th edn. (Freiburg im Breisgau, 1976), no. 1501.
[4] Henry VIII, *Assertio*, pp. 156, 189.
[5] Alexander Alesius, *Of the Auctorite of the Word of God Agaynst the Bisshop of London* ([Strassburg, 1544?]), sigs. A5r–A6v; Diarmaid MacCulloch, *Thomas Cranmer: A Life* (New Haven, CT, 1996), pp. 186–9.

doctors of the Church do entreat and defend the same'. This was repeated in almost identical words in the two fuller doctrinal statements that followed, the 1537 *Institution of a Christian Man* (the Bishops' Book), and the more conservative *Necessary Doctrine and Erudition for any Christian Man* (King's Book) of 1543.[6] This was by no means original: the three creeds were the foundation of sixteenth-century ecclesiastical respectability, as it were, against the radical Reformation, and they regularly appeared in continental Protestant confessions of faith. On that point, the Ten Articles actually reproduced, with minimal changes, the so-called 'Wittenberg Articles', which English ambassadors had lately agreed with Luther and other leading German theologians. But the relation between Scripture and the creeds was not clarified. Other moot points regarded the canon—a standard argument against Protestant *sola scriptura*, which appeared in Henry's *Assertio*, was that it could not be known without tradition—and the interpretation of Scripture. The King's Book added to ambiguity by defining divine faith as the belief that Scripture was infallibly true 'and further also, that all those things which were taught by the apostles, and have been by an whole universal consent of the church of Christ ever sith that time taught continually, and taken always for true, ought to be received, accepted, and kept, as a perfect doctrine apostolic'—an echo of a famous axiom of Augustine: 'whatever is held by the universal Church and has not been instituted by any council but has always been preserved, is rightly believed to be of apostolic authority'.[7]

As a result, views on tradition varied widely within the Henrician Church. In his unpublished *Dyalogue Shewinge what we be Bounde to Byleve as Thinges Necessary to Salvacion, and What Not*, which appears to be related to the vicegerential synod of 1537, the lawyer Christopher St German stressed that 'sayinges of doctoures' ought not to be believed unless they 'be grounded of Scripture and may be deryvied owte thereof in a probable consequence'. To put down the authority of the Fathers, he remarkably used a philological argument: their writings had been subject to interpolations, so that what they really wrote 'cannot be assuredly knowen'. On the other hand, St German maintained that the authority of Scripture was founded on its having been 'canonised by the universall churche'.[8] Sir Thomas Elyot—whom Cromwell significantly suspected of 'not savouring Scripture'—stressed that Scripture has its 'dark' places, and advised therefore to 'consulte with theim, whiche be syncerely exercised therein, or with the bokes of most aunciente and catholike

---

[6] Gerald Bray (ed.), *Documents of the English Reformation* (Cambridge, 1994), p. 164; Charles Lloyd (ed.), *Formularies of Faith put forth by Authority during the Reign of Henry VIII* (Oxford, 1825), pp. 61, 227.

[7] *Formularies of Faith*, p. 221. Compare Augustine, *De Baptismo contra Donatistas*, 4.24.31.

[8] John Guy, 'Scripture as Authority: Problems of Interpretation in the 1530s', in Alistair Fox and John Guy (eds.), *Reassessing the Henrician Age: Humanism, Politics, and Reform, 1500–1550* (Oxford, 1986), pp. 199–220.

doctours'.⁹ Richard Smyth, royal lecturer in theology at Oxford and a future recusant, even held to the full doctrine of 'unwritten verities', which he provocatively propounded in *A brief treatyse settynge forth divers truthes necessary both to be beleved of chrysten people, and kepte also, whiche are not expressed in the scripture but left to ye church by the apostles tradition* (published in 1547, in the first months of Edward VI's reign).

As early as May 1547, the Edwardian authorities commanded Smyth to make a public recantation of his book. The doctrinal statements published under Edward and Elizabeth committed the Church of England much more clearly to a fully Protestant doctrine of the sufficiency of Scripture. Article 5 of the Forty-Two Articles of 1553 (which became the sixth of the Thirty-Nine Articles) expressly stated that 'Holy Scripture containeth all things necessary to salvation'. Dogmatic definitions of general councils were of no authority 'unless it may be declared that they be taken out of Holy Scripture' (twenty-second of the Forty-Two Articles, twenty-first of the Thirty-Nine). The reference to the ancient creeds was maintained but with the explanatory clause that 'they may be proved by most certain warrants of Holy Scripture' (seventh of the Forty-Two Articles, eighth of the Thirty-Nine).[10] There was no explicit discussion of patristic authority, but the Reformed code of canon law prepared in 1551–2 expressed the view of the compilers of the Forty-Two Articles and especially of Thomas Cranmer, who worked simultaneously on both texts: 'the authority of the orthodox fathers is also not at all to be despised, for a great many things are said by them in a most clear and helpful way. Yet we do not allow that the meaning of Holy Writ can be determined by their opinion. For Holy Writ must be our rule and judge for all Christian teaching.'[11]

The canon *Concionatores*, passed in the Convocation of 1571 to order preachers to teach nothing 'but that which is agreeable to the doctrine of the Old Testament and the New, and that which the catholic fathers and ancient bishops have gathered out of that doctrine', did not contradict these principles. It referred to those traditional dogmas, primarily Trinitarian ones, which Protestant divines regarded as scriptural, since they were necessarily 'gathered out of Scripture' (the point was already made in Smyth's recantation of 1547).[12]

The only potential infraction to the principle of *sola scriptura* concerned the canon of Scripture. The Thirty-Nine Articles stated, in a paragraph which was

---

[9] Thomas Elyot, *A Preservative agaynste Deth* (1545), sigs. D4r–D5r; Greg Walker, *Writing under Tyranny: English Literature and the Henrician Reformation* (Oxford, 2005), p. 129 and pp. 468–9n30.

[10] Bray, *Documents*, pp. 287, 289, 297.

[11] Gerald Bray (ed.), *Tudor Church Reform: The Henrician Canons of 1535 and the Reformatio Legum Ecclesiasticarum* (Woodbridge, 2000), p. 183.

[12] Gerald Bray (ed.), *The Anglican Canons 1529–1947* (Woodbridge, 1998), pp. 197–9; Richard Smyth, *A Godly and Faythfull Retractation Made and Published at Paules Crosse in London* (1547), sig. B4r–v.

added in 1563: 'In the name of Holy Scripture we do understand those canonical books of the Old and New Testament, of whose authority was never any doubt in the Church.'[13] This definition was not proper to the Church of England—it was borrowed from the Lutheran *Confessio Virtembergica*—but it certainly departed from continental Reformed confessions of faith, which preferred to follow Calvin and to claim that Scripture was known as such to the faithful by 'the inner witness of the Holy Spirit'. One should not, however, make too much of this clause. In the context of the articles, it was a polemical point against the Tridentine reception of the Apocrypha as a part of Scripture.[14]

THE USES OF CHRISTIAN ANTIQUITY IN SIXTEENTH-CENTURY CONTROVERSIES

The assertion of the principle of *sola scriptura*, if need be in the most uncompromising terms, did not prevent Protestant divines from studying the Fathers and quoting from them. If the status of Christian antiquity was quite clear in practice, its polemical uses were variegated. The continuity with the pre-Reformation past was far greater in this respect. Most patristic proof-texts in Henry's *Assertio* derived from medieval collections, primarily Peter Lombard's *Sentences* and the *Decree of Gratian*. But use was also made of humanist editions lately published on the Continent, such as Erasmus's edition of Jerome. This duality remained characteristic of religious controversy well into the seventeenth century, although the overall tendency was for the range of first-hand quotations to increase. The persistent use of the *Decretum Gratiani* should be stressed, as it was common to both lawyers and theologians. It has become usual to distinguish, among the episcopate of Henry VIII, between those who had received a training in law and those who had been trained as divines. The point was already made by contemporaries, especially by evangelical opponents of Stephen Gardiner. Thus Cranmer, in 1551, dismissed his great rival as entirely dependent on his amanuenses 'in suche waightie matters of scripture and auncyent autours', 'being brought up from [his] tender age in other kyndes of study'.[15] This is to forget that Gardiner was a doctor in canon law. In 1526, when in Wolsey's service, he

---

[13] Bray, *Documents*, p. 287.
[14] Jean-Louis Quantin, *The Church of England and Christian Antiquity: The Construction of a Confessional Identity in the 17th Century* (Oxford, 2009), pp. 47–50.
[15] Thomas Cranmer, *An Answer [...] unto a Crafty and Sophisticall Cavillation devised by Stephen Gardiner [...] agaynst the Trewe and Godly Doctrine of the Moste Holy Sacrament of the Body and Bloud of our Saviour Iesu Christe* (1551), p. 264.

was one of the doctors appointed to dispute with the reformer Robert Barnes, who had preached 'that it was not lawful for one christen man, to sue an other'. Barnes recanted when Gardiner showed him 'a sayenge of saynt Austen'—actually a canon, loosely extracted from Augustine, in the *Decree of Gratian*—'condemn [ing] his Anabaptistical opinions'.[16]

Many of the proof-texts inherited from the Middle Ages were inaccurate or even wholly spurious. Hence the considerable space devoted to critical debates, to the extent that philology became a set of tools for theologians. Religious conservatives had a tendency to be less critical than their opponents, as pseudo-patristic texts, such as the writings ascribed to Pseudo-Dionysius the Areopagite, helped them to date some disputed doctrines and practices to the first centuries. But they also had recourse to philological arguments, if only to demonstrate their scholarly credentials. Gardiner complained in June 1547 that Erasmus had been too bold in his edition of Augustine, to the extent that he had declared spurious some genuine works (a charge which had some justification in fact). Later, however, in his controversy on the eucharist with Cranmer and Peter Martyr—the Italian refugee and keen student of the Fathers whom the Edwardian regime had appointed regius professor of divinity at Oxford—Gardiner (or his scholarly assistants) made critical points, appealing to Erasmus, and pointing out the discrepancies between Gratian's quotations and the 'most correct copies' of Augustine. The controversy also involved comparing various editions and referring to the original of the Greek Fathers in order to correct Latin translations.[17]

Patristic proof-texts indeed played a crucial role in the eucharistic controversy. There was definitely no English originality in this respect. Debates in England had a European impact, but this was mostly due to Peter Martyr. To support his spiritual interpretation of the eucharist, he produced a long series of extracts from the Fathers, first in his Oxford lectures and then in the public disputation which was held in their wake in May 1549. The proof-texts that he introduced, using editions lately printed on the continent and even manuscripts, quickly became Protestant classics.[18] A decade later, at the beginning of Queen Elizabeth's reign, John Jewel, then bishop-elect of Salisbury, preached a sermon in which he listed a number of Roman tenets (most

---

[16] Stephen Gardiner, *A Declaration of Such True Articles as George Joye Hath Gone About to Confute as False* (1546), fos. ii v–iii v.

[17] Stephen Gardiner, *Letters*, ed. J. A. Muller (Cambridge, 1933), p. 314; Stephen Gardiner, *An Explication and Assertion of the True Catholique Fayth, Touching the Moost Blessed Sacrament of the Aulter* [Rouen, 1551], e.g. fos. 56v–57r and 61r–62v; Stephen Gardiner, *Confutatio Cavillationum, quibus Sacrosanctum Eucharistiae Sacramentum, ab Impiis Capernaitis, Impeti Solet* (Paris, 1552), fos. 142r, 143r, 146v; Stephen Gardiner, 'In Petrum Martyrem Florentinum, malae tractationis querela, Sanctissimae Eucharistiae nomine edita', BL, MS Arundel 100, fo. 60v.

[18] Quantin, *Church of England*, pp. 27–30.

of them related to the mass) and defied his opponents to prove them 'by any one clear or plain clause or sentence, either of the scriptures, or of the old doctors, or of any old general council, or by any example of the primitive church' during the first six centuries.[19] The 'Challenge controversy' that followed was essentially devoted to the discussion of patristic testimonies. Neither Jewel's method nor his scholarship differed from those of continental Reformed divines. He had just come back from his exile on the continent and his interest in the Fathers had been much influenced by Peter Martyr.

Antiquity was also appealed to in specifically English controversies, beginning with Henry VIII's 'Great Matter'. In 1529–30, one of the king's agents in Italy, Richard Croke, searched libraries for manuscripts of the Greek Fathers which might support the prohibition of marrying the wife of one's brother. These materials were put to use in the works published to promote the king's case in 1531 (the *Censurae academiarum* and its English version, the *Determinations*), which devoted one chapter to 'the most faithful interpreters of the holy Scriptures'. The 1532 *Glasse of the Truthe* opposed 'the old, ancient doctors' to 'the moderns', and quoted several 'ancient authors', who taught 'according to holy Scripture, that the Pope cannot dispense with other [*sic*] the law of God or nature'.[20]

Extracts from the Fathers and from ancient councils were also compiled by Henry VIII's scholars (in the so-called *Collectanea satis copiosa*) to justify the royal supremacy. One of the main works published in its defence, Edward Fox's 1534 *De vera differentia regiae potestatis et ecclesiasticae*, quoted at length the patristic exegesis of Matthew 16:18 ('thou art Peter, and upon this rock I will build my Church'), to prove that the Church was not built upon the person, but upon the confession, of Peter.[21] In a sermon preached before the king in 1539, Cuthbert Tunstall, bishop of Durham, instanced the case of papal legates at the Council of Carthage of 419, who appealed to a pretended canon of the Council of Nicaea in favour of Roman supremacy: when it was verified that there was no such canon in the genuine acts of Nicaea, 'the hole counsell Carthaginense wrote to Celestine at that tyme beine bysshop of Rome, that [...] they desired him to abstein after to make any more suche demaunde'. The episode was

---

[19] John Jewel, *Works*, ed. John Ayre, 4 vols. (Cambridge, 1845–50), I, pp. 20–1.
[20] Gustavus Przychocki, 'Richard Croke's Search for Patristic MSS in Connexion with the Divorce of Catherine. *De Richardi Croci (Iohannis Flandrensis) Studiis Nazianzenicis*', *Journal of Theological Studies*, 13 (1911–12): 285–95; Jonathan Woolfson, 'A "remote and ineffectual don?": Richard Croke in the Biblioteca Marciana', *Bulletin of the Society for Renaissance Studies*, 17/2 (May 2000): 1–11; Edward Surtz, S.J., and Virginia Murphy (eds.), *The Divorce Tracts of Henry VIII* (Angers, 1988), pp. 76–107; *A Glasse of the Truthe*, in Nicholas Pocock (ed.), *Records of the Reformation: The Divorce 1527–1533*, 2 vols. (Oxford, 1870), II, pp. 399–400.
[21] [Edward Fox], *Opus Eximium de Vera Differentia Regiae Potestatis et Ecclesiasticae* (1534), fos. 7v–11v.

included in the King's Book.²² It was to recur constantly in Protestant polemics, both in England and on the continent. Jewel used it against his Catholic adversaries.²³

Other evidence came from a different type of antiquity: the legendary history of Britain, drawn from medieval historians (primarily Bede and Geoffrey of Monmouth) and from forgeries such as the answer sent by Pope Eleutherius to Lucius, 'king of the Britons' in AD 169 (a fabrication from the beginning of the thirteenth century). In reply to Lucius's request of the Roman laws for his kingdom, Eleutherius was supposed to have told him that newly-converted Britons already had by them the two Testaments, which should be enough; for good measure, he also declared Lucius 'God's vicar in your kingdom'. This anti-Roman version of the origins of Christianity in Britain was fully developed under Elizabeth by Archbishop Matthew Parker, in the preliminary section of his 1572 *De Antiquitate Britannicae Ecclesiae*. According to Parker, Eleutherius's letter proved that Lucius had established Christianity on 'his own authority' and that the Pope had merely provided 'some little help, which came at Lucius's request and wish rather than because of any necessity'.²⁴ At least one additional forgery was produced in this context: the Welsh letter of Dinot, abbot of Bangor, to Augustine of Canterbury, refusing to submit 'to him whom you name to be Pope'. It was first published by Sir Henry Spelman in his edition of British councils.²⁵ While thus championing, at least until the 1680s, a wholly uncritical view of national history, the Church of England gladly used historical criticism against Roman claims. Lorenzo Valla's *On the Donation of Constantine* was translated into English in 1534 by William Marshall, a member of Thomas Cromwell's circle, who claimed that 'there was never better boke made and sett forthe for the defasing of the Pope of Rome'.²⁶

---

²² Cuthbert Tunstall, *A Sermon of Cuthbert Byshop of Duresme, made upon Palme Sondaye Last Past* (1539), fos. D5v-D6r; *Formularies of Faith*, pp. 283-4.
²³ John Jewel, *A Defence of the Apologie of the Church of England*, 1570 preface, in *Works*, III, pp. 126-7.
²⁴ Graham Nicholson, 'The Act of Appeals and the English Reformation', in Claire Cross, David Loades, and J. J. Scarisbrick (eds.), *Law and Government under the Tudors* (Cambridge, 1988), p. 22; Felicity Heal, 'What Can King Lucius Do for You? The Reformation and the Early British Church', *English Historical Review*, 120 (2005): 593-614; [Matthew Parker], *De Antiquitate Britannicae Ecclesiae* ([Lambeth], 1572), 'De Vetustate Britannicae Ecclesiae Testimonia', pp. 6-8.
²⁵ *Concilia, Decreta, Leges, Constitutiones, in re Ecclesiarum orbis Britannici*, I, ed. Henry Spelman (1639), pp. 108-9; Joseph Loth, 'La Prétendue Lettre de Dinoot, Evêque de Bangor à Augustin', *Annales de Bretagne*, 18 (1902-3): 139-40.
²⁶ *A Treatyse of the Donation or Gyfte and Endowment of Possessyons, Gyven and Graunted unto Sylvester Pope of Rhome, by Constantyn Emperour of Rhome* (1534); Wolfram Setz, *Lorenzo Vallas Schrift gegen die Konstantinische Schenkung: De Falso Credita et Ementita Constantini Donatione. Zur Interpretation und Wirkungsgeschichte* (Tübingen, 1975), pp. 181-3.

CHRISTIAN ANTIQUITY AND THE EVOLUTION OF THE EARLY STUART CHURCH

While the sixteenth-century Church of England constantly referred to Christian antiquity, there is little evidence that this appeal was yet made a part of a distinct religious identity. The idea was slow to emerge. In their controversies with puritans on episcopacy and ceremonies, conformist divines quoted the Fathers—as puritans did as well—but they took great care to preserve the principles of *sola scriptura*. In his *Lawes of Ecclesiasticall Politie*, Richard Hooker stressed that there was no need to add traditions to Scripture 'as a part of supernaturall necessarye truth'. Moreover, although he occasionally described the age of the Fathers as the period 'when [the Church of God] most florished in zeale and pietie', Hooker definitely did not make antiquity the standard of orthodoxy: recent institutions, if they were better fitted to recent times, ought not to 'be taken away for conformities sake with the auncientest and first times'.[27] The 'higher conformists', who argued that the superiority of bishops over presbyters was not merely a legitimate institution—Hooker's position—but had in some sense a divine origin, insisted that it had a clear scriptural basis. They only appealed to antiquity as a witness to the true meaning of the Bible. 'We refuse nothing', Thomas Bilson told Presbyterians, 'that the ancient and Primitive church of Christ universally observed and practised as expressed or intended in the Scriptures'.[28] A few years later, in the controversy over Christ's descent into Hell, in which he defended the patristic notion of a literal descent, Bilson accused his Calvinist adversaries of 'pride and disdaine', in as much as they refused to receive the Fathers 'as witnesses of the Scriptures sense'.[29] John Overall, regius professor of divinity at Cambridge, who joined the controversy on the anti-Calvinist side, appealed in this context to the canon *Concionatores*, 'this excellent and truly salutary canon, which is worth its weight in gold'. In his dedication to James I of the collected edition of Jewel's works, in 1609, he again referred to this canon, 'whereby the publike profession of our Church for consent with Antiquitie, in the Articles of Faith and grounds of Religion, doth plainly appeare'. For the first time, this disciplinary prescription was turned into a fundamental theological principle: it henceforth became prominent in conformist discourse.[30]

---

[27] Richard Hooker, *Of the Lawes of Ecclesiastical Polity*, in *Works*, ed. W. Speed Hill and others, 7 vols. (Cambridge, MA, 1977–98), I, pp. 22–4, 129; II, p. 311.

[28] Thomas Bilson, *The Perpetual Governement of Christes Church* (1593), p. 336.

[29] Thomas Bilson, *The Effect of Certaine Sermons touching the Full Redemption of Mankind by the Death and Bloud of Christ Jesus* (1599), p. 349.

[30] Cambridge University Library (CUL), MS Gg.1.29, fos. 23v–24r; John Jewell, *Works* (1609), sigs. ¶2r–¶6r; Anthony Milton, '"Anglicanism" by Stealth: The Career and Influence of John Overall', in Kenneth Fincham and Peter Lake (eds.), *Religious Politics in Post-Reformation England* (Woodbridge, 2006), pp. 159–76.

The notion that the Church of England was uniquely faithful to Christian antiquity was first clearly formulated by continental figures, who felt constrained within the increasingly rigid boundaries of their own Churches. The most famous instance was Isaac Casaubon, a great reader and admirer of the Fathers, especially the Greeks. He was outraged by French Calvinist controversialists, who repudiated patristic authority in the most provocative manner. Catholic apologists, who were aware of his difficulties, urged him to convert. About 1610, although he remained unreconciled to many Catholic tenets, and above all to papal supremacy, there was widespread speculation that he was about to change his religion. He was saved from this state of suspension by James I's invitation to come to England. The Established Church of England struck him as the ideal he had been looking for, and he praised it highly in his letters to his continental correspondents: 'I recognize in this kingdom', he wrote for instance to the Dutch philologist Daniel Heinsius, 'the face of the ancient Church, which I had come to know through the writings of the Fathers'. A few months before his death, Casaubon published a confutation of Cardinal Baronius's *Annales ecclesiastici*, the masterpiece of Counter-Reformation historiography—the work was printed by John Bill, the king's printer, on James I's orders, and had a semi-official character. It opened with a dedication to James, in which Casaubon declared the Church of England closer than any other 'to the shape of the Church as it used to be in its prime'.[31] Another example was Hugo Grotius, who for most of his life regarded the Church of England as the embodiment of many of his aspirations. In his writings of 1615–18, in the context of the Arminian crisis in the United Provinces, he repeatedly quoted the canon *Concionatores*.[32] Both Casaubon and Grotius advocated συγκατάβασις, 'Christian condescension in religious disputes'—the word and idea were borrowed from the Greek Fathers.[33] They thought that the episcopal Church of England, because of its devotion to antiquity, might play a leading role in the reunion of Christendom. No practical results were ever achieved in this direction, but the praises of such figures as Casaubon and Grotius were treasured by apologists of the Church of England.

In England itself, the appeal to antiquity came to characterize so-called 'Arminianism'. Its general formula was propounded by Lancelot Andrewes in a sermon which he preached at court in 1613, and which became famous after its posthumous publication in 1629: 'One Canon of Scripture put in writing by

---

[31] Isaac Casaubon, *De Rebus Sacris et Ecclesiasticis Exercitationes XVI* (1614), sig. 6*4r; Isaac Casaubon, *Epistolae* (Rotterdam, 1709), 2nd pagination, p. 369.

[32] Grotius to Gideon van den Boetzelaer, early Dec. 1615, *Briefwisseling van Hugo Grotius*, 17 vols. (The Hague, 1928–2001), I, p. 431; Hugo Grotius, *De Imperio Summarum Potestatum circa Sacra*, ed. H.-J. van Dam (Leiden, 2001), p. 312.

[33] Casaubon, *Exercitationes*, p. 513: Grotius to Lancelot Andrewes, 19 Nov. 1619, *Briefwisseling*, II, p. 24.

God, two Testaments, three Creeds, the first four Councils, five centuries and the succession of the Fathers therein, three centuries before Constantine, two centuries after Constantine, draw for us the rule of religion.'[34] The context was anti-Roman—Andrewes opposed the 'ancient' rule of faith to 'the new addition of the Roman religion'—and the principle itself was uncontentious. In debates at the Committee of Religion in the Parliament of 1629, the anti-Arminian MP John Hoskins stated that 'the papists and we agree all in the Scripture and differ only in the interpretacion, and for that wee offer to be tryed by the 3 generall Creedes, the 4 first generall Councells, and all the antient fathers that wrote in the first 400 yeares'.[35] But the way this rule was applied by Andrewes's disciples proved deeply divisive, effecting no less than a redefinition of orthodoxy in the Church of England.

A key element of this transformation concerned theological training. In 1616–17 James I sent directions to Cambridge and Oxford, ordering that students in divinity be henceforth 'excited to bestow their time in the Fathers and Councels, Schoolmen, Histories and Controversies, and not to insist too long upon Compendiums and Abbreviators, making them the grounds of their Study in Divinity'. This injunction was renewed in 1622, in the aftermath of the scandal created by John Knight, a young Oxford divine, who had preached a sermon justifying armed resistance against a persecuting monarch, and then claimed to have been inspired by the works of David Pareus, a famous Calvinist professor in Heidelberg. Patristic studies were promoted as a safeguard against the subversive divinity that spread from the continent.[36] In his 1625 *Appello Caesarem*, Richard Montagu professed to have always despised 'moderne [Calvinist] Epitomizers' and to have immediately directed his studies to 'Scripture the Rule of Faith, interpreted by Antiquity, the best Expositor of Faith and applyer of that Rule'.[37] The Scottish Calvinist Robert Baillie called this 'the Englishe method of studie' and lamented attempts to introduce it into Scottish universities.[38]

Even English anti-Arminians, either out of conviction or for tactical reasons, increasingly appealed to antiquity, primarily to Augustine, rather than to modern Reformed authors. Samuel Ward preached at Cambridge a university sermon against Arminianism, in which he exhorted divinity students to read Augustine's polemical writings against the Pelagians and 'Semi-Pelagians'.[39] In the 1630s, Ward's friend, James Ussher, archbishop of Armagh, published extensively on the ancient disputes on grace and predestination.

---

[34] Lancelot Andrewes, *Opuscula Quaedam Posthuma* (1629), p. 86.
[35] Wallace Notestein and Frances Helen Relf (eds.), *Commons Debates for 1629* (Minneapolis, MN, 1921), p. 120.
[36] Quantin, *Church of England*, pp. 160–70.
[37] Richard Montagu, *Appello Caesarem. A Iust Appeale from Two Unjust Informers* (1625), p. 11.
[38] Robert Baillie, *Letters and Journals*, ed. D. Laing, 3 vols. (Edinburgh, 1841–2), I, p. 149.
[39] Samuel Ward, *Gratia Discriminans* (1626), pp. 53–4.

Perceptions of Christian Antiquity   291

He drew on his skills and methods as an antiquarian and critic to demonstrate that strict Augustinianism was orthodoxy and that all its opponents had been heretics. Ussher carefully refrained from pointing out the contemporary implications of his research, so as not to contravene Charles I's 1628 Declaration against controversies, but both friends and foes clearly recognized what he was driving at. In accordance with a common European pattern of the time, historical scholarship was a means of circumventing theological censorship.[40]

Baillie accused Laudians of adopting the 'two engines' of papists against 'the Scriptures absolute perfection': on the one hand, they recognized traditions 'both rituall and dogmaticall, which, beside Scripture with a divine faith must be firmly beleeved'; on the other hand, they made the Fathers authoritative interpreters of Scripture.[41] The second accusation is by far the easier to substantiate. In his conference with 'Fisher' (the Jesuit John Percy), at least according to the 1639 version of his *Relation*, Laud repeatedly professed to believe 'Scripture interpreted by the Primitive Church'.[42] As to the first charge, Montagu indeed appeared, in his provocative pamphlet *A New Gagg for an Old Goose*, to put unwritten traditions on a par with Scripture. Quoting a famous statement of Basil of Caesarea ('of those doctrines and predications which are kept in the Church, we have some from written teaching, some from the tradition of the Apostles [...], and both kinds have the same strength for piety'), he claimed that the Church of England was in full agreement, providing that the traditions in question were genuine.[43] However, when this passage of the *Gagg* was denounced at the York House Conference of 1626, Montagu did not hold his ground, but explained that he had only spoken hypothetically.[44]

Champions of the 'Laudian style' of the 1630s had no such reticence. In their polemical works and sermons, following in the footsteps of Jacobean 'avant-garde conformists', they defended ecclesiastical traditions as ultimately derived from the apostles by uninterrupted succession. Thus Peter Heylyn, echoing Augustine's axiom, counted the eastward position and the placing of communion tables altar-wise among those 'things that have generally beene received in the Church of Christ, [and] are generally conceived to have been derived from Apostolicall tradition, without any speciall mandat, left *in Scriptis*, for the doing of them'. 'This Church', he noted with satisfaction, 'the Lord be thanked for it, hath stoode more firme for Apostolicall and

---

[40] Quantin, *Church of England*, pp. 179–81.
[41] [Robert Baillie], *Ladensium αὐτοκατάκρισις, The Canterburians Self-conviction* ([Amsterdam], 1640), pp. 62–6.
[42] William Laud, *A Relation of the Conference betweene William Lawd, Then, Lord Bishop of St Davids; now Lord Arch-Bishop of Canterbury: and Mr Fisher the Jesuite* (1639), pp. 336, 378, 386.
[43] Richard Montagu, *A Gagg for the New Gospell? No: a New Gagg for an Old Goose* (1624), pp. 42–4.
[44] Quantin, *Church of England*, pp. 197–8.

Ecclesiasticall traditions since the Reformation, than any other whatsoever of the Reformation'.[45]

ANTIQUITY CONTESTED

The whole English Church did not share in this exaltation of antiquity. In his theological lectures at Gresham College in the 1630s, Richard Holdsworth opposed 'true and primitive antiquity' (i.e. Scripture) to the 'adoptive and secondary' antiquity embodied by the Fathers. One could always go back from one Father to another, more ancient and more authoritative, until one came at last to the apostles, from whom there could be no appeal. Holdsworth was an opponent of Arminianism, both in its doctrinal and its ritualist dimensions, whose teaching was rooted in the Reformed theological tradition. He still advised students to begin with continental (Calvinist) textbooks, since 'moderns are more fitted to form childhood, Fathers to confirm adulthood'.[46] But scepticism towards patristic authority could also be found among those who rejected Calvinist orthodoxy. John Hales, whose hostility to dogmatism had been fed by his experiences at the synod of Dort, expressed his distrust of authoritarian appeals to antiquity in a sermon 'Of private judgment in religion'. Appeals 'to Antiquity, thus have our Ancients delivered unto us; or to Universality [...]; or to Synods, Councels, and consent of Churches, [...] all these', Hales declared, 'are nothing else but deceitfull formes of shifting the account and reason of our Faith and Religion from our selves, and casting it upon the back of others'. In a long letter which he addressed in 1636 to William Chillingworth (later printed under the title of *A Tract of Schism*), Hales blamed an excessive reverence for antiquity as the source of the unreasonable dread of schism.[47]

Chillingworth's *The Religion of Protestants a Safe way to Salvation*, which he wrote with the help of his friend Lord Falkland while staying at the latter's seat at Great Tew in Oxfordshire, expressed similar views in a much ampler and more forceful manner. 'The BIBLE, I say, the BIBLE only, is the Religion of Protestants! [...] I see plainly, and with mine own Eyes, that there are Popes against Popes, Councils against Councils, some Fathers against others, the same Fathers against themselves, a Consent of Fathers of one Age against a Consent of Fathers of another Age, the Church of one Age against the Church

---

[45] Peter Heylyn, *Antidotum Lincolniense* (1637), Section II, pp. 87–8; Peter Lake, 'Lancelot Andrewes, John Buckeridge, and Avant-Garde Conformity at the Court of James I', in Linda Levy Peck (ed.), *The Mental World of the Jacobean Court* (Cambridge, 1991), pp. 113–33.

[46] Richard Holdsworth, *Praelectiones Theologicae* (1661), pp. 312–13, 410, 447–52; Quantin, *Church of England*, pp. 205–9.

[47] John Hales, *Sermons Preach'd at Eton* (1660), pp. 11–12; John Hales, *A Tract concerning Schisme and Schismatiques* (1642), pp. 3–4.

of another Age.' Chillingworth accepted that the canon of Scripture could only be determined 'by the Testimonies of the Ancient Churches', but he stressed that this tradition was the only one that could be proved to be of apostolic origin. 'Traditive Interpretations' of Scripture had existed in the primitive Church but 'were all lost, within a few Ages after Christ'. This scripturalism resulted in an undogmatic version of Christianity. Antiquity could no longer guarantee the core of (especially Trinitarian) orthodoxy on which the main Churches agreed. Chillingworth confessed in private that he was 'very inclinable to beleeve, that the Doctrine of Arius is eyther a Truth, or at least no damnable Heresy'.[48]

Falkland, Chillingworth, and other members of the 'Great Tew circle' greatly admired the *Traicté de l'employ des Saincts Peres* by the French Calvinist Jean Daillé, which argued with considerable skill that the Fathers were unfit to serve as 'Judges of the Controversies in Religion at this day betwixt the Papist and the Protestant'. First, it is, 'if not an impossible, yet at least a very difficult thing to finde out' what they held on questions now controverted. Second, even if we could find out, their judgement 'not being Infallible, and without all danger of Errour, cannot carry with it a sufficient Authority for the satisfying the Understanding'.[49] Nowhere had the book such an enduring impact as in England. It is disputable whether Chillingworth already knew it when he wrote *The Religion of Protestants*, but the Tew circle certainly pioneered its use in English religious controversies. Falkland professed that Daillé's work confirmed him in his conviction that no apostolic tradition could be sufficiently proved by patristic testimonies 'except the undoubted books of Scripture, or what is so plainly there, that it is not controverted' between Catholics and Protestants.[50] At the height of the Laudian ascendancy, the Church of England was still able to accommodate such views.

CHRISTIAN ANTIQUITY AND THE SURVIVAL OF THE CHURCH OF ENGLAND

The liberal spirit of Great Tew did not disappear with the civil war. In his 1647 *Liberty of Prophesying*, Jeremy Taylor argued for mutual toleration in all

---

[48] William Chillingworth, *The Religion of Protestants a Safe way to Salvation* [1638], in *Works*, 10th edition (1742), pp. 87, 91, 126, 164, 354 [*sic*]; Thomas Birch, 'The Life of Mr. William Chillingworth' (in the same volume), pp. iv–v.

[49] Jean Daillé, *Traicté de l'Employ des Saincts Peres, pour le Jugement des Differends, qui sont Aujourd'huy en la Religion* (Geneva, 1632); *A Treatise Concerning the Right Use of the Fathers, in the Decision of the Controversies that are at This Day in Religion* (1651).

[50] *Sir Lucius Cary, late Lord Viscount of Falkland, his Discourse of Infallibility, with an Answer to it: And his Lordships Reply* (1651), 'Reply', pp. 202–3.

things 'not necessary', i.e. not clearly expressed in Scripture. The sum of faith was the Apostles' Creed, which Taylor opposed to the 'uncharitablenesse' of the Athanasian Creed. Universal tradition could not be proved for any other doctrine. The questions at present controverted between Christians, Taylor argued, were in any case unknown in the first centuries, so that 'to dispute concerning the truth or necessity of Traditions, in the Questions of our times, is as if Historians disputing about a Question in the English Story, should fall on wrangling whether Livie or Plutarch were the best Writers'.[51] The English translation of Daillé's *Use of the Fathers*, which came out in 1651, originated from the same milieu.

To beleaguered episcopalians, however, this line of argument appeared increasingly ill-advised, for both positive and negative reasons. On the one hand, the appeal to antiquity was foremost in the defence of episcopacy, especially after Ussher had published at Oxford, in 1645, the uninterpolated Latin version of Ignatius of Antioch's letters (what was later called the Middle Recension). There now appeared to be incontrovertible evidence that full-blown monarchical episcopacy was already in force at the beginning of the second century. Presbyterians, Joseph Hall, bishop of Norwich, wrote to Ussher, should be ashamed of themselves.[52] Henry Hammond thought that Ussher's edition had appeared 'not without a special providence of God'.[53] Episcopalians had been vanquished in the battlefield, but they were confident that they were winning the scholarly argument.

On the other hand, Presbyterians, partly as a reaction to the Laudian exaltation of tradition in the 1630s, adopted the most intransigent version of *sola scriptura*. The Westminster Confession of Faith declared that 'the Supreme Judge, by which all controversies of religion are to be determined, and all decrees of councils, opinions of ancient writers, doctrines of men, and private spirits, are to be examined, and in whose sentence we are to rest, can be no other but the Holy Spirit speaking in the Scripture'. The certainty of the canon was founded on 'the inward work of the Holy Spirit, bearing witness by and with the Word in our hearts'.[54] Daillé's *Use of the Fathers* became a favourite of Independents and Presbyterians. John Owen praised it as the last word on 'the Authority of the Ancients in matters of Religion and worship of God'.[55] When Richard Baxter, in 1653, was challenged by a neighbouring minister over the necessity of episcopal ordination, he referred him to Daillé to

---

[51] Jeremy Taylor, Θεολογία ἐκλεκτική. *A Discourse of the Liberty of Prophesying* (1647), pp. 5–18, 53–5, 95.

[52] Hall to Ussher, 25 May 1647, in Richard Parr, *The Life of the Most Reverend Father in God, James Usher* (1686), pp. 516–17.

[53] Henry Hammond, *Dissertationes Quatuor* (1651), p. 57.

[54] *The Westminster Confession of Faith*, ed. S. W. Carruthers (Manchester, [1937]), pp. 91, 93.

[55] John Owen, *The Doctrine of the Saints Perseverance Explained and Confirmed* (Oxford, 1654), sig. B2v.

see how much the Fathers had contradicted each other, so that 'it's hard seeing the Face of the Church universal in this Glass'.[56]

Episcopalian apologists took pains therefore to defend the credit of the Fathers, if not as authoritative teachers, at least as witnesses of the belief and practice of the primitive Church. Hammond insisted that 'the Authority of the Canon of Scripture' was 'taken from the authentick testimony of the Christian Church of the first ages'. And 'the accepting of so great a thing, as is the Canon of Scripture, primarily and fundamentally from this testimony of the ancient Church' was 'a very great presumption, and acknowledgement of the force of the argument drawn from the universal testimony of the first and purest ages of the Church'.[57]

If we are to believe Matthew Scrivener, who published a confutation of *The Use of the Fathers* in 1672, Hammond already called it in private a 'defamatory book'.[58] A revealing clash certainly occurred over the book on confirmation that Daillé published in 1659. The Huguenot divine argued that the laying on of hands and anointing with oil were accessory ceremonies to baptism, which had been first introduced at the end of the second century, when Christians had begun to deviate from primitive simplicity. Only very late and only in the Latin West had confirmation become a sacrament of its own and been appropriated to the bishop.[59] Hammond regarded this as an assault against 'the discipline of the Church of England, or rather of the ancient and purer Church'. He wrote an answer, which was finished in January 1660 but only came out posthumously after the Restoration. According to Hammond, the doctrine of the Church of England, which was borne out by 'very clear testimonies of the Fathers', was that 'the rite of confirmation has come down to us from the pattern of the Apostles'. He felt no qualms about quoting the King's Book of 1543, 'before what we call the reformation of doctrines', which derived confirmation from apostolic practice. The Reformation had made no fundamental change.[60] The appeal to Christian antiquity was thus integrated within a continuous scheme of English Church history, in which the radicalism of the Reformation was largely glossed over. It has been claimed that divines of Hammond's school only viewed Scripture and the Fathers 'through the medium of the sixteenth century as the classical moment for

---

[56] Letter to Martin Johnson, 9 Sept. 1653, in M. Sylvester, *Reliquiae Baxterianae* (1696), Appendix, pp. 36–7.

[57] Henry Hammond, *A Letter of Resolution to Six Quaeres, of Present Use in the Church of England* (1653), pp. 21, 26.

[58] Matthew Scrivener, *Apologia pro S. Ecclesiae Patribus, adversus Joannem Dallaeum De Usu Patrum, etc.* (1672), sig. A2v.

[59] Jean Daillé, *De Duobus Latinorum ex Unctione Sacramentis, Confirmatione et Extrema ut Uocant Unctione Disputatio* (Geneva, 1659).

[60] Henry Hammond, *De Confirmatione, sive Benedictione, post Baptismum, Solenni, per Impositionem Manuum Episcopi Celebrata, Commentarius ex Sententia Ecclesiae Anglicanae* (Oxford, 1661), sig. A2r–v, pp. 34–6 and 174.

the Church of England'.[61] It might as plausibly be argued that they projected back on to the sixteenth century their own doctrine of tradition. It is clear at any rate that devotion to patristic authority was closely associated with a particular reading of the English Reformation.

It remained for Restoration divines to develop this conception to the full, especially in their polemics against Dissenters, but, for episcopalians like Hammond, partly under the influence of adversity, antiquity was already essential to their self-definition. Hammond claimed that the Church of England had consistently taken the primitive Church for its 'standard', and he proudly recalled how Casaubon had praised 'the temper of our Church to his brethren beyond seas, as the [model] of purity and antiquity, which was not else to be found any where'.[62] Conformity to antiquity had become a distinctive mark of the episcopal Church of England.

SELECT BIBLIOGRAPHY

Ford, Alan, *James Ussher: Theology, History and Politics in Early Modern Ireland and England* (Oxford, 2007).

Fox, Alistair and John Guy (eds.), *Reassessing the Henrician Age: Humanism, Politics, and Reform, 1500–1550* (Oxford, 1986).

Hampton, Stephen, 'Richard Holdsworth and the Antinomian Controversy', *Journal of Theological Studies*, 62 (2011): 218–50.

Heal, Felicity, 'Appropriating Histories: Catholic and Protestant Polemics and the National Past', *Huntington Library Quarterly*, 68 (2005): 109–32.

Lake, Peter, 'Lancelot Andrewes, John Buckeridge, and Avant-Garde Conformity at the Court of James I', in Linda Levy Peck (ed.), *The Mental World of the Jacobean Court* (Cambridge, 1991), pp. 113–33.

Lake, Peter, 'The Laudian Style: Order, Uniformity and the Pursuit of the Beauty of Holiness in the 1630s', in Kenneth Fincham (ed.), *The Early Stuart Church, 1603–1642* (Basingstoke, 1993), pp. 161–85.

Marshall, Peter, 'The Debate Over "Unwritten Verities" in Early Reformation England', in Bruce Gordon (ed.), *Protestant History and Identity in Sixteenth-Century Europe*, 2 vols. (Aldershot, 1996), I, pp. 60–77.

Milton, Anthony, '"Anglicanism" by Stealth: The Career and Influence of John Overall', in Kenneth Fincham and Peter Lake (eds.), *Religious Politics in Post-Reformation England* (Woodbridge, 2006), pp. 159–76.

---

[61] Calvin Lane, *The Laudians and the Elizabethan Church: History, Conformity and Religious Identity in Post-Reformation England* (2013), pp. 163, 178 (on Peter Heylyn).

[62] Hammond to Thomas Smith, 4 Jan. 1653, in [Nicholas Pocock], 'Illustrations of the State of the Church during the Great Rebellion', *The Theologian and Ecclesiastic*, 13 (Jan.–June 1852), p. 325.

Milton, Anthony, *Catholic and Reformed: The Roman and Protestant Churches in English Protestant Thought, 1600–1640* (Cambridge, 1995).

Pollmann, Karla (ed.), *The Oxford Guide to the Historical Reception of Augustine*, 3 vols. (Oxford, 2013).

Quantin, Jean-Louis, *The Church of England and Christian Antiquity: The Construction of a Confessional Identity in the 17th Century* (Oxford, 2009).

Tyacke, Nicholas, *Anti-Calvinists: The Rise of English Arminianism c.1590–1640* (Oxford, 1987).

Voak, Nigel, 'Richard Hooker and the Principle of Sola Scriptura', *Journal of Theological Studies*, 59 (2008): 96–139.

16

Protestants and the Meanings of Church History, 1540–1660

W. J. Sheils

When the new national Church broke free from its allegiance to Rome in the 1530s there was a pressing need for it to address its relationship not only with the institution it had just left but also with the Christian past more generally. The ways in which the reformers negotiated the history of the early Church are the subject of another chapter and will not detain us here,[1] except to say that the antiquity of the new Church was a central plank of its justification for breaking with what the reformers considered to be a corrupt institution, that is to say, the medieval Church and papacy. The break with Rome therefore required reformers to examine the past of Christian history in two potentially conflicting ways: firstly, the emphasis on the corruption of the institutional Church since about 1000 CE reminded readers and hearers of the necessity of the break with Rome; alternatively, the search for continuity with the early Church led reformers to seek out a true church existing in England free of Roman influence. This was sought for in two distinct ways, sometimes but not often overlapping, which were to have important consequences for the self-understanding of the Established Church as it grew to maturity in the first half of the seventeenth century.

On the one hand, there were those who sought to find an independent British Church emerging in the post-apostolic centuries separate from the Roman mission of Augustine, and which had come to maturity in the age of Bede, only to be thrust back into Roman obedience following the Norman Conquest.[2] On the other hand there were those who looked for the true Church not in institutions but among those 'gospellers' who gathered in congregations persecuted by the ecclesiastical authorities, and whose beliefs,

---

[1] See Chapter 15, 'Perceptions of Christian Antiquity', in this volume.
[2] Felicity Heal, 'What Can King Lucius Do for You? The Reformation and the Early British Church', *English Historical Review*, 120 (2005): 596–614.

in the eyes of the reformers, prefigured many of their own. These views were not incompatible, and a number of reformers shared an understanding of the existence of an ancient English, or often British Church, with a sense that the true Church had been preserved in England throughout the previous five centuries chiefly by small groups of brave and persecuted 'gospellers', often laity, who stood aloof from the medieval Church. There were tensions, however, between these views, between those who saw continuity through an ancient English Church overlaid by a corrupt foreign papacy and those who saw the preservation of the gospel as existing outside of an institutional framework among gathered communities of Christians. As the English Church moved towards maturity in the first half of the seventeenth century, these tensions became divisions and, by then, the history of the early Reformation had itself become contested territory between the defenders of the Established Church and its puritan critics.

The first task of the reformers, however, was to justify the decision to separate from Rome. This achieved its fullest and most erudite expression in 1562 in John Jewel's *An Apologie, or Aunswer in Defence of the Church of England*, published in both English and Latin. In this, Jewel maintained that the newly established national Church represented a return to the primitive Church of the apostles and of the Fathers, from which the medieval Church and papacy had turned away. Jewel had gone into exile under Mary and was appointed bishop of Salisbury on his return to England in 1560. The *Apologie* was an influential text, directed chiefly at Roman Catholics, which acquired a quasi-official status in setting out the position of the English Church and the legitimacy of its independent ecclesiastical government.[3] Although Jewel rested his defence on the Scriptures and the Fathers, his views about the false claims of the papacy and the corruption of the medieval Church were well known and emerged in print in the following decade during his lengthy and learned dispute with the Catholic exile Thomas Harding.[4] In noting the corruption of the medieval Church, Jewel was following a path already trodden by John Bale, a pugnacious and outspoken critic of the medieval Church, whose history was couched in apocalyptic terms. Bale's historical output from the late 1530s had concentrated on exposing the claims of the medieval papacy, most notably in his play *King Johan*, written in the 1530s, and on printing the testimony of some of those English faithful who had suffered at the hands of clerical oppression, including the Lollard nobleman Sir John

---

[3] John E. Booty (ed.), *John Jewel, An Apologie of the Church of England* (Ithaca, NY, 1963); John E. Booty, *John Jewel as Apologist of the Church of England* (1963), esp. pp. 126-60.

[4] Peter Milward, *Religious Controversies of the Elizabethan Age: A Survey of Printed Sources* (1977), pp. 1-24.

Oldcastle (executed in 1417) and the Henrician martyr Anne Askew (burnt for heresy in 1546).[5]

Bale had been in exile during the 1540s when Askew had suffered under the conservative faction which dominated policy in the last years of Henry's reign, but he returned under Edward VI. His sustained and unsparing attack on the corruptions of the medieval Church, the *Actes, or Unchast Examples of the Englysh Votaryes*, was first published abroad in 1546 and then in London in 1551, and coloured the view of the medieval Church held by more radical reformers for generations. The primary focus of Bale's history was on the supposed miracles of the medieval saints—those 'lyenge and mervelous signes' in the words of the Henrician martyr John Frith—which, according to the great biblical translator William Tyndale, had no place in the Church after the apostolic age. For the reformers, the age of miracles had passed with Scripture, and those claimed by the medieval Church were nothing more than deceptions and frauds, often conjured by the devil or his agent, the Pope.[6] Thus the past was used to undermine a central belief of the Roman Church, the greatest miracle of the medieval Church and one performed every day at mass, the transubstantiation of the bread and wine on the altar into the body and blood of Christ. The attack on transubstantiation lay at the heart of the evangelical criticism of the Roman Church from the very beginning, intellectually in Tyndale's *Answer to More* and more scabrously in the tract *The Burial of the Mass*. The accession of Edward VI brought a deluge of pamphlets attacking the mass, and many of them sought to expose as fraudulent the eucharistic miracles recorded in the lives of the saints.[7] Bale dismissed a popular miracle story attributed to Saint Odo, archbishop of Canterbury in the 950s, claiming that he had used 'legerdemayne' to produce a consecrated host apparently dripping with blood in order to convince those of his clergy who argued that the host was simply a sign of Christ's body and blood. And, according to Bale, such deceits continued to the present, as in the story of John Germes, a priest who pricked his finger at the moment of consecration in order to give the illusion of Christ's blood. For Bale and his fellow reformers, these miracle stories were portrayed both as clerically inspired deceptions of the faithful and as threats to the safety and stability of the realm.[8]

For Bale and others the medieval monks were like the 'soothsayers of Egypt' through whom the pharaohs had kept the people in darkness, and one of the

---

[5] Thomas Betteridge, *Tudor Histories of the English Reformations, 1530–83* (Aldershot, 1999), pp. 68–101; Susan Royal, 'Historian or Prophet? John Bale's Perception of the Past', in Peter D. Clarke and Charlotte Methuen (eds.), *The Church on its Past* (SCH 49, Woodbridge, 2013), pp. 156–67.

[6] Helen Parish, *Monks, Miracles and Magic: Reformation Representations of the Medieval Church* (2005), pp. 24–6.

[7] Parish, *Monks, Miracles and Magic*, p. 63.

[8] Parish, *Monks, Miracles and Magic*, pp. 51, 66–7.

chief sources of this deceit was clerical celibacy, an invention of Antichrist brought into the Church by the monastic orders. Monasteries were often the repositories of relics of the saints, accounts of whose lives and miracles were staple ingredients of medieval piety. These lives had been collected by Jacobus de Voragine, archbishop of Genoa, in the thirteenth century in a popular compilation of 182 chapters entitled *Legenda Aurea*. Widely circulated in translation, *The Golden Legend* was a popular devotional text and became a prime target for the reformers, who inverted the hagiographical tradition to provide evidence of the corruption of the medieval clergy who, in Bale's words, 'in the legends of their sanctyfyed sorcerers diffamed the English posterytie'. Most of the chroniclers of these miracles had been monks and, for Bale and others, their celibacy had been at the root of the corruption of the Roman Church, creating a lustful and hypocritical clergy. Bale's account of the famous sighting by Pope Gregory of the Anglo-Saxon slaves in a Roman market, which was said to have prompted Augustine's mission, implied that the Pope's interest in the young men had not been entirely spiritual.[9] Prior to the Roman mission, so the reformers claimed, the clergy of the early English Church had been married; it was the requirement of celibacy which distorted its vocation, encouraged papal interference in the Church's affairs, and produced an overweening and over-mighty clerical estate, represented most fully in the person of Thomas Becket.

Becket was a national saint and hero of the medieval Church with an elaborate cult around his shrine. His cult had been attacked by Tyndale in 1530 in *The Practice of Prelates*, which drew less than subtle parallels between the saint's worldly career and that of the recently disgraced Cardinal Wolsey. Becket's confrontation with Henry II presaged the conflict between Henry VIII and the Church during the 1530s, and Becket's shrine at Canterbury was dismantled in 1538, the saint being charged with treason and found guilty in his absence. But Henry II's implication in Becket's murder complicated the argument about the rights of Church and state, and some rewriting of the story was required. Bale took up the case, seeking to undermine Becket's widely held reputation as a saint, among both the people and the learned. Firstly, he contrasted the case of Becket with that of the Lollard Oldcastle, claiming the heretic as a martyr of the gospel and the archbishop as a false saint, asking his readers 'which of these two semeth rather to be the martyr of Christ/ and which the Popes martyr'? Furthermore, in the *English Votaries* Bale went on to accuse Becket not only of robbery during his time with the army, but also of rape, and sought to undermine his status as a martyr by claiming that Becket actively sought his own end, thereby exonerating Henry of the crime. Becket's story fitted Bale's schematic account of the rise of papal power and pretensions

---

[9] Benedict S. Robinson, 'John Foxe and the Anglo-Saxons', in Christopher Highley and John King (eds.), *John Foxe and his World* (Aldershot, 2002), pp. 54–72, esp. p. 61.

in the centuries following 1000 CE, and it became the fulcrum of his history, marking the time when Antichrist was loosed upon the earth.[10]

Bale's history of Becket, like his play of King John, used the medieval past to demonstrate the rightness of the contemporary English Church in separating from a corrupt institution headed by the devil's emissary. It was a story which was rehearsed by subsequent generations of English Protestant historians, often in the same apocalyptic terms. The most distinguished of these was John Foxe, who had met Bale while tutoring the Howard family children in 1548. Foxe was younger than Bale, and like him went into exile under Mary, publishing his first historical work, *Commentarii Rerum in Ecclesia Gestarum*, in Strassburg in 1554. This was a history, written in Latin, of the persecution by the Roman Church of John Wyclif, Reginald Pecock, and other late medieval heretics, in which the Church's willingness to persecute the gospel was evinced as proof of its Antichristian character. Subsequently Foxe, having later moved to Frankfurt and then to Basel, where he lodged with Bale, was encouraged by his fellow exiles to collect evidences of the sufferings of the reformers at the hands of the Marian Church with an eye to writing a martyrology. Possibly influenced by Bale, but also following his earlier study, Foxe added a historical dimension to the work, publishing in 1559 his *Rerum in Ecclesia Gestarum... Commentarii* at Basel in six volumes. The work, with the exceptions of Jan Hus and Jerome of Prague, confined itself to English examples: the first volume was largely a reprint of his earlier work on the Wycliffite martyrs, the second volume took the story from the case of the Lollard Richard Hunne in 1515 to the execution of the duke of Somerset in 1552, and books three to six dealt with the Marian martyrs. Although the corruption and evil-doing of the Roman Church was explicit in Foxe's text, its main focus was on the true believers, those English 'gospellers' who suffered for their beliefs, and a link was established between the present sufferings of God's people and the earlier fifteenth-century martyrs. This was an important shift in focus, reflecting the work of continental martyrologists. At the time of writing Foxe was still in exile and the Marian persecutions were continuing but, in the context of those persecutions, Foxe shifted the emphasis of his account from the persecutors to the persecuted; to the heroism of the martyrs rather than to the evil of the ecclesiastical authorities.[11] With the death of Mary and the restoration of a Protestant regime in England, the search for the historical origins of the English Church had begun in earnest. This was not without its problems.

---

[10] Parish, *Monks, Miracles and Magic*, pp. 92–100.

[11] Elizabeth Evenden and Thomas S. Freeman, *Religion and the Book in Early Modern England: The Making of Foxe's 'Book of Martyrs'* (Cambridge, 2011), pp. 45–62, 85–93; Brad S. Gregory, *Salvation at Stake: Christian Martyrdom in Early Modern Europe* (Cambridge, MA, 1999), pp. 165–86.

Foxe returned to England immediately on the accession of Elizabeth and began at once on the compilation of an English version of his history, and in March 1563 his *Actes and Monuments* was published in London by John Day. This was a greatly extended work, almost three times the length of his Latin text, amounting to almost 1,800 folio pages. Foxe both increased the chronological range of the study by taking the history from Wyclif until the accession of Elizabeth, adding an introductory section on the history of the Church, or papacy, from 1000 CE, and incorporated material on non-English martyrs. More significantly, he greatly extended the material on the Marian martyrs by providing more textual evidence, by incorporating eyewitness accounts, and by including his own archival research, particularly in the London diocese where many of the burnings had taken place. The book became known immediately as 'The Book of Martyrs', a name which has stuck, and, despite its size, it was a publishing success which, in varying editions, continued to be hugely influential through to 1660.[12]

In setting the sufferings of the martyrs against persecution by ecclesiastical authorities, Foxe highlighted the divergence between the invisible Church of the gospel and the institutional Church, and, following Bale, he placed that conflict within an apocalyptic framework. Both of these approaches were to prove problematic to the new Church and regime over the next century. The Latin text of 1559 had described the present days as 'postremos et periculosis', echoing the prophecy of the Apocalypse, and the English edition of 1563 went further.[13] By extending his timeframe Foxe chronicled the fall of the gospel from the time of Pope Gregory at the end of the sixth century, when corruption first entered the Church, until the present: in this scheme the critical date was the year 1000 CE when 'Sathanus the old serpent, beying tied up for a thousand years, was losed', and the beast of the Apocalypse was revealed in his true colours in the form of the papacy. Foxe thereby linked history to prophecy, describing the Marian persecutions as among the most heinous of the sufferings imposed on the faithful by Antichrist. In subsequent editions Foxe gave greater emphasis to the apocalyptic elements of his history. In 1570, at a time when such prophetic writing was extensive following the Northern Rebellion and the papal bull against Elizabeth, he extended the historical period back to the Church of the apostles and he incorporated a section on the Ottoman Empire, that other manifestation of Antichrist. This edition was a collaborative effort with Foxe receiving much support from his friends from exile and also from Archbishop Parker and the scholarly circle around him.

---

[12] Evenden and Freeman, *Religion and the Book*, pp. 102–29.
[13] Tom Betteridge, 'From Prophetic to Apocalyptic: John Foxe and the Writing of History', in David Loades (ed.), *John Foxe and the English Reformation* (Aldershot, 1997), pp. 210–32; Katharine R. Firth, *The Apocalyptic Tradition in Reformation Britain 1530-1645* (Oxford, 1979), pp. 69–110.

At this date the *Book of Martyrs*, notwithstanding the criticisms of the queen contained in the prefaces, could be said to represent the officially received understanding of Church history within the Established Church.[14] By the date of the fourth edition in 1583 this was less clearly the case. By then the *Book of Martyrs* had become a contested text within the Church between the proponents of episcopacy and their puritan critics, and Foxe himself was less content with the religious settlement following the suspension of his old friend from exile, Edmund Grindal, archbishop of Canterbury, in 1576 and the emergence of John Whitgift. The divisions within the English Church and the aggressive advance of Catholicism in Europe threatened to overturn the Reformation.[15] Writing in these circumstances, Foxe's prefaces, introductions, and conclusions to the *Actes* were full of references to biblical prophecies, as were the marginal notes to the text, so that the 1583 history could be read not only as a record of the past and present persecutions of the gospel, but also as a prophetic warning of persecutions still to come. Foxe, never entirely comfortable with episcopacy, and by now also at odds with the younger generation of puritans, was deeply engaged in study of the Apocalypse, and this was reflected in his history. The 1583 edition represented the fullest expression of the prophetic, apocalyptic purpose of history to be adopted by the reformers, a purpose which was to reappear in the 1632 edition, published in the context of the Laudian revival of ceremonial.[16]

Foxe's identification of the true Church with the congregations of believers persecuted by the authorities was not unconnected to his apocalyptic interpretation of the past, and was also problematic in the context of the Elizabethan Church. Foxe had identified the Lollards and their friends as the precursors of both the Marian martyrs and the Elizabethan Church, but a narrative which produced a national Church from communities which sat outside of, and were persecuted by, the establishment in earlier times was a problematic one. Foxe himself was aware of this: for example, in his treatment of the Lollards, who existed in the time of suffering before the arrival of the gospel, the varied and heterodox views recorded at their trials were allowed to stand, but in the case of the Marian martyrs, whose sufferings under Mary post-dated the arrival of the gospel in England under Edward VI, eclectic opinions were less acceptable, and Foxe edited the beliefs of some of those martyrs so that the views of the 'free-willers', who were opposed to predestination, were removed. The Marian martyrs therefore appeared as a theologically more coherent group than they actually were; fitting precursors to a

---

[14] Evenden and Freeman, *Religion and the Book*, pp. 135–62, 183–5.
[15] Patrick Collinson, *The Elizabethan Puritan Movement* (1967), pp. 177–91, 257; Diarmaid MacCulloch, *Reformation: Europe's House Divided, 1490–1700* (2003), pp. 322–30, 337–40.
[16] Evenden and Freeman, *Religion and the Book*, pp. 314–19; Daniel Nussbaum, 'Appropriating Martyrdom: Fears of Renewed Persecution and the 1632 edition of *Acts and Monuments*', in Loades (ed.), *Foxe and English Reformation*, pp. 178–91.

national Church within the Reformed Calvinist tradition.[17] If Foxe trimmed the beliefs of the martyrs to the needs of the new Church, his emphasis on the 'congregational' character of their meetings was less helpful to it. What was the proper relation between a national institutional and visible Church, and gathered congregational churches, only recognizable by the beliefs and behaviour of their members? It was a relationship full of tension; expressed by Foxe in his preface to the 1570 edition which was addressed to 'the true and faithful Congregation of Christ's Universal Church with all and singular the members thereof, wheresoever congregated or dispersed throughout the realm', a dedication which sat uneasily with the preface's running headline, 'A Protestation to the whole Church of England'. The nature of that Church, however, remained contested between those who defended the continued use of bishops within the Church and those puritans who sought further reform along more Presbyterian lines. The latter, though most of them still thought in terms of a national Church, identified with the congregational spirit of the martyrs both in their adherence to a less hierarchical church government and because, through their increasing marginalization within the Established Church, they claimed a share in the sufferings of earlier generations.[18] Both Archbishop Whitgift and Thomas Cartwright, his leading puritan opponent, appealed to Foxe for vindication of their positions and, following Foxe's death in 1587, Whitgift sponsored an abridged version of the *Actes* by Timothy Bright, published in 1589. This appeared at the height of the conflict between the episcopate and the puritans following the failure of the puritans in Parliament to push through reform, and in the wake of the scurrilous Marprelate Tracts and the uncovering of the puritan classis movement. The abridgement sought to appropriate Foxe more clearly to the position of the bishops and Bright softened the more radical criticisms of the Church in Foxe's text, especially on two issues of most concern to the puritans, the 'ex officio oath' administered in the ecclesiastical courts, and the use of vestments in the liturgy.[19]

The successive editions of Foxe were both the most influential and the most contested historical texts to emerge in Elizabeth's reign, but they were not the only ones. If it was Foxe's purpose to write the history of the true Church in its struggles with the power of Antichrist, insofar as it affected England, others searched for the past of an established English Church free from Roman

---

[17] Thomas Freeman, 'Dissenters from a Dissenting Church: The Challenge of the Freewillers 1550-1558', in Peter Marshall and Alec Ryrie (eds.), *The Beginnings of English Protestantism* (Cambridge, 2002), pp. 129-56, esp. p. 153; Susan Royal, 'Reforming Household Piety: John Foxe and the Lollard Conventicle Tradition', in John Doran, Charlotte Methuen, and Alexandra Walsham (eds.), *Religion and the Household* (SCH 50, Woodbridge, 2014), pp. 188-98.

[18] Patrick Collinson, 'John Foxe and National Consciousness', in King and Highley (eds.), *Foxe and his World*, pp. 26-8.

[19] Daniel Nussbaum, 'Whitgift's "Book of Martyrs": Archbishop Whitgift, Timothy Bright and the Elizabethan Struggle over John Foxe's Legacy', in David Loades (ed.), *John Foxe: An Historical Perspective* (Aldershot, 1999), pp. 135-53.

influence which was the precursor of the present establishment. The tradition of an ancient British Church, established by King Lucius in the second century, was widespread in scholarly quarters, and the Anglo-Saxon Church was also considered to be a precedent. Both Bale and Foxe alluded to these, albeit uneasily, but they fitted in with the apocalyptic chronology which had Satan entering the world in 1000 CE.[20] The Anglo-Saxon Church was especially problematic, however, as its greatest historian, Bede, had written his account to show how that Church had been brought into conformity with Rome and had overcome local 'British' traditions. Catholic apologists such as Thomas Stapleton, the translator of Bede, had made much of this, and so it was important to establish the Protestant credentials of that Church.[21] A group of scholars emerged in the 1560s around the household of Archbishop Parker who edited and collected surviving manuscripts and texts from the Anglo-Saxon and medieval English Church, publishing some, most notably a life of King Alfred, the Easter sermon of abbot Aelfric, the *Historia Brevis* of Thomas Walsingham, and the *Chronicon Maiora* of Matthew Paris, a thirteenth-century monk of St Albans and critic of the papacy. The purpose of these texts was to establish the ways in which the Anglo-Saxon and medieval English Church resisted Roman encroachment; thus, Aelfric's sermon attempted to demonstrate that the Anglo-Saxon Church had a Protestant view of the eucharist, and Walsingham's chronicle was a source for Wyclif and his followers. Foxe had used these sources too, and printed some of them, but whereas his history was built around the suffering of God's servants at the hands of Antichrist, the documents published by Parker's scholars revealed the resistance of ecclesiastics to interference from Rome.[22] For a Church which retained episcopacy and the structures and some of the ceremonies of the medieval Church whilst changing its theology, this stress on institutional continuity was important. By the 1580s, therefore, the new Church had two accounts of its past; they overlapped and supported each other, but in the context of a religious settlement which remained contested, they also offered alternative readings. The complex interactions of these two approaches were most clearly revealed in the second edition of the classic account of British history, Holinshed's *Chronicles*, published in 1587, in which providential history, incorporating lengthy passages from Foxe, sat uneasily alongside the chronicle tradition, with its sense of ecclesiastical continuity between the pre- and post-Reformation Churches.[23] While Scripture remained the defining test

---

[20] Heal, 'King Lucius', pp. 607–8.

[21] Christopher Highley, *Catholics Writing the Nation in Early Modern Britain* (Oxford, 2008), pp. 84–91; Robinson, 'Foxe and the Anglo-Saxons', p. 65.

[22] May McKisack, *Medieval History in the Tudor Age* (Oxford, 1971), pp. 26–49.

[23] Peter Marshall, 'Religious Ideology', in Ian W. Archer, Felicity Heal, and Paulina Kewes (eds.), *The Oxford Handbook of Holinshed's Chronicles* (Oxford, 2013), pp. 412–19, 425–6, and essays by Walsham, and Freeman and Monta in the same volume.

of the truth of the doctrine of the Elizabethan Church, its history was an important factor in how its governance and liturgy was understood by many of its leading members.

Among the antiquarian scholars associated with Archbishop Parker who also contributed to the second edition of Holinshed was John Stow, a conservative conformist who published *A Summarie of Englyshe Chronicles* in 1565 and a history, *Annals, or a General Chronicle of England* in 1580, before the work for which he is most remembered, *The Survey of London* in 1598. All of these went through many editions in the half century following their publication. Stow was suspected of Catholic sympathies by the more radical Protestants, and his views were certainly sympathetic to the piety of the medieval Church, if not its theology. The *Survey of London* makes this clear in Stow's account of the losses to the city landscape of monuments such as the Cheapside Cross, occasioned by the iconoclastic activities of the reformers.[24] This sense of loss was not new—even Bale remarked on the losses consequent upon the destruction of the great monastic libraries—and by the 1590s these institutions themselves were attracting sympathetic recorders. Stow himself compiled a manuscript list of monastic houses and in 1590 Michael Sherbrooke, vicar of Wickersley in Yorkshire, a county where monasteries were numerous, wrote a defence of the social worth of the religious houses and a lament for the economic consequences of their dissolution. His account of the dissolution of Roche Abbey would have struck a chord with Robert Aske, leader of the Pilgrimage of Grace in 1536.[25] Further north, at Durham, a manuscript compilation of about the same time, subsequently known as the *Rites of Durham*, faithfully recorded the devotional life of Durham priory on the eve of the dissolution and the depredations visited on the cathedral by the reformers, in particular the dismantling of the tomb and shrine of St Cuthbert.[26] This account, probably the product of a Catholic, was to prove influential among clerical scholars of the Church of England in the early seventeenth century.

These conservative voices were in stark contrast to the prevailing Foxeian narrative of a Calvinist like William Harrison, whose *Description of Britain*

---

[24] Ian W. Archer, 'John Stow, Citizen and Historian', in Ian Gadd and Alexandra Gillespie (eds.), *John Stow (1525–1605) and the Making of the English Past* (2004), pp. 13–26; Alexandra Walsham, *The Reformation of the Landscape: Religion, Identity and Memory in Early Modern Britain and Ireland* (Oxford, 2011), p. 275.

[25] Michael Sherbrooke, 'The Falle of Religious Howses, Colleges and Chantreys Hospitalls &', in A. G. Dickens (ed.), *Tudor Treatises* (Yorkshire Archaeological Society, Record Series 125, Leeds, 1959), pp. 89–142 (esp. pp. 123–30).

[26] J. T. Fowler (ed.), *Rites of Durham: Being A Description of all the Ancient Monuments, Rites & Customs Belonging or Being Within the Monastical Church of Durham Before the Suppression: Written 1593* (Surtees Society 107, 1903).

prefaced both the 1577 and the 1587 editions of Holinshed,[27] but they were growing in significance. Furthermore their stress on institutional continuity resonated with a younger generation of scholars who had no direct contact with the heroic years of the pre-Elizabethan Reformation. Pre-eminent among these was Richard Hooker, whose first five books of *Of The Laws of Ecclesiastical Polity* were published in 1593 and 1597. Hooker's theology was firmly scriptural and Calvinist, but he opposed those puritans who demanded scriptural precedent for all ecclesiological matters such as church governance and ceremonial, addressing the preface of the work 'To them that seek (as they term it) the reformation of Laws, and orders Ecclesiastical, in the Church of ENGLAND'. Books two to five challenged the four main assertions of the puritans, that Scripture was the only rule of all things in this life, that nothing could be used in the Church that was not explicitly stated in Scripture, that the English Church was corrupted with popish orders banished from other Reformed Churches, and that public worship of the Church still retained superstitious practices. These were all matters which Hooker considered to be subject to reason, by means of which they would be adjusted to prevailing political circumstances, so that his book, though not a work of history, historicized the ecclesiology of the English Church, and that of all others. Matters of church order and ceremony, where they did not flatly contradict Scripture, were 'things indifferent' or *adiaphora*, to be determined by the appropriate authorities. Thus Hooker was able to argue both that the Genevan Church order was right for the situation in which Calvin constructed it, and that the English Church order was appropriate to the monarchical polity of the country. The work was not widely disseminated at first, but Hooker's analysis came to influence not only his contemporaries' views of the Established Church, but also their views of the Roman Church.[28]

Most importantly, Hooker's principal argument in book four was that a ceremony, such as using the sign of the cross in baptism, was not wrong simply because it was used in the Roman Church, and he went further: 'Where Rome keeps that which is ancienter and better; others whom we much more affect leaving it for newer, and changing it for worse, we had rather follow the perfections of them whom we like not, than in defects resemble them whom we love.' Of course Catholic devotion was full of superstition and rife with error, but as a Church it contained 'perfections' which retained spiritual value. This was a huge shift in emphasis. The identification of the Pope with Antichrist was universally accepted among Protestants (even Whitgift's DD

---

[27] Glyn Parry, *A Protestant Vision: William Harrison and the Reformation of Elizabethan England* (Cambridge, 1987) and his chapter in Archer, Heal, and Kewes (eds.), *Holinshed*, pp. 93–110.

[28] A. S. McGrade (ed.), *Richard Hooker: Of the Laws of Ecclesiastical Polity*, 3 vols. (Oxford, 2013), I, pp. xxxii–xxxiii; Diarmaid MacCulloch, 'The Reputation of Richard Hooker', *English Historical Review*, 117 (2002): 773–812, esp. pp. 773–84.

was on that topic) and the Roman Church was the Babylon of Revelations, but now Hooker was claiming that some of its traditions were more appropriate precedents for the English Church than the practices of continental Protestant Churches. Furthermore, Hooker had argued in book three that, insofar as Rome had retained 'those main parts of Christian Truth', it could be admitted 'to be of the family of Jesus Christ'.[29] Rome, therefore, was no longer the home of Antichrist but was part of the Church, albeit a part steeped in error.

Hooker's historicizing of ecclesiology and liturgical practice coincided with two other new intellectual developments in the English Church, both of which challenged its Calvinist foundations. First, at a Paul's Cross sermon in 1589, Richard Bancroft had suggested that episcopacy was not merely the constitutional basis of the English Church but that it was a form of government with divine origin, a view developed more fully in print the following year by Matthew Sutcliffe and Hadrian Saravia, a Flemish émigré.[30] Second, another émigré, Peter Baro, regius professor of divinity at Cambridge, had published lectures on Jonah in 1580 in which he had questioned the Calvinist doctrine of justification. This had brought responses from the Cambridge puritans, in particular from his fellow professor William Whitaker, and in 1595 Archbishop Whitgift issued the Lambeth Articles clarifying the Church's Calvinist position on predestination. When Baro attacked the articles in a sermon at Cambridge in 1596 the dispute became public, resulting in Baro being removed from his chair. From the late 1590s the dominance of a Calvinist consensus among the intellectual leadership of the English Church no longer went unchallenged.[31] This required a fresh engagement with its past.

In the reign of James I, Protestant churchmen sought to recover a 'visible' Church which had existed before Luther. In this they were answering the criticism of Catholic historians who characterized the 'invisible' gospellers of Foxe and Bale as being heretical congregations rather than a Church. It was important, in this context, to establish a Protestant succession. It was not enough to follow Foxe and find justification in their persecution by the papacy; continuity in doctrine and practice now had to be established. Much effort was put into proving that groups like the Waldensians and the Hussites had preserved an outward ministry of word and sacrament. The greatest defence of the doctrines of the medieval heretics and their conformity with Protestant belief was produced in 1613 by James Ussher, the Anglo-Irish professor of theological controversies at Trinity College, Dublin. His *De Christianarum Ecclesiarum Successione* became a source-book for later Calvinist authors

---

[29] McGrade (ed.), *Hooker*, I, pp. xlix, liii.

[30] Peter Lake, *Anglicans and Puritans? Presbyterianism and English Conformist Thought from Whitgift to Hooker* (1988), esp. pp. 93–6.

[31] Nicholas Tyacke, *Anti-Calvinists: The Rise of English Arminianism c.1590–1640* (Oxford, 1987), pp. 29–33.

seeking to stress the consistency of the views of the major medieval heretical groups. These heretics were far from being invisible, being numbered in their tens of thousands and having, among their followers, a number of landowners and prosperous merchants.[32] Moreover, as the recently published confessions of these 'Churches' showed, they were served by a legitimate, episcopally ordained ministry. These Jacobean histories replaced Foxe's congregations of the godly with doctrinally respectable communities led by clergy. Following Hooker, these historians went beyond Foxe by also including among their predecessors ecclesiastics who had not separated from Rome. Thus Francis Godwin's *Catalogue of the Bishops of England* (1601) had defended the episcopal succession of the Church through biographies of distinguished individuals like Robert Grosseteste, securing a bishopric for the author in the process.[33] It followed from this that some members of the pre-Reformation Roman Church had been saved, an issue which had first brought Hooker into contention with the puritan Walter Travers when he preached on that point in 1587.[34]

The problem was how to allow for salvation within the pre-Reformation Church without admitting it to the contemporary Roman Church. This was resolved by Richard Field who published in 1606 his *Of the Church*, which set out a history of the medieval Church in which he claimed that 'all those Christian Catholic Churches in the West part of the world, where the Pope formerly tyrannized, and where our fathers lived and died, were the true Protestant Churches of God'. The Roman tyranny had never been complete and so the pre-Lutheran Church, despite its errors, contained all things necessary to salvation; it was only at the Council of Trent that papal tyranny over the Roman Church was fully accomplished, thereby rendering it a false Church. In this new historical framework a Calvinist like Ussher could argue that true doctrine had been preserved in the liturgy of the medieval Church, and even an anti-Catholic as vehement as William Crashawe published a *Manuale Catholicorum* in 1611 to show that Protestant doctrine was to be found in popular medieval prayers. If Calvinists like Ussher and Crashawe could find virtue among the corruption of the medieval Church, then by the end of James's reign the growing number of anti-Calvinists reversed the thrust of earlier Protestant histories of the pre-Reformation Church. In 1621 Richard Montagu overturned the Protestant view of Wyclif as hero, deploring his anti-clericalism and his attack on tithes, and he subsequently embarked on

---

[32] Anthony Milton, *Catholic and Reformed: The Roman and Protestant Churches in English Protestant Thought, 1600–1640* (Cambridge, 1995), pp. 281–3; Alan Ford, *James Ussher: Theology, History and Politics in Early Modern Ireland and England* (Oxford, 2007), pp. 36–56, 106–15.

[33] Milton, *Catholic and Reformed*, p. 284.

[34] Richard Bauckham, 'Hooker, Travers and the Church of Rome in the 1580s', *JEH*, 29 (1978): 37–50.

a study of Thomas Becket, that prime example of overweening clerical ambition to earlier evangelicals. By the end of the 1630s Montagu's friend, John Cosin had added Becket's name to the Prayer Book calendar.[35]

By that date the Laudians celebrated the devotional life of the medieval Church as an example for the contemporary Church. In 1627 Cosin published his *Collection of Private Devotions* based on the office prayers of the medieval Church and on the widely used Sarum Missal. With their focus on the 'beauty of holiness' the Laudians brought these private devotions into the public worship of parish church and cathedrals.[36] This was done most fully by Cosin and his associates at Durham Cathedral where, during the 1620s, the church was completely reordered, the communion table was replaced by a marble altar placed at the east end of the church, the font was moved to the west end, the choir was decorated with scarlet and gold angels and an image of Christ, and the altar railed. Candles were introduced on the altar, towards which clergy and people were encouraged to bow, and elaborate vestments were purchased for the main services, which were now enhanced by choir and organ. While undertaking this, Cosin researched the pre-Reformation history of the cathedral, commissioning a copy of the *Rites of Durham* and annotating the text, whilst others were reviving the life and legends of St Cuthbert, whose tomb was visited by Charles I in 1633. The ceremonial and architectural changes at Durham, grounded on medieval practice, were reflected elsewhere, if not so fully.[37] John Pocklington, in his *Altare Christianum* of 1637, praised the devotion of the Middle Ages, when the people donated stained glass windows, bells, belfries, pews, fonts, as well as candles, lights, and statues to their churches, and devotional practices such as Lenten fasting, and even the monastic life, that pit of clerical concupiscence to Bale and Foxe, began to find defenders.[38] Antiquarian scholarship was also interested in the survivals of the Middle Ages, both in manuscript and in masonry, and John Weever's Pevsneresque survey of the *Ancient Funerall Monuments within the United Kingdom of Great Britain and Ireland* (1631) provided a detailed account of the tombs and epitaphs of a time when 'Christian Religion and good literature were propagated over this our Island'. For the Laudians, the medieval centuries were when 'the piety of Princes, and devotion of God's people... gave beauty and wealth to the Churches', and they were to be contrasted with the neglect of the present age.[39]

---

[35] Milton, *Catholic and Reformed*, pp. 286–8, 290, 312–13.

[36] Tyacke, *Anti-Calvinists*, p. 119; Milton, *Catholic and Reformed*, p. 318.

[37] Kenneth Fincham and Nicholas Tyacke, *Altars Restored: The Changing Face of English Religious Worship, 1547–c.1700* (Oxford, 2007), pp. 115–18, 137–9; Diana Newton, 'St Cuthbert: Durham's Tutelarie Deitie', *Recusant History*, 31 (2013): 439–59 (pp. 446–53).

[38] Milton, *Catholic and Reformed*, pp. 316–18.

[39] Graham Parry, *The Trophies of Time: English Antiquarians of the Seventeenth Century* (Oxford, 1995), pp. 190–216, quote at p. 194; Milton, *Catholic and Reformed*, quote at p. 316.

The Laudians did not have things all their own way. Cosin's *Private Devotions* was challenged in print by the puritan lawyer William Prynne and the ex-royal chaplain Henry Burton, and his innovations at Durham by the Calvinist preacher Peter Smart.[40] Conversely, Pocklington's historical defence of the medieval Church required a hasty second edition in response to *The Holy Table, Name and Thing*, published by the Calvinist bishop John Williams in 1637.[41] Calvinist history was still being published: a new edition of Foxe, with extensive additional material on recent Catholic persecutions of Protestants in Europe and Catholic plots in England, was issued in 1632, in response no doubt to the growing influence of the Arminians on royal policy, and possibly also to the king's dissolution of Parliament in 1629.[42] This edition brought Foxe's history up to more recent times, and its view of the Reformation remained dominant among puritans like Henry Burton and John Shawe who, when looking back to the early Reformation, depicted a prophetic Church warning kings and people of the snares of the devil, snares all too apparent to them in the years of the Personal Rule.[43] In this context it was not enough for the Laudians to rehabilitate the medieval Church; they had to reclaim the Reformation. The search for a constitutional Reformation to replace the prophetic one of the puritans was undertaken by the combative pen of Peter Heylyn. Challenging the account of Henry Burton, who used the example of the Edwardian regime to challenge the claims of the episcopate, Heylyn argued that the moderation of the Edwardian Reformation, as exhibited in the First Prayer Book, had been subverted by foreign divines, chief among whom was Calvin, and by the greed of Northumberland's regime. Balance had only been restored by the Elizabethan Settlement, and the subsequent falling away in standards of public worship was due to neglect by the laity, especially its leaders in Parliament, and to the spread of puritanism. The true English Reformation had been preserved in the devotional life of the cathedrals and the royal chapels, and this was the standard to which the Church needed to return. The effect of this, though not made explicit at the time, was to deny that Elizabethan Presbyterians such as Thomas Cartwright had ever been members of the Church, thus making sectaries of contemporary puritans.[44]

---

[40] William Lamont, *Marginal Prynne* (1963), pp. 17–18, 21–2; Henry Burton, *A Tryall of Private Devotions* (1628); Fincham and Tyacke, *Altars Restored*, pp. 137–9.

[41] Tyacke, *Anti-Calvinists*, pp. 209–10; Fincham and Tyacke, *Altars Restored*, p. 155.

[42] Nussbaum, 'Appropriating Martyrdom', pp. 186–91.

[43] Kevin Sharpe, *The Personal Rule of Charles I* (New Haven, CT, 1992), pp. 758–65; William Sheils, 'John Shawe and Edward Bowles: Civic Preachers at Peace and War', in Kenneth Fincham and Peter Lake (eds.), *Religious Politics in Post-Reformation England* (Woodbridge, 2006), pp. 209–23, esp. p. 213.

[44] Anthony Milton, *Laudian and Royalist Polemic in Seventeenth-Century England: The Career and Writings of Peter Heylyn* (Manchester, 2007), pp. 83–7.

The breakdown in relations between the puritans and the regime at the end of the 1630s eventually led to civil wars. In the process a new edition of Foxe was printed with parliamentary support in 1641 and, insofar as the history of the Church played any part in the disputes which followed, it was to Foxe and his followers that the opponents of the king looked.[45] It would be wrong, however, to claim too much, or much at all, for the contribution of these histories to the debates of the 1640s, suffused as they were with religious references. The execution of the king in 1649, coupled with the iconoclasm of the 1640s, and the abolition of episcopacy and of cathedral churches marked the eclipse of the Laudians, and the end of their historical enterprise. Scholarly antiquarian work continued, however. The publication of *Monasticon Anglicanum* by William Dugdale in 1655 addressed what had been a sensitive subject. Largely an edition of charters, it emphasized the integrity of ecclesiastical property, with a title page showing, at the top, Henry III confirming the protection of ecclesiastical property promised in Magna Carta and, below, Henry VIII reneging on that promise. The volume was copiously illustrated with views of monastic ruins which further emphasized the losses that the Reformation had brought with it. In 1658 Dugdale followed this with a copiously illustrated history of another dissolved institution, St Paul's Cathedral. In the context of the 1650s these volumes represented a criticism of the regime and of the destructive power of the iconoclasts, and were a powerful argument for the restoration of an established church.[46]

It was left to a Calvinist supporter of the royalist cause to publish a new church history. Thomas Fuller had published a history of the Crusades in 1639 at a time when, by his own account, he embarked on his *Church History of Britain*, published in 1655. Though a royalist chaplain in the wars, Fuller continued to minister in the parish of Waltham Abbey in the 1650s. Fuller's *History* largely followed the Foxeian narrative for the years up to the Reformation, devoting a long section to Wyclif, and betrayed no sympathy for the medieval Church or its institutions, though he did devote a whole volume to monastic history, praising the hospitality of the monks and their scholarship but decrying their greed and licentiousness. His detailed account of the Reformation focused more on its constitutional aspects than on the sufferings of the martyrs, and he provided an even-handed discussion of the disputes in the Elizabethan Church. The English Church, as it emerged in the reign of James I, exhibited the best practice of Reformed religion, and Fuller was unsparing about the responsibility which Laud and his associates had for the collapse into war.[47] Although not quite Collinsonian in its depth of

---

[45] Evenden and Freeman, *Religion and the Book*, pp. 333–4.
[46] Parry, *Trophies of Time*, pp. 229–39.   [47] Parry, *Trophies of Time*, pp. 267–74.

scholarship, Fuller's *History* was one to which Calvinist supporters of the episcopate could subscribe, and was influential at the Restoration, an event he did not long outlive. It was a Foxeian account without the presence of Antichrist, yet one which did not depart from its moderate Calvinist beliefs; in that sense, it was an Anglican history.

To conclude: we must begin with two caveats. First, it has to be acknowledged that the historical writing discussed here was composed against a background of formidable Roman Catholic scholarly and polemical history from the pens of men such as Thomas Stapleton and Robert Parsons, and the ways in which those writers shaped the debate has not been considered here.[48] Second, the question of reception has hardly been mentioned. How far these writings penetrated beyond the elite remains elusive, except perhaps in the case of Foxe. Even in his case, the extent to which martyr stories circulated among the people is unclear, but we can be confident that it was the acts of hearing these stories told and seeing the woodcut illustrations of the martyrdoms that were most likely to have influenced people's understandings of their religious heritage rather than direct contact with the text.[49] That said, we can draw some other conclusions. To the reformers, the Reformation was essentially about restoring the Church to its primitive purity, and its truth was to be judged by the evidence of Scripture and the Fathers. To the early reformers, insofar as history had a part to play, its role was to demonstrate the falling away from that primitive purity. Disagreements might be had about whether or not particular practices departed from primitive Christianity, but that remained the test. It was not until the 1590s, with Hooker's historicizing of the Church, that history began to be thought of as having a positive contribution to make to ecclesiological understanding, at least by the non-Calvinists. From that date the example of the medieval Church became a battleground, not just between Protestants and Catholics, but among English Protestants themselves. By the 1630s disputes arose about the history of the early Reformation itself, and the lessons drawn by the opposing parties from their competing histories were to contribute significantly to the political and religious upheavals of the mid-seventeenth century.

---

[48] Felicity Heal, 'Appropriating History: Catholic and Protestant Polemics and the National Past', *Huntington Library Quarterly*, 68 (2005): 109–32.

[49] Margaret Aston and Elizabeth Ingram, 'The Iconography of the *Acts and Monuments*', in Loades (ed.), *Foxe and English Reformation*, pp. 66–142, esp. pp. 66–70; Tessa Watt, *Cheap Print and Popular Piety 1550–1640* (Cambridge, 1991), pp. 158–9; Collinson, 'Foxe and National Consciousness', pp. 31–4.

SELECT BIBLIOGRAPHY

Archer, Ian W., Felicity Heal, and Paulina Kewes (eds.), *The Oxford Handbook of Holinshed's Chronicles* (Oxford, 2013).

Betteridge, Thomas, *Tudor Histories of the English Reformations, 1530–83* (Aldershot, 1999).

Evenden, Elizabeth and Thomas S. Freeman, *Religion and the Book in Early Modern England: The Making of Foxe's 'Book of Martyrs'* (Cambridge, 2011).

Fincham, Kenneth and Nicholas Tyacke, *Altars Restored: The Changing Face of English Religious Worship, 1547–c.1700* (Oxford, 2007).

Highley, Christopher and John King (eds.), *John Foxe and his World* (Aldershot, 2002).

Lake, Peter, *Anglicans and Puritans? Presbyterianism and English Conformist Thought from Whitgift to Hooker* (1988).

Loades, David (ed.), *John Foxe and the English Reformation* (Aldershot, 1997).

McKisack, May, *Medieval History in the Tudor Age* (Oxford, 1971).

Milton, Anthony, *Catholic and Reformed: The Roman and Protestant Churches in English Protestant Thought, 1600–1640* (Cambridge, 1995).

Milton, Anthony, *Laudian and Royalist Polemic in Seventeenth-Century England: The Career and Writings of Peter Heylyn* (Manchester, 2007).

Parish, Helen, *Monks, Miracles and Magic: Reformation Representations of the Medieval Church* (2005).

Parry, Graham, *The Trophies of Time: English Antiquarians of the Seventeenth Century* (Oxford, 1995).

Tyacke, Nicholas, *Anti-Calvinists: The Rise of English Arminianism c.1590–1640* (Oxford, 1987).

Walsham, Alexandra, *The Reformation of the Landscape: Religion, Identity and Memory in Early Modern Britain and Ireland* (Oxford, 2011).

17

The Church of England and International Protestantism, 1530–1570

Diarmaid MacCulloch

England's Reformation was remarkably barren of original theologians, at least until the coming of that quietly wayward figure Richard Hooker. English Reformers would not have been too resentful of this assessment, because their outlook was determinedly international: the stars of Reformation thought blazed elsewhere. English insularity might only be said to begin with Hooker, and not just because of his own cooling attitudes towards Reformations outside England. It is remarkable that none of Hooker's writings were translated into Latin. In other words, no one in any other part of the continent could be bothered to read him, so Hooker was left languishing in that baffling and marginal European language, English (which it must be said is particularly baffling when Hooker writes it).[1] Otherwise, the flow of ideas in the Reformation seems at least at first sight to be a matter of imports from abroad, with an emphatically unfavourable English balance of payments. How, therefore, should we relate England's Reformation to the Reformations which sprang from Wittenberg, Zürich, or Geneva? Can we apply labels like 'Lutheran' or 'Reformed' in an English context, and what might they mean here?

The quest must begin with Henry VIII, a king fascinated by theology, because he was convinced that God had put his family on the throne. This was despite the fact (which Henry knew full well but would never acknowledge) that they had a remarkably weak claim by blood to be kings of England. His father had won the crown by God's favour in a battle at Bosworth in 1485. So it mattered what God thought of Henry's actions. His first instinct in the Reformation was that it was a blasphemy against God. He read Martin Luther, another man in a perilously one-to-one relationship with God. Henry's

---

[1] D. MacCulloch, 'Richard Hooker's Reputation', *English Historical Review*, 117 (2002): 773–812, repr. in W. J. T. Kirby (ed.), *A Companion to Richard Hooker* (Leiden and Boston, 2008), pp. 563–612.

negative reaction to Luther's encounter with God was expressed in his ghost-written *Assertio Septem Sacramentorum*, earning both papal gratitude and a riposte from Luther rightly taken as *lèse-majesté*. Luther and Henry never laid aside their mutual loathing, particularly since Luther disapproved of Henry's repudiation of Catherine of Aragon with a good deal more genuine moral fervour than Pope Clement VII.

Yet Henry was still the first king in Europe fully to declare against Rome; all rulers who had previously done so were mere princes or city councils. Not even the newly minted King Gustav Vasa of Sweden made as clean a break as Henry with the Holy See when he set up his untidy alliance with the Reformation from the late 1520s. Henry had to decide what his schism had to do with the Reformations in progress in central Europe. Much is puzzling about his decisions.[2] His Church has often been called 'Catholicism without the Pope'—recent scholars have seen it more as 'Lutheranism without justification by faith' (a formulation invented by Peter Marshall), for the king never accepted this central doctrine of the Reformation.[3] Henry was part of both the old religious world and the new. Throughout the king's reign, the Latin mass remained in all its splendour, and all his clergy had to remain celibate, as did the monks and nuns whose lives he had ruined. On the other hand Henry ceased to pay much attention to the doctrine of purgatory, he destroyed all monasteries and nunneries in England and Wales (and, where he could, in Ireland), and he was positively proud of eliminating English and Welsh shrines and pilgrimages.

It is worth seeing this mixture in a wider context, something classically Anglican historians were never inclined to do. Several northern European monarchs were not enthused by Luther and Wittenberg, yet still made their own pick and mix Reformations, sometimes without breaking with Rome. Besides Gustav Vasa of Sweden, there was the Elector Joachim II of Brandenburg, who had a Lutheran brother-in-law but also a Catholic father-in-law, the king of Poland. Joachim's uncle was Luther's enemy the indulgence-peddling Cardinal Albrecht of Mainz, so it is perhaps not surprising that the Elector had no excessive reverence for the old Church hierarchy. He took it upon himself to enact his own religious settlement for Brandenburg, specifically declaring the settlement temporary until there could be a general settlement throughout the Empire. He made no break with Rome, but confiscated much ecclesiastical land and dissolved monasteries, just as Henry VIII was doing in England, and with almost as much lack of concern to reinvest his winnings in good causes.[4]

---

[2] D. MacCulloch, 'Henry VIII and the Reform of the Church', in D. MacCulloch (ed.), *The Reign of Henry VIII: Politics, Policy and Piety* (Basingstoke, 1995), pp. 159–80.
[3] Cf. A. Ryrie, 'The Strange Death of Lutheran England', *JEH*, 53 (2002): 64–92 (p. 67).
[4] J. Estes, 'Melanchthon's Confrontation with the "Erasmian" *Via Media* in Politics: The *De officio Principum* of 1539', in J. Loehr (ed.), *Dona Melanchthoniana* (Stuttgart, 2001), pp. 83–101 (pp. 93–5).

Equally interesting were the policies of Duke Johann III of the United Duchies of Jülich-Cleves-Berg. In 1532–3 he enacted a *Kirchenordnung* (Church Ordinance) without consulting his clergy, yet also not breaking with Rome. Duke Johann's son succeeded as Duke Wilhelm V in 1539: he was not only brother-in-law of Luther's protector the Elector of Saxony, but more importantly for England, he was Anne of Cleves's brother. So the English political and religious leadership would be particularly aware of what was going on in Jülich-Cleves at the end of the 1530s, when for instance Henry VIII pushed a new doctrinal statement through Parliament, the Six Articles of 1539.[5] Just as in the changes in Cleves, these reaffirmed the traditional liturgical ceremonies of the Church, and yet they did not reverse any of the changes that had so far occurred in England. A keynote of the Cleves changes as embodied in Duke Johann's 1532–3 *Kirchenordnung* was that preaching should be based on Scripture and the early Fathers and should be free of polemics. This was of course also the constant cliché of the Henrician Reformation.

As always, Henry VIII managed to confuse his subjects about his views on the Bible. In 1543 he forced an Act through Parliament which overlooked King Canute's lesson to his courtiers and tried to limit Bible-reading on the basis of social hierarchy. That same year in Scotland, the Scottish Parliament passed very similar legislation about Bible-reading, but this legislation was not restrictive but permissive in its effect; for the first time it permitted landowners to possess the Bible.[6] The Scots were thus newly *allowed* an access to the Bible approximately equivalent to its newly *restricted* access in England: a symptom of a regime which for a moment had decided to undermine the old Church in Scotland and come closer to the religious settlement south of the border. What we are seeing alike in Brandenburg, Jülich-Cleves, England, and the Scotland of 1543 is a whole series of attempts to find a 'middle way'—that phrase which meant so much to King Henry, let alone to others like Archbishop Cranmer who often radically disagreed with him as to precisely what it might mean.[7]

Henry VIII's Reformation represents a march away from an initial Lutheran mould at a much earlier stage than the same development in Scotland. This is because there was more to what Alec Ryrie has termed 'the strange death of Lutheran England' than the familiar story of King Henry's mood-swings.[8] His England had at least two other Reformations: first a Reformation from below,

---

[5] Estes, 'Melanchthon's Confrontation', pp. 96–7.

[6] G. Donaldson, *The Scottish Reformation* (Cambridge, 1969), p. 30.

[7] G. W. Bernard, 'The Making of Religious Policy, 1533–1546: Henry VIII and the Search for the Middle Way', *Historical Journal*, 41 (1998): 321–51.

[8] A. Ryrie, 'The Strange Death of Lutheran England', *JEH*, 53 (2002): 64–92; K. D. Maas, *The Reformation and Robert Barnes: History, Theology and Polemic in Early Modern England* (Woodbridge, 2010).

which was also a Reformation before the Reformation: that of Lollardy.⁹ Admittedly Lollardy was never a unified force, and in the fifteenth and sixteenth centuries it was certainly not identical with the views of John Wyclif: given the way that it had been so effectively persecuted out of the universities and positions of power, that was hardly surprising. Nevertheless, on the eve of the Reformation, one can assemble a 'family resemblance' of beliefs common to most of those who would have thought of themselves (and who were recognized by neighbours and the old Church authorities) as having a distinctive and dissident identity or outlook within English religion: the identity which their detractors labelled Lollardy.¹⁰ When a definite shape emerged for the Protestant Church of England's thought after 1559, it had three major characteristics: a distrust of assertions of the real presence in the eucharist, a deep animus against images and shrines, and a reassertion of the value of law and moral systems within the Reformation structure of salvation. All these three were also characteristic of mainstream early Tudor Lollardy, and all three clashed with Luther's style of Protestantism. It would be crass to assert that the English Reformation was home-grown, or nothing but Lollardy writ large. Nevertheless, the Lollard inheritance cannot be ignored when seeing the choices which early English Reformers made, constrained though they were by the existence of Henry VIII and of competing Reformations on the other side of the North Sea.¹¹

There was yet another English Reformation: the evangelical programme sought and put into effect as far as they dared by the group of politicians and senior clergy who had been rallied by Queen Anne Boleyn, Thomas Cromwell, and Thomas Cranmer.¹² Thanks to that trio, there was something of an evangelical establishment in Church and royal court, with constant if precarious access to power from 1531 right up to the old king's death. This group started close to the beliefs of Martin Luther, because to begin with, Luther seemed to be the only act in town. That soon changed. Cranmer, at the heart of the Henrician and Edwardian Reformations, was in close touch with Martin Bucer and the Strassburg Reformation as early as 1531, and any theological pundit worth his salt in the 1530s would have seen Strassburg as the future of any united Protestant Reformation. So Cranmer veered away

---

⁹ Contrast R. Rex, *The Lollards* (Basingstoke, 2002), esp. ch. 5 and conclusion.
¹⁰ J. P. Hornbeck II, *What is a Lollard? Dissent and Belief in Late Medieval England* (Oxford, 2010); M. Aston, *Lollards and Reformers: Images and Literacy in Late Medieval Religion* (1984); A. Hudson, *Lollards and Their Books* (1985); A. Hope, 'Lollardy: The Stone the Builders Rejected?', in P. Lake and M. Dowling (eds.), *Protestantism and the National Church in Sixteenth Century England* (1988), pp. 1–35.
¹¹ D. MacCulloch, *The Later Reformation in England 1547–1603* (2nd edn., Basingstoke, 2001), pp. 55–65.
¹² D. MacCulloch, *Tudor Church Militant: Edward VI and the Protestant Reformation* (1999), pp. 2, 4.

from Luther towards Strassburg on the important question of the admissibility of images in worship. During the 1530s the evangelicals tortuously smuggled their views on various matters of doctrine into the Church's official doctrinal statements. They made sure that Henry VIII's Church renumbered the Ten Commandments in such a way as to stress the command against graven images, something which Luther did not do, but which had been newly revived in Zürich and Strassburg. It is too simple to see this momentous little change simply as a borrowing from the Swiss Reformation. It suggests the tug of a Lollard agenda already at work even on those who were now bishops and politicians.[13]

Yet throughout the 1530s, the Lutheranism of Henry's establishment evangelicals seemed strong on the vital matter of the eucharist. Throughout Henry's life, England remained officially aloof from the eucharistic theology of Strassburg and Switzerland: establishment evangelicals like Cranmer were just as committed to defending real eucharistic presence as Luther or the king, and in 1538 they even actively engineered the downfall and eventual burning for heresy of their wayward colleague John Lambert, who had denied the real presence.[14] This makes even more surprising a new direct link to the city of Zürich. Between 1536 and 1538 successive young Englishmen, including young evangelical Oxford dons from Magdalen College, travelled to Zürich, and in return Heinrich Bullinger's foster-son Rudolph Gwalther paid a visit to southern England and Oxford in 1537.[15] He never forgot his warm welcome, and it had consequences for the rest of the century.

Cranmer was prominent in the actual organization of the initial visit to Zürich and he continued to take an interest in the English 'exchange students'. But what is striking is how few traceable personal links they had to Cranmer and his Cambridge-educated clerical circle, and how many they had to Thomas Cromwell and the court circle of the Greys, marquises of Dorset, who were Cromwell's earliest patrons in the 1520s after his return from mainland Europe. The explanation for this oddity is surely that while political proprieties dictated that the clergyman Bullinger should deal with the clergyman Cranmer rather than directly with English politicians, Thomas Cromwell was the real driving force behind the Zürich initiative. During 1537 and 1538 Cranmer made clear his strong disapproval of the eucharistic theology of his Strassburg and Zürich contacts. That makes it all the more interesting that Cromwell should ignore his reservations, and should be so heavily and consistently involved with the English friends of Zürich. It is all the more

---

[13] D. MacCulloch, *Thomas Cranmer: A Life* (New Haven, CT, 1996), p. 192.
[14] MacCulloch, *Cranmer*, pp. 232–4.
[15] D. MacCulloch, 'Heinrich Bullinger and the English-Speaking World', in E. Campi (ed.), *Heinrich Bullinger (1505–1575): Leben, Denken, Wirkung*, 2 vols. (Zwingliana 32, 2005), I, pp. 891–934.

clear why Henry VIII was eventually prepared to listen to those who called Cromwell a sacramentarian. When in 1540 Cromwell was executed, it was for what Henry VIII would have considered the right reason: heresy. Cromwell has often been called a Lutheran; he was actually Zürich's best friend in Henry's England. It is striking that this supposedly cynical politician was prepared to invest so much in a perilous initiative towards a city which offered few positive political assets to England, and represented a Reformation detested by King Henry.

When Cromwell was executed in 1540, it should have been a blow to the growing nexus with Zürich. Yet Cromwell's was not the only Protestant martyrdom in England that year: the winter before the vicegerent's fall, King Henry burned England's most prominent and self-conscious Lutheran spokesman, Robert Barnes. Barnes was one of very few major magisterial Reformers to be executed anywhere in the European Reformation, and in one of history's great ironies, he was executed by the Pope's chief enemy in Europe.[16] Now the future of England's Protestantism turned out to lie not in Wittenberg. To find out what it turned out to be, we must meet some more European rulers trying to find a middle way.

One of the most important is Archbishop Hermann von Wied of Cologne. After gradually moving from Roman obedience, von Wied tried to create an autonomous Protestant Church in the lower Rhineland, but he was evicted by Charles V in 1546 after vigorous opposition to his plans from the canons of his own cathedral. Von Wied has often been casually characterized in English-speaking historiography as a Lutheran in his later years, but he did not at all conform to Lutheran doctrinal tramlines (particularly on the matter of images), and he became an inspiration for theologians who equally kept outside the Lutheran fold. One of them was his fellow-archbishop Thomas Cranmer, who seems to have kept in touch with the former archbishop even in von Wied's years of retirement in the 1550s.[17] Von Wied's proposals to reform the liturgy were highly influential in constructing the Book of Common Prayer. He represented one possible future direction for the European Reformation, snuffed out on the mainland by the Holy Roman Emperor's action against him.

Besides von Wied, there is the story of the little imperial territory of East Friesland. This tiny corner of Europe has a disproportionate significance for the course of northern European Reformations in many ways, not least for the early Reformation in England. When its ruler Count Enno II died in 1540, he left his widow Anna von Oldenburg with three young sons. Countess Anna, a

---

[16] A. Ryrie, *The Gospel and Henry VIII: Evangelicals in the Early English Reformation* (Cambridge, 2003).

[17] MacCulloch, *Cranmer*, pp. 393–4, and other index refs. s.v. von Wied, Hermann; J. K. Cameron, 'The Cologne Reformation and the Church of Scotland', *JEH*, 30 (1979): 39–64; R. W. Scribner, 'Why Was There No Reformation in Cologne?', *Bulletin of the Institute of Historical Research*, 49 (1976): 217–41.

resourceful and cultured woman, brushed aside opposition and assumed regency power on behalf of her children, planning to build them an inheritance in East Friesland which might form the basis of greater things for the dynasty. In politics she sought out alliances with rulers who like herself wanted to keep out of religious or diplomatic entanglements.[18] In her domestic religious policy, Countess Anna likewise sought to avoid total identification with either Lutherans or papalist Catholics, just as Henry VIII generally did after his break with Rome. She chose as principal pastor in her little port-capital at Emden an exotic and cosmopolitan figure from the Polish noble caste, Jan Łaski (usually known in his international travels as Johannes à Lasco by non-Polish Latin-speakers trying to get their tongues around Polish pronunciation). Łaski was a humanist scholar, friend and benefactor of Erasmus. When he broke with the old Church in the late 1530s, he remained an admirer of Archbishop von Wied. Łaski was also in friendly contact with Swiss Reformers, and he had views on the eucharist diametrically opposed to Luther—the sort of views which Cranmer was about to develop for himself in England. This cosmopolitan Pole's remarkable career is a symbol of how effortlessly the non-Lutheran Reformation crossed cultural and linguistic boundaries. It is arguable that by the end of his life in 1560, he had become more influential in the geographical spread of Reformed Protestantism than John Calvin. The two men were in any case never soul-mates.[19]

In 1547 Henry's Reformation was swept away when his little son Edward inherited the throne. Edward became the figure-head for an evangelical-minded clique of politicians both lay and clerical, including the now veteran evangelical Archbishop Cranmer. This clique began accelerating religious changes, against the background of a shift in theological stance among the English evangelical leadership. Around the time of the old king's death in 1547, Archbishop Cranmer became convinced that Luther was wrong in affirming eucharistic real presence. One might cynically call this a convenient moment to change his convictions, but we should never underestimate the psychological effect of suddenly being released from the hypnotic power of Henry's extraordinary personality. So after 1547, on both images and the eucharist, the two greatest points of distinction between Lutheran and non-Lutheran Protestants, those in charge of England's religious destiny made a decisive break with Wittenberg.

The king's death also preceded a military and political crisis in mainland Europe. In 1547 the Emperor Charles V defeated leading Protestant German

[18] H. E. Jannsen, *Gräfin Anna von Ostfriesland: eine Hochadelige Frau der Späten Reformationszeit (1540/42–1575)* (Münster, 1998).
[19] A. Pettegree, *Marian Protestantism: Six Studies* (Aldershot, 1996), pp. 80–4; C. Strohm (ed.), *Johannes à Lasco: Polnischer Baron, Humanist und europäischer Reformator* (Tübingen, 2000); C. Zwierlein, 'Der Reformierte Erasmianer a Lasco und die Herausbildung seiner Abendmahlslehre 1544–1552', in Strohm (ed.), *Johannes à Lasco: Polnischer Baron*, pp. 35–100.

princes in the Schmalkaldic Wars. England was suddenly poised to act as a refuge for prominent European Protestants, but not Lutherans, who generally either accepted the 'Interim' compromise imposed by the Emperor (making minimum concessions to Lutherans: permission for clerical marriage and communion in both kinds) or stayed and fought it (and each other) from comparatively safe refuges like Magdeburg. Accordingly from late 1547 Cranmer welcomed to England many overseas reformers displaced by the Catholic victories. The refugees whom he found most congenial were now non-Lutherans; indeed some of the most important were from the vanishing Reformation of Italy, which was for the most part now finding refuge in non-Lutheran strongholds, especially Zürich and Strassburg. Two refugees, the great Italian preacher Peter Martyr Vermigli and some time later the leader of the Strassburg Reformation Martin Bucer, were given the leading professorial chairs in Oxford and Cambridge respectively. In their wake came hundreds of lesser asylum-seekers.

With Strassburg no longer a reforming centre, the chief alternative was Zürich. English contacts with Zürich do not seem to have been close during the Protectorate of the duke of Somerset, but when his colleagues overthrew him in autumn 1549, the new regime included leaders of the Grey family, who had been prominent in the Zürich exchange visits of the 1530s. Bullinger became a good friend of the English Reformation, commending it as the best hope for convening a true General Council, and seeing it as a bulwark against Anabaptism: from 1550, he dedicated parts of his classic collection of sermons the *Decades* successively to King Edward and Henry Grey marquis of Dorset. Bullinger had already become a best-selling English author in the 1540s, although generally anonymously, because of English versions of his treatise on marriage sponsored by Miles Coverdale.[20] By contrast, John Calvin of Geneva had few close friends in Edwardian England, and Calvin kept an obstinate attachment to the fortunes of the duke of Somerset, a stance which embarrassed those who knew England better.[21] An England ruled by Lady Jane Grey would have been increasingly tied in with Zürich, and Geneva would not have enjoyed much benefit.

In 1550 came a significant step: the official foundation of a London 'Stranger Church' intended to embrace all refugees. Its superintendent—in effect, its bishop—was none other than Jan Łaski, who had eventually been forced out of East Friesland in the wake of the Interim. The English government was anxious to use his leadership skills to curb religious radicalism among the refugees, so they gave him a handsome salary and one of the largest churches in the city, Austin Friars. Łaski administered his congregation to show how

---

[20] C. Euler, 'Heinrich Bullinger, Marriage, and the English Reformation: *The Christen State of Matrimonye* in England, 1540–53', *Sixteenth Century Journal*, 34 (2003): 367–94.
[21] MacCulloch, *Tudor Church Militant*, pp. 173–4, 176.

England might gain a pure Reformed Church (this was clearly the intention of several leading English politicians).[22] So Edward's Reformation was marked both by its awareness of being part of international Protestantism, and by its now open move towards the Churches which were consciously not Lutheran—Churches which would soon come to be called Reformed. The English break with Lutheranism was destined to be permanent. At the very end of Edward's reign, the English government tried to entice Philipp Melanchthon from Wittenberg to succeed the late Martin Bucer as regius professor at Cambridge. Indeed they got to the point where they sent Melanchthon his travel expenses and had set a date for him to arrive, in late June 1553—but the young king's death intervened, and Melanchthon had enough warning that he could quietly drop the whole idea (what happened to the English money is not clear). But it is unlikely that Melanchthon would have brought a Lutheran future with him to England. It is more probable that Cambridge would have proved the escape-route from hardline Lutheranism which he sought for much of his career, and that he would have found a new home in Reformed Protestantism.[23]

Before this melancholy coda, Edward VI's short reign had created many of the institutions of the Church of England which survive to the present day. Cranmer was generally careful in orchestrating the pace of change, and his caution in creating his first version of a Prayer Book in 1549 had been justified when a major rebellion in western England in summer 1549 specifically targeted the religious revolution, specifically that first Prayer Book. Not just Catholics objected to the book: no one liked it. It was too full of traditional survivals for Protestants, and it was probably only ever intended to be a stopgap until Cranmer thought it safe to produce something more satisfactory.[24] Cranmer produced his second Prayer Book in 1552 in dialogue with Peter Martyr and Martin Bucer; the theology of the eucharist which its liturgy expressed was close to the major agreement on the eucharist which Zürich had clinched in 1549 with Calvin, what was later called the *Consensus Tigurinus*: formulae which Geneva and Zürich could interpret in their own ways, to express their different emphases within their common acceptance that Christ's presence in the eucharist was spiritual and not corporeal. The creation of the *Consensus* was a crucial moment in the European Reformation. It provided a rallying-point for non-Lutherans and also a point of attack for hardline Lutherans such as Joachim Westphal of Hamburg, thus making permanent the division between the Lutherans and the Reformed. When England aligned with the *Consensus Tigurinus*, it was clear that the English evangelical

---

[22] A. Pettegree, *Foreign Protestant Communities in Sixteenth Century London* (Oxford, 1986), chs. 2–4.
[23] MacCulloch, *Cranmer*, pp. 538–40.
[24] MacCulloch, *Cranmer*, pp. 461–2, 504–8. Contrast A. Jacobs, *The Book of Common Prayer: A Biography* (Princeton, NJ and Oxford, 2013), esp. pp. 50–2.

establishment was by now fully ready openly to reject consciously Lutheran stances in theology. It is significant that there had been no sermon on the eucharist among England's twelve Homilies issued in 1547; while the doctrines of justification and works were clearly and indeed classically set out in Reformation patterns, it was clearly too early to be making up eucharistic definitions. A eucharistic homily promised in 1547 was not delivered until Elizabeth's reign, and Archbishop Cranmer delayed publishing his own extensive treatise on the eucharist until 1550, when the *Consensus* had been safely agreed and published.

In 1552-3 Cranmer further presided over the formulation of a statement of doctrine (the Forty-Two Articles) and a complete draft revision of canon law. This revision was a remarkable witness to Cranmer's vision of England as leader of Reformation throughout Europe: Peter Martyr and Łaski were both active members of the working-party which drafted it—even though Łaski had often vocally disapproved of the slow pace at which England was implementing religious change. With this combination of authors, it is not surprising that the draft scheme of canon law was vocally hostile to Lutheran belief on the eucharist as well as to Roman Catholicism and to radical sectaries like Anabaptists.[25] The canon law reform is admittedly one of the great might-have-beens of English history. It was defeated in Parliament out of sheer spite, because the secular politicians in the regime had badly fallen out with leading Protestant clergy, who accused them of plundering the Church not for the sake of the Reformation but for themselves.[26] As a result, the carefully drafted scheme fell into oblivion—Elizabeth I never revived it when she restored Protestantism. In one of the great untidinesses of the Reformation, the Protestant church courts of England went on using the Pope's canon law. Crucially, the lost legislation had introduced procedures for divorce. Because those arrangements fell, the Church of England was left as the only Protestant Church in Europe not to make any provision for divorce—for no more elevated theological reasons than a politician's malice and Elizabethan inertia. This was the first respect in which the English Reformation diverged from the European-wide norm.

After the five-year ecclesiastical U-turn under Mary Tudor (1553–8), Elizabeth I's parliamentary settlement was a deliberate snapshot of King Edward VI's Church as it had been in doctrine and liturgy in autumn 1552.[27] That meant bringing back the 1552 Prayer Book, not the 1549 Book, which enjoyed

---

[25] G. Bray (ed.), *Tudor Church Reform: The Henrician Canons of 1535 and the Reformatio Legum Ecclesiasticarum* (Woodbridge, 2000), pp. 186–213.
[26] MacCulloch, *Cranmer*, pp. 531–5; J. F. Jackson, 'The *Reformatio Legum Ecclesiasticarum*: Politics, Society and Belief in Mid-Tudor England', DPhil thesis, University of Oxford, 2003, pp. 222–4.
[27] MacCulloch, *Cranmer*, pp. 620–1.

virtually no support from anyone, and which not even the queen attempted to revive.[28] The 1559 legislation made a number of small modifications in the 1552 Book and associated liturgical provisions. Traditionally in Anglican history, these were called concessions to Catholics. That is absurd. How would these little verbal and visual adjustments mollify Catholic-minded clergy and laity, whom the Settlement simultaneously deprived of the Latin mass, monasteries, chantries, shrines, gilds, and a compulsorily celibate priesthood? Clearly they did have a purpose and significance: the alterations were probably aimed at conciliating Lutheran Protestants either at home or abroad. At home, Elizabeth had no way of knowing the theological temperature of her Protestant subjects in 1559, while over the North Sea, the Lutheran rulers of northern Europe were watching anxiously to see whether the new English regime would be as offensively Reformed as the late government of Edward VI (the atmosphere is well-captured in the letters of 1559–61 between Zürich reformers and leading English returned exiles).[29] It was worthwhile for Elizabeth's government to throw Lutherans a few theological scraps, and the change also chimed with the queen's personal inclination to Lutheran views on eucharistic presence.

Nevertheless, the new Church of England was different in tone and style from the Edwardian Church. Edward's regime had wanted to lead militant international Protestantism in a forward-moving revolution. Many Edwardian leaders had gone into exile under Mary to parts of Europe where they saw such change in action, and they expected to carry on the good work now that God had given them the chance to come home. Elizabeth begged to differ. She took particular exception to returning exiles associated with Geneva: she excluded them from high office in the new Church, because she was furious with the Scots Edwardian activist and Genevan enthusiast John Knox—he had written the famously titled *First Blast of the Trumpet against the Monstrous Regiment of Women*, claiming that it was unnatural (monstrous) for a woman to rule. Knox had aimed it against Elizabeth's predecessor Mary; unfortunately the arguments applied to her as well.[30]

One accidental survival from Edward's interrupted Reformation, the retention of cathedrals, was particularly important in the unexpected developments

---

[28] Pace R. Bowers, 'The Chapel Royal, the First Edwardian Prayer Book, and Elizabeth's Settlement of Religion, 1559', *Historical Journal*, 43 (2000): 317–44. Contrast D. MacCulloch, Review of Heal, Felicity, *Reformation in Britain and Ireland*. H-Albion, H-Net Reviews. Sept. 2003, <http://www.h-net.org/reviews/showrev.php?id=8172>; C. Clegg, 'The 1559 Books of Common Prayer and the Elizabethan Reformation', *JEH*, 67 (2016): 94–121.

[29] H. Robinson (ed.), *The Zürich Letters*, 2 vols. (Cambridge, 1842–5); D. MacCulloch, 'Peter Martyr Vermigli and Thomas Cranmer', in E. Campi, F. A. James III, and P. Opitz (eds.), *Peter Martyr Vermigli: Humanism, Republicanism, Reformation* (Zürich, 2002), pp. 173–201 (pp. 199–200).

[30] Pettegree, *Marian Protestantism*, pp. 144–8, 197–9.

of the English Church in subsequent generations. Cathedrals were a hangover from King Henry's Reformation with no parallel anywhere else in Protestant Europe. Not even the more conservative Lutherans preserved the whole panoply of cathedral deans and chapters, minor canons, organs and choristers, and the rest of the life of the cathedral close as the English did. Most northern European Protestant cathedrals survived (where they survived at all) simply as big churches, sometimes retaining a rather vestigial chapter of canons in Lutheran territories. Why the English cathedrals were not dissolved like the monasteries is unclear, but it has a lot to do with the personal preferences of Queen Elizabeth. That made the Church of England unique in European Protestantism. Cathedrals made of Cranmer's Prayer Book something which he had not intended: it became the basis for a regular (ideally, daily) presentation of a liturgy in musical and ceremonial form.

Cathedrals were an ideological subversion of the Church of England as re-established in 1559. Otherwise it was Reformed Protestant in sympathy. If it was Catholic, it was Catholic in the same sense that John Calvin was Catholic, and up to the mid-seventeenth century it thought of itself as a part (although a slightly peculiar part) of the international Reformed Protestant family of Churches, alongside the Netherlands, Geneva, the Rhineland, Scotland, or Transylvania. It had long left Lutheranism behind. Lutherans had not helped their cause by some egregious examples of harassment of Protestant refugees from England in Mary's reign. For example, marked inhospitality had been shown in Scandinavia to members of Jan Łaski's Stranger Church in their second flight, and a little English exile congregation suffered expulsion from the town of Wesel in 1556 because of the exiles' Reformed eucharistic beliefs: in the latter case, Switzerland offered the twice-exiled English from Wesel a safe refuge at Aarau, thanks to the good offices of the government of Bern. The Elizabethan episcopal hierarchy, so many themselves Marian exiles, would not forget that Lutheran inhospitality.[31]

Once historians argued about whether there was a 'Calvinist consensus' in the Elizabethan Church.[32] That debate produced much fruitful thinking, but it was the wrong question to ask. John Calvin had virtually no effect on the Church of Edward VI: in no sense had it been Calvinist, although that description is still sometimes misleadingly found in textbooks. By 1558, however, times had changed. Certainly, Calvin emerged on the English scene as important, but we have to remember that he never became a Reformed pope. His influence was greatest in Protestant Churches created during the popular

---

[31] O. P. Grell, 'Exile and Tolerance', in O. P. Grell and B. Scribner (eds.), *Tolerance and Intolerance in the European Reformation* (Cambridge, 1996), pp. 164–81; H. Robinson (ed.), *Original Letters relative to the English Reformation*, 2 vols. (Cambridge, 1846–7), I, pp. 160–8.

[32] S. F. Hughes, 'The Problem of "Calvinism": English Theologies of Predestination c.1580–1630', in S. Wabuda and C. Litzenberger (eds.), *Belief and Practice in Reformation England* (Farnham, 1998), pp. 229–49.

upheavals of the 1560s—Scotland, France, the Netherlands—and also in the attempted Reformations by certain princes and civic corporations in Germany's 'Second Reformation' later in the century and into the seventeenth century. Even in such settings, the other great non-Lutheran Reformers were read and honoured. Everywhere there was nuance and eclecticism: a spectrum. Just as in England, right across Europe, Heinrich Bullinger, Peter Martyr, Jan Łaski, and also Luther's former colleague Philip Melanchthon had as much shaping effect as Calvin.

What was restored in England in 1559 was a Reformed Church which in Edward's time had been developed in dialogue with theologians of Strassburg and Zürich, not Geneva. The newly titled Supreme Governor presided rather uncomfortably over a frozen tableau of her half-brother's Church, with various remarkable exotic undercurrents permissible beneath her jealous but idiosyncratic gaze, such as the secretive Netherlands imported sect, the Family of Love, or discreetly heterodox refugees like the Spanish putative anti-Trinitarian Antonio del Corro.[33] More conventionally, a strong Zürich flavour continued in the upper reaches of the Church to an extent usually not fully appreciated today. By 1559 Strassburg was out of the picture, no longer a point of reference for Protestant Europe but an increasingly conventional part of the Lutheran world. Zürich by contrast stood firm in its theology, and its influence was now reinforced by its recent generous hospitality to a small group of exiled English clergy, many of whom now became bishops in Elizabeth's Church of England. Virtually all leading former exiles kept in close touch with Zürich. Interestingly some former exiles also chose to join the circus of English correspondence with Zürich even though they had never met the Zürich leadership: notably Edmund Grindal and Richard Cox. Grindal's and Cox's initiative makes all the more surprising the complete silence from Matthew Parker, the first Elizabethan archbishop of Canterbury. Parker was one of the clergy around the queen who had shared her experience of being a 'Nicodemite': though a Protestant, he had served a cure in Queen Mary's Church. Perhaps that made it more difficult for him to join those who had undergone the very different experience of exile in those testing years.[34] Zürich may also have felt the difficulty.

In the next few years, Bullinger and Gwalther's tensions with Geneva inevitably affected their attitude to disagreements developing in England, into which they found themselves being drawn by their former guests in exile. Friends of Zürich chosen as bishops gradually found themselves defending a static settlement in which they had little emotional investment (as we can see exemplified in Bishop Parkhurst's gleeful reaction to the destruction of the

---

[33] D. MacCulloch, 'The Latitude of the Church of England', in K. Fincham and P. Lake (eds.), *Religious Politics in Post-Reformation England* (Woodbridge, 2006), pp. 41–59.

[34] D. MacCulloch, *Silence: A Christian History* (2013), pp. 173–8.

silver crucifix in Elizabeth's Chapel Royal).³⁵ The approval or disapproval of Zürich was a valuable prize for those involved in conflicts about the pace of reform, and so increasingly Zürich came to be a touchstone for measuring the imperfectly Reformed Church of England. It was a two-way process: the warring factions in England sought support from an honest broker, and that role suited Zürich very well in its continuing efforts to maintain its position among Reformed Churches.

Broadly speaking, Bullinger and Gwalther acted in the Elizabethan disputes as they had done in earlier clashes about how quickly the English should make ecclesiastical changes, in King Edward's reign involving John Hooper, and during the Marian exile, the English congregation in Frankfurt: they recommended further reformation, but they did not press uniformity on another Church, and they supported those placed in positions of authority by the civil power.³⁶ They were annoyed and embarrassed when a consortium of bishops at the height of their clash with puritans in 1566 published an English translation of what the Zürich leadership had intended to remain private expressions of opinion to old friends. Yet they were even more annoyed when an angry young puritan, George Withers, visited Zürich with Beza's backing, and so misrepresented the situation in England that the Zürich leadership had written more strongly to their English friends than they later felt warranted.³⁷

Bullinger and Gwalther were all too conscious that this same young puritan had intervened in the dispute over Thomas Erastus's views on excommunication in the Palatinate which ultimately represented a defeat for Zürich's ecclesiology at the hands of Geneva.³⁸ When they met Withers, they met a variety of Reformed Protestant who rejected the model of ecclesiastical superintendency uniting such undoubtedly Reformed Churches as Zürich, England, Hungary, and Transylvania. Such people also rejected the model of close union between the authority of the civil magistrate and the administration and discipline of the Church, which in very different settings and with very different origins united England, Zürich, and the advocacy of Thomas Erastus in Heidelberg.³⁹ So when Bullinger and Gwalther encountered English

---

³⁵ Robinson, *Zürich Letters*, I, pp. 121, 128; R. A. Houlbrooke (ed.), *The Letter Book of John Parkhurst, Bishop of Norwich, compiled during the years 1571-5* (Norfolk Records Society, 43, 1975), p. 62.

³⁶ J. H. Primus, *The Vestments Controversy* (Kampen, 1960); H. Horie, 'The Influence of Continental Divines on the Making of the English Religious Settlement ca. 1547-1590: A Reassessment of Heinrich Bullinger's Contribution', PhD thesis, University of Cambridge, 1991, pp. 243-68.

³⁷ Robinson, *Zürich Letters*, I, p. 357: cf. p. 362.

³⁸ A. Mühling, *Heinrich Bullingers Europäische Kirchenpolitik* (Bern and Frankfurt am Main: Zürcher Beiträge zur Reformationsgeschichte 19, 2000), pp. 116-17.

³⁹ J. W. Baker, 'Erastianism in England: The Zürich Connection', in A. Schindler and H. Stickelberger (eds.), *Die Zürcher Reformation: Ausstrahlungen und Rückwirkungen* (Zürich,

puritans, they felt themselves drawn closer to the bishops of England, to whom they sent a steady stream of warm book dedications during the 1560s. And their ultimate seal of approval on England's polity in Church and state was Bullinger's vigorous riposte in 1571 to a papal bull excommunicating the queen; his text was put into an English translation within a few months of its arrival in England.[40]

Ultimately the issue inclining Bullinger and Gwalther to support the English bishops was more profound simply than considerations of ecclesiastical politics. Bullinger's natural conservatism as a leader of Reformation was sealed from the 1550s by his fraught dealings with anti-Trinitarian radicals in Eastern Europe, whom he saw as threatening all the Reformation's gains. In constructing their revisions of the Christology of the fourth and fifth centuries, these real radicals maintained that whatever was not taught specifically in Holy Scripture should be repudiated. Bullinger and Zürich steadily maintained the opposite principle, that that which cannot be shown to contradict Scripture may be retained even if it is not prescribed by Scripture.[41]

By contrast to Eastern Europe, few such anti-Trinitarians strayed to England. Instead, a different group on the English theological scene might be portrayed as raising an echo of Bullinger's foes in Hungary and Poland. The principle of the Eastern anti-Trinitarians could with a certain justice be represented as that of Elizabethan puritans on matters ranging from clerical dress to the office of a bishop. It was a very shrewd hit of Bishop Horne of Winchester when he wrote to Bullinger in 1573 that the English Church was in less danger from papists than from 'false brethren, who seem to be sliding into anabaptism', by which he meant puritans. That provoked one of Bullinger's last interventions in English ecclesiastical politics before his death in 1575: in his reply to Horne he expressed his disapproval of disruptive behaviour from those 'that will seem most evangelical', and he reminisced ruefully about the beginnings of Anabaptism in Zürich, back at the beginning of his long career in the 1520s.[42] Remarkably, Bullinger was now cast as defender of England's episcopal system, and in 1577 the preface to the first complete publication in English of his *Decades* converted the volumes into a main bulwark of

---

2001), pp. 327–49. NB: K. Rüetschi, 'Rudolf Gwalthers Kontakte zu Engländern und Schotten', in Schindler and Stickelberger (eds.), *Die Zürcher Reformation*, p. 368; Horie, 'Heinrich Bullinger's Contribution', p. 297.

[40] *RSTC* 4044, and see D. J. Keep, 'Bullinger's Defence of Queen Elizabeth', in U. Gäbler and E. Herkenrath (eds.), *Heinrich Bullinger 1504–1575: Gesammelte Aufsätze zum 400 Todestag, Bd. 2: Beziehungen und Wirkungen* (Zürich: Zürcher Beiträge zur Reformationsgeschichte 8, 1975), pp. 231–41.

[41] M. Taplin, *The Italian Reformers and the Zürich Church, c.1540–1620* (Aldershot, 2003), esp. p. 191.

[42] Robinson, *Zürich Letters*, I, p. 276; J. Ayre (ed.), *The Works of John Whitgift D.D.*, 3 vols. (Cambridge, 1851), III, pp. 496–7.

that defence.[43] With that enterprise, we are taken back to Magdalen College Oxford and Gwalther's visit to England in 1537, for the moving spirit in promoting the *Decades* was an anti-puritan colleague of Archbishop Whitgift on the episcopal bench, Thomas Cooper, by now bishop of Lincoln, who had been associated with Magdalen since 1531.[44]

The regular and officially promoted use of the *Decades* in England says something important about the official Elizabethan Church, which distinguished it from the later Arminianism which became part of the Church's identity in the next century. It was able to claim its Reformed Protestant identity because it drew on Bullinger as an alternative to Calvin and Beza. By canonizing the *Decades*, and getting their clergy to read this book as a statement of the Church of England's own theology, Cooper and Whitgift had still committed themselves to unmistakably Reformed Protestant theological positions: they maintained a moderate and nuanced predestinarianism, they considered that there was nothing normative or universal about the institution of episcopacy, they saw the leading role of the civil magistrate in the Church as a positive virtue, and they maintained a spiritual presence view of the eucharist within the broad latitude offered by the *Consensus Tigurinus*, firmly differentiated from confessional Lutheranism. The sort of sacramental theology espoused in Geneva was regarded as rather over-sacramentalist by most English divines (this was certainly the opinion of Samuel Ward, master of Sidney Sussex College, Cambridge).[45] The parallel canonization in English divinity of the English translation of the adopted Züricher Peter Martyr Vermigli's *Common Places* had the same effect.

What emerges from detailed scrutiny of the Elizabethan Church of England is that as late as 1600, it was marching to rhythms set in Zürich between the 1530s and 1550s, even though much of its theological life was increasingly set in different patterns decided by Churches and theologians with a greater allegiance to Geneva and its heirs. That element of the ambiguity of English divinity, a tension *within* the Reformed Protestant tradition, has largely been forgotten in English concentration on later party strife: the great fault-lines between Arminians and anti-Arminians, Restoration conformity and Dissent, and Evangelicals and Anglo-Catholics. Undoubtedly the English ecclesiastical future turned in other directions, set by Richard Hooker. But even in Hooker, that delicate subverter of the Reformed tradition, the theologian of the Elizabethan Church who most resonates with the idiosyncrasies and strong opinions of Queen Elizabeth I, there is generous quotation from Bullinger.

---

[43] Horie, 'Heinrich Bullinger's Contribution', pp. 302–66.
[44] A. B. Emden, *A Biographical Register of the University of Oxford A.D. 1501 to 1540* (Oxford, 1974), p. 135; MacCulloch, 'Heinrich Bullinger and the English-Speaking World', pp. 931–3.
[45] B. D. Spinks, *Two Faces of Elizabethan Anglican Theology: Sacraments and Salvation in the Thought of William Perkins and Richard Hooker* (Lanham, MD, 1999), p. 164.

Moreover, one can find emphases which Bullinger would have recognized and of which he would have approved: Hooker's emphatic affirmation of the place of the civil magistrate in the Church, his relativistic discussion of episcopacy and his maintenance of a Reformed view of the eucharist, still firmly distanced from Lutherans—even his turning away from Calvinistic harshness on predestination would not raise eyebrows in Bullinger's Zürich. The *Ecclesiastical Polity* was much more in the spirit of Bullinger's *Decades* than has often been realized; and that is a perspective on the English Reformation worth preserving.

SELECT BIBLIOGRAPHY

Collinson, P., 'The Fog in the Channel Clears: The Rediscovery of the Continental Dimension to the British Reformations', *Proceedings of the British Academy*, 164 (2010): xxvii–xxxvii.

Heal, F., *Reformation in Britain and Ireland* (Oxford, 2003).

MacCulloch, D., 'The Myth of the English Reformation', *Journal of British Studies*, 30 (1991): 1–19.

MacCulloch, D., *Thomas Cranmer: A Life* (New Haven, CT, 1996).

Pettegree, A., 'The Reception of Calvinism in Britain', in W. H. Neuser and B. G. Armstrong (eds.), *Calvinus Sincerioris Religionis Vindex: Calvin as Protector of the Purer Religion* (Sixteenth-Century Essays and Studies 36, Kirksville, 1997), pp. 267–89.

Trueman, C., *Luther's Legacy: Salvation and English Reformers 1525–1556* (Oxford, 1994).

Tyacke, N., *Anti-Calvinists: The Rise of English Arminianism c.1590–1640* (Oxford, 1987) [see especially introduction to paperback edn., 1990].

Wendebourg, D. (ed.), *Sister Reformations/Schwesterreformationen* (Tübingen, 2010) [see especially D. Wendebourg, 'The German Reformers and England', pp. 94–132].

18

Attitudes towards the Protestant and Catholic Churches

Anthony Milton

The idea that the Church of England occupies a *via media* has for centuries been deeply entrenched in the Anglican psyche. For many historians this *via media* is understood to have lain between Catholicism and Protestantism, with the Church of England playing a mediating role between the two religions. Or at least it is seen as situating the English Church between the extremes of Rome and Geneva. This paradigm has embodied a number of assumptions— including that the English Church is equidistant from Rome and mainstream Protestantism, and that it has held continental Protestantism at arm's length. But for most of the first century of its existence this was certainly not how foreign Churches viewed the Church of England, or indeed how the Church of England viewed itself. If it inhabited a *via media* then this was (as some recent historians have suggested) one that was situated either (at its narrowest) between Lutheran Wittenberg and Calvinist Geneva or (at its widest) between Rome and Anabaptism.[1] Not only was the Church of England seen as unambiguously Protestant, but it was also seen as being ranged emphatically on the Reformed side of Protestantism's own divisions.

The Church of England's Protestant credentials were manifested—apparently unambiguously—in the inclusion of the Thirty-Nine Articles in that symbolic affirmation of Protestant unity, the *Harmony of Confessions*, published in Geneva and sponsored by John Calvin's successor Theodore Beza.[2] The Church of England's presence on the Reformed side of Protestantism that was taken as read by both Roman Catholic and Lutheran commentators was partly a function of its distance from the Lutherans over the doctrine of the eucharist.[3] But

---

[1] V. J. K. Brook, *A Life of Archbishop Parker* (Oxford, 1962), pp. 250, 344–5; D. D. Wallace, '*Via Media*? A Paradigm Shift', *Anglican and Episcopal History*, 72 (2003): 2–21 (pp. 2, 15).
[2] See also Chapter 11, 'Confessional Identity', in this volume.
[3] A. Milton, *Catholic and Reformed: The Roman and Protestant Churches in English Protestant Thought, 1600–1640* (Cambridge, 1995), pp. 383–4.

this also reflected a long history of positive personal contacts between prominent English divines and the foremost theologians of the continental Reformed Churches. These were evident at the time of the Marian exile, of course, but they were sustained by later correspondence and scholarly exchanges, as visitors, exiles, and students travelled to and fro.[4] By the 1580s the generation of exiles had passed on and this doubtless affected the intimacy of the relationship between the Church of England and foreign Reformed Churches to some extent, but the sense of a special relationship continued, partly encapsulated in charitable collections for Geneva (for which some £6,000 was collected in the 1580s when it was threatened by Catholic troops). In the 1590s, Archbishop Whitgift could still repeatedly address Beza as 'dear brother' with no sense of irony, and receive the dedication of a book by the French Calvinist and firm Presbyterian Lambert Daneau.[5] Another lasting symbol of the links forged by religious persecution was the presence of the so-called 'Stranger Churches' of Dutch and French Protestants in London and Norwich, whose assemblies were also frequented by native English Protestants, including two lord mayors of London. Moreover, the fact that ministers from continental Churches were not deemed to require reordination before serving in the Church of England was also a clear recognition of the validity of the orders of the foreign non-episcopal Churches in English eyes.[6]

These links were also evident in the translations of religious literature between England and the foreign Reformed Churches, most notably in the remarkable impact of English practical divinity. In the Netherlands there were 114 editions of sixty translations of works of English practical divinity published between 1598 and 1622, and a further 580 editions of 260 new translations in the rest of the seventeenth century, forming a decisive influence on the personnel and writings of the Dutch *nadere reformatie* (or 'second reformation').[7] *The Practice of Piety* of Lewis Bayly (later bishop of Bangor) went through at least 164 editions in no fewer than eleven languages.[8]

Theological influences worked both ways. Diarmaid MacCulloch has noted the particular influence in Elizabethan England of the Zürich theologian Heinrich Bullinger, whose works were officially promoted.[9] But as Elizabeth's reign continued, this influence paled before the extraordinary popularity of the

---

[4] C. M. Dent, *Protestant Reformers in Elizabethan Oxford* (Oxford, 1983), pp. 74–87.

[5] Milton, *Catholic and Reformed*, pp. 397–404; J. Strype, *The Life and Acts of John Whitgift*, 3 vols. (Oxford, 1821), II, pp. 167, 172, 173.

[6] O. P. Grell, *Dutch Calvinists in Early Stuart London* (Leiden, 1989), pp. 47–8; Milton, *Catholic and Reformed*, pp. 481–2.

[7] W. J. op 't Hof, *Engelse Pietistische Geschriften in het Nederlands, 1598-1622* (Rotterdam, 1987), pp. 626–7, 645.

[8] P. Benedict, *Christ's Churches Purely Reformed* (New Haven, CT, 2002), p. 319.

[9] D. MacCulloch, 'Sixteenth Century English Protestantism and the Continent', in D. Wendebourg (ed.), *Sister Reformations: The Reformation in Germany and in England* (Tübingen, 2010), pp. 7–9.

works of John Calvin. This influence is not merely evidence that English religion was not hermetically sealed from the continent: in fact, Genevan theological works were actually vastly *more* popular in England than in other Protestant countries, with ninety editions of Calvin's works and fifty-six of those of his successor Beza published in English by 1600.[10] But Geneva and Zürich were not the only sources of foreign Reformed influence: the Rhineland Palatinate and its Heidelberg Catechism can lay claim to an equally substantial impact upon English Protestantism. Oxford's Catechetical Statute of 1579 prescribed the Heidelberg Catechism (along with several others) as a set work to be used by all juniors in the university and those without degrees. The catechism was the only catechism to be printed in Oxford University, and the two editions of the catechism published in 1588 were printed with the arms of the university on the title page.[11] Just three years later the catechism was published by the king's printer in Edinburgh with the specific declaration on the title page that it was 'authorized by the Kinges Maiestie, for the use of Scotland'. Copies of the catechism continued to be published in England well into the Jacobean period, and there is evidence of its being used to catechize students in Cambridge well into the 1630s.[12] Another aspect of this formal approval of the Heidelberg Catechism was the enormous popularity of English translations of the commentaries upon the catechism by the Palatine divines Jeremias Bastingius and Zacharias Ursinus. While Bastingius's commentary was published in English translation three times in Cambridge between 1589 and 1595, the English translation of Ursinus's lectures on the catechism went through no fewer than six published editions at Oxford between 1587 and 1601, becoming effectively 'a standard Oxford textbook'. In fact, Ursinus's work went through more English editions between 1587 and 1643 than the English translation of Calvin's *Institutes* (and also through three editions of the Latin version) despite running to over a thousand pages in its quarto editions.[13]

The Church of England's links with the Rhineland Palatinate stretched back to the 1560s, but they were made particularly tangible by the marriage in 1613 of James I's daughter Elizabeth to Frederick, the Elector Palatine.[14] The German churchmen who accompanied Frederick to England forged enduring

---

[10] A. Pettegree, 'The Spread of Calvin's Thought', in D. McKim (ed.), *The Cambridge Companion to John Calvin* (Cambridge, 2006), pp. 210–11.

[11] Dent, *Protestant Reformers*, pp. 81, 87–93, 186–7.

[12] A. Milton, 'The Church of England and the Palatinate, 1566–1642', in P. Ha and P. Collinson (eds.), *The Reception of Continental Reformation in Britain* (Oxford, 2010), p. 140n8; I. Green, *The Christian's ABC: Catechisms and Catechizing in England c.1530–1740* (Oxford, 1996), pp. 199–200.

[13] Dent, *Protestant Reformers*, p. 186; Milton, 'Church of England and Palatinate', pp. 140–1.

[14] D. S. Gehring, *Anglo-German Relations and the Protestant Cause: Elizabethan Foreign Policy and Pan-Protestantism* (2013).

links with leading scholars at Oxford and Cambridge as well as court divines. There was also significant English input into the formal conversion of John Sigismund, the elector of Brandenburg, from Lutheranism to the Reformed faith in the year following the Palatine marriage. Divinity lectures by the archbishop of Canterbury George Abbot were republished in 1616 in Heidelberg by the Elector Palatine's chaplain Abraham Scultetus with a dedication to the Brandenburg court preacher Martin Füssel (who had presided over John Sigismund's conversion ceremony) in which Scultetus explained that these lectures specifically manifested the agreement of the Churches of Great Britain with the French, German, and other Reformed Churches.[15]

The English Church's links with German and Dutch Calvinism were encapsulated in the attendance of the delegation of British divines at the Synod of Dort, an international conference where the tenets of Calvinist orthodoxy were upheld against the theological innovations of the Dutch Arminians. Here was an apparently definitive manifestation of the Church's Reformed identity which has embarrassed most Anglican historians ever since. They have variously depicted the delegates as mere royal representatives, or as uncomfortable guests who sat apart from the other Reformed delegates, alienated by the stringent Calvinist doctrines being asserted, disgusted by the rough treatment meted out to the Arminians, and anxious to leave and to wash their hands of such an unfortunate and demeaning experience. In fact, however, for all their disagreements with some of the other delegations, there is nothing to suggest that the English delegates were uniquely 'moderate' in their behaviour, or that they disapproved of the dismissal of the Arminians, or that their subscription to the canons (which they were happy to defend subsequently) was anything less than sincere. And if they were technically royal appointees, it would nevertheless make a nonsense of the synod's proceedings to suggest that they were not regarded as *de facto* representatives and spokesmen of the Church of England. And far from losing an appetite for engaging with foreign Reformed divines, some of the delegates continued to play a mediating role in divisions among and within the Reformed Churches of the continent in the 1630s.[16]

A further reason why generations of Anglican historians have sought to dissociate their Church from the Synod of Dort takes us into one of the more delicate aspects of the Church of England's relationship with the Reformed Churches, and that relates to church government. There had always of course been a number of idiosyncratic aspects of the Church of England which did not cohere easily with some of the Reformed Churches, and the retention of episcopacy was an obvious sticking point. Small wonder that Anglicans have

---

[15] Milton, 'Church of England and Palatinate', pp. 146–55.
[16] A. Milton (ed.), *The British Delegation and the Synod of Dort (1618–19)* (Woodbridge, 2005), pp. xix–xxi, xxiv–xxvii, xxxvi–lxvii, l–lv.

looked askance at the spectacle of episcopalian clergy (a bishop among them) debating on equal terms with Presbyterian divines at Dort. It has been claimed that there were clashes over church government at the synod itself—indeed, recent ecumenical statements have also (erroneously) maintained this.[17] In reality, events at Dort, and more generally the rather delicate *modus vivendi* between the Reformed Churches and the Church of England over church government, were more complex.

The *Harmony of Confessions* had crept around the problem by appending a careful Presbyterian gloss to the exposition of the power of keys provided in John Jewel's *Apology*.[18] But relations were tested more directly in the 1590s, when more outspoken English defences of episcopacy began to take aim at the Genevan discipline being urged by English Presbyterians. Theodore Beza, Calvin's successor as patriarch of Geneva, complained to Archbishop Whitgift of attacks by authors including Matthew Sutcliffe, whom he dismissed in print as 'rather a peevish reproacher, than a Christian disputer'. Whitgift responded with a rebuke of his own, defending the writings of Sutcliffe and others and accusing Beza of having implicitly and even explicitly urged the reform of church government in England. Beza's defence was that he had not sought to obtrude the Genevan discipline on other Churches and had never criticized the Church of England directly (his strictures being directed only against tyrannical forms of episcopacy).[19] If this was ingenuous, it was nevertheless in everyone's interests to believe it. As long as episcopacy was defended simply as adiaphorous (as Whitgift himself had initially presented it), and foreign divines claimed that their defences of Presbyterianism were not intended to attack England's reformed episcopacy, then there was no obvious problem. Increasingly, however, the idea that episcopacy existed *iure divino* (by divine right)—first proposed by Sutcliffe and Hadrian Saravia (with Whitgift's backing)—became an unofficial orthodoxy in the Church of England. Foreign divines would seem to have been mercifully unaware of this development, to such an extent that the Heidelberg divine David Pareus in his *Irenicum* (1615) listed divine-right episcopacy as a Catholic error that Protestants were united in opposing. Rather than there being a direct clash over the issue of episcopal government at the Synod of Dort, the issue was in fact sidestepped in what was now a familiar fashion. The issue arose only because the assembly was called upon to endorse the articles of the Belgic Confession that defended the Presbyterian church structure. The English delegates publicly stated their rejection of the principle of ministerial parity, and were met by a tactful silence which (they commented) reflected either consent 'or at least approbation of our just and necessary performance of our bounden duty to that Church,

---

[17] Milton (ed.), *British Delegation*, p. xxxiii.
[18] *Harmonia Confessionum*, 'Observationes brevissimae', sig. çiiiv.
[19] Strype, *Whitgift*, II, pp. 105–6, 160–73; III, pp. 300–4.

whereunto they all afforded no small respect, though differing in government from their several Churches'.[20]

It was symbolic of the relative unimportance (in some eyes) of the issue of episcopacy for relations with the foreign Reformed Churches that Beza's bête noire the *iure divino* theorist Matthew Sutcliffe was an enthusiastic supporter of international Calvinism. He published one treatise in Heidelberg in 1606 and dedicated others to the States of Holland and the Prince of Orange, mounting defences of Dutch Calvinists in their controversies with Dutch Jesuits. He also spoke out in defence of 'that reverend Synode' of Dort in 1626 against those English Protestants who dared to attack its doctrinal orthodoxy, and emphasized that episcopacy had never been discussed there.[21] As long as blind eyes were politely turned, and implicit disagreements tiptoed around, a general sense of Reformed unity could be preserved. Medieval survivals in the English Church's liturgy, government, and canons could similarly be passed over with the assumption that they were merely adiaphorous.

There were two things that threatened this deliberate and tactful fraternal agreement to differ. One, as we have seen, was the fact that the foreign Churches were increasingly invoked as a model and exemplar by puritans to support their arguments for further reform of the Church of England. It was the need to combat internal critiques which prompted the first manifestations of a sense of critical distance from foreign Protestantism. Sutcliffe's works have already been mentioned, but still more vitriolic were the writings of the future archbishop Richard Bancroft, whose *Survey of the Pretended Holy Discipline* and *Dangerous Positions* mounted scathing attacks upon the Genevan Reformation. Richard Hooker ventured more ironic backhanded compliments to Calvin, saluting him as 'incomparably the wisest man that ever the French Church did enjoy, since the hour it enjoyed him'.[22] Increasingly, we can find expressed a sense that foreign Protestantism spread dangerous political and ecclesiastical ideas, even if it was the uncritical veneration and utilization of foreign divines by puritans that stirred concerns among the ecclesiastical authorities at this point, rather than the foreign Churches themselves.[23] Prominent conservative churchmen such as Bancroft, Sutcliffe, and Whitgift still drew a stark distinction between the unity that they continued to share with the foreign Reformed in matters of doctrine, and their differences in matters of discipline.

---

[20] David Pareus, *Irenicum* (Heidelberg, 1615), pp. 32, 37–8, 186; *A Joynt Attestation, Avowing that the Discipline of the Church of England was not Impeached at the Synode of Dort* (1626), pp. 8–11.

[21] Emmanuel College, Cambridge, MS II.2.10, nos. 2, 3; Matthew Sutcliffe, *De Indulgentiis et Iubileo* (Heidelberg, 1606); Matthew Sutcliffe, *A Briefe Censure upon an Appeale to Caesar* (1626), pp. 33–4.

[22] R. J. Bauckham, 'Richard Hooker and John Calvin: A Comment', *JEH*, 32 (1981): 29–33 (p. 32).

[23] Milton, *Catholic and Reformed*, pp. 431, 450.

The other threat to the Church of England's affable relations with the Reformed Churches lay not with over-enthusiastic English admirers of foreign Churches, but with those English Protestants who were no longer prepared to treat the Church of England's distinctive structures and ceremonies as merely 'things indifferent'. With the development of 'avant-garde conformity', divines such as Richard Hooker and Lancelot Andrewes sought to place a greater positive emphasis on ceremonies, and on precisely those elements of the Church of England that were most out of harmony with the foreign Protestant Churches. Ceremonies were no longer seen merely as adiaphorous but from Hooker onwards were presented by some divines as positively edifying. Episcopacy was increasingly presented, not just as *iure divino*, but as a separate order altogether that was vital to the very being of the Church, its succession not just an indication of orthodoxy but an indispensable means of conveying grace.[24] Doctrinally, too, things were in flux. Calvinist predestinarianism had constituted a doctrinal cement linking England's ecclesiastical hierarchy with the continent, reflected in the Lambeth Articles that Whitgift had formally approved in 1595, in the publication in translation in 1598 of the Heidelberg professor Jacobus Kimedoncius's *Of the Redemption of Mankind* and *Treatise of God's Predestination*, personally licensed by Bishop Bancroft of London and Bishop Vaughan of Chester (soon to be of London), and in the signatures of the British delegates on the canons of the Synod of Dort.[25] But by the 1620s, avant-garde conformist divines were challenging these same doctrines as 'fatal opinions' that undermined the Church's preaching and external ministry, dissociating themselves from the Lambeth Articles (which did not agree with 'the practice of piety and obedience to all government') and the canons of Dort ('a foreign synod...of such a Church as condemneth...[our] discipline and manner of government').[26] Indeed, these divines felt that the Church of England's integrity had been compromised by its involvement in the condemnation of the Arminians at the Synod of Dort (the idea that the British delegation had been distinctively moderate in its formulations and was alienated from the rest of the Synod was a later development).

At the heart of such attitudes was an increasing tendency among at least some divines to identify foreign Reformed religion as the enemy, and to see the Church of England's path as distinct from that pursued in other reformations. Now, there was nothing unusual in stressing ecclesiastical continuity, in rejecting the appellation 'Calvinist', in acknowledging the importance of the Fathers, and in seeing the Church of England as distinctive in the effectiveness of its moderate and orderly reformation. All these points were argued by

---

[24] Milton, *Catholic and Reformed*, pp. 463–74.
[25] N. Tyacke, *Anti-Calvinists: The Rise of English Arminianism c.1590–1640* (Oxford, 1987), p. 34 (but see sig. a2r).
[26] Tyacke, *Anti-Calvinists*, p. 267.

Bishop Joseph Hall, a firm defender of Dort and of the Church of England's foreign 'Sisters of the Reformation' who (he stressed) were not divided in doctrine at all and barely in discipline.[27] But in the hands of William Laud and his followers, there was more of a tendency to link these features to the Church of England in a newly exclusive way—and puritan attacks upon this trend only intensified the tendency. In the 1630s, Joseph Mede explained to the Polish exile Samuel Hartlib how there was a 'disposition in our Church' to maintain that:

> Our Church...goes upon differing Principles from the rest of the Reformed, and so steers her course by another Rule than they do. We look after the Form, Rites and Discipline of Antiquity, and endeavour to bring our own as near as we can to that Pattern. We suppose the Reformed Churches have departed farther therefrom than needed, and so we are not very solicitous to comply with them; yea, we are jealous of such of our own as we see over-zealously addicted to them, lest it be a sign they prefer them before their Mother.

He assumed Hartlib would have noted that this 'disposition' in the Church of England 'is of late very much increased'.[28] Mede's wording implied that he did not share the sentiment, but this was not strictly true. Mede was no mere Laudian—he had attacked the innovations of John Cosin and lamented that his own determination to identify the Pope as Antichrist and his apocalyptic speculations barred him from any preferment. But he was drawn to the Laudian 'beauty of holiness' in the 1630s and wrote qualified defences of its historical legitimacy, and combined this with an increasing sense that the English Church was distinct from the continent in its reverence for antiquity and its avoidance of the sacrileges of the continental Reformation. The fact that he expressed such opinions bears eloquent testimony to the growing strength of this idea among English Protestants. Similarly, the Book of Common Prayer was starting to find defenders who not only argued that it was legitimate, but presented it as flawless, the 'most absolute for perfection, of any that is used in the Churches reformed at this day'.[29] Not only was the Church of England's reformation thus being seen as more orderly than that of other Protestant Churches, but it was regarded as uniquely perfect. Moreover, the view that episcopacy was integral to the very being of the Church was casting increasing doubt on the validity of non-episcopal orders. English Protestants had habitually dealt with this problem by claiming that such orders might charitably be seen as extraordinary vocations on the grounds that the Reformed Churches had reluctantly been forced to abandon episcopacy by unavoidable necessity, but by the 1630s we can find Laudian writers showing increasing reluctance to weaken the case for episcopacy by allowing this point

---

[27] Joseph Hall, *Works*, ed. P. Wynter, 10 vols. (Oxford, 1863), VI, p. 610.
[28] *The Works of...Joseph Mede*, ed. John Worthington (1664), p. 1061.
[29] William Covell, *A Modest and Reasonable Examination* (1604), p. 179.

(which also rested on a very questionable reading of the history of the continental Reformations).[30]

A concern to avoid the excesses of Calvinism (especially in relation to the doctrine of predestination), an enhanced doctrine of episcopacy, and a preference for more elaborate church decoration could theoretically have led Laudian divines to embrace closer links with the Lutheran Churches. However, although Laud evinced a mild interest in John Dury's attempts to build closer links between the Church of England and the Swedish Church (and a Swedish bishop who had travelled in England would soon begin to draft a new Church Order which included substantial borrowings from the Book of Common Prayer), Laud's followers displayed little curiosity about continental anti-Calvinism at this stage.[31] Theirs was a disquiet with the instinctive association of the Church of England with the Reformed world, rather than a search for alternative ecclesiological alliances.

In the civil war of the 1640s, we might have expected a situation where more conservative royalists increasingly distanced themselves from a foreign Calvinism that might have seemed complicit with puritan resistance, while newly dominant puritans would have finally embraced foreign Reformed influence in a more systematic way. But things were not that straightforward; indeed, in some respects the opposite happened. On the parliamentarian side, despite some initial suggestions, the reform of the Church of England did not follow the example of the Synod of Dort, and delegates from the foreign Reformed Churches were not invited to take part in the Westminster Assembly. The Assembly did—on the instructions of the Commons—seek the explicit written support of the foreign Reformed Churches for its activities at one point, but with such lukewarm success that it would prompt the royalist civil lawyer Sir Edward Peirce to exclaim later in mock bafflement that the exchanges had been played down so much that 'it is scarce at all known whether there were ever any such thing or not'.[32] By contrast, the royalist side sought to emphasize their orthodox European Protestant credentials, and Charles I issued a declaration in 1644 in which he not only emphasized his own firm Protestant faith, but also emphasized that 'this most holy Religion of the Anglican Church' which he practised had been approved and applauded by the most eminent Dutch, German, French, Swiss, Danish, and Swedish Protestant authors. He also recalled the presence of an English bishop at the Synod of Dort.[33] In 1646, Charles told the French ambassador that he was prepared to propose the calling

---

[30] Milton, *Catholic and Reformed*, pp. 475–94.
[31] Milton, *Catholic and Reformed*, pp. 444–5; T. Harjunpaa, 'Liturgical Developments in Sweden and Finland in the Era of Lutheran Orthodoxy (1593-1700)', *Church History*, 37 (1968): 14–35 (pp. 27–31).
[32] Edward Peirce, *The English Episcopacy and Liturgy Asserted* (1660), p. 7.
[33] *His Majesties Declaration, Directed to all Persons of what Degree and Qualitie Soever, in the Christian World* (1644), sigs. A1v–A2r.

of a national synod with other divines 'as the English divines were at the Council of Dort, not excluding the like assistance of the divines of any other reformed churches, if it shall be thought fitt'.[34]

In fact, royalists had much to gain by denying that the Reformed religion had inspired the rebellion, especially after the intervention by the Genevan divine Jean Deodati—a man with close links to England who had been a delegate at the Synod of Dort, and whose annotations on the Bible (some 900 folio pages) had recently been published in translation by order of the House of Commons. Deodati's letter to the Westminster Assembly deplored the failure of earlier hopes for church reform and the desolation of what had been a flourishing Church, and urged both sides to seek unity through the work of a panel composed of the most discreet divines from both sides. This was a letter that Parliament did its best to hush up, but it came into the hands of royalists who not surprisingly made the most of it. It went through three editions in translation with royalist annotations in 1646 and 1647, and became a mainstay of royalist polemic right through to the Restoration and beyond. In fact, a significant strand of royalist thought continued through the 1650s to emphasize the distance of the foreign Reformed Churches from the actions of the English Presbyterians and Independents, and the chaplain to the English exiles in Paris, John Cosin, made a point of developing close fraternal links with the Huguenot pastors of Charenton, whom he saluted as 'very deserving and learned men, great lovers and honourers of our Church'. He prayed and sang psalms with them and heard their sermons, while in turn he baptized many of their children at the ministers' own request, conducted marriages for them, admitted two young Huguenots to English orders, and gave many of the Huguenots communion according to the Anglican rites, and explicitly approved of intercommunion.[35] For their part, Huguenots wrote positive defences for Charles II at the Restoration. Other royalist divines were equally happy to emphasize their continuing sense of identification with foreign Reformed divines. It is notable that when the royalist Thomas Fuller compiled in 1651 a collection of 'worthy Saints' who offered examples of upholding a good conscience in times of strife, 'a grace very worthy of our Imitation, especially in this Age', well over half of the lives were those of continental divines, including recent Palatine theologians such as Scultetus and Pareus, as well as Calvin and Beza (a list that Fuller was happy to take from the puritan Samuel Clarke's recent *Marrow of Ecclesiastical History*), but neither Richard Hooker nor John Donne was included.[36]

---

[34] *State Papers Collected by Edward, earl of Clarendon*, 3 vols. (Oxford, 1767–86), II, p. 210.

[35] John Cosin, *Works*, ed. J. Sansom, 5 vols. (Oxford, 1843–55), IV, pp. 397–8; Isaac Basire, *The Dead Mans Real Speech* (1673), p. 58; *ODNB*, 'Cosin, John (1595–1672)'.

[36] Thomas Fuller, *Abel Redevivus* (1651), sig. A3r; D. H. Woodward, 'Thomas Fuller, the Protestant Divines and Plagiary yet Speaking', *Transactions of the Cambridge Bibliographical Society*, 4 (1966): 201–24.

Other royalists were, however, more hostile towards the foreign Churches: for them, the association between the events of the 1640s and 1650s and Bancroft's earlier warnings of Calvinist republican and regicidal tendencies seemed all too obvious. Cosin had his strong critics among the other exiles in Paris who firmly opposed his links with Charenton. Peter Heylyn and Jeremy Stephens composed vitriolic attacks upon the conduct of the Calvinist Reformations and tied them directly to recent English events (although these works remained in manuscript for the moment). Even in these cases, however, these anti-Reformed sentiments were not leading their authors towards a simple Anglican *via media*: Heylyn at times was tempted to invoke an international anti-Calvinist movement in which the Church of England made common cause with Lutheranism, especially as manifested in the writings of Melanchthon who (it was claimed) had had a notable influence upon English Protestantism. Heylyn's fellow-controversialist Thomas Pierce argued the same point, and also emphasized the English Church's doctrinal common ground with the Dutch Arminians (pursuing a notable correspondence with Philip van Limborch).[37]

Meanwhile, the post-regicidal regimes had provoked a very troubled response among continental Protestants, and for a while England was *persona non grata* in international Protestant circles. Nevertheless, as the protectoral regime became entrenched, gradually some stability in relations was restored. The government's desire to re-establish links with foreign Protestantism was symbolized by its support for the indefatigable professional irenicist John Dury, who began his travels with Cromwell's explicit backing, although this was initially a mixed blessing. However, the Waldensian crisis of 1655 (when troops of the Duke of Savoy massacred Piedmontese Protestants, sparking outrage throughout the continent) witnessed more significant re-engagement of the English with Reformed Europe in the shape of charitable collections and diplomatic pressure.[38] Unsurprisingly, English Presbyterians still preserved links with the foreign Churches, and in the months preceding the Restoration they were suspected of aiming at the calling of an international synod with the assistance of foreign divines, and of trying to gain the Dutch Presbyterians onto their side when travelling over to The Hague to meet the king.[39]

As a counter to such plans, a scheme was launched to induce foreign Protestants to write in support of the restoration of bishops, and even of the Book of Common Prayer. George Morley (soon to be appointed bishop of Winchester) urged Sir Edward Hyde in May 1660 that it was very important 'to draw something from the Dutch and French Presbyterians, though it be an

---

[37] A. Milton, 'A Tale of Two Melanchthons: Melanchthon and English Protestantism 1560–1660', in A. J. Beck (ed.), *Melanchthon und die Reformierte Tradition* (Göttingen, 2016); Bibliotheek van de Universiteit van Amsterdam, MS M35a.

[38] J. M. Batten, *John Dury: Advocate of Christian Reunion* (Chicago, IL, 1944), pp. 143–74; Zürich Staatsarchiv, MS E.II. 457b; Zürich Zentralbibliothek, MS F.64, esp. fos. 45–9.

[39] R. S. Bosher, *The Making of the Restoration Settlement* (1951), pp. 128–9.

acknowledgement only of Episcopal government, which I think none of them will stick at, and that will be enough to oblige the Presbyterians in point of conscience to submit to it'. This built upon a collection of testimonials from Huguenot divines of the king's steadfastness in the Protestant religion, which had been published in early 1660, and letters from French divines in favour of episcopacy were published by the Jersey minister Jean Durel in 1662 (Durel was a good deal more successful in gaining foreign letters of support than the Westminster Assembly had been).[40]

This attempt to emphasize the Reformed credentials of the restored Church of England, however, ran into problems with the countervailing desire to maintain the purity of episcopal discipline, and most of all with the 1662 Act of Uniformity which decreed that foreign clergy must receive episcopal ordination and discipline. And when the Dutch 'Stranger Church' artfully sought to regain the autonomy that it had enjoyed under Edward VI by inviting the new bishop of London, Gilbert Sheldon, to act as their superintendent, it was rebuffed and placed under direct episcopal authority as before. Nevertheless, a readiness to explain away non-episcopal orders as the result of unavoidable necessity, and to turn a blind eye to Reformed doctrines and practices that were ostensibly incompatible with the Church of England, was still apparent in the Restoration Church. If the anomalies seemed more glaring than ever, the continuing sense of identity with the foreign Reformed Churches in the wake of the increasing international threat from Roman Catholicism remained deeply ingrained in English Protestant thinking.[41]

Often, English Protestants' view of the Church of England's relationship with the Reformed Churches was reflective of, or had a knock-on effect upon, their view of the Church of Rome. It should therefore come as no surprise that English Protestants' sense of their Church's relationship with Rome also underwent some notable developments during this period.

In the wake of the Marian persecutions, the Elizabethan and Jacobean Churches upheld a vigorous style of anti-Catholicism. Every Protestant archbishop of Canterbury from Cranmer until Archbishop Laud publicly maintained that the Pope was the Antichrist—a view that was also upheld in sermons, university disputations, Bible commentaries, and popular discourse.

---

[40] Bosher, *Restoration Settlement*, pp. 129–34; John Durel, *A View of the Government and Publick Worship of God in the Reformed Churches Beyond the Seas Wherein is Shewed their Conformity and Agreement with the Church of England, as it is Established by the Act of Uniformity* (1662).

[41] O. P. Grell, 'From Persecution to Integration: The Decline of the Anglo-Dutch Communities in England, 1648–1702', in O. P. Grell, J. Israel, and N. Tyacke (eds.), *From Persecution to Toleration: The Glorious Revolution and Religion in England* (Oxford, 1991), pp. 122–3; T. Claydon, 'The Church of England and the Churches of Europe, 1660–1714', in G. Tapsell (ed.), *The Later Stuart Church, 1660–1714* (Manchester, 2012), pp. 173–94.

This was not just a barometer of Protestant hostility, but had broader implications for the ways in which Rome's errors were viewed. Her idolatry and superstitions were not just deplorable errors, but were imbued with prophetic significance, and necessitated for Protestants a state of inevitable and permanent conflict with her. As Joseph Hall observed, 'Not only in the means and way, but in the end also, is Rome opposite to heaven... Rome [shall pass away] by destruction, not by change'.[42] Given such beliefs it followed that, if Catholic theologians occasionally offered more acceptable doctrinal readings this was evidence not of their laudable and encouraging moderation but merely of their dexterous duplicity; the 'true' Roman position was only to be found in the more extreme and objectionable formulations of other authors.

The Church of Rome and her religion were therefore often depicted as the antithesis of the values and doctrines of Protestantism and of the Church of England. Roman Catholicism was an anti-religion, its faith a form of heathenism, its doctrines a form of blasphemy, and the sin of idolatry the essence of her religion. The juxtaposition of Protestant 'truth' with the errors of Rome provided the indispensable framework for all doctrinal exposition in this period, not just in university disputations and controversial divinity, but in sermons, Bible commentaries, and popular religious literature. The Roman Catholic position was the erroneous extreme that helped to focus and structure people's exposition of English Protestant divinity.

As long as the forces of continental Roman Catholicism also posed a political threat to the crown this meant that, in addition, anti-Catholic writing and preaching were a principal means whereby puritans could present themselves as loyal defenders of Church and state (as well as providing a path to preferment for would-be bishops). Not only was this true under Elizabeth, but in the early years of James's reign it was further confirmed by the king's involvement in public religious controversy with foreign Roman Catholic divines in defence of his oath of allegiance (ostensibly a loyalty oath to be taken by Catholics in the wake of the Gunpowder Plot). Chelsea College was founded in 1610 by Matthew Sutcliffe with the king's explicit support and approval for the systematic production of religious controversy against Rome.

Nevertheless, attitudes towards Roman Catholicism were not necessarily as unthinkingly antagonistic as this might imply. Effective polemical attack could sometimes dictate the use of more subtle weaponry; after all, there was much to be gained by being able to portray oneself as more moderate and reasonable than one's opponent. Moreover, the presentation of Rome as a simple inversion of true religion was only one of the ways in which Protestants depicted that Church. There had always been ambiguities in the English Protestant engagement with Rome: opposition to Rome's claims to catholicity often

---

[42] Hall, *Works*, X, pp. 396–7; Joseph Hall, *Polemices Sacrae...Roma Irreconciabilis* (1611), pp. 189–90.

presented that Church as a branch laying claim to the root; Rome's sacraments and ordination were still recognized as valid, albeit gravely abused by superstitious accretions; and she was still seen as a Church in some sense, although a gravely erring one. The writings of theologians such as Robert Bellarmine often did not fit the crudely antithetical models of some anti-Catholic polemic, but could be cited to illustrate alleged Roman Catholic confusion, disunity, or sophistry. Claiming to have fled Babylon at the Reformation might appeal to many Protestants, but if by contrast they argued that they had been aggressively ejected by Rome rather than having left of their own accord (as King James put it: '*non fugimus sed fugamur*') this gave an air of injured innocence, victimhood, measured restraint, and legitimacy to Protestants' separation from Rome. Moreover, English Protestants were not hostile or allergic to all manifestations of Roman Catholicism. Roman Catholic systematic theology and scriptural exegesis were still prominent in the libraries of even hardline puritans, and Catholic devotional literature was also notably influential.[43]

While this ambiguous engagement with Rome tacitly underlay a good deal of the anti-Catholicism of the Elizabethan and early Stuart periods, some more serious reservations about the prevalent anti-Roman attitudes were also emerging. Already, there was a concern that violent anti-Catholicism could undermine the more tactically subtle defences of the Established Church that were being mounted in controversial divinity. Moreover, extreme anti-Catholicism was increasingly the weapon of choice for those attacking the Church of England itself. By the late sixteenth century, extreme puritan attacks upon the Established Church were generating increasing concerns that harsh anti-Catholicism potentially undermined the Church's own liturgy, and encouraged sacrilege. As puritan separatists justified their own rejection of the Church of England in the same language of justified separation as anti-Catholic polemic used against Rome, so the need to emphasize the orderly, measured, and legalistic aspects of the departure from Rome's communion seemed more acute. As puritans used charges of idolatry to condemn the ceremonies of the Church of England, so there was a counter-tendency among defenders of the Established Church to present Rome's errors as gross and sinful, but not necessarily as idolatrous. By the 1590s we can start to find English Protestant divines rejecting the exclusive identification of the Pope as the Antichrist, which freed them up to emphasize ecclesiastical continuity more wholeheartedly, and the preservation of elements of the medieval liturgy and ceremonial. All of these features can begin to be observed in various combinations among the so-called 'avant-garde conformist' divines of the

---

[43] A. Milton, 'A Qualified Intolerance: The Limits and Ambiguities of Early Stuart Anti-Catholicism', in A. Marotti (ed.), *Catholicism and Anti-Catholicism in Early Modern English Texts* (Basingstoke, 1999), pp. 91–5; *The Answere of Master Isaac Casaubon* (1612), p. 14.

final years of Elizabeth's reign.⁴⁴ But while anti-Catholic writing enjoyed a further boost of favour in the Jacobean period in the face of the oath of allegiance controversy and the king's own delight in polemical debate, royal patronage also embraced those offering this more tactically moderate reading of Rome's errors, especially as this gave implicit support for the king's pursuit of a Spanish Catholic marriage for his son Charles.⁴⁵ Indeed, as royal policy became increasing out of sync with the dictates of anti-Catholicism, so anti-popery came to be a weapon used to attack and criticize royal government rather than to defend it against its foreign enemies.

By the early 1620s, those Protestants who feared that extreme anti-Catholicism was undermining the integrity of the Church of England, and hindering the exploration of the 'beauty of holiness', were gaining increasing political importance, and the onset of Laudianism meant that vehement anti-Catholicism was increasingly seen as a Trojan horse for attacks upon the Established Church and its religion (or at least as a means of attacking the more elaborate ceremonialism that the Laudians themselves were promoting, and in this case they were at least partly correct to identify this danger). By the 1630s, inflammatory anti-Catholic views started to be deleted from books by Laudian licensers. For their part, Laudians tended not so much to condemn Catholic errors as heretical or idolatrous, but rather to criticize the fact that they were imposed as fundamental points of faith. Thus the doctrine of transubstantiation was condemned not as a spur to idolatry, but as an unnecessary imposing as an article of faith of a debatable reading of the mode of divine presence in the eucharist. There was an increasing tendency towards seeing the Pope's claims to universal jurisdiction as Rome's chief error.⁴⁶

None of this need be seen as representing positive thinking towards the current Roman Church as such—it was more a rejection of the constraints that severe anti-Catholicism had placed upon the exploration of non-Reformed doctrinal, liturgical, and ecclesiological options. Archbishop Laud himself was sufficiently aware of the danger that his reforms were being tarred with a pro-Catholic brush that he spoke out strongly against Roman Catholic conversions at court, and published a revised and expanded version of his *Conference with Fisher the Jesuit* in 1639 at the height of his unpopularity. He would leave £100 in his will to have the book translated and sent abroad 'that the Christian world may see and judge of my religion'.⁴⁷

What did Roman Catholics think of Laudianism? Traditionally, they had ranked the Church of England with the Calvinists. It is true that Romanist

---

⁴⁴ Milton, *Catholic and Reformed*, pp. 46–50, 110–12, 187–209, 310–20, 326–45.
⁴⁵ K. Fincham and P. Lake, 'The Ecclesiastical Policy of King James I', *Journal of British Studies*, 24 (1985): 169–207 (pp. 183–4, 198–205).
⁴⁶ Milton, *Catholic and Reformed*, ch. 4.
⁴⁷ William Laud, *Works*, ed. W. Scott and J. Bliss, 7 vols. (Oxford, 1847–60), IV, p. 449.

divines had displayed an increasing tendency to distinguish Hooker and the 'avant-garde conformists' from the more extreme anti-Catholicism of the 'puritans', and to suggest that the two sides upheld what were essentially different religions. But this was of course done merely to sow division among English Protestants and undermine the position of the Church of England—the intention was to argue either that puritans were further away from English Protestants than were Catholics (who therefore deserved formal religious toleration), or to suggest that such 'moderate' divines had effectively undermined the Protestant position and that the logic of their own arguments should impel them to return to Rome (along with their Church, of which they were the authentic spokesmen). But by the 1630s some Catholics became more aware of the liturgical innovations of the Laudians and were ready to praise their anti-puritanism and ceremonialism (albeit with the usual hope that this presaged a return to Rome).[48]

Catholics and Laudians did make some contacts, most notably in the shape of the informal discussions between the papal agent Gregorio Panzani and the Laudian bishop Richard Montagu about the possibility of reconciliation of the Church of England with Rome. They found themselves mostly in agreement, even if reunion would only have been possible if Rome had truly been as flexible as Montagu thought it was, and the Church of England as Catholic-leaning as Panzani thought it was.[49] Perhaps most remarkable was the reading of the Thirty-Nine Articles published at this time by the Franciscan convert Christopher Davenport (Franciscus a Sancta Clara). As we have seen, the inclusion of the articles in the *Harmony of Confessions* was emblematic of the Church of England's Protestant identity. But Sancta Clara instead sought to present the articles as compatible with the Tridentine Church, insisting that while their bare words might seem objectionable in Catholic eyes, yet 'the hidden sense ... [is] not very dissonant from the truth'.[50] Sancta Clara may have been unrepresentative in his irenical enthusiasm, but his work had a major impact at court and among elites, and was reportedly read by the king, Laud, and other divines (indeed, it was the writings of Laudian divines that often provided Sancta Clara with the evidence for his Catholic glosses on the Thirty-Nine Articles). This was also a time when Laudianism was problematizing the limits of what were deemed to be acceptable forms of doctrine and worship. If the bugbear of 'popery' was removed or redefined, then patristic ideas and practices could be embraced with fewer reservations. In some circles,

---

[48] C. Condren, 'The Creation of Richard Hooker's Public Authority: Rhetoric, Reputation and Reassessment', *Journal of Religious History*, 21 (1997): 35–59 (pp. 40–3); M. Questier, 'Arminianism, Catholicism, and Puritanism in England during the 1630s', *Historical Journal*, 49 (2006): 53–78.

[49] Milton, *Catholic and Reformed*, pp. 353–9.

[50] Franciscus a Sancta Clara, *Paraphrastica Expositio Articulorum Confessionis Anglicanae*, ed. and trans. F. G. Lee (1865), p. 116.

the 1630s were therefore a time of liturgical and devotional experimentation, where boundaries could be redrawn and even elements of the Counter-Reformation could creep in. The inventory made in 1644 of the nearly one thousand books kept by John Cosin at Peterhouse, Cambridge, includes no Reformed theology but instead a massive collection of saints' lives, and many works on Roman Catholic liturgy, ministry, canon law, and church government. It also shows evidence of a particular interest in the life and actions of Cardinal Borromeo: the inventory lists several relevant works, including a life of Borromeo, a copy of his provincial decrees, and two copies of that bible of Counter-Reformation churchmanship, the *Acta Ecclesiae Mediolanensis*.[51] As we have seen, his exile helped to draw Cosin closer to foreign Reformed Protestantism, but nevertheless Laudian Cambridge in the 1630s clearly witnessed a remarkable openness to the arts and writings of the Counter-Reformation.

The civil war and Interregnum complicated matters. While the king made determined efforts to recruit Catholic support against the Scottish Covenanters, and was willing to negotiate a deal with the Confederates in Ireland that would grant effective toleration of Catholics and of the Catholic episcopal hierarchy, it was also vital that the king emphasize his Protestant credentials against hostile parliamentarian propaganda, and on the scaffold and in his posthumous *Eikon Basilike* Charles's Protestant beliefs were resoundingly reaffirmed. For their part, while the majority of English Catholics were royalists (and indeed occupied a significant proportion of posts within the ranks of royalist officers), the Catholic hierarchy in Rome and notable Catholic thinkers such as the Blackloists, were not.[52] With the dismantling of some of the structures of the Church of England, there were a few high-profile conversions to Catholicism, including Hugh Cressy (a member of the Great Tew circle). As Cressy explained it, faced with the failure of 'that Church wherein I had been bred', 'I could not finde any [Protestant] Congregation, unto the Communion of which I could without hypocrisy adhere' and so began to rethink his aversion to Rome.[53] These new converts—Cressy, Vincent Canes, John Sergeant, Abraham Woodhead, and Thomas Tylden (alias Godden)—would become a dominant (if not always unifying) force in shaping English Catholicism's engagement with the Church of England in the Restoration period, embracing more tactically moderate and subtle critiques of the English Church, often around the rule of faith, and in some cases portraying Laudianism as a distinctive and praiseworthy development in English Protestantism.

---

[51] Peterhouse Library, Bibliotheca Box, 'The Catalogue of Doctor Cosens bookes'.

[52] P. R. Newman, 'Roman Catholic Royalists: Papist Commanders under Charles I and Charles II, 1642–1660', *Recusant History*, 15 (1981): 396–405; S. Tutino, 'The Catholic Church and the English Civil War: The Case of Thomas White', *JEH*, 58 (2007): 232–55.

[53] Serenus Cressy, *Exomologesis* (Paris, 1653), p. 57.

Despite this smattering of conversions, Catholicism did not make the major inroads among disenfranchised English episcopalian Protestants that it might have hoped for. Nevertheless, its attempts to do so did help to shape some trends in English Protestant apologetic. Thus, in the 1650s a series of Roman Catholic attacks focused on opposing the claims to catholicity of the 'failed' Church of England. These included the work of the French convert Théophile Brachet De La Milletière, who urged Charles II to atone for his Church's act of schism by converting to an irenic, conciliarist form of Roman Catholicism which would best preserve the peace of the Church and the integrity of episcopacy and the monarchy. If this failed to convince Charles II, nevertheless such arguments forced defenders of the English Church into more comprehensive affirmations of the catholicity of the episcopalian Church of England and of the non-schismatical nature of the Reformation—further reinforcing some of the trends in Laudian defences against Rome.[54] Again, these were non-apocalyptic readings of Roman Catholicism, de-emphasizing idolatry and doctrinal error and focusing in particular on issues of authority and jurisdiction. By contrast, there was relatively little sustained anti-Catholic writing among Presbyterian and Independent writers, whose polemical energies were expended more in internal disputes.

Generally, it seems that direct and sustained experience of foreign Catholicism among the English exiles mostly helped to clarify and refine their position against Rome, rather than weakening it. In the Restoration Church, while styles of anti-Catholicism varied, and divines may have considered themselves to be more distant from the Reformed Churches, there was no corresponding warmth towards Rome, especially in the face of Charles II's recurring readiness to contemplate toleration for Roman Catholics. Anti-Catholicism would come increasingly to be a mark of popular Toryism as well as of Whig propaganda.[55]

SELECT BIBLIOGRAPHY

Collinson, P., 'England and International Calvinism 1558–1640', in Menna Prestwich (ed.), *International Calvinism 1541–1715* (Oxford, 1985), pp. 197–223.
Dent, C. M., *Protestant Reformers in Elizabethan Oxford* (Oxford, 1983).
Fincham, K. and P. Lake, 'The Ecclesiastical Policy of King James I', *Journal of British Studies*, 24 (1985): 169–207.
Grell, O. P., *Dutch Calvinists in Early Stuart London* (Leiden, 1989).

---

[54] M. Williams, *The King's Irishmen: The Irish in the Exiled Court of Charles II, 1649–60* (Woodbridge, 2014), pp. 97–115; J. Spurr, *The Restoration Church of England 1646–1689* (New Haven, CT, 1991), pp. 115–19.

[55] T. Harris, *London Crowds in the Reign of Charles II* (Cambridge, 1987), pp. 139–44.

Milton, A. (ed.), *The British Delegation and the Synod of Dort (1618–19)* (Woodbridge, 2005).

Milton, A., *Catholic and Reformed: The Roman and Protestant Churches in English Protestant Thought, 1600–1640* (Cambridge, 1995).

Milton, A., 'The Church of England and the Palatinate, 1566–1642', in P. Ha and P. Collinson (eds.), *The Reception of Continental Reformation in Britain* (Oxford, 2010), pp. 137–66.

Questier, M., 'Arminianism, Catholicism, and Puritanism in England during the 1630s', *Historical Journal*, 49 (2006): 53–78.

Spurr, J., *The Restoration Church of England 1646–1689* (New Haven, CT, 1991).

Tyacke, N., *Anti-Calvinists: The Rise of English Arminianism c.1590–1640* (Oxford, 1987).

Williams, M., *The King's Irishmen: The Irish in the Exiled Court of Charles II, 1649–60* (Woodbridge, 2014).

19

'Puritans' and 'Anglicans' in the History of the Post-Reformation English Church

Peter Lake

As long ago as 1964, in a seminal essay on '"Godly Master Dering"', Patrick Collinson observed that 'what we call Puritanism at this time was nothing but authentic Protestantism'. He added that, contrary to the views of some Anglican interpreters of history, 'the reign of Elizabeth was not a conspicuously post-Reformation age... but the age of the English Reformation *par excellence,* when Protestantism was for the first time taking a strong hold on families of the country gentry and on the urban middle classes'.[1] Collinson saw Dering's career—and much of what subsequently became known as puritanism—as what happened when the core claims of English Protestantism (namely, justification by faith alone; the idolatrous, Antichristian nature of popery; the centrality of the word preached both to the process whereby people were converted from popery to true religion and to the subsequent life of faith) came into contact with the recalcitrantly unreformed structures of the English national Church.

Of course, the fact that those structures remained unreformed was contingent, a function of the refusal of the Elizabethan establishment (by which, to a remarkable extent, we must mean that of Queen Elizabeth herself) to countenance any further changes to the religious settlement of 1559. But there was more at stake here than royal recalcitrance. Historians of a revisionist stamp have emphasized the vitality of what Eamon Duffy termed 'traditional religion', the two-steps-forwards-one-step-back course of the English Reformations, and the indifference and hostility in the face of the 'new learning' expressed by many of the English 'people', or 'folk'.[2] Other scholars, simply

---

[1] 'A Mirror of Elizabethan Puritanism: The Life and Letters of "Godly Master Dering"', reprinted in his *Godly People: Essays on English Protestantism and Puritanism* (1983), pp. 289–323 (p. 292).

[2] Christopher Haigh (ed.), *The English Reformation Revised* (Cambridge, 1987); Christopher Haigh, *English Reformations* (Oxford, 1993); J. J. Scarisbrick, *The English Reformation and the*

answering A. G. Dickens's call to take Reformation studies into the local records, have revealed the paucity of the proselytizing resources at the disposal of the first generation of Elizabethan Protestants.[3] With its transfer of both landed wealth and ecclesiastical patronage to the laity and its consequent diminution of the secular power (and indeed spiritual charisma) of the clergy, the Reformation rendered it harder than ever for the clerical estate either to control its own affairs or to influence (still less, as Protestant ideology insisted that it should, transform) the wider society.

At the best of times, the national Church was not the most nimble of institutions. Its diocesan structures and parochial livings were manned, as often as not, by people who had either been ordained under 'popery', or had weathered the religious tergiversations of the mid-Tudor period by going along to get along. The church courts were presided over by laymen, ecclesiastical lawyers of almost uniformly conservative predilections, who (just like the beneficed clergy) in effect owned their offices and thus could not easily be ordered around (still less removed) even by the new breed of reforming bishops recruited, in large part, from the Marian exiles. And these reforming bishops, whatever their misgivings about the episcopal office they were now entering, saw it as their fundamental mission to preach the gospel, foster a godly preaching ministry, convert the people to true religion and thus face down 'popery'.[4]

The English reformed tradition that confronted these unpromising realities and constraints was itself not without its own internal tensions and contradictions.[5] Since Diarmaid MacCulloch's magisterial account of Cranmer relocated the founding father of 'Anglicanism' within genuinely international reformed strands of thought and feeling,[6] there has been a tendency to regard as normative that strand of moderate, magisterial, and (on certain views of the matter) Bucerian reform that linked Cranmer to Archbishop Edmund Grindal. But as Karl Gunther has argued, there were significant anti-prelatical, even anti-episcopal tendencies to be found in Tyndale and others, and many early reformers (like Hugh Latimer) emphasized the necessarily divisive effects

---

English People (Oxford, 1984); Eamon Duffy, *The Stripping of the Altars: Traditional Religion in England 1400–1580* (New Haven, CT, 1992).

[3] Felicity Heal and Rosemary O'Day (eds.), *Continuity and Change: Personnel and Administration of the Church of England 1500–1642* (Leicester, 1976); Felicity Heal and Rosemary O'Day (eds.), *Church and Society in England: Henry VIII to James I* (1977); Rosemary O'Day, *The English Clergy: The Emergence and Consolidation of a Profession 1558–1642* (Leicester, 1979); Felicity Heal, *Of Prelates and Princes: A Study of the Economic and Social Position of the Tudor Episcopate* (Cambridge, 1980).

[4] Rosemary O'Day, 'Thomas Bentham: A Case Study in the Problems of the Early Elizabethan Episcopate', *JEH*, 92 (1977): 137–59.

[5] Karl Gunther, *Reformation Unbound: Protestant Visions of Reform in England, 1525–1590* (Cambridge, 2014).

[6] Diarmaid MacCulloch, *Thomas Cranmer: A Life* (New Haven, CT, 1996).

of true religion and used the doctrine of 'things indifferent' to emphasize not the peace and unity that must come from obedience to the Christian prince, but rather the obligations on all true believers neither to offend the godly nor to confirm papists or false believers in their errors.[7]

Thus, under Edward VI, far from experiencing the progress of reform and the 'triumph' of Protestantism (at least at the level of theory and officially sanctioned practice) as some sort of vindication, committed Protestants tended to view the crepuscular pace of real change amongst the people, and the self-serving behaviour of the elite, as invitations to divine judgement. Consequently, they continued to regard the inner core of true believers created by the spread of the gospel at least as much as 'a persecuted little flock of Christ' as the avatars of incipient Protestant triumph. Thus when, under Mary, idolatry was reimposed and that core minority of true believers started to suffer various sorts of persecution and even martyrdom, many Protestants saw these developments as confirmation of all the jeremiads launched over the years at the variously sinful, indifferent, or hostile responses that the gospel had elicited from the English.[8]

The resulting tensions were compounded by the experience of persecution and exile, combined with the willingness of many erstwhile Protestants to keep their heads down in the face of Marian persecution. This latter response came to be known as Nicodemism—a pejorative term for the sort of minimal (and entirely formal) conformism that might allow a professor to keep his or her profession of true religion alive on the inside, while doing enough on the outside to stave off the attentions of a hostile or persecuting regime.[9] These tensions were transferred into the early Elizabethan period, since while the Elizabethan Church settlement was designed to restore the public face and unequivocally Protestant profession of the Edwardian Church—the outward face of a commonwealth of Christians—it was also devised and presided over by a triumvirate of Nicodemites. The queen herself, William Cecil, and Archbishop Parker had all stayed in England under Mary and performed various degrees of conformity to the Catholic faith in so doing (it was of course, no accident that, on reaching the end of his tether in 1570, it was to these three central figures that Dering directed his excoriating rebukes about the current condition of the English Church). Not only that, but the settlement itself was administered in a distinctly Nicodemite spirit. Scarcely draconian in its dictates, the law turned out to be even laxer in its application, requiring

---

[7] Gunther, *Reformation Unbound*, ch. 2.

[8] Catharine Davies, '"Poor persecuted little flock" or "Commonwealth of Christians": Edwardian Protestant Concepts of the Church', in Peter Lake and Maria Dowling (eds.), *Protestantism and the National Church in Sixteenth Century England* (1987), pp. 78–102; Catharine Davies, *A Religion of the Word: The Defence of the Reformation in the Reign of Edward VI* (Manchester, 2002).

[9] Gunther, *Reformation Unbound*, ch. 3.

nothing more even of the queen's Catholic subjects than a certain minimal attendance at, and an even more minimal conformity to, the rites and ordinances of the national Church. Certainly, none of this constituted the sort of spiritual discipline that was necessary (in the eyes of hot Protestants) if the saving truths of right religion were to be brought to the mass of the population and England transformed into a truly Christian commonwealth.

Thus at the start of Elizabeth's reign committed Protestants viewed the settlement, much as Cranmer had viewed the Book of Common Prayer itself, not as the last word in religious change—the foundational document of a changeless Anglicanism—but rather as the best that could be achieved under the circumstances and thus as but the opening move in what was expected to be a continuing campaign of further reformation.[10] At least in 1563, the consensus behind further reform had encompassed Archbishop Parker himself, but soon thereafter that consensus started to break down in the face of the queen's increasingly authoritarian insistence on conformity to every jot and tittle of the 1559 settlement.[11]

The story of how the passions aroused, particularly in London and Cambridge University, by the so-called Vestiarian controversy produced the first stirrings of a puritan movement organized around a Presbyterian vision of the national Church—a movement pursued both at the level of formal academic disputation and of more popular pamphleteering and agitation—has been well told by Patrick Collinson and others. Here, we might think, was the point at which the internal contradictions within English Protestantism, between the vision of the Church as 'poor persecuted little flock' and a 'commonwealth of Christians', finally broke apart and the real nature of the divisions between a sect-type puritanism and church-type Anglicanism really started to show. But that was not the case.

THE FOXEIAN SYNTHESIS

To understand why, we need only turn to the career of John Foxe, and of his magnum opus, the *Actes and Monuments*. Foxe's great book was dedicated to a vision of the true Church centred on communities of true believers, often humble laypersons and dissident clerics, who were consistently subject to the persecutory attentions of the great powers of this world, of prelates, popes, and princes, who almost always found themselves fighting on the side of Antichrist

---

[10] MacCulloch, *Cranmer*, pp. 615–18.
[11] David Crankshaw, 'Preparations for the Canterbury Provincial Convocation of 1562–63: A Question of Attribution', in Susan Wabuda and Caroline Litzenberger (eds.), *Belief and Practice in Reformation England* (Aldershot, 1989), pp. 60–93.

in his campaign against the little persecuted flock of Christ.[12] Culminating in its famous account of the Marian persecution, Foxe's narrative was intended to defend a national Church, with a secular prince at its head, run by bishops who looked rather more like lordly prelates than preaching pastors. This created certain tensions between Foxe's vision of the true Church and the current structures and claims to unity and uniformity of the Elizabethan national Church. Thus Patrick Collinson has pointed to the stark contrast between what he terms 'the congregational' elements in Foxe's work and other passages in which, as Collinson puts it, Foxe sounds just like Richard Hooker.[13] Even when, on the subject of the royal supremacy and Elizabeth's status as a new Constantine, Foxe seems at his most laudatory, he can also be detected subtly altering his materials between editions, mobilizing apparent praise in order to criticize and counsel the queen to embrace his own vision of further reformation and of the Church as a proselytizing machine designed to defeat popery, convert the ungodly, and to sustain the godly.[14] His elastic notion of 'episcopacy' enabled Foxe to describe Rowland Taylor, the martyred minister of Hadleigh in Suffolk, whom he somewhat optimistically presented as the model 'reformed pastor',[15] as a 'true bishop' on the Pauline model.[16] This was a vision of what episcopacy could mean and what bishops should be that recalls the schemes for modified episcopacy canvassed in the early Elizabethan period, not to mention Lord Burghley's commendation of the situation in Denmark, where a large number of bishops lived, not as heavily endowed lordly prelates, but as state-salaried pastors.[17]

Foxe enjoyed a decidedly ambiguous relation to the Elizabethan ecclesiastical establishment. He never allowed himself to take a fixed parochial cure and retained an intense dislike for the ceremonies imposed by the Church on its clergy. But he retained very close ties to William Cecil, Lord Burghley, and Burghley's two clients, Thomas Norton and the printer John Day, ties which not only enabled the production of the *Actes and Monuments* in the first place, but also conferred on that text, with all its ambiguities and subtle shifts of emphasis and inflection, the status of pseudo-official propaganda. Foxe's close

---

[12] Jane Facey, 'John Foxe and the Defence of the English Church', in Lake and Dowling (eds.), *Protestantism*, pp. 162–92; Patrick Collinson, 'John Foxe and National Consciousness', reprinted in his *This England: Essays on the English Nation and Commonwealth in the Sixteenth Century* (Manchester, 2011), pp. 193–215.

[13] Collinson, 'John Foxe and National Consciousness', p. 205.

[14] Thomas Freeman, 'Providence and Prescription: The Account of Elizabeth in Foxe's "Book of Martyrs"', in Susan Doran and Thomas Freeman (eds.), *The Myth of Elizabeth* (Basingstoke, 2003), pp. 27–55.

[15] John Craig, 'Reformers, Conflict and Revisionism: The Reformation in Sixteenth Century Hadleigh', *Historical Journal*, 42 (1999): 1–23 (p. 13).

[16] John N. King (ed.), *Foxe's Book of Martyrs: Select Narratives* (Oxford, 2009), p. 73.

[17] Patrick Collinson, 'Episcopacy and Reform in England in the Later Sixteenth Century', reprinted in his *Godly People*, pp. 154–89; Heal, *Prelates*, p. 207.

collaboration with Norton in a move to have Parliament legally confirm the *Reformatio Legum Ecclesiasticarum* and revise the Prayer Book reveals his practical commitment to further reformation of a moderate puritan stamp, as do his later attempts to mitigate the disputes over conformity sparked by Whitgift's Three Articles in 1583/4.[18]

For all its areas of actual or potential contradiction and instability, the Foxeian synthesis thus represents a sustained attempt to maintain an evangelical Protestant, reformed vision of the national Church, with the community of the godly at its heart. As such it has a claim to represent the hegemonic, evangelical Protestant, even 'moderate puritan', vision of the early and high Elizabethan Church, a vision fundamentally challenged by the advent of Presbyterianism and the subsequent debate between the proponents of the discipline and their hardline conformist opponents.

Foxe, of course, deeply disapproved of the young firebrands of the Presbyterian movement, but they too, just like Foxe himself, enjoyed very close ties to some of the leading lights of the lay establishment. Burghley, Francis Walsingham, the earl of Leicester, and Sir Henry Mildmay all had close ties to leading Presbyterian divines like Thomas Cartwright, John Field, Laurence Chaderton, and Walter Travers. This, of course, does not make them supporters of Presbyterianism per se, but it does mean that despite both their own rather different views of church polity, and the unstinting efforts of various conformist ideologues to portray Presbyterianism as the quintessence of sedition, disaffection, and disobedience, these pillars of the lay establishment all continued to regard even their most notoriously Presbyterian clients as godly learned divines, of very considerable value to the Elizabethan state in its great confrontation with Antichrist and the threat represented by both international and domestic Catholicism.[19] And, of course, it was no accident that, from William Fulke through Cartwright to William Whitaker, Andrew Willet, and William Perkins, it was puritan divines, both radical and moderate, Presbyterian and conforming, who were at the forefront of the defence of the English Church from popery; a position which, of course, allowed them to construe the position of that Church according to their own doctrinal commitments and preferences, as Richard Montagu was to lament in 1624.

---

[18] Elizabeth Evenden and Thomas Freeman, 'Print, Profit and Propaganda: The Elizabethan Privy Council and the 1570 Edition of Foxe's "Book of Martyrs"', *English Historical Review*, 119 (2004): 1288–307; Catharine Davies and Jane Facey, 'A Reformation Dilemma: John Foxe and the Problem of Discipline', *JEH*, 39 (1988): 37–65.

[19] Simon Adams, 'A Godly Peer? Leicester and the Puritans', in his *Leicester and the Court: Essays on Elizabethan Politics* (Manchester, 2002), pp. 151–75.

PRESBYTERIANISM, THE NATIONAL CHURCH, AND THE 'MONARCHICAL REPUBLIC OF ELIZABETH I'

It is, therefore, important not to take the characterization of Presbyterianism produced by the clerical defenders of the status quo simply at face value. What they portrayed as a subversive assault on the basic structures of Church and state, the first step on a slippery slope that led inexorably to schism and sectarian excess, was intended by the proponents of the discipline as no such thing. For them, Presbyterianism represented not a repudiation of the national Church, but rather an attempt to take it over for their own urgently evangelical and disciplinary purposes. For them the discipline represented the final coping stone of the arch of reformation, the foundations of which had been laid by Henry VIII in the 1530s. Here was the final extension, to the realm of church government, of the same scripturalist impulse that had already conferred on the Church of England right doctrine and the pure administration of the sacraments.

Moreover, since the discipline was the form of church government intended by God for His Church, its (re)institution in Elizabethan England represented the keeping of Protestant England's covenant with its God, and as such a guarantee of continuing divine favour, and even of final victory over the forces of sin, superstition, and popery. To hear Laurence Chaderton tell it, the discipline was not only the best way to convert the population to true religion, it was the ultimate surveillance system; an almost fool-proof way to control sin, detect and confute religious error and superstition, unmask popery, and defeat seditious plots against the crown and the gospel.[20]

The Presbyterian platform addressed the long-term tension, inherent in the English reformed tradition, between the godly minority and the variously unconverted, crypto-popish, superstitious, profane, or indifferently lukewarm mass of the population by creating an institutional mechanism whereby the former could be given power over the latter. It was the visibly godly who would provide the active membership of the Church, the deacons and elders who would help elect the ministers and aid them in the exercise, over their fellow Christians, of a tightly focused spiritual discipline.

While in theory they held that the governing structures of Church and state were independent and distinct, the one precisely *not* having to mirror or model the other, in practice, the Presbyterians held that the government of the Church and that of Elizabethan England were both mixed monarchies. In

---

[20] Peter Lake, *Anglicans and Puritans? Presbyterianism and English Conformist Thought from Whitgift to Hooker* (1988), chs. 1 and 2; Peter Lake, *Moderate Puritans and the Elizabethan Church* (Cambridge, 1982), pp. 25–35; Peter Lake, 'Presbyterianism, the Idea of a National Church and the Argument from Divine Right', in Lake and Dowling (eds.), *Protestantism*, pp. 193–224.

the Church, the monarchical element was provided by Christ himself. Presbyterians conceived of his role as the head of his mystical body, the Church, being actualized through the workings of the discipline, which was itself also often conceptualized as another version of Christ's body. Through the application to the workings of the discipline of the organic, corporeal, and corporate imagery which the Elizabethans habitually used to address issues of order in Church and commonwealth, the Presbyterians were able to argue that only through the institution of the Presbyterian platform could Christ be truly established in his tripartite role as prophet, priest, *and* king.

As for the aristocratic element, this was provided by the elders and ministers and the democratic element by the people. In the state, the monarchical element proceeded, of course, from the queen, the aristocratic from the Council, and the democratic from the Parliament. In this Thomas Cartwright's vision of the Elizabethan state coincided perfectly with that of William Cecil, and many another of Professor Collinson's 'monarchical republicans', albeit not with that of either Queen Elizabeth or Archbishop Whitgift who continued to view England not as any sort of mixed or elective monarchy, but rather as, in James I's famous phrase, a 'free' and hereditary monarchy.[21] This happy coincidence allowed the Presbyterians to argue that, *contra* the claims of their conformist opponents, there could and would be no clash between the workings of monarchical authority in the state and the operation of the discipline in the Church, and explains why at least some of the Elizabethan establishment appears to have agreed with them.

This was not the only way that Presbyterianism mirrored the lineaments of the 'monarchical republic.' At moments of political crisis, spooked by their incapacity either to apprehend where the religio-political loyalties of the mass of the population lay or to identify the core groups of really reliable supporters who would enable the Protestant state to survive the death of the queen with Mary Stuart still above ground, the circles around Burghley produced a number of devices to enable the state to do precisely that. These culminated in the Bond of Association, and the interregnum scheme (designed by Burghley and his kitchen cabinet to recall the previous Parliament and thus to manage the succession should the queen die suddenly) that followed it. However, even after the failure of the interregnum project, Thomas Digges, for one, persisted in thinking up ways to identify both the regime's core supporters, and its most dangerous Catholic enemies, while squeezing the soggy middle between the good offices of the godly magistrate and minister.[22] But these, of course, were

---

[21] Patrick Collinson, 'The Monarchical Republic of Queen Elizabeth I', reprinted in his *Elizabethan Essays* (1994), pp. 31–57; Patrick Collinson, 'The Elizabethan Exclusion Crisis and the Elizabethan Polity', reprinted in his *This England*, pp. 61–97.

[22] Thomas Digges, *Humble Motives for Association to Maintaine Religion Established* (1601).

all outcomes that Chaderton had proclaimed that the Presbyterian platform would achieve at a stroke.

Viewed in this light, therefore, Presbyterianism emerges as a comprehensive vision of a fully reformed national Church, a properly Christian commonwealth. As such, it had at least as good a claim as any of the positions canvassed by the conformist opponents of the discipline, not only to realize the full implications and potentials of the English Protestant tradition, but also to deliver political ends and effects long desired by central elements in the Elizabethan regime. Presbyterianism thus deserves a rather more central place within the history of the English national Church than it is often accorded. Certainly, its return in the 1640s as the only viable version of a genuinely reformed and national Church on offer deserves to be analysed as something more than a merely contingent effect of a preternaturally high level of Scottish involvement in English affairs.[23]

EDIFICATION AND ITS DISCONTENTS, OR THE CONFORMIST DEFENCE OF THE NATIONAL CHURCH AND THE PROTESTANT IMPULSE

At stake here is the pervasive assumption that, being 'Anglican', the national Church was necessarily, and must always remain, in its very essence, an episcopal Church. But that was by no means obvious or inevitable at this point in its history. Even as late as the 1590s, Whitgift opined that, unlike the stalwart Bancroft, some of those recently preferred to bishoprics and deaneries had 'been formerly inclined to faction' and that most of them had stood 'as neuters' on the issue of further reformation, 'so that they might, as things should fall out, run with the time'.[24]

Moreover, when Presbyterianism announced itself, the dominant rationale for episcopacy was based on the claim that church government was one of the many areas of religious life left indifferent by Scripture. As such, it was to be determined by the relevant secular authority, which, in the English case, was the Christian prince. Church government, the argument ran, should mirror that of the state, and in a monarchy like England that meant that rule by

---

[23] Nicholas Tyacke, 'The Fortunes of English Puritanism, 1603–40', reprinted in his *Aspects of English Protestantism, c.1530–1700* (Manchester, 2001), pp. 111–31; Eliot Vernon, 'A Ministry of the Gospel: The Presbyterians in the English Revolution', in Christopher Durston and Judith Maltby (eds.), *Religion in Revolutionary England* (Manchester, 2006), pp. 115–36; Peter Lake, 'Reading Clarke's *Lives* in Political and Polemical Context', in Kevin Sharpe and Steve Zwicker (eds.), *Writing Lives: Biography and Textuality, Identity and Representation in Early Modern England* (Oxford, 2008), pp. 293–318.

[24] Albert Peel (ed.), *Tracts Ascribed to Richard Bancroft* (Cambridge, 1953), p. xix.

bishops was the best option, not only because the semi-monarchical rule of bishops and archbishops paralleled the structure of the monarchical state, but also because, conceived as royal officials, the bishops both embodied and maximized the control of the Church by the secular ruler. As defenders of *iure humano* episcopacy were to argue well into the next century, to deny this, by conferring on episcopacy a necessity for the well-being, or, even worse, the mere being, of a true Church was to impose worryingly popish, indeed frankly seditious, restraints on the royal supremacy.[25]

Where the Presbyterian position resolved the tensions between the godly community and the national Church by, in effect, giving the former control over the latter, Whitgift collapsed the so-called godly into the surrounding mass of professing Christians who constituted the national Church, the barriers to the membership of which Whitgift kept as low as possible. Only overt recusants were to be excluded, and only the most notorious excommunicated sinners kept from the sacrament. Whitgift maintained that the puritans' insistent division between the godly and the ungodly, and their propensity to denounce many of their fellow Christians as ignorant, superstitious, or crypto-Catholic, betokened a dangerous confusion between the Churches militant and triumphant, visible and invisible. The result was the puritans' belief that the visible Church could aspire to levels of purity that were simply unattainable in a fallen world—all of which, to Whitgift, smacked of Anabaptism.

Whitgift underpinned his defence of the national Church with a rather wintry predestinarianism, which maintained that in a Church blessed, as the Church of England undoubtedly was, with right doctrine and the lawful administration of the sacraments, salvation was, in effect, on offer to all baptized members of that Church. In those circumstances the double decree could be relied upon to do its work, with the elect being called to an effectually saving faith and the reprobate left to their fate. In a remarkable passage, Whitgift even used a variation of this argument to justify pluralism and non-residence.[26]

The result was a decidedly downbeat account of the evangelical mission of the national Church and a consequently attenuated notion of 'edification'. Coolidge suggests that conformist defenders of the English Church simply did not understand the notion of edification in the full, properly Pauline, sense. Rather, they rendered it synonymous with the mere transfer of information:

---

[25] W. D. J. Cargill-Thompson, 'Sir Francis Knollys's Campaign against the *Iure Divino* Theory of Episcopacy', in C. R. Cole and M. E. Moody (eds.), *The Dissenting Tradition* (Athens, OH, 1975), pp. 39–77; Lake, *Anglicans and Puritans*, pp. 88–97; William Lamont, *Marginal Prynne, 1600-1669* (1963); William Lamont, *Godly Rule: Politics and Religion 1603-60* (1969), chs. 2 and 3; Mark Goldie, 'Danby, the Bishops and the Whigs', in Tim Harris, Mark Goldie, and Paul Seaward (eds.), *The Politics of Religion in Restoration England* (Oxford, 1990), pp. 75–105.

[26] Lake, *Anglicans and Puritans?*, pp. 37–42.

the making available to the laity, through the iterative reading of the service book, the Scriptures, and the Homilies, of the basic saving truths of right doctrine, in the hope that, in combination with the sacraments rightly administered, those various readings would save the elect and render the reprobate both inexcusable before the justice of God, and unable to blame their slide towards damnation on the imperfections of the national Church.[27]

But what was at stake here was not so much the impoverished theological imaginations of the conformists, but rather a set of structural and conceptual constraints inherent in their position as defenders of the ecclesiastical status quo. The dean of Salisbury John Bridges, for one, displayed a properly Pauline understanding of edification and even made intermittent attempts to wrest the notion back from his puritan opponents, accusing them of misunderstanding or misappropriating the concept by simply equating it with the adoption of the Presbyterian platform, when in fact it referred solely to the 'edifying in mutual faith and love' of the Christian community that constituted 'the mystical body of Christ, which is his house or church'.[28] However, just like all the other apologists for the ecclesiastical status quo, Bridges was committed both to the defence of a reading ministry and to a rationale for the controverted ceremonies conceived solely in terms of their capacity to project and defend order and uniformity, and not to edify in any recognizably positive sense of the word. He also had to defend an ecclesiastical establishment that connived at a good deal of pluralism and non-residence and contained many a (often impropriated) living too poor to maintain a preaching minister and many a minister entirely unable to preach. This rendered it all but impossible for him successfully to claim any but the most impoverished notion of edification as a positive conformist value. All this ensured that, whatever the personal preferences or formal theological views of individual writers—and, as his Paul's Cross sermon of 1571 so eloquently shows, Bridges, for one, was no merely credal Calvinist—the conformist defence of the national Church could have little to say to what we might term the spiritual and affective core of English Protestantism.

Essentially the same point can be made about the anti-popery espoused by conformist divines like Whitgift. They might subscribe to the Pope's identity as Antichrist with the same certainty and intensity as their puritan opponents, but the expansive definition of the Christian community to which their defence of the ecclesiastical status quo committed them, did not allow them to use the insidious ubiquity of popery to underwrite the vision of the community of the godly as a fused group of the quintessentially non-popish that was so dear to the hearts even of moderate puritans, like William Whitaker, let alone of radicals like William Bradshaw. While, on the puritan side of

---

[27] John S. Coolidge, *The Pauline Renaissance in England* (Oxford, 1970), esp. ch. 2.
[28] Lake, *Anglicans and Puritans?*, p. 120.

the equation, an expansive vision of popery and crypto-popery prompted a tightly defined vision of the godly community, on the conformist side of the argument, a tightly defined definition of popery underpinned an expansive vision of the Christian community, one, of necessity, coterminous with the formal membership of the national Church. On topics like this, formal doctrinal consensus did not lead to anything like real agreement.[29]

But it would not be until the 1590s, and in particular until the publication of Hooker's *Laws*, that these radical differences of assumption and action would be turned into doctrinal change and the beginnings of more properly theological disagreement, not to mention a more spiritually fervent, devotionally intense, defence of the ecclesiastical status quo. And tellingly when that happened, the innovators would be accused of popery, just as Hooker had attempted to label previously commonly held Protestant assumptions as 'puritan'.[30]

'PURITAN' PRACTICAL DIVINITY?

As Alec Ryrie has recently emphasized, the highly emotive, deeply internalized, spiritually strenuous, prayerful piety peddled by Dering and Foxe had its roots in the Protestantism of the earlier Reformation period. While predestinarian in its theological underpinnings, this style of divinity was not characterized by too close a concern with, or too enthusiastic a propagation of, the doctrine of predestination. Thus Collinson points out that Dering's primary concern was with the doctrine of justification and its consequences, and suggests that John Foxe's enthusiasm for 'some of Luther's more practical and "comfortable" works' stemmed from anxieties about 'the negative pastoral', indeed the 'divisive', 'implications of an excessively experimental Calvinism'.[31]

However, as Elizabeth's reign went on, the interior lives of the godly came increasingly to be organized around a series of recognizably predestinarian concerns. We might attribute this development at least in part to changes within Reformed theology, the notional emergence of a style of 'Protestant scholasticism' centred more firmly on the double decree than the theology of earlier reformers had been. However, as Michael Winship has argued, it was probably just as much a response to the all too successful dissemination of the

---

[29] Peter Lake, 'The Significance of the Elizabethan Identification of the Pope as Antichrist', *JEH*, 31 (1980): 161–78; Peter Lake, 'William Bradshaw, Antichrist and the Community of the Godly', *JEH*, 36 (1985): 570–89.

[30] Peter Lake, 'Business as Usual? The Immediate Reception of Hooker's "Laws of Ecclesiastical Polity"', *JEH*, 52 (2001): 456–86.

[31] Alec Ryrie, *Being Protestant in Reformation Britain* (Oxford, 2013); Collinson, 'John Foxe and National Consciousness', p. 204.

basic Protestant doctrine of justification by faith. For, by the 1580s, Winship suggests, many a layperson had learned to turn aside the urgent appeals to repent, amend, and make their assurance sure emanating from the pulpit, or at least from those pulpits that were occupied by godly learned preachers, with a stripped-down and rote-learned version of basic Protestant orthodoxy. Similarly, as the letters of spiritual counsel written to a number of mostly female correspondents by Edward Dering show, the pursuit of genuinely saving faith could plunge other, more intently godly, professors into a dizzying spiral of doubt and even despair. Following Winship, we might see the clergy responding to these different but virtually contemporaneous developments with a discourse centred on the question of how to tell a true from a false faith, and how to achieve and sustain a settled sense of one's own assurance of salvation, without falling, on the one hand, into a hypocritical, indeed a pharisaical, pride and presumption, and, on the other, into some form of melancholy, or even a potentially damning despair.[32]

It used to be claimed that it was only with the failure of the Presbyterian movement in the early 1590s that 'the puritans' turned to the pursuit of further reformation through the more incremental, gradualist methods of practical divinity. This is to attribute too monolithic a decision-making structure to a puritan 'movement' that, in its most coherent and aggressive Presbyterian form, only ever encompassed a small minority of those considered by themselves, and their contemporaries, puritan. Rather it now seems that practical divinity, the propagation of a highly affective, zealous, both intensely introspective and reformation-of-manners-centred style of piety had been a long-term feature of puritan religion. Many of the classic works of practical divinity which started to make their way into print in increasing numbers in the 1590s had been written years earlier. Manuscript sermon notes and commonplace books, as well as printed sermons, from the 1570s, 1580s, and 1590s all show this aspect of puritan piety being pursued by a range of divines, many of whom, like Thomas Wilcocks, Laurence Chaderton, Thomas Cartwright, and, even at the very end of his life, Edward Dering,[33] had been not only nonconformists and, like Richard Greenham, Presbyterian fellow travellers, but central figures in the agitation for the Presbyterian platform.[34] The fact that the sort of zealous, deeply affective, prayerful, but also angst-ridden piety, recently defined as characteristic of the experience of 'being Protestant', is to be found overwhelmingly concentrated in the printed works, and indeed,

---

[32] Michael P. Winship, 'Weak Christians, Backsliders and Carnal Gospellers: Assurance of Salvation and the Pastoral Origins of Puritan Practical Divinity in the 1580s', *Church History*, 70 (2001): 462–81.

[33] Lake, *Moderate Puritans*, pp. 16–24.

[34] Collinson, '"Godly Master Dering"'; Ryrie, *Being Protestant*; Kenneth L. Parker and Eric J. Carlson, *'Practical Divinity': The Works and Life of Revd Richard Greenham* (Aldershot, 1998); Lake, *Moderate Puritans*, ch. 7.

where they survive, in the diaries and life writings, of persons notorious, both at the time and subsequently, as 'puritans', makes the point well enough.[35]

Moreover, if we accept, as the quintessence of moderate puritanism, the argument that precisely because they were indifferent, the controverted ceremonies ought to be accepted as the lesser of two evils (that is, if the result of rejecting them would be the loss of the ministry, and thus disobedience to the direct divine injunction to preach the word in season and out), then it is surely significant that such a position was first outlined, within puritan circles, in the early 1570s, by none other than Thomas Cartwright, the leading ideologue of the Presbyterian movement. On this account, the division between moderate and radical puritans, and between puritanism as a spiritual, pietistic phenomenon and as a political movement, an agitation for liturgical and institutional change, has been overdrawn.[36]

It is undoubtedly the case that some were driven to separate by the pincer movement produced, by, on the one hand, the refusal of the authorities in Church and state to pursue further reformation and, on the other, by increasingly strident Presbyterian claims about the Antichristian nature of episcopacy and the criminally unreformed state of the English Church. Thus, as myriad conformist polemicists from Whitgift on claimed, there was indeed a logical and emotional connection between certain strands of radical puritanism and separation. However, Presbyterianism itself represented not a step towards separatist fragmentation, but rather a bid to embody and fully realize the ideal of a genuinely Protestant, *Reformed*, national Church. Later, even as a variety of radical puritans took ship for New England, they stopped short of condemning the Church in England as a false Church and insisted that, however far they might diverge from its internal organization and practices, they remained in communion with the Churches in England.[37]

But if, throughout the period, separation represented a bridge too far for even the most radical puritans and aggressive nonconformists,[38] the spectre of schism remained a subject fraught with difficulty for the godly. On one view, separatists were erring brethren, godly persons who had fallen into dangerous error and who therefore ought not to be outed to the authorities, or publicly excoriated, but rather admonished and reclaimed for the path of virtue. On another, such people seemed to confirm the claim that puritanism represented the first step on a slippery slope that led straight to schism and heresy; a claim

---

[35] Ryrie, *Being Protestant*. [36] Cf. Lake, *Moderate Puritans*.
[37] Michael P. Winship, *Godly Republicanism* (Cambridge, MA, 2012), pp. 168–9.
[38] Patrick Collinson, 'Sects and the Evolution of Puritanism', in his *From Cranmer to Sancroft: English Religion in the Age of Reformation* (2006), pp. 129–43; Patrick Collinson, 'Towards a Broader Understanding of the Early Dissenting Tradition', in his *Godly People*, pp. 527–62. For Bradshaw see Lake, *Moderate Puritans*, ch. 11; Peter Lake, 'The Dilemma of the Establishment Puritan: The Cambridge Heads and the Case of Francis Johnson and Cuthbert Bainbrigg', *JEH*, 29 (1978): 23–35.

consistently reiterated over the decades, by a host of conformist attack-dogs and professional anti-puritans, ranging from Whitgift and Bancroft, their clients and epigone, to multiple Laudians.

More often than not, therefore, puritans tried to handle this and related issues behind closed doors, in exchanges which, while they demanded 'public' discussion within the confines of the godly community, were not intended for the public domain described by print and formal polemical exchange.[39] But as often as not, when called out by the separatists, or put under pressure by conformist authority, even radical puritans like William Bradshaw were forced into print to explain just why it was that separatism was wrong and their own views did not lead to separatist conclusions. However, too easy a recourse to such means and modes—still less, active collaboration with the authorities in bringing separatists, or even some of the more actively heterodox members of the godly community, to book—could get the perpetrators into serious trouble with at least portions of godly opinion.[40]

THINKING WITH PURITANS, OR WAS THERE MORE THAN ONE WAY OF 'BEING PROTESTANT' IN POST-REFORMATION ENGLAND?

But for all its commitment to the English national Church, for all its integral links to the core doctrines and attitudes that defined the English Protestant impulse, this does not mean that the emergent style of strenuous, deeply affective piety, traditionally regarded as 'puritan', can simply be collapsed into the consensual mainstream of 'the religion of Protestants'.[41] Rather, as the decades passed, and this style of piety became more and more widely disseminated in pulpit and press, and more and more intensely internalized and aggressively asserted by various groups of laypeople, both humble and elite, it also became, if anything, more rather than less distinctive, since the more it spread, the more it prompted a variety of often hostile reactions. And

---

[39] David Como and Peter Lake, 'Orthodoxy and its Discontents: Dispute Settlement and the Production of "Consensus" in the London (Puritan) "Underground"', *Journal of British Studies*, 39 (2000): 34–70; David Como and Ian Atherton, 'The Burning of Edward Wightman: Puritanism, Prelacy and the Politics of Heresy in Early Modern England', *English Historical Review*, 120 (2005): 1215–50.

[40] Lake, 'Dilemma of the Establishment Puritan'; Peter Lake, 'Robert Some and the Ambiguities of Moderation', *Archiv für Reformationsgeschichte*, 71 (1980): 254–79; Lake, *Moderate Puritans*, ch. 5; Peter Lake, *The Boxmaker's Revenge; 'Orthodoxy', 'Heterodoxy', and the Politics of the Parish in Early Stuart London* (Manchester, 2001); Collinson, 'Sects and the Evolution of Puritanism'; Collinson, 'Towards a Broader Understanding'.

[41] Patrick Collinson, *The Religion of Protestants: The Church in English Society 1559–1625* (Oxford, 1982); Ryrie, *Being Protestant*.

these were reactions produced not only in the tedious works of polemic produced by learned defenders of the ecclesiastical status quo, but also at far more popular levels of thought and action.

Ironically, some of our earliest and best sources for these developments are to be found in the works of the puritans themselves. Thus in 1583, despite his best intentions, which were to denounce what he termed derisively 'the country divinity' as ignorant, irreligious, and tinged with popery, the puritan divine George Gifford succeeded in outlining what was in effect, a rival version of the role of the clergy and the Christian community. At stake was a vision of social unity based on various forms of sociability and recreation viewed by the godly as simply sinful.[42] Here the ideal clergyman either does not preach or, if he does, does not preach 'damnation' in the style of the puritans.[43] Rather, he seeks to preserve peace and good neighbourhood amongst his flock,[44] going along to get along, by joining his parishioners in the harmless recreations of the ale bench or May game.[45]

The representative anti-puritan (named 'Atheos') is no moral idiot; he knows 'when I do well' and 'when I do evil',[46] but he trusts that 'God will not require more at my hands than I am able to do'[47] and takes comfort from his own efforts 'to live honestly, serve God and think no man any harm'.[48] 'I am no thief, no murderer, nor traitor, I pay every man his own. I think this is God's bidding.'[49] In terms of formal religious profession he has conned 'the ten commandments, the lord's prayer and the articles of faith'.[50] But his is no simple works theology. He knows that he is a sinner, as are all men, and he takes comfort from the fact that in a fallen world the best that anyone can do is 'repent, call for mercy and believe'.[51] 'Because Christ shed his blood for us I look for to be saved by him, what would you have me more?'[52] 'The mercy of God must save all and what should you have a man care for more than to be saved?'[53] On that basis he claims that 'I trust I believe as well as any scripture man of them all.'[54]

While, under the rubric of 'love', such people look back with nostalgia to a lost golden age of good neighbourhood, located safely before the rise of puritan preaching,[55] they have no truck with the Pope or 'popery' and, while excoriating the disobedience of the puritans, express their own loyal subjection to the current queen in matters religious.[56] They might have conformed under

---

[42] George Gifford, *A Brief discourse of Certain Points of Religion which is among the Common Sort of Christians, which may be termed the Country Divinity* (1583), p. 5a.
[43] Gifford, *Brief discourse*, pp. 24a, 34.   [44] Gifford, *Brief discourse*, pp. 18a–19.
[45] Gifford, *Brief discourse*, pp. 2, 7.   [46] Gifford, *Brief discourse*, p. 31.
[47] Gifford, *Brief discourse*, p. 32.   [48] Gifford, *Brief discourse*, p. 16a.
[49] Gifford, *Brief discourse*, p. 12a.   [50] Gifford, *Brief discourse*, p. 29.
[51] Gifford, *Brief discourse*, p. 70a.   [52] Gifford, *Brief discourse*, p. 79.
[53] Gifford, *Brief discourse*, p. 66.   [54] Gifford, *Brief discourse*, p. 20.
[55] Gifford, *Brief discourse*, pp. 65a, 46a–47.   [56] Gifford, *Brief discourse*, p. 22.

Catholicism, but they did not mean it, having preserved their inner convictions from the polluting idolatry implied by their outward actions. Insofar as theirs is a 'works theology', it bears none of the signature characteristics of traditional (Catholic) religion. There is no trace of purgatory, of the cult of the saints, of the necessity for intercessory prayer, or spiritual sacrifice to be found here. The hopes of such people for salvation are located entirely outside anything resembling a Catholic economy of grace or penitential cycle. Their profession of Christian belief revolves around a somewhat desultory and attenuated version of justification by faith and involves loud protestations of the belief that a merciful God would not damn to hell any Christian who repented for his sins and expressed a complete faith in Christ.

Whatever else this is, it is neither merely conservative nor a case of simple continuity with the Catholic past, but rather a creative response, not only to the religious tergiversations of the mid-Tudor decades, but also to the insurgent aggression of puritan (or perfect Protestant) evangelism. We have here the outlines of an alternative way of 'being Protestant', and as such we might regard the spread of such attitudes as one of the most important (unintended) consequences, we might even say achievements, of what emerges from Gifford's text as the 'puritan' impulse.

And, by the 1590s, Richard Hooker could be found, in effect, agreeing with Gifford's character Atheos that the 'things necessary to all men's salvation... are in scripture plain and easy to be understood' and therefore that preaching, at least as the puritans understood it, was not 'the necessary means of salvation'. On Hooker's view, as (in effect) on Atheos's, regular, decorous, and fervent participation in the style of public worship laid out in the Book of Common Prayer—centred as it was (at least on Hooker's rendition), on public prayer and the sacraments, rather than on the word preached—would do nicely. Thus, Hooker concluded, ordinary believers were not wrong if they believed that, having 'virtuously... behaved themselves' during public worship and been 'fervent' both in 'their devotion and zeal in prayer' and in 'their attention to the word of God' (read as well as preached), 'they have performed a good duty'.[57]

Thus was what the godly tended to regard as 'mere conformity' given a positive, both theological and devotional, meaning, and thus were the popular anti-puritan attitudes, habitually organized by godly commentators like George Gifford under the signs of irreligion, profanity, and crypto-popery, infused with theological depth, coherence, and polemical bite. And thus we might say was something that subsequent commentators have tended to call 'Anglicanism' created by, or rather in reaction against, 'puritanism'.

---

[57] Lake, *Anglicans and Puritans*, pp. 163, 168.

Thus, *pace* Collinson, the stereotype of the puritan as a distinctively zealous, self-regarding, and aggressive opponent of all true piety, social unity, and obedience long *preceded* the outbreak of printed and performed anti-puritan satire and stereotyping provoked, in the early 1590s, by the Marprelate affair. Indeed, the fact that we find the first printed accounts of anti-puritanism of this sort within the works of the godly themselves demonstrates all too clearly just how integral to their own self-image the notion of puritanism and the popular hostility that it attracted had become, at least by the early 1580s. However, this is most definitely not to deny that, as the careers not only of Ben Jonson and William Shakespeare but also of countless hack-writers and polemicists all show from the 1590s onwards, a variety of anti-puritan stereotypes and tropes did indeed establish themselves, both at court and in the country, as hardy perennials of popular print and both popular and court performance. As such, they constituted established ideological or polemical quantities, conceptual and symbolic means, through which a range of contemporaries, from James I downwards, could interpret events, and frame their policies and pitches for support.[58] Just as anti-popery turned Catholicism into 'popery', so anti-puritanism played an equally large role in turning the leading edge of English Protestant zeal into 'puritanism'.[59]

A JACOBEAN SYNTHESIS?

It might be tempting to see these developments as the emergence of the coherent 'Anglican' other, opposition to which underwrote the coherence of 'puritanism' and even presaged puritanism's incipient (and now, if not before, inevitable) expulsion from the mainstream of the national Church. But that would be a mistake. For all that these developments among the conformist avant-garde in the 1590s anticipated central features of the styles of piety and of anti-puritanism pushed by the likes of Lancelot Andrewes, John Buckeridge, Samuel Harsnett, and John Overall in the reign of James I, and even presaged the Arminianism and Laudianism of the 1620s and 1630s,[60] in

---

[58] Patrick Collinson, 'Ecclesiastical Vitriol: Religious Satire in the 1590s and the Invention of Puritanism', in John Guy (ed.), *The Reign of Elizabeth I: Court and Culture in the Last Decade* (Cambridge, 1995), pp. 150–70; Peter Lake and Michael Questier, *The Antichrist's Lewd Hat: Protestants, Papists & Players in Post-Reformation England* (New Haven, CT, 2002), chs. 12, 13, 14.
[59] Peter Lake, 'Anti-Popery: The Structure of a Prejudice', in Richard Cust and Ann Hughes (eds.), *Conflict in Early Stuart England: Studies in Religion and Politics 1603–1642* (Harlow, 1989); Peter Lake, 'Anti-Puritanism: The Structure of a Prejudice', in Kenneth Fincham and Peter Lake (eds.), *Religious Politics in Post-Reformation England* (Woodbridge, 2006), pp. 80–97.
[60] Peter Lake, 'Lancelot Andrewes, John Buckeridge and Avant-Garde Conformity at the Court of James I', in Linda Levy Peck (ed.), *The Mental World of the Jacobean Court* (Cambridge,

the short- to medium-term the future did not belong to Hooker and his heirs. Indeed, despite Bancroft's elevation to Canterbury in 1604, it did not even belong (definitively) to a Bancroftian conformity.

As a number of historians have argued, after the initial agitation for further reformation that culminated in Hampton Court and the fuss generated by the subsequent conformist crackdown had subsided, in certain times and in certain places, the desire of even quite radical puritans to continue their evangelical calling within the ministry of the national Church combined with the broadly reformed, anti-popish evangelical zeal of many a Jacobean bishop and Calvinist conformist to create the ideal conditions in which the household worship, the 'conventicles' held to repeat the heads of sermons, the private fasts, the lectures by combination that many historians have seen as characteristic of the godly, could be integrated within the overarching structures and proselytizing agenda of the national Church.[61] Kenneth Fincham has shown that, under James, the predominant policy was to insist on subscription by ministers, but not thereafter to enforce every jot and tittle of conformity upon them.[62] Such latitude was often extended even to radical puritan nonconformists—that is to say, not those ministers who subscribed but whose subsequent performance of conformity was either patchy, or virtually non-existent, but rather those who, like John Dod or Arthur Hildersham or William Bradshaw or John Cotton, became notorious for adamantly refusing to conform. Such radical figures nevertheless continued—albeit sometimes only intermittently, under duress, and with the help of powerful lay interests or sympathetic diocesans—to exercise some sort of ministry within the national Church as well (of course) as exerting very considerable personal authority within the godly circles that sustained them.

Thus with Presbyterian reformation off the table, and with the rise of *iure divino* episcopalianism, and of the *iure divino* argument for tithes, as new or emergent orthodoxies, and with sabbatarianism widely accepted amongst both the moderate puritan clergy and many of the episcopate, a moment arrived when apologists for the reformed Church of England could reasonably claim that, under the rule of a divinely ordained prince and a similarly divinely ordained episcopal order, the English were committed—in theory at least, and it was to be hoped increasingly in practice—to giving to God and his Church a tenth of their substance and a seventh of their time, just as the word of God

---

1991), pp. 113–33; Peter Lake, 'The Laudian Style', in Kenneth Fincham (ed.), *The Early Stuart Church* (Basingstoke, 1993), pp. 161–85; Anthony Milton, '"Anglicanism" by Stealth: The Career and Influence of John Overall', in Fincham and Lake (eds.), *Religious Politics*, pp. 159–76.

[61] Collinson, *Religion of Protestants*, ch. 6; Patrick Collinson, 'The English Conventicle', in his *From Cranmer to Sancroft*, pp. 145–72.

[62] Kenneth Fincham, 'Clerical Conformity from Whitgift to Laud', in Peter Lake and Michael Questier (eds.), *Conformity and Orthodoxy in the English Church c.1560–1660* (Woodbridge, 2000), pp. 125–58.

required them to do. If we factor in the 'Calvinism' that passed for orthodox amongst the majority of the educated clergy and in both universities, together with the commitment to a godly learned ministry that united most parts of the ecclesiastical establishment, and a virulent anti-popery, then we can quite see how elements in the ecclesiastical establishment could plausibly claim that this was the best *reformed* church in the world.[63]

While it would be absurd to claim that even moderate puritans—many of whom almost certainly remained committed to *iure humano* rather than *iure divino* versions of episcopacy—bought into this vision entirely, it remains the case that, under the right circumstances, there was more than enough on offer within both the theory and the practice of the Jacobean Church to keep such people more or less happy.

But of course, the circumstances were far from always right. Throughout the period, the bench of bishops contained dedicated conformists and hardline anti-puritans. Some, like Harsnett or Overall or Andrewes or Richard Neile, were now armed with a fully-formed avant-garde conformist or proto-Laudian sensibility. Others, like Thomas Ravis or Bancroft, while doctrinally Calvinist, retained a very developed sense of what they took to be the puritan threat to order, uniformity, and obedience. To these men, and their lay backers and allies—and that meant in some moods, although not in others, James I himself—the integration of moderate, and even some radical, puritans into the structures of the national Church looked anything but benign. To them the conventicles and household worship, the private fasts and exercises, the aggressive sabbatarianism and the endless extempore prayers and sermons of the godly did not look like benign supplements to the public ministry and worship of the national Church, but rather cells of dissidence and seedbeds of division. The capacity of moderate puritans to accommodate themselves to the demands of conformity without fully conforming themselves, and while conniving at the nonconformity of their flocks or patrons, looked, not like the containment or de-fanging of the puritan threat, but rather more like the creation of a dangerous fifth column. The cosy relationship enjoyed by many puritan local elites with the puritan ministry appeared to committed conformists not to be a major bulwark of provincial order, an instrument of moral and spiritual reformation, but rather the infiltration of the structures of the Church by sinister lay interests and of local government by elements whose loyalty and obedience, particularly at moments of crisis, like the fuss over the projected match between Prince Charles and the Spanish infanta, could not be relied upon.

---

[63] Nicholas Tyacke, 'Calvinism, Arminianism and Counter-Revolution', in Conrad Russell (ed.), *The Origins of the English Civil War* (1973), pp. 119–43; Collinson, *Religion of Protestants*, esp. chs. 1, 2, and 3; Lake, 'Presbyterianism and the Idea of a National Church', pp. 207–19; Lake, *Anglicans and Puritans*, pp. 96, 100.

Similarly, to those on the receiving end, 'the reformation of manners', particularly when it was attended with the polarizing rhetoric beloved of many a puritan minister, continued to look and feel not like the pursuit of order and the suppression of sin, but rather more like the breach of long-standing norms of social unity and neighbourliness by self-regarding and self-selecting godly elites;[64] hence the burgeoning reputation of the godly for positively pharisaical levels of spiritual pride and hypocrisy, and hence, too, the continuing salience at both popular and elite levels of an often virulent anti-puritanism.

Nor did the course of high politics always run smooth when it came to maximizing the integration of the most godly elements within the national Church. Two areas of difficulty stand out. Firstly, James's policies towards Catholicism and his projected marriage alliances with Catholic powers remained extraordinarily inflammatory and divisive. Secondly, his plans for the Scottish Church retained their capacity to cause alarm in England, as well as in his northern kingdom.[65] Moreover, much to James's chagrin, whenever Parliament was in session, bills intended to ease the lot of various nonconformist divines continued to percolate their way up through the House of Commons,[66] and whenever the king found himself confronted by recalcitrance or defiance in the Commons, even on issues seemingly unconnected with the classic puritan concerns of conformity or ecclesiastical reform, he tended to resort to a rhetoric of 'popularity' with a vision of puritan dissidence somewhere near its heart.[67]

We find all of these factors—tensions over local versions of the reformation of manners, the king's policy towards the Scottish Church, and his attitude towards Catholicism—coming together first in 1617, over the Book of Sports. But the real crisis arrived with the events in central Europe that culminated in the outbreak of the Thirty Years War and the Spanish match, the virulent opposition to which gave the language of anti-puritanism and the notion of a populist (puritan) threat to royal authority new salience. As the likes of Archbishop George Abbot as well as puritans like Thomas Scott and Samuel Ward of Ipswich made their opposition to the match clear,[68] a group

---

[64] Kenneth Fincham, *Prelate as Pastor: The Episcopate of James I* (Oxford, 1990).

[65] Alan R. MacDonald, *The Jacobean Kirk, 1567–1625* (Aldershot, 1998); Alan R. MacDonald, 'James VI and I, the Church of Scotland and British Ecclesiastical Convergence', *Historical Journal*, 48 (2005): 885–903.

[66] Nicholas Tyacke, 'The "Rise of Puritanism" and the Legalising of Dissent, 1571–1719', reprinted in his *Aspects of English Protestantism*, pp. 61–89.

[67] Richard Cust, 'Charles I and Popularity', in Thomas Cogswell, Richard Cust, and Peter Lake (eds.), *Politics, Religion and Popularity in Early Stuart Britain* (Cambridge, 2002), pp. 235–58, esp. pp. 239–42.

[68] Peter Lake, 'Constitutional Consensus and Puritan Opposition in the 1620s: Thomas Scott and the Spanish Match', *Historical Journal*, 25 (1982): 805–25; Kenneth Fincham, 'Archbishop Abbot's Defence of Protestant Orthodoxy', *Historical Research*, 61 (1988): 36–64.

of avant-garde conformist clergy sought to play on James's now rampant antipuritanism by associating Calvinism with puritanism in order to exclude both from the pale of respectability and preferment within the national Church. And so the Jacobean moment of reformed consensus, the stable hegemony of Collinson's 'religion of Protestants', did not, in fact, last for more than about the ten years that stretched from c.1606–7 to c.1618. This (admittedly) was a great deal better showing than anything achieved by its Grindalian precursor, but it did not a seamless web of Protestant consensus make.

Here is not the place to retell the convoluted story of the factional *coup de main* and ideological and cultural *renversement* that has been styled (variously) the 'rise of Arminianism' and the triumph of 'Laudianism' in the Caroline Church.[69] This is a topic that is relevant here only to the extent that it transformed the relationship of the puritan godly, if not to the national Church as they understood and wanted it to be, then certainly to that Church as it existed in the minds, and increasingly in the policies, of Laud and Charles I. While, to the godly, the ecclesiastical policies of the Personal Rule looked like persecution and popery, to the proponents and agents of those policies they represented merely a much-needed reformation, a 'thorough' purging of a national Church literally infested with both puritanism and Calvinism. Either way, those policies drove many puritans to New England. They reopened old debates about the lawfulness or unlawfulness of conformity, the meaning of which, many of the godly claimed, had been transformed by the policies being pursued by Laud and Charles. The Laudian drive to achieve the beauty of holiness drove some into separation, or into acts and positions that to their godly colleagues seemed dangerously close to separation. Even for more 'moderate' (in the sense of moderate *puritan*) spirits, like the tirelessly zealous William Prynne, it rendered the language of anti-popery and evil counsel threateningly salient and drove even notably careful stalwarts of various local godly establishments, like Samuel Ward of Ipswich, into a variety of overt gestures of dissent and critique.[70]

The Laudian push also opened, reopened, or, at the very least, exacerbated and exposed to view, a number of divisions amongst the godly, with what were to be fatal consequences during the 1640s and 1650s. It was, for instance, no accident that one of the major bones of contention between, the famous Presbyterian heresy hunter Thomas Edwards and his Independent enemies was what Edwards claimed had been their very different responses to Laudian

---

[69] Nicholas Tyacke, *Anti-Calvinists: The Rise of English Arminianism, c.1590–1640* (Oxford, 1987); Kenneth Fincham and Nicholas Tyacke, *Altars Restored: The Changing Face of English Religious Worship, 1547–c.1700* (Oxford, 2007), chs. 4–6. Contrast Kevin Sharpe, *The Personal Rule of Charles I* (New Haven, CT, 1992).

[70] *ODNB*, 'Ward, Samuel (1577–1640)'.

popery and persecution.[71] As David Como has proved, it was the impact of Arminianism and what appeared to some to be the weak response thereto of many puritans that precipitated what Como calls the first antinomian crisis in the late 1620s.[72]

PURITANISM, IN OR OUT OF THE 'MAINSTREAM'?

Once again some of our best sources for the resulting tensions and conflicts come from the godly themselves, who continued not only to talk about the relations between themselves and their more hostile or critical neighbours in the most uncompromising and polarized terms, but also to root their own self-image as the godly, the last best hope of the English nation in its attempts to preserve true religion and keep its covenant with its God, in the hostility evidenced towards them as 'puritans' by those they persisted in writing off as the 'profane' or the 'ungodly'.[73] Using a range of local sources and court records, a variety of historians, ranging from Christopher Haigh to David Underdown and Ann Hughes, have shown that these tensions and animosities were anything but invented.[74] We are decidedly not dealing here just with the fevered imaginations of puritans, high on their own singularity and godliness, and determined to use the hostility of the children of this world to demonstrate their status as the children of God. This is not mere 'preachers' talk'.

But equally we should not take this heavily polarized vision of the relations between the godly and the ungodly as simply true, the outcome of some sort of value-free social reportage. Clearly, such tensions did exist, and in the right circumstances could flare up into a variety of local and even national disputes. But again, in different circumstances, where the balance of local forces favoured the godly, those tensions could be contained or dissipated. Our leading historian of 'prayer book Protestantism' has sought to find this often elusive prey in anti-puritan presentments and complaints in the church courts. These, of course, turned on specific charges about discrete acts of nonconformity, the necessary implication of which was that, these particular charges

---

[71] Ann Hughes, *Gangraena and the Struggle for the English Revolution* (Oxford, 2004), pp. 22–49.

[72] David Como, *Blown by the Spirit: Puritanism and the Emergence of an Antinomian Underground in Pre-Civil-War England* (Stanford, CA, 2004).

[73] Peter Lake and Isaac Stephens, *Scandal and Religious Identity in Early Stuart England: A Northamptonshire Maid's Tragedy* (Woodbridge, 2015), esp. part I.

[74] Christopher Haigh, *The Plain Man's Pathways to Heaven: Kinds of Christianity in Post-Reformation England* (Oxford, 2007); David Underdown, *Fire from Heaven: Life in an English Town in the Seventeenth Century* (1992); Ann Hughes, 'Religion and Society in Stratford upon Avon, 1619–1638', *Midland History*, 19 (1994): 58–84; Lake and Stephens, *Maid's Tragedy*.

apart, even ministers as (allegedly) obnoxiously nonconformist as these, were, for the most part, using (at least parts of) the Book of Common Prayer.[75] We might conclude that the most zealously protestant 'prayer book Protestantism' of the period was to be found amongst various sorts of moderate puritan, and that one of the more prevalent styles of piety to be found in the national Church was comprised of prayer-book worship, spliced together with (or perhaps slightly modified or adapted to accommodate) the zealously elaborated preaching style, the intermittently extemporized prayers, the predestinarian piety (and perhaps the non- or partially conformist scruples) of the godly clergy and at least elements in their flock.

And for every one such who found himself up before the church courts, there were many more who slipped through the net, presumably because their pastoral style satisfied the needs, or at the very least, did not seriously alienate the sensibilities, of even the most zealously conformist of their flock. As Isaac Stephens has shown, even Elizabeth Isham, a passionate devotee of the pastoral style and spiritual advice of that notoriously recalcitrant nonconformist, John Dod, could develop a deeply affective style of personal piety, laced with references to the Book of Common Prayer, while experiencing not a twinge of incongruity as she did so.[76]

A great deal turned on questions of personality. The powers and prerogatives of the powerful preacher gave the terminally fractious and self-important, but formally moderate (i.e. conforming) puritan minister, Stephen Dennison, ample opportunity to create all sorts of animosities and divisions, both in his parish and the wider London godly community.[77] In the hands of more skilled or emollient pastors, the same claims to spiritual authority and charismatic power could have very different outcomes. Isham found the notorious nonconformist John Dod so effective a doctor of the soul not because of his 'puritanism'—she herself was studiously moderate on the topic of conformity—but because, as she put it, 'Mr Dod had a delightful, easy way, which was very effectual.'[78] As Eamon Duffy has explained, the range of epithets devised by puritan ministers to characterize their often appallingly unsatisfactory auditories could run the gamut from 'sons of Belial', to 'mere civil honest men' and 'formal professors'. Taken one way, this terminology could merely perpetuate a simple godly/ungodly binary, but taken in another, it could serve to distinguish between different sorts of parishioner and form

---

[75] Judith Maltby, *Prayer Book and People in Elizabethan and Early Stuart England* (Cambridge, 1998).
[76] Isaac Stephens, 'Confessional Identity in Early Stuart England: The Prayer Book Puritanism of Elizabeth Isham', *Journal of British Studies*, 50 (2011): 24–47.
[77] Lake, *Boxmaker's Revenge*.
[78] Elizabeth Isham's *Book of remembrance*, fol. 15r, cited from the online edition by Elizabeth Clarke and Erica Longfellow: <http://www.Warwick.ac.uk/English/perdita/Isham/index bor.htm>.

the basis for a far more modulated pastoral style than some of the ministers' harsher rhetoric might seem to imply.[79]

Much turned, too, on the local structures of power, and the relation of godly groups to the local ruling elites. Dod had to be invited into the Isham household and his godly strictures remained subject to the veto or qualification of the Isham paterfamilias. Where the godly had achieved a certain primacy or hegemony, even after quite sharp initial conflicts, thereafter deep resentments could be hidden, or dissipated, until some change in the political circumstances enabled dissidents to voice their complaints and appeal to higher authority. Such shifts in both local and central politics, and in the interactions between them, came to the fore during the later 1620s and 1630s as power at the centre, and then in at least some of the localities, passed into Laudian hands, and various anti-puritan groups and individuals, some nursing grievances that went back years or even decades, gained renewed access to central backing.

In the absence of a concerted puritan movement of the sort tracked by Patrick Collinson through Elizabeth's reign, historians of early Stuart puritanism have tended to trace the social and patronage networks of the godly, talking of 'sociability' amongst the ministers, of links of patronage, mutual respect, and even friendship between the laity and the clergy. Such studies have been focused sometimes on particular localities, sometimes on the unit of the family and its ramifications, sometimes on more ideologically inflected affinities.[80] All these connections and networks were decidedly Janus-faced; they could be read either as centripetal or centrifugal, or alternately as both. In the right circumstances, they could act to integrate the godly into the structures of the Church and the workings of the social order. But equally they might provide enclaves in which ideas and assumptions at odds with current orthodoxy could be sustained or developed. Thus between the 1590s and 1640s a residual Presbyterianism, the first stirrings of what would become Independency, and doctrinal trends and tensions organized around familism both name and thing, that would culminate in the emergence of antinomianism, were all preserved, and even fostered, within the godly community.[81]

---

[79] Eamon Duffy, 'The Godly and the Multitude in Seventeenth Century England', *Seventeenth Century*, 1 (1986): 31–55; Lake and Stephens, *Maid's Tragedy*, pp. 128–36.

[80] John T. Cliffe, *The Puritan Gentry: The Great Puritan Families of Early Stuart England* (1984); Jacqueline Eales, *Puritans and Roundheads: The Harleys of Brampton Bryan and the Outbreak of the English Civil War* (Cambridge, 1990); Tom Webster, *Godly Clergy in Early Stuart England: The Caroline Puritan Movement, c.1620-1643* (Cambridge, 1997), esp. parts 1 and 2; Frank Bremer, *Congregational Communion: Clerical Friendship in the Anglo-American Puritan Community, 1610–1692* (Boston, 1994); Peter Lake, 'The "Court", the "Country" and the Northamptonshire Connection: Watching the "Puritan Opposition" Think (Historically) about Politics on the Eve of the English Civil War', *Midland History*, 35 (2010): 28–70.

[81] Polly Ha, *English Presbyterianism, 1590–1640* (Stanford, CA, 2011); Tyacke, 'Fortunes of English Puritanism'; Murray Tolmie, *The Triumph of the Saints: The Separate Churches of*

Similarly, godly circles might nurture and perpetuate a nexus of political assumptions about mixed monarchy, active citizenship, and the right to resist, that if it only turned overtly 'republican' in New England, nevertheless retained throughout a distinctly oppositionist hue, and was certainly entirely at odds with the political theology being peddled by the first two Stuarts.[82]

If the political circumstances proved adverse, these networks could work to protect the godly against the hostile attentions of authority, or even, as the Feoffees for Impropriations scheme shows, provide the basic structures necessary to organize resistance.[83] Should the political winds turn favourable, the same solidarities and connections could provide the basis for rapid political mobilization. When the crisis hit, they could get themselves 'ready and organised first'.[84]

CONCLUSION

Thus, for anyone interested in the history of the post-Reformation national Church—or 'Anglicanism' as that topic is sometimes described—puritanism matters. It matters because it was in and through the areas of tension and disagreement that have come to be organized under the sign of 'puritanism' that the Protestant impulse worked its way through the national Church and English society in the decades after the Elizabethan Settlement. It matters because the vast majority of those regarded, either by themselves or by their friends and enemies, as puritans, sought to work out their religious calling within the structures and strictures of the national Church. Of course, that did not alter the fact that, under the wrong circumstances—and for the godly the circumstances were nearly always, in some sense, wrong, 'the world' always, of necessity, against them—separation was one of the possible places to which the puritan impulse could lead, and mainstream puritans always found that an extremely uncomfortable fact. Nevertheless, the vast majority of the people

---

London, 1616–1649 (Cambridge, 1977); Lake, *Boxmaker's Revenge*; Michael Winship, *Making Heretics: Militant Protestantism and Free Grace in Massachusetts, 1636–1641* (Princeton, NJ, 2002).

[82] Lake, 'Thomas Scott and the Spanish Match'; Lake, 'The "Court", the "Country" and the Northamptonshire Connection'; Nicholas Tyacke, 'The Puritan Paradigm in English Politics, 1558–1642', *Historical Journal*, 53 (2010): 527–50; Winship, *Godly Republicanism*.

[83] Ann Hughes, 'Thomas Dugard and his Circle in the 1630s: A "Parliamentary-Puritan" Connexion', *Historical Journal*, 29 (1986): 77–93; John Fielding, 'Opposition to the Personal Rule of Charles I: The Diary of Robert Woodford, 1637–41', *Historical Journal*, 31 (1988): 769–88; Lake, 'The "Court", the "Country" and the Northamptonshire Connection'; Webster, *Godly Clergy*, esp. part 3.

[84] Tyacke, 'Fortunes of English Puritanism'; Conrad Russell, *The Fall of the British Monarchies* (Oxford, 1991), p. 22.

known as puritan were, and wanted to remain, active members of the national Church. Indeed, as Collinson and others have insisted, in some places and at some times, theirs might even become the dominant style of evangelism operating within that Church.

But puritanism also belongs at the centre of any account of 'Anglicanism' because some of the most significant indeed defining elements in that bundle of attitudes and beliefs that have come to be associated with that moniker were developed against what we might term the defining other of puritanism. Anti-puritanism, like anti-popery, could operate as a mere prejudice, a series of crude stereotypes, and conspiracy theories, but it could also be a much more positive force, a way of formulating (through an intensely adversarial, but also essentially dialectical, process of claim and counter-claim) a positive vision, both of the English Church and of true, English, Protestant religion.[85] This is self-evidently true of the work of Richard Hooker, but even what have too often been taken to be wholly devotional or edificational works, like the sermons of Lancelot Andrewes, in fact drew a great deal of their emotional energy and ideological resonance from their overtly stated and insistently reiterated opposition to an image of religious error and deviance, labelled puritan.[86] (As ever the attempt to distinguish definitively between the 'polemical' and the 'devotional' not merely breaks down, but proves to be almost entirely obfuscatory.)

Puritans, in short, were good to think with. Over the period from the 1570s, puritanism operated as the sand within the oyster of the national Church, providing an irritating, noxious, and even, on the most extreme view of the matter, a polluting presence that stimulated the production of a series of often, if not mutually exclusive, then certainly competing, visions of the national Church, the descendants of which remain in contention for the soul of the Church of England to this day; nearly all of them still seeking a legitimating myth of origin in one version or other of the post-Reformation.[87]

The result is something of a paradox, for we are dealing here with a process of conformist differentiation whereby, even as what had been something like the leading edge of English Protestant evangelism was achieving virtual hegemony at least in parts of England, it was also becoming more, rather than less, distinctive, controversial, and divisive. On this view, the rise of Laudianism is best seen, not as some wholly exogenous factor, visited by the

---

[85] Lake, 'Anti-Popery'; Lake, 'Anti-Puritanism', pp. 80–97; Lake and Stephens, *Maid's Tragedy*, esp. pp. 52–167.

[86] Lake, *Anglicans and Puritans*, ch. 4; Lake, 'Lancelot Andrewes, John Buckeridge and Avant-Garde Conformity at the Court of James I'.

[87] Cf. Ryrie, *Being Protestant*; Maltby, *Prayer Book and People*; Peter White, *Predestination, Policy and Polemic: Conflict and Consensus in the English Church from the Reformation to the Civil War* (Cambridge, 1992); Ian Green, *Print and Protestantism in Early Modern England* (Oxford, 2000).

political contingencies of Charles I's reign on an otherwise consensual English Protestantism, the seamless unity of which stretched back uninterrupted into the 1520s, but rather as the culmination of a dialectical process of challenge and response, of mutual self-definition and othering, with its roots in the 1560s and early 1570s (indeed, if Karl Gunther is to be believed, in the 1530s); a process to which puritanism both name and thing had always been central.

Not that the puritans would have agreed that their main significance lay in provoking their enemies into new heights of theological creativity, devotional fervour, and political and polemical activism. On the contrary, when the fears and hopes, the excitements and anxieties, of the 1640s were over, and the famous puritan martyrologist Samuel Clarke had to contemplate the prospect of living first under Independent and then under episcopalian rule, he constructed, out of the lives of the puritan dead, a version of puritan tradition as the epitome of English Protestant zeal, the animating spirit of the English national Church, a vibrant *via media*, defined against the noxious extremes of Laudian (but not only Laudian) prelacy on the one hand, and of sectarian extremism, on the other.[88] He defined puritanism, in short, as a form of 'Anglicanism', and so should we.

SELECT BIBLIOGRAPHY

Collinson, Patrick, *The Elizabethan Puritan Movement* (1967).
Collinson, Patrick, *Godly People: Essays on English Protestantism and Puritanism* (1983).
Collinson, Patrick, *The Religion of Protestants* (Oxford, 1982).
Como, David, *Blown by the Spirit: Puritanism and the Emergence of an Antinomian Underground in Pre-Civil-War England* (Stanford, CA, 2004).
Gunther, Karl, *Reformation Unbound: Protestant Visions of Reform in England, 1525–1590* (Cambridge, 2014).
Lake, Peter and Maria Dowling (eds.), *Protestantism and the National Church in Sixteenth Century England* (1987).
Ryrie, Alec, *Being Protestant in Reformation Britain* (Oxford, 2013).
Seaver, Paul, *Wallington's World: A Puritan Artisan in Seventeenth-Century London* (Stanford, CA, 1986).
Tyacke, Nicholas, *Anti-Calvinists: The Rise of English Arminianism, c.1590–1640* (Oxford, 1987).
Winship, Michael P., *Godly Republicanism* (Cambridge, MA, 2012).

---

[88] Lake, 'Reading Clarke'.

20

'Avant-Garde Conformity' in the 1590s

Peter McCullough

The coining of a new epithet so fine that it immediately passes as current in ecclesiastical history is a rare thing. Indeed, historiography of the early modern Church of England over the past three decades has recalled or qualified almost all of the hallmarks used by previous practitioners—'Anglican', 'puritan', 'Reformed', and 'Catholic' can now most often be struck only with cautionary inverted commas or question marks.[1] But with 'avant-garde conformity' Peter Lake minted in pure gold. The phrase appeared only in the title and last sentence of his seminal article, 'Lancelot Andrewes, John Buckeridge, and Avant-Garde Conformity at the Court of James I'.[2] Lake did not labour the new terminology, perhaps because he did not need to, since it perfectly captured the sum total of his epitome of the churchmanship of Lancelot Andrewes (1555–1626) and his protégé, John Buckeridge (d. 1631). Lake first surveyed the impressive list of 'what Andrewes hated' about mainstream English Protestantism: speculative divinity, faith as intellectual assent, the cult of the sermon, predestinarian presumption, popularity, and neglect of ceremonies.[3] He then turned to 'what [Andrewes] liked': deep Christocentrism, faith forged in cooperation with works, soteriological preaching, the superior efficacy of prayer and sacraments (supremely, a sacrifical eucharist), and strict ceremonial and liturgical observance.[4] Under these headings Lake marshalled generous quotation from Andrewes's and Buckeridge's Jacobean court sermons to reveal what he called 'the avant-garde conformist cause'. Scholars were quick to see the taxonomical usefulness of 'avant-garde conformity'.

---

[1] Cf. Peter Lake, *Anglicans and Puritans? Presbyterianism and English Conformist Thought from Whitgift to Hooker* (1988); Anthony Milton, '"Anglicanism" by Stealth: The Career and Influence of John Overall', in Kenneth Fincham and Peter Lake (eds.), *Religious Politics in Post-Reformation England: Essays in Honour of Nicholas Tyacke* (Woodbridge, 2006), pp. 159–76.

[2] Linda Levy Peck (ed.), *The Mental World of the Jacobean Court* (Cambridge, 1991), pp. 113–33.

[3] Lake, 'Avant-Garde', pp. 115–20.   [4] Lake, 'Avant-Garde', pp. 120–31.

Before it appeared in print, Debora Shuger had hailed it as 'a splendid paradox'—even if she went on to demur, 'which I will not steal but hope it catches on'.[5] It did catch on, not least because it provided an escape from the anachronistic application of terms like the post-Restoration 'High Church' or the Victorian 'Anglo-Catholic' to something so peculiarly early modern. It also avoided, at least for Andrewes, the chronological misnomers 'Caroline divine' and 'Laudian'. But perhaps most usefully, it resisted the impulse then current to divide the early Stuart church along the single doctrinal binary of 'Calvinist' vs. 'Arminian' (or 'anti-Calvinist').

Andrewes's 'avant-garde conformity' was a package of things which, individually, had native antecedents, but which when found together were, in terms of the Jacobean mainstream, daring, counter-cultural—'avant-garde'. But Andrewes at the same time was a scion of discipline and order, light-years away from either crypto-popery or Presbyterianism, and hence (the second part of Lake's 'splendid paradox') 'conformist'. But was he original? Lake's essay posited Andrewes not as *sui generis*, but as a narrow bridge spanning two far-flung shores. On one side was Richard Hooker, who 'invented' the avant-garde 'style of piety', and occupied 'a somewhat exposed and lonely position during the 1590s'. On the other, perhaps less surprisingly, were 'the ecclesiastical policies pursued by Charles I, Laud, and their supporters' in the 1630s.[6] In the governing terms of Lake's piece (religion at the English court of James VI and I) Andrewes certainly was the Jacobean bridge between those two poles, one Elizabethan and the other Caroline. But was Hooker—and avant-garde conformity with him—really so unique and isolated in the 1590s? This remains a question to ask even after Lake's thoughtful re-articulation of his claims for Hooker's distillation of an 'Anglican moment' in the 1590s.[7] We might start by reconsidering Hooker and Andrewes alongside one another, because twists of biographical and bibliographical fate can give the false impression that Hooker was Andrewes's intellectual progenitor. The majority of Hooker's *Lawes*, and all of the books indisputably left as he wished them to be printed, were late Elizabethan monuments. Books I–IV appeared in 1593. The year 1597 saw the publication of Book V, Hooker's careful exposition of worship according to the 1559 Book of Common Prayer. Scholars disagree over the extent to which the fifth book was simply an eloquent defence of the status quo, or nothing less than the very invention of 'Anglicanism'. But a balanced view of 'what was individual' about it is that Hooker 'deliberately and at some length reemphasised the role of the sacraments and liturgical prayer at

---

[5] Debora Kuller Shuger, *Habits of Thought in the English Renaissance: Religion, Politics, and the Dominant Culture* (Berkeley and Los Angeles, CA, 1990), p. 8n25.

[6] Lake, 'Avant-Garde', pp. 113–14.

[7] Peter Lake, 'The "Anglican Moment"? Richard Hooker and the Ideological Watershed of the 1590s', in Stephen Platten (ed.), *Anglicanism and the Western Christian Tradition: Continuity, Change and the Search for Communion* (Norwich, 2003), pp. 90–121.

the expense of preaching'.[8] That is, Hooker was the first to articulate in print the core characteristic of avant-garde conformity. But he died on 2 November 1600, aged only forty-six. His early death froze him in the historical mind's eye as a great *Elizabethan*. Andrewes, however, published almost nothing in English at all in his lifetime, except a handful of court sermons squeezed out of him by King James. His bibliographical monumentalizing had to wait until the posthumous *XCVI Sermons* and *Opuscula Quaedam Posthuma*, edited by Laud and Buckeridge and published by Charles I's command in 1629. As if that were not enough to pull Andrewes towards the Stuart end of the avant-garde bridge, Laud and Buckeridge also packed *XCVI Sermons* with court orations preached after his consecration as bishop (1605). Andrewes, then, particularly if seen only in the spotlight shone by Lake on the pulpit performances for King James, is too often thought of as a great *Jacobean*—and therefore the successor of Hooker.

But Andrewes was not Hooker's junior, and both had debuted as avant-garde conformists by 1590. In age they were near-exact contemporaries. Hooker was born in early April 1554. Although we know only that Andrewes was born in 1555, no more than sixteen months, and as few as four, could have separated them in age. Accordingly, Hooker and Andrewes proceeded in tandem through Oxford and Cambridge respectively: BA 1574 and 1575, MA 1577 and 1578. Andrewes (1575) beat Hooker (1577) to the prize of a college fellowship, and they even had in common as patron of their early studies Sir Francis Walsingham (no avant-garde conformist he). Hooker was ordained deacon in August 1579, and Andrewes deacon and priest ten months later. In the early 1580s, their roads diverged slightly, with Andrewes remaining in Cambridge for higher degrees (BD 1585, DD 1590) while Hooker took his first benefice (1584) and then appointment as Master of the Temple (1585). At this point, we encounter a variable in the genesis of avant-garde conformity to which we will return—London. No sooner had Hooker taken his Temple pulpit, preaching in a pastoral mode deemed too indulgent of weak or even false beliefs, than he found himself locked in battle with the rigid Reformism of Walter Travers. Their pulpit tussle was deemed so unseemly by Archbishop Whitgift that he silenced both men in 1586. Hooker forthwith channelled his convictions, or his pique, into writing the *Lawes*. And two years after that row at the Temple, Andrewes returned to his native London. Thanks to the combined efforts of Walsingham (who feared Andrewes would be wasted in a country parish) and Lettice Knollys (who held the right of presentation of a prebendal stall at St Paul's from her recently deceased husband, the earl of Leicester), Andrewes joined the Chapter of London's cathedral (May 1589). He had already been given its most populous London living, St Giles

---

[8] Diarmaid MacCulloch, 'Richard Hooker's Reputation', in Torrance Kirby (ed.), *A Companion to Richard Hooker* (Boston, 2008), p. 571.

Cripplegate (September 1588). With his ensuing election as Master of his Cambridge college, Pembroke Hall (September 1589), and to Residentiary status at St Paul's, Andrewes could be said to have pulled well ahead of the Master of the Temple in the preferment stakes. And from this date both men were firmly in the orbit of Whitgift—Andrewes as his chaplain, and Hooker as recipient of his patronage. The seeds of Andrewes's esteem for Hooker expressed at the latter's death—'Almighty God comfort us over him!... with inward and most just honour I ever honoured him since I knew him'—must have been sown, and probably well watered, by 1590.[9]

A perhaps unanswerable, but still pertinent question is, what happened to make these two men avant-garde? Coming face-to-face with radicalized puritanism seems to be at least an important part of an answer. The eruption of anti-establishment satire from the presses of Martin Marprelate in 1588–9 must have rankled with both, though, intriguingly, neither was a target. Hooker was only grazed by one bullet in Martin's opening salvo, the *Epistle*, in its appeal to Whitgift to 'Let the Templars have Master Travers their preacher restored again unto them, he is now at leisure to work your priesthood a woe I hope.'[10] Andrewes, as yet unpublished, and after only a few months in London, had probably not yet shown his hand. But if for Hooker puritanism incarnate took the form of Walter Travers, for Andrewes it was the perhaps more daunting person of his and Hooker's erstwhile patron, Walsingham. Writing in 1608, Sir John Harington (an avant-garde conformist himself)[11] said that Andrewes's 'Patron that studied proiects of pollicy as much as precepts of pietie' called for him 'and dealt earnestlie with him, to hold vp a side that was even then falling, and to maintaine certayn Statepoints of Puritanisme'. Harington continued with something which should qualify Lake's opinion that Andrewes 'was a man chronically devoid both of political sense and gumption': 'he had too much of the [man] in him to be skard with a Councellors frown', and 'answeared him playnly they were not only against his learning but his conscience'. So, having no sooner brought Andrewes to London, Walsingham found that his man was not 'to be taught in a Closet what he should say at Pouls'.[12]

Soon, too, Andrewes would confront a form of religious radicalism that would make Travers look, by comparison, conservative: the imprisoned separatists Henry Barrow and John Greenwood. In the spring of 1590, Andrewes was deployed by Whitgift in one of the many waves of clergy sent over the top

---

[9] Andrewes to Henry Parry, 7 Nov. 1600, in J. P. Wilson and J. Bliss (eds.), *The Works of Lancelot Andrewes*, 11 vols. (Oxford, 1841–54), XI, p. xli.

[10] Joseph L. Black, *The Martin Marprelate Tracts: A Modernized and Annotated Edition* (Cambridge, 2008), p. 26.

[11] Jason Scott-Warren, *Sir John Harington and the Book as Gift* (Oxford, 2001), ch. 7.

[12] Sir John Harington, *A Supplie or Addicion to the Catalogue of Bishops to the Yeare 1608*, ed. R. H. Miller (Potomac, MD, 1979), p. 139; Lake, 'Avant-Garde', p. 132.

to argue conformist sense into the two. But, as with the many others before him, Andrewes was mown down by Barrow's unflagging denunciation of everything from set forms of prayer to the parochial system itself, and, it seems, Andrewes's flawed New Testament Greek. Andrewes's impotent rage was revealed in his infamous snide remark to Barrow's face that confinement in the vile Fleet Prison was an enviable scholarly retreat. Scholars ever since have surely been right to cheer Barrow's response: 'You speake philosophically but not christianly.'[13] But also important, indeed more important here, are the startlingly avant-garde arguments which Andrewes dropped into his debate with Barrow, arguments which many conventional conformists themselves would have cringed to hear. He dismissed the validity of scriptural interpretation by any 'pryvat spyrit'; rejected Barrow's equation of Catholics with 'infidells' by asserting, 'We thinke more reverently of the papists than so, though they be idolaters'; repeatedly insisted that full membership in the body of Christ was available without the ministry of preaching; 'especially' claimed that 'Scriptures ought to be judged and interpreted by the ancyent fathers' wrytings, and not by other Scriptures'; and, when referred to a Geneva Bible, said that 'he utterly rejected both that translation and the notes thereuppon'.[14] Not only do we find here—in March 1590—Laudianism *avant la lettre*, but we also have avant-garde conformity *avant The Lawes of Ecclesiasticall Polity*.

Harington's parenthetical remark about Andrewes not being told what to do or say at St Paul's was also very to the point, for it was there, from 1589, that Andrewes attracted attention for practising what he preached to Barrow. In fact, Harington's contemporary biographical miniature of Andrewes anticipates by four hundred years Lake's list of Andrewesiana, and also makes clear that it constituted avant-garde conformity at the St Paul's of the 1590s, long before it was such 'at the court of James I'. Harington noted Andrewes's high view of learned but not excessive preaching ('his studie was not as most mens are... to get a little superficiall sight in devinity by reading two or three of the new wryters... and vp into the pulpet'); his revival at St Paul's of auricular confession keyed to the liturgical year ('espetiallie in Lent time... in one of the yles of the Church'), and defence of it by an avant-garde interpretation of the Prayer Book ('expressed and required *in a sort* in the Communion booke'; my emphasis); and his high view of the eucharist expressed bodily in ritual gesture ('his reverent speaking of the highest misterie of our faith, and heavenly foode the lords supper, which some... hold yt Idolatrie to receaue it kneeling'). For all of this, Andrewes was 'barked at' and 'quarrelld by divers'.[15]

What Andrewes was saying in the St Paul's pulpit, as well as doing in its aisles and at its altar, was all unusual, at least in the City of London, and has

---

[13] Leland H. Carlson (ed.), *The Writings of John Greenwood 1587–1590* (1962), p. 143.
[14] Carlson (ed.), *Writings of John Greenwood*, pp. 141, 149, 154–6, 158.
[15] Harington, *Supplie*, p. 140.

begun to receive scholarly attention. Nicholas Tyacke was the first to turn to the matter of Andrewes's London cathedral and parish sermons of the 1590s, which survive as very full notes printed in 1657, with a preface by the shrill Laudian Thomas Pierce, as ΑΠΟΣΠΑΣΜΑΤΙΑ SACRA ('Holy Fragments'). Of particular interest is the extended series of exegetical lectures on Genesis 1–4:26, dated as preached in two runs separated by some six years: on Genesis 1:1–3:13 (from the Creation through Eve's confession) preached from 13 October 1590 to 12 February 1592 at St Paul's; and on Genesis 3:14–4:26 (from God's punishment of Adam and Eve through the curse upon Cain) from 18 June 1598 to 17 February 1599 at St Giles. Tyacke observes the prominence of 'un-Calvinist' notes in the first run, but calls particular attention to Andrewes's thoroughgoing demolition of predestined reprobation in the later lectures on Cain and Abel.[16] In twenty lectures preached from February 1598 to February 1599, Andrewes interpreted Cain's loss of God's favour, his murder of Abel, and God's curse upon him not as the result of his having been a predestined reprobate, but solely as the result and then the punishment of his own wilful rebellion. Moreover, Andrewes understood Cain as compounding his own misery solely by his 'doubt of the forgivenesse of sinne', something always available to him, and to all sinners.[17] Tyacke sees Andrewes's decision to decamp for the Cain and Abel lectures from the 'much more public auditory' of St Paul's to St Giles after a six-year gap, as a tactful step likely taken to avoid attracting controversy. There may have been more mundane reasons for the hiatus, such as a period of dangerous ill-health suffered sometime in the decade.[18] But we find elsewhere support for the view that Andrewes put his head farther above the parapet in parish than in cathedral.

In 1592, with his Genesis lectures in full swing in St Paul's, he was in St Giles concurrently delivering a lecture series on the Ten Commandments, only two of which survive.[19] One of these, given the editorial title 'Of the Worshipping of Imaginations' in the Laudian edition, is a scathing rebuttal of the entire nonconformist and Presbyterian agenda, animated by the satirical conceit that whereas the Reformation had rightly abolished images, the Church's present detractors were simply replacing them with equally idolatrous 'imaginations'. It is a performance worthy, in places, of the tone and content of the latter stages of the Marprelate controversy. But Andrewes's critique extends far

---

[16] Nicholas Tyacke, 'Lancelot Andrewes and the Myth of Anglicanism', in Peter Lake and Michael Questier (eds.), *Conformity and Orthodoxy in the English Church, c.1560–1660* (Woodbridge, 2000), pp. 13–14; Peter McCullough (ed.), *Lancelot Andrewes: Selected Sermons and Lectures* (Oxford, 2005), pp. xviii–xix, 347–8.

[17] Lancelot Andrewes, *ΑΠΟΣΠΑΣΜΑΤΙΑ SACRA* (1657), pp. 363–499; quoting p. 449.

[18] Henry Isaacson, *An Exact Narration of the Life and Death of... Lancelot Andrewes* (1650), sig. *2v.

[19] William Laud and John Buckeridge (eds.), *XCVI. Sermons... by Lancelot Andrewes* (1629), pt. 2, pp. 25–48.

beyond mere anti-puritanism. To be sure, it condemns '*æquality* in the *Clergie*' and Presbyterian appeals to church government and ministry by '*Lay-elders*', '*Pastors* and *Doctors*', and '*Deacons* too: that they should be men of occupation and trade'. But Andrewes also attacked 'imaginations' about proper worship. He made the deliberately inflammatory suggestion that extempore prayers were often 'as long as a whole *Rosarie*' and just as full of 'fond *repetitions, tautologies*' and '*inconsequences*'; disdained the preference for newly written songs over Psalms and canticles appointed by the Prayer Book; and insisted that the '*partaking of* CHRIST's *true bodie*' was more than merely 'a *Signe, figure* or *remembrance* of it' which 'the Church ... should do better to celebrate more often', and for which, with 'the old Writers use no lesse, the word *Sacrifice*, then *Sacrament*; *Altar* then *Table*'.[20] So, while the *Lawes of Ecclesiasticall Polity* were as yet pen and ink on paper, Andrewes was already preaching the gist of Hooker on church government, ceremonies, liturgy, and eucharist, if not going beyond it. And both men, as MacCulloch has observed of Hooker, had decided not to drop tools after the routing of the Presbyterian *classes* movement by Whitgift in 1591.[21] On the contrary, there was still a common enemy for both and that enemy was not (at least not urgently) Roman Catholicism. Nor was it only the kind of Presbyterianism or separatism that, as Patrick Collinson has brilliantly shown us, drove Richard Bancroft's increasingly bug-eyed anti-puritan campaigns in the same decade.[22] Rather, Andrewes, like Hooker (but more in practice than on the page), had turned his sights on what had been, only decades before, entirely conventional high Elizabethan piety and practice.

It would be inaccurate, though, to give the impression that Andrewes, any more than Hooker, was the only begetter of avant-garde conformity. Or, perhaps more exactly, inaccurate to say that they should be credited with more than being at the right place at the right time to see their ecclesiastical style become a major force in the post-Reformation English Church. Pockets of sentiment and even practice did exist which, for decades before Andrewes and Hooker, could be described as anticipating all that those two men would articulate, but lacking the wider social and political circumstances for its open expression and wider imitation that they began to exploit in the 1590s. It should also be borne in mind how much historical narratives are at the mercy of the haphazard survival of evidence. I have already suggested how even the dates of publication of Andrewes's and Hooker's major works can subtly influence which period we associate each with. More dramatically, there is a great danger in privileging print evidence *tout court*. How different, for example, would our picture of Andrewes be in the 1590s without the chance

---

[20] Laud and Buckeridge (eds.), *XCVI. Sermons*, pt. 2, pp. 33–7.
[21] MacCulloch, 'Reputation', p. 568.
[22] Patrick Collinson, *Richard Bancroft and Elizabethan Anti-Puritanism* (Cambridge, 2013).

survival of his St Paul's and St Giles lectures? Or, for that matter, why should the idea of 'influence', or even 'publication' of avant-garde ideas be judged any less influential if published orally from a pulpit but not issued in print?

Kenneth Fincham and Nicholas Tyacke have kept many of these issues in mind in their application and extension of Lake's thesis in their survey of 'Avant-Garde Conformity and the English Church, c.1590–1625'.[23] Not least, they have called attention to avant-garde conformity having a home not only at the court of James I, but also of Elizabeth I. Whitgift's (and, after him, Bancroft's) anti-Presbyterian campaign had desperate need of conformist apologists, avant-garde or otherwise, and Hooker and Andrewes were preferred and encouraged accordingly. Still, Whitgift had little interest in pushing the boundaries either of liturgy or Calvinist doctrine beyond the inherited status quo. But the queen herself had consistently, if tactfully, been toeing what could be called an avant-garde conformist line since 1558. She did all she could, repeatedly, to keep a crucifix and candles on her Chapel Royal altar, and was capable of shouting down preachers who dared to object. She also preferred as her first Chapel dean George Carew, who had been content, though married, to accept preferment at the hands of her Catholic sister Mary. For the other senior clergy appointment in the royal household, the lord almonership, she preferred Bishop Edmund Guest who, in two sermons preached *coram regina* in 1561, explicitly commended the real presence of Christ in the eucharist, asserted universal grace, and insisted that all had the free will to accept or lose salvation. To complete the pattern, she appointed as Guest's successor as almoner in 1572 Edmund Freke, who as bishop of Norwich purged the diocese of radical preachers and earned the enmity of the godly gentry. Perhaps alone amongst the other higher clergy in the first decades of the reign who held similar views, was Bishop Richard Cheney of Gloucester. Without court office, his experience of pulpit attacks on him (to which Archbishop Parker was sympathetic) for his views of the real presence suggests that without Elizabeth's direct protection, these ancestors of later avant-garde conformity were not only rare birds, but also sitting ducks.[24]

But such was clearly not the case by the time that the last of these men, Freke, died in 1591. As the Whitgiftian establishment had become ever more conservative in defence of conformity, and with the deaths of more progressively Protestant counsellors like Leicester (1588) and Walsingham (1590) opening the way for the increasing influence of Whitgift and the Cecils, younger clergy like Andrewes, and Hooker perhaps, found greater scope to venture their avant-garde opinions. Lake in particular has recently stressed how the confluence of shifts in political power at court and the anti-puritan

---

[23] Kenneth Fincham and Nicholas Tyacke, *Altars Restored: the Changing Face of English Religious Worship, 1547–c.1700* (Oxford, 2007), ch. 3.
[24] Fincham and Tyacke, *Altars Restored*, pp. 75–9.

polemic unleashed in the Marprelate controversy made possible the 'further ideological and doctrinal change' pressed by Hooker, Andrewes, and others in the 1590s.[25] Although such pragmatic explanations are useful, they run the risk of obscuring additional prompts for change, such as personality, belief, and conviction. For example, as MacCulloch has observed, 'the accumulated vision of Hooker's work is uncannily close to what we can glean of the idiosyncratic private religious opinions' of Elizabeth.[26] She was evidently also impressed by Andrewes, making him one of her twelve select chaplains sometime in the early 1590s, and offering him no fewer than two bishoprics (which he declined, taking exception to the proferred terms) in the middle of the decade. Harington said that learned sermons like his 'that smelt of the Candle' appealed to her.[27] And he preached a eucharistic theology, strongly inflected by Lutheranism, which had not been heard of from the higher clergy since the days of Guest and Cheney. And Elizabeth herself was one of the few people still living who had not just heard it before, but had countenanced it.[28]

Members of the universities were also getting in on the avant-garde act, at least in its doctrinal aspects, by the 1590s, which raises further questions of just when and where this 'style' had its origins. The most well-known evidence is the *cause célèbre* of the Cambridge heads' prosecution in the spring and summer of 1595 of William Barrett for a university sermon which denied the predestinarian doctrine of assurance.[29] Within days of his sermon, Barrett found himself in the university's consistory court facing prosecution by a group of college heads, led by the rigid Calvinist William Whitaker. Barrett was required to recant publicly in terms of pure supralapsarianism, including that 'the reprobation of the wicked was from eternity'.[30] But since Barrett read his recantation with tongue firmly in cheek, he was summoned again, and both sides soon ran crying to Whitgift. On the advice of his chaplains, Andrewes and Hadrian Saravia, Whitgift queried the necessity of most of Barrett's recantation, which only sparked further ire from an even larger group of dons. The resulting 'Lambeth Articles', drafted by Whitaker, but carefully adjusted by Whitgift in light of advice from his chaplains and archbishop of York Matthew Hutton, were stopped short of fully official doctrinal status outside of Cambridge by the intervention of the queen. Meanwhile, Cambridge Calvinists had turned their sights in July on the anti-Calvinist Lady Margaret Professor of Divinity Peter Baro, who held Barrett's views. Both he and Barrett had left Cambridge within a year. Interpretation of these events still divides scholars. Nicholas Tyacke saw in Barrett and Baro the beginnings

---

[25] Lake, '"Anglican Moment"', pp. 105–8.   [26] MacCulloch, 'Reputation', p. 573.
[27] Harington, *Addicion*, p. 139.   [28] McCullough (ed.), *Andrewes*, p. 381.
[29] H. C. Porter, *Reformation and Reaction in Tudor Cambridge* (1958), pp. 314–90.
[30] Peter White, *Predestination, Policy and Polemic: Conflict and Consensus in the English Church from the Reformation to the Civil War* (Cambridge, 1992), p. 102.

of a sharply defined, reactionary anti-Calvinist movement; Peter White holds Whitaker and the other Cambridge heads' brand of 'high Calvinism' to be as avant-garde as Barrett and Baro's anti-Calvinism, and argues that Whitgift, Andrewes, Hooker, and Hutton occupied a moderate, carefully qualified Calvinist middle-ground. And most recently, Peter Lake has repositioned the entire episode by seeing Barrett and Baro's contributions as salvoes fired only after opening rounds in London by Samuel Harsnett and Andrewes, with Whitaker's move against them as defensive, not offensive.[31]

But if, as I have suggested, part of the worth of the very term 'avant-garde conformity' is to avoid the defining of this distinctive and influential style simply in doctrinal terms, then an impatience with Calvinist predestinarianism (however articulated) is only one constituent part of that style. By the same token, espousing any other single component part of the Andrewesian avant-garde package does not an avant-garde conformist make. So, for example, Richard Bancroft's anti-puritanism and assertion of episcopacy by divine right (like his patron, Whitgift's) never joined hands with ceremonialism or sacramentalism, nor was he ever anything other than routinely Calvinist in theology—thus very much more a disciplinarian than an avant-garde conformist.[32] And the strongest roots of avant-garde conformity seem to me to be less in the theology of election, than in the (admittedly not unrelated) deep suspicion of sermon-centred piety, renewed investment in corporate liturgy (particularly choral and eucharistic), and changes to the apparatus of worship and the status of the clergy who presided over it all. Hooker rightly gets the credit for articulating these positions in the commanding prose of the *Lawes*. But on all of these scores, Andrewes was out in front putting them in practice, and also managing somehow (like Hooker again) to avoid involvement in anything as public or unseemly (or fatal to him) as the Barrett and Baro controversy.

Under the possible cover of academic display—and Latin—he had chosen his divinity act, or lecture upon taking his doctorate in June 1590, to wield a very sharp double-edged sword. Broadly a defence of tithes as belonging to the clergy by divine right (itself a claim unheard of since the reign of Mary Tudor), Andrewes struck out not only at new Presbyterian schemes to replace tithes with stipends administered by lay elders, but also at the present system, instituted by Henry VIII and grossly exploited by Elizabeth, of alienating church property to the crown for both its own profit and for dispensing as patronage to lay favourites. His breath-taking exordium used the thin allegorical cover of the story of building Solomon's Temple to condemn the Tudor establishment's denuding of the Church and clergy for the sake of '*Court*

---

[31] Nicholas Tyacke, *Anti-Calvinists: The Rise of English Arminianism, c.1590–1640* (Oxford, 1987), pp. 29–34; White, *Predestination*, pp. 101–23; Lake, '"Anglican Moment"', p. 109.
[32] *ODNB*, 'Bancroft, Richard (1544–1610)'.

Vanities' and to line the pockets of *'Court-Ratts'*. The victim of 'our *Clergy-Devourers*' was not simply the wealth of the clergy (albeit, he said, 'the *condition* of the *Clergy* ought to be...nearer *Envy,* then *Mercy*'), but also the quality of the clergy. When beholden to lay patrons for impoverished livings with revenues that amounted to little more than 'a *piece of silver,* and *a bit of bread*', the *'consecrated Priest*', he said, was 'even of the *lowest of the people'.* Thus denigrated, so the avant-garde logic followed, ministers pandered to the lay patrons' impoverished view of priesthood which held that 'any, that can but *weare a long Gowne,* and *prate by the houre-glasse, and huddle out much, no matter what, to the purpose or beside,* shall bee a fit *PROPHET* for Us'. And when Andrewes used architectural terms as a metaphor for this ruination of the clergy, he hinted strongly at the neglect of church buildings and the apparatus of worship: 'truly the *wasts* and *ruins* of the *Church* are manifest...I see the *decaies, and dilapidations'*.[33] Lake has identified the investment of ceremonies with a spiritual status greater than mere things indifferent as one of Hooker's most important innovations in Book V of the *Lawes* (1597) and as a hallmark of the Jacobean Andrewes's avant-garde reorientations of conformity; Fincham and Tyacke's research adds that in 1597 and 1598 John Howson of Oxford would preach up building and furnishing churches; and John Overall would do the same in private correspondence in 1605.[34] But in 1590 Andrewes had already declared that not just ceremonies, but even church fabric and funds, were nothing less than holy: 'it is evident that *things may be consecrated to Holy use,* even under the *Gospel*' (for which read, 'even under the Reformation').[35] He even took similar sentiments to court in a sermon preached before the queen in Lent 1593. Without apology, but with some strategic compliments to the queen, he compared any objection to endowing the church to Judas Iscariot's scorning of Mary Magdalen for anointing Christ's feet. He added that to spoil or steal from the Church was 'plaine sacrilege', and (ever with his eye on perceived hypocrisies in conformist thought) that sin, he said, 'is (if not worse, yet) as bad as *Idolatrie*' (and tightened the screw even further by explicitly citing 'Saint Paul... Rom. 2.22').[36]

It should be little surprise, then, that we find Andrewes a pivotal figure in a 1594 parochial case which had at its heart both a church endowment and the chance to privilege choral liturgy over preaching (again, positions that had to wait until 1597 for Hooker to express in print). Fincham and Tyacke discovered the important incident of Christ Church Newgate Street's long-running Elizabethan tussle over its Henrician foundation's provision of five

---

[33] McCullough (ed.), *Andrewes,* pp. 83, 89, 97–8.
[34] Lake, '"Anglican Moment"', p. 102; Lake, 'Avant-Garde', p. 130; Fincham and Tyacke, *Altars Restored,* pp. 86–7, 89.
[35] McCullough (ed.), *Andrewes,* p. 94.
[36] Laud and Buckeridge (eds.), *XCVI. Sermons,* p. 291.

singing ministers. The churchwardens complained in 1580 that 'the auditory and parishioners' were 'not edified' by either the singers or the organs, prompting over a decade's worth of back-and-forth between traditionalists and progressives, the one for music, the other for sermons. Finally coming before the High Commission in 1594, Whitgift appointed a committee of two— Andrewes and the powerful ecclesiastical lawyer Sir Edward Stanhope—to hear the case. Unsurprisingly, the two upheld the original intent of the endowment and choral worship by recommending the reinstatement of the singers. The Commission duly enforced their view upon the parish in March 1595. Not insignificantly, either, Fincham and Tyacke attribute Andrewes's appointment to the committee as likely stemming from his appointment as commissary of the diocese of London on 6 June 1594; that is, Andrewes exercised episcopal jurisdiction in the diocese during the vacancy between the death of bishop John Aylmer on 5 June and the election of his successor, Richard Fletcher, on 30 December.[37] And was Andrewes defending parochial choral worship with one avant-garde hand while he was using the other to promulgate avant-garde anti-Calvinism? Just months before making his recommendation in the Christ Church case, Andrewes had gone so far as to coin the new word 'imperseverant' to hold up, in a sermon before the queen, Lot's wife (turned into a pillar of salt for disobeying God's orders not to look back on Sodom) as proof positive of how salvation was not secure for those who did not constantly exercise their own will and moral fortitude in cooperation with God's grace.[38] And in the same year Andrewes's fellow collegian, Samuel Harsnett, preached what has long been recognized as one of the decade's most vehement attacks on double predestination. But not noticed has been the fact that the date of its delivery—27 October 1594—falls precisely within Andrewes's active service as commissary of the diocese. Since appointment to preach at Paul's Cross was made by the bishop of London, might Andrewes, as commissary, not very well have been responsible for appointing his younger, outspoken colleague to do the dirty deed of avant-garde preaching in the rough-and-tumble arena that was Paul's Cross?[39]

Mention of a parish church and the civic pulpit of Paul's Cross brings me, then, to what must be the most urgent need for further research on the origins of avant-garde conformity and its growth in the 1590s. Andrewes and Hooker must be well established now as the catwalk stars of the new style. But who was

---

[37] Fincham and Tyacke, *Altars Restored*, pp. 95–6; *The Clergy of the Church of England Database* (theclergydatabase.org.uk, accessed 3 Mar. 2014), record ID 241672; Joyce M. Horn, 'Bishops of London', *Fasti Ecclesiae Anglicanae 1541–1857: volume 1: St. Paul's, London* (1969), pp. 1–4.

[38] McCullough (ed.), *Andrewes*, pp. 108–21, 353–65; Fincham and Tyacke, *Altars Restored*, p. 84.

[39] Fincham and Tyacke, *Altars Restored*, pp. 84–5; Mary Morrissey, *Politics and the Paul's Cross Sermons, 1558–1642* (Oxford, 2011), pp. 26–7.

applauding at their feet? Enthusiastically approving of Andrewes's intervention at Christ Church Newgate Street was the antiquary Edmund Howes and his father, and a network of rich merchant taylors including Robert Dow and the brothers William, Robert, and John Parker. The elder two would in the next reign further endow music-making at Christ Church and in their native Staffordshire, and grace the north choir aisle of St Paul's Cathedral with windows depicting the life of its patron; and the youngest would in 1626 be entrusted as executor of the vast estate left by Andrewes. If, as Fincham and Tyacke suggest, 'avant-garde conformism would appear to have run in the Parker family', we need more studies of families like them.[40] The receptivity of some kinds of Londoners to Andrewes's arresting ministry in parish and cathedral is not wholly undocumented. Surely significant is that the first praise of him as a preacher came from the pen of one under-employed and overly-educated writer who truly deserves the epithet 'avant-garde', Thomas Nashe, upon the recommendation of another, John Lyly:

> Doctor *Androwes*: who (if it bee no offence so to compare him) is *tanquam Paulus in Cathedra*, powerfull preaching like *Paul* out of his chaire; and his Church another *Pantheon*, or *Templum omnium deorum*, the absolutest Oracle of all sound Deuinitie heere amongst vs; hee mixing the two seuerall properties of an Orator and a Poet both in one, which is not onely to perswade, but to win admiration.[41]

A surviving manuscript copy of Andrewes's Genesis lectures bears on its flyleaf the seventeenth-century testimonial that it was bound and owned by Sir Paul Pindar, who, it says, '*had noe Pictshure in his house But the Pictshure of Docter Andrewes*'.[42] And Pindar—trained as an apprentice to a London haberdasher whose agent he was in Venice, and then leading ambassador and financier—was a prime patron of early Stuart avant-garde church building and decoration.[43] Andrewes's household steward and later biographer, Henry Isaacson, along with his domestic chaplains the Wren brothers Matthew and Christopher, were all sons of liverymen of the London Painter-Stainers Company.[44] All of this, taken together with several scholars' work on the distinctly avant-garde tradition of churchmanship in the Elizabethan city and abbey of Westminster that was nurtured by its dean Gabriel Goodman and the Cecil family, must pose the question of whether the seeds of avant-garde conformity

---

[40] Fincham and Tyacke, *Altars Restored*, pp. 98–9.
[41] Thomas Nashe, *Have With You to Saffron Waldon* (1596), in R. B. McKerrow (ed.), rev. F. P. Wilson, *The Works of Thomas Nashe*, 5 vols. (1958), III, pp. 105, 107.
[42] P. G. Stanwood, 'Lancelot Andrewes's "Orphan Lectures": The Exeter Manuscript', *English Manuscript Studies*, 13 (2008): 35–46. Formerly in private ownership, the manuscript was purchased in 2013 by Pembroke College Cambridge.
[43] Fincham and Tyacke, *Altars Restored*, pp. 166–7, 231–2.
[44] *ODNB*, 'Isaacson, Henry (1581–1654)', 'Wren, Matthew (1585–1667)'.

flourished when they fell on a field whose fertility was as much, broadly speaking, artistic and aesthetic as theological or political.[45] And there, perhaps, lies another of Lake's great insights—that avant-garde conformity, like any of the perennials in the various garden of 'churchmanship' through the ages, is as much about style as it is about substance. Andrewes's style had its heyday late in his own life when indulged by King James, and posthumously when that style became the substance of Laudianism under King Charles. But in Laud's dirigiste hands it fuelled a civil war. Although Andrewes was, after the Restoration, often coupled with Hooker in the stakes to define and assert a quintessential 'Anglicanism', Andrewes never proved as malleable to diverse interests as did Hooker—nineteenth- and twentieth-century evangelicals have not fought to claim Andrewes's legacy from 'catholic' Anglicans like they have Hooker's. Here perhaps we have the final proof that Andrewes's avant-garde conformity was always more 'avant' than Hooker's, and that if his more advanced guard in the 1590s constituted anything quintessentially 'Anglican', it was in marking out one of the many perennially contested territories of what became Anglicanism.

SELECT BIBLIOGRAPHY

Andrewes, Lancelot, *XCVI. Sermons*, ed. William Laud and John Buckeridge (1629).
Andrewes, Lancelot, *ΑΠΟΣΠΑΣΜΑΤΙΑ SACRA* (1657).
Andrewes, Lancelot, *Selected Sermons and Lectures*, ed. Peter McCullough (Oxford, 2005).
Andrewes, Lancelot, *Works*, ed. J. P. Wilson and J. Bliss, 11 vols. (Oxford, 1841–54).
Collinson, Patrick, *Richard Bancroft and Elizabethan Anti-Puritanism* (Cambridge, 2013).
Fincham, Kenneth and Peter Lake (eds.), *Religious Politics in Post-Reformation England: Essays in Honour of Nicholas Tyacke* (Woodbridge, 1996).
Fincham, Kenneth and Nicholas Tyacke, *Altars Restored: The Changing Face of English Religious Worship, 1547–c.1700* (Oxford, 2007).
Harington, Sir John, *A Supplie or Addicion to the Catalogue of Bishops to the Yeare 1608*, ed. R. H. Miller (Potomac, MD, 1979).
Hooker, Richard, gen. ed. W. Speed Hill, *The Folger Library Edition of the Works of Richard Hooker*, 7 vols. (Cambridge, MA, 1977–89).
Lake, Peter, 'The "Anglican Moment"? Richard Hooker and the Ideological Watershed of the 1590s', in Stephen Platten (ed.), *Anglicanism and the Western Christian Tradition: Continuity, Change and the Search for Communion* (Norwich, 2003), pp. 90–121.

---

[45] Julia F. Merritt, *The Social World of Early Modern Westminster* (Manchester, 2005), pp. 75–80; Fincham and Tyacke, *Altars Restored*, p. 84.

Lake, Peter, *Anglicans and Puritans? Presbyterianism and English Conformist Thought from Whitgift to Hooker* (1988).

Lake, Peter, 'Lancelot Andrewes, John Buckeridge, and Avant-Garde Conformity at the Court of James I', in Linda Levy Peck (ed.), *The Mental World of the Jacobean Court* (Cambridge, 1990), pp. 113–33.

MacCulloch, Diarmaid, 'Richard Hooker's Reputation', in Torrance Kirby (ed.), *A Companion to Richard Hooker* (Boston, 2008), pp. 563–612.

Merritt, Julia F., *The Social World of Early Modern Westminster* (Manchester, 2005).

Porter, H. C., *Reformation and Reaction in Tudor Cambridge* (1958).

Shuger, Debora, *Habits of Thought in the English Renaissance: Religion, Politics, and the Dominant Culture* (Berkeley and Los Angeles, CA, 1990).

Tyacke, Nicholas, *Anti-Calvinists: The Rise of English Arminianism, c.1590–1640* (Oxford, 1987).

Tyacke, Nicholas, 'Lancelot Andrewes and the Myth of Anglicanism', in Peter Lake and Michael Questier (eds.), *Conformity and Orthodoxy in the English Church, c.1560–1660* (Woodbridge, 2000), pp. 5–33.

White, Peter, *Predestination, Policy and Polemic: Conflict and Consensus in the English Church from the Reformation to the Civil War* (Cambridge, 1992).

21

Early Modern English Piety

Jessica Martin

In the 1530s the meaning of life changed. Every marker of community and identity altered its significance, even if the marker itself stayed the same shape. Here are only some of those markers: what it meant to die, to be sorry, to be redeemed, to be a family, a nation; the nature of days and seasons and the passing of time; what it meant to mourn, to feast, to remember. Some ways of living changed suddenly and radically, some with more reluctance and slowly. Some were intermittent and external; others altered root as well as branch.

Some ways of living—among them the visible, agreed shape of lived-out personal piety—changed less than one might suppose. But this concealed a most radical transformation: the events of personal holiness were no longer unambiguous signs of salvation, either in exemplary or in personal terms. It was not that they ceased to be powerful. It was that the extent of their power was contested and uncertain. With the dismantling of stable systems of penitence and its external acts (and with the rise of rigid doctrines of predestination) there were no clear signs available. Forgiveness and remembrance, in particular, had become completely different and much more ambiguous processes.[1] Lives lived around them (both are fundamental to the medieval sensibility) had become fragmented, splintered into small communities. Universally agreed sacramental meanings for life events broke up. In this period they did not disappear (or not for everyone involved) but their reach shrank and cracked. Some of what came through the cracks was violence, and some of it was a kind of freedom, but because the freedom and the violence were bound up with each other each individual soul became an undefended field of interpretation which might at any time become a hermeneutic battleground.

This is the world of early modern English piety. It was not, in our late modern sense, a fully private or individuated world, although the Reformed

---

[1] Sarah Beckwith, *Shakespeare and the Grammar of Forgiveness* (Ithaca, NY, 2011); Peter Marshall, *Beliefs and the Dead in Reformation England* (Oxford, 2002).

emphasis on a personal engagement with Scripture, especially as it was conveyed through the English Calvinism imported from Geneva by the Marian exiles from the mid-sixteenth century, fostered a sense of the work of salvation as one expressed through the formally unreliable or occluded medium of private experience. (Calvinism's emphasis upon the particular soul's salvation might indeed indicate the beginning of our current understanding of the 'private' as an authentic state of withdrawal, a space for individual flourishing which imagines the solitary self to be complete. Its flip-side is the personal alienation to which much late modern cultural attention is directed.)[2] Even if so, privacy in this sense was only beginning; and early modern piety is deeply imbued with the politicized battles over public modes of worship and religious identity at the same time as this individuated (and, in soteriological terms, profoundly untrustworthy) sensibility is on the rise.[3] By the 1620s the potentially nightmarish components of modern privacy were fully assembled. These are eloquently demonstrated by John Donne's portrait of individual alienation in his *Devotions on Emergent Occasions* of 1624, which he constructs to be a bridge between isolated disease and the healing properties of *koinonia* (Christian community) mediated by Christ the Physician.[4] The book's most famous phrase—'No man is an island entire of itself'—should be read against this alienated setting. Donne intends his imagination in the *Devotions* to be monstrous, and the picture of forced isolation he paints is figured as a life-crisis—a fever of soul as well as body, which is both as everyday and as singularly cataclysmic as the regular bouts of life-threatening ague or fatal plague which formed part of the grain of early modern life.

What follows, then, discusses piety not only or even mainly as a 'private' practice, but as it is implicated in the many fault-lines of the public religious life of the Church of England in this period. I consider it as it is manifested in the practices of remembrance and holy imitation, the habits of prayer and the experience of conversion, engagement with Scripture, and the approach to death.

REMEMBRANCE, IMITATION, AND VIRTUE

Jacobus de Voragine, writing in the thirteenth century about the Feast of All Saints in his influential medieval collection *The Golden Legend*, has this to say about his readers' relation to the saints:

---

[2] E.g. Charles Taylor, *Sources of the Self* (Cambridge, MA, 1989); Brad S. Gregory, *The Unintended Reformation: How a Religious Revolution Secularized Society* (Cambridge, MA, 2012).

[3] Erica Longfellow, '"My Now Solitary Prayers": *Eikon Basilike* and Changing Attitudes towards Religious Solitude', in Jessica Martin and Alec Ryrie (eds.), *Private and Domestic Devotion in Early Modern Britain* (Farnham, 2012), pp. 53–72.

[4] John Donne, *Devotions upon Emergent Occasions* (1624).

> When we honor the saints, we are taking care of our own interests and procuring our own honor. Their feast day honors us. When we pay tribute to our brothers, we honor ourselves, since love makes all things to be in common, and all things are ours, in heaven, on earth, and in eternity.[5]

For Voragine, honouring the saints is a collective act of virtuous self-interest, operating within the complete and single world of the communion of saints, a world which builds the spiritual health of the living upon a partnership with the dead. It is both a two-way ladder between heaven and earth assisting personal holiness (we honour them, they intercede with God for us) and an expression of cross-temporal Christian solidarity. His remark expresses with particular neatness what confidence is felt in this integrated vision: 'all things are ours, in heaven, on earth, and in eternity'.

Compare this to the Collect for the Second Sunday after Easter as it appears in the 1549 Book of Common Prayer:

> ALMIGHTIE God, whiche haste geven thy holy sonne to bee unto us, bothe a sacrifice for synne, and also an example of Godly life; Geve us the grace that we maie alwaies moste thankfully receive that his inestimable benefite, and also dayely indevour ourselfes to folow the blessed steppes of his moste holy lyfe.[6]

This is a much more equivocal understanding of the relationship between honour (or worship) and personal sanctity. It is a balancing act. In the wake of Easter, the faithful contemplate their sole means to salvation, Christ's sacrifice recently marked in Holy Week. Yet their attention on the unique event of his death and resurrection is counterpoised by a different kind of focus on Christ's life. The Collect leaves the implicit *sola gratia, sola fide* theme to consider the daily labour of pious imitation, an endeavour marked by a submerged image of pilgrimage: we 'folow...blessed steppes'. As those steps apply to the days of Christ's own life they are the steps of a journey rather than gradated accretions of holiness; but as they apply to the hearer the meanings merge. Here the hard cumulative work of traditional piety makes an uneasy pact with a reformed emphasis on grace. As the Prayer Book was revised across the period, this Collect, and its equivocations, stayed almost exactly the same, its balancing act a cameo of the position that was in time to be called 'Anglicanism'.

The Collect's survival, even in the face of a dominant reformed insistence that the works of piety had nothing definite to say to salvation, suggests an ineradicable desire across all the shades of reform for the worked-out practice of holy living. And indeed the reformed sensibility went to work to reinterpret accumulating virtue as the fruit, rather than the means, of grace, via the

---

[5] Jacobus de Voragine, *The Golden Legend: Readings on the Saints*, trans. William Granger Ryan, 2 vols. (Princeton, NJ, 1993), II, p. 274.

[6] Brian Cummings (ed.), *The Book of Common Prayer: The Editions of 1549, 1559, and 1662* (Oxford, 2011).

Lutheran distinction between justification and sanctification. The pastoral, and even the argumentative base for such arguments wobbled sometimes, but the trajectory was clear: 'daily procede further and further' wrote John Brinsley in 1608, 'from vertue to vertue'.[7] Everyone was in any case soaked in an Aristotelian understanding of virtue as *character*, or (literally) engraved impression, developed through the repeated, socialized practice of disciplines of body and mind. Acquiring the habit of virtue was, in practice, something that all shades of conformists would put a mind to, although the theological justification for it would vary across the spectrum from ceremonialist and sacramental understandings of grace to rigidly predestinarian ones.

With the desire to accumulate virtue went the need for models upon which holy living might be based and with whom the pious might identify and join themselves as part of an unambiguous cross-temporal Christian community, but the integrated world expressed by Voragine's remark had been dismantled, the channels of communication between the dead and the living cut. The huge array of medieval saints had largely been pruned from the Calendar—the saints' days of the Book of Common Prayer only commemorate the apostles (plus a couple of notable women) recorded in the New Testament. In an article published in 1942, Helen C. White remarks that the 'two clearest casualties' in mid-sixteenth-century religious publishing in England were the saint's life, and the contemplative treatise.[8] But the impulse to imitation and indeed to honour was not to be diminished easily. As quickly as the rites and places associated with the great array of medieval saints were suppressed and destroyed, new models arose for—sometimes problematically interpreted—veneration and imitation.

The reformers themselves were textually reconstructed to become examples of holiness. John Bale translated an account of the death of Luther into English in 1546 and John Stradling did the same service for Theodore Beza's life of Calvin in 1564.[9] Most startlingly, John Foxe's hugely influential *Actes and Monuments* of 1563, itself deliberately constructed to integrate the Marian martyrs with the body of the martyred Church across the ages in a mode designed to eclipse Voragine, had at the front of its slimmer first edition a 'Kalendar'. This echoed the form of the medieval saints' Calendar, with black- and red-letter days for lesser and greater saints across the year, but in the names written upon it those of the Marian martyrs predominated. New saints had been invented to replace the old. The 'Kalendar' itself disappeared in the

---

[7] Alec Ryrie, *Being Protestant in Reformation Britain* (Oxford, 2013), pp. 409–16; John Brinsley, *The True Watch, and Rule of Life* (1608), p. 162.

[8] Helen C. White, 'Some Continuing Traditions in English Devotional Literature', *PMLA*, 57 (1942): 966–80 (p. 969).

[9] Justus Jonas and others, *The True Hystorye of the Christen Departynge of D. Martyne Luther*, trans. John Bale (Marburg, 1546); Theodore Beza, *A Discourse...Conteyning in Briefe the Historie of the Life and Death of Maister Iohn Calvin*, translated by I.S. (1564).

expanded edition of 1570.[10] By then, though, digests of Foxe had emerged and were selling well, further fuelling the pious need for models of martyrdom.[11]

For in the popular imagination the Protestant martyrs of Foxe and others remained a powerful influence comparable to that of the pre-Reformation saint. They retained a kind of soteriological force for many readers,[12] though no doubt for others prurience joined forces with piety. Martyrdoms, unlike other forms of popular anti-Catholic literature within the broadside ballad tradition, survive well into the seventeenth century in the repertoire of the pedlar's pack, especially if the martyr were a woman. Anne Askew was persistently popular.[13] Foxe's *Actes* itself moved from a central established position in the sixteenth century to inspire new generations of different kinds of dissenter to imitative martyrdoms (not necessarily fatal ones) over the course of the seventeenth century, eventually finding its spiritual home in the formal nonconformities recognized after 1663.

Scriptural templates for holiness were, of course, many. There were readymade 'characters' for the behaviour of the clergy and of bishops, used across the spectrum of churchmanship—in, for example, the requirements set out in the third chapter of the first letter of Timothy, widely used throughout the period.[14] The vexed but widespread practice of proto-biographical funeral sermons encouraged a kind of marriage of the scriptural ideal with particular historical exemplars. If anything, the battle (waged as part of the Admonition controversy of the 1570s) over ensuring that funeral sermons had a properly homiletic rather than purely eulogistic focus, further encouraged preachers to press together scriptural and individual details into an exemplary alloy.[15]

For some preachers this was just eulogy by other means. For others the scriptural expression was the main point, the historical detail a potentially sinful distraction. The relation between 'honour' and edification was by now anything but integrated. Yet there are moments of unexpected unity. The author (probably Richard Sibbes) of 'A Triall of Sinceritie', preached at the funeral of a woman in the 1630s, finds his subject's identity delineated fully through his scriptural text. She chose what he should preach on, Isaiah 26:8–9: 'the sweet Swan-like song of our deceased Sister... there not being in the

---

[10] John Foxe, *Actes and Monuments* (1563), sigs. *iii–*v; Foxe, *Actes and Monuments* (1570), sigs. Ciiir–Civr.

[11] E.g. Clement Cotton, *The Mirror of Martyrs* (six editions, 1613–37).

[12] Ryrie, *Being Protestant*, pp. 422–7.

[13] Tessa Watt, 'Piety in the Pedlar's Pack', in Margaret Spufford (ed.), *The World of Rural Dissenters* (Cambridge, 1995), p. 245n46.

[14] E.g. Edward Leigh, 'Epistle Dedicatory' to William Whateley, *Prototypes, or the Primary President Precedents out of the Booke of Genesis* (1640), sigs. A3r/4; John Barwick, *The Fight, Victory and Triumph of St Paul. Accommodated to the Right Reverend Father-in-God, Thomas* (1660), p. 141.

[15] Patrick Collinson, *Godly People: Essays on English Protestantism and Puritanism* (1983), p. 519.

whole Scripture, a portion that will afford a fitter Character...for her person'.[16] Its words bring together the longing soul and the recollection of God: 'in the way of thy judgements, O Lord, have we waited for thee; the desire of our soul is to thy name, and to the remembrance of thee'. This woman is remembered in her remembrance of God; her name (now lost) becomes his name, and as the text itself stands for her essence, so it also comes very close to confirming her felicity—as, perhaps, its chooser trusted that it might.

Like a number of exemplary commemorations for women, this one demonstrates a measure of self-determination for female piety both in its conduct and in the mediation of that conduct through commemoration.[17] But generally in commemorations for women or the young the line between exemplary self-fashioning and homiletic appropriation is not so much fine as blurred. Within the medium of print (the less culturally defined world of manuscript or even manuscript publication is a different matter) it is rare for an unambiguously expressed female act of remembrance to be allowed to emerge. (Women did not, of course, preach sermons; and funeral sermons constitute the main source for remembrances.) The closest parallel is the 'mother's legacy' genre, where a mother writes and publishes pious advice to an unborn child, a form which offers a less circumscribed canvas for the expression of female piety but which nevertheless tends to enjoy a freer expression in manuscript.[18]

This tense and difficult relationship between remembrance and the exemplary was characteristic of the Church of England's attitude towards its own reformation. Its ambivalences show early in the conflicted attitude to physical remembrances of the dead, especially the noble dead, in the mid-sixteenth century, where church monuments were sometimes defaced or destroyed and sometimes honoured and preserved.[19] Another, somewhat later version of reformed corkscrew thinking on remembrance also emerges in the double bluff commonly resorted to by the exemplary commemorators of the hotter sort of divine. So it was that when the puritan John Carter died, he required of his commemorator, Samuel Ward, that nothing should be said of his virtues in his funeral sermon. Yet his wish was circumvented by having them preached upon by Ward in Ipswich shortly after his funeral, and his modesty in forbidding any mention of his virtues was celebrated by Carter's biographer Samuel Clarke in his *Lives of Twenty-Two Godly Divines* (1661–2).[20]

---

[16] 'A Triall of Sinceritie; or, the Desire of the Faithfull', in *The House of Mourning* (1640), p. 299.

[17] Peter Lake, 'Feminine Piety and Personal Potency: The "Emancipation" of Mrs Jane Ratcliffe', *The Seventeenth Century*, 2 (1987): 143–65.

[18] E.g. *Mothers' Advice Books*, selected and introduced by Betty A. Travitsky (Aldershot, 2000): the collection includes Dorothy Leigh, *The Mother's Blessing*; Elizabeth Gymeston, *Miscelleanea, Meditations, Memoratives*; Elizabeth Joscelin, 'A Mother's Legacie to her Unborne Child'.

[19] Marshall, *Beliefs and the Dead*, pp. 93–123.

[20] Collinson, *Godly People*, p. 520.

For the first generation of worshippers in the newly reformed Church of England, and for recusant families induced to conformity later than that, the question mark over the salvation of their forefathers added a bitter and difficult extra emotional layer to the practice of remembrance. This is the place for Hamlet's ghost-father, whose relation to Hamlet's agonies of identity is so ambiguous.[21] Whereas the doctrine of purgatory had systematized the inevitable uncertainties about the dead's final destinations, its loss left few mechanisms for determining what in this world might be imitable, holy, or venerable in the lives or deaths of any person at all. Perhaps the rise in popularity of the 'Character' book, and the employment of the 'how to' form for administering life-advice to clergy, provided theologically safer forums for recommending qualities without implicating particular persons; and both the character and the advice genre do influence exemplary commemorations. The most famous example of an advice book which crosses over towards the life-writing genre is seen in the transformation of sections of George Herbert's *The Country Parson* (published in Barnabas Oley's *Herbert's Remaines* [1652]) into narrative sections of Izaak Walton's *Life of Mr George Herbert* (1670).[22]

Only over the person of Christ could there be no question mark, though in practice the narrated experiences of conversion and assurance could offer a measure of confidence as to whether someone were saved. It makes sense, then, to move to consider the person of Christ as a pattern for imitation, and the dynamics both of conversion and of pious habit in this period.

Christ is both the only secure subject for imitation and an extremely problematic one. How to imitate the inimitable? There is still mileage in J. Sears McGee's remark that the notion of Christ as exemplary model was an 'Anglican' (by which he means relatively high church Arminian) one, whereas the 'puritan' sensibility would prefer to talk of having an 'interest and portion' in him.[23] The reasoning is that only those who thought such imitation to be within the compass of human effort—that is to say, not Calvinists—would think like this. Added to this is the problematic, dangerously iconic history of regarding Christ as a devotional spectacle, particularly in relation to his passion and crucifixion.[24] Long ago M. M. Knappen remarked on the puritan tendency to cite the Old Testament and the epistles rather than the gospels; this also alters the scriptural relationship of readers to what they read from a concentration on the events of Christ's life and death to a concentration (especially in reading the epistles) on the narrative of their own potential regeneracy.[25]

---

[21] Stephen Greenblatt, *Hamlet in Purgatory* (Princeton, NJ, 2001).
[22] Jessica Martin, *Walton's Lives* (Oxford, 2001), pp. 82–9, 218–22.
[23] J. Sears McGee, *The Godly Man in Stuart England* (New Haven, CT, 1976), p. 107.
[24] Jessica Martin, 'Reformed Responses to the Passion', in Martin and Ryrie (eds.), *Private and Domestic Devotion*, pp. 115–34.
[25] M. M. Knappen, *Tudor Puritanism* (Chicago, IL, 1939), p. 376.

That said, there is a smaller but significant body of work which shows a more varied readership for Christological devotion, including Passion devotions, than this would assume. William Perkins, so central to English Calvinism, wrote a highly visualized devotional tract on the crucifixion, *The True Manner of Knowing Christ Crucified* (1596).[26] The history of the medieval contemplative treatise *Imitatio Christi*, traditionally ascribed to Thomas a Kempis, is significant here. A text of restricted circulation before the Reformation, it became a best-seller in the last quarter of the sixteenth century in its translation by the Calvinist conformist Thomas Rogers; by 1730 it had gone through seventeen editions.[27] Yet Rogers's translation is also an adaptation to Protestant devotional needs—mediated not so much through the nature of the main translation as through the scriptural citations he adds. These are indeed very largely from the epistles and the psalms (each couched in the devotional, the passionate, the anxiously ratiocinating 'I') rather than from the gospels, so that between the *sententiae* of the text and its scriptural marginalia there is an invitation to experiential spiritual autobiography, the process of which supplants gospel devotional spectacle almost entirely. Rogers's *Imitation* is not, after all, an exemplary text exactly, but one of anxious, first-person sensibility; more than a little puritan.

The directly exemplary account of Christ as model emerges with Jeremy Taylor's (also best-selling) volume *The Great Exemplar of Sanctity and Holy Life*, published in the significant year 1649.[28] Taylor's instructions on how to read it are firmly in the 'blessed steps' tradition, for like King Wenceslas's pageboy (and Taylor gives this very example in his preface) its reader is invited to step in Christ's footmarks to ease his own struggles in life's journey.[29] Taylor's text draws explicitly on medieval models, especially Nicholas Love's *Myrrour of the Blessed Lyf of Jesu Christ* (c.1400). And for Taylor, practising the habits of virtue begets more virtue, of a highly civic and achievable kind; his Christ is also highly civic, modelling a life Taylor calls 'holy' but 'ordinary'. (Taylor had never had much time for an over-insistence on the paralysing effects of original sin.)[30] At the same time its form is designed to be immersive for the reader, even transformative: moving from narrative to reflection to prayer; reading as action.

---

[26] Martin, 'Reformed Responses', p. 125.

[27] Ian Green, *Print and Protestantism in Early Modern England* (Oxford, 2000), p. 656; Roger Lovatt, 'The *Imitation of Christ* in Late Medieval England', *Transactions of the Royal Historical Society*, 5th ser., 18 (1968): 97–121 (p. 114); Maximilian von Hapsburg, *Catholic and Protestant Translations of the Imitatio Christi, 1425–1650* (Farnham, 2011), pp. 49–178.

[28] Green, *Print and Protestantism*, pp. 325, 663 (but note Wing T342).

[29] Jeremy Taylor, *The Great Exemplar of Sanctity and Holy Life* (1649), sig. A4r.

[30] Andrew Harvey, 'Original Sin, Grace and Free Will in the Works of Jeremy Taylor', PhD thesis, University of Birmingham, 2012; *ODNB*, 'Taylor, Jeremy (1613–1667)'.

CONVERSION, HABIT, AND SCRIPTURE

In the preface to his short devotional book *The Golden Grove*, a manual designed to inculcate and foster Christian habit, Jeremy Taylor deplores the religious regime of the Commonwealth, contrasting past 'devotions... regular and constant' under Establishment with the rule of 'impertinent and ignorant preachers, who think all religion is a sermon'.[31] His sense that religious disciplines and behaviours suffer with the loss of liturgy and the rise of inflammatory demonstrative rhetoric is, of course, polemically exaggerated. However, there certainly is a tension between the see-saw modes of a faith built around an often endlessly receding personal hope of election, and one based—in effect, cumulatively—on daily patterns of virtuous striving.

Not that this tension can be simply divided into 'Anglican' behaviours and 'puritan' feeling. Pious behaviour and soteriological anxiety subsisted together for most people—in all but the most extreme antinomian end of pious practice; indeed, the particular combination of Calvinist sensibility and a lively sense of liturgical efficacy in domestic observance are the main ingredients for a distinctive emergent 'Anglican' pious tradition. But the relative proportions of each ingredient in the mix were very far from stable, varying across the religious spectrum and changing assumptions of the period. The relationship between the religious dynamics of conversion and the disciplines of habit is delicate, and not necessarily inimical.

We cannot know what people did in private prayer as certainly as we know what they did in public worship. We can only recover what is a matter of record: so, for example, we can know that in many households spontaneous prayer was offered and how it was received, but we cannot know what was said; and we know that in other households only set prayers were admitted.[32] Before 1640 there was a broad consensus that some prayers must be set (the debate was rather what should be in them than whether they should be written) and that some prayer was extempore—by no means the same thing as unprepared or halting:[33] it was only after that date that the need for set prayers at all was seriously questioned. In that respect the landscape for domestic prayer reflected the religious divisions of public worship, though operating with the greater latitude which goes with less comprehensive oversight. Even genuinely solitary praying would usually be uttered, rather than silent ('use thy tongue if thou canst' recommends Lewis Bayly in his manual

---

[31] Jeremy Taylor, 'To the Pious and Devout Reader', prefacing *The Golden Grove* (1655), pp. viii–ix.

[32] Ian Green, 'Varieties of Domestic Devotion in Early Modern English Protestantism', in Martin and Ryrie (eds.), *Private and Domestic Devotion*, pp. 9–31; Virginia Reinburg, 'Hearing Lay People's Prayer', in Barbara Diefendorf and Carla Hesse (eds.), *Culture and Identity in Early Modern Europe, 1500–1800* (Ann Arbor, MI, 1993).

[33] Ryrie, *Being Protestant*, pp. 214–21.

of prayer)[34] and gesture and posture were of great importance, with kneeling and looking upward with folded hands commanding a broad consensus.

However, many manuals produced to assist private devotion are built on the Morning and Evening Offices of the Book of Common Prayer, and the evidence is for its widespread use, at least as a structure and (especially earlier in the period) often verbatim, in household prayers.[35] The backbone of domestic devotion, then, was the liturgical form used in churches, itself a reduction and adaptation of the pre-Reformation monastic offices to the use of people in secular employments. The Lord's Prayer (it gradually acquires this name across the period, though the familiar pre-Reformation 'paternoster' fades slowly) is also of widespread use, in its verbatim form and as a ground for extended prayer under headings; like the martyrs' digests, it finds its way into the pedlar's pack for use by any who have access to literacy.[36] Its repeated use within the Book of Common Prayer made it the prayer anyone, literate or non-literate, could confidently say.

This Cranmerian reduction in the liturgical offices to a couple of basic, memorable forms, met a growing awareness of secular devotional needs from the early to the mid-sixteenth century onwards, for people for whom times of set prayer would be only one among the many employments of life. Manuals of prayer for householders are a medieval genre category but they swell in numbers, diversity, and importance after the 1530s, when monastic prayer is superseded by prayer within the secular communities of the nation. From the 'professed brother of Syon' Richard Whitford's *Godly Werke for Housholders* of 1530, through the reformed Edward Dering's *Godly Private Praiers for Housholders* of 1572, to the thick, immensely successful manuals of daily prayer in every human circumstance Bishop Lewis Bayly's *Practice of Pietie* and Daniel Featley's *Ancilla Pietatis* in the first decades of the seventeenth century, this shift of prayerful emphasis from a dedicated body of clerks to the bulk of the people is significant.[37] It is also worth noting that texts such as Bayly's had a wide circulation on the continent; if this was emergent Anglicanism, its influence was broad and its characteristics recognizable.[38]

With the shift to a secular (rather than a monastic-based) prayerfulness came more specialized and tailored texts for particular kinds of circumstance. Lewis Bayly's manual provides prayers for every vicissitude—when travelling,

---

[34] Lewis Bayly, *Practice of Pietie* (1626), fol. L12r.
[35] Green, 'Varieties of Domestic Devotion', pp. 19–20.
[36] Tessa Watt, *Cheap Print and Popular Piety, 1550–1640* (Cambridge, 1991), pp. 246–8; Ryrie, *Being Protestant*, pp. 227–32.
[37] Lewis Bayly, *Practice of Pietie* (the first surviving edition is 1613); Daniel Featley, *Ancilla Pietatis* (1626); Helen C. White, *The Tudor Books of Private Devotion* (Madison, WI, 1951), pp. 157–69.
[38] Philip Benedict, *The Faith and Fortunes of France's Huguenots, 1600–85* (Aldershot, 2001), p. 166, table on p. 168.

when sick, at different times of day or night, upon the approach to death, and so on. It met a deep and widespread need.[39] Just as the walls of houses might be decorated with appropriate scriptural texts or images, or a chamber pot be inscribed with a *memento mori*, so the smallest action (for example passing from one room to another) could have its devotional accompaniment.[40]

Different authors aimed at a kind of 'full life coverage' in different ways, with some of the more reformed—Dering, for example—choosing an implicitly linear order to human time and ignoring or even opposing the cycle of the church year (to the elect all days are holy, and only Sabbaths mark the biblical command to special time). Others, like Daniel Featley in his *Ancilla Pietatis*, used and explicitly defended the Church's cycle as an aid to particular kinds of remembrance or devotion, joining sacred event and daily experience.

While these different approaches do indeed mark different doctrinal positions and shades of churchmanship, the drive to 'prayer coverage' spans them. That might be a mutation of the monastic perception of life as underpinned by the habit of prayer (later Laudian and post-Laudian prayer books, such as that of John Cosin, reinstate 'Anglican' forms of the monastic offices);[41] but it might also reflect some of the pervading anxiety, the emotional see-saw which Protestant piety brings with it.[42] Any given mood might, or might not, be a sign tending to election or to reprobation; either way, it needed nourishment and reflection. The continual search for a stability which could not arrive often brought discouragement, 'dryness', or even despair. Helen C. White comments upon a prayer in Dering's collection 'for constant Perseverance', which expresses this sense of desperation, seeing in it an individual 'candor' and freshness; no doubt she is right, but it may also be there because the state it describes is close to universal for the praying Protestant:

> I call upon thee in the day time, and in the night season doe I poure out prayers unto thee, and yet for all that I feel mee nothing released, but oftentimes worse and worse, which maketh mee oftentimes deere Father, almost to doubt of thy goodness.[43]

Some of this is attributable to soteriological uncertainty; some, as Alec Ryrie reminds us, might equally be attributed to the universal belief in the power of Satan.[44] Either way, the psychological impact of doctrines of predestination

---

[39] Green, *Print and Protestantism*, p. 599.

[40] Tara Hamling, 'Old Robert's Girdle: Visual and Material Props for Protestant Piety in Post-Reformation England', in Martin and Ryrie (eds.), *Private and Domestic Devotion*, pp. 135–64, at p. 161.

[41] John Cosin, *A Collection of Private Devotions: in the Practice of the Ancient Church, called the Hours of Praiers. As they were Much after this Manner Published by the Authoritie of Queen Elisa. 1560* (1655).

[42] Ryrie, *Being Protestant*, esp. pp. 17–91.

[43] Edward Dering, *Godlie Private Praiers for Housholders* (1609), sig. Fiiv; White, *Tudor Books*, p. 169.

[44] Ryrie, *Being Protestant*, pp. 32–9.

really did not help. The urge to foreclose on despair rather than to endure uncertainty is tackled by a number of notable preachers, including the pastorally minded Richard Sibbes.[45] Perhaps its finest example is Richard Hooker's *Of the Certaintie and Perpetuitie of Faith in the Elect*:

> ...an Errour groweth, when men in heaviness of Spirit suppose they lack faith, because they find not the sugred joy and delight which doth indeed accompany Faith... Better it is sometimes to go down to the pit with him, who beholding darkness... cryeth from the bottom of the lowest Hell, *my God, my God, why hast thou forsaken me?* than continually to walk arm in arm with Angels.[46]

Hooker's choice of the opening line of Psalm 22, the line Christ calls from the cross, reminds the sufferer that to feel forsaken is to follow in Christ's 'blessed steps' after all.

It is also a characteristic use of a psalmic line as a place for a reader to speak, to *inhabit*—even when doing so puts that person in the place and *persona* of their suffering Lord. Prayer and Scripture merged amongst early modern petitioners—Scripture being the best and the safest utterance when one was not sure how to speak by the Holy Spirit—and the psalms retained a privileged place.[47] This too was a continuity from medieval and monastic piety—and the seven penitential psalms continued to be heavily used also[48]—but the dynamic for many had shifted. Psalms spoke the ups and downs of a life in the first person, talked towards God from every variety of mood, and delineated personal stories of salvation. Dering's prayer for perseverance also begins with a direct echo of Psalm 22: 'I cry in the day-time, but thou hearest not, and in the night-season also I take no rest'. He chooses the second verse rather than the first—approaching the cross, as it were, without daring to inhabit it.[49] The typologies of suffering and despair, and likewise of praise and delight, are channelled through the psalms into the salvific narratives of a life narrated via Scripture but unique in its detail; an autobiography ghost-written by God.

This is the period (and especially the seventeenth century) of the rise of the spiritual diary, telling and being told via the scripture which performs so much of the work of identity and definition for the early modern sensibility.[50]

---

[45] Richard Sibbes, *Complete Works*, ed. A. Grosart, 7 vols. (Edinburgh, 1862–4), IV, p. 449; R. T. Kendall, *Calvin and English Calvinism to 1649* (Oxford, 1981), p. 103.

[46] Richard Hooker, *Of the Certaintie and Perpetuitie of Faith in the Elect*, in *Of the Lawes of Ecclesiasticall Politie* (1676), pp. 527–32, at p. 529.

[47] Beth Quitslund, *The Reformation in Rhyme: Sternhold, Hopkins and the English Metrical Psalter, 1547–1603* (Aldershot, 2008); Ryrie, *Being Protestant*, pp. 225–6.

[48] Hannibal Hamlin, 'Sobs for Sorrowful Souls: Versions of the Penitential Psalms for Domestic Devotion', in Martin and Ryrie (eds.), *Private and Domestic Devotion*, pp. 211–36.

[49] Dering, *Godlie Private Praiers*, sig. Fiiv.

[50] Andrew Cambers, 'Reading, the Godly, and Self-Writing in England, circa 1580–1720', *Journal of British Studies*, 46 (2007): 796–825; Margo Todd, 'Puritan Self-Fashioning: The Diary of Samuel Ward', *Journal of British Studies*, 31 (1992): 236–64.

No wonder that the most 'godly' of the biblical translations, the Geneva Bible, was also the one thickest with annotations, in order to limit hermeneutical variation. The Bible, as the central book for making sense of lives, spoke in voices both authoritative and dangerously malleable; clerical unease was widespread, if often unacknowledged, about the latitude of lay reading.[51] So it is that the gentlewoman Elizabeth Isham, writing in the mid-seventeenth century, not only tells her own tale but expresses her apprehension of its gaps and puzzles of salvific meaning, in the collated words of Scripture:

> I have often desired that the evill which I am borne to by nature, thou wouldest reforme by thy grace: for thou makest them that conjecture fooles and turnest the wise men backward, and make there knowledge foolishnesse, \Isa 44.25/ Yea Lord thou doest many things which wee can give no reason for. thy wayes are past finding out. \Rom. 11.33/ neither is \it/ fitt for us to plead whether thou makest this vessell to honner or that to disshoner \Rom 9.21/ these tentations which I have bene trobled with I find it the safest way to resist in the consepion but *as for me*it is good for me to or to put my trust hold me fast cleve fast to the Lord my God and to trust in him: \psal 73.28/[52]

When you are not your own Author, you cannot be privy to your own plot. For those who afforded God sole agency in the writing-partnership, a continual problem (and the one Hooker was attempting to fix in *Of the Certaintie and Perpetuitie*) was not knowing when you had come to your turning-point, your conversion. For many, all the exercises of piety, all self-examination, fasting, watching (keeping yourself awake), reading, all the heady emotional experiences of high-temperature rhetoric afforded by sermon-gadding—all these were in the service of finding out whether that conversion experience had indeed happened, or whether it was another false dawn.

In a curious switchback, one book which seemed to offer many Calvinists, from the late sixteenth century onwards, a process to 'fix' the moment of repentance was provided by the Jesuit author Robert Parsons in a book written for English recusant Catholics, *The Christian Directory*. Parsons aimed at a book which would guide his Catholic reader to the point of 'resolution'—a decision for amendment of life analogous to conversion. His text was 'Protestantized' by the moderate puritan Edmund Bunny under the title *A Booke of Christian Exercise Appertaining to Resolution* and became an instant hit, going into multiple editions.[53] Bunny had recognized that the penitential,

---

[51] Kate Narveson, '"Their Practice Brings Little Profit": Clerical Anxieties about Lay Reading in Early Modern England', in Martin and Ryrie (eds.), *Private and Domestic Devotion*, pp. 165–88.

[52] Elizabeth Isham, *Book of Rememberance*, fo. 18r, <http://www.warwick.ac.uk/english/perdita/Isha./bor_p18r.htm>.

[53] James F. Keenan, S.J., 'Jesuit Casuistry or Jesuit Spirituality? The Roots of Seventeenth Century Practical Divinity', in John W. O'Malley, S.J., Gauvin Alexander Bailey, Steven J. Harris, and T. Frank Kennedy, S.J. (eds.), *The Jesuits: Cultures, Sciences and the Arts 1540–1773* (Toronto, 1999), pp. 627–40 (p. 630).

transformative process (with largish doses of the threat of hell) was an ideal medium for the kind of cathartic life-change the anxious Calvinist longed for. Because it invited an interior process, it was curiously independent of its own theological and ecclesiastical origins.[54] (Bunny's venture also spawned imitative Protestant works which attempted to replicate its mix of threat and promise.)[55] Richard Baxter and John Wesley were both to be profoundly influenced by it.[56]

It was against such extremes of experience that the steadying influence of pious habit was set—whether by those sympathetic to the *sola fide* doctrine setting the roller-coaster in motion but aware that some underpinning was vital, or whether by those who thought the Lord readier to accept some modicum of human effort on trust as an earnest of good intentions and pious hopes. This was the role of the daily prayer books, designed to inculcate habits of praise and finite frameworks for penitence; also of the volumes such as Thomas Becon's *Pomander of Prayer*, or Joseph Hall's *Meditations and Vowes* which taught the techniques needed to sustain the habit of prayer and sought to find glimpses of the presence of God in the world.[57] Catholic devotional texts like the *Imitatio*, Gaspar Loarte's *The Exercise of a Christian Life* (first Englished in 1557), or the work of François de Sales, supplied the initial gap in the devotional/contemplative market for Protestant readers.[58]

Catechetical works, from the highly sophisticated to the catechisms used to educate the wider population in the basics of Protestant religion, along with the Apostles' Creed, form the backbone of what one might expect to be taught as a child and to use throughout life.[59] And every shade of Protestant, including those who disapproved on principle of much of what was contained within the Book of Common Prayer, would nevertheless extract and use prayers from it as part of their own internal prayer discipline, just as they might select prayers for use from any other source.[60]

Preparative manuals for receiving the holy communion are an interesting case. They bring together soteriological anxiety and the rewards of habit into a point of crisis—the moment of receiving in bread and wine. To be a communicant was

---

[54] Keenan, 'Jesuit Casuistry or Jesuit Spirituality?' [55] Ryrie, *Being Protestant*, p. 284.

[56] Matthew Sylvester, *Reliquiae Baxterianae* (1696), I, p. 3. See Brad S. Gregory, '"The True and Zealous Service of God": Robert Parsons, Edmund Bunny, and *The First Booke of the Christian Exercise*', *JEH*, 45 (1994): 238–68.

[57] Thomas Becon, *The Pomander of Prayer* (1558); Joseph Hall, *Meditations and Vowes Divine and Morall* (1605).

[58] White, *Tudor Books*, pp. 149–73; Ryrie, *Being Protestant*, pp. 286–91; Louis Martz, *The Poetry of Meditation: A Study in English Religious Literature* (New Haven, CT, 1962), pp. 156–7.

[59] Ian Green, '"For Children in Yeeres and Children in Understanding": The Emergence of the English Catechism under Elizabeth and the Early Stuarts', *JEH*, 37 (1986): 397–425; Ian Green, *The Christian's ABC: Catechisms and Catechizing in England c.1530–1740* (Oxford, 1996).

[60] Ryrie, *Being Protestant*, pp. 232–8.

both required as a regular commitment (which might mean once or twice a year and would at its oftenest mean once a month) and fraught with peril. The words of St Paul on receiving unworthily being to eat and drink one's own destruction[61] bit deep, and manual after manual offer guidance as to how to walk the narrow line between potentially receiving your own damnation with the Host and the sin of not communicating.[62] The question of what and how much to feel, and the spirit in which one made one's preparation (curiously, the nonconformist manuals which proliferate after 1660 are most at ease with encouraging sacramental affect in their readers),[63] concentrated all the paradoxes of the semi-reformed Church of England into the narrowest of needle's eyes. The mental torture instruments for the great lexicographer Samuel Johnson's agonized preparation for his Easter communion were set up almost two centuries before his birth.[64]

Around death and deathbeds the ambiguous nature of external signs was, if anything, even more problematic than it was for holy communion. There were no clear signs to point watchers to the final destination of the dying person. A good life, full of the works of virtue, was not definitive: grace, not works, saved souls. On the other hand, deathbed repentances were problematic too; how sincere were they, and was it really all right for reprobates to get to heaven so lazily? The pre-Reformation *ars moriendi* tradition was still a powerful one, and therefore deathbeds were instinctively seen as a potentially edifying spectacle, in the seventeenth century as in the sixteenth.[65] Preachers could argue until they were blue in the face that *modes* of death said nothing about the dying person's salvation, but the lesson tended to be quietly ignored. The argument's most eloquent proponent, John Donne, in his 1632 sermon *Deaths Duell*, nevertheless set up his own death as a fully staged spectacle of edification; and the sermon itself was preached (according to his biographer Izaak Walton) as much in his 'decayed body, and dying face' as in the words he spoke.[66]

The difficulty was that while an edifying death might say nothing about the salvation of the one dying, it could preach to those who watched—and by extension, to those who received it in its vivified textual or preached form.

---

[61] 1 Cor. 11:23-32.

[62] For example, William Bradshaw, *A direction for the weaker sort of Christian...By W.B. Whereunto is Adioined a Verie Profitable Treatise of the Same Argument, By Way of Question and Answer, Written by Another [Arthur Hildersham]* (1609).

[63] Margaret Spufford, 'The Importance of the Lord's Supper to Dissenters', in Spufford (ed.), *World of Rural Dissenters*, pp. 86-102.

[64] Samuel Johnson, *Prayers and Meditations* (Dublin, 1785).

[65] Thomas Lupset, *A Compendious and Very Frutefull Treatyse Teachynge the Waye of Dyenge Well* (1541); Desiderius Erasmus, *Preparation to Deathe: a Boke as Devout as Eloquent* (1543); Jeremy Taylor, *The Rule and Exercises of Holy Dying* (1651); Christopher Sutton, *Disce Mori: Learn to Die* (1601).

[66] John Donne, *Deaths Duell: or, a Consolation to the Soule, against the Dying Life, and Living Death of the Body* (1632); Izaak Walton, *Life of Dr John Donne*, in *Lives*, ed. George Saintsbury (Oxford, 1927), p. 75.

Even (and perhaps especially) the spiritual struggles of the dying might convince readers; and to this end was published the best-selling account of the agonized deathbed doubts and fears of the godly Katherine Brettergh.[67] With her final hours comes also the restoration of her faith, so the work operates to scotch salvific doubts: blown out of the storm and into the calm harbour of assured salvation. For the popular market, the broadside ballad known as *The Godly Clerk* offered a comparable approach to an assured end, though in this case it is his settled faith rather than his settled doubts which mediate the reader's comfort.[68]

Every report of an edifying death gives rise to the life of faith: its text figures itself as a resurrection. 'The dead yet speaking', culled from Hebrews 11:4 was a frequent trope especially for the eloquent dead, the preachers and writers of the period; but even the eloquence of the 'godly clerk' worked the same way. In the faith (and sanctified imitation) of readers, the dead rose, and the living joined them in the communion of saints. Voragine's vision, mediated through more oceans of text than he could have imagined, was re-inscribed.

CONCLUSION

Only a dangerously heavy reliance on hindsight provides any unambiguous narrative of the beginnings of a distinctive 'Anglican' sensibility and pious observation before 1663. Between the English Reformation and the Restoration devotional practices converge, borrowing and appropriating with eclectic confessional permeability; but the meanings of those practices diverge. (There was, after all, a lot to be said—from the point of view of the early modern person at prayer in a constantly altering religious climate—for devotions which did not either reveal or fully define their inner meanings.) Piety is therefore informed, but not necessarily shaped, by public doctrinal division.

Yet the visible continuities of observance were to create a ground for a seductive narrative (or several different competing seductive narratives) of homogeneity and continuity. It is important to see these sceptically, and to continue to problematize them. Within this earlier period, the loudest narratives of the post-regicidal nation are not yet authoritative; some are barely visible. With the Restoration—as with the Reformation itself—hindsight may be inevitable, but its advantages require circumspection.

---

[67] William Harrison, *The Life and Death of Mistris K. Brettergh* (1612).
[68] Watt, *Cheap Print*, pp. 104–8 (p. 107).

SELECT BIBLIOGRAPHY

Duffy, Eamon, *The Stripping of the Altars: Traditional Religion in England 1400–1580* (New Haven, CT, 1992).
Green, Ian, *The Christian's ABC: Catechisms and Catechizing in England c.1530–1740* (Oxford, 1996).
Gregory, Brad S., *The Unintended Reformation: How a Religious Revolution Secularized Society* (Cambridge, MA, 2012).
Martin, Jessica and Alec Ryrie (eds.), *Private and Domestic Devotion in Early Modern Britain* (Farnham, 2012).
Martz, Louis, *The Poetry of Meditation: A Study in English Religious Literature* (New Haven, CT, 1962).
Molekamp, Femke, *Women and the Bible in Early Modern England: Religious Reading and Writing* (Oxford, 2013).
Perry, Nandra, *Imitatio Christi: The Poetics of Piety in Early Modern England* (Notre Dame, IN, 2014).
Quitslund, Beth, *The Reformation in Rhyme: Sternhold, Hopkins and the English Metrical Psalter, 1547–1603* (Aldershot, 2008).
Ryrie, Alec, *Being Protestant in Reformation Britain* (Oxford, 2013).
Walsham, Alexandra, *The Reformation of the Landscape: Religion, Identity and Memory in Early Modern Britain and Ireland* (Oxford, 2011).
Watt, Tessa, *Cheap Print and Popular Piety, 1550–1640* (Cambridge, 1991).
White, Helen C., *The Tudor Books of Private Devotion* (Madison, WI, 1951).

22

The Bible in Early Modern England

Lori Anne Ferrell

It is a commonplace that the Bible has been the cornerstone of the English Church since that institution's reformation under the Tudors. Recalling the words of William Chillingworth, who declared it to be the 'religion of Protestants' in 1637, the heirs of a Restoration settlement forget the unsettled world that Chillingworth addressed.[1] The Bible may well have been the religion of Protestants, but if this was the case we may be obliged to take a different view of early modern English Protestantism.

The vernacular Bibles appointed by English monarchs in 1539, 1568, and 1611 for use in the Church over which they claimed a supreme, if terrestrial, authority mark an increasingly wary path away from the passionate bibliocentrism that had characterized evangelical reform in the early sixteenth century. This is a shift presaged in the fraught history of Henry VIII's commissioning of the 'Great Bible', complicated by the proliferation and popularity of private Bibles and Bible-reading in the second half of the reign of Elizabeth I, and, finally, exemplified in the elegant—and anodyne—revisions that gave the English-speaking world what it now calls, with no little reverence, the 'King James Bible'. The Protestant Bible's spiritual authority, buttressed by its translation into the vernacular and expressed in the familiar phrase *sola scriptura*, often posed more problems than it solved for the English Church's exercise of secular authority.

A closer examination, one that applies a reasonable hermeneutics of suspicion to the claims made about Scripture's authority in either of the English Reformation's two great flashpoint decades—the 1530s or the 1630s—reveals that the Bible's relation to the Church of England was always a more contested and uncertain thing than even its advocates were willing to acknowledge. In England, as on the continent, the vernacular Bible provided as succinct a

---

[1] William Chillingworth, *The Religion of Protestants a Safe Way To Salvation* (Oxford, 1638), sig. Rr.

synonym for 'Protestantism' as the doctrine of justification by faith. (Perhaps more so: Catholics and Protestants alike recognized the centrality of faith to salvation, after all, and only differed on the quality and quantity of human effort expended in the exchange; on the other hand, they disagreed markedly about the primacy of Scripture.) But by the reign of Charles I, the Church of England's increasingly conflicted relationship with the Protestantism of its continental co-religionists exposed a mounting anxiety over the authority of Scripture, especially in matters of worship.

That the Bible would have a central role to play in the drama eventually called 'The Reformation' was due not only to its unquestioned status as Christianity's sacred text, but also to social and cultural developments in the late medieval period, chief among them the advent of humanism in the fourteenth century and the Western invention of movable type in the fifteenth. Translators had been writing vernacular scripture throughout the later Middle Ages, but these budding attempts to render the Bible into the language of the people were innovatory only insofar as the language was not Latin: the copy-text remained the Vulgate. In England, then, the Wycliffites challenged the language, not the idiom, of the Catholic Church's version of Scripture. They were adjudged heretics nonetheless and treated accordingly, under the provisions of the statute written precisely for them in 1401: *De haeretico comburendo* ('Regarding the burning of heretics', 2 Hen. 4 c. 15).

When scholars decided to dispute the validity of the biblical text itself, they posed a far greater threat to tradition and orthodoxy. Citing the Vulgate's inaccuracies (accreted over generations of hand-transcription since the fourth century of the common era), as well as its post-dated sources, humanists claimed access to earlier, and therefore arguably more accurate, versions of both testaments to translate. By the 1520s, William Tyndale could draw upon the acclaimed second edition of Erasmus of Rotterdam's Greek New Testament and Martin Luther's German-language translation of the Old Testament to produce the first great English translation of Scripture 'dylygently corrected and compared' by humanist method.

Now this *was* extraordinary. Translation is not exactly original scholarship—in fact it could be argued that, at least in spirit, it is quite necessarily the opposite. But the process invariably cracks the interpretive spine of the original and thus can be neither wholly disinterested nor entirely preservative. In an unsettled age, the energy released by the deconstructive work of translation sparked combustible theological reconstructions that Tyndale decided should be 'set [as] light in the margent' of his translations.[2] Such work trained a newly critical lens on the sacred text. The truth of Scripture was no longer a matter of trust established in tradition; it had to be earned, through correct

---

[2] William Tyndale, *The Newe Testament, Dyligently Corrected and Compared with the Greke by Willyam Tindale* (Antwerp, 1534), sig. *ivr.

application of scholarly method—chiefly, translation and revision. The Word so central to Protestant doctrine and authority had taken on a kind of sanctioned instability, in the process becoming an uncanny *synecdoche* for the era itself.

Another source of the vernacular Bible's cultural currency in the sixteenth century was its smart, symbiotic relationship to new technologies of the book: with movable type, bibles could finally be made and distributed in bulk. Even mechanical reproduction could not, however, guarantee the stability of the Word. Presses, and the people who worked in and on them, were simply too wayward to produce standardized texts in multiples: there are myriad variants to be found in even a single early modern print run.[3] What print did fix, permanently, was a powerful abstract: Scripture as easily *producible*, if not pristinely *re*producible, for mass distribution.

These qualities made the press a fortuitous medium for the infant religion of Protestants. Printed in thick black-letter font, *incunabula* looked like the hand-made books they were beginning to supplant (manuscripts continued to circulate, healthily, throughout the era): manuscript books, after all, were what early printers assumed all books were supposed to look like. But they, and their authors, recognized and seized the opportunities offered them: something in the way sheets could be impressed onto *formes* and assembled into quires inspired equally dexterous techniques of page design. New possibilities in formatting led to novel approaches to spatial organization, making strange, startling, and difficult ideas *look* familiar, persuasive, and accessible. This sea-change in how books were made thus led to remarkable innovations in how they were handled—and understood.[4]

In an undereducated age, however, neither innovation of form nor accessibility of language could make the *contents* of the Bible any easier to grasp. Far fewer ploughboys than priests ever learned to read the Bible in English. And while they had the benefit of a classical education, clerics had their own vernacular learning to undergo in order to mull over Scripture and doctrine in English as readily as they could in Latin, long the argot of ecclesiastical life. (The works of the late sixteenth-century English theologians testify, ineloquently, to the fact that graceful thinking in Latin can produce astonishingly awkward writing in English.)[5]

And then there were the politics of scriptural translation to consider. As humanist and evangelical ideas flourished on the continent, finding increasingly enthusiastic receptions in his insular realm, Henry VIII was glorying in

---

[3] Charlton Hinman, *The Printing and Proof-Reading of the First Folio of Shakespeare*, 2 vols. (Oxford, 1963), I, pp. 3–14.

[4] Lori Anne Ferrell, 'Grasping the Truth', in Kristin De Troyer and Christine Helmer (eds.), *Truth: Interdisciplinary Dialogues in a Pluralistic Age* (Leuven, 2003).

[5] David Daniell, *The Bible in English* (New Haven, CT, 2003), pp. 342–3.

the papal title *Defensor Fidei* ('Defender of the Faith'), earned in 1521 for commissioning a tract condemning Martin Luther. For a while it seemed that Henry, with an early modern monarch's healthy fear of popular movements (and the Protestant doctrines that inevitably seemed to foment them), would continue to deserve the accolade. But on 22 June 1530, when the king commanded his subjects to surrender outlawed English Bibles to their local bishops within fifteen days, he ended on an intriguing note:

> Albeit if it doth appear hereafter to the king's highness that his said people do utterly abandon and forsake all perverse, erroneous, and seditious opinions, with the New testament and the Old corruptly translated in the English tongue now being in print, and that the same books... be clearly exterminate and exiled out of this realm of England forever: his Highness intendeth to provide that the Holy Scripture shall be by great, learned, and Catholic persons translated into the English tongue, if it shall then seem to his grace convenient to be.[6]

Thus the king proclaimed, not translation in itself, but the act of translating *without royal approval*, as criminal. And as tantalizing reward for their obedience, Henry's subjects would have a Bible in their own language, in a future that only the king could command.

The illicit Bibles that worried Henry were William Tyndale's early translations of the New Testament, recently published on the continent, and produced in small formats (undoubtedly to facilitate smuggling). The printing of Tyndale's translations began in Cologne in 1525, but authorities swiftly stepped in and halted the work at the gospel of Matthew. In exile, condemned by both Roman Church and English government, Tyndale went on working. But not for long: for his work of translating and publishing religious texts—but more importantly, for doing these things without the approval of Church or king, an offence under English statute since *De haeretico*—Tyndale was executed in Belgium in 1536. A woodcut from John Foxe's *Actes and Monuments* depicted Tyndale's ordeal at the stake in unsparing detail, reporting his final, prescient words: 'Lord, open the king of England's eyes.'[7]

At this time Henry VIII had moved on to a greater matter: his divorce from Catherine of Aragon and marriage to Anne Boleyn. Supported by Thomas Cranmer, archbishop of Canterbury, and Thomas Cromwell, secretary of state and vicegerent for ecclesiastical affairs, the English Bible project stammered through a succession of interim solutions. Tyndale's assistant, Miles Coverdale, was allowed to continue, unmolested, the work to which his infamous master had apprenticed him. Translating from the Latin Vulgate and consulting Tyndale's scriptures, Coverdale completed the first full English Bible in

---

[6] Paul L. Hughes and James F. Larkin (eds.), *Tudor Royal Proclamations*, 3 vols. (New Haven, CT, 1964–69), I, pp. 193–7.

[7] John Foxe, *Actes and Monuments* (1570), sig. DDDiiir.

1535 under the new queen's short-lived patronage. With a dedication to the king declaring his loyalty and suggesting that access to the vernacular scriptures would make Henry's subjects obedient to both God and their divinely protected monarch, Coverdale's Bible was first printed in London, with tacit monarchical approval, in 1537.

That same year the king, urged by Cranmer and Cromwell, licensed another English translation, the pseudonymous 'Matthew's Bible', a textual collaboration between the quick and the dead. Its contents combined Tyndale's printed translations; the smuggled manuscript copies of his uncompleted work on the Old Testament; and Coverdale's translations of everything else. In 1538, Cromwell issued an injunction requiring every church in England to purchase a copy of the Bible in English and 'set it in a convenient place… whereas your parishioners may most commodiously resort to the same and read it'.[8] He probably had Coverdale's or Matthew's Bible in mind; both were now being printed in England, in folio.

But the political issue at hand was one of tone as well as translation. Both Coverdale's and Matthew's Bible had retained two things which Henry's conservative bishops (and they were many and still powerful) loathed: Tyndale's translations and, worse, Tyndale's trenchant marginal commentary. Cromwell, whose political star was now rapidly on the wane (in small part because of his advocacy of religious reform) remained committed to his Injunction: he consequently ordered Miles Coverdale to revise Matthew's Bible.[9] Coverdale had neither Greek nor Hebrew, but he did have Latin, with which he smoothed over the more objectionable of Tyndale's verses by a judicious application of the Vulgate, translated and accommodated to the patterns of English speech. The margins were largely wiped clean; this was to be a Bible for public reading in church, not private consultation by curious laypeople.

The Byble in Englyshe (1539) was then printed and distributed with royal authority: a validating claim that, like the anti-vernacular legislation that had preceded it, again set the English experience of scriptural reform apart from the continental. It also set this particular Bible—which in subsequent ecclesiastical injunctions was called the 'Great Bible' or the 'Bible of the largest size'— apart as the only version of the Bible in English that has ever been, in fact, 'authorized'. (Although the 1611 Bible is often called, incorrectly, the 'Authorized Version', James I never officially authorized its use, nor did he finance its production.)

The publication of Henry's Bible thus marked the beginning of the long association of state, Church, and Scripture in England. The 1539 Bible gave

---

[8] G. R. Elton, *Policy and Police: The Enforcement of the Reformation in the Age of Thomas Cromwell* (Cambridge, 1972), pp. 254–5, 258–60.

[9] Daniell, *Bible in English*, pp. 200–1.

not only legislative but also iconic proof of Henry VIII's claim to be Supreme Head of the Church in his realm, with the king's determination to control the pace and tenor of reformation in his Church and realm depicted in the striking imagery of the title page. In this masterstroke of bilingual propaganda, Henry hands copies of the Bible, identified by the words *Verbum Dei*, to the churchmen and scholars kneeling at his left and right. And below, a man preaches to a cross-section of the people of England—young and old, male and female, free and imprisoned—who receive his words with upturned hands and grateful cries of... *vivat Rex*.

Vivat Rex is the most significant image on the Great Bible's title page, in which nearly every word is in Latin. Its meaning would have been unmistakable to the essential minority of men for whom it was intended. The interior contents of the Church's new Bible may have been translated into the language of Henry's lay subjects, but—given its costly production in folio, the reality of mass illiteracy amongst the king's subjects, and the fact that it had been ordered into every church, cathedral, and deanery in the realm—this eloquent Latin legend was obviously meant for Henry's priests, all of whom had begun their careers as Catholic priests beholden to Rome, many of whom were no fans of royal supremacy, and most of whom kept their own counsel as regards translated Scripture.[10]

Henry soon repented his sponsorship of a Bible for his people and soon his 1543 Parliament passed an act forbidding poor men and most women from reading Scripture. A conservative in matters of the spirit, the king was, perhaps, not entirely unjustified in his concern that in some unruly circles the 'true... exposition' of Scripture was being 'subvert[ed]'.[11] The Bible was too confusing and radical a document simply to be handed over to a priesthood made up of *all* believers. Most English parish priests were not prepared, either, to trade in a life of celebrating mass for one devoted to exegetical preaching.

Luckily they did not have to: the mass, stripped of references to the Pope but otherwise familiar to English ears since time out of mind, remained at the centre of worship in Henry's Church of England.[12] The Great Bible may have been, then, the signal achievement of the Henrician Reformation, but at the time of the old king's death in 1547 its prospects, like those of England's Protestantism, looked about as puny and puerile as the heir to the supremacy. The daunting work of Protestant reformation had been left to Henry's nine-year-old son.

He and his Lords Protector embraced the task with unprecedented enthusiasm. Under Edward VI, the provision of lay Scripture was revitalized, with

---

[10] Lori Anne Ferrell, *The Bible and the People* (New Haven, CT, 2008), pp. 76–8.
[11] 34° & 35° Hen. VIII. c. 1, *The Statutes of the Realm*, 12 vols. (1810–28), I, p. 894.
[12] Lucy Wooding, 'The Marian Reformation and the Mass', in Eamon Duffy and David Loades (eds.), *The Church of Mary Tudor* (Aldershot, 2006), pp. 232–3.

forty editions of the English Bible issuing from the press during the six short years that the young king ruled. The reforming government of 'England's Josiah' (to his father's long-stymied Protestant clerics)[13] also ordered all parish churches to buy a copy of the biblical paraphrases of Desiderius Erasmus.[14] These expansions of and commentaries on the scriptural text were to be set up, like the Bible, 'in some convenient place' so that parishioners could 'resort unto the same and read the same'. Edward's subjects would thus not only hear but also *learn* Scripture, and, perhaps as important, learn that the Bible was a text best studied with the help of other books. In Edward's Church, lay reading became part of the public apparatus of worship—a significant part of that worship, in fact, once the Church abolished the Latin mass and offered a revised version in vernacular, scripted in the Book of Common Prayer, in 1549 and 1553.

The reformation of the mass had long been Cranmer's ambition, not simply in terms of the liturgy but also in view of how this familiar structure of weekly worship could be expropriated to foster lay education. His original plan for the scriptural reformation of the Church linked common prayer to an ambitious programme of Bible-reading: every book of both testaments, 'entire and unbroken', to be read at service, so congregants would have heard it all, in order, by year's end, and with all psalms covered monthly. In his preface to a new Book of Common Prayer, Cranmer explained why:

> [I]f a man would search out by the ancient fathers, he shall find that ... [divine service] was not ordained, but of a good purpose, and for a great advancement of godliness: For they so ordered the matter, that all the whole Bible (or the greatest parte thereof) should be read over once in the year ... and further, that the people (by daily hearing of holy scripture read in the Church) should continually profit more and more in the knowledge of God ...

At some point between the 1530s draft (British Library, Royal MS 7B.IV) and the publication of the 1549 Prayer Book, the reading of the Bible 'entire and unbroken' became only the 'greatest parte thereof'.[15] Considering the extent of biblical illiteracy in Edward's reign, this was still a highly ambitious plan.

But such painstaking attention to and provision for lay biblical literacy was to cease upon the young king's death in 1553. Vernacular bible printing also ceased during the five years' reign of Edward's Catholic sister Mary I, whose attempts to return England to the faith (if not the statutes) of her father began with an immediate repeal of Henry's 1534 Act of Supremacy and restoration of the Latin mass. The English Bible (unlike, perhaps, persistent

---

[13] Diarmaid MacCulloch, *Tudor Church Militant: Edward VI and the Protestant Reformation* (1999), pp. 14–15.

[14] W. H. Frere and W. M. Kennedy (eds.), *Visitation Articles and Injunctions of the Period of the Reformation*, 3 vols. (1910), II, pp. 117–19.

[15] *The Booke of the Common Prayer and Administracion of the Sacramentes* (1549), sig. ∞.i.r.

and provocative Protestants) was not subjected to the fires of faith—at least not in great numbers. Mary's bishops—a mix of conformists, Henrician stalwarts, and new appointees (to replace Edwardian loyalists now deprived, confined to prison, condemned for heresy or treason, or fled to the continent or to the safety of obscurity)—were content simply to remove it from the Church. Some priests preached against it, but few ordered its outright confiscation or destruction. Many experienced churchwardens—those thrifty veterans on the front lines of Tudor reform whether Protestant or Tridentine—quietly placed copies in church cupboards safely away from public view.[16]

They knew, of course, that they might well be needed in future. With the succession in 1558 of Mary's younger sister Elizabeth I to the English throne (the Tudors were as mutable in religion as they were incapable of producing viable heirs), Mary's version of English Catholicism was outlawed. In the same year the Roman Church, at the Council of Trent, explicitly prohibited the translation of the Vulgate into the vernacular for the first time. Elizabeth claimed to be reviving the faith of *her* father, something she made clear in a swift reissue of the Act of Supremacy. But she resembled Henry most in the sceptical caution with which she regarded continental-style Protestantism, and in her consistent determination to temper the unrulier spirits, Protestant as well as Catholic, in Church and state.

With the return of royal supremacy came the reinstatement of the English Bible. The Elizabethan *Book of Certaine Canons*, which covered the specific responsibilities of every member of an episcopal polity and was published by royal decree in 1571, opened: 'All bishops shall diligently teach the gospel... principally they shall exhort their people to the reading and hearing of the Holy Scriptures'. Every bishop was expected to own both a bible (and Foxe's *Actes*) and to place these 'either in the hall or in the great chamber, that they may serve to the use of their servants and of strangers'. The same applied to deans, cathedral residents, and archdeacons, who were to 'buy the same books every one for his own family and... lay them in some fit place, either in the hall or in the chamber'. The canons enjoined all licensed ministers to preach 'the word of God'. Just how diligently was spelled out in further injunctions and articles. Preachers were to 'take heed, that they teach nothing in their preaching which they would have the people religiously to observe and believe, but that which is agreeable to the doctrine of the Old Testament and the New'. They were to teach that the 'articles of Christian religion agreed upon by the bishops in... convocation [and commanded by the queen]' were 'undoubtedly... gathered out of the holy books of the Old and New Testament, and in all points agree with the heavenly doctrine contained in them... also [that] the book of common prayers... contains nothing repugnant to the same'. This was

---

[16] David Loades, 'The Marian Episcopate', in Duffy and Loades (eds.), *Church*, p. 52.

reformation by Scripture's lights, whereby the parliamentary statutes that reinstated England's Protestant polity, worship, and doctrine were granted protected status by virtue of their agreement with Holy Writ. The injunctions were reissued in at least five more editions before 1600.[17]

Elizabethan statute required parish churches to replace or restore their copies of 'the largest Bible in the English language', but the contents of the Great Bible had become as sadly outdated as its pages had become worn with use, less capable to lend expression to the heady sense of evangelical survival and progressive hopes that the queen's providential accession had inspired. Elizabeth's spiritually ambitious subjects turned to a new translation, one that better reflected the culture of England's Protestantism in the second half of the sixteenth century. That Bible was licit, but it was not appointed for use in Church of England services. Its language was English but the cast of its Protestantism spanned the Channel. Translated and annotated on the continent by men who had fled the government of Mary I, this Bible was a product of exilic culture, its presentation of the Word characterized by a singular mix of freedom, fear, and profound homesickness.

The Bible and Holy Scriptures conteyned in the Olde and Newe Testament was first printed in the reformed city of Geneva in 1560, and while it was soon issuing from England's presses, its common name, the 'Geneva Bible', stuck, lending foreign flavour to an otherwise domestic product. The earliest English Bible to be printed in clear roman type and with numbered verses, the Geneva also featured extensive notes, engraved maps, and useful tables and indexes. These helps, along with its compact quarto size, made it the first Bible obviously designed to assist private readers.

The Geneva also boasted plentiful, printed marginal notes designed to provide on-the-spot commentary on difficult passages. The introduction by its translators made it clear that this Bible was generally intended for educated clergymen, not untutored laypeople—who, the writers insisted, 'pretended' they could not understand the meaning of Scripture and so needed to be brought to its study without excuse.[18] The Geneva's margins bristle with equally sceptical, unsolicited advice to rulers, warn darkly of the consequences of ungodliness, place unmistakably Calvinist glosses onto Scripture, and mutter irritated admonitions against intestine enemies—lines that reveal as much about power struggles in small voluntary congregations as they do about the politics of religion in an age of confessional violence. But poignant words of spiritual comfort also abound in the margins of the Geneva. They may fume, impoliticly, against bad queens (at II Kings 9), but they also weep, affectingly, by the waters of Babylon (at Psalm 137).

---

[17] Gerald Bray (ed.), *The Anglican Canons 1525–1947* (Woodbridge, 1998), pp. 173–83, 187, 197–9.

[18] *The Bible and Holy Scriptures* (Geneva, 1562), sig. a iiij r.

Not only its user-friendliness, then, but also the Geneva's tone of confessional dislocation, of keeping faith in an uncertain age, explains its popularity in the Protestant culture of late sixteenth-century England. It spoke out of the private congregation: the voluntary assembly of like minds and mutual helps. The Geneva was primarily a domestic Bible, Scripture meant for edification more than for declamation. It offered material proof that the instilling and maintenance of true religion was effected by education, especially insofar as Scripture served as the basis for Protestant preaching, and so it found a place in many libraries, private and ecclesiastical. Bishops and puritans alike consulted the Geneva Bible; even anti-Calvinists kept copies close to hand, perhaps because of its excellent scholarly notes, probably because they found its translations more up to date than the Great Bible's.[19]

As before, however, the devil was in the margins. Elizabeth I's bishops preferred their official Bibles to be translated and issued under royal authority, and designed to be read aloud, publicly and decorously, in the state-regulated worship of a conforming, visible Church (with no shouting from the sidelines). In 1568 the last Tudor queen became the second Tudor monarch to proclaim guardianship of the Church of England by putting her name and face on the title page of a new Bible. *The. Holie. Bible. conteynyng the olde Testament and the Newe* was intended to revise the Great Bible and in so doing replace it. But this implied, of course, that it was destined to replace the Geneva, whose linguistic superiority, especially in terms of Hebrew translation, had so exposed the Great Bible's deficiencies that ministers were increasingly using the Geneva version in church, in lieu of a formal alternative.[20]

Too hastily produced, Elizabeth's Bible still ended up resembling its accidental rival in some telling measures of pedagogical style. Like the Geneva, the 'Bishops' Bible' (so-called because it was the brainchild and *magnum opus* of Matthew Parker, archbishop of Canterbury, who engaged a team of bishops to assist him in the translating) featured many textual helps, and four handy maps (three of which came straight out of the Geneva Bible). It had more marginal commentary than the Great Bible, although it also boasted many more, and more pleasingly scenic, illustrations than did the Geneva. Nonetheless it would seem that the archbishop and his translators were bent on producing a text for public worship, not private reading.

If so, they failed in both spheres. Archbishop Parker's Bible had few admirers and was criticized—especially in godly circles for whom translational accuracy had become the watchword for *sola scriptura*—for its textual inaccuracies. But beyond the quibbles of precisians, the mistakes included 'not obedient' for 'not *dis*obedient' in Psalm 105:28 (surely an essential doctrinal

---

[19] Peter McCullough (ed.), *Lancelot Andrewes: Select Sermons and Lectures* (Oxford, 2005), p. lvi.

[20] A. W. Pollard, *The Holy Bible... with Illustrative Documents* (Oxford, 1911), p. 287.

distinction), and 'prayed' for 'executed judgment' in Psalm 106:30 (a significant deviation if not exactly a heterodox offence).[21] But perhaps the most distinctive thing about the Bishops' Bible was its sheer infelicity of language. Parker's patristic learning was prodigious, but he and his translators had better Latin than they had Hebrew and Greek. In many tortuous passages, they apparently had better Hebrew and Greek than they had English.

So the Bishops' Bible didn't teach, but it also couldn't wax lyrical, and in the end no one, save Parker, seemed to care for it at all—not even the queen for whom it was devised. In the end, churchwardens were only required to purchase this new translation if 'convenient'; it appears that many parishes managed to scrape by with crumbling copies of the Great Bible and occasional dips into the Geneva. What Parker could do for his Bible was make sure it enjoyed a monopoly; as archbishop, he oversaw the printing of religious books and held an enviable authority over the Stationers' Company.[22] No Geneva bibles were printed between 1565 and 1575, the year Parker died. But even after a decade of market advantage, the archbishop's Bible proved no true competitor to the Geneva. It enjoyed healthy print runs from 1575 until the King James Version, which eventually benefited from the terms of its own monopoly.[23]

At the same time, persistent English Catholics, whose hide-in-plain-sight ardour could not be entirely dampened by Elizabeth's government, sponsored an English-language Bible of their own. Translating strictly from the Vulgate (rather than older Hebrew and Greek texts, making this version not unlike those produced by the Wycliffites a century and a half earlier), Gregory Martin, with the assistance of members of the exiled English Catholic college at Douai, completed this version of the New Testament in Rheims in 1578 (their translation of the Old Testament appeared in 1610 from Douai). The work was overseen by Cardinal William Allen: missionary to England, eloquent author of Catholic polemic, and, along with men like Robert Parsons, determined fomenter of plots to re-establish Catholicism in England along the new, provocative lines issued at the Council of Trent.

Martin's superiors did not intend *The New Testament of Jesus Christ, translated faithfully into English, out of the authentical Latin* (1582) to be read by laypeople. Indeed its preface satirized Protestant claims to be reviving the purity of the early Church, by reminding its readers that, while times might have changed, the condition of the laity and the nature of its favoured haunts and employments had not:

---

[21] William Barlow, *The Summe and Substance of the Conference at Hampton Court* (1605), sig. G3r-v.
[22] Cyndia Clegg, *Press Censorship in Elizabethan England* (Cambridge, 1997), pp. 36–43.
[23] Daniell, *Bible in English*, 340–7.

> [W]e must not imagine that in the primitive Church... that the translated Bible into vulgar tongues were in the hands of every husbandman, artificer, prentice, boys, girls, mistress, maid, man: that they were for table talk, for ale benches, for boats and barges, and for every profane person and company...[24]

The acid tone of the preface continued unabated in the margins of this translation—which, while *its* complaints about wicked Jezebels, heretics, and backsliders aimed at a different English queen, confession, and underground religious community, made it look and sometimes even sound uncannily like the Geneva. (Like the Geneva as well, of course, the Rheims claimed its origin out of a religious community in exile.) Despite intentions, the initial publication of the Rheims New Testament came to five thousand copies, a healthy print run.[25]

A seeming affront to both Christian confessions, the Rheims was not reprinted with anything like regularity until the nineteenth century. More than any other Bible of this century, however, this Bible offers material evidence that scriptural culture had finally begun to triumph in England. It was designed to assist recusant priests and Jesuit missionaries to debate prooftexting Protestants; their long argument was now conceived in, and proceeding on, vernacular terms.

Whether the Rheims might keep the Catholic faithful in England from straying to the pages of the Geneva or resorting to a convenient place in the parish church to consult a Bible of the largest size, or even lure lukewarm Protestants back into the Church of Jerome, were questions made hypothetical by the swift appearance of its content in radically different format: William Fulke's 1589 *The Text of the New Testament of Jesus Christ, translated out of the vulgar Latin by the papists of the traiterous Seminary at Rheims... Whereunto is added the Translation out of the Original Greek commonly used in the Church of England*. This was, as its irascible title (here *greatly* shortened) promised, a parallel-text edition, reprinting every line of the Rheims against the same in the Bishops' Bible, with all of it accompanied by a steady tirade of anti-Catholic commentary. Fulke's treatment did more than any Jesuit missionary to spread the gospel according to Rheims. The original was a smuggled text, risky to possess. Loyal—and even not-so-loyal—English subjects could, however, purchase copies of *Traiterous Seminary* with impunity. The chances are that they did not procure it for the Bishops' Bible inside.

In short, the last two decades of the sixteenth century and the first of the seventeenth were very good years for what we might call The Unauthorized Version. The call to *sola scriptura* was fulfilled in the two great *un*official English-language Bibles of the age: the refugee Geneva Bible of 1560 and the

---

[24] *The New Testament of Iesus Christ, Translated Faithfully Into English out of the authentical Latin* (Rhemes, 1582), sig. a iij r.
[25] Alfred C. Southern, *English Recusant Prose, 1559–1582* (1950), p. 235.

renegade Rheims translation of the New Testament of 1582. On the domestic front, the Sidneys, Sir Philip and Mary, Countess of Pembroke, translated the Psalms into English metrical verse that circulated, in manuscript, amongst a sophisticated and privileged clientele.[26] More widely broadcast were the translations of the Old Testament undertaken by the intemperate and unconventional Hugh Broughton (whose work as a Hebraist was considered the best of his age, but whose truculent personality kept him off the roster of King James's translators). Broughton's *Concent of Scripture*, a work made up of equal parts disinterested scholarship and immoderate self-advertisement, may not have gained attention at court but it found favour with the public. Soon Broughton was lecturing on the subject of translation and the Bible to audiences so expansive that he was forced to change venues several times.[27] John Donne, a man of divers pulpits including St Paul's, was known to cite the Coverdale, Great, Geneva, Bishops', Vulgate, and the 1611 Bible in a single sermon. In so doing, moreover, he was little different—only, perhaps, slightly more flamboyant—than other well-known and learned preachers of his day.[28]

The extraordinary variety of unregulated Englished Scripture on offer by the end of the sixteenth century, coupled with the heady sense that acts of translation could simultaneously free the Word and tie it closer to its original meaning, made the Bible the unparalleled engine of England's literary and dramatic output, sacred and secular, in this, its first golden age of letters. And it is in this context—of Scripture subject to the conformist purposes of a national Church and at the same time open to the many poetic, dramatic, and pedagogical forces thriving outside the bounds of ecclesiastical conformity—that we should assay England's best-known version of Holy Writ.

The Holy Bible, conteyning the Old Testament, and the New: newly translated out of the originall tongues: & with the former translations diligently compared and reuised, by his Maiesties speciall commandement (1611) was not, as its title is at pains to explain, intended to be a brand-new translation, but a conservative revision of the Bishops' Bible. Its translators consulted older English Bibles and even the Vulgate as delivered in Rheims, but in reworking what were still mostly Tyndale's words to achieve a stately, Latinate cadence, the 'King James Version' (KJV) gradually claimed its own distinctive style. Its tone and timbre owe much to the method by which it was devised. Six translation teams, each comprising eight or nine clerics and scholars, laboured cooperatively to produce the KJV. The members ran the gamut of conformist style in the Jacobean Church—not the longest trajectory, perhaps, but longer

---

[26] H. Hamlin, M. G. Brennan, M. P. Hannay, and N. J. Kinnamon (eds.), *The Sidney Psalter* (Oxford, 2009).

[27] Hugh Broughton, *A Concent of Scripture* (1590); J. Lightfoot, *The Works of the great Albionean Divine... Hugh Broughton* (1662), sig. a2r–v.

[28] George Potter and Evelyn Simpson, *The Sermons of John Donne*, 10 vols. (Berkeley, CA, 1953–62), X, pp. 295–401.

than would obtain in a succeeding reign, and so worth noting for its intent.[29] Most tellingly, a final quality control check was to test each passage by reading it aloud. This was a Bible designed to make rough places plain, in politics as well as in public speaking. It was also designed to sound venerable and thus authoritative: the KJV's characteristic and now-beloved 'thees' and 'thous' were archaisms in the seventeenth century.[30]

The KJV now enjoys an unparalleled reputation for literary style and textual ubiquity (it still holds title as the most widely bought, read, distributed, and *stolen* book in the history of printed books; these titles will be hard to maintain, however, long into the twenty-first century), but its seventeenth-century history grants only a tantalizing glimpse of such future greatness. Like the Bishops' Bible, the KJV was a product of its time, commissioned and designed to be appointed for use in Church of England worship. Its origins also lie in the unexpected outcomes of what can only be called a political shellacking. The heir to the childless Elizabeth was James VI of Scotland, the most obvious claimant and a Protestant. But exactly what *kind* of Protestant was a question that exercised James's new bishops, who feared that the king of Scots' youthful training in Calvinist doctrine, reputed preference for preaching over liturgical prayer, and politic disinterest in forcing full-scale episcopacy onto his native Church might be characteristics unbecoming a supreme head of the Church of England. (Other equally concerned observers noted that this was the son of the papist Mary Queen of Scots and recalled the younger king's turning to a Catholic favourite, his cousin Esmé Stuart, when besieged by over-mighty, and Protestant, northern nobles.)[31] So when the king called a conference at Hampton Court in 1604 to discuss the state of religion in his fractious new realm—a call prompted by clamorous, anti-Catholic petitioning—he made a lot of important English ecclesiastics very anxious indeed.

They needn't have lost sleep. England's conservative bishops ('conservative' meaning 'anti-puritan', men resolute against the excessive demands of the hotter sort of Protestant in the previous reign) packed the conference. The puritan cause was represented by proxy: voiced by establishment figures whose concerns (that the full Calvinist reform of the Church had been hampered by overweening attention to matters of conformity in the latter half of the previous reign) had made them sympathetic to the godly. Dr John Rainolds (1549–1607), dean of Lincoln, president of Corpus Christi College

---

[29] Ward Allen, *Translating for King James: Notes made by a Translator of King James's Bible* (Nashville, 1969); Ward Allen, *Translating the New Testament Epistles 1604–1611: A Manuscript from King James's Westminster Company [Lambeth MS 98]* (Nashville, 1977).

[30] E. C. Jacobs, 'King James's Translators: The Bishops' Bible's New Testament', *The Library*, 6th ser., 14 (1992): 100–26.

[31] Patrick Collinson, *The Elizabethan Puritan Movement* (1971), pp. 448–9; David M. Bergeron, 'Writing King James's Sexuality', in Daniel Fischlin and Mark Fortier (eds.), *Royal Subjects: Essays on the Writings of James VI and I* (Detroit, MI, 2002), p. 345.

Oxford, and a man known for his strenuous advocacy of reform despite Elizabeth I's increasing irritation with him, headed this delegation of moderate conformists.

Rainolds brought the case compiled under four familiar and seemingly unimpeachable heads: that the doctrine, preaching, government, and liturgy of the Church of England be brought up to the standards set by 'God's word'. Despite delivering his petitions in the language of the Elizabethan Injunctions, he got nowhere. In fact, according to some (granted, hostile) accounts, he antagonized his interlocutors. The king and his bishops—especially the bishop of London Richard Bancroft (a great hammer of those he considered puritans, as well as of those who had the temerity to defend them)—apparently considered the expression *according to God's word* a stealthy puritan provocation, and proceeded to shout down, upstage, and even mock Rainolds and the rest of his delegation. Rainolds then tried one last gambit, which also kept the Bible firmly at the core of its concerns and even flattered his sovereign: he asked for a new translation of the Bible, owing to the 'corruptness' of the version produced in previous reigns. Disarmingly, the king promptly agreed, remarking to Rainolds that he, too, found the Bible currently in use a disgrace. Rainolds referred, of course, to the Bishops' Bible; King James, however, spoke of the Geneva.[32]

With this agreement, the Church of England got a new Bible and its bishops' triumph over puritanism was nearly complete. The margins of the 1611 Bible are free of commentary, its few notes dealing with matters of disputed translation rather than theology. With its sonorous cadences and lack of study aids, it was not designed for private study and personal instruction but to be an adjutant to the Church's worship as scripted in the Book of Common Prayer. Organized and redacted to complement and facilitate uniformity of worship, it has played the supporting role to the liturgy ever since. This, of course, is exactly what a state Church's liturgy is meant to do: express a corporate and visible, not private and individual, religious culture.

The decision at Hampton Court to commission a Bible signalled the end of a century of biblically oriented reform in the Church of England. At the very moment that James I acceded to the puritans' best representative, the bedrock assumption of their reforming hopes—that the principle of *sola scriptura* did not simply mean that the Bible was sufficient to salvation, but that this sufficiency extended to form a 'measuring rod' for orthodoxy and practice—was, effectively, doomed. An explicitly articulated privileging of the Word was the foundation on which the Elizabethan Church was first reconstructed, but the world looked very different in 1604 than it had in 1558. In the early years of the Elizabethan settlement, the phrase *sola scriptura* seems to have carried a

---

[32] Barlow, *Summe*, sigs. G3v–G4v.

capacious and active meaning: that the Bible was not merely sufficient to the simple doctrine of salvation by faith (which would establish the Church invisible) but was also the literal standard against which the visible Church, its doctrines and practices, was to be judged—a book which all Christians were to 'embrace, believe, and follow if they look to be saved', but also that 'they may the better know their duties to God, Queen, and [to] their neighbour'.[33] This is a broad endorsement of the power of Scripture that links the Christian life in and out of church—an expression of faith in its power to rebuild parish congregations lost to persecution and exile, and with the state constituted out of those congregations.

By the reign of Charles I, however, the Bible can appear as the Church's problem: the telling synonym for *preaching* which had itself become a synonym for *puritan*; the potentially unruly text which, if studied privately, could be used to challenge the authority of the Church of England and its monarch. William Tyndale might remind us that this was no new thing. Stephen Gardiner, who grimly survived the Protestant flirtations of Henry VIII and the reforming reign of Edward VI to become Mary I's Lord Chancellor, remarked in 1547 that any man with a vernacular Bible could claim to be 'a Church alone' and constitute a threat to the religious polity.[34] Access to the vernacular Bible was tempered by John Whitgift, Elizabeth I's archbishop of Canterbury, whose 'Articles Touching Preachers' of 1583 restricted not only preaching, but also 'interpretation of the scriptures' to licensed clergy.[35] Bancroft, whose elevation to archbishop came soon after his routing of Rainolds at Hampton Court, crafted metropolitical visitation articles in 1605 that pointedly enquired whether parishioners claimed that the form of ordaining bishops and priests was 'repugnant to the word of God'.

So when Matthew Wren's visitation articles of 1635 demanded whether 'any preach, speak, or declare, that the book of common prayer containeth anything that is repugnant to holy scripture' the bishop could claim precedent of long standing. But he and his fellow Laudians also now held unprecedented power, so much so that not only puritans, but even conforming Calvinists began to fear that England's Protestant identity, along with its fidelity to *sola scriptura*, was in danger.[36] The consequences, as all students of Britain's civil wars know, were devastating—but also short-lived. In the 1640s and 1650s, loyalists met privately to read the Prayer Book, not the Bible, to keep the Established Church alive in an age of public directories and Cromwellian Independency.

---

[33] *Articles to be Enquired of in the Visitation of the Church* (1559), sig. A3r–v: Item 6.

[34] Stephen Gardiner, *A Declaration of Such True Articles as George Joye hath gone about to Confute as False* (1546), sig. L5r.

[35] G. W. Prothero, *Select Statutes* (Oxford, 1898), p. 212.

[36] Kenneth Fincham (ed.), *Visitation Articles and Injunctions of the Early Stuart Church*, 2 vols. (Woodbridge, 1994–8), I, p. 6; II, p. 130.

As befitted that age of extremity and experiment, the KJV went on to thrive in unofficial formulations: John Canne, a religious Independent and printer, added his own marginal notes, drawn in part from the Geneva, to the 1611 Bible, dedicating it, 'his owne work', to the Parliament.[37] Canne's notes were licensed in 1653, but even after the KJV was reappointed and reinstated in the Restoration Church, enterprising rogue printers got around the powerful copyright privileges held by royal printers in Oxford, Cambridge, and London by simply adding a clutch of fairly worthless footnotes on the bottom margin that could be easily cut away before the book was bound. As printers and readers worked out how to tailor Scripture for private uses, the KJV became the Bible of choice for former roundheads as well as for once and future royalists.

The larger idea—that the Bible was the religion of Protestants, or at least the measure by which purity of doctrine and worship could be assayed—also went on to thrive, in the denominations of an America opposed to one national form of Christianity and later, in the global strategies of missionaries American and British. In post-1660s England, however, its progress stalled upon that era's intention to claim and then craft a distinctly English style of Protestantism. Mindful of the power of puritan revolution, the Restoration Church viewed its official liturgy, not its appointed version of Scripture, as a reliable guarantor of conformity and the still-enduring representative of English Reformation.

Because it signals the omega rather than the alpha of scripturally based Protestantism in England, the Bible ordered into existence by King James I provides us with the best example of the place of Scripture in the post-Reformation Church of England. Except for some minor editing, the 1611 KJV was not significantly revised until the introduction of the notoriously unpopular and short-lived English Revised Version of 1881. King James's Bible had silenced arguments about translations and their accuracy or efficacy; banished the heady memories of sixteenth-century martyrdom to the shadowy realms of time out of mind; sidelined the reforming optimism, both theological and pedagogical, that had characterized Elizabethan and early Jacobean Calvinist consensus; and drew an unassailable and permanent distinction between private and public scriptural education. The 1611 Bible thus signalled the end of the reformation of Scripture even as this Good Book settled into its long afterlife as literary masterpiece and premier transmitter of the English language to the rest of the world. For this reason, it does not, indeed cannot, represent either the promised end to which fifteenth- and sixteenth-century vernacular translating energy pointed, nor provide us with the cornerstone on which was built an inevitable and essential English Protestant identity—unless we consider a certain resistance to *sola scriptura* one of the defining hallmarks of what we now call 'Anglicanism'.

---

[37] David Norton, *The King James Bible: A Short History from Tyndale to Today* (Cambridge, 2011), pp. 147, 164.

SELECT BIBLIOGRAPHY

Cressy, David, *Literacy & the Social Order: Reading & Writing in Tudor & Stuart England* (Cambridge, 1980).

Daniell, David, *The Bible in English* (New Haven, CT, 2003).

De Hamel, Christopher, *The Book: A History of the Bible* (2001).

Ferrell, Lori Anne, *The Bible and the People* (New Haven, CT, 2008).

Greenslade, S. L. (ed.), *The Cambridge History of the Bible: The West from the Reformation to the Present Day* (Cambridge, 1963).

Gutjahr, Paul, *An American Bible: A History of the Good Book in the United States, 1777–1880* (Stanford, CA, 1999).

Hamlin, Hannibal and Norman W. Jones (eds.), *The King James Bible after 400 Years: Literary, Linguistic, and Cultural Influences* (Cambridge, 2010).

MacCulloch, Diarmaid, 'The Myth of the English Reformation', *Journal of British Studies*, 30 (1991): 1–19.

Metzger, Bruce, *The Bible in Translation* (Grand Rapids, MI, 2001).

Norton, David, *A History of the English Bible as Literature* (Cambridge, 2000).

23

The Westminster Assembly and the Reformation of the 1640s

Chad van Dixhoorn

By the outbreak of the civil war, a majority of members in the Long Parliament saw it as their duty to renovate the Church of England, bringing it both into line with a more biblical code and up to date with the best Reformed Churches. Aspects of this transformation, chiefly the work of demolition, the Lords and Commons were willing to direct themselves. But while ready to dismantle aspects of church life and ministry, neither house was eager, and together they were unable, to generate a new design for the Church. It is for that reason that the Long Parliament formed an assembly of divines, a kind of ecclesiastical architectural service, to which it could contract the task of planning a remodelled Church.

The Westminster Assembly of divines, taking its name from the abbey in which it met, was comprised of approximately thirty Members of Parliament and 120 ministers, the latter, almost to a man, clergy of the Church of England. But instead of following a more familiar pattern of permitting the clergy to elect members to this 'convocation', the Commons nominated, vetted, and elected to the Assembly two members from each English, and one from each Welsh shire, and the House of Lords appointed a proportionate number, with each house giving the other a veto over its choices.[1]

Virtually all who were invited, including a few bishops, were self-acknowledged Calvinists, well-connected to leaders in the two houses of Parliament. Many were vocal opponents of Archbishop William Laud, some would testify at his trial, and a handful had fled to the Netherlands or America during the latter part of Charles I's Personal Rule. The kind of men who were *invited* varied from the theological tenor of the English clergy as a whole. The

---

[1] For the narrative spine of this chapter, see C. van Dixhoorn (ed.), *The Minutes and Papers of the Westminster Assembly, 1643–1652*, 5 vols. (Oxford, 2012). Hereafter *MPWA*.

men who ultimately *attended* were even more distant from the average clergyman in that those who came were intent on reform, and willing to obey the summons to meet at Westminster in the face of the king's command that they must not.

Members were allotted four shillings per day and taxpayers worried that, equipped with a favourite cushion, these clergymen would be happy to sit in session until Christ returned.[2] As it happened, the gathering held almost 1,400 working sessions from 1 July 1643 until the demise of the Long Parliament in 1653. Ironically, the task that consumed more time than any other was one which the Parliament's summoning ordinance for the Assembly never envisaged: examining ministers. In many congregations in the 1640s the most tangible evidence of the Assembly's reformation was the insertion of a new minister in a local parish. The Long Parliament had assumed the task of ejecting morally scandalous and politically 'malignant' ministers from the Church. Additional vacancies were caused by ministers fleeing their parishes or being captured by rival armed forces. The task assumed by the Assembly was to consider replacements for the clergy of the Church of England who had been sacked by the Committee for Scandalous Ministers, to facilitate relocations for clergy displaced by the war, and to assess fresh recruits for congregations without pastors. It was the greatest shift in parochial personnel in any decade of the history of the English Church, and almost all of it 'off the grid' covered by normal diocesan records. Joel Halcomb estimates that the Westminster Assembly 'conducted as many as 5,000 examinations' of men for positions within the Church and the two universities—'an astonishing number considering that there were 8,600 parishes in England and perhaps 10,000 ordained clergy in England and Wales'.[3] No doubt there was an element of self-selection among those coming to the Assembly rather than seeking clandestine ordination from a bishop, or simply choosing to remain in one place rather than risk the scrutiny of loyalties and behaviour that was unavoidable at the Assembly. Nonetheless, given the Assembly's reputation for exactitude in life and doctrine, a surprisingly small number of examinees were ever rejected for service in the reforming Church of the 1640s.

While the Assembly was willing to examine ordinands and ministers it was unwilling, as an ad hoc assembly appointed by Parliament, to ordain them. Thus it is easy to see, with hindsight, that the Assembly would eventually have to turn its attention to the subject of the ordination of ministers. But the first assignment handed to the Assembly was not so practical. Instead, the gathering was charged by Parliament to 'vindicate' the Thirty-Nine Articles.

This initial task typified the Assembly's approach to all that it did. A committee reported with the most reliable copies of the Thirty-Nine

---

[2] *Mercurius Clericus*, 1, 17–24 Sept. 1647.   [3] *MPWA*, I, p. 218.

Articles. The Assembly then carefully debated each clause of each article, also insisting that some kind of scriptural support be found for every statement. A couple of articles remained unchanged by the Assembly (1 and 12); a few were given stylistic adjustments only; others were simplified or supplemented. 'Christian men' was changed to 'Christians'; Christ's descent into hell was explained; the Apocrypha were no longer recommended; the dubious claim that no Old or New Testament books were 'ever doubted' was removed. For the Assembly, the sacrosanct sections of the articles were those teaching the Christian doctrine of God and classic Christology. The most heavily revised articles were the ninth article, on sin, and the eleventh article, on justification. Calvinist claims were stiffened in both, and after weeks of debate, the Assembly added a statement about the basis for justification and an anti-antinomian conclusion about the need for penitence.[4] The gathering was always thorough. And it was always slow. After more than three months of full-time study, the Assembly had only debated the first fifteen articles.

During these summer months the Assembly made dozens of modifications to words and phrases. To the untrained eye these must have seemed trivial since, in the judgement of the House of Lords, even the Assembly's later confession of faith was proof to Churches abroad and people at home 'that the Parliament did never intend to innovate Matters of Faith'.[5] The gathering clearly endeavoured a sympathetic revision of the fifteen articles rather than a wholesale replacement. Indeed, in revising the English (1571) text the Assembly would, where possible, choose a preferred reading from the Latin (1563) text before offering its own (for example, inserting a translation of *'renatis et credentibus'* in place of 'believe and are baptized' in the revised Article 9). Even in the most extensively altered paragraphs, the wording and phrasing of the articles is largely retained.

The impression given is that the Assembly was reluctant to alter the articles. Historians now know that the summer of 1643 was fractious and heated, with a moderate party in the abbey wanting minimal changes and a more radical party calling into question the use of creeds, forms in worship, and time-honoured theological phrases. While these specific concerns remained the property of a minority of members, four years later the Assembly authored a memo indicating that the body's discontent with the articles had only grown. In a note to the House of Lords, the Assembly explained that since its members were charged with only 'cleering and vindicating' the Thirty-Nine Articles, it had made 'fewer alterations in them and additions to them, then otherwise we should have thought fit to have done'. The gathering judged that 'many things yet remaining' were 'defective' and that there were 'other expressions also fit to bee changed'. This comment was, in part, a reflection on

---

[4] *MPWA*, V, pp. 323–8 (Doc. 122). [5] *LJ*, VIII, p. 558.

their own revision of 1643 that they could now see 'was severall ways imperfect'. Nonetheless, the memo is clear that it was also a comment on the historic articles themselves.[6]

Work on the Thirty-Nine Articles might have continued if the by now critical shortage of men for pastoral ministry had not coincided with a political development: the two houses of Parliament (having consulted with the Westminster Assembly) signed a solemn political alliance and religious covenant with the rebel Presbyterian authorities in Scotland. The primary motivations behind the alliance probably differed between the English and the Scottish representatives who drafted the declaration, and the politicians and pastors who signed it. Likewise, the directions that the Solemn League and Covenant sent to the Assembly vis-à-vis the texts and practices of the Church of England were not more radical than Parliament's original ordinance calling the Assembly. Nonetheless, its immediate effects for the Assembly's tasks were clear: it was no longer tenable to revise the Thirty-Nine Articles, or any text 'relating onely to the Church of England' (and Wales).[7] It stretched the Assembly's original task to include a reformation of the Churches of Scotland and Ireland too. The Assembly's new responsibilities were now wider in scope, a reality that members embraced with varying degrees of warmth. Nonetheless, the records of the Assembly reveal that English members continued to privilege their own national reformation and were determined that the newly reformed Church must be recognizable as the Church of England itself, and not some part or new incarnation of it.

Members insisted that the Church of England as constituted was already a true Church. They made the point publicly in a justification for their actions, sent to Reformed Churches in Europe. Nineteen different regional Churches in Europe received a self-justifying circular from the Assembly explaining why they were effecting 'a more thorow Reformation of Religion in the Church of England, according to the Word of God'.[8] Although six Scottish commissioners to the Westminster Assembly signed the text alongside the names of the Assembly's own English officers, the letter mentioned 'the Church and Kingdome of Scotland' almost as a postscript.[9] The focus of the letter was England's reformation, but the Scottish commissioners did not consider this to be a slight; their Church was, as they saw it, in better spiritual shape. Indeed, they encouraged a preoccupation with an English reformation since many of their own troubles at home were caused by the English 'presumption' to 'impose upon the whole Kingdome of Scotland a new Popish book of Service, Rites, and Ceremonies; and a book of Canons' and, in earlier decades, an episcopal form of government.[10] Nor was this commitment to the Church of England as

[6] *MPWA*, V, pp. 323–4 (Doc. 122).   [7] *MPWA*, V, p. 324 (Doc. 122).
[8] *MPWA*, V. p. 34 (Doc. 14).   [9] *MPWA*, V. pp. 39, 41 (Doc. 14).
[10] *MPWA*, V, p. 36 (Doc. 14).

a true Church only for the members of and commissioners to the Assembly: members required a statement of allegiance to the continuing Church of England from the ordinands and ministers who came before them for examinations, questioning each examinee on the subject.[11]

Shortly after the Solemn League and Covenant was signed, the Westminster Assembly turned its attention to church government, and then to the production of a directory for ordination to replace the old ordinal. As a new system of government had not been erected to replace the old, these efforts had a provisional nature and were intended to be used in England only. Nonetheless, the Scots threw themselves into the effort, probably presuming (rightly, as it turned out) that with some adjustments, the text would be incorporated into a directory for church government that could be used in all three kingdoms.

Debates over ordination were typical of the Assembly's constructive work, and the gathering's intention to reform the Church without replacing it with something entirely alien. This concern directed many of the Assembly's debates: could the vestiges of the idea of a ruling elder be present in the office of churchwarden?[12] (Perhaps.) Should the gathering continue the historic requirement of an ordination to the diaconate prior to an ordination to the presbyteriate? (No.) Would existing deacons, as before, need to be ordained specifically to a presbyterial ministry before they would be permitted to assume a pastoral charge?[13] (Yes.) Would ordination by a single bishop or his suffragan be considered valid in a Church where future ordinations would be conducted by a plurality of presbyters? Should the Church distinguish between the form and the substance of such an action? (Yes.)[14]

The directory was a test balloon for parliamentary and Scottish opinion of the Assembly's work, and the Assembly knew it.[15] In England, the political atmosphere made predictions of favourable acceptance unreliable. The majority in Parliament, in this instance, without demurring from the Assembly's basic approach, objected to many of the details of the document, and deleted its doctrinaire introduction, preferring to argue for the expediency and not the divine warrant of the Assembly's proposals. It edited the text along similar lines and issued a revised directory for ordination as a civil ordinance valid for one year.[16] The Assembly was deeply disappointed both with the heavy-handed revisions and with the almost total elimination of Presbyterian polity from their original text. They also had to deal with the fallout that came from candidates who felt that the ordinance for ordination cheapened their entrance into the ministry: legislation with a twelve-month expiry date inspired

---

[11] *MPWA*, II, pp. 305–11 (Sess. 94, 13 Nov. 1643); John Lightfoot, *Works*, ed. J. R. Pitman, 13 vols. (1822–5), XIII, pp. 48–9.
[12] *MPWA*, II, pp. 356–7 (Sess. 101, 22 Nov. 1643).
[13] *MPWA*, V, p. 114 (Doc. 40, pt. 1). [14] *MPWA*, V, p. 67 (Doc. 20, pt. 10).
[15] *MPWA*, V, p. 63. [16] *MPWA*, V, pp. 63–9 and pp. 75–7 (Docs. 20 and 28).

the same kind of confidence as jobs with a twelve-month contract.[17] The text was eventually issued with the authority of Parliament in October 1644, reissued in November 1645, and finally incorporated into a settled system of government in August 1646.

Each of the Assembly's subsequent efforts extended the reformation that had begun with the directory for ordination. In December 1644 the Assembly completed a Directory for Public Worship to replace the Book of Common Prayer; it was revised by Parliament and printed a few months later. Preaching, in particular, was given a new prominence in the Assembly's new 'liturgy'. Indeed, parts of the Directory are ordered with respect to this central part of the worship service, such as 'the prayer before the sermon' and 'the prayer after the sermon'. The Directory offered the most visible victory of the reformists. For displaced bishops and committed users of the Prayer Book, their new existence as nonconformists was a nightmare from which they had little hope of waking. For the Assembly and Parliament, it marked the high point of harmony in their relationship and their concurrence on church reform.

An ordinance for the Lord's Supper was completed in 1645, revised, printed, recalled, and finally ordered in 1646. It permitted elderships, with the assistance of Parliament if need be, to determine who could attend the eucharist in parochial congregations. This, and the ordinal, were coupled with a directory for church government, authored by the Assembly in 1645, revised and then ordered by Parliament in 1646. The directory for church government was intended to replace with a Presbyterian structure the episcopal statutes and canons previously directing the government of the Church. For historians, this 'Presbyterianism' needs significant qualification. The Church was not a pure Presbyterianism: the Assembly's work was reshaped by an anti-clerical Parliament. In most parts of England it was a paper Presbyterianism only: an idea, promulgated by Parliament, requiring the establishment of an egalitarian government of elders and clergy in every parish, but only practised in London and in counties where ministers put themselves forward as potential participants in the grand experiment. None of this would be disputed by the reformers in the abbey, and much of it would be lamented. They had been handed what Laud had inherited: a working relationship with a House of Commons that was all too willing to take to itself what the clergy saw as the prerogatives of the Church.

The directories were followed by four other texts. In 1647 a Psalter, translated by a member of the House of Commons and revised by the Assembly, was approved by the Assembly as a replacement for the traditional English Sternhold and Hopkins; it won few points north of the border and was never officially sanctioned by Parliament since the House of Lords (and many

---

[17] *MPWA*, V, pp. 114–15 (Doc. 40).

members of the Assembly) preferred a rival psalter. Appearing in stages through 1646 and 1647, the Assembly's Confession of Faith replaced the Assembly's fifteen revised articles of 1643 which had been used, sporadically, in place of the Thirty-Nine Articles.[18] Virtually all the doctrines discussed in the Thirty-Nine Articles found their place in the confession's thirty-three chapters, as did some of their tone and style. For example, the sole anathema in the Thirty-Nine Articles is repeated in the confession,[19] and the Assembly suggested that Scripture proofs were inappropriate for their confession because they were not present in the Thirty-Nine Articles.[20] As well, the revisions made in the fifteen articles found their way into the finished confession of 1646: a new emphasis on regeneration and the effectiveness of God's grace became a discussion of effectual calling; a comment introduced on the subject of Christian liberty became a chapter. The Assembly's final work was to replace Thomas Norton's long catechism with its own Larger Catechism in 1647 and, in the same year, the Church's small catechism, designed for confirmation, with a much longer Shorter Catechism.

Of course no mere examination of texts can convey the concerns evident in the abbey. Whatever the topic or text under consideration, the Assembly always debated the implications of their proposals for the Church of England's members and ministers. Was it every minister's duty to visit the poor? In theory, perhaps, but in the Church of England some parishes were so wealthy that it might not be fitting to stipulate this as a regular duty in unqualified terms.[21] Was it a minister's responsibility to visit prisoners? Maybe, but many ministers did not live near major gaols and prisons.[22] The Assembly was attempting a national reformation, and each text needed to be suitable for London or Lancashire. Again, quite strikingly, the Assembly never asked what was suitable for Edinburgh or Aberdeen. But also because it was a reformation of a national Church, all that could be retained would be retained. Past baptisms would be recognized, and the normative pattern of infant baptism was upheld. Members were, in theory, assumed to be fitted for the Lord's Table—they needed merely to be free from scandalous sin and ignorance. Deacons would be repurposed, but existing deacons were recognized to be men on track for pastoral ministry, and not mercy ministry per se. Priests episcopally ordained were to be seamlessly admitted as presbyters, and only these clergy were permitted to administer the sacraments.

Calculating points of continuity is a fractious endeavour; the points of comparison along a line of reform seem infinite. A case can be made for connections between the Church of the 1640s and the Church at other points since the Reformation, connections that are substantial in both senses of the

---

[18] *CJ*, V, p. 533 (14 Oct. 1647). [19] Art. 18 and *Westminster Confession of Faith* X.4.
[20] *MPWA*, V, p. 310 (Doc. 113). [21] *MPWA*, II, p. 477 (Sess. 119, 20 Dec. 1643).
[22] *MPWA*, II, p. 475 (Sess. 118, 19 Dec. 1643).

word. Nonetheless, for at least six reasons (explained below), a long history of historical writing loyal to the Church of England has emphasized the alien nature of the Assembly, arguing that the reform offered by this strange synod is not a legitimate chapter in accounts of the Church of England itself, but rather a sideshow while the 'real' Church continued operating underground.

This perspective has seemed plausible, first, because from the start of the civil war in 1642, reforms were chiefly negative. This is not an essay on Parliament and the reform, but on the Assembly and reform, and yet the constructive work of the latter is inexorably tied to the destructive work of the former. And what Parliament did in its early years was to advertise, with enthusiasm, the pending suspension or abolition of aspects of church life, worship, and government without offering anything concrete in their places. Parliaments are not usually evaluated for their pastoral wisdom, but this was pastorally irresponsible, even if it had its purposes in terms of public policy and rhetoric.

Second, but probably first in the mind of many people in the 1640s, the Assembly's legitimacy as a reforming body of the Church could never be accepted by those who were economically disadvantaged by ecclesiastical reforms. Even though it was a gradual development, and not tied to any of the Assembly's reforms per se, Parliament effectively assumed the rights and duties of many patrons, and rewarded its own members, and members of the Assembly, with the profits that came from the sale of episcopal property and the ejection of royalist clergy. So long as they kept away from the plunder, Assembly members retained some credibility. But when, after Daniel Featley was framed for treason, Philip Nye received part of his property, and John White, another Assembly member, was granted his library, their intentions were open to negative readings.[23] When Stephen Marshall and Cornelius Burges were rewarded with rich livings, and when Assembly members were given livings that once belonged to their opposites, motives for reform were inevitably questioned.[24]

Third, in constituting this gathering of clergy in an unconventional way, Parliament had sacrificed credibility on the altar of control. The House of Commons knew that an election similar to the formation of a synodical body of the English Church could give the Assembly more integrity among the clergy, but the two houses were even more eager to have a body that they could direct in all of its details. Unsurprisingly, the gathering was criticized in the press as a puppet of Parliament.[25] The Assembly itself, knowing how things were normally done in the Church of England and elsewhere, was conscious of

---

[23] *MPWA*, I, pp. 117, 130; *CJ*, III, pp. 262, 289 (3, 26 Oct. 1643).
[24] A. Hughes, *Gangraena and the Struggle for the English Revolution* (Oxford, 2004), p. 232; T. Webster, *Stephen Marshall and Finchingfield* (Chelmsford, 1994).
[25] *Observations upon the Ordinance... for Ordination* (Oxford, 1645), pp. 1–7.

its purely civil origin and embarrassed by it. In writing to the General Assembly of the Church of Scotland they humbly admitted their inexperience, acknowledging that 'we walk in paths that have hitherto been untrodden by any Assembly in this Church'.[26] Yet never, in all of its communications with Reformed Churches, did the gathering mention the presence of Members of Parliament among them in their working sessions, or circulate its summoning ordinance from Parliament. Indeed, on only one occasion did it even mention that it had been summoned by Parliament.[27] By contrast, the Assembly did refer Reformed Churches to the Solemn League and Covenant, which it appears to have appended to at least one piece of public correspondence.

The fourth and related reason why the Westminster Assembly has appeared out of accord with the history of the Church of England is due to its relationship with the Church of Scotland and the presence of Scottish commissioners in the Assembly. The Solemn League and Covenant proved a stumbling block for some of the Assembly's members, even after the gathering offered a very careful defence of its legitimacy.[28] The irony is that the Assembly, as noted above, never swerved from its principal preoccupation with England. Indeed, members like Cornelius Burges—who was so outspoken in his opposition to the Covenant that he was, for a time, suspended from the Assembly—eventually managed to use the Covenant as a way of insisting on the legitimacy of the historic English Church.[29]

Although it was never explicitly stated in the Assembly (where minutes were kept and Scottish commissioners were present) all of the gathering's work was designed for the Church of England with the expectation that it could be adopted, and in some cases adapted, by the Church of Scotland. If the suitability of documents for the Church of Scotland is rarely mentioned, their usefulness for the Church of Ireland would have been entirely forgotten by the English if it had not been for occasional reminders from the Scottish commissioners.[30] But the Assembly's preoccupation with England was never visible outside the abbey, and was further obscured by the Assembly's failure to offer enduring solutions to pre-war problems. This preoccupation has been invisible to historians, too, because most of the Assembly's programmatic texts were officially adopted by the Church of Scotland only, and often saw the light of day in England solely because they were printed in Edinburgh for distribution in the south.

The unconventional setup and circumstances of the Westminster Assembly have made it easy to ignore in the annals of the Church of England. But doubts adhere not only to the Assembly as a whole, but also to its parts. Indeed a fifth reason for doubting that the Assembly has a proper place in the history of the

---

[26] *MPWA*, V, p. 71 (Doc. 21).   [27] *MPWA*, V, p. 38 (Doc. 14).
[28] *MPWA*, V, pp. 44–8 (Doc. 15).   [29] *MPWA*, II, p. 310 (Sess. 94, 13 Nov. 1643).
[30] *MPWA*, V, p. 178.

Church of England is its members' strong identity with past dissidents. The theologians of the Assembly were the kind of people who quoted William Ames more than Lancelot Andrewes, and William Fulke more than Richard Field.[31] Prior to the civil war, this fascination with the eddies and avoidance of the mainstream had marginalized the Assembly's future members. Within the Church they could, like William Gouge, be openly ambivalent about their minority status as 'puritans', or even embrace it.[32] Members identified themselves as part of a self-conscious party within the Church, as did Daniel Cawdrey and his audience when, preaching before the Assembly, he made the 'sad observation that the professing part of the church of England ware like a faire looking glasse, all of one peece, but one Image to be seen in it—but now looke: all in pieces'.[33]

Nonetheless, in spite of this complicated history, all but a few Assembly members considered themselves to be, most basically, not mutineers in, but faithful ministers of, the Church of England. This claim, insisted on by the Assembly for itself and others, was sporadically contested during the decade of the Assembly's existence. Repeatedly, the majority refused to give up their history and identity as a component part of the Church.[34] As the Assembly-member Edmund Calamy would explain on one of these occasions, 'if the question ware whether the church of Rome ware a true church, it would admitt of a debate'.[35] There could be no real debate about the legitimacy of the Church of England—although unlike Archbishop Laud, Assembly members saw themselves as belonging to a tradition of protest precisely because they understood the Church of England to belong to the family of Reformed Churches. By way of contrast to their own situation, no mere adjustments could be made to Catholic, Lutheran, or Anabaptist churches; those were communions to flee, not to amend; to denounce, not to defend. The Reformation in England, on the other hand, was an overt attempt to bring their beloved Church into greater conformity with 'the best Reformed Churches'. That this endeavour was pursued whole-heartedly is a statement of loyalty often overlooked.

Assertions of solidarity with the pre-1640s Church took many forms. Members would routinely stress that they held the same doctrine as the rest of the Church of England, and they were pleased to cite comments by

---

[31] *MPWA*, I, pp. 148, 155.
[32] W. Gouge, *Guide to Goe to God* (1626), p. 255; W. Gouge, *The Sabbaths Sanctification* (1641), pp. 30-1; 'A Narrative of the Life and Death of Doctor Gouge', unpaginated, in W. Gouge, *A Learned and Very Useful Commentary on the Whole Epistle to the Hebrews* (1655).
[33] *MPWA*, IV, p. 111 (Sess. 635, 6 May 1646).
[34] E.g. *MPWA*, III, p. 29 (Sess. 203, 18 Apr. 1644), p. 250 (Sess. 274, 29 Aug. 1644), p. 275 (Sess. 280, 6 Sept. 1644); and *MPWA*, V, p. 87 (Doc. 31).
[35] *MPWA*, II, p. 308 (Sess. 94, 13 Nov. 1643).

Archbishop Sandys, King James, and Lancelot Andrewes to that effect.[36] In burning a book by the Congregationalist John Archer, the Assembly emphasized, among other things, that critics 'might justly insult over us, and publish to the world, that now in the Church of England it was openly, and impunely [i.e. with impunity] maintained, That God is the Author of Sin' (Archer's particular error).[37] Members of the Assembly, furthermore, protested their dedication indirectly, when they insisted that they were faithful patriots. In lobbying for change, they were as loyal as their neighbours to the crown, even if they criticized the bishops.[38] But here too, they considered themselves to be steadfast sons of the Church. The problem with Laudianism was, in large part, its tainted associations with Catholicism. The discipline, ceremonies, and pastoral care of the Laudians was problematic because it left the Church unprotected from what was supposed to be a common enemy of all parties in the Church. Assembly members argued that what contact people did have with the Laudian bishops actually drove them away from productive pastoral care. This collective understanding of self, of late-arriving reformers who were against the establishment because they were for the Church, was expressed by John Arrowsmith in a sermon before the Assembly, in which he told his fellow Assembly members that they were continuing the work of the Waldensians and Albigensians, of Martin Luther, Henry VIII, and Edward VI.[39] It was a blend of 'heretics', heroes, and kings that would have horrified Henry himself, or Archbishop Laud, but there was nothing incongruous about this religious pedigree for Arrowsmith's hearers.

What may be the final and most substantial opposition to the Assembly's integration into the history of the Church of England is the fact that the Assembly's reforms seem out of proportion to godly grievances. These seventeenth-century reformers were convinced that prelacy had been used to abuse parishioners and preachers alike, and was not well-founded on the Scriptures. But actions speak louder than words and Parliament, with the Westminster Assembly's enthusiastic support, abolished the whole system of episcopacy, root and branch, and by 1644 the Assembly had made it obvious that it would offer, as a replacement, a simplified, non-hierarchical model of ministry. Gone were the archbishops, bishops, deans, and archdeacons. What remained were ministers and elders, with ordinations effected by a plurality of other ministers, and not by a higher order of minister. In some cases, members went even further. While they would speak of the Church which they were reforming with terms of endearment that would have stretched the English

---

[36] *MPWA*, II, p. 73 (Sess. 48, 7 Sept. 1643).   [37] *MPWA*, V, pp. 226–7 (Doc. 80).

[38] E.g. T. Thorowgood, *Digitus Dei: New Discoveryes; with Sure Arguments to Prove that the Jews (a Nation) or People Lost in the World for the Space of near 200 Years, Inhabite Now in America* (1652), p. 81; W. Twisse, *Of the Morality of the Fourth Commandment* (1641), pp. 37–4 [sic].

[39] *MPWA*, III, p. 93 (Sess. 221, 17 May 1644).

Protestant Reformers to use of their own forebears, members held more animosity towards Archbishop Laud than did some Reformers towards their Catholic antecedents, and their testimony at Laud's trial was ugly, and in some cases, arguably unfair.

Again, for those with access to the Assembly's debates, it is obvious that almost no change was proposed by the Assembly without some party taking up cudgels in defence of the status quo. Care was taken to defend the continuity of the Church in matters as 'arcane' as Henry VIII's interpretation of consanguinity and affinity, or as significant as thoroughgoing opposition to separatism, or as awkward as opposition to the House of Commons. Nonetheless, the result was comprehensive change—not exhaustive, but still extensive.

For example, many of the godly were offended by the liturgy of the Church of England, and found its ceremonies redolent of Catholicism; the Laudian elevation of the ceremonial, the enforcement of unpopular canons, and other attempts to strengthen conformity during Charles I's reign only increased their concerns. As Stephen Marshall would say, 'they did so mix their humane Inventions with Gods Institutions, that we could not have the worship of God according to the pattern, but must wound our consciences if pertake of the Ordinances'.[40] And yet the truth was that before the civil war most of the wounded consciences would have been content with a revision of the Book of Common Prayer. After all, the Assembly itself could find elements of a reforming agenda actually mandated within the book, such as a justification for church discipline 'in the Rubrick before the Sacrament'.[41] Members also acknowledged that the Church, especially in the West, was committed to the book.[42] Nonetheless, the Assembly supported its abolition.

Where the Book of Common Prayer was removed and replaced by the Directory for Public Worship, the change in church life would have been striking. Not only were the weekly services of worship so entirely altered that even phrases that Scottish Presbyterians could tolerate were excised,[43] but every turning point in life was given a new script: from birth to burial, no part of the pattern of a person's spiritual journey was left untouched. The paradox of apologetics from prior decades was that successful arguments of the past now made reform in the 1640s more difficult, for it raised the bar in the conscience of reformers; it put gradual reform that much more out of reach once the godly were actually allowed to offer amendments.

It is no accident that the Assembly's most extensive comment on the Church of England from the days of Edward VI to their own day is found in

---

[40] S. Marshall, *The Power of the Civil Magistrate in Matters of Religion, Vindicated* (1657), p. 24.
[41] *MPWA*, V, p. 234 (Doc. 83).   [42] E.g. *MPWA*, III, p. 433 (Sess. 314, 31 Oct. 1644).
[43] E.g. *MPWA*, III, p. 174 (Sess. 249, 2 July 1644 and Alexander Henderson's comments on the *sursum corda*).

its preface to the Directory for Public Worship.[44] While giving thanks for the history of the Reformation in England and repeatedly highlighting the piety and good intentions of the men behind the Book of Common Prayer, the Assembly offered a catalogue of abuses that had arisen through the use of the book, concluding that its original authors 'were they now alive... would joyne with us in this work' of continued reformation.[45] To consider the Assembly's continuing reformation, or even to say that the Assembly in league with Parliament reformed the Church, is inevitably to be imprecise: the Assembly was created by Parliament and could perform few positive changes without it. Nonetheless, after it was created the body did achieve a kind of independent existence that its inventor had not envisaged and did everything it could to prevent. Few contemporaries of the Assembly could plausibly have denied that the Assembly became a reforming organism in its own right. Whether people today appreciate those short-lived reforms or consider them a freak of history is a matter of doctrinal conviction or personal taste. The question raised in this chapter, and by its presence in this volume, is whether the Assembly should be accepted as one part of the history of the Church of England. In the mind of the Westminster Assembly itself, the answer to that question was never in doubt.

SELECT BIBLIOGRAPHY

Bower, J., *The Larger Catechism: a Critical Text and Introduction* (Grand Rapids, MI, 2010).

Bradley, R. D., 'Jacob and Esau Struggling in the Womb: A Study of Presbyterian and Independent Religious Conflicts, 1640–1648, with Particular Reference to the Westminster Assembly and the Pamphlet Literature', PhD thesis, University of Kent, 1975.

Carruthers, S. W., *The Everyday Work of the Westminster Assembly* (Philadelphia, 1943).

Coates, W. H., A. S. Young, and V. F. Snow (eds.), *The Private Journals of the Long Parliament: 3 January to 5 March 1642* (New Haven, CT, 1982).

Morrill, J. S., *The Nature of the English Revolution* (1993).

Paul, R. S., *The Assembly of the Lord: Politics and Religion in the Westminster Assembly and the 'Grand Debate'* (Edinburgh, 1985).

Powell, H., *The Crisis of British Protestantism: Church Power in the Puritan Revolution, 1638–1644* (Manchester, 2015).

Shaw, W. A., *A History of the English Church during the Civil Wars and under the Commonwealth, 1640–1660*, 2 vols. (1900).

---

[44] *MPWA*, V, pp. 118–20 (Doc. 42).   [45] *MPWA*, V, p. 120 (Doc. 42).

van Dixhoorn, C. (ed.), *The Minutes and Papers of the Westminster Assembly, 1643-1652*, 5 vols. (Oxford, 2012).

van Dixhoorn, C., 'A New Taxonomy of the Westminster Assembly (1643-49): The Creedal Controversy as Case Study', *Reformation and Renaissance Review*, 6 (2004): 82-106.

van Dixhoorn, C., 'Politics and Religion in the Westminster Assembly and the "Grand Debate"', in R. Armstrong and T. O'hAnnrachain (eds.), *Alternative Establishments in Early Modern Britain and Ireland: Catholic and Protestant* (Manchester, 2013), pp. 129-48.

van Dixhoorn, C., 'The Strange Silence of Prolocutor Twisse: Predestination and Politics in the Westminster Assembly's Debate over Justification', *The Sixteenth Century Journal*, 40 (2009): 395-418.

24

The Cromwellian Church

Ann Hughes

It might seem misguided or eccentric to include a chapter on the Cromwellian Church in a volume devoted to the history of Anglicanism. If 'Anglican' is taken to mean a national episcopal Church, with a set liturgy defined in a Book of Common Prayer, then the Anglican Church as an institution was dismantled in the 1640s and restored along with the monarchy between 1660 and 1662. In most narratives of Anglican history the Interregnum reveals the capacity of the 'Anglican community ... to survive shorn of establishment'; it was in these years of eclipse and persecution that the essential character of a 'self-conscious Anglicanism' was debated and constructed, perhaps for the first time.[1] But if we were to foreground the issue of 'establishment', then, following the break with Rome, Anglicanism could arguably be equated with the legal arrangements operating at any time to organize a national Church of England. In this sense, at least, it could be argued that the Cromwellian Church could plausibly claim to be the 'Anglicanism' of the 1650s. Certainly, as Peter Lake and Michael Winship among others have insisted, many puritan ministers, characteristically nonconformists but not separatists before the civil war, supporters of modified episcopacy or Presbyterianism in the 1640s and 1650s, and mostly ejected in 1662, bitterly resented the claim of restored episcopalian Anglicans to embody the 'Church of England'. The writings of Richard Baxter and Samuel Clarke presented moderate puritans as central to a national Church tradition going back to the godly preaching Calvinist bishops and nonconformist pastors of the Elizabethan and early Stuart era.[2]

---

[1] Jacqueline Rose, 'Kingship and Counsel in Early Modern England', *Historical Journal*, 54 (2011): 47–71 (p. 63); Judith Maltby, 'Suffering and Surviving: The Civil Wars, the Commonwealth and the Formation of "Anglicanism", 1642-60', in Christopher Durston and Judith Maltby (eds.), *Religion in Revolutionary England* (Manchester, 2006); John Spurr, *The Restoration Church of England, 1646–1689* (New Haven, CT, 1991).

[2] Michael P. Winship, 'Defining Puritanism in Restoration England: Richard Baxter and others Respond to *A Friendly Debate*', *Historical Journal*, 54 (2011): 689–715; Peter Lake, 'Reading Clarke's *Lives* in Political and Polemical Context', in Kevin Sharpe and Steven

There is, however, another preliminary difficulty to be addressed. It was not men of Baxter's or Clarke's stamp who dominated religious policy under Protector Oliver Cromwell, but 'Independents' or (to use their self-designation rather than the label given by their opponents) 'Congregationalists' such as Thomas Goodwin, John Owen, and Philip Nye who insisted on the autonomy of the individual congregation. It might be thought that these men had little concern for a national Church that incorporated both the precious and the vile. For Congregationalists, voluntary gatherings of the godly were the true visible Churches on earth. As they explained in the 1658 declaration from a general meeting of the gathered congregations at the Savoy: 'the members of these churches are Saints by calling, visibly manifesting and evidencing (in and by their profession and walking)' their suitability for admission to the church. Members 'willingly consent to walk together, according to the appointment of Christ... in professed subjection to the Ordinances of the Gospel'. On this basis, 250 churches had been established by 1660.[3] Perhaps we should refer to the Cromwellian *churches*, rather than to a Cromwellian *Church*. But this verdict also is too hasty, for mainstream Congregationalists had complex, perhaps even contradictory, relationships with the concept and practice of a national Church, as suggested by the description—'magisterial Independents'—given to them by many historians. A commitment to some sort of non-compulsory official or national Church (or a 'public profession' as they termed it), combined with an elevated notion of the role of the civil magistrate, divided men like Nye and Owen from more radical separatists throughout the Interregnum. At the Whitehall debates of winter 1648 between army officers, civilian Levellers, and prominent pastors of gathered congregations, the crucial divisions were over the proper role of the civil magistrate in supporting true religion, and over the difficult balance between combating error and defending religious liberty.[4]

The mainstream Congregationalist view of the magistracy was summed up at Savoy. Magistrates were 'bound to incourage, promote and protect the Professors and Profession of the Gospel' and 'to take care that men of corrupt minds and conversations do not licentiously publish and divulge Blasphemy and Errors in their own nature subverting the faith, and inevitably destroying the souls of them that receive them'. Yet men of good conscience, 'holding the foundation' and not disturbing others were to be protected even if they

---

N. Zwicker (eds.), *Writing Lives: Biography and Textuality, Identity and Representation in Early Modern England* (Oxford, 2008).

[3] 'Of the Institution of Churches and the Order Appointed in them by Jesus Christ', appended to *A Declaration of the Faith and Order Owned and practised in the Congregational Churches in England* (1659); Joel Halcomb, 'A Social History of Congregational Practice during the Puritan Revolution', PhD thesis, University of Cambridge, 2009.

[4] Rachel Foxley, 'Freedom of Conscience and the "Agreements of the People"', in Philip Baker and Elliot Vernon (eds.), *The Agreements of the People, the Levellers and the Constitutional Crisis of the English Revolution* (Basingstoke, 2012).

differed from the 'public profession' over 'the Doctrines of the Gospel, or ways of the worship of God'.[5] Most moderate Congregationalists were willing to take public or state money (usually derived ultimately from tithes) as salaried lecturers, while many also held parish livings. Thomas Brooks at St Margaret, New Fish Street, London, for example, preached to the whole parish while administering the sacrament of the Lord's Supper to those fit and willing to join his gathered congregation. The Suffolk minister John Philip emigrated to New England but returned to his parish living in 1641, gathering a congregation there in 1650 while continuing to serve his broader flock until his death in 1660. Ministers like Philip saw the gathered church as an exemplar that would prompt reformation in the wider parish community. The latest research suggests that 80 per cent of all pastors of Congregational Churches relied on state funding; some from lectureships but most (85 per cent) through parochial livings.[6]

It is thus not surprising that the Instrument of Government, the written constitution establishing the Protectorate in December 1653, declared 'That the Christian religion, as contained in the Scriptures, be held forth and recommended as the public profession of these nations', even though this was not to be compulsory. The Cromwellian regime gave consistent attention to this 'public profession', involving a broad range of opinion, and building on Commonwealth policies to defend a learned, preaching ministry and to combat error. Before looking at the workings of the Cromwellian Church in detail, we need to take brief stock of religious developments in England between 1642 and 1653. Parliament's initial religious aims were for a reformed national Church, not for religious liberty or Protestant pluralism. Victory in the civil war promised not only the opportunity to dismantle the quasi-popish and clericalist innovations associated with Charles and Laud but also a chance at last to complete the reformation of a Church left, in puritan eyes, but 'halfly reformed'. True reformation involved moderating the hierarchical episcopal government of the Church; securing uncompromising Calvinist doctrine and purified worship with zealous preaching at its heart; and creating a structure that would ensure effective religious and moral discipline of the population.

Once initial plans for a regulated or moderated episcopacy had floundered in the early 1640s, the obvious alternative for a national Church within the Reformed tradition was a Presbyterian government of parochial elderships, classes, and synods, and the Parliament's alliance with the Scots increased pressure in that direction. The synod summoned by the Parliament in 1643, the Westminster Assembly of Divines, worked slowly and painfully to draw up a church settlement. Their plans were delayed by complex internal divisions particularly over church government, and by Parliament's anxieties over

---

[5] *A Declaration of the Faith and Order*, pp. 17–18.
[6] Halcomb, 'Social History', pp. 39–40, 65, 104, 111.

clerical domination, anxieties that came to focus especially on the vexed question of who had the ultimate authority to exclude from the sacrament parishioners whose religious understanding or way of life fell short of godly expectations. Beyond the Assembly, in an atmosphere of enthusiastic speculation and experimentation, and in the absence of church government with effective coercive powers, the fissiparous tendencies within English puritanism came to fruition with the emergence of separatist Churches, and attacks on Calvinist orthodoxy, and the status of a learned ministry. Episcopal government had collapsed in the early 1640s although it was not formally abolished until 1646; some 3,000 ministers were excluded from their livings although something like a third found other posts. The Book of Common Prayer was banned and replaced by the Assembly's Directory for Public Worship although it is not clear how widely it was adopted. Disruptive religious change, upheaval at the universities, and uncertainty over the survival of tithes, meant that in many areas it was difficult to find parish clergy. It is likely that most of the population regretted the loss of familiar services and their old ministers but the most dangerous threats to a national Presbyterian Church came from elsewhere. Hostility to compulsory Presbyterianism, and support for a thoroughgoing religious liberty for Protestants, came to be associated particularly with London radicals and Parliament's own New Model Army. The legislation for a Presbyterian Church, obstructed and revised in any case by Parliament, was slowly worked out between 1645 and August 1648, but never fully implemented. The measures were never formally repealed but after the army-backed coup of December 1648 they never received effective backing from the civil power. Functioning provincial assemblies operated only in the Presbyterian strongholds of Lancashire and London, and these were essentially (and paradoxically) voluntary bodies dependent on the commitment of individual ministers and elders. No national synod met in revolutionary England. The Commonwealth regime repealed the Elizabethan legislation requiring attendance at parish worship and an era of unprecedented religious liberty was inaugurated along with republican civil government.

Nonetheless, the basic parish structure of the English Church survived the upheavals of the 1640s, as (more surprisingly) did lay patronage (except for convicted royalists who had not made their peace with the new regimes) and compulsory payment of tithes. Many Congregationalists regretted this last but it was not easy to find alternatives, and attacks on tithes threatened the property rights of many laypeople and secular institutions. The Rump Parliament continued and elaborated 1640s measures to support a preaching ministry, to create a more effective parochial structure and to combat error. The clauses of the Instrument of Government and the early legislation of the Protectorate built on these initiatives, while also drawing on the more thoroughgoing discussions between army officers, London radicals, and ministers in the winter of 1648/9. The religious clauses of the Instrument of Government were modelled closely on the compromise Officers' Agreement of January 1649.[7] These declared: 'That the Christian religion, as contained in the Scriptures, be held forth and recommended as the public profession of these nations; and that, as soon as may be, a provision, less subject to scruple and contention, and more certain than the present, be made for the encouragement and maintenance of able and painful teachers, for the instructing of the people, and for discovery and confutation of error, heresy, and whatever is contrary to sound doctrine.' Until an alternative could be found, the 'present maintenance' through tithes was not to be taken away. No one was to be compelled to follow the 'public profession' but rather 'endeavours' should be used 'to win them by sound doctrine and the example of a good conversation'. A broad toleration was enacted: 'such as profess faith in God by Jesus Christ (though differing in judgment from the doctrine, worship or discipline publicly held forth) shall not be restrained from, but shall be protected in, the profession of the faith and exercise of their religion; so as they abuse not this liberty to the civil injury of others and to the actual disturbance of the public peace on their parts'. The necessity for professing faith in God by Jesus Christ was taken to exclude Socinianism, rapidly becoming the focus for puritan anxiety about orthodoxy, while liberty was explicitly withheld from 'Popery or Prelacy' and from 'such as, under the profession of Christ, hold forth and practise licentiousness'. What constituted prelacy was not always clear, and definitions varied anyway with the political climate, while the last phrase targeted 'Ranters', a group that prompted disproportionate alarm amongst the orthodox.[8]

The legislation of the Protector and Council in the first months of the Protectorate brought commendable order to structures supporting the personnel of the 'public profession'. The Commonwealth regime had organized comprehensive parish surveys, identifying poor, tiny, or unmanageably large parishes, and assessing the quality of the ministry. In Lancashire, for example, the survey concluded that the county's sixty-two existing enormous parishes should become 185, in order to support a learned, preaching, reforming ministry. In Blackburn hundred, it was proposed that five ancient parishes should be divided into twenty-eight based mainly on existing chapelries. These ambitious proposals were by no means fully implemented. In Lancashire only twenty-nine new parishes were planned for the county, and only four of these had actually been established by 1660.[9] Cromwell and his Council continued

---

[7] Ann Hughes, '"The Public Profession of these Nations": The National Church in Interregnum England', in Durston and Maltby (eds.), *Religion in Revolutionary England*, pp. 95–6.

[8] Samuel R. Gardiner, *Constitutional Documents of the Puritan Revolution* (Oxford, 1906), p. 416, clauses 35–8; Blair Worden, 'Oliver Cromwell and the Instrument of Government', in Stephen Taylor and Grant Tapsell (eds.), *The Nature of the English Revolution Revisited* (Woodbridge, 2013).

[9] Alex Craven, 'Ministers of State: The Established Church in Lancashire during the English Revolution, 1642–1660', *Northern History*, 45 (2008): 51–69 (pp. 67–8).

to approve measures for the division of unwieldy parishes and the amalgamation of small ones, usually responding to local initiative, founded on the evidence of the church survey. A crucial Cromwellian ordinance rationalized procedures for the augmentation of the livings of preaching parish ministers and lecturers through the establishing of 'Trustees for the Maintenance of Ministers'. A series of mechanisms to improve livings had been inaugurated in the 1640s, using tithe income confiscated from royalists and other church property, but the measures had become increasingly ramshackle and uncertain. Local studies suggest that under Cromwell, augmentations were more securely paid, albeit to fewer clergy. These policies were the most effective attempts to improve the maintenance of the parish clergy before Queen Anne's bounty.[10]

Two further measures addressed the chaotic context for the approval of ministers and the removal of unsatisfactory clergy, creating bodies commonly known as the 'Triers' and the 'Ejectors'. The Triers (formally the Commissioners for the Approbation of Public Preachers) were a central body of thirty-eight men, who approved the appointment of all ministers to positions in receipt of public maintenance (including established figures seeking new posts). Ministers had to provide testimonials to their abilities, and a legal presentment from a patron. The 'Ejectors' were local committees for purging 'scandalous' and 'insufficient' ministers, made up of laymen assisted by panels of ministers. There is evidence for activity by Ejectors in more than two-thirds of English counties, although few ministers seem to have been removed, at least before Major-Generals were appointed in the summer of 1655 to intensify general drives for godly reformation.[11]

These measures were based on proposals submitted to the Rump by John Owen and other leading Congregationalists in February 1652, although they reversed Owen's initial plans for national Ejectors and local approval of ministers. The character and success of the Cromwellian ordinances have been credited to the influence of 'magisterial Independents' and seen as a triumph for centralizing authority.[12] This was not the Protector's own view: Cromwell saw the Triers as 'persons, both of the Presbyterian and Independent judgments, men of as known ability, piety, and integrity, as I believe any this nation hath' and his definitions of orthodoxy were consistently generous, encompassing Presbyterians, Independents, and 'many under the form of Baptism, who are sound in the Faith, only may perhaps be different in

---

[10] Craven, 'Ministers of State', p. 63; Rosemary O'Day and Ann Hughes, 'Augmentation and Amalgamation: Was there a Systematic Approach to the Reform of Parochial Finance, 1640–1660?' in Rosemary O'Day and Felicity Heal (eds.), *Princes and Paupers in the English Church, 1500–1800* (Leicester, 1981).

[11] Hughes, 'Public Profession'.

[12] Jeffrey R. Collins, 'The Church Settlement of Oliver Cromwell', *History*, 87 (2002): 18–40. Contrast Hughes, 'Public Profession'.

judgment on some lesser matters'.[13] The argument of this chapter is that Cromwell's claim was justified: the Cromwellian Church was characterized by broad participation, encouraged by the Protector's attitudes, while the regime's flexibility and openness to local and personal initiatives was crucial to its success. Most of the Triers were magisterial Independents, including Owen, Philip Nye, and William Greenhill, but eminent Presbyterians such as Thomas Manton and Anthony Tuckney also served alongside moderate Baptists like Daniel Dyke and John Tombes. At a county level many Presbyterians were nominated as clerical assistants to the ejecting commissions, particularly in the later years of the Protectorate as anxiety over the spread of error and religious division intensified. In London, Edmund Calamy was nominated alongside William Jenkyn who had been implicated in the royalist–Presbyterian plot that cost the Presbyterian minister Christopher Love his life in August 1651. Presbyterian clergy provided many testimonials for their colleagues to present to the Triers, sometimes supporting godly ministers who differed from them on many issues; thus Calamy set his name to a testimonial for the Stepney Congregationalist Greenhill, and Ralph Josselin of Earls Colne testified to the fitness of his neighbour William Sparrow of Halstead, despite profound disagreements over church government. In exercising the Protector's extensive religious patronage, Cromwell and his Council usually responded to local initiatives, taking little account of precise affiliations as long as ministers had godly credentials, and many of the Council's augmentation orders were in effect rubber-stamping measures worked out locally. In 1654, for example, a petition from twenty-one men from Mansfield in Nottinghamshire asked the Council to approve an augmentation of £94 a year arranged for their minister John Firth, 'a man of most gracious qualifications and spiritual abilities'.[14]

The Triers were relaxed about approving ministers who had episcopal ordination, and Robert Skinner—one of the most active Interregnum ordainers amongst the bishops—signed a testimonial for one minister examined by the Triers, albeit in his guise as a provincial parish minister. Despite the formal exclusion of 'prelacy' from the benefits of the religious liberty established by the Instrument, it is clear from the research of Ken Fincham and Stephen Taylor that the Cromwellian Church turned a blind eye to many of the quasi-underground activities of episcopalians. Significant numbers of aspirant ministers were episcopally ordained throughout the Interregnum by an energetic minority of bishops, and it seems likely that John Thurloe, Cromwell's secretary of state and intelligencer, was well aware of this. Yet no one was ever prosecuted. Was this an accidental by-product of the commitment to religious liberty for peaceable Protestants, an attempt to win over former political enemies, or (most

---

[13] Hughes, 'Public Profession', pp. 98, 102.   [14] Hughes, 'Public Profession'.

intriguingly) a deliberate policy to balance Presbyterian influence within the national Church? As Cromwell complained to the corporation of London in 1654: 'I have had boxes and rebukes on one hand and on the other, some envying me for Presbytery, others as an in-letter to all the sects and heresies in the nation.' Certainly the ex-royalist earl of Bridgewater thought it worthwhile seeking Cromwell's approval for his presentation of the episcopalian Nicholas Bernard to a Shropshire living through an attack on the Presbyterian incumbent Robert Porter as a Scottish-sympathizing enemy of the regime. Cromwell responded that he was willing to leave the nomination to Bridgewater as long as he intended the 'real good of the people', although in the end Porter survived until the Restoration.[15]

This 'public profession' of the Protectorate was thus a very broad and flexible Church. It provided encouragement and effective practical support for a godly preaching ministry in parishes and public lectureships, and although 'magisterial Independents' were at its heart, Presbyterians were not marginalized; the practical functioning of the Cromwellian Church depended on their sustained participation at local and national level, and, for much of the time on the tacit 'toleration' of ceremonial episcopalians. As a national Church, of course, the Cromwellian settlement had its limitations. No agreement was ever reached on the doctrinal basis for the public profession, despite the broadly Calvinist affiliations of most of its leading figures, and in spite of significant support for the doctrinal elements of the Westminster Assembly's Confession of Faith and Shorter Catechism even from those who rejected Presbyterian ecclesiology. The emerging 'Arminianism' of Richard Baxter and John Goodwin should nonetheless be noted. The sustained attempts to achieve doctrinal unity remain significant although they were not ultimately successful.[16] John Owen was a prominent figure in most of these moves. In December 1652 the 'Humble Proposals' of Owen and other ministers included a list of doctrines against which no one was to preach or teach. These doctrines were broadly Trinitarian but open-minded on predestination, so that those more sceptical about Calvinism were still comprehended within definitions of orthodoxy. Nonetheless, the measures were blocked by the lobbying of Baptists and others who feared that defining orthodoxy would prompt unacceptable restrictions on religious liberty. During the first

---

[15] Kenneth Fincham and Stephen Taylor, 'Vital Statistics: Episcopal Ordination and Ordinands in England, 1646–60', *English Historical Review*, 126 (2011): 319–44; Hughes, 'Public Profession', pp. 103, 106–7.

[16] Carolyn Polizzotto, 'The Campaign against The Humble Proposals of 1652', *JEH*, 38 (1987): 569–81; Sarah Mortimer, *Reason and Religion in the English Revolution: The Challenge of Socinianism* (Cambridge, 2010); John Coffey, 'A Ticklish Business: Defining Heresy and Orthodoxy in the Puritan Revolution', in David Loewenstein and John Marshall (eds.), *Heresy, Literature and Politics in Early Modern English Culture* (Cambridge, 2006); Tim Cooper, *John Owen, Richard Baxter and the Formation of Nonconformity* (Farnham, 2011).

Protectorate Parliament, a committee of Presbyterian and Congregationalist ministers met to discuss a 'confession of faith'. They drew on the earlier proposals, but Owen, in particular, was now more anxious about both Arminianism and Socinianism; these proposals were more strictly Calvinist and more specifically Trinitarian. The early dissolution of the Parliament meant that no legislation was passed to define public doctrine.

The second Protectorate Parliament moved in more conservative directions, with the offer of the crown to Cromwell, and attempts to limit religious liberty in the face of rising alarm at the spread of Quaker activism as well as Socinian doctrine. The Humble Petition and Advice modified the religious clauses of the Instrument, stressing the importance of the 'Public Profession' and qualifying the commitment to religious liberty. Clause 10 asked that Cromwell, 'out of your zeal to the glory of God, and the propagation of the gospel of the Lord Jesus Christ' give consent to laws against those who 'do openly revile' or disturb godly ministers and their assemblies. The brief doctrinal statement of the Instrument, commending faith in God by Jesus Christ, was given a restrictive and overtly Trinitarian gloss. A confession of faith was to be drawn up and no one was to 'be suffered or permitted, by opprobrious words or writing, maliciously or contemptuously to revile or reproach the Confession of Faith to be agreed upon as aforesaid'. Beyond the public profession, only those who professed 'faith in God the Father, and in Jesus Christ His eternal Son, the true God, and in the Holy Spirit, God co-equal with the Father and the Son, one God blessed for ever, and do acknowledge the Holy Scriptures of the Old and New Testament to be the revealed Will and Word of God' were to be granted religious liberty 'so that this liberty be not extended to Popery or Prelacy, or to the countenancing such who publish horrid blasphemies, or practise or hold forth licentiousness or profaneness under the profession of Christ'. Ministers who did not agree over 'matters of faith' (rather than matters of government, worship, or discipline) with the public profession would not be able to receive public maintenance.[17]

The Humble Petition and Advice thus called for the production of an elaborate confession of faith that would not have been compulsory but was protected from public criticism. Again, though, Parliament did not produce the necessary legislation. It may be that the doctrinal conclusions of the Congregationalist meeting at Savoy in 1658 constituted an abortive attempt to provide a national confession of faith. The conclusions bear the marks of Owen's rising anxiety about Socinianism: 'In the unity of the God-head there be three persons of one substance, power and eternity, God the Father, God the Son, and God the Holy Ghost... Which Doctrine of the Trinity is the foundation of all our Communion with God, and comfortable Dependence

---

[17] Gardiner, *Constitutional Documents*, pp. 454–5.

upon him'.[18] But this declaration too had no formal authority within the broader Cromwellian Church, and was not universally welcomed. While the preface to the printed Savoy Declaration insisted that 'the differences that are between Presbyterians and Independents' were 'differences between fellow-servants', the Presbyterian bookseller and collector George Thomason wrote on his copy that it had been drawn up by 'Philip Nie and his Confederat Crew of Independants'.[19]

The effectiveness of Interregnum puritanism in implementing a broad programme of godly reformation has been much debated by historians, with the latest research suggesting some success in regulating drinking, sexual morality, and general deportment, even if the highest hopes of the godly were, inevitably, disappointed.[20] On such matters Presbyterians, Congregationalists, and episcopalians were usually united in their support for the magistracy. The implementation of more intimate discipline over doctrine and behaviour within parishes was fraught, however, with division and obstruction. The Presbyterian framework for discipline depended on a functioning parish eldership overseeing admission (and exclusion) from the sacrament, supported by broader local and regional assemblies. Conscientious catechizing of the congregation (adults as well as young people) was necessary if ignorance was to be grounds for exclusion. Many parishioners did not meet the expectations of zealous clerics, but exclusion was deeply resented. The veteran London preacher Thomas Gataker complained that parishioners excluded from the sacrament would not pay tithes, while in Covent Garden plans to administer the sacrament after a long interval prompted the worried assistant minister to seek the advice of Richard Baxter. The Cheshire minister Adam Martindale explained how one young man excluded on moral grounds simply went off to join the Quakers.[21] There was no national system for supporting ministers who sought to impose a controversial discipline, and the religious pluralism of the 1650s meant that acceptance of ministerial authority was voluntary. Few were as willing as Martindale's parishioner to accept their exclusion from parish worship, but no minister could compel attendance at his services. There was some compensation for the lack of a national disciplinary structure, however, in the emergence in the 1650s of some eighteen regional associations of ministers, usually based on counties,

---

[18] *A Declaration of the Faith and Order*, p. 3; Halcomb, 'Social History'; Cooper, *John Owen, Richard Baxter and the Formation of Nonconformity*.

[19] BL, E 968 (4); Cooper, *John Owen, Richard Baxter and the Formation of Nonconformity*, p. 237.

[20] Bernard Capp, *England's Culture Wars: Puritan Reformation and its Enemies in the Interregnum, 1649–1660* (Oxford, 2012).

[21] Hughes, 'Religion 1640–1650', in Barry Coward (ed.), *A Companion to Stuart Britain* (Oxford, 2003), p. 361; Julia F. Merritt, *Westminster 1640–1660: A Royal City in a Time of Revolution* (Manchester, 2013), pp. 240–2; *The Life of Adam Martindale Written by Himself* (Chetham Society, 4, 1845), p. 114.

and influenced by the pioneering Worcester Association established by Richard Baxter. All these associations offered encouragement and advice to parish ministers over catechizing and administration of the sacrament in particular; most used or adapted the Westminster Assembly's Directory of Worship, Confession of Faith, and Shorter Catechism as guides. The precise character of the associations varied, however. Most involved compromises between Presbyterians and Congregationalists; some like Cheshire's were essential forms of 'voluntary' Presbyterianism; others such as Devon's genuinely brought together Presbyterian, Congregationalist, and episcopalian ministers, while Baxter's Worcestershire Association was so flexible in its approach to discipline that Thomas Hall (a confirmed and 'rigid' Presbyterian) shunned it, preferring to participate in the smaller but more focused Kenilworth Classis in the neighbouring county of Warwickshire.[22]

Finally, we know too little about the nature of worship in this national Church. The observance of saints' days, Christmas, and other festivals not validated by Scripture was forbidden. The administration of the sacraments was disrupted in many parishes and marriage became a civil matter. Judith Maltby's pioneering study stresses that the Assembly's Directory for Public Worship involved a radically extreme rejection of set prayers within the Protestant tradition. It offered guidance for what ministers might say rather than any formulas; even the Lord's Prayer was only recommended rather than required, although some specific words and scriptures were suggested for the administration of the sacrament of the Lord's Supper. This framework for worship demanded a great deal of the clergy who, in theory at least, had to construct prayers and choose psalms for every occasion, and it also, again in theory, left nothing for the congregation to say following the banning of the set responses of the Book of Common Prayer. But many godly parishioners did participate in the discussion and repetition of sermons with ministers beyond the Sunday services as the memoirs and diaries of ministers such as Baxter, Martindale, and Josselin reveal. It is also clear that use of the Book of Common Prayer was mostly winked at, except for occasional drives against royalist gatherings at politically sensitive times, such as the dispersal of a London celebration of Christmas attended by John Evelyn in 1657.[23] The marriage of Cromwell's own daughter Mary to Lord Fauconberg was apparently celebrated according to the Book of Common Prayer (following a public civil ceremony). The precariousness of episcopalian fortunes is dramatically illustrated, however, by the execution of John Hewitt, the clergyman who

---

[22] Hughes, 'Religion'; Halcomb, 'Social History', pp. 217–26.
[23] Judith Maltby, '"Extravagancies and Impertinencies": Set Forms, Conceived and Extempore Prayer in Revolutionary England', in Natalie Mears and Alec Ryrie (eds.), *Worship and the Parish Church in Early Modern Britain* (Farnham, 2013); Hughes, 'Religion'.

performed the marriage in 1658. He had been implicated in royalist plotting and refused to plead at his trial.[24]

For all its contradictions and omissions, the 'public profession' of the Cromwellian religious settlement worked well in practice. A broad spectrum of Protestant opinion participated in the formal structures established to regulate and support the ministry, and a range of informal associations and networks supported individual ministers. Prelacy was outlawed but many episcopalians were left to minister more or less as they wished. Presbyterians were more prominent than might be expected. Presbyterians and Independents found it easier to work together once there was no likelihood of an authoritarian national Presbyterian Church being established. After 1649 and especially after 1653, working with a partial, optional public profession was the best option for Presbyterians, while the orthodox Calvinist godly had genuine shared interests in promoting godly reformation and defending 'orthodoxy' against aggressive Quakers and dangerous Socinians. At the heart of power, Thomas Manton was close to the Protector and many of his Council, while in the regions, a more sceptical figure like Adam Martindale would later look back nostalgically on the many opportunities that he had for preaching in the 1650s, and on the productive fellowship fostered with his most godly parishioners in 'worke-day conferences'.[25]

This broad coalition faltered after Cromwell's death and disintegrated at the Restoration, for Congregationalists and Presbyterians tended to adopt different stances during the political upheavals of 1659–60. The restoration of an episcopal or 'prelatical' Anglicanism was a closer run process than we might imagine, and prompted regret as well as rejoicing. In the weeks before the Restoration of the monarchy, Presbyterianism was briefly restored to ascendancy and the resolution of the dilemmas of the previous fifteen years in their favour seemed, fleetingly, to be at hand. In March 1660 the Convention Parliament entrusted the review of 'An Act declaring the Publick Confession of Faith of the Church of England' to the moderate episcopalian Edward Reynolds and the senior Presbyterians Edmund Calamy and Thomas Manton; a mostly Presbyterian commission for approving public preachers was appointed; the Directory for Public Worship was to be compulsory in parish worship; and it was declared that the ordinance of 29 August 1648 establishing Presbyterian government in the Church 'shall stand, and be in force, and put in execution'. Justices of the Peace were to consider how classical presbyteries should be established in counties where they did not already exist. But the

---

[24] Edward Hyde, Earl of Clarendon, *History of the Rebellion*, ed. W. D. Macray, 6 vols. (Oxford, 1888), VI, p. 61.

[25] *Register of the Consultations of the Ministers of Edinburgh*, ed. William Stephen, 2 vols. (1921–30), II, pp. 107–10; *Life of Adam Martindale*, pp. 104, 110.

Convention was dissolved two days later.[26] Most, but not all, of the ministers who wielded influence in the Cromwellian Church lost their positions between 1660 and 1662; many looked back at the 1650s as a golden age for a godly ministry within a national Church, and many continued to insist to 1689 and beyond that they represented the best of English or Anglican church traditions. They were not merely a sect or a denomination. On the other hand, many men of similar views remained within the episcopal Church to form a more familiar 'Low Church' Anglicanism.

SELECT BIBLIOGRAPHY

Coffey, John, 'A Ticklish Business: Defining Heresy and Orthodoxy in the Puritan Revolution', in David Loewenstein and John Marshall (eds.), *Heresy, Literature and Politics in Early Modern English Culture* (Cambridge, 2006), pp. 108–36.

Collins, Jeffrey R., 'The Church Settlement of Oliver Cromwell', *History*, 87 (2002): 18–40.

Cooper, Tim, *John Owen, Richard Baxter and the Formation of Nonconformity* (Farnham, 2011).

Fincham, Kenneth and Stephen Taylor, 'Vital Statistics: Episcopal Ordination and Ordinands in England, 1646–1660', *English Historical Review*, 126 (2011): 319–44.

Halcomb, Joel, 'A Social History of Congregational Practice during the Puritan Revolution', PhD thesis, University of Cambridge, 2009.

Hughes Ann, '"The Public Profession of These Nations": The National Church in Interregnum England', in Christopher Durston and Judith Maltby (eds.), *Religion in Revolutionary England* (Manchester, 2006), pp. 93–114.

Hughes, Ann, 'Religion 1640–1650', in Barry Coward (ed.), *A Companion to Stuart Britain* (Oxford, 2003), pp. 350–73.

Maltby, Judith, '"Extravagancies and Impertinencies": Set Forms, Conceived and Extempore Prayer in Revolutionary England', in Natalie Mears and Alec Ryrie (eds.), *Worship and the Parish Church in Early Modern Britain* (Farnham, 2013), pp. 221–44.

Maltby, Judith, 'Suffering and Surviving: The Civil Wars, the Commonwealth and the Formation of "Anglicanism", 1642–60', in Christopher Durston and Judith Maltby (eds.), *Religion in Revolutionary England* (Manchester, 2006), pp. 158–80.

Mortimer, Sarah, *Reason and Religion in the English Revolution: The Challenge of Socinianism* (Cambridge, 2010).

Winship, Michael P., 'Defining Puritanism in Restoration England: Richard Baxter and others Respond to *A Friendly Debate*', *Historical Journal*, 54 (2011): 689–715.

---

[26] *CJ*, VII, pp. 862, 874; C. H. Firth and R. S. Rait (eds.), *Acts and Ordinances of the Interregnum*, 3 vols. (1911), II, p. 1459.

25

Episcopalian Identity, 1640–1662

Kenneth Fincham and Stephen Taylor

By 1640 episcopacy, the Book of Common Prayer, and the royal supremacy had been central characteristics of the *Ecclesia Anglicana* for over eighty years. Only when they came under attack, however, following the collapse of Charles I's Personal Rule, do we see the emergence of individuals and groups who began to define their religious identity in terms of their adherence to these features of the old order. The temptation to describe these people as 'Anglicans' should be resisted. Not only is the label anachronistic, but it also has connotations which can be deeply misleading. The alternative preferred here, 'episcopalian', has some contemporary warrant: while their opponents often labelled them the 'prelatical party', Robert Sanderson called himself an 'episcopal divine', and Abraham Wright referred to those of the 'episcopal perswasion'. It offers a neutral and accurate shorthand for the combination of doctrines and practices that its adherents believed was fundamental to the historic Church of England.[1] The story of the remarkable collapse, 'persecution', revival, and triumph of that Church between 1640 and 1662 is well known. What is less familiar is how we conceptualize and understand the identity and experience of episcopalians in these years. Two models dominate the literature. On the one hand, in what is in many respects still a strikingly rich and compelling book, *The Making of the Restoration Settlement*, Robert Bosher presents a picture of intransigent withdrawal into country houses to wait for better times—what emerged in 1660–2 as Anglicanism was forged by a small minority of committed Laudians.[2] On the other hand, John Morrill and Judith Maltby have emphasized the importance of 'religious traditionalists', people who, when confronted by the emergence of a state religion that had embraced the destruction of prayer books, fonts, and church monuments,

---

[1] R. Sanderson, *XXXIIII sermons* (1657), sig. (A2)r; A. Wright, *Five sermons* (1656), sig. A4iir.
[2] R. S. Bosher, *The Making of the Restoration Settlement: The Influence of the Laudians 1649–62* (1951).

adhered doggedly to known forms and practices.³ Recently, this picture has been amplified and complicated, most notably by our own work on conformity and nonconformity, revealing that the majority of episcopalians to a greater or lesser extent conformed to the state Church in the 1650s, and by Anthony Milton's careful uncovering of some of the varieties of episcopalian thought in the 1640s.⁴ But this work still offers little more than a few insights into episcopalian identity. The aim of this chapter, then, is to provide a new overview, arguing in particular that episcopalian identity in this period is best understood not as mere survival, a defensive response to radical change, but rather in terms of processes of formulation and reformulation.⁵ Change is a key theme, and for this reason the chapter is organized chronologically. First, we consider the emergence of a distinctive and self-conscious episcopalian identity in response to the collapse of the old order in the 1640s. The second section explores the complexities and ambiguities that emerged in the 1650s as episcopalians came to terms with the new order, and the final section on the period from 1660 to 1662 examines the working out of those complexities as episcopalianism was again reshaped at the Restoration, eventually resulting in the creation of a new identity that can be described as Anglican.

1640–49

In the 1640s the historic Church of England underwent a religious revolution, culminating in 1649 with the execution of its supreme governor, Charles I. In turn, this revolution provoked a conservative reaction among Laudians, Calvinist conformists, moderate puritans, and refugees from Scotland and Ireland, all, to a greater or lesser extent, committed to checking, moderating, or reversing these waves of destruction and radical reform. For them, 1640–49 proved to be a protracted period of uncertainty and adaptation as well as loss and bereavement.

---

[3] J. Maltby, *Prayer Book and People in Elizabethan and Early Stuart England* (Cambridge, 1998), p. 237; J. Maltby, '"The Good Old Way": Prayer Book Protestantism in the 1640s and 1650s', in R. N. Swanson (ed.), *The Church and the Book*, SCH 38 (Woodbridge, 2004), pp. 233–56; J. Morrill, 'The Church in England, 1642–1649', in J. Morrill (ed.), *Reactions to the English Civil War 1642–9* (1982), pp. 89–114.

[4] K. Fincham and S. Taylor, 'Episcopalian Conformity and Nonconformity, 1646–60', in J. McElligott and D. L. Smith (eds.), *Royalists and Royalism during the Interregnum* (Manchester, 2010), pp. 18–43; K. Fincham and S. Taylor, 'Vital Statistics: Episcopal Ordination and Ordinands in England, 1646–60', *English Historical Review*, 126 (2011): 319–44; A. Milton, 'Anglicanism and Royalism in the 1640s', in J. Adamson (ed.), *The English Civil War: Conflicts and Contexts, 1640–49* (Basingstoke, 2009), pp. 61–81.

[5] Cf. J. Spurr, *The Restoration Church of England* (New Haven, CT, 1991).

The attack on the traditional structures of the Church of England in the 1640s is well known, and need not detain us long. It began in the summer of 1640, during Charles I's ill-conceived war against the Scottish Covenanters, and gained momentum after the opening of the Long Parliament on 3 November 1640. A potent combination of widespread hostility to Laudian reforms of the 1630s, heightened puritan expectations for further reformation, and the collapse of royal and episcopal authority, all led to upheaval and change. These included bouts of popular and official iconoclasm, the overthrow of Laudian ceremonialism, the imprisonment of Laud himself, the investigation of parochial clergy for scandalous or popish conduct, and, most significantly, calls for the 'root and branch' reform of episcopal government and the abolition of the established liturgy. A full religious settlement in 1641–2 proved to be elusive. Parliament itself was divided on the question, and the king offered few real concessions; after the outbreak of civil war in August 1642, the future of the Church bulked large in the unsuccessful negotiations between royalists and parliamentarians at Oxford (1643) and Uxbridge (1645). This deadlock was broken in 1645–6 by parliamentary ordinances and military victory over the royalists. The Directory for Public Worship replaced the Prayer Book, the office and jurisdiction of bishops were abolished, and a new formulary of faith, the Westminster Confession, was intended to supplant the Thirty-Nine Articles. Meanwhile the noose tightened for disaffected clergy and dons: a significant minority were sequestrated from their livings in the mid-1640s, and both universities were purged, first Cambridge in 1644–5 and then Oxford in 1647–9.

Many came to oppose this sustained attack on the historic Church in the 1640s. Rather than being a fixed constituency of 'Prayer Book Protestants' or 'Anglican survivors' attached to a fast-disappearing world of common-prayer worship and popular festivities, these episcopalians, as we shall call them, were men and women forced, by their reading of events and imminent threats to the religious and social order, to define their loyalties and defend their interests. For many, the royal supremacy, episcopacy, and Prayer Book had been settled and unquestioned landmarks in their religious landscape, and only when all came under direct challenge did they come to own and articulate their allegiance to them, and stand up against changes in the parish or across the nation. The reshaping of the religious world in 1640–2 with the collapse of Laudian rule, the rise of militant puritans, the emergence of sectaries, and the mobilizing and polarizing of opinion through preaching and the press, saw a range of religious viewpoints adopt a common defensive attitude towards radical change. Among episcopalians we find past and present Laudians, conformist critics of Laudianism, former moderate puritans alarmed at sectarian excesses, and an unknown number of refugees from the religious troubles in Scotland after 1638 and from civil war in Ireland after 1641; never a homogeneous group, they were loosely and temporarily united by a conservative ideology, and expressed their views in a number of ways, from private criticism and acts of defiance to active opposition.

This episcopalian voice can be heard in the petitions in favour of bishops and the Prayer Book compiled in 1641–2 in the teeth of counter-petitioning. Some went beyond a mere defence of the established government and liturgy to endorse cathedrals and the church courts, and many condemned 'the great increase of late of schismaticks and sectaries' and 'bitter invectives divulged and commonly spoken by many disaffected persons', egged on by both seditious preaching and 'ill-affected pamphlets which fly abroad in such swarmes'.[6] Parishioners, often in large numbers, signed petitions or testified in support of ministers under threat of sequestration for ceremonialism, misconduct, or royalism: in London, for example, thirty-four vestrymen and 'chief inhabitants' backed Edward Layfield of All Hallows Barking, but presumably there was a broader social mix among more than 200 signatures for John Squire, vicar of St Leonard, Shoreditch, and 600 of 'the ablest men' for John Piggott, lecturer at St Sepulchre. Intruders who replaced sequestered clergy sometimes faced hostile parishioners who refused to pay their tithes and did their best to reinstate the excluded minister or another of his ilk.[7] Episcopalian clergy themselves were quick to use the pulpit and the press to make their case, producing an enormous literature in manuscript and print which is only beginning to be explored. A representative publication was Thomas Cheshire's sermon, popular enough to warrant a second edition, preached at St Paul's Cathedral in October 1641. Cheshire argued that 'many of our pulpits now a days do ring of the doctrine of devils' and went on to condemn false teaching, profaning of churches, iconoclasm, extempore prayer, and the abuse of the ministry, and wondered 'what will become of us' if the governors of the Church were not able to restore order. He also sprang to the defence of the Prayer Book and episcopacy. Punish bishops who may have erred but, he urged, leave well alone their innocent office.[8] After 1642, similar messages were heard in many cathedral and parish pulpits and particularly at

---

[6] J. Maltby (ed.), 'Petitions for Episcopacy and the Book of Common Prayer on the Eve of the Civil War 1641–1642', in S. Taylor (ed.), *From Cranmer to Davidson: A Church of England Miscellany* (Woodbridge, 1999), pp. 103–67.

[7] I. M. Green, 'The Persecution of "Scandalous" and "Malignant" Parish Clergy during the English Civil War', *English Historical Review*, 94 (1979): 507–31 (pp. 521–2); K. Fincham and N. Tyacke, *Altars Restored: The Changing Face of English Religious Worship, 1547–c.1700* (Oxford, 2007), pp. 269–72; *An Answer to a Printed Paper Entituled Articles Exhibited in Parliament against Mr John Squier* (1641), pp. 10–12; [L. Womock], *Sober Sadnes* (1643), p. 32. For testimonies, see F. McCall, *Baal's Priests: The Loyalist Clergy and the English Revolution* (Farnham, 2013), pp. 127–9, 202–4, 208; R. Ashton, *Counter-Revolution: The Second Civil War and Its Origins, 1646–8* (New Haven, CT, 1994), ch. 7.

[8] T. Cheshire, *A Sermon Preached in Saint Paules Church the tenth of October 1641* (1641), pp. 11–15; T. Westfield, *A Sermon Preached in the Cathedrall Church of S. Paul* (1641), pp. 19–23.

Charles I's headquarters in Oxford, where there were sermons preached each Sunday to the royalist Parliament and twice weekly to the king as well as on the monthly fast-day. A number of these were then published.[9] One obvious target was Presbyterian government, that 'new-sprung out-landish weede of mans invention', according to Bishop Williams of Ossory, which, another preacher claimed, would 'set up a pope with a conclave of lay cardinalls' in every parish. A second was the Directory for Public Worship. Its chief critic was Henry Hammond, in a pamphlet which ran through three editions in 1645-6, who attacked the parliamentary ordinance imposing the directory for not just abolishing a Prayer Book 'so piously and discreetly framed by those who have seal'd our Reformation with their bloud' but also for its unprecedented removal of all form of liturgy, 'the only way of security to Gods worship'. Hammond confidently predicted that the directory's deficiencies would 'within very few years' lead to the restitution of a liturgy.[10] But Hammond and other court divines at Oxford also had to combat the enemy within, those royalists prepared to sacrifice episcopacy and church lands so as to ease Charles I's return to power; both Hammond and Henry Ferne had this group in mind when in 1645 they urged in print that abolishing bishops would endanger religion.[11]

For much of the 1640s, the outcome of the religious revolution remained in the balance. Episcopalians must have taken strength from the knowledge that until the mid-1640s the governors of the Church still exercised some authority, primarily in those parts of the country controlled by royalists. It is true that the start of war in 1642 saw the disciplinary machinery of the church courts grind to a halt in many dioceses, particularly in those controlled by Parliament.[12] But until 1646 diocesan government was less moribund than some historians have implied. Visitations by bishops and archdeacons occurred in several dioceses, as at Bristol in 1644 and Exeter in 1642, 1644, and 1645.[13] The church courts went on issuing marriage licences and handling probate cases;[14] almost all bishops

---

[9] J. Eales, 'Provincial Preaching and Allegiance in the First English Civil War', in T. Cogswell, R. Cust, and P. Lake (eds.), *Politics, Religion and Popularity in Early Stuart Britain* (Cambridge, 2002), pp. 185-207; Christ Church Oxford Archives, CC DP ii C 1; F. J. Varley, *The Siege of Oxford* (1932), p. 26; F. Madan, *Oxford Books volume II... Oxford Literature 1450-1640 and 1641-1650* (Oxford, 1912), pp. 258-422.

[10] G. Williams, *A Sermon Preached at the Publique Fast the eighth of March in St Maries Oxford* (Oxford, 1644), p. 36; Bodl., MS Rawlinson E 115, fos. 3v-4r; H. Hammond, *A View of the New Directorie and a Vindication of the Ancient Liturgy of the Church of England* (3rd edn., Oxford, 1646), sig. Br, pp. 9, 94, 102.

[11] Milton, 'Anglicanism and Royalism', pp. 68-72.

[12] Morrill, 'Church in England', p. 99; D. Cressy, *England on Edge: Crisis and Revolution 1640-1642* (Oxford, 2006), pp. 187-8.

[13] R. Standfast, *Clero-laicum Condimentum. Or, a Sermon Preached at a Visitation in Saint Nicholas Church in Bristoll, April 16. an. D. 1644* (Bristol, 1644); Devon RO, A/E/V/5-7.

[14] C. Kitching, 'Probate during the Civil War and Interregnum. Part I', *Journal of the Society of Archivists*, 5 (1974-7): 283-93 (p. 284); Worcestershire RO, b 778.713-BA.2700; Gloucestershire RO, GDR 207A-B.

continued to admit clergy to livings, and, while most ordained just a handful, a small number did so regularly, notably Hall of Norwich, Skinner of Oxford, Towers of Peterborough, and Winniffe of Lincoln, operating from Buckden manor in Huntingdonshire where he was surrounded by parliamentary forces.[15] Cathedral chapters met periodically at Carlisle until 1644, Worcester and Llandaff until 1645, Exeter until 1646, and Norwich until 1649.[16] Throughout the first civil war, Charles I also remained an active supreme governor. He worshipped in the Chapel Royal, now installed in Christ Church Cathedral at Oxford, with its customary rich diet of ritual and music. He was a busy ecclesiastical patron, appointing bishops until 1644, parochial clergy (although a vastly reduced number) until at least 1645, and cathedral deans and royal chaplains until 1646.[17] The king also created a new monthly fast in 1643, with its form of prayer, and issued other state prayers of thanksgiving and intercession for the royalist cause.[18] After the recapture of Cornwall in 1644, Charles sent instructions to the chancellor of Exeter diocese, bypassing the absentee bishop, to re-establish order and obedience in the south-west. Clergy were to avoid scandalous conduct, use the Prayer Book 'with all reverence and devotion', observe the monthly fast, confer privately with 'men who have benne misled' and participate in combination lectures 'to teach the people their duty towards God and the kinge'. Incumbents who supported Parliament were to be ejected.[19] The royal supremacy, of course, became a cipher on the royalists' defeat in 1646. Nevertheless, an element of uncertainty remained so long as negotiations over religion (and much else) continued with the captive king, while there was even the faint prospect, in the spring of 1648, of royalist success in the second civil war which could have led to a return of episcopal government and the old liturgy. Indeed, defence of the old religious order featured in several of the insurgents' demands and, in Kent, the widespread revolt was precipitated by a riot in Canterbury against the 1647 prohibition on celebrating Christmas.[20]

The shifting ecclesiastical politics of the 1640s meant that at times some episcopalians advocated change, either from conviction or necessity. Amid the

---

[15] Norfolk RO, DN/REG/18 Book 24; Oxfordshire RO, Oxf. Dioc. Papers e.13; Northamptonshire RO, X959/4; Lincolnshire Archives Office, Reg. XXXI; *CSPD 1654*, p. 56.

[16] Worcester Cathedral Library, A75, fos. 156r–61v, A116; Carlisle Archive Centre, D&C 1/7, pp. 132–40; National Library of Wales, LLCh/4, pp. 142–51; Exeter Cathedral Library, MSS 3557–8: Norfolk RO, DCN 24/2.

[17] Hampshire RO, 35M48/6, pp. 122–3; Wiltshire and Swindon RO, D1/18/5 [Alton, 25 Apr. 1645]; John Le Neve, *Fasti Ecclesiae Anglicanae 1541–1857*, ed. J. M. Horn and others., 13 vols. (1969–2014), II, p. 7, VII, pp. 11, 111; Corpus Christi College Oxford, MS 306, fo. 45r.

[18] N. Mears, A. Raffe, S. Taylor, and P. Williamson, with L. Bates (eds.), *National Prayers: Special Worship since the Reformation, Volume 1* (Woodbridge, 2013), pp. 387–8, 401, 402–9, 412–13, 427–32, 445.

[19] Devon RO, Chanter 57, fos. 46r–7r.

[20] Ashton, *Counter-Revolution*, pp. 240–1, 452; *The Declaration of Col. Poyer and Col. Powel* (1648), pp. 4–5.

Laudian backlash of 1640–1 was an episcopalian push for moderate reform, led by Bishop Williams of Lincoln's committee of religion to reform liturgy and doctrine, and by Archbishop Ussher's proposal to 'reduce' episcopacy, which was revived by Bishop Hall in 1644 in a vain attempt to block the advance of Presbyterianism.[21] Some calls for change were probably tactical, such as those in pro-episcopal petitions of 1640–1, but in any case the rising pressure for wholesale reformation quickly eroded this reformist stance.[22] The need to make significant concessions in 1646–8 forced Charles I and his advisers to contemplate suspending episcopacy for three years, alienating church lands and ceding toleration. Jeremy Taylor's open advocacy of religious toleration in 1647 indicates how changed circumstances led some episcopalians to rethink their views on the proper ordering of religion, a theme which we will encounter again in the 1650s.[23]

Episcopalians met the loss of office with a mixture of resignation, defiance, and covert resistance. Some ousted ministers proved to be adaptable and resilient. Thomas Holbech was ejected from Epping in November 1643 but, as he wrote years later, he had 'noe mind to cast off' his calling. Accordingly, he kept his ministry alive by weekly sermons, as we learn from his preaching diary of 1643–5. Many of them were delivered at Copt Hall near Epping where evidently he continued to serve as domestic chaplain to the earl of Middlesex, but others in nearby parishes in Hertfordshire, Essex, and Cambridgeshire.[24] On the abolition of their jurisdiction in October 1646, most bishops went quietly into the night, but not all: nine defied the ordinance and continued to ordain, although much the most active were two exiled Irish bishops, Thomas Fulwar and Robert Maxwell. More strikingly, Hall of Norwich continued to institute some clergy until 1648, while the Exeter diocesan registry exercised its authority in the bishop's name up to 1649, and Ralph Brownrigg, its non-resident bishop, still exacted traditional oaths affirming the old church government and liturgy from a handful of clergy taking office until 1648.[25] About half of Oxford's academics were expelled by the parliamentary visitors in 1647–9, and shortly afterwards some of the ejected commissioned hundreds

---

[21] C. Russell, *The Fall of the British Monarchies 1637–1642* (Oxford, 1991), pp. 249–52; A. Ford, *James Ussher: Theology, History and Politics in Early Modern Ireland and England* (Oxford, 2007), pp. 235–56; J. Hall, *A Modest Offer* (1644).

[22] P. Lake, 'Puritans, Popularity and Petitions: Local Politics in National Context, Cheshire, 1641', in Cogswell et al. (eds.), *Politics, Religion and Popularity*, pp. 276–7 and fn. 30; McCall, *Baal's Priests*, pp. 93–4.

[23] A. Milton, 'Sacrilege and Compromise: Court Divines and the King's Conscience, 1642–1649', in M. J. Braddick and D. L. Smith (eds.), *The Experience of Revolution in Stuart Britain and Ireland* (Cambridge, 2011), pp. 146–51.

[24] McCall, *Baal's Priests*, ch. 6 and p. 233; A. G. Matthews, *Walker Revised* (Oxford, 1948), pp. 154–5; Centre for Kentish Studies, U269/Q13/6.

[25] Norwich RO, DN/REG 18.24 ii., fos. 67r–70r, PRE/21 [1648–9], ANW/19/1 [1647–8]; Devon RO, Chanter 44, pp. 102–3, 57 fos. 49r–51r; Lichfield RO, B/A/4/19, i. pp. 6–8.

of silver and brass medals to commemorate their steadfastness, bearing the words 'in pious memory of the university of Oxford' on the obverse, as though it no longer existed, and on the reverse 'a sacrifice for God, the church and the prince'. They were worn on ribbons by the ejected, and scholars, still at Oxford, expressed their solidarity by having the words woven in ribbon and pinned on their hats—to the irritation of Presbyterian dons such as Francis Cheynell. Here was a clear statement of episcopalian and royalist sentiments, a memorial to shared suffering and a shared understanding of that experience; in short, the fashioning of an identity.[26]

1649-60

A calamitous decade for episcopalians peaked on 30 January 1649 with the execution of their supreme governor, Charles I. In retrospect, however, that devastating blow proved to be the culmination of a period of revolutionary change, and the more settled times of the 1650s allowed a distinctive episcopalian identity to flourish. This transition is captured well in the record of a private prayer composed by William Sancroft in c.1649-50:

> The Apostolicall discipline of thy Churches is indicted; the daily sacrifice of praier, and praise in Our Sacred Liturgy is forbidden, and declaimed against, as superstitious; the Preaching of thy Word is embased with a great mixture of error, and vanity; thy Blessed Sacraments are contemned, thy Sabbaths, and Holy Festivalls neglected, thy Sanctuaries profaned, and instead of Priests, bold intruders (raised up from among the meanest of the people) execute about Holy things.

Its content mirrors the profound despondency many episcopalians felt as they surveyed the ruins of their Church.[27] Yet the prayer was composed as part of a private fast on behalf of Church and crown, and thus points to an activist mentality which characterized many of the key factors at work shaping episcopalian identity in the 1650s. Four of these deserve analysis: the concept of persecution, antipathy to other Protestant groups, preaching and publications, and charitable support.

First, the concept of 'persecution' is central to any understanding of episcopalian identity, developing through the 1640s and into the 1650s. This is not to deny the reality of persecution, as vividly recorded more than a generation

---

[26] A. Wood, *The History and Antiquities of the University of Oxford*, ed. J. Gutch, 2 vols. (Oxford, 1792-6), II, p. 614; E. Hawkins (ed.), *Medallic Illustrations of the History of Great Britain and Ireland* (1979), nos. 15-17 and plate XXX.

[27] Bodl., Sancroft MS 118, fos. 28v, 29v. For similar sentiments, see W. Stampe, *A Treatise of Spirituall Infatuation* (1650), sig. A5r.

later by John Walker in his *Sufferings of the Clergy*, nor to overlook the fluctuations in its intensity, but to emphasize the importance of the belief of persecution and its meanings to the construction of episcopalian identity. Episcopalians drew on familiar tropes from Scripture and the whole history of the Church to sustain themselves in adversity: as a court preacher at Paris noted in 1650, 'all that will live godly in Christ Jesus must suffer persecution' and 'there was never sailing to heaven in a calm'. They were captive, like the Jews in Babylon, weeping 'when we remembered thee O Sion' (Psalm 137:1); like early Christians, they were driven to worship secretly in dens, caves, and upper rooms. Gilbert Sheldon noted that the episcopate was now 'in the state and condition of primitive bishops', John Evelyn denounced Cromwell as a second Julian the Apostate, and John Hacket proclaimed that the Church of England, like the primitive Church, was being refined by its sufferings.[28] Others maintained that the Church itself was in eclipse, just as it had been before Luther. Persecution had to be borne with fortitude: as Jeremy Taylor urged his readers, 'let us do charity to the afflicted, and bear the crosse with noblenesse'. Joseph Hall proposed that 'orthodox and genuine sonnes of the Church of England' should create a 'Holy Fraternity of Mourners in Sion' to offer 'fervent prayers and teares' in hope of obtaining seasonable redress from God and to prevent final destruction 'which threatens this miserable church'. The call to repentance for national sin, the invitation to powerful petitioning which would offer 'a sacred violence to the throne of grace', held out the comforting promise that Sion would be restored in all her beauty at a time of God's choosing.[29] For Sion, the historic Church of England, was not destroyed but 'disordered and eclipsed', or, as John Bramhall put it, like a tree in winter, awaiting the spring. The most potent symbol of this were the great cathedrals, damaged or dilapidated but still standing, and much commented on by contemporaries, and not just episcopalians.[30]

It followed that hostility to the enemies of the historic Church of England helped to sharpen this episcopalian identity. As Henry Ferne explained, the Church of England was assaulted both by its old foe, the Church of Rome, and by those he simply called 'sectaries', its Protestant sons who had turned on their mother in the early 1640s with such disastrous results. Episcopalian

[28] Maltby, '"The Good Old Way"', pp. 249–50; BL, Add. MS 78364, fos. 6, 26r; 78298, fo. 66v; J. Hewitt, *Repentance and Conversion* (1658); W. Nicholson, *Ekthesis Pisteos* (1661), pp. 519–29; L. Andrewes, *Apospasmatia Sacra* (1657), sig.)()()()(iv; J. Taylor, *The Golden Grove* (1655), sig. A3r; Bosher, *Restoration Settlement*, pp. 9, 19, 33, 41; John Hacket, *A Century of Sermons* (1675), p. xxviii.

[29] Stampe, *Treatise*, p. 50; J. Taylor, *XXVIII sermons* (1654), p. 135; BL, Add. MS 78364, fos. 3v, 31r, 35r; J. H[all], *The Holy Order* (1654), pp. 1–4, 23; Nicholson, *Ekthesis Pisteos*, p. 527.

[30] BL, Add. MS 78364, fo. 2; J. Bramhall, *A Replication to the Bishop of Chalcedon* (1656), pp. 109–10; I. Atherton, 'Cathedrals and the British Revolution', in Braddick and Smith (eds.), *Experience of Revolution*, pp. 112–14. For comments by episcopalians, see BL, Harleian MS 3783, fo. 165r, 6942, no. 107.

clergy in England or in exile missed few opportunities in their sermons and treatises to draw attention to the consequences of what William Nicholson called the 'fractions and factions' of the godly, resulting in 'confusion, unhallowed deformity, lyes and errours, irreverence, licentiousness, discord, dissension, malice and hatred'. This disdain was matched by laymen such as the London lawyer, Richard Smith, who censured the opponents of bishops as 'a multitude of arrogant, ambitious and envious adversaries' supported by 'a rabble of illerat and rude mechanicks'.[31] But often episcopalians singled out Presbyterians as their greatest rivals and nemesis, the root of all the troubles from 1640, who aimed to erect a state Church on the ruins of episcopacy. Bishop Tilson in 1653 condemned local Presbyterians who were petitioning to establish an 'illimited jurisdiction' in place of what they called 'the tirannicall governement of the prelates', while in 1657 Taylor complained how Presbyterians were pressing Cromwell's Council to oppress episcopalians further. Bishop Duppa saw both Jesuits and Presbyterians united in 'their infinite malice toward this poor church', but he put the greater blame on Presbyterians, an attitude which may explain the retribution visited on them in the Restoration settlement in 1660–2, as we shall see. The real winners of this inter-Protestant quarrel, as Robert Sanderson and others feared, would be their joint enemy, the Church of Rome.[32]

A remarkable outpouring of sermons and publications in the 1650s also helped to shape and sustain an episcopalian identity. Some episcopal clergy still in livings, such as Sanderson, were busy preachers in and beyond their cures; while many ejected clergy 'pray'd and preach't', as we observe from the sermon notebooks of the earl of Bridgewater and John Evelyn, and from the diary of Anthony Blagrave. During the 1650s, a significant number were re-admitted to livings and took control of the parish pulpit.[33] Some of these sermons were then published. Taylor went into print to combat what he saw as a paucity of preaching across the nation (an indication perhaps that many livings remained vacant) so that 'this publication may be esteemed but like preaching to a numerous auditory...I make use of all the wayes I can to minister to the good of souls'. Taylor's sermons usually avoided current controversies and centred on the perennials of Christian life, but others directly attacked heterodox teaching, including Robert Mossom's eight sermons against 'the present heresies and schisms', with which he intended 'not

---

[31] H. F[erne], *A Compendious Discourse* (1655), pp. 1–2; BL, Add. MS 78364, fos. 2r, 15; H. Byam, *XIII Sermons* (1675), esp. pp. 6, 36–8, 91–2, 99–100; Nicholson, *Ekthesis Pisteos*, pp. 179, 423; Folger Shakespeare Library (hereafter FSL), V.a.510(1), fo. 8v.

[32] Bodl., MS Eng Hist b 205, fo. 3r, Tanner MS 52, fos. 106v, 216; Sanderson, *XXXIIII Sermons*, sigs. (D2)v–(D2)iv, E(2)iir.

[33] Bodl., MSS Eng th f 63, fos. 34r, 48v, 56v–7v, Eng Misc E 118; R. Mossom, *An Apology in the Behalf of the Sequestred Clergy* (1660), pp. 4–5; Huntington Library, EL 8008; BL, Add. MS 78364, fos. 2r–76v; Fincham and Taylor, 'Episcopalian Conformity', pp. 25–7.

so much to confute the Adversary, but to confirm the Orthodox', and Abraham Wright's censure of preachers who lacked a university education, especially lay preachers recruited from the shops and stalls of London.[34] Contemporary sermons were but a small part of a veritable flood of writings by episcopalians, penned in exile or at home, or else from deceased luminaries. These included polemics by Hammond, Bramhall, Ferne, John Cosin, and others defining and defending the primitive discipline and doctrine of the historic Church of England against the pretensions of Rome and the Presbyterians; accounts of public disputations against Fifth Monarchists, Independents, Baptists, and Catholics by Clement Barksdale, Matthew Griffith, Peter Gunning, and John Pearson; treatises and sermons mostly composed before 1640 by prominent divines such as Sanderson, Peter Heylyn, Richard Gardiner, and Thomas Jackson, and by deceased bishops such as Lancelot Andrewes, Laud, Samuel Harsnett, and Thomas Westfield; a rubrical account of the Prayer Book by Anthony Sparrow; and a substantial corpus of devotional writings led by Taylor and Richard Allestree, which included editions of private prayers by Andrewes and Laud.[35] Perhaps the most popular devotional work was *Eikon Basilike*. We usually regard this as a royalist text, sustaining a monarchical ideology through the dark days of the 1650s, and significant in religious terms for presenting Charles I as a martyr for the Church. Yet the *Eikon* was also devotional: each chapter justifying an aspect of the king's conduct in civil wars was accompanied by prayers, many couched in general terms which could be applied to the challenges of the 1650s. Thus in the chapter on the Irish rebellion, the devout episcopalian joins with his executed king to pray: 'In the sea of our Saviour's blood drown our sins; and through this Red Sea of our own blood bring us at last to a state of piety, peace, and plenty.'[36] The sheer scale of this episcopalian output indicates that it was ignored by the censors, who evidently targeted overt political opposition rather than religious debate. Publishers were quick to recognize the buoyant market for episcopalian works, a sizeable number of which were reprinted: the best-known publisher of this literature was Richard Royston, but there were others including Humphrey Moseley, Henry Seile, and Timothy Garthwaite whose private sympathies for the historic Church ran in parallel with their commercial instincts. The new practice of publishers appending backlists of recent publications was used to direct readers to works likely to be of interest; hence in Sparrow's *A Rationale upon the Book of Common Prayer* Garthwaite advertised writings by Cosin and Jackson. Royston himself used at least one regional bookseller, William Ballard in Bristol, for the distribution and

---

[34] J. Taylor, *XXV Sermons* (1655), sig. A3r–ir; J. Taylor, *XXVIII Sermons*, sig. ¶2ir; R. Mossom, *The Preachers Tripartite* (1657), 'To the ingenuous readers' and part 3; Wright, *Five Sermons*, sigs. A2r–A4iiiv.
[35] Bosher, *Restoration Settlement*, pp. 33–9; Fincham and Tyacke, *Altars Restored*, pp. 291–6.
[36] P. A. Knachel (ed.), *Eikon Basilike* (Ithaca, NY, 1966), p. 68.

sale of his works, and through these various means, the appetite for episcopalian works was both fed and stimulated.[37] Among the many readers of this literature was Richard Smith, who used some of it in his unpublished chronology on the English episcopate, and the Kentish gentleman Henry Oxinden, who extracted works by Taylor and Andrewes into his commonplace book.[38]

An extensive charitable network for impoverished clergy also contributed to episcopalian identity. The benefactors were usually aristocrats and gentry, offering employment as chaplains or schoolmasters to ejected clergy, and relying on trusted intermediaries or 'almoners' to distribute money to distressed ministers or their dependants. The ministers themselves might be sequestrated in England or in exile overseas, but equally might be struggling to survive in a single poor living. Bishop Warner of Rochester drew on his private income to become the greatest donor amongst the clergy. Other funds were raised by public subscription—on Anthony Farindon's forced removal from St Mary Magdalen Street, London, the congregation on two successive Sundays contributed an astonishing total of £400. The will of John Horne, an ejected fellow of Oriel College, Oxford, proved in 1658, demonstrates how widespread and reciprocal this charity could be. Horne left legacies as 'acknowledgements of more kindness received by me from them' than from his nearest kin 'in my greatest extremity'—namely after his ejection from Oxford—to many ejected clergy including Gilbert Sheldon, Bruno Rives, John Birkenhead, George Wilde, Richard Bayly, and Thomas Triplett, and also to lay episcopalians at Sonning and elsewhere. But in addition, Horne gave donations to several named ministers, and gave more to Wilde, Rives, and others to distribute to 'ministers of Christ' in need.[39] The fact that in many of these charitable transactions the benefactor and beneficiary were often unknown to each other must have deepened that sense of identity with a wider, national community of episcopalians.

Episcopalians, we are suggesting, made sense of themselves and the disjointed world of the 1650s, as members of a persecuted Church, holding fast to their beliefs in opposition to threats from Protestant and Catholic opponents,

---

[37] J. McElligott, *Royalism, Print and Censorship in Revolutionary England* (Woodbridge, 2007), pp. 141–7, 210, 216–17; P. Lindenbaum, 'Publishers' Backlists in Late Seventeenth-Century London', *The Library*, 7th ser., 11 (2010): 381–404 (p. 394); J. C. Reed, 'Humphrey Moseley, publisher', *Oxford Bibliographical Society Proceedings and Papers*, 2 (1929): 61–142; A. Sparrow, *A Rationale upon the Book of Common Prayer* (1657), sig. A3iiiv; [J. Taylor], *A Short Catechism* (1652), [pp. 58–60]; J. Peacey, *Print and Public Politics in the English Revolution* (Cambridge, 2013), p. 61; *A Catalogue of the Most Vendible Books in England* (1657).

[38] FSL, V.a.510(1), fo. 12r, (2); V.b.110, pp. 150–1, 162–7, 449–53; R. Chiswell (ed.), *Bibliotheca Smithiana* (1682), esp. p. 377 no. 65.

[39] Fincham and Taylor, 'Episcopalian Conformity', pp. 27–8; Bodl., Walker MS c.2, fo. 199v; TNA, PROB/11/281, fos. 209r–10r. Non-episcopalian ministers also contributed to this charity: N. Cox, *Bridging the Gap: A History of the Corporation of the Sons of the Clergy over 300 Years, 1655–1978* (Oxford, 1978), pp. 1–11.

taking sustenance from sermons and from a lively market of printed works championing their practices and traditions, and participating as benefactors or beneficiaries of charity to support suffering clergy and their families. Yet episcopalian identity contained inherent tensions and complexities, which we can best explore by examining attitudes towards pillars of the old order in a new age: the royal supremacy, episcopacy, the Prayer Book, and clerical conformity.

Most obviously, the royal supremacy meant different things to different episcopalians. For clergy and laity who had followed Charles II into exile, it had a vestigial reality, with the Chapel Royal maintaining the traditional ritual, liturgy, and prayers for the royal family, served by chaplains who had the prospect, were the king to be restored, of advancement to senior posts in the revived Church. Yet no English bishop resided at court, and only a handful of Scottish and Irish bishops (Sydserf, Bramhall, and Leslie) occasionally attended on Charles II, although James I, for one, had regarded bishops as 'the best companions for princes'.[40] Nor did the king usually exercise his ecclesiastical authority, beyond pressing, intermittently, for new bishops to be consecrated. The supremacy was a reality of a different kind for the circle around Sheldon in England, essential to the nature and constitution of the Church of England, but almost impossible to envisage being used without incurring the wrath of the Interregnum regimes. This is most evident in the debates over the consecration of new bishops in 1655 and 1659. The group warmly welcomed the idea in principle, but were keenly aware that to participate might be read by the government as an act of political subversion, and were unable to contemplate a way forward which did not involve a royal nomination.[41] Elsewhere, as we shall see, some clergy who were illegally ordained took the oath of supremacy. Prayers may still have been made for the king in parish churches, or more likely at home, using the Prayer Book or devotional works. Taylor, for one, published a prayer for Christian kings, commending them as 'nursing fathers to the church'.[42] Yet for others, with the removal of the coat of arms from church interiors, the royal supremacy may have been little more than a receding memory. There had also emerged a critical questioning of the Stuarts' credentials as defenders of the faith, fanned by Charles II's temporary embrace of the Covenant in Scotland in 1650-1, albeit for reasons of expediency. Some went so far as to appeal to Cromwell, as supreme power rather than supreme governor, to establish some order in the Church. In 1653 Godfrey Goodman, bishop of Gloucester, requested action against blasphemers, and in 1655 proposed that senior dons in the universities be entrusted with conferring

---

[40] K. Fincham, *Prelate as Pastor: The Episcopate of James I* (Oxford, 1990), p. 35.
[41] Bosher, *Restoration Settlement*, pp. 89-100.
[42] J. Hewitt, *Prayers of Intercession for their Use who Mourn in Secret* (1659), pp. 14-17, 24; Taylor, *Golden Grove*, p. 113.

ordination and institution to livings. It would be easy to dismiss this as another eccentric action by a wayward bishop, who died in 1656 under the suspicion of conversion to Rome; but we also know that in 1657 the Laudian Peter Heylyn invited Cromwell to appoint bishops who would restore religious peace.[43] Both Goodman and Heylyn were bypassing the royal supremacy as irrelevant to the pressing problems of the 1650s.

As for bishops, the memory of episcopacy burned strongly for some. The London lawyer Richard Smith, best known as an obituarist, revered the antiquity of the order and the learning of the bishops of his time, and in the late 1650s began to compile a supplement to Francis Godwin's *Catalogue of Bishops* from 1616 to the present day of 'these venerable prelates', the 'illustrious angels' of the Church, whose deeds would otherwise have been forgotten. Curiously, though, there is no sign in his writings that Smith was personally acquainted with any bishop. Episcopalian manuals of devotion also contained prayers for bishops.[44] Yet for many episcopalians, bishops had become marginal to their religious practices and experience. As Duppa noted in 1656, the historic Church of England was 'dispersed and scattered *in capite et membris*', and its dwindling number of bishops was criticized by some contemporaries (and following them, by some historians) for going to ground, neglecting their sees, and offering no leadership to the wider Church. Certainly, they failed to agree on a common policy towards the use of the Prayer Book in 1653, leaving individual ministers to devise their own solution to this pressing problem.[45] If we study patterns of episcopal residence and the evidence for ordination, it is clear that the north and west of England, and probably also Wales, saw little or nothing of bishops across the 1650s. The notable exception was in Yorkshire, where Tilson, Irish bishop of Elphin, was the incumbent of Cumberworth in the West Riding, where he preached weekly, ordained ministers, and even consecrated the neighbouring church of Meltham.[46]

The picture was rather different in the south and east of the country. The best-documented example here is Joseph Hall of Norwich. Having been unceremoniously evicted from his palace in 1647, Hall settled at Higham, just a mile south-west of the city, and for the next nine years until his death in 1656 he preached in the church (several of these sermons were later printed)

---

[43] Bosher, *Restoration Settlement*, pp. 15–16, 68–9; Maltby, '"The Good Old Way"', pp. 253–5; G. G[oodman], *The Two Great Mysteries of Christian Religion* (1653), sig. A3ir; *To His Highness my Lord Protector... Godfree Goodman, Bishop of Gloucester* (1655); A. Milton, *Laudian and Royalist Polemic in Seventeenth-Century England* (Manchester, 2007), pp. 165–70.

[44] *ODNB*, 'Smith [Smyth], Richard (1590–1675)'; FSL, V.a.510(1), fos. 1r–8v, (2); R. Allestree, *The Practice of Christian Graces* (1658), p. 652; Taylor, *Golden Grove*, p. 113.

[45] Bodl., Tanner MS 52, fo. 107r; Bosher, *Restoration Settlement*, pp. 16–27.

[46] C. L. Berry, 'Henry Tilson, Bishop of Elphin, and his Ministry during the Suppression of the Church', *Church Quarterly Review*, 132 (1941): 54–68.

and ordained candidates in his parlour, sometimes calling on the assistance of neighbouring ministers. Hall also continued to confirm, even from his sickbed, and one of more than a dozen works he published as an ejected bishop was a defence of the rite of confirmation. He berated its neglect as an 'apostolicall institution' and argued 'how infinitely advantageous' its revival might be 'to the church of Christ'. The book was a quarto, eighty-four pages long, aimed at a popular audience, and in fact the first tract in English to be devoted to the subject. Hall was always accessible to local people, so much so that 'many persons of honour, learning and piety... came to crave his dyeing prayers and benediction'. A few weeks after Hall's death, he was commemorated in a sermon by the rector of Higham in St Peter Mancroft, the principal civic church in Norwich. There is a strong case, then, for seeing Hall as a diocesan bishop to his dying day, notwithstanding his loss of jurisdiction, lands, and title, and as a clear example of a 'primitive' bishop operating without coercive powers.[47] Other bishops living in the south and east matched some of Hall's activities. Perhaps as many as 2,500 men were illegally ordained in 1646-60, chiefly by Bishops Fulwar, Maxwell, and Tilson (all Irish bishops, the first two peripatetic), but also in significant numbers by Skinner in Oxfordshire, Brownrigg in Berkshire and London, Duppa in Surrey, King in Buckinghamshire, and Morton in Northamptonshire. Confirmation was very popular, as Hall remembered from his time as bishop of Exeter in the 1630s, and was conferred by Skinner, Duppa, Fulwar, and Warner, the latter of whom later claimed to have sometimes celebrated it publicly in 'orthodox congregations'.[48] Several were tireless preachers: Ussher preached regularly to packed audiences at Lincoln's Inn and in the provinces, while Skinner recalled that he had preached every Sunday for fifteen years, presumably principally at his cure at Launton in Oxfordshire; Brownrigg was probably as assiduous, and ended his career as preacher at the Inner Temple.[49] None, however, came close to matching Hall's numerous publications. Bishops also offered spiritual counsel to their immediate circle of friends and acquaintances, Warner, for example, advising Sir John Oglander to avoid taking the Engagement in 1650. Some clergy looked to their bishop for advice, with Anthony Farindon continuing to

---

[47] J. Whitefoot, *Israea Agchithanes, Deaths Alarum* (1656), pp. 68-72, 78; J. Hall, *The Shaking of the Olive-Tree* (1660), sig. A2ir-iir, pp. 140-235; J. Hall, *Cheirothesia, or a Confirmation of the Apostolicall Confirmation of Children* (1651), sig. A2v; Bodl., Tanner MS 52, fo. 97; Fincham and Taylor, 'Vital Statistics', pp. 333-4; Bosher, *Restoration Settlement*, p. 25.

[48] Fincham and Taylor, 'Vital Statistics', pp. 323, 326-7; Hall, *Cheirothesia*, pp. 16-17; Bodl., MSS Tanner 48, fo. 25r, Carte 145, p. 155, Rawlinson D 158, fo. 18r, Eng Hist b 205, fo. 25r.

[49] A. G. H. Bachrach and R. Collmer (eds.), *Lodewijick Huygens: The English Journal 1651-1652* (Leiden, 1982), pp. 74, 79; M. Stieg (ed.), *The Diary of John Harington MP, 1646-53* (Somerset Record Society, 74, 1977), pp. 63-85; G. Isham (ed.), *The Correspondence of Bishop Brian Duppa and Sir Justinian Isham, 1650-60* (Northamptonshire Record Society, 17, 1954), p. 13; Bodl., Tanner MS 48, fo. 25r; BL, Harleian MS 3783, fo. 220; J. Gauden, *A sermon preached... at the funeral of... Dr Brounrig* (1660), pp. 224, 228.

regard Duppa as his 'diocesan' to whom he owed obedience.[50] There would have been many other encounters, now lost to us: we only know of the regular appearances of Bishop Juxon at Sonning in Berkshire in 1651-2, dining, hunting, and attending communion, thanks to the diary of Anthony Blagrave, while Fulwar later claimed to have consecrated a church, as yet unidentified, sometime during the decade.[51]

With the Prayer Book outlawed, what place did public worship play in expressing and sustaining episcopalian identity in the 1650s? Some episcopalians such as John Allington argued that clergy should observe their oaths and continue to use the Prayer Book, even at the risk of sequestration, while others led by Sanderson proposed a more pragmatic approach, using as much or as little as circumstances permitted. Some incumbents, such as John Hacket and George Bull, memorized large portions of the text and impressed puritans with their ostensibly fluent extempore praying. Others largely put aside the Prayer Book but retained particular offices: the marriage service was regularly celebrated at Maid's Moreton in Buckinghamshire, and elsewhere funeral services were sometimes held in defiance of the Directory. Thomas Hassall, a Hertfordshire incumbent, prayed for divine forgiveness for abandoning the traditional liturgy, and at his request was buried in 1657 with a sermon and according to the Prayer Book.[52] So might we suppose that for many episcopalians in the 1650s, the Prayer Book was confined to household devotions?

In fact, there were parishes where something of the old order was preserved, as minister, vestry, and perhaps the local gentry colluded to evade the official proscription, use common prayer, and invite episcopalians to preach; in short, to practise what we may call episcopalian congregationalism. In the absence of church courts and annual visitations, parishes in the 1650s were largely left to their own devices, and some episcopalians took full advantage of this. At Harrold in Bedfordshire, the Prayer Book was used without interruption from 1646 to 1659; at Llandrinio in North Wales, it was alleged in 1653 that the incumbent George Griffith retained the Laudian altar and at Easter admitted any people from neighbouring parishes to communion; at Wardley in Rutland, John Allington finally lost his living in 1655 for using the Prayer Book in worship and for 'cringing, bowing, and kneeling to the altar and

---

[50] Isle of Wight RO, OG/CC/84 (a reference we owe to Jason Peacey); Bodl., Tanner MS 52, fo. 210r.

[51] Bodl., MSS Eng Misc E 118, fos. 17v, 33v, 35v, 39r, 48v, 52r, 69v, 70r; Carte 145, p. 155.

[52] J. Allington, *A Brief Apologie for the Sequestred Clergie* (1649), pp. 6–17; W. Jacobson (ed.), *Works of Robert Sanderson*, 6 vols. (Oxford, 1854), V, pp. 37–57; Maltby, '"The Good Old Way"', pp. 141–2; B. Capp, *England's Culture Wars: Puritan Reformation and Its Enemies in the Interregnum, 1649-1660* (Oxford, 2012), pp. 118–21; Buckinghamshire RO, PR 139/1/1, pp. 30, 32; Byam, *XIII Sermons*, pp. 215–63; S. Doree, *The Parish Register and Tithing Book of Thomas Hassall of Amwell* (Hertfordshire Record Society, 1989), pp. xxiv, 3.

sacrament'. At St Peter, Paul's Wharf in London, a congregation from across the city attended prayer-book services and monthly communions, and listened to visiting preachers such as Jeremy Taylor and the assistant minister Robert Mossom, an ejected cleric. Two illegal ordinations were performed in the church in 1649. Soldiers disrupted worship in September 1649, and in 1652 Mossom was temporarily forced to quit and his congregation, unparalleled for its 'reverence, charity and devotion', was temporarily dissolved. Prayer-book services were later resumed and Mossom returned as preacher.[53] Such 'episcopalian gadding' was obviously much harder outside towns. The freedom to appoint lecturers allowed several London parishes to employ episcopalians: St Gregory by St Paul's chose Bishop Brownrigg in 1653, which he declined, while in 1654 St Clement Eastcheap hired John Pearson, whose weekly sermons led to the publication of his *Exposition of the Creed* in 1659.[54] Outside London, some parishes welcomed sequestrated episcopalians in their pulpit: at Sonning they included George Wilde (former chaplain to Laud), two chaplains to Bishop Juxon, and John Horne, the ejected fellow of Oriel College, Oxford. The incumbent was Thomas Saxby or Sexby, appointed in the 1630s, and a close friend was Anthony Blagrave, a local gentleman and vestryman, who observed the Prayer Book offices of baptism and churching at home, with Saxby officiating, although there are few signs here, unlike Harrold or St Peter Paul's Wharf, that the old liturgy was used in public worship. Relatives of Bishop Juxon lived in the parish, and in 1654 the manor was purchased by Thomas Rich, episcopalian and friend of Bishop Brownrigg, who often visited Sonning in the later 1650s. Saxby died in 1656 and his successor, Samuel Reyner, was later to refuse to accept the Act of Uniformity in 1662, so episcopalian preachers may have ceased to occupy the parish pulpit in the later 1650s.[55]

There was scope, too, for liturgical experimentation. In 1658 Taylor published his *A Collection of Offices or Forms of Prayer*, which was effectively an alternative version of the Prayer Book, adapted from eastern liturgies, for use in parishes where common prayer had been put aside and where 'every man uses what he pleases, and all men do not choose well'. It contained many new offices and prayers, particularly for women, and one to be 'said in the days of

---

[53] Spurr, *Restoration Church*, pp. 14–18; Bodl., MS Walker c.2, fo. 97r; *A Relation of a Disputation between Dr Griffith and Mr Vavasor Powell* (1653), pp. 2–3 (a reference we owe to Judith Maltby); J. Allington, *A Review of a Brief Apology* (1678), sig. G2v; *CSPD 1658–9*, pp. 13–14; Matthews, *Walker Revised*, pp. 260–1; Bodl., Tanner MS 49, fos. 59, 52, 144r; Mossom, *The Preachers Tripartite*, 'To the ingenuous readers'; Lichfield RO, B/V/1/89A [Mark Hope and Samuel Cryer].

[54] London Metropolitan Archives (hereafter LMA), MSS 1336/1 fo. 37v, 978/1 [18 August 1654]; Bodl., Tanner MS 52, fo. 14r.

[55] Bodl., MS Eng Misc E 118, fos 69v, 80r, 89r; Spurr, *Restoration Church*, pp. 1–2, 16–17; Bodl., Tanner MS 52, fo. 178r; BL, Harleian MS 3783, fo. 194r; A. G. Matthews, *Calamy Revised* (Oxford, 1934), p. 408.

persecution of a church, by sacrilegious or violent persons', all intended to be 'useful to the present or future necessities of the sons and daughters of the Church of England'. The fact that it went through a second edition in 1658 suggests that the *Collection of Offices* addressed a genuine need. A year later there appeared John Hewitt's posthumous *Prayers of Intercession*, described as 'very necessary and useful in private families, as well as in congregations' and it included a prayer for 30 January, the anniversary of Charles I's execution.[56] The impression from the parishes is of diversity, as episcopalian congregations developed their own pathways according to the rather different circumstances they faced.

Tensions over clerical conformity also complicated episcopalian identity. First and foremost, opinion differed sharply on whether or not to serve in the state Church of the 1650s. A small minority of unyielding nonconformists, led by Hammond and Sheldon, would have no dealings with what they regarded as an illicit and schismatic Church, and instead chose exile abroad or service in England as private chaplains or schoolmasters to the upper classes; by contrast, the majority of episcopalians in the parish ministry, where they could, remained in post. They were joined, in the early 1650s, by numerous clergy ejected from their livings in the 1640s, often desperate for a regular income and keen to resume their ministry. Among them was Bishop Piers of Bath and Wells, who in 1655 unsuccessfully petitioned for a post as lecturer or curate 'to keep him from starving'.[57] How did they justify working in a Church without the government and liturgy which they had sworn to obey? Many would have been familiar with Sanderson's influential opinion in 1652 in favour of conducting worship without using the Prayer Book, which could be extended to service in the ministry as a whole: we do so, he wrote,

> neither in contempt of our lawful governors, or of the laws, nor out of base compliance with the times, or other unworthy secular own ends...but merely enforced thereunto...to the glory of God and the public good, for the preservation of our families, our flocks...and that with the good leave and allowance...of such as have power to dispense with us and the laws...

The last clause was not entirely wishful thinking: though the bishops had not granted such a dispensation, some at least accepted the need for accommodation with the law as it now stood.[58] The motives of the estimated 2,500 ordinands receiving episcopal orders between 1646 and 1660 are also worth pondering. Ordination involved, as far as we can tell, taking traditional oaths to the old order. Skinner of Oxford claimed in 1662 that all those he had

---

[56] J. Taylor, *A Collection of Offices* (1658), sig. C4i and 'Advertisement'; Hewitt, *Prayers of Intercession*, title page, pp. 74–8.

[57] W. Prynne, *Some Popish Errors* (1658), pp. 32, 56. For examples of sequestered clergy readmitted to livings in the 1650s, see Matthews, *Walker Revised*, pp. 54–5, 97, 112, 154, 229.

[58] Jacobson, *Works of Sanderson*, V, p. 55; Bosher, *Restoration Settlement*, pp. 17–21.

admitted to orders accepted the Thirty-Nine Articles and the royal supremacy, and the sole surviving certificate for one of his ordinands, for 1648, states exactly that. A chance survival is the nugget that Tilson of Elphin required an ordinand in 1650 to subscribe to the royal supremacy. (The only ordination certificate surviving for Brownrigg unusually makes no mention of any oaths, perhaps because none was tendered, or perhaps because the standard clause was deliberately omitted to protect bishop and ordinand were the letters to fall into hostile hands.)[59] So to choose to take orders illegally from a deprived bishop seems a clear-cut statement of identity; in practice, however, it was read in several different ways. A few hedged their bets and took both Presbyterian and episcopal orders, and a small number of others were to be ejected in 1660-2, which suggests that it was the absence of ecclesiastical discipline after ordination which made it so attractive in the 1650s.[60] Most others were committed episcopalians, but differed over the purpose of their ordination. A minority, such as John Dolben and George Davenport, needed orders to serve as chaplains outside the state Church; many, however, were ordained shortly before taking up a parochial cure or, in some cases, after several years' work in an incumbency, and saw no contradiction between their new orders and their service in a non-episcopal Church. Nor, it seems, did the bishops who laid hands on them.

Attitudes towards county associations, dominated by Presbyterians and Independents, were another fault-line in episcopalian identity. The abolition of episcopacy in 1646, and the failure to establish a nationwide system of Presbyterian classes by 1650, meant that many areas of the country lacked any structure of ecclesiastical discipline for clergy and laity. This situation the association movement of the 1650s attempted to remedy, as well as to combat the rising tide of sectarianism. As Richard Baxter discovered in Worcestershire, some episcopalians, led by Hammond and Gunning, refused to join what they branded 'a schismatical combination' and warned off others. In Herefordshire, episcopalians wanted 'the old episcopacy' and nothing else.[61] But a small number of episcopalians broke ranks and joined associations in Worcestershire, Cambridgeshire, Devon, and elsewhere. All had been episcopally ordained, one of them (Thomas Whitehand) as recently as 1654,[62] and all were to accept the Act of Uniformity in 1662. Several had been sequestrated

---

[59] Fincham and Taylor, 'Vital Statistics', p. 323n17; Bodl., MSS Tanner 48, fo. 25r, Ch. Somerset 165A; H. J. Morehouse, *The History... of Kirkburton* (Huddersfield, 1861), p. 127; Bodl., MS Charters Camb.a.1 fo. 25r.

[60] Fincham and Taylor, 'Vital Statistics', pp. 339-40, 342.

[61] M. Sylvester, *Reliquiae Baxterianae* (1696), I, pp. 97, 149-50, appendix I; N. Keeble and G. Nuttall (eds.), *Calendar of the Correspondence of Richard Baxter*, 2 vols. (Oxford, 1991), I, p. 343.

[62] W. A. Shaw, *A History of the English Church... 1640-1660*, 2 vols. (1900), II, p. 441; Clergy of the Church of England Database (hereafter CCEd), 'Thomas Whitehand' (Clergy ID 14389).

in the 1640s and some, either side of 1640–60, were prominent figures in the episcopalian Church. John Gandy had been chaplain to Bishop Davenant and canon of Salisbury in the 1630s, while Roger Ashton was a prebendary of Exeter after the Restoration. At least seven episcopalian clergy, including Gandy and Ashton, were members of the Devon association, and signed up to thirty articles, several of which formally crossed their episcopalian practice: namely, that admission to the holy communion should be selective, that no one should disparage the Westminster confession of faith, and that groups of ministers had the power of ordination. Episcopalians and Presbyterians could sometimes be found cooperating to provide testimonies for ministers appearing before the Triers.[63] These different forms of collaboration by some episcopalians point to their desire for unity among moderate Protestants and for the imposition of some order in the parishes, thereby creating a bulwark against sectarian excesses.

1660–62

It is evident, therefore, not only that episcopalianism was surviving despite the destruction of the old order, but also that it was maintaining a distinctive, quasi-denominational identity, setting it apart from other religious groups of the period. Tensions and complexities abounded; it would have been surprising had they not, as individuals responded in different ways to the challenges of the 1640s and 1650s. But these tensions and complexities do not appear to have led to the fragmentation of episcopalian identity. More than that, episcopalianism was adapting and developing, and, as the memory of the traditional structures of the historic Church began to fade, it assumed a variety of new and often surprisingly vibrant forms. Viewed from this perspective, we are able to look at the events of 1660–2 in a new light.

This is not the place to recount the making of the Restoration settlement in the Church. The recent consensus is that it was a gradual process, dominated by debates with the nonconformists about ordination, episcopacy, and the liturgy, and that the key decisions took place late: only in autumn 1661 were proposals for a modified episcopacy and significant revisions to the Book of Common Prayer finally rejected.[64] In fact, the religious landscape began to change quickly and dramatically after the king's return to London at the end of May 1660 in a manner that represented the triumph of a small group of

---

[63] Spurr, *Restoration Church*, pp. 25–6; CCEd, 'John Gandy' (Clergy ID 7625), 'Roger Ashton' (19705); Matthews, *Walker Revised*, pp. 77, 112; *Report and Transactions of the Devonshire Association*, 9 (1877), pp. 279–83; Fincham and Taylor, 'Vital Statistics', pp. 340–1.

[64] I. M. Green, *The re-establishment of the Church of England 1660–1663* (Oxford, 1978).

episcopalians who had spent the Interregnum in the purity of internal or external exile. Very rapidly, in the summer and autumn of 1660 (as we shall demonstrate more fully elsewhere), decisions were taken that would have a profound effect on the character of the religious settlement and that would ensure the return of those three central pillars of episcopacy, liturgy, and the royal supremacy in forms strikingly similar to those of the early seventeenth century.

The royal supremacy, almost irrelevant to the functioning of episcopalianism in England in the 1650s, was vigorously reasserted. Within days of Charles's return, presentations were being made to livings in the king's gift and a public day of thanksgiving for the Restoration was ordered throughout the kingdom. These acts were echoed in an enthusiastic response in many parishes where royal coats of arms were among the first parts of the fittings to be restored.[65] That episcopacy would be re-established alongside the monarchy was apparent from the moment of the king's return. Moreover, while discussions with the Presbyterians about some form of Ussherian 'reduced episcopacy' continued well into 1661, the reality was that something more reminiscent of the pre-civil war hierarchy was being recreated. Mass ordinations were celebrated publicly from as early as June 1660; from the summer of 1660, bishops were insisting on episcopal ordination as a condition of institution to livings; and, in the autumn of 1660, the consecration services for new bishops were conducted in a manner that presented a consciously 'high' vision of the office.[66] These services were performed using the pre-civil war Ordinal, which was reprinted for the purpose, and, while the Book of Common Prayer was not *imposed* until the passage of the Act of Uniformity in 1662, it immediately began to be used for services in the Chapel Royal, it was quickly adopted in the royal peculiars of Westminster Abbey and St George's Chapel, and soon its familiar cadences were being heard again in many parishes across the country.[67]

Thus, in 1660–2 we see the beginnings of the articulation of an Anglican identity, in which the centrality of supremacy, episcopacy, and Prayer Book was asserted more self-consciously than ever before. All three played a key role in the definition of the Church of England as a *via media* between, and against,

---

[65] E.g. Cheshire RO, P8/13/4; P40/13/1; Northamptonshire RO, 94P/22; LMA, 1179/1, p. 175.

[66] K. Fincham and S. Taylor, 'The Restoration of the Church of England, 1660–1662: Ordination, Re-ordination and Conformity', in S. Taylor and G. Tapsell (eds.), *The Nature of the English Revolution Revisited* (Woodbridge, 2013), pp. 200–2, 213–21; J. Sudbury, *A Sermon Preached...on Sunday 28 October at S. Peters Westminster* (1660); W. Sancroft, *A Sermon Preached in S. Peter's Westminster* (1660); D. Laing, *The Diary of Alexander Brodie 1652–80* (Aberdeen, 1863), p. 233.

[67] Edward, earl of Clarendon, *The History of the Rebellion and Civil Wars in England*, ed. W. D. Macray, 6 vols. (Oxford, 1888), VI, p. 232; LMA, 6047/1, fo. 124v; Wiltshire and Swindon RO, 1076/19, fo. 53r.

Catholicism and dissent, a theme which assumed a new prominence in Anglican ecclesiology in this period. But what influence did episcopalian identity, as it had evolved during the previous two decades, have on this emerging Anglican identity? To what extent was Anglicanism a radical revision or rejection of mid-century episcopalianism? At first sight, it appears that the Restoration saw the triumph of the vision of one narrow stream of episcopalianism, represented by the two key figures in the restored hierarchy, Gilbert Sheldon, dean of the Chapel Royal and then bishop of London, and George Morley, a royal chaplain and then bishop of Worcester. Both had been Interregnum nonconformists who shared, despite Morley's moderate Calvinism, a distinctively Laudian view of order and discipline in the Church. Many even of the laity, at least as represented in the Cavalier House of Commons, appear to have embraced this vision; in May 1661 the Commons required all its members to take communion according to the forms of the Prayer Book. That a narrow Anglican identity triumphed at the Restoration was certainly the view of many of those excluded from the Church after St Bartholomew's Day 1662, who blamed the intrigues and betrayals of 'hierarchists', intent on recreating a intolerant Church on the Laudian model, for the failure to create a broader, more comprehensive Anglicanism.[68] It would, however, be a mistake to equate Restoration Anglicanism with the episcopalianism of Sheldon, Morley, and their allies.

There is no doubt that some of the most ambiguous developments of the 1650s, those that flowed from the collapse of the structures of the old order, were not only abandoned, but also purged from the collective memory of the Restoration Church. Primitive or reduced episcopacy, which had played a central part in debates about reform in the 1640s and, with its emphasis on confirmation, ordination, and preaching, might be seen as having characterized the behaviour of some of the surviving bishops through the 1650s, was a major thread in Presbyterian accounts of the Restoration settlement, but it seems to have had little purchase on even more moderate episcopalians, although Gauden did choose to ordain with the assistance of presbyters in Exeter and Reynolds of Norwich self-consciously presented himself as a bishop who acted in consultation with his presbyters on the 'antient' model.[69] County associations vanished, leaving little visible trace of cooperation across hardening denominational boundaries. The re-establishment of the structures of visitation and the church courts took some years, but there appears to have been little appetite for the preservation of the parochial

---

[68] S. Taylor (ed.), *The Entring Book of Roger Morrice. IV: The Reign of James II 1687–1689* (Woodbridge, 2007), pp. 39, 46, 266, 434.

[69] J. Gauden, *Consilia et Voce et Scripto Tradita XLIIII Fratribus Filiisque, Sacris Ordinibus per Ipsum Episcopum et Primores Presbyteros* (1661), pp. 15–16, 25; E. Reynolds, *Preaching of Christ* (1662), dedicatory epistle.

autonomy that characterized 'episcopalian congregationalism'. Even enthusiasm for liturgical innovation seems to have withered, or was perhaps shut down. This may be one of the most surprising aspects of the process of settlement, as much of the experimentation had come from the higher end of the theological spectrum and from clergy not out of sympathy with the aims of the Sheldon circle. Yet the amendments to the Prayer Book, as agreed in 1662, were both minor and overwhelmingly conservative.

But if some of the complexities of episcopalian identity disappeared in the melting pot of 1660–2, others, sometimes transformed, became more deeply embedded, ensuring the construction of an Anglican identity that was richer and more paradoxical than that conveyed by the notion of the 'restoration' of the Church of England. One major reason for this was the complex and often opaque attitude of Charles II as Supreme Governor. On the one hand, the king's personal religious preferences appear to have accorded quite closely with those of Sheldon, and he had no qualms about demonstrating his commitment to order, ceremony, and the old liturgy publicly and unequivocally from the moment of his return. On the other hand, he repeatedly used the royal supremacy to pursue policies that suggested a desire for a broad settlement, in the Church as much as in the state. Uncertainty about Charles's commitment to the Church, dating back to his dalliance with Presbyterianism in 1650–1, was reinforced by his readiness to contemplate policies of both comprehension and toleration, embracing even Roman Catholicism. There were repeated reminders of his preference for a more comprehensive settlement through 1660–2, illustrated by offers of bishoprics to Richard Baxter and Edmund Calamy, the promotion of the moderate Presbyterian Edward Reynolds to the see of Norwich, and the appointments of Robert Sanderson and John Gauden—both Interregnum conformists and noted moderates—to the bishoprics of Lincoln and Exeter respectively. Royal preference thus ensured that the Restoration Church was broader and more comprehensive than it might otherwise have been, and Anglicans were firmly reminded in 1663 and 1672 that the 'liberty to tender consciences' granted in the Declaration of Breda was never a matter of mere expediency for the king. Suspicion of the Supreme Governor remained a strong undercurrent in Anglican identity, culminating in the crisis of 1686–8.

Doubts about the Supreme Governor might be seen as a destabilizing element in Anglican identity after 1660; other aspects of the inheritance of the 1650s were more positive. The circumstances of that decade stimulated the emergence of the Book of Common Prayer as a resource for lay piety, a staple of private and family worship, as much as a liturgical manual for congregational worship. These practices of private prayer-book devotion also informed the stream of works of practical, non-controversial divinity produced by authors such as Richard Allestree, Henry Hammond, and Jeremy Taylor. Some of these—notably *The Whole Duty of Man* (1658), the *Practical*

Catechism (1644), and *Holy Living* (1650)—quickly established themselves as popular devotional manuals right across the Church, reaching out well beyond the strand of intransigent episcopalianism whence they had originated.[70] Episcopalian charitable networks were also maintained and developed after 1660. A service at St Paul's Cathedral in 1655, at which the preacher was George Hall, the son of the deprived bishop, and a collection was taken for distressed clergy and their families, provided the model for the Sons of the Clergy, established in 1674, and thus arguably for the corporate philanthropy which was to be one of the distinguishing features of Anglicanism through the next century.[71]

Finally, it is important to remember that Anglican identity at the Restoration was forged not only by the Church's leaders, but also by its members, both clerical and lay. Many were suddenly empowered to react to the sufferings of two decades of persecution. The sometimes brutal settling of scores in the parishes was recorded in dissenting martyrologies and, despite some official efforts to encourage healing, hostility to dissent was institutionalized in Church and state through legislation. While this was regretted by some, it was to be an important feature of Anglican identity for two generations and more, finding expression in outbreaks of popular violence, such as those orchestrated by the Hilton gang in the 1680s, as well as in countless sermons. Alongside this, the experience of the 1650s for a significant group of episcopalians had been one of harmonious and sometimes fruitful cooperation in the national Church, creating a section of the clergy temperamentally inclined to seek reconciliation and the strengthening of a broad Protestant interest through comprehension.[72] Even more striking was the inclusion within the Church of some who could not be described as episcopalians during the previous two decades, many of whom had been Presbyterians. The loss of most of the classis records means that it is impossible to estimate the number of such men serving in the Church after 1660, but, of those known to have received Presbyterian ordination between 1646 and 1660, at least a quarter were reordained in 1660–2.[73] The boundaries of Anglican identity were stretched even further by those gentry who felt able to combine conformity with the maintenance of dissenting chaplains in their households.[74] Developments such as these ensured that the puritan heritage enriched the Restoration

---

[70] Spurr, *Restoration Church*, ch. 6; I. Green, *Print and Protestantism in Early Modern England* (Oxford, 2000), pp. 351–9.

[71] G. Hall, *Gods Appearing for the Tribe of Levi* (1655); Cox, *Bridging the Gap*, chs. 1–2.

[72] M. Goldie, 'The Hilton Gang and the Purge of London in the 1680s', in H. Nenner (ed.), *Politics and Political Imagination in Later Stuart Britain* (Rochester, NY, 1997), pp. 43–73; E. Stillingfleet, *Irenicum* (1660).

[73] Fincham and Taylor, 'Restoration', pp. 222–3.

[74] J. T. Cliffe, *Puritans in Conflict: The Puritan Gentry During and After the Civil Wars* (1988), pp. 194–6.

Church after 1662. Moreover, the experience of episcopalian congregationalism and the absorption of former Presbyterians into the church contributed to an enduring distrust of clericalism, often expressed most vigorously in a critique of the *power* of the bishops, that was manifested strikingly at points in the 1670s and 1680s, and then sustained throughout the eighteenth century, and was articulated not only by the laity but also by some of the clergy.

CONCLUSION

To state that the period from 1640 to 1662 was one of quite extraordinary flux and change is a truism; to portray it as a period of dramatic formulation and reformulation of episcopalian identity is more novel. Traditionally, the episcopalian response to the destruction of the old order has been portrayed either as steadfast opposition in exile, at home and abroad, or else a conservative adherence to traditional forms and practices. The central argument of this chapter, by contrast, is that episcopalian identity was not static; it was forming, evolving, and developing through the 1640s and 1650s. In some senses, a distinctive episcopalian identity only emerged in the later 1640s, as both clergy and laity defined themselves in terms of what was being lost: the royal supremacy, episcopacy, and the Prayer Book. Through the 1650s episcopalians held fast to these pillars of faith, seeing themselves as members of a persecuted Church. At the same time, however, episcopalian identity was multi-faceted, containing tensions and complexities as different individuals and groups responded to the religious revolution of the 1640s and the challenges of the 1650s in different ways. In particular, the decade following the execution of the Supreme Governor was a period of remarkable and often fertile experimentation and adaptation, as episcopalians found ways of sustaining their identity despite the partial or total disappearance of episcopacy, the supremacy, and the Prayer Book. As a result, it was impossible simply to turn the clock back following the restoration of the monarchy in 1660. Instead, that event, while accompanied by the rapid return of the king, the bishops, and common prayer, was followed by a further intense period of reformulation and adjustment, influenced by the experiences of 1640–60, and culminating in time with the creation of a distinctively Anglican identity.

SELECT BIBLIOGRAPHY

Bosher, R. S., *The Making of the Restoration Settlement: The Influence of the Laudians, 1649–62* (1951).

Braddick, M. J. and D. L. Smith (eds.), *The Experience of Revolution in Stuart Britain and Ireland* (Cambridge, 2011).

Cogswell, T., R. Cust, and P. Lake (eds.), *Politics, Religion and Popularity in Early Stuart Britain* (Cambridge, 2002).

Fincham, K. and S. Taylor, 'The Restoration of the Church of England 1660–1662: Ordination, Re-ordination and Conformity', in S. Taylor and G. Tapsell (eds.), *The Nature of the English Revolution Revisited* (Woodbridge, 2013), pp. 197–232.

Fincham, K. and S. Taylor, 'Vital Statistics: Episcopal Ordination and Ordinands in England, 1646–60', *English Historical Review*, 126 (2011): 319–44.

Green, I., *The Re-establishment of the Church of England 1660–1663* (Oxford, 1979).

McCall, F., *Baal's Priests: The Loyalist Clergy and the English Revolution* (Farnham, 2013).

Maltby, J., '"The Good Old Way": Prayer Book Protestantism in the 1640s and 1650s', in R. N. Swanson (ed.), *The Church and the Book*, SCH 38 (Woodbridge, 2004), pp. 233–56.

Milton, A., 'Anglicanism and Royalism in the 1640s', in J. Adamson (ed.), *The English Civil War: Conflicts and Contexts, 1640–49* (Basingstoke, 2009), pp. 61–81.

Morrill, J., 'The Church in England, 1642–9', in J. Morrill (ed.), *Reactions to the English Civil War 1642–9* (1982), pp. 89–114.

Spurr, J., *The Restoration Church of England* (New Haven, CT, 1991).

Index

Abbey Dore church 202
Abbot, Archbishop George 69, 70, 98, 100, 111, 336, 372
Aberdeen Doctors 260, 264
Actes and Monuments ('Book of Martyrs') 11, 47, 303–5, 312, 313, 314, 355–7, 356, 398–9, 415, 419
Act for Kingly Title 246
Act for Confirming Ministers (1660) 81
Act for the English Order, Habit and Language (1536) 250
Act in Restraint of Appeals (1533) 18, 30, 104, 105, 106, 111–12, 168
Act of Exchanges (1559) 90–1, 98
Act of Submission of Clergy (1534) 18, 104, 112
Act of Supremacy (1534) 18, 28, 30–1, 33, 89, 95, 104, 150, 418
Act of Supremacy (1559) 49, 89, 95, 105, 419
Act of Uniformity (1549) 41–2, 89, 95, 149, 153
Act of Uniformity (1553) 156
Act of Uniformity (1559) 49, 52, 54, 89, 95, 158
Act of Uniformity (1662) 21, 82, 89, 95, 344, 475, 477
Adair, Archibald 261
Adamson, Archbishop Patrick 253
adiaphora 56, 107–8, 115, 260, 308, 337, 338, 339, 365
Admonition Controversy 56, 399
Admonition to the Parliament 56, 159, 231
Advertisements (1566) 177, 213
advowsons 16, 71, 134–5
Aelfric 306
Albigensians 440
Alesius, Alexander 281
Alfred, King 306
Allen, William, cardinal 54, 118, 422
Allestree, Richard 467, 479
Allington, John 472–3
altars 67–8, 156
  bowing towards 72, 163, 311, 472
  railed 17, 70, 74, 141–2, 201, 207, 208, 472
  use of term 71, 386
Ames, William 439
Amicable Grant (1525) 29
Anabaptism 116, 212–13, 214, 323, 325, 330, 361
Andreae, Jacob 216

Andrewes, Lancelot, bishop 8–9, 60, 67, 70, 73, 98, 162, 195, 198, 201, 289–90, 339, 369, 371, 378, 380–93, 439, 440, 467, 468
'Anglican moment' 381
Anglicanism
  anachronistic use of term 7–8, 27, 28–9, 58, 227, 457
  assumed values/beliefs 1, 5, 8, 10, 14–15, 122, 360
  reading of 1640s–1650s 18–19, 436–7, 444
  and *via media* 1, 4, 5, 6, 23, 26–7, 49, 89, 228–9, 230, 280, 333, 343
Anglo-Catholics 52, 381
Anglo-Saxon Church 306
Anna, countess of East Friesland 23, 321–2
anti-Arminianism 290, 292, 331
anti-Calvinism 14, 24, 343, 373, 381, 388–9, 391, 447
anti-catholicism 3, 36, 37, 54–5, 71, 116, 240, 256, 262, 264, 300–3, 325, 344–6, 347, 353, 357, 362–3, 369, 370, 371, 373, 378, 399, 423, 466, 467
Antichrist, Pope as 3, 21, 61, 69, 251, 256, 257, 263, 303, 306, 308–9, 340, 344, 346, 352, 357, 362, 365
anti-clericalism 113, 310, 435
anti-episcopalianism 38, 74, 77, 181, 244, 253, 260, 261–2, 365, 440, 455, 459
anti-Laudianism 2, 16, 74–5, 76, 440–1
antinomianism 270, 374, 376
anti-popery *see* anti-catholicism
anti-Presbyterianism 386, 387, 461, 466
anti-puritanism 8, 10, 16, 59, 73, 182, 183, 348, 365–6, 367–9, 371, 372, 373, 374–6, 378, 385–6, 387–8, 389, 425–6
anti-Trinitarianism 80, 328, 330 *see also* Socinians/Socinianism
Antwerp Mannerism 194
Apocrypha 284, 432
Apologeticall Narration 79
Apostles' Creed 281, 294, 408
Aquinas 88
Archbold, Nicholas 244, 261
archdeacons 94, 108, 124, 419
Archer, John 440
Arminianism 60, 66, 68, 69, 72, 74, 97, 99, 100, 101, 270, 289, 290, 312, 331, 336, 339, 343, 369, 373, 451, 452
Arminius, Jacobus 25, 60

484 Index

Arrowsmith, John 440
ars moriendi 409
Arthington, Henry 117
Arthur, Prince 29
Articles of Perth 67, 74, 161–2, 254–5, 257,
    259, 260
Articles of Religion 2–3
    Forty-Two Articles 3, 40–1, 51, 176, 177,
        212–13, 283, 325
    Six Articles 2, 36–7, 247, 318
    Ten Articles 2, 35, 212, 281–2
    Thirty-Nine Articles 3, 14–15, 19, 40–1, 51,
        52, 56, 57, 70, 77, 79, 89, 102, 178, 179,
        212, 213–17, 219–27, 251, 257, 273,
        283–4, 333, 348, 419, 436, 459, 475
        reform of 431–3
    Twelve Articles 249–50
Ascension Day 255
Ash Wednesday, abolition of 154
Ashton, Roger 476
Aske, Robert 307
Askew, Anne 300, 399
Association movement 20, 453–4, 475–6
Aston, Margaret 187
Athanasian Creed 281, 294
'Atheos' character 132, 367–8
Atherton, Ian 13–14
augmentations 449, 450
Augustine of Canterbury 149, 162, 168, 287,
    298, 301
Augustine of Hippo 216, 282, 285, 290, 291
auricular confession 257, 280, 384
Austin, William 139
avant-garde conformity 8–9, 10, 13, 67, 69,
    73, 162, 198, 291, 339, 346–7, 348, 369,
    371, 373, 380–93
Aylmer, John, bishop 94, 97, 391

Bacon, Sir Francis 58
Bacon, Nicholas 92, 134
Bagshaw, Edward 112, 113
Baillie, Robert 290, 291
Balcanquahall, Walter 73
Bale, John, bishop 36, 60, 247–8, 299–302,
    303, 306, 307, 309, 398
    King Johan 299, 302
Ballard, William 467
Baltinglass revolt 245
Banastre, Sir Robert 202
Bancroft, Richard, archbishop 19, 59, 60, 64,
    72, 87, 97, 98, 99, 119, 138, 174, 181,
    253, 254, 309, 338, 339, 343, 360, 366,
    369, 370, 371, 386, 426
baptism 125, 164, 225, 255, 268, 274, 275, 276,
    277–8, 295, 436
    infant baptism 80–1

lay baptism 63
sign of cross in 56, 63–4, 76, 81, 107, 137,
    156, 182, 222, 308
Baptists 452, 467
Barbados 22, 266, 279
Barksdale, Clement 467
Barlow, William, bishop 161, 220
Barnes, Richard, bishop 93
Barnes, Robert 33, 285, 321
Baro, Peter 24, 60, 309, 388–9
Baron, Robert 260
Baronius, Caesar, cardinal 289
Barrett, William 60, 388
Barrow, Henry 160, 383, 384
Basel 47, 302
Basil of Caesarea 291
Bastingius, Jeremias 335
Baxter, Richard 82, 115, 116, 134, 165, 277,
    294–5, 408, 444–5, 451, 453, 454,
    475, 479
Bayly, Lewis, bishop 334, 403–5
Beale, Robert 210
'beauty of holiness' 2, 70, 73, 141–2, 162, 204,
    207, 234, 257, 311, 340, 347, 373
Becket, Thomas 36, 149, 151, 301–2, 311
Becon, Thomas 408
Bede 149, 287, 298, 306
Bedell, William, bishop 66
Belgic 17, 222, 337
Bellarmine, Cardinal Robert 346
benefit of clergy 171–2
Berkeley, Sir William 271
Bermuda 266, 271
Bern 222, 327
Bernard, Nicholas 451
Bernard, Richard 65, 132, 140
Beza, Theodore 218, 219, 221, 333–4, 335,
    337, 338, 342
Bible 17–18, 31, 32, 63, 193, 226, 292, 318,
    412–28
    Bishops' Bible 194, 421–2, 424
    Coverdale's Bible 416, 424
    Gaelic translation 250, 256
    Geneva Bible 18, 47–8, 194, 384, 407,
        420–4, 426, 428
    Great Bible 2, 150–1, 412, 416–17, 421
    King James Bible 18, 24, 79, 161, 416,
        424–8
    'Matthew's Bible' 37, 416
    Rheims New Testament 423–4
    Tyndale's translation 37
    Vulgate 413, 415, 416, 419, 424
bible illustration 193–4
Bill, John 289
Bilney, Thomas 32
Bilson, Thomas, bishop 98, 109, 288

Index

bishops *see also* episcopacy; episcopalian identity
   activities in 1650s 465, 469, 470–2
   administrator bishops 99–80, 108–11, 175, 221
   and Charles I 100–2
   as civil servants 84–6, 99, 100
   and Elizabeth I 3, 88–97, 99
   financial plight of 91–2
   in House of Lords 77, 94, 100
   and James I 98–102
   pastoral function of 93, 99
   on Privy Council 13, 64, 85, 97, 98, 100, 101
   reforming bishops 53, 328–9, 353
   in royal court 85, 98–101
   Scottish 161, 164, 254, 255, 258, 259
   as superintendents 99
   and universities 87–8
Bishops' Book 3, 281, 282, 335
Black Acts (1584) 253
black-letter inscriptions, Puddletown 191–2
Blackloists 349
'Black Oath' 261
'Black Rubric' 51, 158
Blagrave, Anthony 466, 472, 473
Boleyn, Queen Anne 35, 37, 319, 415
Bond of Association 359
Bonner, Edmund, bishop 46
Book of Common Prayer 2, 4, 14, 15, 19, 23, 43, 45, 74, 75, 76, 77, 78, 122, 124–5, 159, 225, 255, 258, 321, 340, 341, 362, 368, 374–5, 384, 398, 404, 408, 426, 427, 441, 442, 454, 459, 460, 461, 462, 477, 478, 481
   (1549) 21, 41–2, 51, 148–9, 153–5, 157, 158, 162, 163, 166, 248, 258, 260, 312, 324, 325, 397, 418, 470
   (1552) 42, 47, 49, 51, 156, 157, 176, 324, 325, 326, 418
   (1559) 6, 49, 51, 56, 57, 74, 79, 157–9, 178, 216, 325–6, 381, 419
   (1662) 112, 166, 428, 479
   clandestine use of 20, 22, 144–5, 164–5, 427, 435, 454, 469, 472–3, 479
   Latin edition (1559) 158
   petitions in favour of 76, 261, 460
   reform of 63, 82, 159–61, 165, 223, 476
   Scottish Prayer Book (1637) 21, 74, 163–4, 259, 260, 261, 433
   use in Ireland 250, 256, 257, 258, 262
   use in North America 271
   use in Scotland 255, 258, 261
Book of Discipline, First Scottish 230
Book of Discipline, Second Scottish 230
Books of Homilies 3, 14, 16, 50, 72, 73, 74, 96, 187–8, 214, 325, 362

Homily against the Peril of Idolatry 3, 16, 74, 186
'Book of Martyrs' see *Actes and Monuments*
Book of Sports (Caroline) 66, 71
Book of Sports (Jacobean) 68, 372
Borromeo, Charles, cardinal 349
Bosher, Robert 457
Bossewell, John 235
Boston 273, 274
Boughen, Edward 137
Bourne, Gilbert, bishop 86
Bowers, Roger 151–2
Boyle, Richard, earl of Cork 257
Bradshaw, William 362, 366, 370
Bramhall, John, bishop 22, 110, 256–7, 258, 260, 261, 262, 263, 465, 467, 469
Bramston, Sir John 144
Brancepeth church 205
Brandenburg 317, 318, 336
Bray, Gerald 12, 13, 19
Brenz, Johann 216
Brettergh, Katherine 410
Bridgeman, Anthony 92–3
Bridges, John 59, 109, 362
Bridgewater, John Egerton, earl of 451, 466
Bright, Timothy 305
Brinsley, John 398
Bristol 32
   diocese of 86, 461
   see of 90
Brooks, Thomas 446
Broughton, Hugh 424
Browne, George, archbishop 247
Brownrigg, Ralph, bishop 463, 471, 473, 475
Bucer, Martin 3, 153, 155, 221, 223, 319, 323, 324
Buckeridge, John, bishop 369, 380, 382
Bull, George 472
Bullinger, Heinrich 3, 23, 105, 218, 223, 320, 323, 328–32, 334
   Decades 3, 323, 330–2
Bunny, Edmund 240, 407–8
Burges, Cornelius 226, 437, 438
Burghley, lord 48, 50, 53, 55, 57, 87, 95, 179, 354, 356, 359
Burton, Henry 312
Bury St Edmunds 116
Byrd, William 50

Calamy, Edmund 77, 439, 450, 455, 479
Calvin, John 3, 23, 25, 48, 49, 54, 56, 72, 159, 188, 193, 211–12, 218, 219, 220, 224, 312, 323, 324, 327–8, 335, 342, 398
Calvinism 14, 24, 25, 56, 60, 65, 68, 69, 73, 133–4, 162, 180, 199, 211, 244, 288, 336, 338, 363, 371, 373, 396, 432

'Calvinist consensus' 56, 68, 309, 327
Cambridge Platform (1649) 273–4
Cambridge University 24, 32, 40, 89, 97, 155, 158, 290, 309, 323, 324, 335, 336, 349, 355, 382, 388, 459
  canon law faculties 169, 176
  choirs and organs in 239
  college chapels 196–8, 207, 208
  college founders and visitors 88
Cambridge University colleges
  King's College 239
  Peterhouse 162–3, 201, 349
  Trinity College 239
Camden, William 11, 73
Canes, Vincent 349
Canne, John 428
canon law 2, 3, 12, 41, 95, 168–84, 325
canons 2, 12, 31, 74, 99, 112
  (1571) 77–8, 179, 180, 213–14, 221, 283, 288, 289, 419
  (1576) 178, 179
  (1584) 179, 180
  (1597) 179, 180
  (1604) 63–4, 65, 66, 67, 69, 71, 88, 98–9, 138, 181–3, 191, 199, 214, 225, 257, 273, 288
  (1606) 3, 175
  (1640) 21, 72, 75, 175, 183
  'Henrician' 176–7
  Irish 21, 250, 257
  and Parliament 64, 112, 174, 183
  Scottish 74, 175, 259–60, 433
Canterbury 462
  cathedral 13
  province of 31, 97, 100, 171
Carew, George 89, 387
Carleton, George, bishop 100–1, 107, 215
Carlisle
  bishop of 92
  cathedral 92
  chapter of 462
  diocese of 96
  see of 94
Carter, John 400
Cartwright, Thomas 56, 115, 305, 312, 357, 359, 364, 365
Casaubon, Isaac 24, 289, 296
catechisms 47, 58, 63, 74, 77, 138–9, 221, 248, 335, 408, 436, 451, 454
  Gaelic 249–50
  Nowell's 74, 221
  Prayer Book 161, 221
  Westminster Larger 77, 436
  Westminster Shorter 77, 436, 451, 454
catechizing 128, 138–9, 452, 454

cathedrals 13–14, 29, 55, 86–7, 92, 93, 182, 228–42, 312, 326–7, 462, 465
  abolition of 93, 230, 231, 241
  centres of learning 237–9
  collegiate churches 237
  defence of 460
  diversity of 237
  Elizabethan establishments 92
  Henrician establishments 237
  Laudianism and 70, 74, 162–3, 201, 208, 230, 234, 241, 311
  parliamentary opposition to 241
  promotion of preaching 179, 239–40
  puritan criticisms of 230–2
  puritan prebendaries 240
  Scottish 230
  survival of 13–14, 55, 234–5, 239, 326–7
Catherine of Aragon, Queen 29, 30, 46, 168, 415
Catholic Church, perceptions of 60–1, 68, 256, 300, 308–9, 344–50, 439
Catholic devotional literature 346, 407, 408
Catholics 35, 36, 40, 41, 45–6, 54–5, 61, 68, 69, 104, 105, 118, 119, 129–30, 180, 181, 182, 189, 194, 211, 314, 324, 326, 347–8, 349, 350, 355, 359, 372, 384, 401, 413, 422–3, 479
  in Ireland 250–1, 256, 262, 264
  in North America 271
  recusancy 54, 96, 130, 256, 361
Caudrey's Case (1593) 113
Cawdrey, Daniel 439
Cecil family 392
Cecil, Sir Robert see Salisbury, Robert Cecil, earl of
Cecil, Sir William see Burghley, lord
ceremonies perceived as edifying 60, 67, 70, 339, 390
Chaderton, Laurence 161, 238, 357, 358, 360, 364
Chaderton, William 238
Chadwick, Henry 1
'Challenge controversy' 10, 52, 285–6, 299
chancel screen 205
chantries 127
chapels, decoration of 16–17, 194–9, 201, 207, 208
Chapel Royal 50, 53, 65, 89, 98, 157, 162, 163, 186, 195, 196, 312, 329, 387, 462, 469, 477
  Holyrood 67–8, 195, 254, 255, 258
Chappuis, Jean 170
Charenton, French Church at 342, 343
charity 126–7
Charles I, King 2, 18, 68, 69, 77, 79, 84, 94, 98–102, 105, 110, 113, 163, 180, 183,

214, 225, 238, 245, 248, 258, 311,
    341–2, 347, 348, 349, 373, 427, 431,
    459, 461–3, 467
  Royal Declaration for the Peace of the
    Church (1628) 72, 214–15, 225, 291
  Royal Instructions (1629) 138
Charles II, King 77, 79, 81, 82, 110, 119, 245,
  263, 276, 277, 342, 350, 469, 479
Charles V, Emperor 30, 321, 322–3
Chatham 207–8
cheap print 58
Cheapside Cross 307
Chelsea College 239, 345
Cheney, Richard, bishop 90, 387, 388
Chertsey Abbey 154
Cheshire, Thomas 460
Chester
  cathedral 234
  diocese of 86
Cheynell, Francis 464
Chichester, diocese of 90
Child, Robert 272
Chillingworth, William 292–3, 412
choirs 17, 158, 163, 231, 235, 238–9, 311, 327,
  390–1
chrism 175
Christ
  descent into hell 288, 432
  imitation of 401
  pictures of 196, 197, 201, 311
Christchurch, Dublin 258
Christmas 126, 143, 161–2, 164, 255, 454, 462
Christological devotion 402
Christopherson, John 114
church ales 126
church attendance 123–4, 129, 180, 273
church courts 6, 12, 55, 63, 71, 75, 94, 97,
  124, 130, 142, 169, 171–2, 353, 460,
  461, 478
church fees 131–2, 179, 180
church history, English Protestant views
  of 298–314
Church of England
  confessional identity of 14, 24–5, 210–27,
    327, 331, 333–5
  divergence from foreign Protestantism 35,
    55, 59, 119, 156, 284, 292, 308, 325,
    326–7, 338–41, 343 see also Lutherans/
    Lutheranism
  links with foreign Protestantism 3–4, 14,
    23, 40, 43, 47–8, 51, 105, 162, 210–13,
    215–22, 223, 227, 320, 321, 323–5,
    327–8, 329–32, 333–6, 342, 353, 439
  non-English views of 22–6, 211, 244, 337,
    342, 347–8
  Reformed defence of 329–31, 343–4

Church of Ireland 21, 225, 243, 247–52,
  256–65, 433, 438
  bishops appointed 252, 263
Church of Scotland 175, 195, 230, 243, 248,
  252–65, 372, 438
  General Assembly 253–5, 259, 260, 438
'church popery' 55, 119, 129 see also Catholics
churching 56, 125, 473
churchwardens 40, 124, 130, 136, 143, 182–3,
  419, 422
civil lawyers 97, 100, 171
civil magistrate, authority of in religious
  affairs 79, 103–20, 329, 331, 332,
  445–6
Clarendon, Edward Hyde, earl of 80, 343
Clarendon Code 277
Clarke, Samuel 342, 379, 400, 444–5
Clement V, Pope 170
Clement VII, Pope 30, 317
clergy
  appointment of 47, 134–5
  as JPs 99
  ejection of 18, 77, 82, 142, 145, 166,
    431, 447
  graduate 141, 178, 290
  non-residence of 93, 131, 231, 240,
    361, 362
  ordination of 182, 219–20, 334, 340–1,
    344, 431, 434, 450, 462, 463, 469,
    470–1, 473, 474–5, 477, 480 see also
    Ordinal
  pastoral role of 132–4, 138, 364, 367
  pluralism 93, 131, 179, 240, 361, 362
  relationship with parish vestry 136–7
  training of 290
Clerke, Francis 181
Coke, Sir Edward 107, 113
Colchester 135
collegiate churches 236
Collinson, Patrick 5, 13, 65, 93, 95, 96, 352,
  355, 356, 359, 363, 369, 373, 376,
  378, 386
Colloquy of Bern (1588) 224
Colloquy of Montbéliard (1586) 217–18
Cologne 32, 177, 415
Commandments board, St Saviour 200
commemorations, for women 399–400
Commission on Fees 132
Committee for Scandalous Ministers 431
common law, and canon law 168–9, 172
communion 50–1, 67, 70–1, 87, 124–5, 128,
  130–1, 134, 141, 144, 154, 156, 157–9,
  162, 163, 182, 216–17, 255, 342, 349,
  408–9 see also eucharistic presence
  exclusion from 79, 113, 143–4, 182, 271,
    435, 447, 453

communion (*cont.*)
  kneeling at 51, 56, 58, 67, 81, 107, 137, 156, 158, 162, 222, 255, 263, 384, 472
  preparation manuals for 408–9
communion tables, placing of 50, 70, 74, 102, 130, 141–2, 155, 163, 164, 195, 201, 234, 255, 257, 291, 311 *see also* altars
Como, David 374
Concordat of Leith (1572) 253
Confession of Augsburg 211
Confessio Virtembergica 284
confirmation 67, 263, 281, 295, 471
Congregationalists/Congregationalism 26, 82, 113, 144, 271–2
  in 1650s 445–6, 453
  'episcopalian congregationalism' 20, 80, 472, 479, 481
  in Foxe's works 356
  Marian martyrs 305
  New England 267–75
Congregational synods 268–9, 277
Connecticut General Court 274
Consensus Tigurinus 324–5, 331
consociations 277
conventicles 245, 255, 260, 370, 371
Convocation 3, 12, 18, 51, 53, 64, 70, 75, 85, 86, 95, 98–9, 104, 112, 165, 166, 173–5, 183, 213, 281, 283
  of Canterbury 31, 85, 172–3, 174, 175, 176, 177, 178, 183, 184
  Henrician 281
  Irish 246, 251, 257
  of York 85, 172–3, 174, 184
Coolidge, John S. 361–2
Cooper, J. P. D. 152
Cooper, Thomas, bishop 331
Coppinger, Edmund 117
Corbet, John 119, 261
Cornwall 155, 462
Cornwall family 190
Corro, Antonio del 24, 60, 328
Cosin, John, bishop 70, 74, 162–3, 166, 201, 205, 311, 312, 340, 342, 343, 349, 405, 467
  Collection of Private Devotions 70, 311–12, 405
Cotton, John 270, 370
Council of Carthage 286
Council of Niceae 286
Council of State 448–9, 455, 466
Council of the North 86
Council of Trent 47, 95, 213, 281, 284, 310, 419, 422
Counter-Reformation 47, 205, 349
Court of Augmentations 36
Court of Delegates 172

Court of High Commission 64, 74, 75, 77, 113, 129, 172, 183, 391
  Irish 250
  Scottish 254, 261
Court of Star Chamber 100
Covenanters *see* Scottish Covenanters
Coverdale, Miles 323, 415–16
Cowell, John 100
Cox, Richard, bishop 47, 87, 328
Cranmer, Edmund 39
Cranmer, Thomas, archbishop 3, 5, 9, 15, 23, 33, 38, 39, 40, 42–3, 47, 52, 56, 148, 151, 152–5, 156, 176, 232, 283, 284, 285, 318, 319–22, 324, 325, 353, 355, 404, 415–16, 418
Crashawe, William 310
Cressy, Hugh 349
Croke, Richard 286
Cromwell, Mary 454
Cromwell, Oliver 79, 165, 246, 248, 343, 445, 448–51, 455, 465, 469–70
Cromwell, Richard 115
Cromwell, Thomas 13, 35, 37, 86, 97, 173, 246, 281, 319, 320–1, 415–16
Cromwellian Church 19, 117, 444–56
crucifix 39, 53, 158, 163, 186, 195, 258, 387
Culmer, Richard 207
Cummings, Brian 166
Cuthbert, St 149, 151, 307, 311

Daillé, Jean 11, 293, 294, 295
  The Use of the Fathers 294, 295
Dale, Valentine 92
Daneau, Lambert 334
Datheen, Petrus 159
Davenport, Christopher *see* Sancta Clara, Franciscus a
Davenport, George 475
Davenport, John 270
Day, John 11, 153, 303, 356
deacons 47, 160, 220, 358, 386, 434, 436
deans 87, 89, 92, 179, 419
  laymen appointed as 92
death/deathbeds 409–10
Declaration of Breda (1660) 81, 165, 479
Declaration of Indulgence (1672) 145
De Dominis, Marco Antonio, archbishop 24
De haeretico comburendo 413, 415
De La Milletière, Théophile Brachet 350
Denmark, Church of 356
Dennison, Stephen 132, 375
Deodati, Jean 342
Dering, Edward 352, 354, 363, 364, 405, 406
Devon Association 475–6
Dickens, A. G. 6, 353

Diet of Speyer (1529) 32
Digges, Thomas 359
Dinot, abbot of Bangor 287
diocesan chancellors 90, 94, 95–6
diocesan synods 12, 75
dioceses
  changes under Elizabeth I 88–97
  changes under Henry VIII 86–7
  numbers of 235–6
Directory for Public Worship 2, 77, 78, 142, 164, 262, 435, 441–2, 447, 454, 455, 459, 461
'Dissenting Brethren' 78–9 see also Independents
divorce 12, 176–7, 180, 325
Doctors' Commons 171
Dod, John 370, 375, 376
Dolben, John 475
Donne, John 17, 342, 396, 409, 424
Dort see Synod of Dort (1618–19)
Douai 422
Dow, Robert 392
Dowsing, William 189, 207
Dublin 250–1
Duffy, Eamon 352, 375
Dugdale, William 11, 313
Duppa, Brian, bishop 466, 470
Durel, Jean 344
Durham Book 166
Durham
  bishops of 99
  cathedral 70, 74, 149, 151, 162–3, 201, 208, 234, 307, 311, 312
  diocese of 96
  see of 94
Durham House Group 70, 162, 165–6
Dury, John 25, 26, 341, 343
Dutch Arminians 68, 343
Dutch Calvinists 10, 25, 338, 343, 344
Dutch Reformed Church 191
Dutch Second Reformation 25–6, 334
Dyke, Daniel 450

Easter 161–2, 164, 175, 255, 397
  communion 124, 128, 141, 472
  election of officials 136
East Friesland 321–2, 323
East Knoyle church 204
'edification' 360–3, 378, 399
Edinburgh, diocese of 258
Edward the Confessor 151
Edward VI, King 2, 3, 6, 19, 39–41, 84, 102, 104, 114, 118, 157, 187, 220, 236, 322, 356, 440
  as Josiah 39, 418

Edwardian Reformation 2, 3, 5, 6, 23, 39–41, 72, 152–7, 187, 211, 236, 247, 312, 322–4, 354, 417–18
Edwards, Thomas 373–4
Eikon Basilike 77, 349, 467
Ejectors 79, 117, 449–50
elders 114, 143, 269, 359, 389, 435, 453
Eleutherius, Pope 287
Eliot, John 278
Elizabeth I, Queen 2, 3, 6, 13, 48–50, 53, 56, 65, 88–97, 101, 102, 105, 111, 118, 157, 160, 173, 178, 179, 186, 195, 210, 211, 235, 236, 248, 249, 252, 304, 325–6, 327, 331, 352, 354, 377, 388, 419, 426
  change of title to 'Supreme Governor' 49, 105, 107, 157, 213
  papal bull of excommunication of (1570) 54, 119, 177, 247, 303, 330
  semper eadem motto 2, 53
Elizabethan Church 3, 4, 5, 7, 9, 15, 24, 48–61, 74, 158–9, 187, 210–11, 219, 327–32, 358–60, 426–7
Elizabethan Reformation 2, 3, 4, 5, 45–6, 48–61, 353
Elizabethan Settlement 2, 7, 11, 21, 45, 48–53, 60, 63, 72, 78, 84, 102, 105, 157–61, 180, 186, 191, 249, 312, 325–6, 352, 354–5, 377, 426–7
Elizabeth of Bohemia 68, 335
Elphinstone, Kenneth, bishop 171
Elyot, Sir Thomas 282
Endicott, John 269
episcopacy
  as apostolic 109
  in Church of England 13, 20, 21, 22, 45, 55–9, 66, 75, 79–82, 108–10, 220, 263, 294, 336–7, 338, 340–1, 356, 360–1, 459, 469, 470–2, 477, 481
  in Church of Ireland 251–2, 256–7
  in Church of Scotland 67, 98, 244, 253–4, 258, 433
  iure divino 13, 24, 59, 66, 75, 100, 105, 109–11, 288, 309, 337–8, 339, 370, 371, 389
  iure humano 361, 371
  'limited episcopacy' (Scotland) 253
  primitive episcopacy 21, 81, 478
  'reduced episcopacy' (also modified/moderated episcopacy) 21, 75–6, 81, 99, 116, 240, 264, 356, 444, 446, 463, 476, 477, 478
  Reformed defence of 55–6, 330, 343–4
episcopalian identity (1640–62) 457–81
  (1640–9) 458–64
  (1649–60) 464–76
  (1660–2) 476–81

episcopalian identity (1640–62) (*cont.*)
  antipathy towards other Protestant groups 464, 465–6
  charitable support 468
  clandestine ordination 431, 450, 469, 470–1, 474–5
  clerical conformity 474
  'episcopalian congregationalism' 20, 80, 472, 479, 481
  interaction with other Protestant groups 453, 454, 475–6
  persecution 464–5
  preaching and publications 466–8
  and royal supremacy 469–70 *see also* royal supremacy
  toleration 450–1, 454–5
Erasmus, Desiderius 6, 284, 285, 413
  Paraphrases on the New Testament 6, 418
Erastianism 13, 113, 119, 244, 273
Erastus, Thomas 329
etcetera oath 75, 110, 183, 259
eucharistic presence 35, 39, 41, 47, 50–1, 154, 156, 212, 213, 216–17, 319, 320, 326, 331, 347, 387
  transubstantiation 37, 51, 154, 300, 347
Evangelicals (Victorian) 26
Evelyn, John 454, 465, 466
excommunication 30, 112, 113, 116, 129, 177, 179, 180, 214, 269, 329
Exeter
  diocese of 96, 461
  see of 98
ex officio oath 64, 305
extempore prayer 137, 371, 386, 403–4, 460

Falkland, Lucius Cary, viscount 292–3
Family of 43, 328, 376
Farindon, Anthony 468, 471–2
fasting 139, 259, 268, 311, 371, 462, 464
Fathers (Church) 10–11, 71, 282, 284, 288, 290, 291, 292–6, 299, 314, 318, 348, 384
Featley, Daniel 404, 405, 437
female piety 400
Feoffees for Impropriations 71, 134, 377
Ferne, Henry, bishop 461, 465, 467
Ferrar, Robert, bishop 47
Ferrell, Lori Anne 17, 18
festival communions 141
Field, John 159, 357
Field, Richard 217, 310, 439
Field, Thomas 56
Fiennes, Nathaniel 101
Fincham, Kenneth 7, 20, 21, 22, 93, 370, 387, 390–1, 392
Firmin, Giles 144
First Bishops' War 75

Firth, John 450
Fisher, John, bishop 31, 87, 104
Fitzgerald, Thomas, lord 246
Fletcher, Richard, bishop 391
fonts 164, 311, 457
Forced Loan (1627) 100
Forest, Friar John 36
Form of Prayers (1556) 159, 160, 161, 163, 164
Formula of Concord 210–11, 216–17, 218
Foster, Andrew 12, 13
Fox, Edward, bishop 286
Foxe, John 11, 60, 102, 159, 302–6, 309–10, 355–7, 363, 398–9, 415 *see also Actes and Monuments*
Frankfurt 47, 302, 329
Frederick V, Elector Palatine 68, 335–6
'free-willers' 47, 304
Freke, Edmund, bishop 387
French Calvinists 289, 343–4 *see also* Huguenots
French Confession (1559) 218, 220, 222
Frith, John 32, 300
Froude, Hurrell 4
Fulke, William 193, 423, 439
Fuller, Thomas 97, 101, 313–14, 342, 357
Fuller, William 195
Fulwar, Thomas, bishop 463, 471, 472
funeral monuments 59, 73, 126, 129, 190, 207, 400, 457
funeral sermons 133, 399–400
Füssel, Martin 336

Gaelic Irish 245, 247, 251
Gaelic Prayer Book 256
Gaelic translations 249–50
Galloway, Patrick 161
Gandy, John 476
Gardiner, George 240
Gardiner, Richard 467
Gardiner, Stephen, bishop 32–3, 35, 46, 87, 102, 107, 154, 284–5, 427
Garnet, Henry 130
Garthwaite, Timothy 467
Gataker, Thomas 453
Gauden, John, bishop 478, 479
Geneva, Reformed Church of 14, 23, 24, 36, 47, 48, 49, 51, 55–6, 58, 222, 227, 308, 324, 326, 328, 331, 333, 337, 338, 396
Geoffrey of Monmouth 287
Germes, John 300
Gibson, Edmund 177
Gifford, George 57–8, 132, 133, 134, 367–8
Gilby, Anthony 159
Gledstanes, George, archbishop 254
Gloucester
  cathedral 201, 234

Index

diocese of 86
see of 90
Goad, Thomas 73
Godly Clerk, The 410
godly/ungodly division 132–4, 361, 374
Godwin, Francis, bishop 310, 470
Golden Legend, The 301, 396–7
Good Friday 255
Goodman, Christopher 118, 119
Goodman, Gabriel, dean 60, 392
Goodman, Godfrey, bishop 469–70
'good neighbourhood' 114, 132, 367–8
Goodwin, John 451
Goodwin, Thomas 445
'gospellers' 31, 299, 309
Gouge, William 439
Gratian 170, 284–5
Great Tew circle 11, 292–3, 349
Greenham, Richard 133, 364
Greenhill, William 450
Green, Ian 159, 241
Greenwood, John 160, 383
Gregory I, Pope 301, 303
Gregory IX, Pope 170
Gregory XIII, Pope 119
Gresham College 239, 292
Grey family 320, 323
Grey, Jane 46
Griffith, George 472
Griffith, Matthew 467
Grindal, Edmund, archbishop 8, 53, 56–7, 93, 111, 136, 178–9, 223, 304, 328, 353
    clash with Queen Elizabeth 56–7, 111, 178–9
Grosseteste, Robert, bishop 310
Grotius, Hugo 289
Guest, Edmund, bishop 387, 388
Gunning, Peter, bishop 467, 475
Gunpowder Plot 126, 345
Gunther, Karl 353, 379
Gurnay, Edmund 206–7
Gustav Vasa, King 317
Gwalther, Rudolf 223, 320, 328–31

Hacket, John, bishop 465, 472
Hacket, William 117
Haigh, Christopher 16, 235, 373, 374
Hailes, Blood of 36
Halcomb, Joel 431
Hales, John 292
Hall, George 480
Hall, Joseph, bishop 294, 339–40, 345, 408, 462, 463, 465, 470–1
Hall, Thomas 454
Hamilton, Patrick 245
Hamling, Tara 193

Hammersmith 135
Hammond, Henry 199–200, 201, 294, 295, 296, 461, 467, 474, 475, 479
Hampton, Christopher, archbishop 254
Hampton Court Conference (1604) 63, 69, 82, 98, 161, 220, 223–4, 251, 253, 370, 425–6
Hampton, Stephen 14, 23, 24
Harding, Thomas 299
Harington, Sir John 93, 99, 383–4, 388
Harley, Sir Robert 135, 207
Harmony of Confessions 211, 221, 333, 337
Harrison, William 189, 307–8
Harrold 472
Harsnett, Samuel, bishop 100, 195, 369, 371, 389, 391, 467
Hartlib, Samuel 25, 26, 340
Hassall, Thomas 472
Hatfield House chapel 195–6
Hatton, Sir Christopher 59, 95
Heal, Felicity 16, 17, 91
Heath, Nicholas, archbishop 86, 89
Heidelberg 336, 338, 339
Heidelberg Catechism 3, 335
Helmholz, R. H. 12
Henrician Reformation 1–2, 5, 6, 7, 13, 18, 28–39, 72, 84, 86, 104, 106, 111–12, 149–52, 236, 244, 281–2, 316–19, 321, 322, 417
Henry II, King 30, 301, 313
Henry IV, Holy Roman Emperor 30
Henry VII, King 29
Henry VIII, King 2, 3, 6, 12, 13, 18, 19, 28–39, 50, 84, 87, 102, 104, 106, 111–12, 151, 152, 153, 168, 173, 176, 237, 246, 264, 280, 301, 313, 316–19, 321, 322, 414–17, 440, 441 *see also* Henrician Reformation
    Assertio Septem Sacramentorum 280, 281, 282, 284, 317
Henson, Hensley, bishop 228
Herbert, George 401
Herbert, John 92
Hereford
    cathedral 234
    diocese of 96
heresy, executions for 31–3, 36–7, 54–5, 245, 300, 320, 321, 413, 415
Hewitt, John 454–5, 474
Heylyn, Peter 101, 291, 312, 343, 467, 470
Heynes, Simon 240
Hieron, Samuel 132–3, 189
Higham, Florence 7
Higham, Sir John 134
High Court of Admiralty 171
High Court of Chivalry 171

Hildersham, Arthur 370
Hill, Robert 133–4
Hobbes, Thomas 118
Hoby, Lady Margaret 139
Holbech, Thomas 463
Holdsworth, Richard 292
Holgate, Robert, bishop 86
Holinshed, Ralph 159, 306–7, 308
Hooker, Richard 1, 4, 6, 8–9, 23, 60, 73, 89, 103, 109, 198, 217, 222, 223, 288, 308–9, 310, 314, 316, 331–2, 338, 339, 342, 356, 363, 368, 378, 381–93, 406, 407
   Laws of Ecclesiastical Polity 4, 60, 288, 308, 332, 363, 381, 382, 384, 386, 389, 390
Hooker, Thomas 270
Hooper, John, bishop 42, 47, 52, 155, 329
Horne, John 468, 473
Horne, Robert, bishop 330
Hoskins, John 290
Houlbrooke, Ralph 94
household worship 139, 194, 370, 371, 404, 472
Howes, Edmund 392
Howson, John, bishop 198, 390
Hughes, Ann 20, 374
Huguenots 342
Humble Petition and Advice (1657) 452
Humble Proposals (1652) 451
Hungary, Reformed Church in 23, 221, 329
Hunne, Richard 302
Hus, Jan 302
Hussites 309
Hutchinson, Anne 270
Hutton, Matthew, archbishop 8, 86, 388–9
Hyde, Dr Edward 80
Hyde, Sir Edward *see* Clarendon, Edward Hyde, earl of

iconoclasm 2, 3, 11, 16–17, 20, 39–40, 49, 50, 53, 73, 77, 142, 186–9, 190, 207, 247, 313, 320, 322, 345, 346, 459, 460
Ignatius of Antioch 294
images 35, 36, 39, 67–8, 186–208, 319, 320
   see also religious art, post-Reformation
   abused imagery 16, 39, 186
Imitatio Christi 402, 408
impropriations 91, 134–5, 181, 231, 256, 258, 389–90 *see also* Feoffees for Impropriations
Independents 78, 79, 116, 117, 164, 294, 445, 449–50, 451, 452, 455, 467, 475
Ingram, Martin 94
Ingram, Sir Arthur 201
Injunctions
   (1536) 35, 150, 173
   (1538) 150–1, 152, 173, 416
   (1554) 173

   (1559) 6, 16, 50, 52, 74, 105, 110, 115–16, 196, 426
Inns of Court, Tudor 113, 114
Institution of a Christian Man see Bishops' Book
Instrument of Government (1653) 446, 447–8, 452
Interregnum 20, 63, 117, 241, 349, 444–56
   Cromwellian Church 444–56
Irish Articles (1615) 3, 21, 67, 70, 74, 225, 251, 256, 257
Irish Confederates 349
Isaacson, Henry 392
Isham, Lady Elizabeth 15, 375, 407

Jackson, Thomas 467
Jacobean Church 5, 9, 12, 24, 65–8, 74, 369–73, 424–5
James VI and I, King 2, 63–4, 67–8, 69, 76, 84, 94, 98–102, 105, 161–3, 174, 175, 180–4, 195, 211, 214, 224, 248, 251–2, 253, 264, 289, 290, 345, 346, 347, 371, 372, 382, 393, 425, 440, 469
   Directions to Preachers (1622) 214
James VII and II, King 264
Jeanes, Gordon 152, 154
Jenkyn, William 450
Jermyn, Sir Robert 134
Jerome of Prague 302
Jessop, Constant 66
Jesuits 54, 119, 193, 338, 423, 466 *see also* Catholics
Jewel, John, bishop 4, 5, 9, 10, 52, 67, 74, 89, 211, 217, 221, 251, 285–6, 287, 288, 299, 337
   Apologia pro Ecclesia Anglicana 4, 211, 299, 337
Joachim II, elector of Brandenburg 317
Johann III, duke of Jülich-Cleves 318
John XXII, Pope 170
John of Atton (Ayton) 170
John Sigismund, elector of Brandenburg 336
Jones, Lewis, bishop 262
Jonson, Ben 369
Joseph of Arimathea 202
Josselin, Ralph 144, 450, 454
justification, doctrine of 35, 37, 58, 69, 212, 317, 325, 352, 363–4, 368, 398, 413, 432
Juxon, William, bishop 100, 101, 472

Keble, John 4
Kempis, Thomas a 402
Kenilworth Classis 454
Kidderminster 165
Kildare rebellion 246
Kimedoncius, Jacobus 339

Index

King, Henry, bishop 471
King's Book 3, 248, 282, 287, 295
King's Litany (1545) 152, 153
King's Primer (1545) 152
Kitchen, Anthony, bishop 49
Knappen, M. M. 401
Knewstubbs, John 161
Knight, John 290
Knollys, Lettice 382
Knox, John 47, 49, 119, 159–60, 244, 248, 252, 254, 326

Lake, Arthur, bishop 65
Lake, Peter 8, 9, 10, 115, 380–1, 387–8, 389–90, 393, 444
Lambert, John 36, 320
Lambeth Articles (1595) 3, 14, 21, 60, 67, 74, 224, 225, 251, 309, 339, 388
Lambeth Palace chapel 207
Lancashire 78, 143, 447, 448
Lanfranc, Archbishop 259
Langland, John, bishop 87
Łaski, Jan 322, 323–4, 325, 327, 328
Latimer, Hugh, bishop 32, 47, 118, 353
Laudians/Laudianism 2, 4–5, 9–10, 12, 14, 17, 21, 24, 70–5, 105–6, 113, 141–2, 163–4, 198, 201, 204–5, 207, 230, 234, 241, 271, 291, 304, 311, 312, 313, 340–1, 347–8, 349, 366, 369, 373, 376, 378–9, 384, 393, 427, 440, 457, 459, 463, 478
Laud, William, archbishop 66, 70, 71, 77, 87, 91, 94, 100, 101, 105, 106–7, 135, 141, 162, 163–4, 182, 183, 194, 197, 201, 207, 234, 255, 256, 258–9, 261, 291, 340, 347, 348, 373, 393, 430, 440–1, 459, 467
Layfield, Edward 460
Lehmberg, Stanford E. 151
Leicester, Robert Dudley, earl of 57, 87, 357, 382, 387
Lent 311, 384
Leo X, Pope 247
Leslie, Henry, bishop 261, 469
Lever, Christopher 105
Ley, John 78
Library of Anglo-Catholic Theology 4, 5
Lichfield cathedral 241
Lincoln
 cathedral 86, 233
 diocese of 90
Lincoln's Inn 198
Litany (1544) 151–2, 155
Loarte, Gaspar 408
Lollardy 304, 306, 319, 320, 413, 422
Lombard, Peter 284

London 32, 40, 55, 78, 125, 128, 133, 135, 143, 144–5, 157, 160, 198–9, 307, 334, 355, 375, 382, 389, 435, 447, 454, 473
 diocese of 90
 see of 59
London parishes
 All Hallows, Barking 460
 All Hallows, Staining 136
 Christ Church, Newgate St 390–1, 392
 St Botolph Aldersgate 127
 St Christopher le Stocks 136
 St Clement Eastcheap 473
 St Faith under St Paul's 157
 St Giles Cripplegate 382–3, 385–6
 St Giles in the Fields 132
 St Katherine Cree 205, 206
 St Leonard Shoreditch 460
 St Margaret New Fish St 446
 St Martin Orgar 131
 St Mary le Bow 171
 St Mary Magdalen Milk St 144, 468
 St Mildred Bread St 199
 St Olave Jewry 137
 St Peter, Paul's Wharf 473
 St Saviour, Southwark 199
 St Sepulchre Newgate 460
 St Stephen Walbrook 199
Longland, John, bishop 38
'Lords of the Congregation' 249
Louis VI, Elector Palatine 210, 216
Love, Christopher 450
Love, Nicholas 402
Lucius, King 107, 254, 287, 306
Lutherans/Lutheranism 6, 23, 41, 51, 152, 154–5, 156, 187, 194, 210–11, 216–17, 249, 284, 317, 317–28, 331, 332, 333, 336, 341, 343, 388, 398
Luther, Martin 32, 43, 280, 282, 316–17, 320, 322, 363, 398, 413, 415, 440
Lyly, John 392
Lyndwood, William 170, 176

McCafferty, John 21
MacCulloch, Diarmaid 15, 23, 24, 229–30, 334, 353, 386, 388
McCullough, Peter 8, 9
MacDonald, Alan 253
McGee, J. Sears 401
MacMullen, Ramsey 149–50
Mainz 177
Major-Generals 449
Maltby, Judith 15, 16, 160, 374–5, 454, 457
Manchester collegiate church 233, 236, 238
manducatio impiorum 216, 217
Mansfield 450
Manton, Thomas 450, 455

Marian Church 47, 114
Marian episcopate 49, 111
Marian exiles 47–8, 53, 105, 118, 159, 248,
    299, 302, 326, 327, 328, 334, 353, 354,
    396, 420
Marian persecution/martyrs 47, 54, 302–5,
    344, 354, 356, 398–9
Marian Reformation 46–7
Marprelate controversy 369, 385, 388
Marprelate Tracts 58–9, 305, 383
marriage 125, 179, 472
    use of ring in 56, 156
Marshall, Stephen 437, 441
Marshall, William 287
Martindale, Adam 453, 454, 455
Martin, Gregory 422
Martin, Jessica 15
Martyr, Peter *see* Vermigli, Peter Martyr
Mary, Queen of Scots 49, 54, 57, 252
Mary I, Queen 2, 46, 85, 86, 87, 102, 104,
    114–15, 118, 157, 168, 173, 177, 236,
    245, 248, 302, 325, 326, 354, 418
Maryland 271
Mason, Sir John 87
Massachusetts Churches 267–79
Massachusetts General Court 272, 273–4,
    275, 277
Massacre of St Bartholomew (1572) 54
mass, the Latin 35, 37, 40, 46, 48, 49, 126, 152,
    153, 154–5, 157, 233, 248, 252, 285–6,
    300, 317, 417, 418
Mather, Richard 270
Matthew, Tobie, archbishop 65, 99, 254
Maxwell, John, bishop 261
Maxwell, Robert, bishop 463, 471
Mede, Joseph 340
medieval church 11–12, 40, 59–60, 67, 71,
    107, 124, 125, 126, 130, 139, 149, 162,
    169–70, 180, 194, 205, 298–314, 346,
    396–7, 398
medieval devotion 402, 404, 406, 409
medieval heretics 309–10
Melanchthon, Philip 153, 324, 328, 343
Melville, Andrew 253, 259
memorialization 126, 190, 398–401
Merbecke, John 156
Merritt, Julia 13, 16
Middleburg Book 159–60
Mildmay chapel (Apethorpe) 196
Mildmay, Sir Henry 357
millenarianism 212
Millenary Petition 63, 98, 161, 253
Milton, Anthony 198, 458
monarchical republic, Elizabethan 358–60
monasteries, dissolution of 34, 36, 86, 155–6,
    232–3, 247, 313, 317

monasticism
    defence of 311, 313
    mutation of 405, 406
Montagu, Richard, bishop 69–70, 74, 215,
    224, 225, 290, 291, 310–11, 348, 357
Montague, James, bishop 65, 98
More, P. E. 4
More, Sir Thomas 31, 33, 104
Morley, George, bishop 343–4, 478
Morrill, John 457
Morton, Thomas, bishop 471
Moseley, Humphrey 467
Mossom, Robert 466–7, 473
mothers' legacy genre 400
Munday, Anthony 199
Munroe, Robert 261
music, in churches 17, 50, 53, 155–6, 158–9,
    199, 201, 231, 238–9, 327, 390–1, 462

Nashe, Thomas 392
National Covenant (1638) 260
Neale, Sir John 93
Necessary Doctrine and Erudition for any
    Christian Man see *King's Book*
Negative Confession (1581) 253, 260
Neile, Richard, archbishop 70, 95, 98, 100,
    162, 194, 234, 371
Nericius, Laurentius Petri, archbishop 23
Newcastle, William Cavendish, marquess
    of 263
New England 266–79
    Congregational structures in 267–72
    'expanded baptism' in 267–72
    mission to Indians 278
Nicanor, Lysimachus *see* Corbet, John
Nicene Creed 281
Nicholson, William 466
Nicodemism 48, 55, 119, 328, 354–5
Nine Worthies 193
Nine Years War 245
North America 266–79
Northern Rising (1569) 54, 303
Northumberland, John Dudley, duke of
    41, 86
Norton, John 275
Norton, Thomas 356–7, 436
Norwich cathedral 233
Nowell, Alexander 195, 221
Nye, Philip 437, 445, 450

Oath of Allegiance (1606) 105, 107, 345
O'Devaney, Cornelius, bishop 245
Odo, archbishop 300
Officers' Agreement (1649) 448
Oglander, Sir John 471
Oldcastle, Sir John 299–300, 301

Old English (in Ireland) 245, 246, 247, 250, 251, 256
Oldenburg, Countess Anna von 321-2
Orange, Prince of 68, 338
Orarium 158
Ordinal 2, 5, 23, 178, 213, 220, 435, 434, 477
Ordinance for the Lord's Supper 435
ordination of clergy 182, 219-20, 434, 450, 462, 463, 471, 473, 474, 477, 480
  Catholic 346
  clandestine episcopalian 431, 450, 469, 470-1, 474-5
  directory for 434
  non-episcopal 334, 340-1, 344
  re-ordination 480
organs 17, 163, 195, 201, 207, 231, 238-9, 327, 390-1
Ormond, James Butler, duke of 262
Othobon, cardinal 170
Otho, cardinal 170
Ottoman Empire 303
Overall, John, bishop 60, 67, 133, 162, 175, 198, 288, 369, 371, 390
Owen, David 119
Owen, John 25, 445, 449, 450, 451
Oxford
  diocese of 86, 93
  royalist base 77, 461, 462
  see of 88, 90, 91
Oxford colleges
  Christ Church 32, 237, 462
  Lincoln 197, 198
  Magdalen 201, 320, 331
  Magdalen Hall 80
  Queen's 198
  St John's 197
  University 198
  Wadham 196-7, 198
Oxford University 24, 32, 40, 89, 101, 155, 158, 198, 201, 285, 290, 335, 336, 382, 459, 463-4
  canon law faculties 169, 176
  college chapels 196-8, 201
  college choirs and organs 239
  college founders and visitors 88
Oxinden, Henry 468

Palm Sunday procession, abolition of 154
Panzani, Gregorio 348
papal authority 2, 30-1, 38, 41, 46, 55, 107, 169-70, 286
Pareus, David 290, 337, 342
'parish Anglicans' 16, 122, 140, 145
Paris exiles 343
parish churches 40, 49, 53, 130-1, 143, 156, 163, 420

church seating 128, 130, 142
music in 17, 138, 144, 158
repair and decoration of 16-17, 94, 126, 140, 198-9, 202-3, 207-8
royal coat of arms in 116, 190, 191, 469, 477
surveys of 98, 198-9, 448
parishes 40, 117, 122-46, 447
  amalgamations 128, 449
  and Catholics 129-30
  church attendance 123-4, 129
  church fees 131-2
  clerical appointments 134-5
  communion
    celebration of 158-9
    reception of 124-5, 133, 182
  covenanting groups 139-40, 144
  feasts and customs 125-66
  'festival communions' 141
  lectureships 135, 137, 142
  parish community 123-7, 130
  'parish religion' 16, 57-8, 122, 127-41, 145-6
  'particularizing' 132
  Prayer Book services 19, 138, 140, 144-5
  see also Book of Common Prayer
  Rogationtide processions 50, 125-6, 141
Paris, Matthew 306
Parker Certificates 94
Parker, John 392
Parker, Matthew, archbishop 5, 11, 48, 55, 56, 95, 109, 213, 251, 287, 303, 306, 307, 328, 354, 355, 387, 421-2
  De Antiquitate Britannicae Ecclesiae 11, 287
Parker, Robert 392
Parker Society 5
Parker, William 392
Parkhurst, John, bishop 105, 328-9
Parkyn, Robert 149
Parliament, English 18, 28, 46, 64, 69, 78, 104, 105, 111-14, 117, 173, 174, 181, 183, 251
  House of Commons 74, 81, 82, 174, 195, 226, 232, 341, 372, 430, 435
  House of Lords 76, 85, 100, 430, 432, 435-6
  sessions of
    (1529-36) Reformation 30-1, 174, 175
    (1539) 36-7
    (1543) 417
    (1552) 325
    (1610) 112
    (1614) Addled 100
    (1629) 290, 312
    (1640) Short 75, 112, 175, 272
    (1640-53) Long 64-5, 75, 81, 100, 101, 106, 112, 115, 207, 241, 248, 261, 430-2, 446-7, 459

Parliament, English (*cont.*)
   (1648–53) Rump 447, 449
   (1654–5) First Protectorate 451–2
   (1656–8) Second Protectorate 452
   (1660) Convention 455
   (1661–79) Cavalier 112, 478
Parliament, Irish 250, 256, 261
Parliament, Scottish 249, 318
Parsons, Robert 56, 407, 422
Passenham church 202
patristics *see* Fathers (Church)
Paul's Cross sermons 119, 239, 309, 362, 391
Peacham, Henry 196
Pearson, John 226, 467, 473
Pecock, Reginald 302
Peirce, Sir Edward 341
Pembroke, William Herbert, earl of 88
Pentecost 255
Percy, John 291
Perkins, Sir Christopher 92
Perkins, William 25, 133, 193, 194, 357, 402
Peterborough, diocese of 86
Philip II, king of Spain 46, 114
Phillip IV, king of France 30
Philip, John 446
Pierce, Thomas 343, 385
Piers, William, bishop 474
Piggott, John 460
pilgrimages 39, 149–50, 234, 317
Pilgrimage of Grace 36, 307
Pindar, Sir Paul 392
Pocklington, John 311, 312
Poland-Lithuania 23, 221
Pole, Reginald, cardinal 46, 48, 87, 111, 115, 177
Ponet, John, bishop 99
poor relief 123, 126, 179
Pope, as Antichrist 3, 21, 61, 69, 256, 257, 263, 303, 306, 308, 344, 346, 357, 362, 365
Porter, Robert 451
Poullain, Valerand 159
practical divinity 25, 334, 364–5, 366
Practice of Piety 334, 403–5
praemunire 31, 106, 110
'Prayer Book Protestantism' 16, 140, 374–5, 459
'Prayer Book puritanism' 15
prayer for the dead 156, 189
prayer for the sick 125
prayer of consecration 164, 166
predestination/predestinarianism 3, 41, 47, 58, 60, 65, 68, 72, 132, 133–4, 162, 217–19, 224, 251, 290–1, 309, 331, 332, 339, 361, 363, 385, 388, 391, 395, 405–6, 451
Presbyterianism 56, 57, 77, 109, 110, 114, 273, 376

   (1640s–1650s) 78–9, 143, 273, 435, 446–7, 455–6
   Elizabethan 305, 312, 337, 355, 357, 358–60, 364, 365
   in Ireland 261
   in New England 272
Presbyterians 79, 81, 82, 108, 109, 113, 115, 116, 117, 144, 145, 294, 343, 449–50, 451, 455, 466, 475, 480, 481
Pre-Tractarian High Churchmen 6, 26
Prideaux, John, bishop 215, 224
primers 152, 156, 158, 249–50
primitive church 10–11, 37, 110, 280, 286, 288, 291, 292, 295, 296, 299, 423, 465
private baptism 178, 255
private communion 255
private fasts 139, 259, 371, 464
private prayer 403–4
Privy Council 40, 95, 99, 213, 222
   bishops on 13, 64, 85, 97, 98, 100, 101
   Irish 256
'prophesyings' 56–7, 65, 111, 179
Protector, Lord *see* Cromwell, Oliver
Protestant, use of term 31–2, 47, 58
Prynne, William 70, 113, 234, 312, 373
psalms 138, 160, 386, 402, 406, 418, 424
psalm-singing 138, 144, 158, 231, 245, 255, 268, 316, 342
Pseudo-Dionysius the Areopagite 285
'public profession' 445–6, 448, 451, 452, 455
Puddletown, black-letter inscriptions 191–2
purgatory 35, 37, 40, 213, 317, 368, 401
puritans/puritanism 7, 8, 10, 12, 15, 16, 26, 55, 56, 58, 59, 61, 63, 65, 66, 67, 68, 69, 71, 79, 94, 95, 98, 132–3, 137, 139, 159, 174, 178–9, 180, 199, 219, 223, 230–2, 240, 267–8, 271–2, 273, 275–6, 288, 304, 305, 309–13, 329–30, 338, 345, 346, 348, 352–79, 383, 425, 426, 439, 444, 452, 459, 480–1 *see also* Cromwellian Church
Pym, John 259

Quakers 275–6, 279, 452, 453, 455
Quantin, Jean-Louis 10, 11, 18

Rainolds, John 161, 220, 223–4, 425–6, 427
Ranters 448
Ravis, Thomas, bishop 371
Read, Sophie 161
Reeve, Edmund 225
Reformatio Legum Ecclesiasticarum 3, 12, 41, 56, 176–7, 283, 325, 357
'reformation of manners' 372
Reformed tradition, diversity of 24–5, 218–19, 327–8, 331

relics, destruction of 36
religious art, post-Reformation 190–208
resistance theory 118–20, 377
Restoration 7, 11, 63, 81, 82, 226, 241, 263–4, 275–6, 296, 314, 342, 349, 350, 393
Restoration Church of England 17, 166, 344, 428, 444, 456, 478–9, 480–1
Restoration settlement 21, 145, 183–4, 466, 476–81
  Oath of Supremacy 49, 80
Reynolds, Edward 455, 478, 479
Rhineland Palatinate 222, 329, 335–6
Rhode Island Churches 270
Ridley, Nicholas, bishop 5, 42, 47, 52, 155
Ripon minster 238, 240
Rites of Durham 307, 311
Rives, Bruno 468
Rochester cathedral 234
Rogationtide processions 50, 125–6, 141
Rogers, John 37, 65
Rogers, Richard, bishop 93
Rogers, Thomas 179, 214–15, 402
Rose, Jacqueline 18
royal supremacy 18, 20, 28, 29, 30–4, 39, 45–50, 57, 77, 79–80, 87, 88, 96, 101, 103, 104–16, 119, 157, 173, 181, 213, 214, 221, 222, 244, 246, 257, 264, 286, 356, 459, 462, 469–70, 475, 477, 479, 481
Royal Visitations 87–8, 89, 102, 186
Royston, Richard 467
rural deaneries 92
Ryrie, Alec 318, 363, 405

sabbatarianism 26, 255, 370, 371
sacrilege 11–12, 20, 34, 67, 71, 91, 101, 181, 340, 346, 390
St Basil, liturgy of 165
St George's chapel (Windsor) 477
St German, Christopher 112–13, 282
St Giles, Edinburgh 258, 260
St James, liturgy of 165
St Paul's cathedral 124, 156, 229, 241, 258, 313, 382, 384, 385, 392, 460, 480
saints 149–50, 155, 189, 396–7, 398
  invocation of 151, 156
  lives of 349
  veneration of 35, 149–50, 397
saints' days 454
Sales, François de 408
Salisbury, Robert Cecil, earl of 195–6
Sallabass, Melchior 190–1
Salvart, Jean-François 211, 221
Sancroft, William 464
Sancta Clara, Franciscus a 348
Sander, Nicholas 188

Sanderson, Robert, bishop 166, 457, 466, 467, 472, 474, 479
Sandys, Edwin, archbishop 187, 439–40
Sanhedrin 111
Sanquhar Declaration 119
Saravia, Hadrian 24, 109, 309, 337, 388
Savoy Conference (1661) 165
Savoy Declaration (1658) 117, 445–6, 452–3
Saxby, Thomas 473
Schleitheim Confession 212
Schmalkaldic Wars 323
Scottish commissioners (at Westminster Assembly) 433, 438
Scottish Covenanters 77, 259–62, 349, 459
  and Charles II 77, 79, 469, 479
Scott, Thomas 372
Scrivener, Matthew 295
Scudamore, Sir John, viscount 202
Scultetus, Abraham 336, 342
Second Bishops' War 75
Second Commandment, graven images in churches 187, 191–2, 320
Second Helvetic Confession 217, 218, 220, 222, 224
Seile, Henry 467
Selden, John 101, 181
separatists 65, 116–17, 160, 180, 264, 267, 270, 346, 365–6, 377, 383–4, 386, 441, 447
Sergeant, John 349
sermon-repetition 139, 370, 454
Shagan, Ethan 3
Shakespeare, William 369
Sharp, James 263
Shawe, John 312
Shaw, W. A. 19
Sheils, Bill 11
Sheldon, Gilbert, archbishop 166, 344, 465, 468, 469, 474, 478, 479
Sherbrooke, Michael 307
shrines, destruction of 151
Shuger, Debora 381
Sibbes, Richard 399–400, 406
Sidney, Mary, countess of Pembroke 424
Sidney, Sir Henry 249–50
Sidney, Sir Philip 424
Sigismund, John 336
Skinner, Robert, bishop 450, 462, 471, 474–5
Slingsby, Sir Henry 196
Smart, Peter 163, 312
Smith, Richard 466, 468, 470
Smith, Sir Thomas 92
Smyth, John 140
Smyth, Richard 283
Socinians/Socinianism 117, 183, 448, 452, 455

sola scriptura, principle of 10, 18, 177, 282, 283, 284, 288, 294, 412, 421, 423, 426–7, 428
Solemn League and Covenant 81, 262, 264, 433–4, 438
Solomon's Temple 71, 115, 389
Somerset, Edward Seymour, duke of 39, 302, 323
Sonning 468, 472, 473
Sons of the Clergy 480
Spanish Match 68, 195, 256, 347, 371, 372–3
Sparkes, Thomas 161
Sparrow, Anthony 467
Sparrow, William 450
Spelman, Sir Henry 73, 181, 287
Spinks, Bryan 15
spiritual diaries 406
Spolsky, Ellen 188
Spottiswoode, John, archbishop 254
Squire, John 460
stained glass 30, 126, 196, 198, 199, 202, 205, 208, 311
Stanhope, Sir Edward 391
Stapleton, Thomas 306
state *see also* royal supremacy
   relationship to Church of England 29, 30, 42, 43, 55, 69–70, 96, 101, 126, 301, 358–60
   relationship to Church of Ireland 246, 249–50, 252, 256–7, 259
   relationship to Church of Scotland 249, 252–5, 258, 259
   relationship to New England churches 269
Stephens, Isaac 15, 375
Stephens, Jeremy 343
Sterne, John, bishop 93–4
Sternhold and Hopkins metrical psalms 158, 159, 435
Stillingfleet, Edward 107, 108
Stokesley, John, bishop 281
Stow, John 11, 307
Stradling, John 398
stranger churches 159, 323–4, 327, 334, 340, 344
Strassburg 159, 302, 319, 323, 328
Stubbe, Henry 111
Suarez, Francisco 211, 212
subscription (to the Three Articles) 71, 88, 219–20, 370
Suffolk 134
suffragan bishops 93–4
surplice 55, 56, 65–6, 88, 107, 137, 159, 182, 253, 255 *see also* vestments
surveys of the ministry 93, 94, 131
Sutcliffe, Matthew 109, 309, 337, 338, 345
Swan, John 130

Sweden, Church of 341
Swift, Daniel 160–1
Sydserf, Thomas, bishop 469
Synod of Dort (1618–19) 4, 6, 25, 68–9, 73, 74, 211, 224, 255, 292, 336–8, 339, 340, 341–2
   canons of 70, 74, 339

Tallis, Thomas 50
Taylor, Jeremy, bishop 165, 263, 293–4, 402, 403, 463, 465, 466, 473–4, 479
Taylor, John 85
Taylor, Rowland 356
Taylor, Stephen 20, 21, 22, 450
Temple Newsam 201
Terling 140
Thirty Years War 68, 372
Thomason, George 453
Thornborough, John, bishop 100
Thorndike, Herbert 79–80
Three Articles *see* Whitgift, John, archbishop
Throckmorton, Job 57, 58
Thurloe, John 450
Tilson, Henry, bishop 466, 470, 475
tithes 79, 131, 144, 181, 260, 310, 447, 448, 453, 460
   iure divino 13, 100–1, 370, 389
Toleration Act (1650) 79
Tombes, John 80–1, 450
tombs 59, 190–1, 207, 311
Towers, John, bishop 462
Tractarians 4, 5, 7, 9, 26
traditions, unwritten 280–3, 290–1, 294
Transylvania, Reformed Church in 329
Travers, Walter 310, 357, 382, 383
Tresham, Sir Thomas 119
Triall of Sinceritie, A 399–400
Triers 79, 117, 449–50, 476
Trinitarian doctrine 451, 452–3
Trollope, Anthony 229
Trustees for the Maintenance of Ministers 449
Tuckney, Anthony 450
Tuke, Thomas 137
Tunstall, Cuthbert, bishop 32, 46, 85, 86, 286
Tyacke, Nicholas 385, 387, 388–9, 390–1, 392
Tylden, Thomas 349
Tyndale, William 32, 37–8, 300, 301, 353, 413, 415, 416, 427

ubiquitarianism 51, 217
Ulster 260
Underdown, David 374
Ursinus, Zacharias 3, 335
Usher, Brett 91

Ussher, James, archbishop 21–2, 66, 76, 81, 251, 254, 257, 259, 290–1, 294, 309–10, 463, 471
Utrecht 13

Valla, Lorenzo 287
van Dixhoorn, Chad 19
van Limborch, Philip 343
van Linge, Abraham 197, 198, 201
van Linge, Bernard 197, 198, 201
Vaughan, Richard, bishop 339
Vermigli, Peter Martyr 3, 155, 223, 285, 286, 323, 324, 325, 328, 331
Vestiarian Controversy 55, 223, 251, 329, 355
vestments 42, 47, 51–2, 66, 87, 108, 130, 155, 156, 157, 158, 177, 178, 182, 198, 222, 249, 305, 311
vestries 16, 22, 128, 135–8, 143, 266, 472
via media 1, 4, 5, 6, 23, 26–7, 49, 79, 84, 89, 228–9, 230, 280, 318, 333, 343, 379, 477–8
Vicars, John 206
Virginia 22, 271, 275, 279
  General Assembly 266
Virgin Mary 151, 156
von Wied, Hermann, archbishop 23, 153, 321, 322
Voragine, Jacobus de, archbishop 301, 396–7, 410

Waldegrave Book 159–60
Waldensian crisis (1655) 343
Waldensians 309, 440
Walker, John 465
Walsingham, Sir Francis 357, 383
Walsingham, Thomas 306
Walton, Brian 131
Walton, Izaak 401, 409
Ward, Samuel 66, 215, 224, 290, 331
Ward, Samuel, of Ipswich 372, 373, 400
Warham, William, archbishop 85, 87
Warner, John, bishop 468, 471
Watt, Tessa 193
Weever, John 73, 190, 311
Wells
  cathedral 233
  deanery of 92
Wells-Cole, Anthony 194
Wentworth, Thomas 256, 258, 261
Wesel 327
Wesley, John 408
Westfield, Thomas, bishop 467
Westminster Abbey 13, 39, 48, 60, 151, 233, 236, 239, 392, 477
Westminster Assembly of Divines 19, 77, 78, 106, 112, 115–16, 164, 225–6, 272, 341, 342, 430–42, 446–7, 451, 454

Westminster Confession 19, 20, 77, 81, 226, 251, 294, 432, 436, 451, 454, 459, 476
Westminster, diocese of 86, 236
Westminster, parishes
  St Margaret 140
  St Martin in the Fields 131
  St Paul Covent Garden 128
Westminster Psalter 435–6
Weston, Robert 92
Westphal, Joachim 324
Whitaker, William 309, 362, 388, 389
Whitehall debates (1648) 445
White, Helen C. 398, 405
White, John 115, 133, 437
White, Peter 389
Whitford, Richard 404
Whitgift, John, archbishop 3, 8, 9, 56, 57, 58–9, 60, 64, 91, 93, 94, 95, 97, 98, 109, 174, 179, 181, 198–9, 214, 224, 237, 253, 304, 305, 309, 334, 337, 339, 357, 359, 360, 361, 366, 382, 383, 386, 388, 404, 427
  Three Articles of 57, 64, 214, 357, 427
Whittingham, William 159
Wilcocks, Thomas 364
Wilcox, John 56
Wilcox, Thomas 159
Wilde, George 468, 473
Wilhelm V, duke of Jülich-Cleves 318
Willet, Andrew 223, 240, 357
Williams, Griffith, bishop 461
Williams, Isaac 229
Williams, John, bishop 76, 98, 100, 197, 312, 463
Williams, Roger 269
Winchester, see of 98
Winniffe, Thomas, bishop 462
Winship, Michael 22, 363–4, 444
Withers, George 329
Wittenberg 33
'Wittenberg Articles' 282
Wolsey, Thomas, cardinal 85, 102, 170, 235–6, 301
women, commemorations for 399–400
Woodford, Robert 163
Woodhead, Abraham 349
Wooley, Sir John 92
Worcester
  cathedral 86, 234
  diocese of 96
  see of 85
Worcestershire Association 454, 475
Worcester House Declaration 81–2, 165
Worksop 140
Wotton, Lady 129
Wren, Christopher (dean) 202, 392

Wren, Matthew, bishop 166, 392, 427
Wren, Sir Christopher 208
Wright, Abraham 457, 467
Wriothesley, Charles 156–7
Wyclif, John 302, 303, 306, 310–11, 313, 319
Wycliffites *see* Lollardy

Yates, John 201
York
  diocese of 96
  province of 85, 170, 171, 172–3, 184

York House Conference (1626) 70, 291
Young, Thomas, bishop 86

Zanchi, Girolamo 217, 220
'Zelotes', character 132
Zürich, Reformed Church in 3, 14, 23, 51, 211, 222, 223, 227, 320, 323, 324, 326, 328–9, 330, 331
Zwinglianism 211
Zwingli, Huldrych 32

Printed and bound by CPI Group (UK) Ltd, Croydon, CR0 4YY